JOHN DONNE

Essays in Celebration

JOHN DONNE

Essays in Celebration

Edited by
A. J. SMITH

METHUEN & CO LTD
London

First published in 1972
by Methuen & Co. Ltd.
11 *New Fetter Lane, London, EC4.*
© 1972 *Methuen & Co. Ltd.*
except Ch. 6 © 1972 *Brian Vickers*
Printed in Gt. Britain
by T. & A. Constable Ltd.
Hopetoun Street, Edinburgh

SBN 416 75960 2

Distributed in the USA by
HARPER & ROW PUBLISHERS INC
BARNES & NOBLE IMPORT DIVISION

Contents

page

Preface   vii

1   Donne's Reputation   1
    A. J. Smith

2   The Circulation of Donne's Poems in Manuscript   28
    Alan MacColl

3   *Musa Iocosa Mea*: Thoughts on the *Elegies*   47
    Roma Gill

4   Thinking and Feeling in the Songs and Sonnets   73
    Barbara Hardy

5   The Dismissal of Love   89
    A. J. Smith

6   The 'Songs and Sonnets' and the Rhetoric of   132
    Hyperbole
    Brian Vickers

7   'As Through a Looking-glass'   175
    Margaret M. McGowan

8   Not, Siren-like, to tempt   219
    Brian Morris

9   Donne and the Limits of Lyric   259
    John Hollander

10 Courtiers out of Horace   273
    Howard Erskine-Hill

11 Donne and the Poetry of Patronage   308
    Patricia Thomson

CONTENTS

12   Hermetic Elements in Donne's Poetic Vision   324
      Eluned Crawshaw

13   More Machiavellian than Machiavel   349
      Sydney Anglo

14   The *Devotions* Now   385
      D. W. Harding

15   John Donne's *Critique of True Religion*   404
      Dominic Baker-Smith

16   Donne's Sermon to the Virginia Company   433
      W. Moelwyn Merchant

      Index   453

Preface

John Donne was born in London between January and June 1572. As far as records tell this is the first time a centenary of his birth has been celebrated or as much as remarked. One can't conceive now that a time will come again when the names of Shakespeare, Milton, Wordsworth, Keats are honoured but the name of Donne is not.

In 1931 a notable collection of critical essays commemorated the tercentenary of Donne's death. Introducing that *Garland for John Donne* its editor, Theodore Spencer, said that he had aimed at 'partiality to contemporary interests' as a way of expressing the peculiar debt of gratitude his generation owed to Donne; for 'not all of Donne's activities really concern us'. Four decades later our emphasis has noticeably shifted, partly no doubt because we can now take our debt to the poet for granted. We pay homage to John Donne in 1972 by trying to see him as he was and see him whole. Most of the collaborators in the present volume have set themselves to relate Donne's writing to the circumstances in which he produced them. Had it proved possible there would have been consideration, as well, of other aspects of his work which have been too little regarded up to now, not just for the sake of completeness but because they seem important to a shaping vision such as we are only just beginning to glimpse in Donne.

Studies of Marvell and other seventeenth-century poets have shown us how much their poems need a historical context. Donne's writing too is intimately involved with the life of its time. No one in our century has much attended to *Satyres II* and *V*, the *Metempsychosis*, the complimentary verse letters, the funeral poems, perhaps because these writings quite peremptorily point us to Donne's society and the impulses, realised and unrealised, which moved it. Those contributors to the collection that follows who work in other disciplines than

English literature amply show what literary studies have to gain by seeking help elsewhere. With luck there might have been more of them, and a more consistent attempt to follow Donne's imagination back to the life that fed it. But our own demanding times work against completeness. An editor may count his blessings indeed when he has such generous support and interest as his collaborators have shown in this celebration of the quatercentenary of a great writer's birth.

A.J.S.

1

Donne's Reputation

A. J. SMITH

The history of Donne's reputation as a poet is a vivid index of changing critical attitudes over three hundred years.[1] Successive commentators, and times, define themselves for us by what they make of Donne. The following brief sketch says little of the prose writings, whose fortunes of favour, by and large, followed those of the poems even in the middle of the nineteenth century when sermon-fodder was most in demand. Nor does it take account of the manuscript evidence from Donne's own day, such as Mr MacColl discusses elsewhere in this volume. It does try to bring out what is clearly there, a sharp pattern or response in which we too have our place and which may even tell us something about Donne. For perhaps we are too ready to believe that he is the peculiar property of this age. The people who brought him back from oblivion or worse, well over a hundred years ago, deserve our attention though they don't write of him in our terms. Some of the best things ever said about Donne come from the nineteenth century.

The seventeenth century

The record of publication speaks for itself. There were seven editions of Donne's poems in the thirty-six years from 1633 to 1669, three of them within eight years of Donne's death. Another edition, based on 1669, appeared in 1719. After that no one edited the poems afresh for over a hundred and thirty years, though they were reprinted, largely from 1719, in the

[1] Comments on Donne used in this survey have been traced with the help of directions by G. Keynes, A. H. Nethercot, Mrs K. Tillotson, R. G. Howarth, J. E. Duncan, C. W. Moulton, W. Milgate, F. Eldredge and others.

standard collection of old authors such as Bell (1779), Anderson (1793), and Chalmers (1810).

Evidence abounds of Donne's reputation and esteem in his own day. Many other poets borrowed from his work quoting phrases and epithets, using his distinctive traits of diction and the like. John Webster, for one, has more than a dozen such borrowings from Donne in his plays.[1] Some half a dozen contemporary musical settings of his poems survive.[2] Ben Jonson addressed him as 'Donne, the delight of Phoebus, and each Muse' and particularly emphasised the continuing esteem of even his early writings; moreover Jonson of all people sent his own poems to Donne for criticism and the seal of magisterial approval.[3] William Drummond reported that Ben Jonson 'esteemeth John Donne the first poet in the world in some things'.[4] Drummond himself placed Donne 'Second to none, and far from all Second' as a writer of 'Anacreontick Lyricks' though in other kinds of poetry he thought that Donne didn't excel Alexander or Sidney.[5] Other contemporaries evidently found Donne difficult or obscure – King James himself is alleged to have said that 'Dr. Donns verses were like ye peace of God they passed all understanding'[6].

It's the recurrent strain of writers in the 1630s that Donne isn't to be compared with contemporary poets, whose wit and power don't approach his. The Dutch poet Huygens in 1630 spoke of the high esteem in which Donne was held as Dean of St Paul's, and 'still higher for the wealth of his unequalled wit, and yet more incomparable eloquence in the pulpit'[7]. For T.

[1] They are listed in R. W. Dent, *John Webster's Borrowing*, Berkeley and Los Angeles, 1960.

[2] Given in *Poèmes de Donne, Herbert et Crashaw mis en musique par leurs contemporains*, introduced by J. Jacquot, Paris, 1961.

[3] Who shall doubt, DONNE, where I a *Poet* bee,
When I dare send my *Epigrammes* to thee? . . .

[4] *Conversations with Drummond*, in *Ben Jonson*, ed. C. H. Herford and P. Simpson, Oxford, 1925, i, p. 135.

[5] *Heads of a Conversation betwixt the Famous Poet Ben Johnson, and William Drummond of Hawthornden*, January 1619, in Drummond, *Works*, Edinburgh, 1711, p. 226.

[6] Archdeacon Plume, in his notebook. See P. Simpson, letter to *The Times Literary Supplement*, 25 October 1941, p. 531.

[7] See H. J. C. Grierson, *The Poems of John Donne*, Oxford, 1912, ii, p. lxxvii.

Pestell around 1633 Donne was the 'Black prince of witts'.[1] 'Incomparable' is the strain of the funeral elegies which celebrated his death in 1631; in them his brother poets not only laud his wit, secular and divine alike, in high hyperbole but speak of him as a man whose authority and standing as a poet and preacher are unique and unquestionable. The 'Printer to the Understanders' which prefaced the 1633 edition of the poems said simply that the best judgements in England take it for granted that Donne's poems are 'the best in this kinde, that ever this Kingdome hath yet seene'.[2] Carew put Donne above Virgil, Lucan, Tasso in poetic worth.[3]

Walton published his *Life of Donne* in 1640 and in it reported the opinion of some critics that no Greek or Latin poet ever equalled 'A Valediction: forbidding Mourning'.[4] Cowley's *Mistress*, 1647, has dozens of echoes of Donne and clear imitations of him too.[5] Dryden's *Upon the Death of Lord Hastings*, 1649, drew heavily upon Donne. For the editor of the Cartwright memorial edition in 1651 Donne was 'The highest Poet our Language can boast of'.[6] In 1652 Pestell called Donne the '*Prince of Wits*' who 'rapt Earth round with *Love* and was its *Sun*'.[7] For J. Collop in 1656 he was 'our Seraphick Donne'.[8] And in fact Donne was still familiarly quoted and praised on all sides down through the 1650s.

Shipman hailed Cowley in 1667 as dividing the field of poetic fame with Donne and Waller; but Cowley, he said, 'Outglitters *Waller*, and ev'n dazzles *Donne*'.[9] A year later Dryden remarked that Donne gives us 'deep thoughts in common language, though rough cadence'[10]; and attitudes to Donne

---

1 'Elegie on the noble Eliz: Countess of Hunt.', in *The Poems of Thomas Pestell*, ed. H. Buchan, Oxford, 1940, p. 7.
2 Grierson, i. p. 1.
3 'In Answer of an Elegaical Letter upon the Death of the King of Sweden.'
4 Published with Donne's *LXXX Sermons*. Ed. G. Saintsbury (1927), 1950, p. 42.
5 See J. Sparrow, *The Mistress, with other select Poems of Abraham Cowley 1618-1667*, 1962, especially p. xvi.
6 *To the Reader*, in *Comedies, Tragi-Comedies, with other Poems*.
7 *Preface to Benlowe's Theophila, ed. cit.*, pp. 83-4.
8 *Poesis Rediviva: or, Poesie Reviv'd*, 1656, A3ʳ
9 'Gratitude. 1667', in *Carolina, or, Loyal Poems*, 1683, pp. 120-2.
10 *An Essay of Dramatic Poesy*, 1668, ed. G. Watson, 1962, i. p. 40.

had clearly begun to change. E. Phillips in 1675 said that Donne's 'more brisk and Youthful Poems' are 'rather commended for the heighth of Fancy and acuteness of conceit, then for the smoothness of the Verse'.[1] R. Wolseley in 1685 advised the would-be poet that his verses should walk like Virgil's or run like Ovid's not 'stand stock still like Dr. Donne's'.[2] The anonymous preface to *The Second Part of Mr Waller's Poems*, 1690, advised anyone who wanted to see how harsh and untunable English poetry was before Waller to 'read ten lines in *Donne*, and he'll be quickly convinc'd'.[3]

W. Walsh in 1692 seems to anticipate Johnson when he allowed Donne great wit but denied him much feeling: 'Never was there a more copious Fancy or greater reach of Wit, than what appears in Dr. Donne', he said, but in common with other wits Donne lacks 'softness, Tenderness, and Violence of Passion'.[4] Such distinctions perhaps clarify Dryden's celebrated judgment in the same year – 'Doctor Dunn the greatest Wit, though not the best Poet of our Nation'.[5] Dryden kept coming back to distinguish between Donne's native talent and his manner of writing, as when he used Donne as a foil to the Earl of Dorset in a flattering address in 1693: 'Donne alone, of all our countrymen, had your talent, but he was not happy enough to arrive at your versification; and were he translated into numbers, and English, he would yet be wanting in the dignity of expression . . . you equal Donne in the variety, multiplicity, and choice of thoughts; you excel him in the manner and the words'.[6] Plainly there's more here even than a sense that Donne is by now an old and outmoded author. Dryden looks at him across the gulf that separates modern English from the older mode of the language and can say of the writers of his own day that 'if we are not so great wits as Donne, yet certainly we are better

---

[1] *Theatrum Poetarum*, pp. 106-7.
[2] Preface to Rochester's *Valentinian*, 1685, b3*b*.   [3] A6.
[4] *Letters and Poems, Amorous and Gallant* (1692), 1716, p. 338.
[5] 'To the Right Honourable the Earl of Abingdon &c', *Eleonora: A Panegyrical Poem* . . .
[6] *A Discourse concerning the Original and Progress of Satire*, 1693, ed. G. Watson, 1962, ii, p. 75.

poets'.[1] Being better poets had to do with decorum too, and expectations seem to have much changed when Dryden can tell the Earl of Dorset that he reads him and Donne 'with the same admiration, but not with the same delight. He affects the metaphysics not only in his satires but in his amorous verses, where nature only should reign; and perplexes the minds of the fair sex with nice speculations of philosophy, when he should engage their hearts, and entertain them with the softnesses of love.'[2] By 1697, when C. Wernicke contradicted Hofmann-swaldau's account of the most noted English poets, the gulf seems absolute: 'Of the English writers he mentions with admiration Donn and Quarles, whom no Englishman ever reads'.[3]

The eighteenth century

Apart from Tonson's edition of the poems in 1719 and the inclusion of the poems in Bell's and Anderson's collections there wasn't much to keep Donne before the public in the eighteenth century. Pope 'versified' two of Donne's *Satyres* (*II* and *IV*) about 1713, and published revised versions separately in 1733 and 1735. Parnell 'versified' *Satyre III* before 1718.

Pope wrote to Wycherley in 1706 that 'Donne . . . had infinitely more Wit than he wanted Versification: for the great dealers in Wit, like those in Trade, take least Pains to set off their Goods'.[4] *The Guardian* in 1713 made Donne's excess of wit itself a matter for censure: 'But of all our Countrymen, none are more defective in their Songs, through a Redundancy of Wit, than Dr. Donne and Mr. Cowley.' Donne's wit dazzles the reader's attention by 'the continual sparkling' of the imagination so that you find 'a new Design started in almost every Line, and you come to the end, without the Satisfaction of seeing anyone of them executed'.[5]

---

[1] *Ibid.*, ii, p. 144.

[2] *Ibid.*, ii, p. 76.

[3] *Auf die Schlesische Poeten.* Hofmannswaldau had spoken of the 'learning, art and elegance' to be found in 'the religious poems of Quarles and Don' among other works (preface to *Deutsch Übersetzurgen und Gedïchte,* 1679). See G. Waterhouse, *The Literary Relations of England and Germany in the Seventeenth Century,* 1914, p. 119.

[4] *The Correspondence of Alexander Pope,* ed. G. Sherburn, Oxford, 1956, i, p. 16.

[5] XVI, Monday 30 March, 1713.

Adverse criticism now began to harden into dismissal, as when Oldmixon censured seventeenth-century preachers and poets alike for punning and buffoonery: 'Thus it was that Dr. *Donne* and Mr. *Cowley* confounded Metaphysicks and Love, and turn'd Wit into Point'.[1] By 1728 Oldmixon could cite Donne as an example of a wit who subtilises so much that he loses himself in his own thoughts, and whose extravagance is such that 'there's hardly any Thing that's agreeable, or one Stroke which has any Likeness to Nature'. In good Johnsonian fashion Oldmixon found 'The Broken Heart' an extraordinary way of writing about falling in love; and his comment on the last four stanzas of 'A Valediction: forbidding Mourning' is worth pondering: 'What Woman's Heart in the World could stand out against such an Attack as this, after she once understood how to handle a Pair of Compasses'.[2]

In 1730 Spence reported Pope's comment that 'Donne had no imagination, but as much wit I think as any writer can possibly have', and that Davenant was a better poet than Donne.[3] Spence's own view was uncompromising. About 1732–3 he wrote a brief historical account of English poetry which held Donne up as one of the chief architects of the bad taste of the previous century when 'All was full of plays on words, of glittering thoughts, of strange comparisons and of outlandish metaphors'. It was in this 'interregnum of good sense' that Donne stood as the Prince of Wit so that he is full of 'a puerile affectation of seeking to say something fine' and 'the majority of his pieces are nothing but a tissue of epigrams'. Donne's versification was very bad too, Spence thought.[4] Warburton, commenting on Pope's version of *Satyres II* and *IV*, said that in Donne's originals 'the lines have nothing more of numbers than their being composed of a certain quantity of syllables'. Yet Warburton held that *Satyre III* is 'the noblest work not only of this but perhaps of any satiric poet'.[5]

---

[1] *The Arts of Logick and Rhetoric*, 1728, p. vi.

[2] *Ibid.*, p. 333.

[3] *Spence's Anecdotes*, ed. J. M. Osborne, Oxford, 1966, i, p. 187–9.

[4] *Quelques Remarques Hist: sur les Poets Anglois*, Given in J. M. Osborne, 'The First History of English Poetry', in *Pope and his Contemporaries*, ed. J. L. Clifford and L. A. Landa, Oxford, 1949, p. 247.   [5] *Pope's Works*, 1766, iv, p. 241.

Theobald took up the attack on the vicious wit of Shakespeare's age whose faults he traced to an 'ostentatious Affection of abstruse Learning' such as Donne notably exemplified: 'Thus became the Poetry of DONNE (tho' the wittiest Man of that Age,) nothing but a continued Heap of Riddles'.[1]

John Wesley appears to be one reader to whom Donne still meant something, for he wrote some lines from *A Hymne to God the Father* in his journal during a sea voyage from America in 1738.[2] Moses Browne introducing an edition of Walton's *Compleat Angler* in 1750 went as far as to speak of Donne as one 'whose Writings are at this day very justly admired',[3] but he gave no indication of who actually admired them.

Birch in 1753 said that Donne's poetical works 'show a prodigious fund of genius under the disguise of an affected and obscure style and most inharmonious versification'.[4] In Hume's *History of England*, 1754–62, Donne again appears as a striking example of the prevailing bad taste and decadence of his times; Hume allows Donne's satires some flashes of wit and ingenuity, 'but these totally suffocated and buried by the hardest and most uncouth expression that is any-where to be met with'.[5] Joseph Warton, 1756, allowed that Donne and Swift 'were undoubtedly men of wit, and men of sense'; but he asked 'what traces have they left of PURE POETRY?'.[6] And he later condemned Donne altogether as a corrupter of taste, reprehensible not only in his numbers but because 'He abounds in false thoughts, in far-sought sentiments, in forced unnatural conceits. He was the corrupter of Cowley.'[7] In the same year a reviewer of Warton's book rounded on Warton for attributing any poetical genius at all to one who had in fact left no trace of pure poetry: 'Did any man with a poetical ear, ever yet read ten lines of Donne without disgust? or are there ten lines of poetry in all his works? No.'[8]

---

[1] *Preface to the Works of Shakespeare*, 1734, p. xlvi.
[2] Entry for 24 January 1738. See M. W. England and J. Sparrow, *Hymns Unbidden*, New York, 1966, p. 3.
[3] p. vi.
[4] *The Life of the Most Reverend Dr John Tillotson*, pp. 26-7.
[5] 1813, vi, p. 171-5.
[6] *An Essay on the Writings and Genius of Pope*, 1756, i, p. iv.
[7] *Op. cit.*, 1782, ii, pp. 353-4.
[8] *The Monthly Review*, XIV, Jan.-June 1756, p. 535.

A. Kippis in the *Biographia Britannica*, 1778, as emphatically answered 'Yes', and cited the last four stanzas of 'A Valediction: forbidding Mourning' as 'sixteen lines which, notwithstanding their quaintness, may be read without disgust, and have in them a true spirit of poetry'. But Kippis also remarked of Donne that 'none of his poetical works are read at present', and he allowed that his versification is 'intolerably harsh'.[1] In 1776 Bishop Hurd spoke of 'a great Poet of the last century, I mean Dr. DONNE', and praised the *Metempsychosis*, as well as a simile from *Satyre V* (lines 28-30).[2]

Samuel Johnson used Donne as one of the sources of words for his Dictionary, 1755, though his quotations from Donne are sparse indeed compared with those from Shakespeare, Dryden, Milton, and even Spenser and Sidney. Some twenty-five years later, in 1779-81, Johnson gave examples from Donne in a celebrated account of metaphysical poetry, setting them out to show their extravagant ingenuity with such comments as 'Confusion worse confounded', 'Who but Donne would have thought that a good man is a telescope?', and, once, 'too scholastic [but] . . . not inelegant'. Johnson's comment on the last sixteen lines of 'A Valediction: forbidding Mourning' is typical: 'To the following comparison of a man that travels and his wife that stays at home with a pair of compasses, it may be doubted whether absurdity or ingenuity has the better claim'. And he concluded that 'In all these examples it is apparent that whatever is improper or vicious is produced by a voluntary deviation from nature in pursuit of something new and strange, and that the writers fail to give delight by their desire of exciting admiration'.[3]

V. Knox in 1787 returned to Donne's supposed roughness of verse and 'harsh numbers', remarking that 'It is scarcely possible that a writer who did not studiously avoid a smooth versification could have written so many lines without stumbling on a good one'. Knox characterised Donne, with Jonson and Cowley, as poets who neglected the graces of composition and 'will therefore soon be numbered among those celebrated

---

[1] pp. 334-8.   [2] *Horatius Flaccus*, pp. 97-8.
[3] *Life of Cowley*, in *The Lives of the English Poets*, ed. G. Birkbeck Hill, Oxford, 1905, i, pp. 18-35.

writers, whose utility now consists in filling a vacancy on the upper shelf of some dusty and deserted library'.[1]

Donne evidently wasn't easily accessible reading at the time in any case for one finds Cowper, who was proud of his connection with Donne's family, asking a relative to bring Donne's poems with him when he visits 'for I have not seen them many years, and should like to look them over'.[2] Anderson introduced Donne's poems in 1793 as full of wit and subtlety, and displaying a prodigious richness of fancy and elaborate minuteness of description – 'but his thoughts are seldom natural, obvious, or just, and much debased by the carelessness of his versification'.[3] Right at the end of the century one Nathan Drake tried to dismiss Donne for good as one who utterly neglected the attempt to please, whose 'dissonance and discord' it is 'scarce possible for a human ear to endure', and whose thoughts are hardly worth the decoration Pope gave them.[4]

It is revealing enough in any case, and quite typical of the time, that Drake appeared to know Donne only as a satirist. When he returned to the corpse some twenty years later he at least recognised that Donne had produced more than that, but his opinion of him hadn't changed: 'A more refined age, however, and a more chastised taste, have very justly consigned his poetical labours to the shelf of the philologer. A total want of harmony in versification, and a total want of simplicity both in thought and expression, are the vital defects of Donne. Wit he has in abundance, and even erudition, but they are miserably misplaced; and even his amatory pieces exhibit little else than cold conceits and metaphysical subtleties. He may be considered as one of the principal establishers of a school of poetry founded on the worst Italian model. . . .'[5]

The nineteenth century

Detractions of Donne on the familiar eighteenth-century lines, as a representative of the decadence of his times, a corrupter of

---

[1] *Essays, Moral and Literary*, iii, pp. 167-8 and 440.
[2] Letter to John Johnson, 31 July 1790, in *The Correspondence of William Cowper*, ed. T. Wright, 1904, iii, p. 478.   [3] *Poets of Great Britain*, iv, pp. 3-5.
[4] *Literary Hours, or Sketches Critical and Narrative*, 1798, p. 170.
[5] *Shakespeare and his Times*, 1817, i, p. 615.

taste, a crude versifier, a frigid wit-monger, persist throughout the nineteenth century though they soon begin to look reactionary and out of touch in a very different climate of opinion. In the Coleridge circle itself Kirke White[1] and Southey found extravagant new ways of putting the old charges. Southey thought that 'Nothing indeed could have made Donne a poet, unless as great a change had been worked in the internal structure of his ears, as was wrought in elongating those of Midas'.[2] Twenty-four years later Southey included over thirty of Donne's poems in an anthology but he ventured a moral judgement on the rest, saying that Donne's son 'would have shown himself more worthy of such a father, if he had destroyed a considerable part of them'.[3]

In 1814 Sir E. Brydges spoke of Donne's 'metaphysical subtlety, and tasteless and unfeeling ingenuity' which produced 'execrable distortions in him and his imitators so opposite to all that is attractive or valuable in the Muse.'[4] J. Fry in the same year commented that Donne had 'long been deservedly forgotten', and spoke of his poetry as 'worthless trash' – 'Donne never can be admired, nor ever obtain a second perusal from any mind imbued with the slightest particle of taste, or fancy, or feeling.'[5] Thomas Campbell in 1819, giving three Donne poems and a fragment of another in an anthology, thought that Donne 'addresses the object of his real tenderness with ideas that outrage decorum' and adds 'The life of Donne is more interesting than his poetry'; but he does find, too, 'a beauty of thought which at intervals rises from his chaotic imagination, like the form of Venus smiling on the waters'.[6] Hazlitt considered that Donne lacked Cowley's fancy and spoke of the poems as harsh, disagreeable, full of thoughts 'delivered by the Caesarian operation. The sentiments, profound and tender as they often are, are stifled in the expression; and "heaved pantingly forth" are "buried quick again" under the ruins and

---

[1] See *Melancholy Hours*, in *Remains*, ed. R. Southey, 1806, ii, p. 286.
[2] *Specimens of the Later English Poets*, 1807, pp. xxiv-xxv.
[3] *Select Works of the British Poets from Chaucer to Jonson*, 1831, pp. 714-31.
[4] *Restituta; or, Titles, Extracts, and Characters of Old Books in English Revived*, ii, p. 9.
[5] *Pieces of Ancient Poetry, from unpublished manuscripts and scarce books*, 1814, p. 76.
[6] *Specimens of the British Poets*, iii, p. 73.

rubbish of analytical distinctions' (1819).[1] G. H. Lewes thought Donne's writings a 'wondrous mind-fragment' and praised his wit, subtlety, fancy; but only after finding that his poems 'are not really poems at all' and that in them there is 'an almost total deficiency of imagination, or any feeling of art'.[2]

Literary historians, notably one 'M. M. D.',[3] Hallam,[4] Taine (1863-4),[5] and Welsh[6] continued to relate Donne's writings to the manners and morals of a corrupt era in Europe altogether. Welsh was typical in finding little to admire in Donne and nothing to love, for 'farfetched, similes extravagant metaphors, are not here occasional blemishes, but the substance. He should have given us simple images, simply expressed; for he loved and suffered much: but fashion was stronger than nature'. As late as 1900 R. P. Halleck dismissed Donne as a decadent,[7] and an anonymous reviewer in *The Quarterly* thought him 'more a rhetorician than a poet'.[8] F. E. Schelling put this kind of pseudo-judgement in its place in 1910: 'We may give over expectation of a time when popular histories of literature will not discuss "the metaphysical poets" in eloquent passages expanded from Dr Johnson's "Life of Cowley"'.[9]

It was still possible in 1853 for an intending editor of the poems, Barron Field, to speak of them as 'so little read'[10]; and C. D. Cleveland only three years before that said that Donne is 'almost entirely forgotten'.[11] But by then such remarks were beginning to rebound on their makers.

[1] *Lectures on the English Comic Writers*, in *Complete Works*, ed. P. P. Howe, 1930-4, vi, pp. 49-53.

[2] 'Retrospective Reviews. – No. VII. Donne's Poetical Works', *The National Magazine and Monthly Critic*, ix, April 1838, pp. 374-8.

[3] 'Essay on the Genius of Cowley, Donne and Cleveland', *The European Magazine*, August 1822, pp. 108-12.

[4] *Introduction to the Literature of Europe*, 1837-9, iii, pp. 488-95.

[5] *Histoire de la litterature anglaise*, transl. H. van Laun, Edinburgh, 1872, pp. 201-5.

[6] *The Development of English Literature and Language*, 1882, i, pp. 413.

[7] *A History of English Literature*, p. 186.

[8] 'John Donne and his Contemporaries', *The Quarterly Review*, cxcii, 1900, pp. 220-35.

[9] *English Literature during the Lifetime of Shakespeare*, 1910, p. 364.

[10] See R. F. Brinkley, *Coleridge on the Seventeenth Century*, 1955, pp. 519-20.

[11] *A Compendium of English Literature*, 1850, p. 165.

For these adverse opinions were quite overborne by the sheer volume and vehemence of interest in Donne's writing. Unquestionably it was the nineteeth century that rediscovered Donne, and one sees the drastic change almost as soon as the century turned. Lamb is said to have read Donne to his friends with his face suffused with passion.[1] Coleridge astounded his guests at Highbury with his admiration for such poems as the *Metempsychosis*,[2] which he shared with De Quincey and Browning among the later writers.

The marginal annotations Coleridge made in Lamb's copy of Donne in 1811 show a quality of understanding and sympathy that is altogether new and, in fact, not of an age but for all time. He assumed Donne's greatness and uniqueness without question and didn't hesitate to put him with Shakespeare and Milton in some respects, though he thought him equally capable of grandeur and 'execrable stuff'. His admiration for particular poems or bits of poems is unbounded – 'One of my favourite poems' ("The Canonisation"); 'I should never find fault with metaphysical poems, were they all like this, or but half as excellent' ("The Exstasie"); 'I am tired of expressing my admiration; else I could not have passed by "The Will", "The Blossom", and "The Primrose", with "The Relique"; 'An admirable poem, which none but Donne could have written' ("A Valediction: forbidding Mourning"); 'A grand poem' ("The Undertaking"); 'But for the last stanza, I would use this poem as my Love-creed' ("Loves Deitie").

Coleridge's private jottings weren't published until 1853[3] but he championed Donne privately and publicly throughout his life in terms that went flat counter to Johnson. There's plenty more evidence that Donne was coming back into people's familiar lives. Jane Austen's brother took a famous phrase from *The second Anniversary* to describe his dead sister, in 1817[4]; George Eliot used stanzas from two of the *Songs and Sonnets*

---

[1] W. Hazlitt, 'Persons one would wish to have seen', *Complete Works*, ed. P. P. Howe, 1930-4, xvii, pp. 124-5.

[2] See *A Memoir of Baron Hatherley*, ed. W. R. W. Stephens, 1883, i, pp. 51-2.

[3] In *Notes Theological*, 1853, pp. 249-55, and *The Literary World*, New York, 1853, xii, pp. 349-50, 393, 433.

[4] Henry Austen, *Biographical Notice of the Author*, prefixed to *Northanger Abbey* and *Persuasion*, 1818. Austen dates it 13 December 1817.

as chapter-mottoes in *Middlemarch*, 1871-2, ascribing them to 'Dr. Donne'[1]; an anonymous author, talking to his children about the English poets in 1841, praised Donne's 'rich and picturesque fancy'[2]; Robert Browning and Elizabeth Barrett used fragments of Donne almost as a private code in their early correspondence and when they were planning their elopement, 1845-6[3]; Thoreau read Donne during a trip on the Concord and Merrimack Rivers in 1849 and quoted him several times in the book he wrote about the journey;[4] Longfellow, visiting Lowell in 1846, read Donne while his host went down to feed the chickens.[5] Landor, Wordsworth, Tennyson, Fitzgerald, and Yeats were among those who said they admired particular poems or aspects of Donne's writing.[6] D. G. Rossetti wrote to W. M. Rossetti in 1880, 'I have been enjoying Donne, who is full of excellences, and not brimming but rather spilling with quaintnesses'.[7]

More striking is the fact that further notable champions of Donne now declared themselves. Emerson got interested in his poetry as an undergraduate at Harvard in 1815, and some fifty-four years later included selections from him in programmes of readings he gave at Chickerings Hall.[8] J. R. Lowell's devotion

---

1 The last three stanzas of 'The Undertaking' for Chapter xxxix, lines 8-11 of 'The Good-morrow' for Chapter lxxxiii.

2 *Lectures on the English Poets*, pp. 27-8.

3 *The Letters of Robert Browning and Elizabeth Barrett Barrett, 1845-6*, ed. R. B. Browning, 1899, i, pp. 27, 145, 196; ii, p. 116.

4 *A Week on the Concord and Merrimack Rivers*, 1849. Thoreau quotes from *To the Countess of Huntingdon* ('That unripe side of earth'), and both *Anniversaries*.

5 Diary entry for 29 May 1846. In S. Longfellow, *The Life of Henry Wadsworth Longfellow*, Boston, 1886, ii, p. 40.

6 W. S. Landor, An *Imaginary Conversation* between Walton, Cotton, and Old-ways, in *Complete Works*, ed. T. E. Welby and S. Wheeler, 1927-36, iv, pp.164-71, *The Letters of William and Dorothy Wordsworth: the later years*, ed. E. de Selincourt, Oxford, 1939, ii, p. 652. 'Personal Recollections by F. T. Palgrave' in H. Tennyson, *Alfred Lord Tennyson: A Memoir by his Son*, 1897, ii, p. 503. *The Letters and Literary Remains of Edward Fitzgerald*, ed. W. A. Wright, 1902, ii, pp. 132-3. *The Letters of W. B. Yeats*, ed. A. Wade, 1954, pp. 570-1.

7 Letter of Sunday 22 February 1880. In *Dante Gabriel Rossetti: His Family Letters, with a Memoir by William Michael Rossetti*, 1895, ii, p. 356.

8 Letter to William Emerson, 2 and 3 June 1815, in *The Letters of Ralph Waldo Emerson*, ed. R. L. Rusk, New York, 1939, i, p. 10. For the programmes at Chickerings Hall see *Letters*, vi, pp. 52-3.

to Donne, consummated finally in the Grolier Club edition of 1895, expressed itself in casual quotations and references everywhere in his writings and in some memorable things he said about the poetry. Lowell thought that Donne wrote 'more profound verses than any other English poet save one only'.[1] Donne is 'one of the subtlest and most self-irradiating minds that ever sought an outlet in verse', and 'full of salient verses that would take the rudest March winds of criticism with their beauty'. One such verse is 'A bracelet of bright hair about the bone' ('The Relique'), which 'still shines there in the darkness of the tomb after two centuries, like one of those inextinguishable lamps whose secret is lost. . . . To open vistas for the imagination through the blind wall of the senses, as he could sometimes do, is the supreme function of poetry.'[2]

Swinburne frequently referred to Donne after being bowled over by the *Anniversaries*, which he thought 'a magnificent and enthralling poem. . . . overflowing with glories of thought and word . . . rich in deep grave harmonies of splendid and sonorous sadness'.[3] As Lowell had done he wondered at the arbitrariness of literary reputation, which made Gray's odes 'familiar to thousands who know nothing of Donne's *Anniversaries*. . . . And yet it is certain that in fervour of inspiration, in depth and force and glow of thoughts and emotion and expression, Donne's verses are . . . far above Gray's.'[4]

But by far the most zealous – indeed notorious – of Donne's champions in the nineteenth century was the poet whom his contemporary critics so often (and so misguidedly) compared with Donne, Robert Browning. As a boy, we're told, he essayed a musical setting of 'Goe, and catche a falling starre'.[5] His devotion to Donne must soon have become public knowledge for in 1842 someone presented him with a copy of the 1719

[1] 'James Gate Percival', in *The Writings of James Russell Lowell*, Riverside edition, 1890, ii, p. 160.

[2] 'Wordsworth', *Writings*, vi, pp. 107-8. 'Shakespeare Once More', *Writings*, iii, p. 35. 'Dryden', *Writings*, iii, pp. 107 and 170-1.

[3] Letter v, to Theodore Watts-Dunton, 15 March 1876. In *Autobiographical Notes by Algernon Charles Swinburne*, ed. T. J. Wise, 1920, p. 19.

[4] *A Study of Ben Jonson*, 1889, p. 129.

[5] A. Orr, *Life and Letters of Robert Browning*, 1908, p. 41.

edition of Donne's poems,[1] and a few years later Elizabeth Barrett spoke of 'your Donne' when she wrote to him.[2] We hear of his impressing London literary circles with his curious admirations, 'Coming out once with a long, crabbedly fine screed from John Donne' (the *Elegie on Mistris Boulstred* in fact)[3] or speaking 'with great enthusiasm of a poem by Donne named *Metempsychosis*.'[4] In *The Two Poets of Croisic*, 1878, Browning actually incorporated three lines of the *Metempsychosis* in a stanza which expresses humble reverence for their author:

> Better and truer verse none ever wrote . . .
> Than thou, revered and magisterial Donne.

And in a pseudo-historical knockabout called *Epps*, 1886, he compared his own pipe with the 'trumpet-sound' of Donne and (oddly) Dekker.[5] In some ways we don't seem to have caught up yet with these nineteenth century enthusiasms for the sonorous and magisterial Donne, perhaps because Grierson didn't share or communicate them. A reviewer of the edition of 1912, reprehending the editor for being out of sympathy with some sides of Donne, slipped in a claim that hasn't been much heard in this century: 'He misses the point of that superb and extraordinary satiric poem "The Progress of the Soul", and he undervalues "The Second Anniversary", one of the greatest long poems in English'.[6]

Plainly the new spirit of the nineteenth century brought in a revival of serious concern with Donne's writing which expresses itself in more formal ways too. Despite the lack of a good text, poems and bits of poems by Donne soon began to appear in

[1] It came up for sale at Sotheby's in May 1913 among the effects of R. W. B. Browning who had died in the previous year, and is listed in the catalogue of the sale – *The Browning Collections*, 1913.

[2] *Letters, loc. cit.* She herself wrote of Donne as one 'having a dumb angel, and knowing more noble poetry than he articulates'. *The Book of the Poets, 1842-63*, in *Life, Letters and Essays*, New York, 1887, ii, p. 50.

[3] S. Colvin, *Memories and Notes of Persons and Places, 1852-1912*, 1921, p. 82.

[4] W. M. Rossetti, diary entry for 7 January 1869. In *Rossetti Papers 1862-70*, ed. W. M. Rossetti, 1903, p. 378.

[5] First printed in the *Cornhill Magazine*, and the *New York Outlook*, October 1913. Given in F. G. Kenyon, *New Poems by Robert Browning and Elizabeth Barrett Browning*, 1914, pp. 56-9.

[6] 'John Donne, the Elizabethan', *The Nation*, 15 February 1913, pp. 825-6.

anthologies. *Elegy: Loves Warre* was published for the first time ever in 1802.[1] Bits of verse letters and samples of the Divine Poems came up in collections from the first decade of the century on. When Dyce was putting together his *Specimens of English Sonnets*, 1833, Wordsworth wrote to him and advised the inclusion of 'Death be not proud' which, said Dyce, 'he thought very fine'.[2] An anthology of sacred poetry in 1836 devoted some twenty-three pages to Donne's verse,[3] and *The Book of Gems* in the same year gave nine of the *Songs and Sonnets*.[4] There was a whole volume of selections from Donne published at Oxford in 1840.[5] Sir J. Simeon published what he took to be some twenty hitherto unpublished pieces by Donne in 1856-7.[6] Thereafter Donne turned up regularly in the anthologies and his religious poetry in particular got a very good showing. Palgrave omitted him from *The Golden Treasury* in 1861 but included him in his *Treasury of Sacred Song* (1889); and marks on Palgrave's copy of Grosart's edition of the poems show that he considered him for the second series of *The Golden Treasury* (1896).[7]

There was a growing concern with the text of all Donne's writings and with getting right the facts of his life and career. As early as 1820 J. P. Collier had some characters in a dialogue discuss at length the printed texts and known manuscripts of Donne's poetry, and one of them says that he has made an attempt at collation which enables him to correct some bad

---

[1] By F. G. Waldron in *A Collection of Miscellaneous Poetry*.

[2] What Wordsworth actually wrote was that the sonnet 'is so eminently characteristic of his manner, and at the same time so weighty in thought and vigorous in the expression, that I would entreat you to insert it, though to modern ears it may be repulsive, quaint, and laboured'. *The Letters of William and Dorothy Wordsworth: the later years*, ed. E. de Selincourt, Oxford, 1939, ii, p. 652.

[3] R. Cattermole and H. Stebbing, *Sacred Poetry of the Seventeenth Century*, ii, 1836.

[4] Ed. S. C. Hall.

[5] *Selections from the Works of John Donne D.D.*, Oxford, 1840.

[6] *Unpublished Poems of Donne*, in *Miscellanies of the Philobiblon Society*, iii, 1856-7, pp. 8-9.

[7] The marks occur chiefly against the Divine Poems, three of which Palgrave included in his *Treasury of Sacred Song*, 1889. But there are pencilled crosses on the 'Song. Sweetest love, I do not goe' and 'The Anniversarie', and vertical lines against the first stanza of 'The Anniversarie' and lines 13-20 of 'The Exstasie'.

readings in the 1633 edition.[1] Henry Alford published his edition of the *Works of Donne* in six volumes in 1839. Barron Field prepared an edition of the *Songs and Sonnets* for the Percy Society about 1853, though the project failed and the work remained in manuscript.[2] Jessop published an edition of the *Essay in Divinity* in 1855. Two editions of the poems came out in America some thirty-six years apart, one of them, in 1819, based on the 1719 edition, but the other, in 1855, a genuine attempt to edit the text afresh from some of the early printed versions.[3] Throughout the second half of the century collectors and students of the manuscripts were preparing the way for an adequate edition of all the poems – Dyce, O'Flaherty, Lord Houghton, Gosse, Dowden, Norton, and others. In 1868 W. C. Hazlitt, publishing a note of some variant readings between an unnamed manuscript and the 1669 edition of Donne's poems, called for 'some competent person' to undertake 'A good edition of Donne . . . *con amore*'; and he was answered by 'Cpl' (probably the Rev. T. R. O'Flaherty of Capel near Dorking), who said that he had 'made large collections for his life and works, but I cannot find time or courage to carry out my intention'.[4]

In 1872-3 the Rev. A. B. Grosart produced his edition of the poems, which he dedicated to Browning, 'The Poet of The Century For Thinkers', and introduced as an unashamed attempt to restore a right opinion of 'Donne's incomparable genius'. Other editions quickly followed: by Lowell and Norton in 1895, and E. K. Chambers – with Saintsbury's near-idolatrous introduction – in 1896. Jessop published a short life of Donne in 1897, and two years later Gosse brought out his *Life and Letters of John Donne* which hasn't even yet been altogether superseded.

The sheer bulk of writing about Donne in the nineteenth century is impressive evidence of a new kind of interest in him.

---

[1] *The Poetical Decameron or Ten Conversations on English Poets and Poetry* . . ., 1820, i, pp. 153-60.

[2] See R. F. Brinkley, *Coleridge on the Sevententh Century*, 1955, pp. 519-20.

[3] *The Works of the British Poets with Lives of their Authors*, ed. E. Sanford, Philadelphia, 1819. *The Poetical Works of Dr John Donne*, Boston, 1855.

[4] *Notes and Queries* 1868, pp. 483-4 and 614.

In the literary journals, and in the popular encyclopaedias and magazines too, enthusiasts took him up here and there as an author well worth the earnest consideration of the times. The romantic circumstances of his marriage soon attracted the attention of such sentimentalists as Mrs Jameson, and from her *Memoirs of the Loves of the Poets*, 1829, to Edward Thomas's vastly better *Feminine Influence on the Poets*, 1910, one finds people taking the *Songs and Sonnets* for a direct account of the poet's sentimental life.

But there were some good discussions of the poetry for its own sake, started off by a striking essay in the *Retrospective Review*, 1823, which found Donne very unequal but powerfully imaginative and worthy of comparison with Shakespeare here and there.[1] De Quincey saw Donne as 'the first very eminent rhetorician in the English Literature' (1828), a writer who 'combined – what no other man has ever done – the last sublimation of dialectial subtlety and address with the most impassioned majesty. Massy diamonds compose the very substance of his poem on the Metempsychosis. . . .'[2] *The Penny Cyclopaedia* in 1837 declared that Donne 'had a rich vein of poetry' and that some of his lyrics 'are absolute music'.[3] An article in *Chambers Cyclopaedia of English Literature*, 1844, while repeating the old account of Donne's frigid conceits, yet allowed that his reputation 'has latterly in some degree revived'; and it generously added that 'It seems to be now acknowledged that, amidst much rubbish, there is much real poetry, and that of a high order'.[4] The first number of *Lowe's Edinburgh Magazine*, 1846, inaugurated a 'Gallery of Poets' with a study of Donne which judged that while Donne could never be popular his devotees would always value his poems as 'lumps of precious golden ore, touched here and there, with specks of richest gold'.[5]

More striking evidence of the way things were going is a

---

[1] VIII, 31-55. It is a review of the 1669 edition of Donne's poems.

[2] *Rhetoric*, first published in *Blachwood's Magazine*, XXIV, 1828. In *Collected Writings*, ed. D. Masson, 1897, x, pp. 96-102.

[3] Anon., 'John Donne', IX, p. 85.

[4] Anon., 'John Donne' (1844), 1858, i, pp. 114-15.

[5] Anon., pp. 228-36.

study by J. A. Langford, 'An Evening with John Donne', in *The Working Man's Friend, and Family Instructor*, 1850.[1] The esoteric Donne was now becoming a necessary part of a literary education; even though de Quincey could still speak of him in 1851 as 'a man yet unappreciated'.[2] Accounts in *Temple Bar*, 1861 and 1876,[3] G. MacDonald's *England's Antiphon*, 1868,[4] and *The Athenaeum*, 1873,[5] simply took his stature for granted. W. Minto in an essay on Donne in *The Nineteenth Century*, 1880, said that 'there is no poet of the Shakespearian age to whom it would be more inappropriate to deny the rank of genius, in any conceivable acceptation of the term'.[6] A sentimental rhapsody on Donne in *The Argosy*, 1881, also spoke freely of 'His genius as a poet'.[7] E. Dowden's long lecture on Donne's poetry which was first printed in *The Fortnightly Review*, 1890, started from the proposition that 'The study of a great writer acquires its highest interest only when we view his work as a whole'[8]; and it's evident that the serious academic study of Donne had begun.

An anonymous reviewer of Chamber's edition of the poems in *The Dial*, 1896, declared that 'Whoever can write anything which shall give a true and sufficient idea of John Donne, such an idea as will make the general reader of poetry understand why he is regarded as a poet of surpassing genius, may deem himself no longer an apprentice in the art of criticism'.[9] *The Academy*, 1897, urged its readers to 'read him, read all he wrote, for he is a mine of rough but priceless ore', though it warned them too that the 'typical modern, who wants to lie and let the plums of poetry fall into his mouth, had better hold aloof from

---

[1] Supplementary number for December 1850, pp. 18-21.
[2] 'Lord Carlisle on Pope', first published in *Tait's Magazine*, April to July 1851. In *Collected Writings*, ed. D. Masson, 1889-90, xi, p. 110.
[3] Anon., 'Donne the Metaphysician', *Temple Bar*, III, 1861, pp. 78-89.
Anon., 'The First of the English Satirists', *Temple Bar*, XLVII, 1876, pp. 337-50.
[4] Chapter vii is devoted to an account of Donne's religious poetry.
[5] A. Jessop, 'Donne's Epigrams', pp. 81-2, followed by a controversy with A. B. Grosart and others, pp. 148, 179-80, 210-11.
[6] 'John Donne', VII, pp. 846-63.
[7] A. King, 'John Donne', XXXII, pp. 300-5.
[8] 'The Poetry of John Donne', o.s. LIII, pp. 791-808.
[9] 'Briefs on New Books', XX, p. 280.

Donne'.[1] In the same year an anonymous historian of taste in *The Quarterly Review* very oddly placed Donne with Sterne and Keats as one of the 'Fathers of Literary Impressionism in England'.[2]

Edmund Gosse had a piece on Donne's poetry in *The New Review*, 1893,[3] and devoted a chapter to the poetry in his *Jacobean Poets*, 1894.[4] His biography of Donne (1899) prompted extended discussion of Donne in all the leading literary journals and there's no doubt that Donne had ceased to be an eccentric or an esoteric taste – 'Criticism has come round to the recognition of Donne' (Francis Thompson, 1900).[5] 'His poetry, long forgotten, has in our days again become an influence with poets and students, if not with general readers'.[6] Donne now tended to be invoked as a matter of course in discussions of all kinds of poetry – epithalamions, pastorals, sonnets, religious verse, as well as satire and lyric.[7] Before the end of the century even the literary historians, a class professionally committed to the repetition of Johnson's judgements, were beginning to speak of Donne as 'a man possessed of genuine poetic fire'[8] and 'a thoroughly original spirit and a great innovator' whose fancies 'are still modern in all their distinction and ardour'[9]

Grierson's edition of 1912 didn't then burst like a bomb upon an unsuspecting literary world. It seems to have come, rather, as the completion of the process which had started with Coleridge and Lamb a century before. But there's no mistaking its

[1] LII, p. 475.

[2] clxxxv, pp. 175-81.

[3] 'The Poetry of John Donne', IX, pp. 244-7.

[4] Chapter iii, 'John Donne', pp. 47-67.

[5] In *Literary Criticisms by Francis Thompson*, ed. T. L. Connolly, New York, 1948, p. 149.

[6] Anon., 'Mr. Gosse's Life of Donne', *The Academy*, 4 November 1899, pp. 505-6.

[7] See E. K. Chambers, *English Pastorals*, 1895, pp. xvii-xix; F. E. Schelling, *A Book of Elizabethan Lyrics*, Boston, 1895, pp. xxi-xxiii; Leigh Hunt and S. Adams Lee, *The Book of the Sonnet*, 1867, i, pp. 78 and 117; Leigh Hunt, 'Epithalamiums', *The British Miscellany*, April 1841, in *Leigh Hunt's Literary Criticism*, ed. L. R. and C. W. Houtchens, 1956, pp. 497-8.

[8] J. C. M. Bellew, *Poet's Corner. A Manual for Students in English Poetry*, 1868, p. 189.

[9] F. I. Carpenter, *English Lyric Poetry, 1500-1700*, 1897, p. lviii.

reviewers' sense that something new had happened, as perhaps it had: 'The modern revival of John Donne is an event of some importance, something to remark as we turn from an old year to a new. Speaking to this age under every disadvantage that time can bring – a confused tradition, a debased text, an obsolete cosmology – he has suddenly become to many readers and lecturers the most exciting poet of his century'.[1] 'Of all the great English poets, his name is least known beyond "literary" circles; but he is certainly "getting there". If one has entered, any time these last years, a railway carriage, and found some studious vagabond deep in a little blue book, it generally turns out to be Mr Chambers's invaluable edition. . . . Donne's glory is ever increasing.'[2] 'The reputation of Dr. John Donne has sensibly advanced during the last decade. Possibly it now stands higher than ever it did since a new manner of writing first displaced him as a model for the versifiers of the Restoration. And this revaluation . . . now receives its appropriate seal in Professor Grierson's elaborate and critical volumes.'[3]

What did the revaluation actually amount to in the nineteenth century? Drastic revisions of eighteenth-century ideas of Donne, as of other old authors, followed from the changed spirit of the new era though they remained pioneering attitudes for a long time. Coleridge's marginal observations on the way Donne's poems move, still not adequately followed out in fact, show that he had simply grasped the principle of Donne's rhythms and could have dismissed for good the old charge that Donne is a crude versifier: 'in poems where the writer *thinks*, and expects the reader to do so, the sense must be understood in order to ascertain the metre'. He recognised, too, that all the copies of Donne he had ever seen were likely to be 'grievously misprinted'.[4] As it was, Donne's apologists thereafter tended to argue that his intrinsic unevenness was shown here too, in that he knew all about rhythm and could write most harmoniously

---

[1] Anon., 'The Poems of John Donne', *The Times Literary Supplement*, 30 January 1913, pp. 37-8.
[2] Anon., 'John Donne, The Elizabethan', *The Nation*, 15 February 1913, pp. 825-6.
[3] E. K. Chambers, *The Modern Language Review*, IX, 1914, p. 269.
[4] 1811. Published in *The Literary World*, New York, 1853, pp. 349-50.

when he chose but often didn't choose to. *The Retrospective Review* critic in 1823 spoke of Donne's 'exquisite ear for the melody of versification'.[1] C. E. Norton, in 1895, remarked his 'grave faults of art'[2] which included an 'indifference to perfection of rhythmical form'; though Norton had modified this opinion by 1905 when he allowed that 'some of the faults of ryhthm attributed to him are due to the reader rather than to the poet'.[3] In 1906 W. F. Melton, another lifelong devotee, claimed in a thesis to have discovered the secret of Donne's rhythms and at least showed that people were now expecting to find a principle there.[4]

Donne the cold conceit-monger soon became an inadequate stereotype among people who actually read him, and a very different understanding of his wit emerged. The *Retrospective Review* man in 1823 set out specifically to replace Theobald's 'continued heap of riddles' fancy with the idea of a poet of 'a most active and piercing intellect – an imagination, if not grasping and comprehensive, most subtle and far-darting – a fancy rich, vivid, picturesque, and, at the same time, highly *fantastical*, . . . a mode of expression singularly terse, simple, and condensed . . . and a wit as admirable as well for its caustic severity as its playful quickness'.[5] Donne's shaping power of imagination struck many Victorian critics: 'throughout it was the exercise of the imaginative faculty on the material supplied now by amorous, now by religious experience, that dominated wantonness and spiritually alike'.[6] De Quincey in 1828 flatly rebutted Johnson's account of Donne as a corrupter of taste (which went the rounds for another seventy years nonetheless): 'No criticism was ever more unhappy than that of Dr. Johnson's which denounces all this artificial display as so much perversion of taste. There cannot be a falser thought than this. . . .'[7] A year later Coleridge scribbled a note on wit in a copy of Chalmers's

[1] p. 31.
[2] *The Poems of John Donne*, 1895, pp. xvii-xxxii.
[3] *The Love Poems of John Donne*, Boston, 1905, pp. vi-viii.
[4] *The Rhetoric of John Donne's Verse*, Baltimore, 1906; especially Chapter iii.
[5] p. 31.
[6] Anon., review of Gosse's *Life and Letters of Donne*, in *The Athenaeum*, 11 November 1899, p. 645.
[7] *Rhetoric, ed. cit.*, x, p. 101

Works of the English Poets which seized the truth that Johnson had not remotely sighted: 'Wonder-exciting vigour, intenseness and pecularity of thought, using at will the almost boundless stores of a capacious memory, and exercised on subjects, where we have no right to expect it – this is the wit of Donne'.[1]

It's remarkable in fact how quickly the old idea was reversed. Suddenly Donne became not frigid but passionate, a poet whose 'fault, far from being coldness, is too much erotic fervour'.[2] Lamb in 1808 saw the error of denying Donne and Cowley 'Nature or feeling' just because they were more witty than other men: 'whereas, in the very thickest of their conceits, – in the bewildering mazes of tropes and figures, – a warmth of soul and generous feeling shines through . . .'[3] Leigh Hunt in 1841 found Donne's marriage poems – the work of a 'great wit and intellect, who is supposed, by some, to be nothing but a bundle of conceits' – at times superior in depth and feeling to Spenser's.[4] By the 1890s Donne is the poet *par excellence* who has rendered every extreme of human passion: 'But, for those who have experienced, or who at least understand, the ups-and-downs, the ins-and-outs of human temperament, the alternations not merely of passion and satiety, but of passion and laughter, of passions and melancholy reflection, of passion earthly enough and spiritual rapture almost heavenly, there is no poet and hardly any writer like Donne'.[5]

In an essay by Arthur Symons three years after that the modern Donne begins to emerge:

> Donne's quality of passion is unique in English poetry. It is a rapture in which the mind is supreme, a reasonable rapture, and yet carried to a pitch of actual violence. . . . This lover loves with his whole nature, and so collectedly because reason, in him, is not in conflict with passion, but passion's ally. His senses speak with unparalleled directness. . . . Ecstatic reason, passion justifying its intoxication by revealing the mysteries that it has come thus to

[1] *Miscellaneous Criticism*, ed. T. M. Raysor, Cambridge, Mass., 1936, p. 132.
[2] Anon., 'John Donne', *The Penny Cyclopaedia of the Society for the Diffusion of Useful Knowledge*, 1837, IX, p. 85.
[3] *Mrs Leicester's School and other essays* (1808), 1885, pp. 358-9.
[4] 'Epithalamiums', *ed. cit.*, pp. 497-8.
[5] G. Saintsbury, in *The Poems of John Donne*, ed. E. K. Chambers, 1896, p. xxxii.

apprehend, speak in the quintessence of Donne's verse with an exalted simplicity which seems to make a new language for love. . . .

It may be, though I doubt it, that other poets who have written personal verse in English, have known as much of women's hearts and the senses of men, and the interchanges of passionate intercourse between man and woman; but, partly by reason of this very method of saying things, no one has ever rendered so exactly, and with such elaborate subtlety, every mood of the actual passion. . . .[1]

One of Coleridge's visitors in January 1829 thought his host's enthusiasm for Donne's poetry unaccountable but was much struck by a single stanza of the *Metempsychosis*; the rest of the poem however 'seemed the effusion of a man very drunk or very mad'.[2] Coleridge himself assumed that Donne is a grossly unequal poet – 'All the preceding verses are detestable'[3] he says after admiring the last two lines of *A Fever* (1811) – and the idea of a flawed genius, unable to tell the sublime from the abysmal in his own work, seized even Donne's greatest admirers throughout the nineteenth century. Gilfillan in 1860 spoke of 'great genius ruined by a false system'[4]; *Chambers Cyclopaedia of English Literature* allowed Donne 'much real poetry' amidst 'much rubbish'.[5] At the end of the century his most devoted academic admirers, Dowden, Saintsbury, Norton, Minto, Gosse, Grierson, Sanders, all still take it for granted that he is a poet of 'strange bad taste' whose 'verse must be sifted with a coarse sieve'[6]; or to put it another way, that 'the power of the furnace' is seldom equal for more than a few lines or stanzas at a time to 'the volumes of ore and fuel that are thrust into it'.[7] Norton expressed it concisely: 'few poets are so unequal as Donne; few, capable of such high reaches as he, sink lower than he at times descends'.[8] We're well into the present century before this view is directly contested. In 1913 an anonymous reviewer of

[1] 'John Donne', *The Fortnightly Review*, n.s. LXVI, 1899, pp. 734-45.
[2] *A Memoir of Baron Hatherley*, ed. W. R. W. Stephens, 1883, i, pp. 51-2.
[3] Marginal jotting, 2 May 1811. *The Literary World*, New York, 1853, loc. cit.
[4] *Specimens with Memoirs of the Less-Known British Poets*, 1860, i, p. 203.
[5] Anon., 'John Donne' (1844), 1858, i, pp. 114-15.
[6] C. E. Norton, *The Poems of John Donne*, 1895, pp. xvii.
[7] G. Saintsbury, *op. cit.*, pp. xviii.
[8] *The Poems of John Donne*, p. xvii.

Grierson's edition of Donne's poems brushed aside Grierson's half-heartedness over the hyperboles in the *Anniversaries:* 'here apologies are out of place; one must either reject wholly or accept wholly; Donne is either revolting or magnificent'.[1]

When Donne lost his standing as a corrupter of taste new ways of placing him historically had to be found. He had long been claimed, of course, as the first this or that in England – satirist, great rhetorician, impressionist or what. Donne the intellectual rebel first appeared in 1899 when Gosse painted a vivid portrait of a man of arrogant self-sufficiency who had no interest in his immediate literary predecessors and wouldn't have turned his head to see Spenser pass.[2] Here in fact was the defiant scoffer at all received pieties, the antiplatonic anti-petrarchan revolutionary whom Grierson would formally en-shrine for us in the edition of 1912.

Courthope in 1903 offered a different and more compre-hensive view. For him the 'School of Metaphysical wit' was only one late form among several such of a habit of mind which prevailed in Europe at least from the time of Dante, and was now subject to all manner of local pressures in its decline.[3] Courthope's account of Donne's wit as one among the various forms of European wit in the seventeenth century allowed too little to Donne's own distinctive genius but it is plainly nearer truth than the Gosse-Grierson theory which gained acceptance. For one thing it can easily accommodate both sides in the argument whether Donne was an Elizabethan or a seventeenth century writer, which F. E. Schelling inaugurated in 1910 when he stood out firmly against the view then coming in. To Schelling 'Donne is an Elizabethan in his poetry in the strictest acceptance of that term', and he is in no sense a 'metaphysical' poet; if we see him as 'the forerunner of a remarkable movement, not soon assimilated or even imitated by his immediate con-temporaries', that is not because he had revolutionary intent but because he was an original genius who transformed the common matter in his own way.[4]

---

[1] 'The Poetry of John Donne', *The Spectator*, CX, 1913, p. 103.
[2] *The Life and Letters of John Donne*, 1899, ii, p. 330.
[3] *A History of English Poetry*, 1903, pp. 147-68.
[4] *English Literature during the Lifetime of Shakespeare*, pp. 364-71.

For the Romantics and the Victorians Donne was a poet of passions he struggled to control, and his wit had to be separately explained or ignored. The relation of mind to heart in his writing only gradually struck commentators as special, though that sense is implicit in some of the criticisms already quoted such as De Quincey's and Symon's. A literary history in 1903 put Donne with Shakespeare alone as a love poet in whom 'the true note of absolute passion is struck'; but it added that Donne's lyrics are poems not of pure passion but of 'transcendental sensuality, highly intellectualized'.[1] Grierson in 1906 spoke of the conjunction in Donne of an 'abstract and intellectual element' with passionate feeling, so that the passion itself quickens the intellect 'to intense and rapid trains of thought'.[2] W. B. Yeats, acknowledging Grierson's gift of the edition of Donne's poems in 1912, said he noticed 'that the more precise and learned the thought the greater the beauty, the passion; the intricacies and subtleties of his imagination are the length and depth of the furrow made by his passion'.[3]

Reviewers of Grierson's edition all fastened on this aspect of Donne. One of them remarked of him that 'dialectical quibbling was the natural language of his most passionate love'.[4] 'Everything we have', said Walter de la Mare, 'mind body, soul – he invites to his intimacy'.[5] The *T.L.S.* reviewer, tacitly amending a phrase of Grierson's, called Donne the poet of 'the metaphysic of sex'.[6] A reviewer in *The Nation* remarked that Donne 'belonged to an age when men were not afraid to mate their intellects with their emotions'.[7] A few months later the sense has strikingly sharpened: 'He is the most *intellectual* poet in English . . . when passion shook him, and his being ached for utterance, to relieve the stress, expression came through the intellect. . . . Donne feels only the idea . . . saw everything through his intellect.' The reviewer was Rupert Brooke, who

[1] T. Seccombe and J. W. Allen, *The Age of Shakespeare*, 1903, i, p. 29.

[2] *The First Half of the Seventeenth Century*, pp. 139-64.

[3] *Letters, ed. cit.*, pp. 570-1.

[4] Anon., 'The Poetry of John Donne', *The Spectator*, CX, 1913, p. 103.

[5] 'An Elizabethan Poet and Modern Poetry', *The Edinburgh Review*, 444, 1913, pp. 372-85.

[6] Anon. 'The Poems of John Donne', 30 January 1913, pp. 37-8.

[7] Anon. 'John Donne, The Elizabethan', 15 February 1913, pp. 825-6.

added that other love poems look flat and unreal beside Donne's, 'For while his passion enabled him to see the face of love, his humour allowed him to look at it from the other side'.[1]

T. S. Eliot's celebrated dicta, which inaugurated modern criticism of Donne, came within eight years of that in a *T.L.S.* review of another edition by Grierson: 'there is a direct sensuous apprehension of thought, or a recreation of thought into feeling, which is exactly what we find in Donne'; [Tennyson and Browning] 'do not feel their thought as immediately as the odour of a rose. A thought to Donne was an experience; it modified his sensibility.'[2] Elsewhere that year Eliot found that metaphysical wit involves 'a recognition, implicit in the expression of every experience, of other kinds of experience which are possible'.[3] Plainly this is what some part of our own century has seen and valued most in Donne. But in the year of the quatercentenary of Donne's birth we're as far removed in time from those formulations as Saintsbury was from Southey, and it seems well to consider what we make of him now.

1 'John Donne', *Poetry and Drama*, I, June 1913, pp. 185-8.
2 *The Times Literary Supplement*, 20 October 1921, pp. 669-70; reprinted in *Selected Essays* (1932), 1948, pp. 281-91. In *The Sacred Wood*, published a year earlier, Eliot attributed to Donne and some of his contemporary writers 'a quality of sensuous thought, or of thinking through the senses, or of the senses thinking, of which the exact formula remains to be defined', and went on to speak of 'a period when the intellect was immediately at the tips of the senses' (1934 edn., pp. 22-3, 115, 128-9).
3 'Andrew Marvell', *The Times Literary Supplement*, 31 March 1921, pp. 201-2; reprinted in *Selected Essays* (1932), 1948, p. 303.

2

The Circulation of Donne's Poems in Manuscript[1]

ALAN MacCOLL

While a good deal of information is now available about the critical fortunes of Donne's poetry from the eighteenth century to the present, our knowledge of the course of his reputation as a poet in his own time is still comparatively sketchy. Scholars have usually been content to generalise. The editor of the widely read 'Nonesuch' edition of Donne's works refers to 'the popularity he enjoyed, both as a poet and a divine'. F. P. Wilson is more specific: observing that it seems to have been 'Donne the vivid realist and the witty and humorous satirist' who appealed most to his contemporaries, he speaks of Donne's fame as a poet as being 'firmly and widely established' by 1607. For Dr R. A. Bryan, in a paper discussing the occurrence of poems by Donne in some manuscript miscellanies, his 'great popularity as a poet during and shortly after his lifetime' is 'a fact now well known'. Only a few scholars have gone into the matter in any great detail. Reviewing early references to Donne, Professor W. Milgate finds more evidence to support F. P. Wilson's distinction, and concludes that Jonson (who according to Drummond thought that his friend's best pieces were those he wrote before he was twenty-five, had 'The Bracelet' by heart, and liked 'in his merry humour' to try and pass off the epigram 'Phryne' as his own) was representative in preferring 'the epigrammatic, the satiric, the rhetorical and witty' aspects of Donne's verse. Indeed, Professor Milgate surmises, contemporaries may have been familiar only with such early poems as the *Satyres* and the

---

[1] This essay is based on material used in an unpublished B.Litt. thesis (Oxford, 1967) done under the supervision of Dame Helen Gardner. I should like to express my gratitude for all her help.

Elegies; the dearth of references to the *Songs and Sonnets* may mean that Donne 'exercised some discrimination in deciding to what extent certain of his poems were to be allowed to circulate'.[1]

For Professor Milgate the matter is 'one of speculation'. I think it is possible to be rather more definite, for while the evidence of the early references alone is not enough to go on, there remains a large body of material which has not yet been closely examined for the light it can throw on the circulation of Donne's poems: that is, the extant manuscripts. Only a handful of the poems were printed during his lifetime, and until the appearance of the 1633 edition the bulk existed in manuscript only. A remarkable number of manuscripts of Donne's verse has come down to us: some forty collections of varying size, and over a hundred miscellanies in which his poems appear amongst those of other authors. Since it was in such manuscripts that his contemporaries read his verse, a systematic study of them seems the obvious foundation for any attempt to chart the course of his literary reputation.

The subject is one where bibliography can fruitfully be related to literary history. On an elementary level, a simple census should give as reliable an indication as we are likely to get of the relative popularity of the poems. And a study of the manuscripts should go some way towards settling questions like the one raised by Professor Milgate: did some categories of Donne's poems long remain almost unknown to his contemporaries because he did not want them to be widely read, or should we explain the absence of early references to the *Songs and Sonnets*, for example, by an appeal to taste? Does analysis of the manuscripts support the view that Donne was, as J. B. Leishman called him, 'a coterie poet'? Does it offer grounds for John Buxton's assertion that he was the sort of poet 'for whom poetry was merely the means of giving evaporations to his wit', whose verses were something 'to be pulled

---

1 F. P. Wilson, *Elizabethan and Jacobean*, Oxford, 1945, pp. 54-6. R. A. Bryan, 'John Donne's Poetry in Seventeenth-Century Commonplace Books', *English Studies*, 43, 1962, pp. 170-4. W. Milgate, 'The Early References to John Donne', *Notes & Queries*, May, June, July, September 1950, pp. 229-31, 246-7, 290-2, 381-3.

from the folds of a man's doublet and read to a gay, convivial company'?[1]

Neither the elegies on Donne's death nor the known earlier references to his verse offer good reason for accepting Walton's lament that his secular poems were 'loosely, God knows, too loosely, scattered in his youth' at face value. Donne seems to have gained an early reputation as a satirist, and by 1598 had been paid the compliment of imitation by Everard Guilpin. But just how widely he was known as a poet is difficult to say. Half a dozen references to the *Satyres*, one or two to the *Elegies*, and the repeated misquotation of the epigram 'A Lame Beggar' amount to less than solid evidence of fame.[2] A couple of references do however suggest that the *Satyres* and 'The Storme' at least were fairly widely read. In *A Knights Conjuring* (1607) Dekker quotes two lines from the latter poem in terms indicating that he expected the quotation and its author to be recognized:

> This battaile of *Elements*, bred such another *Chaos* that
> (not to bee ashamde to borrow the wordes of so rare an
> *English Spirit*,)
>
> Did not GOD say
> Another Fiat, It had n'ere been day.

Again, when Joseph Wybarne, in *The New Age of Old Names* (1609), quotes six lines from *Satyre IV*, ascribing them to 'the tenth Muse her selfe' and adding the marginal note 'Dunne in his Satyres', we may infer that he could count on the *Satyres* being known, or at least known of. This need not be taken to mean that everybody was reading them. The epigram Jonson sent to Lady Bedford with a copy of the *Satyres* suggests otherwise:

> If workes (not th'authors) their owne grace should looke,
> Whose poemes would not wish to be your booke?
> But these, desir'd by you, the makers ends
> Crowne with their owne. Rare poemes aske rare friends.
> Yet, *Satyres*, since the most of mankind bee
> Their vn-auoided subiect, fewest see;

---

[1] *Elizabethan Taste*, 1963, p. 317.

[2] Apart from Jonson, the examples in this and the following paragraph are Professor Milgate's in the article cited.

> For none ere tooke that pleasure in sinnes sense,
> But, when they heard it tax'd, tooke more offence.
> They, then, that liuing where the matter is bred,
> Dare for these poemes, yet, both aske, and read,
> And like them too; must needfully, though few,
> Be of the best: and 'mongst those, best are you.

Jonson clearly regards the *Satyres* as connoisseur's poems, 'rare' in both senses. His stress on this is of course partly for the purpose of flattery, and also no doubt because he wanted to make the poems look as desirable as possible. Yet he could scarcely have made so much of the point if they had in fact been freely available.

Be that as it may, even if the *Satyres*, and perhaps the *Elegies* and 'The Storme' and 'The Calme' had attained some currency by the first decade of the century, there is nothing to suggest that many of Donne's other poems were at all widely circulated. There are no known early references to the Divine Poems, and the only apparent mention of the *Songs and Sonnets* during Donne's lifetime is the entry 'Ihone Dones lyriques' in a list of books read by William Drummond in 1613. There seems, indeed, to have been a general ignorance of the very existence of the lyrics.

The same story is told by the elegies on Donne's death, whose authors show little sign of first-hand acquaintance with the poems.[1] Thus although the poet's wit is his most praised characteristic it is not those poems that manifest it most which get special mention. The stress is on the Divine Poems (*A Litanie*, *La Corona* and the hymns; no one refers to the *Holy Sonnets*). The *Satyres* are accorded some loyal but not particularly appropriate praise by Walton:

> Was every sinne,
> Character'd in his *Satyres*? made so foule
> That some have fear'd their shapes, and kept their soule
> Freer by reading verse?

The verse was there now for everyone to read, but we should hardly expect the authors of memorial verses on the Dean of

---

[1] Grierson, *The Poems of John Donne*, Oxford, 1912, i, pp. 371-93.

St Paul's to direct attention to the love poems of his greener days. They lurk disguised in Walton's lines

> Did his youth scatter *Poetrie*, wherein
> Was all Philosophie?[1]

and they are touched on in Sir Lucius Carey's decorous 'Then let his last excuse his first extremes'. But only Thomas Browne is tactless enough to comment outright on what must for many readers of the first edition have been one of its compelling attractions: 'The *Promiscuous* printing of his Poems, the *Looser sort*, with the *Religious*'. Browne's stanzas were excluded from the 1635 edition. It would be hard to argue that these elegies tell us much about the contemporary popularity of Donne's verse.

The inference to be made from this body of evidence, that during the greater part of Donne's lifetime few of the poems reached a very large audience, is reinforced by an analysis of probable manuscript dates. From these alone it would appear that the bulk of the poems scarcely began to circulate to any great extent until well into the second decade of the century. Most of the collections belong to the 1620s and early 1630s, and a great number of the manuscript miscellanies that include Donne items were compiled after his death.

We do not have to look far to find a likely reason for these facts. The very infrequency with which Donne mentions his poems suggests that he was close about them, and the few references he does make tend to confirm this. In all his surviving letters there is only one passage that refers to his actually writing out and distributing copies of a poem. Writing to Goodyer about *A Litanie*, he says that his own litany is 'for lesser Chappels, which are my friends', promising to let Goodyer have the first copy he makes.[2] What seems to be the sole record of his giving someone a collection of his verse is in a letter sent to Sir Robert Ker along with a manuscript of *Biathanatos* just before his trip to Germany in 1619, when he writes, 'But besides the Poems, of which you took a promise, I send you another Book. . . .'[3] Even at an early date he appears to have

---

[1] Later altered to 'Lay Loves Philosophy'.

[2] Quotations are from *Letters to Several Persons of Honour*, 1651, pp. 33, 21; *John Donne: Selected Prose*, chosen by Evelyn Simpson, ed. Helen Gardner and T. Healy, Oxford, 1967, p. 131; *Letters*, 1651, pp. 36, 88, 238, 75, 103-4.

[3] *Selected Prose*, p. 152.

been anxious that his poems should not become too well known. In a letter, which seems to have been written about 1600, accompanying some of the *Paradoxes*, he asks his correspondent for an assurance 'upon the religion of your friendship . . . that no coppy shalbee taken for any respect of these or any other my compositions sent to you'. 'To my satyrs there belongs some feare,' he adds, 'and to some elegies, and these perhaps, shame.'[1] On the subject of his verse Donne usually speaks in tones ranging from diffidence to disapprobation. A song sent to Goodyer with the letter cited above is a 'trifle,' an 'evaporation'; another is a mere 'ragge of verses'. As time went on, he seems to have grown increasingly embarrassed by the difficulty of reconciling his activities as poet and wit with his ambitions for a public career. The printing of the *Anniversaries* gave him almost instant cause for regret, and he twice expresses his shame at having 'descended to print anything in verse': 'I do not pardon my self,' he writes, 'but confess that I did it against my conscience, that is, against my own opinion, that I should not have done so.'[2] Before long we find him very uneasy even at the idea of using his poetic talents discreetly for private patronage. Goodyer seems to have suggested that he write a verse epistle on the subject of the picture of an unnamed countess (perhaps the Countess of Huntingdon). One of Donne's objections is revealing:

> That that knowledge which she hath of me, was in the beginning of a graver course then of a poet, into which (that I may also keep my dignity) I would not seem to relapse.

Although he overcame his reluctance, he expresses the hope 'that by this occasion of versifying, I be not traduced, nor esteemed light in that Tribe, and that house where I have lived'.[3]

The letters, then, reveal Donne as careful that his reputation as a poet should not become too widespread. In the early 1590s, a period from which no prose letters survive, his attitude was no doubt different. For instance, 'The Triple Foole' suggests (if we dare nowadays read any of his poems as autobiographical) that he expected some of his verse to be set to music:

> Some man, his art and voice to show,
> Doth set and sing my paine,

---

[1] ibid., p. 111.   [3] *Selected Prose*, p. 148.
[2] Gosse, *Life and Letters of Donne*, i, p. 306.

According to the authorative Group II manuscripts, three songs ('The Message', 'Sweetest love' and 'The Baite') were written 'to certain airs which were made before', and the associated manuscript *DC* brings a further three under the same heading ('Communitie', 'Confined Love' and 'Goe, and catche'). Settings are extant for all of these except 'Communitie' and 'Confined Love'. 'Breake of Day', 'The Message', 'Sweetest love' and 'The Baite' appear frequently in manuscript miscellanies, which may be regarded as additional evidence that they were allowed to circulate without restriction. 'Breake of Day' and 'The Expiration' (which was also set to music) were among the very few Donne poems to get into print before the publication of the 1633 edition. Nevertheless, even the *Satyres* may not have reached a very great audience, and an analysis of manuscript dates suggests that the same was true of many of the other poems.

Who then first read Donne's verse, and who were the agents through whom it eventually attained an extensive circulation? If we cannot identify many of them as the owners of surviving manuscripts, we can still be fairly certain that the earliest readers of much of his poetry belonged to 'that short Roll of friends' he speaks of in an early verse letter.[1] By the time Donne had written most of his secular verse its members included Goodyer, Wotton, Hoskins, the Woodwards, the Brookes, and the Roes. He corresponded in verse with nearly all of these men. They must have exchanged other kinds of poems as well, which is presumably why pieces by Sir John Roe, Hoskins and others appear so often in the Donne collections. There is, however, very little specific evidence about the early readership. Christopher Brooke may be the 'C. B.' who had a copy of the *Satyres* referred to by Drummond in the Hawthornden MS, and Rowland Woodward evidently possessed a manuscript including the *Satyres* and the *Elegies* dating from before 1603.[2] Two further readers were Everard Guilpin and Joseph Hall: Guilpin imitated the opening of *Satyre I* in *Skialetheia* (1598) and there seem to be echoes of the *Elegies* both in this and in Hall's *Virgidemiarum* (1597). In 1607 Donne sent some 'holy

[1] 'To Mr. I. L.'
[2] See Helen Gardner, *John Donne: The Divine Poems*, Oxford, 1952, p. lxxix.

hymns and sonnets', probably *La Corona*, to Mrs Herbert, and a couple of years later he appears to have sent six of the *Holy Sonnets* to the Earl of Dorset.[1] It is likely too that he exchanged poems with Sir Edward Herbert and Lady Bedford.[2]

Only about a third of the manuscript collections contain any apparent clue to their original provenance, and most of them are too late to offer evidence about Donne's early readers. There are some interesting possibilities regarding the origin of Groups I and II, though. Dame Helen Gardner has made the plausible suggestion that Group I derived ultimately from a collection of his verse put together by Donne in 1614 for publication at Somerset's request. Evidently Donne did not have copies of all his poems, for he had asked Goodyer for the loan of an 'old book' (that is, a manuscript volume of poems) for the purpose[3]. I have argued elsewhere that Group II originated in a collection of poems sent by Donne to Sir Robert Ker in 1619.[4] A letter from Drummond to Ker in 1621 suggests that this collection was a full one, perhaps consisting of all the poems in Donne's possession at the time:

> Though I have no sute at Court to trouble you with, yet so long as Daniell lastes (who, dying as I heare, bequeathed to you his scrolls) or Done, who in his trauells lefte you his, I will euer find a way of trafficking with yow by letters.[5]

Nearly all of the identified first owners of the existing manuscript collections were noblemen. *H 49* (compiled about 1630) almost certainly belonged to William Cavendish, first Earl of Newcastle, and *Lec* to Henry Percy, ninth Earl of Northumberland. A fragment which duplicates a few pages of *Lec* is part of a volume of papers belonging to Edward, second Viscount Conway. No particular connection between Cavendish and Donne is known, but Percy was a close friend: it was he who was entrusted with the task of breaking the unwelcome news to Sir George More

[1] *Ibid.*, pp. xlviii-xlix.
[2] See Helen Gardner, *John Donne: The Elegies and the Songs and Sonnets*, Oxford, 1965, pp. 248-51, 255-7.
[3] *Letters*, 1651, pp. 196-7.
[4] 'The New Edition of Donne's Love Poems', *Essays in Criticism*, 17, 1967, pp. 258-63.
[5] *Correspondence of Sir Robert Ker first Earl of Ancram*, ed. D. Laing, Edinburgh, 1875, i, p. 24.

that Donne had married his daughter. R. C. Bald gives good reasons for thinking it 'not unlikely' that Donne was in touch with Percy during the latter's imprisonment in the Tower between 1606 and 1621.[1] Donne had a lifelong acquaintance with Conway's father Sir Edward, later first Viscount Conway'.[2] *TCC* may have belonged to Sir Thomas Puckering, son of Lord Keeper Puckering, and its copy *A 18* to some member of the family of the Earls of Denbigh. Of the remaining manuscript collections whose first owners can be identified, the only ones whose provenance is of any great interest are *B*, which belonged to John Egerton, first Earl of Bridgewater, the son of Donne's early employer, and Milton's patron, and *W*, which is in the hand of Donne's friend Rowland Woodward. Grierson says of *B*, 'I had hoped that it might prove, being made for those who had known Donne all his life, an exceptionally good manuscript, but can hardly say that my expectations were fulfilled'.[3] *W*, on the other hand, is distinguished by its purity of text and canon, and is the sole witness for three of the *Holy Sonnets*.

Most of the Donne manuscripts fall into two clearly distinguishable classes: collections wholly or primarily of his verse, and miscellanies. The relationships of the former are complex and often obscure, and the question of their origins and growth can be treated only summarily here.[4]

The likelihood is that many of the extant collections reached their final form through the accretion not for the most part of copies of single poems but of sets of poems. This process can be seen most clearly in the case of Group I (*C 57*, *D*, *H 49*, *Lec*

---

[1] *John Donne: A Life*, Oxford, 1970, p. 229. [2] Ibid., *passim*.

[3] Grierson, *Poems, ed. cit.* ii, p. xcix.

[4] For detailed accounts, upon which this discussion draws, see Helen Gardner's editions of *The Divine Poems and Elegies* etc., and W. Milgate's edition of *The Satyres*, etc. Sigla are as used in these editions, with the addition of *Ee* (Cambridge University Library MS Ee. iv. 14), *W 53* (National Library of Wales MS 5308E), and *Wed* (National Library of Scotland MS 6504). I follow Dame Helen Gardner in using the symbol *H 40** to denote the miscellany shared by MS Harl. 4064 and *RP 31*, and *H 40* to denote the Donne collection which was added by the compilers of Harl. 4064 to the common stock. *HK 2** is likewise used to mean the miscellaneous part of Huntington MS MH 198 part 2, and *HK 2* the Donne collection embedded in it. See *Elegies*, etc., pp. lxv-lxvii, lxxv-lxxvii. I have classed *Ee*, *HN*, *La*, *RP 117*, *S 962* and *W 53* as collections.

and *SP*) and its associated manuscript *H* 40.[1] The Group I manuscripts descend from a lost manuscript *X*. It's compiler seems to have possessed a small collection of Donne's poems like that preserved in *H* 40, and also his own copy of the *Satyres*, when a large and comprehensive collection (probably copied from the poet's papers) came into his hands. What he evidently did was add to his own set from the latter. Since *C* 57 and *Lec* have a different version of the *Satyres* from the rest of the Group, we can deduce that the copyist of *X³* (their immediate source) did the same sort of thing. The scribe of *C* 57 added *La Corona* and the *Holy Sonnets* (apparently missing from *X³*) to the poems he was copying, and also *The Progresse of the Soule*.

A like process operated in the case of Group II (*TCC*, *TCD* and their copies *A18* and *N*). *TCC* and *TCD* had a common original *Y*, whose scribe had a set of poems mostly by Donne like that found in *L* 74. This he added to from a much bigger collection, also probably taken from Donne's own papers. The scribe of *TCD* was able to make further additions, notably a full set of verse letters to noble ladies.

We can deduce less about the origins and growth of Group III (*Dob*, *Lut*, *S* 96, and *Lut's* copy *O'F*), which differ widely from one another in content, order and physical appearance. However, since *Dob* and *Lut* agree in presenting the poems more or less systematically according to kinds, it seems a fair inference that in this respect they reflect the lost original of the Group, and that the disorder of *S 96* represents a degeneration. This would make it unlikely that the Group came into being through the bringing together of copies of single poems, or handfuls of them. A similiar point may be made about the Group *Cy*, *O*, *P* and the related manuscript *HK 2*. It is probable that *HK 2* derived from a small collection of poems mostly by Donne, and that this collection was copied and expanded to make up the original of the Group. If *HK 2* had not survived, we might assume from the appearance of the *Songs and Sonnets* in *Cy*, *O* and *P*, which are very haphazardly set out, that they had been gathered together piecemeal; but it seems clear from *HK 2* that they were acquired as a distinct set of poems.

[1] M. Crum, 'Notes on the Physical Characteristics of Some Manuscripts of the Poems of Donne and of Henry King', *The Library*, xvi, 1961, pp. 121-32.

Most of the remaining collections are a motley lot, unreliable as regards both text and canon. The outstanding exception is *W*, which has uniquely high authority. Grierson suggested that it was probably a fair copy of two small collections, the first consisting of the *Satyres*, thirteen elegies, a set of early verse letters, the Lincoln's Inn Epithalamion, the *Paradoxes*, the *Epigrams*, and a solitary lyric, 'A Jeat Ring Sent', and the second containing *La Corona* and the *Holy Sonnets*. *W* is another example of a manuscript put together from substantial sets of poems. Other partial exceptions are *A 25* and *JC*, which although as a whole quite unlike *W*, preserve the same set of elegies in the same order. The Wedderburn MS (*Wed*), which has a good text, offers further evidence that some of the *Songs and Sonnets* may have circulated independently in quite large sets. I have argued elsewhere that it was put together from a small stock of poems common to it and *HN*, and another collection made up almost wholly of lyrics.[1] By and large, however, the uncertain pedigree of most of the unclassified collections, and the evident remoteness of the majority from Donne's originals, rule out their use as evidence of the way the poems first went about.

Turning to the numerous manuscript miscellanies including poems by Donne, the first point to make is that only a few of them are early. I would date twenty-eight of them before 1625. Of these, only two are likely to have been written before 1605,[2] ten between 1605 and 1615,[3] and sixteen between 1615 and 1625.[4] The majority of the miscellanies come between 1625 and 1650. These figures have to be compared with those for the collections, of which thirty could conceivably have been

[1] 'A New Manuscript of Donne's Poems', *RES*, n.s. XIX, 1968, pp. 293-5.
[2] Bodleian: Rawl. poet. 212; British Museum: Add. 34744.
[3] Bodleian: Add. B. 97, CCC 327, Rawl. poet. 26 (first Donne item), Rawl. poet 31; British Museum: Add. 23229 (first and second Donne items), Add. 27407, *H* 40*; Huntington: *HK* 2*; Rosenbach: 1083/15.
[4] Bodleian: Don. c. 54, Eng. poet. e.14, Mal. 19; British Museum: Add. 5956, Add. 21433, Add. 25303, Add. 34324, Harl. 3910, Harl. 4888; Cambridge University: *C* 57 (2); Emmanuel College Cambridge: 1.3.16; Folger: V.a.103; Huntington: HM 172; Nottingham University: Welbeck MS; Pierpoint Morgan: Holgate MS. Few manuscripts were given dates by their compilers. I have dated most on the basis of the latest datable item.

written before 1625. Only five may be dated before 1605: three manuscripts of the *Satyres* (*D 16, H 51* and *Q*) and two of *The Progresse of the Soule* (*G* and *H 39*). Seven others may belong to the years between 1610 and 1615 (*H40, L74, HK 2, Cy, Ee, HN* and *Wed*), and a further eighteen to the years 1615-25 (*D, SP, C57, Lec, DC, Dob, S96, O, P, A25, B, C, JC, K, La, S, W, W53*). Thus the majority of the miscellanies are ante-dated by a large number of collections.

The twenty-eight miscellanies just mentioned include copies of some seventy Donne poems (rather over a third of the canon). The commonest are some of the *Elegies:* 'The Anagram' (seven times), 'The Perfume' (five), and 'The Bracelet' (four). There are four copies of 'The Autumnall'. All but seven of Dame Helen Gardner's first group of lyrics (that is, those she thinks were probably composed before 1600) appear in two or three copies each. The most frequently occurring, doubtless because they were set to music, are 'Breake of Day', which appears five times, and 'The Message, and 'Sweetest love', which occur four times each. Of the twenty-seven lyrics making up her second group (which she would date after 1602), on the other hand, only eight appear in these miscellanies: 'A Valediction: forbidding Mourning' and 'Twicknam Garden' (each four times), 'A Feaver', 'The Good-morrow', 'The Sunne Rising' and 'The Dreame' (each twice), and 'Loves Growth' and 'Loves Alchymie' (each once). Most of the remaining poems appear only once each: half-a-dozen epigrams, twelve verse letters (ten of them early), the three epithalamions, six funeral poems and seven divine poems.

Such considerations make it impossible that existing miscellany copies of the poems should be ancestors of those in the collections. They also make it unlikely that the former preserve independent textual traditions to any significant extent. This is confirmed by the texts themselves, which are mostly derivative and poor. The main exceptions are some copies of elegies, verse letters and occasional poems. Verse letters and occasional poems are the very kinds which by their nature must have circulated separately.

While most of the miscellanies have little value for Donne's editors, they are of interest to literary historians for the light they throw on his early reputation as a poet. The evidence can be expressed in statistical form. If we plot the number of all miscellanies containing poems by Donne against a time scale covering the first half of the seventeenth century, we find that the resulting graph approximates to a normal distribution curve, with the number rising rather steeply to a peak in the years 1625-35 (to which about 60 per cent of the miscellanies belong). Another 20 per cent or so can be dated 1635-45. Thus some four-fifths of the existing miscellanies date from the years 1625-45. After the middle of the century the number declines rapidly. The collections naturally show a different pattern. About three-quarters of them can be dated between 1615 and 1632 (the date of $O'F$). After the appearance of the first edition there would be less need for this sort of compilation (though one suspects that some cachet would still attach to the possession of a manuscript), and only $RP\ 117$ and $S\ 962$ can certainly be dated after 1633. Taking the editions into account, and bearing in mind that one is likely to date most of the manuscripts too early rather than too late, it would appear that Donne's verse enjoyed its highest popularity in the second quarter of the century and that it was not very widely known before this. The peak seems to have come in the ten years or so following the publication of the first edition.

Just over ninety of Donne's poems appear in the miscellanies as a whole – about half of the canon. The commonest are 'The Anagram' and 'Going to Bed', which boast twenty-five copies each. Next come 'Breake of Day' (seventeen), and 'The Bracelet' and 'A Valediction: forbidding Mourning' (sixteen). The epigram 'A Lame Beggar' appears fourteen times, 'The Message, thirteen, 'The Baite' and 'The Apparition' twelve, 'The Perfume' and the epigram 'A Licentious Person' eleven, and 'The Autumnall', 'Loves Diet' and 'Sweetest love' ten. Six lyrics appear in eight copies each: 'Goe, and catche', 'The Legacie,' 'The Broken Heart', 'The Flea', 'The Will' and 'Twicknam Garden'. There are seven copies each of 'Loves Warre' and 'A Hymne to God the Father', six of the elegy on Lady Markham and 'Epitaph on Himselfe', and five of 'The Comparison', 'Natures lay idiot', 'On his Mistris', 'His Picture', 'The Good-morrow', 'To the Countess of Bedford' ('You that are she and you'), the Palatine Epithalamion, the Hamilton elegy and 'The Crosse'. Thus only thirty-three of the poems appear five times or more. The most notable omissions are in the *Songs and Sonnets* and the *Divine Poems*. Several of Dame Helen Gardner's first group of lyrics appear frequently, but nine of them occur only once, twice or three times, and four do not appear at all. With her second group the picture is different. Only three ('A Valediction: forbidding Mourning', 'The Good-morrow', and 'Twicknam Garden') are often found in miscellanies, and fourteen, including such modern favourites as 'Aire and Angels', 'The Anniversarie' and 'The Exstasie', do not appear at all. The only *Divine Poems* to appear at all frequently are 'The Crosse' (an early work) and 'A Hymne to God the Father', presumably because it was set to music.

The above figures have to be treated with some care. It would I think be wrong to interpret them merely as indicating the relative appeal of Donne's poems to readers of the first half of the century, and equally misleading to see them only as reflecting the extent to which the poet himself permitted or restricted the circulation of various pieces. Both factors appear to have been at work. Thus the large number of copies of the *Elegies* lends some support to the view that initially Donne allowed these poems to go about more freely than he did some of his others. At the same time, the relative figures for the *Elegies* tell us something about contemporary taste. There is a marked preference for the witty or erotic; serious love elegies like 'His Picture' were less popular. Again, it can hardly be a coincidence that three of the four lyrics most common in miscellanies are among the few that were set to music; nor, surely, can it have been just because people did not like them that so many of the lyrics placed by Dame Helen in her second group should be absent or occur only rarely. The comparative infrequency of these poems, as of nearly all the Divine Poems, may ultimately have been due in part to restriction by Donne.

A survey of the manuscript collections and miscellanies tends to reinforce the evidence of Donne's letters that, with the exception of verse letters and occasional pieces he rarely gave out copies of single poems. Much of his verse seems rather to have come into circulation divided into more or less substantial sets according to genre, and it appears to have been in terms of such sets that the copyists of the collections often worked. The *Satyres* undoubtedly first appeared, and continued to circulate for a time, as a 'book' in themselves. Two such books still exist: *D 16*, which has the five satires, 'The Storme' and 'The Calme', and *Q*, which also includes 'The Curse'. A third manuscript, *H 51*, contains satires I-III only. The compiler of *X³*, the common original of *C 57* and *Lec*, seems to have possessed a separate book of satires too, since these two collections have a different version from that of the rest of Group I. And Jonson's epigram to Lady Bedford 'with Mr Donne's Satires' shows that such a book was presented to her.

Although no manuscript exists containing the *Elegies* alone, the indications are that they too first circulated as a book. It is likely that *W*, along with *A 25* and *JC*, preserves the set in its original form. It has great authority, and this section of it was probably copied from papers made at an early date. *A 25* provides good evidence for the separate circulation of the *Elegies*, since it has most of them together in the same order as *JC* and *W* in spite of its otherwise haphazard appearance (this same order is also preserved to some degree by manuscripts as diverse as *Lut* and *Hd*). The elegies transcribed by scribe B of *A 25* are numbered 2-12, lacking the first and the last items ('The Bracelet' and the funeral elegy 'Sorrow, who to this house') of the set found in *W*. He would thus seem to have been copying from a set of numbered elegies on papers from which the first quire and the last leaf had been lost. Unlike the *Satyres*, the *Elegies* also circulated singly, and some of them very widely, in miscellanies. Copies of two of them, 'The Bracelet', in Bodleian MS Rawl. poet. 212, and 'The Anagram', in Bodleian MS Add. B.97, are among the earliest known of any of Donne's poems.

The *Songs and Sonnets* are a more complicated and uncertain case. There is no manuscript consisting only of lyrics, and the collections which include them vary considerably in the number they contain and the order in which they are presented. Some have them scattered amongst other poems; others treat them as a set. On balance, however, the evidence is that with some exceptions they did not go about singly, but rather came into circulation in fairly large sets. Analysis of *H 40*, *L 74*, *HK 2* and

Wed lends some support to this view. *H 40* (MS Harl. 4064) includes a small collection of poems which were added by its compilers to a stock shared by this manuscript and the miscellany *RP31*. Thirty-nine of the additional poems are by Donne, and of these thirty-four are lyrics. Again, there is a sequence of thirty-four poems in *L 74* which is set out as a discrete Donne collection. Three of them are by other authors, and twenty-five of the remainder are lyrics. *HK 2's* small Donne collection consists mostly of lyrics. It has thirty-nine, including twenty-three of the *L 74* set in a related but inferior text. And if we subtract from *Wed* the poems also found in *HN*, we are left with a collection made up of twenty-seven of the *Songs and Sonnets* and seven other poems.

Although some scribes group the Divine Poems together, the only ones to circulate consistently as a distinct set were *La Corona* and the *Holy Sonnets*, which are nearly always found together. *La Corona* occurs without the *Holy Sonnets* in *Hd*, *K* and *S*, but there is no manuscript containing the *Holy Sonnets* without *La Corona*. They appear together without any of the other Divine Poems in *W*, and they are lacking together from *Lec*. In common with most of the Divine Poems they do not occur in miscellanies.

Most of the remaining poems are verse letters and occasional items, and would thus in the first instance have been put out by the author individually. A number of verse letters, however, do occur together in groups, notably a set of early ones to men friends in *W* and, in a closely related text, in *TCC*, *TCD*, *DC* and *Lut*, and another of letters to noble ladies in *TCD*, *DC* and *Lut*. Whether or not such groupings derived from Donne's own papers we cannot say; Professor Milgate remarks that he 'does not seem normally to have kept copies of his verse letters'.[1] The most commonly occurring of the letters in manuscript are 'The Storme' and 'The Calme', which are almost always found together and had an early circulation along with the *Satyres*.

It should no longer be possible to speak without qualification of Donne's 'great popularity' as a poet. He did not seek public acclaim for his poems, and he at once regretted his only major poetic venture into print. Even in his youth, when he had little

[1] *John Donne: The Satyres, Epigrams and Verse Letters*, Oxford 1967, p. lxvii.

need to be cautious, his verse seems to have been confined to a smallish audience. At any rate, if he had been at all free with the distribution of his poems in his 'youth's giddiest days', he seems to have ceased to be so after he entered Egerton's service; we find him anxiously requesting a correspondent to allow no copies to be taken of the *Paradoxes*, 'or any other my compositions sent to you'. He is aware of the dangers of exposing poems written for a circle of like-minded readers to the public gaze: 'To my satyres there belongs some feare and to some elegies, and these perhaps, shame'.[1] The absence of early references to the *Songs and Sonnets* and the pattern of their appearance in manuscript make it likely that their circulation was restricted in the same way, no doubt for similar reasons. As I have tried to show, he did not make a habit of freely distributing copies of individual lyrics. What seems to have happened in the case of most of the *Songs and Sonnets* is that he occasionally allowed copies of sets of lyrics to be taken from his papers; or it may be that some sets were amassed by a few close friends from copies of poems shown then over a period by Donne. The collections of lyrics in *H 40, L 74, HK 2* and possibly *Wed* look like the surviving results of some such practice. With two explicable exceptions, the circulation of the Divine Poems appears also to have been restricted.

So far as we can infer, Donne twice allowed large collections of his poems to leave his hands, one probably giving rise to the Group I manuscripts and the other to those of Group II. Towards the end of the second decade of the century other collections also began to multiply, probably put together in the first instance by friends from books of the *Satyres* and *Elegies*, sets of lyrics, occasional poems and so on which they had kept over the years. As collections proliferated, the canon became confused and the text increasingly corrupt. Aware of the latter, some compilers made matters worse in a busy round of conflation and sophistication. The whole process was summed up in 1630 by the diplomat Constantine Huygens: 'Many rich fruits from the green branches of his wit have lain mellowing among the lovers of art, which now, when nearly rotten with age, they are distributing'.[2]

[1] *Selected Prose*, p. 111.   [2] Grierson, *Poems, ed. cit.*, ii, p. lxxvii.

Donne's policy of limited circulation had predictably failed, and it may have been when he became aware of this that (as Jonson told Drummond in 1619) he 'repented highly, and sought to destroy all his poems' – a threat which he seems not to have carried out, though. As his fame as a preacher grew, so did the number of copies of his verse. In the late 1620s, nearly forty years after the earliest of them had been written, Donne's poems were at last reaching a large audience. For twenty years or so, from about 1625 until the mid-1640s (and especially during the ten years following the first edition), they are among the commonest items in manuscript miscellanies, though the poems on which this popularity was chiefly founded are rather limited in number and type. Towards 1650 the flood dwindles to a trickle. It is perhaps significant that John Donne Junior seems to have had to use the sheets from one printing of the poems twice, in 1650 and 1654.[1] The Donne fashion was over.

Donne was a 'coterie poet' not because the public did not appreciate his work but because for a long time it was available only to a small number of readers. From the time he went into Egerton's service one of his main reasons for shunning publicity was that which he expressed to Goodyer in 1614; he did not want to suffer 'many interpretations'.[2] He also seems increasingly to have come to regard a reputation for writing poetry as unsuitable for a man seeking or occupying a public position – an opinion shared by at least one contemporary, John Chamberlain, who wrote of Donne's verses on the death of the Marquis of Hamilton (1625), 'Though they be reasonable wittie and well don yet I could wish a man of his yeares and place to geve over versifieng.'[3]

It would be wrong to conclude from this that he never took his verse seriously, though in his later years he seems to have felt something of the sober Christian remorse for ill-spent time and talents voiced by other great poets before him. Further conjecture about his motives will depend on our reading of the

---

[1] Geoffrey Keynes, *A Bibliography of Dr John Donne*, third edition, Cambridge, 1958, pp. 162-5.

[2] *Letters*, 1651, p. 197.

[3] *The Letters of John Chamberlain*, ed. N. E. McClure, Philadelphia, 1939, ii. p. 613, cited in Helen Gardner's *The Divine Poems*, p. 78.

poems themselves. It has sometimes been held that the exclusiveness of Donne's circle was that of the self-consciously avant-garde. But in fact it is not until after his death, when his verse was approaching the height of its popularity, that we find such an attitude openly expressed: in Carew's often-quoted lines, and in those of his fellow elegist Jasper Mayne, for whom a worthy epitaph for Donne must be 'so high above its reader' that 'wee are thought wits, when 'tis understood'. There is no evidence that the Donne circle, like some early admirers of Pound and Eliot, 'thoroughly despised such recent poetry as had been popular'.[1] If he sometimes mocks the terms and attitudes of 'whining poetry', as did Astrophil, there is no record of his showing anything like Jonson's intolerance of his fellow-writers. Modern criticism has been dogged by Gosse's fancy about the man who would not have turned to see Spenser go by, or have bothered to drop in at the Mermaid to catch some of Shakespeare's conversation.

In attempting to confine his verse to a small group of readers, Donne was after all conforming to the practice of Wyatt, Sidney, Raleigh, and a host of other Tudor and Stuart poets including Shakespeare, who according to Francis Meres circulated his sonnets 'among his private friends'. During the greater part of his poetic career he seems to have observed the advice Jonson gave him in his epigram 'To John Donne': 'A man should seeke great glorie, and not broad'.

---

[1] Patrick Crutwell, 'The Love Poetry of John Donne', in *Metaphysical Poetry*, ed. Malcolm Bradbury and David Palmer, 1970, p. 34.

3

Musa Iocosa Mea

Thoughts on the *Elegies*

ROMA GILL

Donne, after boasting of the independence of his heart, was
suddenly subjugated by the beauty of a married lady . . . and
. . . composed – we dare not allow ourselves to overlook the
fact – some of the most sensual poetry written in the history of
English literature by any poet of eminence.[1]

When Edmund Gosse in 1899 read the story of Donne's life
into his poetry he found the stuff of a torrid love-affair 'scarcely
veiled'[2] in the *Elegies*; these could not have been published at
the time of writing, or even while the author was still alive
because, Gosse explained, this 'would have been to court an
instant, and probably a very distressing scandal'[3]. Gosse ig-
nored the letter (although he prints it in the *Life*) from Donne
to Sir Robert Ker in which the poet, by this time Dean of St
Paul's, excuses himself by claiming that he wrote best 'when I
had least truth for my subjects'.[4] This letter of 1625 appears to
contradict the embarrassment of some twenty-five years earlier
when Donne, writing perhaps to Sir Henry Wotton, forbade
the copying of some of his works, among them the *Elegies*, and
confessed to feeling some 'shame' about them.[5] Scholarship
after Gosse has preferred to accept the Dean's statement, even
though it was written at some remove from the poems and at a
time when, with ecclesiastical dignity to take into account, he
would have every reason to deny the truth of the matter. So
instead of seeing Donne as a libertine who wrote from personal
experience, we now accept him as a scholar engaged in the
respectable academic pursuit of imitating Ovid, with whom he can

[1] Edmund Gosse, *The Life and Letters of John Donne*, 1899, i, pp. 67-70.
[2] *Ibid.* i, p. 67.　　[3] *Ibid.* i, p. 78.　　[4] *Ibid*, ii, p. 215.
[5] *John Donne Dean of St Paul's: Complete Poetry and Selected Prose*, ed. J. Hayward
(1929), 1945, pp. 440-1.

say '*vita verecunda est, Musa iocosa mea*'.[1] But it is now twenty
years since J. B. Leishman's masterly analysis of the *Elegies*
established Ovid as the mastermind of the poems,[2] and after
such a time it is perhaps permissible to question the usefulness
of the label 'Ovidian', asking not only how Donne's poems are
like those of Ovid but also whether there are any significant
differences which the label obscures.

Thirteen of Donne's poems are grouped together as 'Elegies'
and of these two, perhaps three, have no title to that position.
'The Comparison' and 'The Anagram' demand examination
in the light of modern (i.e. Renaissance) Italian writing rather
than that of ancient Rome, while a third, 'The Autumnall' is
aptly described as 'a witty series of variations on an ancient
theme'.[3] Like the two other outsiders it is static, lacking the
logical progression through an argument or episode which
characterises the remaining poems and gives them something
of the nature of dramatic monologues. The three are linked with
the real elegies only through their verse form, the heroic
couplet, which was introduced by Marlowe in his translations
of Ovid's *Amores* and gained acceptance as the English equiv-
alent of the elegiac couplet. The two couplets, however, are
by no means identical in their effects. The Latin form, where
the hexameter is followed by a pentameter, was described (and
enacted) by Coleridge:

> In the hexameter rises the fountain's silvery column;
> In the pentameter aye falling in melody back.[4]

Acutely self-aware, the Roman poets provide enough comments
on the elegiac couplet for us to appreciate the effect aimed at and
to measure Marlowe's and Donne's substitute against it. The
Latin movement is a delicate one: Ovid speaks of '*blanditias
elegosque levis*'[5] and Domitius Marsus in his funeral elegy on

---

[1] *Tristia*, ii, 354; the line was used, in translation, by Herrick for the epilogue to
Hesperides: 'Jocond his Muse was; but his Life was chast'.
[2] *The Monarch of Wit*, 1951.
[3] By Helen Gardner in *The Elegies and the Songs and Sonnets*, 1965, p. 147.
[4] 'The Ovidian Elegiac Metre described and exemplified'.
[5] *Amores*, II.i.21. All quotations from Ovid, Propertius and Tibullus are taken
from the Loeb editions of their works; where the sense of the Latin is not imme-
diately clear from the context, a translation follows the quotation.

Tibullus laments that there will be none after him to croon the songs of love:

> *ne foret aut elegis molles qui fleret amores.*[1]

The elegy is always compared with more martial poetry, and with the epic. Ovid tells us that he was in fact preparing to write of great exploits in appropriate verse –

> *arma gravi numero violentaque bella parabam*   I.i.1

when love came upon him and forced him to write elegy by docking his second line of one metrical foot:

> *risisse Cupido*
> *dicitur atque unum surripuisse pedem.*   I.i.3-4

Propertius loyally explains that if indeed he had the gift for writing martial poetry, he would use it in praise of Caesar; but since this gift has not been vouchsafed, he must instead speak of lovers' struggles on their narrow beds:

> *nos contra angusto versantes proelia lecto.*   II.i.45

From observations like these one begins to think of the Roman couplet as a delicate and subtle creation; and experience of the poems themselves shows the great variety of which the form is capable, and how it is suited to the inflected language. The English couplet, on the other hand, is still (in the 1590s) a somewhat clumsy vehicle, and its demands for rhyme led Marlowe into some very odd convolutions of meaning and syntax.[2] Donne, because he is not translating, does not suffer in this way, and only occasionally does it appear that a word has been mainly for sound and not sense – as in 'The Comparison':

> As the sweet sweat of Roses in a Still,
> As that which from chaf'd muskats pores doth trill.

At other times, most noticeably in 'The Perfume', the rhymes are a witty device for enforcing comic meaning:

> So am I, (by this traiterous meanes surpriz'd)
> By thy Hydroptique father catechiz'd.
> Though he had wont to search with glazed eyes,
> As though he came to kill a Cockatrice,

---

[1] *Catullus, Tibullus and 'Pervigilium Veneris'*, Loeb, 1924, p. 338.
[2] In his translation of III.ii.29-30, for example:
> Swift *Atalantas* flying legges like these
> Wish in his hands graspt did Hippomenes.

But comedy like this would be out of place, being too heavy-handed, in the Latin elegies; and it is an indication of the coarsening the form has undergone in translation. The heroic couplet, as Marlowe was not slow to discover in writing *Hero and Leander*, has great potential for satire of all degrees, gentle or vicious; but love poetry written in this form very easily carries an overtone, however slight, of cynicism. Certainly Donne's *Elegies* could never merit the description of Propertius' collection: *'meus . . . mollis in ore liber'* ('my book that is so sweet to the taste'; II.i.2).

Nor, I think, can Donne's scattering of poems be viewed as a projected collection, a 'book of Elegies'[1] such as Ovid and Propertius have left. It is not simply their being few that disqualifies them, but also their seeming quite independent of each other: the girl in 'The Perfume' has only her poet-lover in common with the citizen's wife in 'Jealousie'. The Roman poets keep one mistress (or the name of one mistress) through most of their poems and this gives the collection the impression, at least, of unity and sequence. Ovid certainly intended some of his poems to be read together: II.vii, for instance, where he voices injured innocence at Corinna's suspicion that he is making love to her maid, Cypassis, must for a full enjoyment of the lover's effrontery, be followed by II.viii, addressed to Cypassis and asking how Corinna could have learned of their doings. In so far as their poems cohere into a greater whole, the Roman elegists could be said to describe the different phases of a single relationship; in this respect their collections have more in common with the Elizabethan sonnet-sequences than with Donne's thirteen poems.

That the whole is not Ovidian – or, to be less precise at this point, Roman – does not, of course, mean that the separate parts cannot be. A comparison of the poems of Tibullus, Propertius and Ovid on the one hand, and those of Donne on the other, should give some idea of the extent to which Donne's poems can properly be called 'Roman'.

At first sight, and read only in the works of a single author, the Roman elegy seems highly personal and its critics have at

[1] Helen Gardner puts this as a possibility in the introduction to *The Elegies and the Songs and Sonnets*, p. xxxi.

times felt with Gosse the urge to trace the writer's life in his works, or at least to identify Ovid's Corinna. But when the *genre* and not the individual author is studied, it becomes clear that the elegy is an exceedingly conventional form in which not only metre is constant from one poem to the next. The same ideas, situations and images recur with surprising frequency, especially in the works of Propertius and Ovid. Both of them, for instance, chafe against the celibacy imposed by religious rites (*Elegies* II.xxxiii and *Amores* III.x); both refer to the two days' night required for the procreation of Hercules in the same context of boasting their own virility (II.xxii and I.xiii); and both revile the bawds Acanthis and Dipsas who endeavour to teach their mistresses the arts of a prostitute (IV.v and I.viii). A convincing explanation for this is given by A. W. Allen:

> When the elegist took for his material traditional commonplaces or erotic literature, he did so because those commonplaces were the repository of a practised attitude toward love and because through them the poet established a community of experience with his readers.[1]

The technique is similar to that of musical composition; the notes are the same, but the arranging is different:

> When by the Gamut some Musitions make
> A perfect song, others will undertake,
> By the same Gamut chang'd, to equall it.
>
> ('The Anagram')

Unlike the musical scale, however, the conventions of poetry are largely dictated by the society for which the poetry is written, and because of this they are not easily shared, especially when time, country and religion intervene. Yet Ovid tells us that he is writing for all young lovers: his emotions are not his alone but will be recognised and shared by the young who will ask in amazement

> quo . . . ab indice doctus   II.i.9-10
> conposuit casus iste poeta meos?

[From whom has this poet learned of my troubles, that he can write of them?]

---

[1] 'Sunt Qui Propertium Malint', *Critical Essays on Roman Literature: Elegy and Lyric*, ed. J. P. Sullivan, 1962, p. 146.

Donne, with his firm belief that

> Love, all alike, no season knowes, nor clyme,
> Nor houres, dayes, months, which are the rags of time.
>
> ('The Sunne Rising')

should not have found it difficult to fit into the Roman lovers' world.

The Roman poets are involuntary lovers who say with Catullus *'Odi et amo'* ('I hate and I love'). Love is slavery, and Cupid is a tyrant, but it is *Amor* that gives purpose and meaning to their existence. Ovid admits his defeat by Cupid and tries to placate the conqueror:

> *En ego confiteor! tua sum nova praeda, Cupido;*
> *porrigimus victas ad tua iura manus.*
>
> I.ii.19-20

[Look, I admit that you've won. I am your new conquest, Cupid, and I hold out my hands to be tied, in obedience to your laws.]

The frustrated Propertius, deprived of Cynthia, finds love a fitting punishment to be wished on his enemies:

> *hostis si quis erit, amet ille puellas*   II.iv.17

Tibullus prays to Venus to have pity on him, since he is her confessed slave and in hurting him she is doing herself harm:

> *at mihi parce, Venus: semper tibi dedita servit*
> *mens mea: quid messes uris acerba tuas?*   I.ii.97-8

Yet each rejoices in the glad possession of his Corinna, Cynthia or Delia, and even more in the cunning purchase of her. The paradoxical situation is summed up in Ovid's oxymoron *'usque adeo dulce puella malum est'* ('a girl is so sweet an evil', II.ix.26). In some of the *Songs and Sonnets* Donne exhibits the same ambivalence towards love, silencing his own complaints at the end of 'Loves Deitie' with the threat that 'Love might make me leave loving'. In the *Elegies*, however, he is always the masterful lover, fully in command of the situation even when the odds are against him. It seems to me likely that Donne recognised the limitations of his heroic couplet, and kept the lover's less dominant postures for the 'whining Poëtry' of lyrics like 'The Triple Foole'. For the lyric poetry too Donne reserved his protestations of fidelity – although these are hardly comparable to the extravagant vows of the Romans who, having once accepted the role of lover, are not unlike their English medieval counterparts. At the beginning of his career Ovid begs to be taken into Corinna's service and outlines his qualifications:

> *Accipe, per longos tibi qui deserviat annos;*
> *accipe, qui pura norit amare fide.*   I.iii.5-6

[Take one who would be your slave throughout long years; take one who knows how to love with a pure faith.]

Taught by Cynthia, Propertius has become an expert who can give guidance to a novice friend:

> *is poterit felix una remanere puella,*
> *qui numquam vacuo pectore liber erit.*
>
>   I.x.29-30

[That man can be happily assured of one girl who never wants to be free and heart-whole.]

Such sentiments are quickly paralleled from the English poetry of courtly love; this stanza of Wyatt's, for instance, reads like a translation of Propertius but is representative of his attitude and of the current conventions:

> Ye know my herte, my ladye dere,
> That sins the tyme I was your thrall
> I have bene yours both hole and clere,
> Tho my reward hathe bene but small.[1]

Servitude like this can only be professed when there is no connection between love and marriage: adultery is as much a characteristic of Roman elegy as it is of medieval love poetry. But the resemblance between these two forms ends at this point, for the Christian writers cannot share the pagan enjoyment of the situation. Donne seems to have found some piquancy in illicit love, if we are to judge by the inventive vigour of his three elegies on the subject, 'The Perfume', 'Tutelage'

---

[1] XLI in *The Collected Works of Sir Thomas Wyatt*, ed. Kenneth Muir and Patricia Thompson, 1969.

and 'Jealousie', but even his is not the refined taste of Ovid, who cannot love without a husband's suspicions to add flavour:

> *Si tibi non opus est servata, stulte, puella,*
> *at mihi fac serves, quo magis ipse velim.*

II.xix.1-2

[If you yourself, idiot, don't feel any need to guard your wench, at least guard her for my sake, to make me want her even more.]

From the collections of Propertius and Ovid it is possible to extract a reasonably clear impression of the *domina* to whom each gives his allegiance. There is little evidence about her appearance – although we do know that the wires growing on Corinna's head were neither gold nor black but a mixture of the two (*mixtus uterque color*', I.xiv.10). There is, however, plenty of information about what she does. From Propertius we learn that Cynthia is fond of fine clothes and jewels (I.ii). plays the lyre (II.i), and dances well (II.iii). From Ovid we get a very detailed portrait of Corinna, who is given to more extravagant and outrageous actions than Cynthia. Corinna dyes her hair until it falls out (I.xiv), attempts to induce an abortion (II.xiii), is obedient to Ceres' injunction of festal chastity (III.x), and owned a parrot that has just died (II.vi). These two (Tibullus' Delia is a more shadowy, unreal figure) give the impression of freedom and independence; they would make amusing companions, although they are not especially well-educated (when Ovid sends a message to Corinna he leaves only a little room for her reply – why should she tire her fingers with writing? *'Quid digitos opus est graphio lassare tenendo?'* (I.xi.23). Donne gives us much less information; we know that one woman is married, that another – or perhaps the same – is well dressed, and that yet another comes from a large family. Although in his elegies he is speaking to the lady and even, sometimes, answering her comments, she is never more than an imagined voice. A frequent tone of exasperation and scorn, unknown to the Romans, suggests that none of these women is an ideal companion. The pupil in 'Tutelage' is 'Nature's lay Ideot' and the account of her accomplishments before she came under Donne's tuition is a frightening indictment of Elizabethan education for girls:

And since, an houres discourse could scarce have made
One answer in thee, and that ill arraid
In broken proverbs, and torne sentences.

The wife in 'Jealousie' is brusquely addressed as 'Fond woman',
and the mock-courtliness of 'Come, Madame, come' at the
beginning of 'Going to Bed' verges upon rudeness and prepares
for the insult at the end of the poem when the lady is roundly
told to abandon all pretences at modesty and

cast all, yea this white linnen hence.
Here is no pennance, much lesse innocence.

In these three poems and also, but less obviously, in 'Loves
Warre' and 'Loves Progress' Donne shows little respect or
regard for women. They are compared to territories that must
be explored and possessed, colts to be broken, and cities to be
captured: in other words, they are always thought of as objects.
There is an adolescent crudeness about such an attitude which
is very different from the suave sophistication of Ovid. The
Romans, professing devotion and distraction, are all the time
conscious of playing an elaborate game, abiding by strict rules
which they formulate themselves. In this game tenderness is
permissible, and so too is the outraged anger of a misunder-
stood or cheated lover, but there is no place for scorn: the lover
is cast as slave, and the loved one must be always and completely
the mistress. The lover's conduct in the elegies (whether he is
Tibullus, Propertius or Ovid himself) is that approved by Ovid
in the *Ars Amatoria*. And this, Professor C. S. Lewis observed,
was to Roman eyes 'shameful and absurd' which

is precisely why he [Ovid] recommends it – partly as a comic
confession of the depths to which this ridiculous appetite may
bring a man, and partly as a lesson in the art of fooling to the top
of her bent the last baggage who has caught your fancy.[1]

Donne, it would seem, had not learned the Romans' politeness
and deceiving charm from his reading of their elegies; he
cannot hide his contempt for the women he is using as mere
sexual objects, although sometimes he manages a little jocu-
larity, and at other times he tries to flatter.

[1] *The Allegory of Love*, (1936), 1967, p. 7.

Such contempt seems to me to be one of the major differences between Donne and the classical elegists that is ignored or evaded when we call his poems 'Roman'. And the difference does not end with this attitude. The basic assumption, the *sine qua non* of the Roman poets, is one which Donne tries very hard to share – but unsuccessfully. However watchful the husband, and however incorruptible the porter at the gate, the poet and his mistress will find a time – many times – for the consummation of their love. This is the right true end; to be alone in bed is a curse for one's enemies:

> *hostibus eveniat viduo dormire cubili*
> *et medio laxe ponere membra toro*
> (*Amores* II.x.17-18)
> [Let it fall to the lot of my enemies to sleep in an empty bed and to stretch languidly in the middle of the couch.]

Leishman claims that from Ovid, Donne 'caught . . . the assumptions about the true nature and end of love'[1] but this, I think, is very far from the truth. Ovid's sexual relations are happy ones; if there are moments of failure to be recounted, there are also many more moments of success to be recalled (cf. III.vii). Nowhere is there a sense of guilt, and he only finds it necessary to justify himself when he is in love with more than one girl at a time (as in II.iv). Furthermore, Roman mistresses may often be 'cruel' – but they are not so by being chaste, and they need no logical arguments to entice them to the lover's bed. The argument in 'Loves Progress' would have been unintelligible and quite unnecessary to the Romans:

> I, when I value gold, may thinke upon
> The ductillness, the application,
> The wholesomeness, the ingenuity,
> From rust, from soyle, from fyre ever free,
> But if I love it, 'tis because 'tis made
> By our new Nature, use, the soule of trade.
>   All these in women wee might thinke upon
> (If women had them) but yet love but one. . . .

The argument here, the dirty jokes in 'Loves Warre', the persuasion in 'Going to Bed' – these all show how very far

[1] *Op cit.*, p. 54.

Donne is from sharing the Roman 'community of experience'
otherwise than superficially. In Christian Elizabethan England,
with thinking men ever more conscious of the dilemma of being
'Borne under one law, to another bound',[1] the basic assumption
of the Romans cannot be made. Donne intended to shock when
he started off his lecture in a matter-of-fact tone with

> Who ever loves, if hee doe not propose
> The right true end of love,

but the sentiment can only shock in a social context where the
right true end is denied. Such bold, self-conscious uneasiness is
very different from Ovid's casual and comic sensuality when,
for instance, he contemplates dying in the very act of love, as an
appropriate end to his life:

> *at mihi contingat Veneris languescere motu,*
> *cum moriar, medium solvar et inter opus;*
> *atque aliquis nostro lacrimans in funere dicat:*
> *'conveniens vitae mors fuit iste tuae'.*   II.x.35-8

Without wishing to present the Donne of the *Elegies* as a
guilt-ridden neurotic, I feel that another quality of these poems
needs to be remarked, and that is their preoccupation with
fairly irrelevant nastiness. Again, this is something that Ovid
and the other Romans are innocent of, but it places Donne
firmly in his period and connects him with writers like Webster
and with plays like *Troilus and Cressida*. The suspicious husband
in 'Jealousie' is visualised on his death bed,

> His body with a sere-bark covered. . . .
> Ready with loathsome vomiting to spue
> His Soule out of one hell, into a new,

Later he is compared to a beast who

> swolne and pamper'd with great fare,
> Sits downe, and snorts, cag'd in his basket chaire,

The unpleasantness affects the poet and his mistress, and we are
told that they used to

> flout openly,
> In scoffing ridles, his deformitie;

[1] Fulke Greville, *Chorus Sacerdotum* from the end of *Mustapha*, 1632.

In 'The Perfume' it is the girl's father who is given this crude treatment: he is dropsical ('Hydroptique') and he peers round the room with bleary ('glazed') eyes; the smell of Donne's perfume alerts him with its sweetness, whereas

> Had it beene some bad smell, he would have thought
> That his owne feet, or breath, that smell had wrought.

And 'Loves Progress', after its clever geography of the female body, ends with the gratuitous illustration that the man who does not take the shortest way to full sexual satisfaction makes a mistake

> as greate
> As who by Clyster gave the stomach meate.

Such observations work like the undercurrent of imagery in poetic drama, leaving a dirty smudge on some of Donne's best-known elegies.

Turning now to individual poems, I want to examine various aspects of Donne's writing that might be called 'Roman', beginning with 'Loves Warre', the most obviously Roman poem of all the elegies. One can say with confidence that here Donne is heavily indebted to a tradition, if not to a particular poem in that tradition. For most of the time he assumes the Roman attitude in a discussion of the commonplace love/war antithesis: the first line of the poem,

> Till I have peace with thee, warre other men,

sounds like an attempt at Ovid's style, with its graceful balance and symmetry. After the traditional opening Donne proceeds to an account of current affairs – an account which is not especially striking in itself and which damages the rest of the poem in being grossly disproportionate. It may, nevertheless, have been the part of the poem that he most enjoyed writing, since its interest is immediate and not dictated by convention. Admittedly, he makes little good use of his freedom, falling back on tired puns when he explains that France

> relies upon our Angels well,
> Which ne'r retourne; no more then they which fell.

After twenty lines of such comment he returns to the Roman

manner, although his puns and *doubles entendres* suggest the
English student and not the Latin gallant:

> Here let mee warre; in these armes let mee lye;
> Here let mee parlee, batter, bleede, and dye.

Propertius is restrained when he says simply that the tussle
with his mistress is quite enough for him –

> *sat mihi cum domina proelia dura mea*   III.v.2

– and Ovid has the purpose in his argument that every lover is
a warrior (*'Militat omnis amans'*, I.ix.1) of convincing Atticus
that it is not cowardly and spiritless to be in love; the dialectic
of his poem is directed towards its closing line:

> *qui nolet fieri desidiosus, amet.*   I.ix.46

The Roman poets give the impression that their wars and their
mistresses are equally real. Donne, in the 'current affairs'
section of his poem, mentions campaigns that are easily identi-
fied, and his horror of being mewed in a ship, 'a swaggering
hell', is unmistakingly genuine. But the mistress is not there.
The details of war must be balanced by details of love. Ovid gives
details of neither, sticking to generalities and achieving thereby
a polished performance that neither offends nor excites. At
times it reads like a dutiful exercise in a too familiar convention,
and the antitheses, elsewhere so delicately poised, often here
seem laboured or obvious:

> *ille graves urbes, hic durae limen amicae*
> *obsidet; hic portas frangit, at ille fores.*   I.ix.19-20

Donne's contrasts are even more ponderous, and are made
worse by the feeble jokes:

> Those warres the ignorant, these th'experienc'd love;
> There wee are always under, here above.

The theme dictated the style, and Ovid, writing in an inflected
language, was able to achieve a measure of success that eluded
Donne. In Donne's poem the heavy oppositions of 'Those'/'these'
'There'/'here' suggest that the English language is barely
tolerant of the antithetical style; and where the style cannot be
translated, the matter will resist. 'Loves Warre' is an example of

the slavish following of a convention which, when there is not enough personal pressure to revivify it, becomes tedious imitation.

Still in the Roman tradition but much more successful is 'Tutelage', although to find in this poem the complexity of relationship and feeling that is usual in the Latin elegy it is necessary to agree that the 'lay Ideot' is a married woman – the original country wife in fact. This Helen Gardner denies: suggesting a debt to Tibullus I.vi.5-14 she insists that Donne's poem 'is more innocent', adding that 'Only "Jealousy" among Donne's *Elegies* is concerned with adultery'.[1] But some explanation must be given for lines 20-23:

> Thou art not by so many duties his,
> That from the worlds Common having sever'd thee,
> Inlaid thee, neither to be seene, nor see,
> As mine. . . .

Clearly the woman belongs to *somebody*, to a man who has made her his personal property. He may not, it is true, be her husband: the image of 'the worlds Common' suggests *The Alchemist* and Face's promise to Dol:

> thou shalt sit in triumph,
> And not be styled DOL Common but DOL Proper,
> DOL Singular: the longest cut, at night,
> Shall draw thee for his DOL Particular.   I.i.186-9

This creates the triangle that is constant in Ovid's *Amores*: the girl, her watchful lover, and her 'husband' (to whom she may, or more probably may not, be married). That she should be unfaithful to her husband is taken for granted, practising 'The mystique language of the eye [and] hand' in order to communicate with the lover in the husband's presence. The mistress in *Amores* I.iv is given full instruction in the signs and their meanings:

> *cum tibi succurret Veneris lascivia nostrae,*
> *purpureas tenero pollice tange genas.*
> *siquid erit, de me tacita quod mente queraris,*
> *pendeat extrema mollis ab aure manus.*   I.iv.21-4

[When our sports with Venus come into your mind, touch your rosy cheeks with a delicate finger; and if you have in your mind

---

[1] *The Elegies and the Songs and Sonnets*, p. 126.

some silent grievance against me, hold the bottom of your ear
gently with your hand.]

The same triangle exists in Tibullus' poems, and in I.vi, when
Delia has cheated him with another lover, he addresses the
husband and warns him to watch for the tell-tale signs:

> neu te decipiat nutu, digitoque liquorem
> > ne trahat et mensae ducat in orbe notas.   I.vi.1920

[she may deceive you with a nod, or she may betray you by taking
wine on her finger and writing notes on the round table.]

Donne had given his lady much the same education, teaching
her the language of flowers,

> how they devisefully being set
> And bound up, might with speechlesse secrecie
> Deliver arrands mutely,'and mutually.

Unless there is a husband to be deceived, such subtlety is
wasted,[1] and the irony of the situation, which is the same one
that Tibullus and Ovid find themselves in, is lost. The deceptions
which the lovers have taught for use on the husbands now
return to plague the inventors. Tibullus laments Delia's false-
ness and blames himself for her craftiness:

> ipse miser docui, quo posset ludere pacto
> > custodes: heu heu nunc premor arte mea.   I.vi.9-10

[It was I, poor wretch, who taught her how to evade her guards;
and now I am overcome with my own craft.]

Ovid's mistress communicates silently with another lover in
his sight:

> multa supercilio vidi vibrante loquentes;
> > nutibus in vestris pars bona vocis erat.   II.v.15-16

[I saw your quivering eyebrows converse, and your nods spoke
volumes.]

And Donne, less direct in his accusations but with the same tone
of injury and resentment, asks if he is destined to

> Chafe waxe for others seales? breake a colts force
> And leave him then, beeing made a ready horse?

---

[1] A case could be made out for the deception of the girl's parents, as in 'The
Perfume', but it seems to me that this reduces the manoeuvres to the level of
adolescent games.

'Tutelage' is not mere imitation of the Roman letter; it catches the spirit, half-amused and half-resentful, of Ovid and adds to this the witty and mimetic but non-Roman reminder of the lady's social and amatory inadequacies. By so doing Donne makes an English poem out of a Latin form, extending and giving new life to a tradition.

A third poem demands attention, the elegy 'To his Mistris Going to Bed', of which Leishman says it 'may perhaps have been suggested by the fifth in Ovid's First Book [of *Amores*]'.[1] Even bearing in mind Helen Gardner's very necessary warning that 'With Donne a suggested source never provides more than a starting-point',[2] I can see no resemblance between the two. Ovid's Corinna, wearing only a '*tunica . . . recincta*' and with her hair loose on her shoulders, calls in his room during the afternoon siesta. He leaps from his couch, rips off the scanty dress (she makes only a coquettish attempt to stop him) and embraces her:

> *et nudam pressi corpus ad usque meum.*   I.v.24
> [and held her naked body close to mine.]

The rest is passed over in silence: '*Cetera quis nescit?*' In the last line of the short poem Ovid hopes for, and looks forward to many more such afternoons:

> *proveniant medii sic mihi saepe dies.*   I.v.26

Until the satisfied slow peace of this line the poem moves rapidly, with mounting excitement, By contrast Donne's poem, after its abrupt opening words –

> Come, Madame, come, all rest my powers defie,

– becomes a slow titillation as each Elizabethan garment is removed with deliberation and relish. The verse almost gives time for the clothes to be folded:

> Your gownes going off such beauteous state reveales
> As when from flowery meades th'hills shadow steales.

Corinna is compared to other women – to Semiramis and Lais – and she is always and only a woman, composed of shoulders, breasts, thighs and belly; and needing no persuasion,

---

[1] *Op. cit.*, p. 73.   [2] *The Elegies and the Songs and Sonnets*, p. 112.

only a show of force to get her into the lover's arms. Donne's unnamed mistress is modest (although we learn at the end that this is only an appearance and that after all 'Here is no . . . innocence'). She must be coaxed and told she is one of the Good Angels, to be distinguished from evil spirits in that the latter 'set our haires, but these the flesh upright'. After that little joke she becomes his 'America, [his] new found lande', then a 'myne of precious stones', and lastly a 'mystique booke' to be studied only by the elect. While Ovid sketches a background for his action – the sultry afternoon, a room with half-open shutters letting in a dim light, and the couch – Donne gives no such details: the bed is the only indication of place, and it may be night, although the 'harmonious chime' which announces 'bed time' may be betraying the lady. Ovid narrates in the past tense a single action, complete with beginning, middle and end; but such action as there is in Donne's poem is double and incomplete—in fact only a prelude. The verbal undressing of the lady in the first twenty-four lines is followed by the speaker's own undressing while he talks glibly, to distract her attention, of exploration and the philosophy of nakedness; finally he turns to her to reveal that

> To teach thee, I am naked first: Why than
> What need'st thou have more covering than a man.

If a classical source is needed for this poem it is to be found in Propertius rather than Ovid. A celebration of nakedness, Helen Gardner notes,[1] can be read in *Elegies* II.xv; and Propertius is even closer to Donne's thought in an earlier poem, I.ii, where he tries to dissuade Cynthia from artificial adornments –

> *naturaeque decus mercato perdere cultu,*
> *nec sinere in propriis membra nitere bonis*   I.ii.5-6

[spoiling your natural charms with purchased ones, and letting your limbs shine with a glory not their own.]

– by reminding her of the heroines who, as he would have her do, conquered with their own unaided beauties:

> *facies aderat nullis obnoxia gemmis*   I.ii.21

[their faces owed nothing to jewels.]

But even if we admit Propertius rather than Ovid as the classical

[1] *Op. cit.*, p. 132.

begetter of this poem, we are no nearer to an explanation of its appeal. Like most of the elegies, 'Going to Bed' is probably an early poem. The jokes about 'where my hand is set my seal shall be' and the sexual effects of Good Angels are deserving of Wilbur Sanders' censure that 'for so sophisticated a courtier, Donne's humour has a surprising schoolboy bathos'.[1] Against this, against the inert metaphor of 'flowery meades' and the confused mythology of 'Atlanta's balls' must be set the active rhythm of

> Licence my roving hands, and let them goe
> Behind, before, above, between, below.

and the mock-solemnity of the final section with its sudden descent from the 'mystique bookes' to the 'midwife' and its change in tone from reverent (if assumed) flattery to plain, even insulting statement. But these alone are not enough to make the poem any more than a young man's efforts at erotic verse (whether or not sanctioned by classical authorty). What is important in 'Going to Bed' is the image of 'my America, my new found lande' – not because it is surprising or daring, but because it is one of the earliest suggestions of that most magical of Donne's concepts, the power of love to annihilate space, making 'one little roome, an every where', as in 'The Good-morrow' or, as in 'The Sunne Rising', so contracting the world that 'both the' India's of spice and Myne' lie in one bed with him. Donne's images of maps and globes, the geography of the female body in 'Loves Progress', and the description in the 'Funeral Elegy' of the dead man's soul as 'rigg'd . . . for heavens discoverie' draw their strength from the period. Donne's sense of blessedness 'in this discovering thee' owes more to Drake and Hawkins, who made possible the pun in 'discovering' than to Ovid and Propertius.

The complicated and careful patterning of the Roman elegies calls for admiration of the craftmanship rather than participation in the feelings. An obvious example of this is Ovid's *Amores* I.vi where the lover's complaint at being locked out from his mistress is punctuated every eight lines by the ritual refrain,

> *tempora noctis eunt; excute poste seram!*
> [Night is passing away; unbolt the door.]

[1] *John Donne's Poetry*, 1971, p. 41.

The formality of this is in direct contrast with the apparent formlessness of Donne's elegies, which seem not to have been planned at all, but to move with the movements of his mind – or, rather, of the speaker's mind. It is here most of all that I feel Gosse's reading of the elegies has failed him. For while the Latin elegists are the same from one book to another – Ovid is constant as *'ille ego nequitiae Naso poeta meae'* ('Naso, the well-known poet who writes of his own naughtiness', II.i.2) – Donne's 'I' is always different, The speaker in each of the elegies, as in Browning's dramatic monologues, is a consistently created *persona*; and not one of them, in all probability, is the real Donne. In 'The Perfume' he is the epitome of Herbert's 'brave Glorie puffing by/In silks that whistled, who but he',[1] and amusedly conscious of the possible misinterpretation that might be laid on his aftershave lotion when he upbraids the perfume

> By thee, the greatest staine to mans estate
> Falls on us, to be called effeminate;

Such an accusation would never be levelled at the lover in 'Jealousie', who is an altogether tougher, even brutal man pointing out the hypocrisy behind the woman's tears:

> If swolne with poyson, hee lay in'his last bed. . . .
> Thou would'st not weepe, but jolly,'and frolicke bee,
> As a slave, which to morrow should be free;
> Yet weep'st thou, when thou seest him hungerly
> Swallow his owne death, hearts-bane jealousie.
> O give him many thanks. . . .

The speaker in 'Tutelage' is a professional, taking pride not only in the seduction of the country wife but also in her education:

> Thy graces and good words my creatures bee;
> I planted knowledge and lifes tree in thee,

And in 'The Bracelet' he has something of Eliot's small house agent's clerk, lamenting the loss of the chain not for any sentimental value, the 'seely old moralitie', but because of 'the bitter cost'. When he creates characters like these, Donne is

---

[1] 'The Quip'.

much closer to native dramatic tradition (it cannot be forgotten that he was 'a great frequenter of Playes'[1]) than to the classical and elegiac. The minimal stage-setting which I commented upon earlier in 'Going to Bed' is, in stage terms, the right one: the bed is all that is needed to indicate place in the theatre – as the stage direction from *Massacre at Paris* shows: '*Enter the* Admirall *in his bed*'.[2] The stunning exhibition, at the end, of the lover 'naked first' is a legitimate (if censorable) *coup de théâtre*. In writing 'The Bracelet' Donne was almost certainly inspired by another man's play, Kyd's *Soliman and Perseda*, and he treats with mock-seriousness the trivial incident that sparks off the play's melodramatic action. 'The Bracelet' is the most dramatic of the elegies, constructed with spaces, if not lines, for a second actor's part. Unobtrusively this second actor, the woman, is characterised as being more mundane and practical than her lover. Whenever his rhetoric reaches the heights, her observation brings it down to earth again:

> Oh be content.
> Receive from him the doome ungrudgingly
> Because he is the mouth of Destiny.
> Thou say'st (alas) the gold doth still remaine
> Though it be chang'd, and put into a chaine . . .

The poem is a battle of wills between the lover, reluctant to part with his 'twelve righteous Angels', and the women, determined that he shall make 'satisfaction' for the loss of her bracelet.

The forceful opening lines (much remarked upon) of the elegies command attention like the first words of a play, whether as in 'The Bracelet' they appear to be continuing a dialogue – 'Not that in colour it was like thy haire' – or beginning the argument *ab initio*, as in the peremptory 'Come, Madame, come'. For the most part the language of the elegies is to perfection that described by Quintilian as 'urbanitas':

Nam et urbanitas dicitur, qua quidem significari video sermonem praeferentem in verbis et sono et usu proprium quendam gustum urbis

---

[1] Sir Richard Baker, *A Chronicle of the Kings of England*, 1643, p. 156.
[2] Scene iv.

*et sumptam ex conversatione doctorum tacitam eruditionem, denique cui
contraria sit rusticitas.*[1]

The classical allusions in 'Loves Progress' are perhaps a little
showy for Quintilian's taste, sounding like learning indulged
for its own sake − or perhaps a little joke to amuse the audience
with the comic aptness of

> the straight Hellespont between
> The Sestos and Abydos of her brests,

Looked at it in this way, it becomes yet another dramatic
characteristic of the elegies. In each one the language is
adapted, however slightly, to fit the speaker. Abstract, scholarly
words are at the speaker's command in 'Loves Progress' when
he refers to 'The ductillness, the application' of gold; and of
course he is conversant with navigation charts. 'Loves Progress'
is more like a lecture than a dramatic speech: no 'thee' is
addressed, and the lecturer drops easily into a plural form with
the arch mock-intimacy of 'our Cupid is not there'. The lover
in 'Loves Warre' talks breezily but in clichés of Ireland and its
troubles, using the sort of medical terminology that is readily
available to the layman, and making old-wife-ish comments:

> Sick Ireland is with a strange warre possest,
> Like to'an Ague, now rageinge, now at rest,
> Which time will cure; yet it must do her good
> If she were purg'd, and her heade-veine let blood.

The masterful lover of 'Jealousie' is a plain blunt speaker, and a
preponderance of one-syllable words in his idiolect gives extra
power to the occasional longer word. In the lines

> Nor at his boord together being satt,
> With words, nor touch, scarce lookes adulterate.

the word 'adulterate' is unexpected after the simple foregoing
words; reinforced by the rhyme it carries heavy overtones of
legal and moral prohibition. But for me it is 'The Perfume'
which best demonstrates Donne's mastery, even at this very

---

1 *Institutio Oratoria*, VI.iii.17: *urbanitas* 'denotes language with a smack of the
city in its words, accent and idiom, and further suggests a certain tincture of
learning derived from associating with well-educated men: in a word, it represents
the opposite of rusticity' (Loeb, ii. 446-7).

early stage in his career, of language, and his sensitivity at once to the rhythms of speech and to those of the couplet. The iambics of the first line ensure that the stress is laid on the first 'Once' and then on the 'but' (whereas speech might tend to stress the repeated word), while speech and metre coincide in the stressing of 'suppos'd' to give great weight – supposed? or real? and supposed by whom? There is a light fantasy in the speaker's playing with words, especially in the enjoyment with which he lingers over the massive adjectives in 'thy Hydroptique father' and 'thy immortall mother'. As with Dickens, the language gives life to *things:* the silks can be 'taught' not to whistle, the shoes are 'opprest' and the perfume wilfully betrays him:

> And unsuspected hast invisibly
> At once fled unto him, and staid with mee.

Through verbal caricature the 'grim eight-foot-high iron-bound servingman' achieves a Dickensian super-existence – a real life and a fantasy life in the hell of nightmares. The lover's apostrophe to the perfume – 'Base excrement of earth' – strikes just the right histrionic note, appropriate to his character and suitably climactic to introduce the poem's last section.

There is, however, one kind of language used obsessively throughout the elegies, and that is the language of religion – more often than not of Roman Catholicism. 'Recusancy' is the obvious illustration of this, with its reference to 'purgatory' and its whole argument directed towards the concluding threat

> thus taught, I shall
> As nations do from Rome, from my love fall.
> My hate shall outgrow thine, and utterly
> I will renounce thy dalliance: and when I
> Am the Recusant, in that resolute state,
> What hurts it mee to be'excommunicate?

In its modern sense 'dalliance' seems a trivial word in an important place and the promise 'I will renounce thy dalliance' almost mock-heroic; but for Donne it was able to combine the two meanings (*O.E.D.* 1 and 2) of 'serious conversation or discussion' and 'amorous toying' so that, like 'Going to Bed' and 'The Bracelet' the poem ends with a play on words, combining its ambiguities. 'The Bracelet' is in fact a better poem

than 'Recusancy' with which to illustrate Donne's linguistic
obsession, since it is not structurally determined by the love-
religion metaphor. Once the pun on 'angels' has established
itself, Donne's thought – although it wanders from English
coins to foreign currency, thence to alchemy and the 'Conjurer'
– never quite lets go of it. To begin with, the coin aspect of the
'angels' is uppermost, but by the time they are 'these Martyrs'
near the end of the poem the currency is almost forgotten. They
reach their elevation to martyrdom through an accumulation
of religious associations – they are twelve, like the disciples,
they have not fallen but are still in 'the first state of their
creation', and they can even perhaps atone for the sins of others,
being 'punisht for offences not their own' and by their elevation
they raise the lover and his mistress to the confusedly blas-
phemous heights of lines 79-82:

> But thou are resolute; Thy will be done.
> Yet with such anguish as her only sonne
> The mother in the hungry grave doth lay,
> Unto the fire these Martyrs I betray.

The mistress thus becomes God the Father (having previously
been the 'dread Judge' of Old Testament rigour) and the lover
seems to share the obedience of Christ in the Garden and the
agony of the Virgin of the Deposition. All that stops the
allusions here from being offensive is their confusion; there
is no scheme by which they are systematically employed, and
the reader can applaud each one individually for its cleverness
and pass on to the next. In other poems Donne uses religious
terminology with more restraint and more effectively – as in
the opening lines of 'Change':

> Although thy hand and faith, and good works too,
> Have seal'd thy love which nothing should undoe,
> Yea though thou fall backe, that apostasie
> Confirme thy love. . . .

The double meaning is made almost explicit in the third line,
which can sustain both the bawdy jest and the technical term
'apostasie', and it reflects back on the two preceding and at
first sight innocuous lines. Familiarity has robbed 'mystique' of
much of its esoteric meaning, but in speaking of the 'mystique

language of the eye [and] hand' in 'Tutelage' and designating women in 'Going to Bed' as 'mystique bookes' Donne is, in his slightly off-beat way, returning to the Middle Ages and what C. S. Lewis called their 'religion of love' where

> The more religiously she [the lady of the love poems] is addressed, the more irreligious the poem usually is.[1]

At the same time it might be suggested – without risk of the accusation of reading life into works – that this predilection for the language of religion sprang from Donne's being vitally concerned at the time he was writing the elegies with his own religious problems and allegiance.

Donne's elegies, then, are a mongrel breed, numbering among their ancestors the Latin elegists, Marlowe as translator of Ovid and sponsor of the heroic couplet and, especially in their use of language to display character, the native dramatic tradition. Up to this point I have, wherever possible, avoided the description 'Ovidian' in favour of the more general 'Roman' – as though Ovid were substantially the same as Propertius. The two, as I showed earlier, have much in common, the 'community of experience' which they shared with their readers and which afforded the situations, characters and images of their superficial resemblances. But the difference between these two is vast, although it can be simply stated: where Propertius wrote with passion, Ovid introduced wit. In Ovid's hands the elegy reached its highest formal perfection; and after him no Latin writer could imitate the wit or bring back the passion. It was left for Donne to achieve this, and we can see a whole tradition at once in a brief comparison of four aubade poems.

The first one, by Propertius (II.xviii), is not strictly an aubade, but in that it tells of the love of Aurora for Tithonus it may be allowed to qualify. Although he was old, Aurora did not scorn her lover –

> *at non Tithoni spernens Aurora senectam*   II.xviii.3

– and she grieved that she had to leave him, complaining that day returned too soon:

> *maturos iterum est questa redire dies.*   II.xviii 12

[1] *Op. cit.,* p. 22.

Ovid's elegy (I.xiii) turns this situation on its head: it is the lover in the poem who utters the famous words *'lente currite noctis equi'* ('gallop slowly, horses of the night') while he is berating Aurora for her infidelities, accusing her of wanting to get smartly away from Tithonus because he is old:

> *illum dum refugis, longa quia grandior aevo,*
> *surgis ad invisas a sene mane rotas.*   I.xiii.37-8

Ovid introduces the theme of the cruelty of the morning – that it compels farm-labourers, women, soldiers and schoolboys to the day's hated tasks. The translation of this is one of Marlowe's best; and it is unusual to find him sympathetic to the downtrodden when he lists the morning's wrongs, which include the charge

> Thou cousenst boyes of sleepe, and doest betray them
> To *Pedants* that with cruell lashes pay them.   17-18

Finally Donne, in 'The Sunne Rising', caught Ovid's tone of witty exasperation with the early morning, turned the farm-labourers with a characteristic pun into 'countrey ants' and remembered a word from Marlowe when he wrote

> Sawcy pedantique wretch, goe chide
> Late schoole boyes, and sowre prentices,

The first stanza is almost pure Ovid; the second, on the power and brightness of love when the lovers are all the world to each other, owes no debts except perhaps to this cliché. But the third, contracting the world to a bed and princes to poor players, returns passion to the elegy. The strong assurance of

> Nothing else is.

is an achievement which Ovid cannot match.

Those of Donne's elegies that are witty and unfeeling have these qualities in common with Ovid's poems, although the inability to share without protest the Roman assumption about the right true end of love introduces a note, often dominant, of unease. But there yet remains for comment one elegy, 'On his Mistris', whose mood and tone are quite unlike those of the poems so far discussed. It has a quiet, yet passionate tenderness which is otherwise lacking in the elegies; and where the other

71

lovers adopt a certain bravura stance, speaking as it were to be overheard, this poem is so private and personal that to read it is like eavesdropping. For once in the elegies Donne (in his dramatic character of the leave-taking lover) is thinking of someone else and not of the impression that he, the speaker, will make when he tells the lady

> Thou shalt not love by meanes so dangerous.

and it is not a selfish fear that is apprehensive of her discovery by the 'Men of France', 'Th'indifferent Italian' or the 'spungie hydroptique Dutch'. At the end of the poem a nightmare vision – the lover going 'Ore the white Alpes, alone' – and daytime matter-of-factness coupled with wry humour –

> Augere mee better chance, except dreade Jove
> Think it enough for mee, t'have had thy love.

– are juxtaposed in a way not unlike that of Shakespearean tragedy, where the last scene or the last lines supply the calm after the storm. An early tribute to the warmth of feeling and the 'truth' of the emotion generated here is the subtitle given (erroneously) in the Bridgewater MS to this poem: 'His wife would have gone as his Page'. One can speak of a writer's 'truth' or 'sincerity' without referring to the facts of his life, for in such a context 'sincerity' is a quality of style, not of personality. In almost all his poems Donne has this sincerity of style, a scrupulous fidelity to the emotion he is communicating. The emotion in 'On his Mistris' is a rare one; the poem may be composed of Donne's usual ingredients, with the popular stage suggesting transvestism, and Propertius (I.viii) or Ovid (II.xi) the idea of forbidding the mistress to undertake a dangerous journey. But in the final analysis it is Donne's own emotion, imagined with sincerity and communicated with honesty, that makes the poem so moving. For evidence of its infectiousness we have the words of Hazlitt when he described Lamb's reading of the poem 'with suffused features and a faltering tongue.[1] Making all due allowance for the foreign language, it is still impossible to imagine any poem of Ovid's being read in this way.

---

[1] 'Persons one would wish to have seen', *Complete Works*, ed. P. P. Howe, 1930-4, xvii, pp. 124-5.

4

Thinking and Feeling in the
Songs and Sonnets

BARBARA HARDY

Great lyric poetry like Donne's, makes us see what D. H. Lawrence meant when he complained that 'we have no language for the feelings'.[1] Lyric creates individual forms of emotional experience, freeing us from the fixities and definites of naming and classifying. Donne's shorter poems renew, recreate, and accessibly record the life of the passions, keeping faith with the way the passions grow, move, shift, combine, and relate to intelligence and sensation. Donne's very wide-ranging love-poems can be broken down into a catalogue of passions: they construct and elucidate desire, affection, fondness, closeness, tenderness, certainty, loving identification, yearnings, grief, exultation, celebration, longing, deprivation, loss, bitterness, scorn, contempt, loathing, hostility, frustration, jealousy, spite, revulsion, delight, excitement, bliss, rest. Such naming, how-ever truthfully multiplied, is hopelessly inadequate, and I essay it in order to show its misleading crudity. It not only tells us very little, if anything, about the poetry, but goes right against the grain of poetry's passionate eloquence. Lyric creates a language for the passions by not naming, by showing those limits and falsities of naming which Lawrence derided:

> We see love, like a woolly lamb, or like a decorative decadent panther in Paris clothes: according as it is sacred or profane. We see hate, like a dog chained to a kennel. We see fear, like a shivering monkey. We see anger like a bull with a ring through his nose, and greed, like a pig . . .[2]

[1] 'The Novel and the Feelings', in *Phoenix*, ed. E. D. McDonald, 1936, p. 757.
[2] *Op. cit.*

I want to look at three groups of poems in the light of this approach to lyric, my grouping being solely one of convenience. I shall look at one poem of satisfied and secure love, a few poems of hostility and frustration, and one poem which gives expression to a complex passion which affirms faith and entertains doubt. I want to suggest that all these poems, and others like them, insist on the complexity and fluidity of states of passion. Some of Donne's most secure assertions include or imply the negation of fulfilment, while some of his most hostile poems reveal the springs of cynicism in tenderness and caring. His poems are immensely concentrated, yet almost always speak from the total experience. They keep pace with the particularity of moment-to-moment existence, and also show the richness, and fulness, of the energetic imagination. His total eloquence speaks intelligently even in irrational or extreme states of passion, is playful when most profound, sensuous when most conceptual. This poetry is formally various too, possessing the advantage of lyric in being able to refuse or bypass the history and analysis of drama and narrative, and so productive of intensities and fluidity, yet using dramatic and narrative forms eclectically and realistically, as our consciousness outside art uses drama or story to shape its passionate recordings and desires. George Eliot said 'there is no human being who having both passions and thoughts does not think in consequence of his passions',[1] and Donne not only illustrates this truth but shows an explicit awareness of it. For he is not only one of the most energetic lyric poets but also one of the most self-conscious. His poems are often shattering, like a blow without an excuse or an embrace without a problem, but they are also, as we know, vastly learned and self-aware. As Walton observed: 'His fancy was unimitably high, equalled only by his great wit; both being made useful by a commanding judgment.' The commanding judgment, however, is that of a poet.

Two quotations from Donne will be more economical than any reminders of T. S. Eliot on the united sensibility. In *The Progresse of the Soule* Donne speaks of 'the tender well-arm'd feeling braine' and in 'The Blossome' of 'A naked thinking heart'. These phrases perfectly express what we can call the

---

[1] *Middlemarch*, Chapter 47.

'interinanimation'[1] of passions and intellect. They draw attention, or may be used to draw attention, to the nakedness and vulnerability which we feel in some of these poems. History, psychology, and moral judgment are bypassed, we are strongly rooted in present time, the stress and rush of feeling is preserved, not lost to the 'commanding judgment': accordingly, we have a special sense of the exposure of human beings in their relationships. This is a feeling which also forms part of the response to Shakespeare's sonnets, for instance, or to Lawrence's *Ship of Death* poems; and in these works is found the other quality which is central to Donne, the sense of pride, triumph, delight and power, felt by the artist but on behalf of a prowess and energy larger than the experience of art. Donne answers beautifully to Coleridge's description of Shakespearean wit as the overflow of artistic power, creativity exulting and scattering its energies, in a virtuosity which is never merely virtuosity.

'Loves Growth' shows Donne's wit, seriousness, sensuousness, profundity, and play. It is a restrained, though not narrow poem, remembered for its assertion that 'Love's not so pure, and abstract, as they use/To say, which have no Mistresse but their Muse', a couplet no reader or critic of Donne can afford to forget. If we try to describe the tones of feeling we find that the beginning of the first stanza is deceptively and teasingly cynical, drily beginning, 'I scarce beleeve my love to be so pure' and not revealing its certainty and praise until the end of the sixth line. It reverses the pattern of many of the so-called cynical poems, which begin with deceptive praise or trust, to move disturbingly into rejection. The false start here belongs to a fine blend of levity and deep gravity which marks the whole poem. It is a poem which seems surprised by joy, and permitted by surprise and joy to play, delightedly and exhilaratingly:

> I scarce beleeve my love to be so pure
>> As I had thought it was,
>> Because it doth endure
> Vicissitude, and season, as the grasse;
> Me thinkes I lyed all winter, when I swore,
> My love was infinite, if spring make'it more.

[1] See 'The Exstasie'.

75

This upward lift, from play to seriousness, is something that recurs through the poem, but one of the things that Donne teaches his reader is the danger of so fixing patterns of feeling. There are the recurring upward movements, but their differences are as important as their resemblances. The poem's second movement of rising is one which depends more on a contrast of images than on a suspension of argument. And the range of feeling covered is individual; the quick, almost painful glance at love's pain is remarkable for its stabbing brevity, and is present rather in the aside or parenthesis that insists on taking in the whole truth, than in any bold antithetical relation to the health, energy, and joy in the sun's 'working vigour'. The first stanza continues:

> But if this medicine, love, which cures all sorrow
>   With more, not onely bee no quintessence,
>   But mixt of all stuffes, paining soule, or sense,
> And of the Sunne his working vigour borrow,
> Love's not so pure, and abstract, as they use
> To say, which have no Mistresse but their Muse,
> But as all else, being elemented too,
> Love sometimes would contemplate, sometimes do.

The third upward lift, in these final four lines, is again new, being altogether lighter, more amused than anything we have had up to now, and concluding in the blunt simplicity of 'do' with that kind of rough 'masculine' force so characteristic of the third, eighteenth and nineteenth *Elegies*. The heart of the poem seems to lie in the beginning of the second stanza, where the upward movement is most whole and most joyous:

> And yet not greater, but more eminent,
>   Love by the spring is growne;
>   As, in the firmament,
> Starres by the Sunne are not inlarg'd, but showne.
> Gentle love deeds, as blossomes on a bough,
> From loves awaken'd root do bud out now.

The movement here is a gentle stir, like the particular sexual movement which is being invoked. It seems to emerge from the movement from argument and scientific example, that of stars and sun, to the natural and self-evident comparison with

76

blossom; from the tiny lift from simile (blossoms) to metaphor (root) which seems to blur the metaphorical into the literal; and from the emphasis on the gentle stirring after the vigour, working, and 'doing' of the previous stanza. In the concluding lines of the poem, there is a change from sensuousness to formality, generalisation and argument. Such a change is appropriate to the enlargement of time in the look at the future of winter and other springs, and the enlargement of scale in the look at the public world. We move into a new thought, that of a continuing increase through the years, and a new claim, purchased after a harder look at the seasonal conceit and a refusal to take the calendar's analogy too literally. There is also the vigorous new spurt of wit in the ironic joke about taxes; an unflattering argument, this, but immediately followed by the serene and grave assurance of the last line:

> And though each spring doe adde to love new heate,
> As princes doe in times of action get
> New taxes, and remit them not in peace,
> No winter shall abate the springs encrease.

Each lifting motion is distinct, the whole poem consisting of a series of separated lifts, climbing like a smooth moving-stair. But we should be giving a very abstract account of the lyrical movement unless we said that there the praises, claims, and vows, are made in markedly differing moods, teasing, playful, witty, moving up to and away from the poem's heart, where the feeling is most sensuous, most gentle, most creative of beauty. The softness here seems to create a special intimacy, despite the total lack of personal address, and the intimate impression is ensured by the final movement into a larger area of wit and reference. The poem seems to achieve its unity by a final triumphant reach towards new and disparate material, ending on a flourish and a reassurance.

It is a staggering example of Donne's capacity for dropping and picking up wit and fancy, or, to put it another way, for using flights of wit and fancy audaciously, simply, and always passionately. His love-lyrics, like love, are eloquent both in extravagance and restraint. The quietest and most peaceful part of this poem depends on the surrounding vigour. It depends too on that literal invocation of the seasons with which the poem begins. The real world of nature is undescribed but taken for granted in the quiet references to 'season' and 'the grasse', which have not only the air of assuming what is present but also of assuming every man's common experience, every man's spring after his winter. But nature becomes more particularised in the sun's 'working vigour' and the imagery of stars, blossom, bough, and root. It is not very easy to say how the particularity is created, since there is no description, and all the natural items are barely mentioned, neither elaborated or personified. Donne seems to interinanimate human nature and the larger vegetable and mineral world of the spring by blending his appreciation of both worlds. He rejoices in the sun's working vigour and the gentleness of the growth of flowers, blurring simile into metaphor by the spread of feeling for the beauty and tenderness of human sex and the beauty and tenderness of non-human fertility. The phallic feeling in 'loves awakened root' is astonishingly gentle, and belongs to a quiet feeling for the body's movement which is continued in the 'stir'd' of the water's ripples. The poem creates a rare impression by its very familiar seasonal image, succeeding in using the sun, flower, and water to enlarge, define and praise sexuality, but also in bestowing a sexual beauty on the non-human world. In the 'working vigour' and in 'loves awaken'd root' there is a phallic beauty which seems to appreciate the phenomenal world, and to convey an impression of unity and kinship. This sense of fusion is not only an imaginative achievement, in the most precise sense of the term, but a proof, palpable and splendid, of the poem's hopeful celebration of love's growth.

It is not a hopeful salute to wholeness made at the expense of dispassionate wisdom. The winter life, the public world, the future seasons, are all there too, not only because, as Empson reminds us, things suggest their opposites but because Donne's frequent achievement is to remind us of opposition. He is always aware of the rest of experience, can combine passionate with dispassionate appraisal. Such acknowledgement of the other side of celebration is there in the sidelook at love's pain, which cures sorrow 'with more'. It is there too in the last airy flight of wit, which creates a movement away from the intimate physical tenderness into the ordinary testing world, a flight earned and licensed by assurance and delight. On reflection, the final excursion seems also to continue the proof that love is 'mixt of all stuffes'. Donne's love-poetry, like love, is mixed of 'all stuffes', embracing aesthetic praise, sexual energy, urgency, gentleness, rest, ease, bluntness, gravity, play. Like so much great poetry, this is a poem aware of itself; its image of the water's spreading ripples applies to the poem's own outward reach and centre, its circles being also 'all concentrique'.

Donne's poetry of certain love has this inclusiveness. 'Sweetest love', 'The Good-morrow', 'Lecture upon the Shadow', 'The Computation' and 'The Relique', amongst other poems, all have this capacity for concentration and breadth. 'The Relique's' most gravely delighted tribute can include the 'cynical' parenthesis about womankind being 'to more then one a Bed'; the theme of that extraordinary poem, 'Negative Love', is in a way demonstrated in Donne's positive declarations, which show an awareness of the difficulty and danger of love in the larger world. At the same time, these positive love-poems particularise intimacy with changing passion and sensuousness. The sensuousness is various, to be sure, and at times resides less in local life of a detail than in a diffuse musicality, as in 'The Paradox', an almost abstract piece of witty argument where physicality is that of ordered sound, not that of invoked experience. Physicality, of one kind or another, is the rule in Donne. It belongs, however, not only to the positive love-poetry but also to what we may like to describe, albeit crudely and temporarily, as Donne's poetry of destructive and rejecting passion. 'Loves Diet' is a destructive poem, both in theme and passion, but has a purchase on wholeness. If 'Loves Growth' conveys the knowing, marginal sense of pain, winter, and dishonesty, 'Loves Diet' hurls its scorn so as to reveal scorn's loving origins. The way the poem moves (in both senses of that word) is through wit, ironic and derogatory, and repulsive sensations. Wit and sensation work together in the images of obesity – 'combersome unwieldinesse', 'burdenous corpulence' – in the idea of sucking sweat instead of tears. Such images are presented as unattractive, visually and tactilely, and are also contemptuously argued: 'made it feed upon/That which love worst endures, *discretion*', or 'I let him see/'Twas neither very sound, nor meant to mee'. Sometimes the stroke of wit depends entirely on the strong sensations, as in the last stanza, where love can be called 'my buzard love', without argument, fitting in immediately with the imagery of flight, recall, and sport, but taking its contempt and its offensiveness in its culminating definition of the food of love as carrion. The poem is a most serious act of rejection, and also in a sense about itself. It works through great control and economy, forcing resentment out in these physical and cerebral ways, until the release of the last stanza. At the end the imagery of the diet is dropped once the 'buzard' makes its logic felt. The feeling is one of release, the poem now exhibiting the ease and heartless play it has been attempting in the diet:

> Thus I reclaim'd my buzard love, to flye
> At what, and when, and how, and where I chuse;
>   Now negligent of sport I lye,
>   And now as other Fawkners use,
> I spring a mistresse, sweare, write, sigh and weepe:
> And the game kill'd, or lost, goe talke, and sleepe.

The state of not caring, of cutting love down to size, of 'lowering' it, has only been achieved slowly, through the whole poem, and the marked disappearance of contempt and irony in the sense of freedom makes it very clear that the 'odi' is part of the 'amo'. In contrast and change it has created for us the sense that value has existed, and must be destroyed. The hostile feeling, and the devaluation of love shows the process of cynical feeling, and creates an apology for it. Better a buzzard than this kind of falcon?

Donne's so-called cynical poems seem to reveal cynicism, to show it as something created. I am not trying to argue it out of existence in order to claim a life-affirming creativity, but rather to suggest that destructiveness is shown as the other side of love, in the poetic process.

Donne gives an anatomy of his passions, analytic and dissecting. He does much more than convey the knowledge that jealousy and cynicism are love soured, frustrated, or cheated.

He creates the process of the passion, writing about starving his love, and dramatising the effort and the success in active verse. Another example is 'The Blossome', much less sensuous than 'Loves Diet' but also a very dynamic poem. It begins very playfully and coolly, describing the blossom which has no knowledge of its brief mortality. Then it slowly moves into a statement of passion in the second stanza, which describes the heart through the parallel with the flower, the more coolly and slowly for separating the means from the end. It is a much more quietly reasoning poem of rejection than 'Loves Diet'. Its argument is made at first more in pity than in anger, using the sad self-conscious reflection, 'But thou which lov'st to bee/ Subtile to plague thy selfe'. Love was a passive, non-answering character in 'Loves Diet' and the drama was one of action, not debate. This is a poem of dramatic argument, working through question and answer, though with a strongly embodied physicality. One of its achievements is that of making the concept physical, in 'A naked thinking heart'. It also makes the physical scornfully present by the understatement, 'Practise may make her know some other part'. And there is one line of direct sensuality, 'thou shalt see/Mee fresher, and more fat, by being with men,/Then if I had staid still with her and thee'. Once more the last verse casts off the effort, though here in a forecast, not a recorded achievement. We seem to be still mastered by the emotion that tries to reason itself out of existence:

> For Gods sake, if you can, be you so too:
> I would give you
> There, to another friend, whom wee shall finde
> As glad to have my body, as my minde.

Donne's drama allows him to acknowledge the complex sensibility. He calls the heart 'subtile' and 'thinking', avoids a dialogue between mind and heart, discusses parts and organs, but plainly speaks from and to human complexity. The dramatic form is made particularised and generalised through wit. Wit says that the 'naked thinking heart, that makes no show' can have no meaning for a woman who has no experience of such purity. But wit is also strikingly absent

81

in the simple direct thrust of 'naked thinking heart'. The
wit may be subtle, as in the comment about subtlety, or
crude, as in the aggressive joke about 'some other part' or in
the quieter stroke,

> You goe to friends, whose love and meanes present
> Various content
> To your eyes, eares, and tongue, and every part.

The word *'double-entendre'* tells us nothing about Donne's
sexual references out of context, since each one works locally
and particularly, as an 'organ to the whole'.

'The Blossome' ends with a clearing away of wit in plain
statement, and seems at least about to achieve a victory. The
all-important conclusion to Donne's poems has been emphasised
by Helen Gardner in the quotation from Donne's sermon, 'the
force of the whole piece is for the most part left to the shutting
. . . the last clause is as the impression of the stamp'. We
often find this kind of reduction of wit, sometimes as here with
the conclusion of a particular debate or argument, just before
the poem ends, sometimes as, in 'A Valediction: of my Name in
the Window', with an extremely self-conscious reflection about
wit, like the epilogue to a play. At times the end is coterminous
with the very last word, as in another poem of hostile love, 'The
Legacie'. This is also a poem where a bizarre physicality of
description plays in with the wit. The 'naked thinking heart'
combines two meanings: that of 'naked and yet thinking' with
'nakedly thinking'. 'The Legacie' also plays elaborately with
the conceit of the heart, with a detailed psychology and physio-
logy. The wit, drama, and sensuousness all belong to Donne,
but all also singularly and uniquely belong to this poem. The
speaker here assumes something of that clarity, purity, and
innocence which belonged to the heart in 'The Blossome',
and achieves a double impact: it impersonates a purely believing
love and makes way for the knowing disillusionment. In
'The Legacie' the speaker never loses the innocence, though
the poem's last line has that kind of Swiftian irony which makes
it possible for us to take the speaker either as innocently not
reflecting on the irony, or as sophisticatedly assuming it.

The poem begins quietly, explanatorily, deceptively, sounding simply the tones of what might be happy love, a sadness belonging to any separation:

> When I dyed last, and Deare, I dye
> As often as from thee I goe,
> Though it be an houre agoe,
> And Lovers houres be full eternity . . .

There follows, still without showing its hand (or heart) the first conceit about the imagined (or dreamed) death, legacy, executor, and will. Only when the poem is complete do we know the full significance of the death and of the brilliantly blurred self-excusing and other-accusing, 'Tell her anon,/That my selfe, that's you, not I,/Did kill me'; of the legacy of the heart; of the goodwill and astonishment of the executor who tried to locate the legacy and 'could there finde none'. The striking feature of the movement here is its extreme slowness, as the speaker demonstrates the difference between real hearts and false ones, false ones being really so unlike the real thing that they cannot be mistaken for it by the anatomist:

> But I alas could there finde none,
>   When I had ripp'd me,'and search'd where hearts should lye;
> It kill'd mee'againe that I who still was true,
> In life, in my last Will should cozen you.

> Yet I found something like a heart,
>   But colours it, and corners had,
>   It was not good, it was not bad,
> It was intire to none, and few had part.
> As good as could be made by art
>   It seem'd, and therefore for our losses sad,
> I thought to send that heart in stead of mine,
> But oh, no man could hold it, for twas thine.

The physical violence in the action of ripping and searching, and the emotional violence in the description of artifice, are the more forceful for being presented in the tones of quiet innocence, goodwill, pain, and patient examination. The quiet thoughtfulness not only draws out the tension but also makes its own innocence eloquently felt, in the bewildered, step-by-step discovery: first there is no heart where there should have been one, in the usual place, then, after all, 'something like' a heart. The description, 'colours it and corners', belongs to the scrutiny of the patient examining eye, while loudly sounding the duplicities. The distance travelled is so great that the final explanation comes with tremendous force. Added to the force is that also of the completed argument: the heart was artificial, it was impossible for any man to hold it, 'for twas thine'. The double argument re-doubles climax, one point taken in a moment after another. The heart's physical substance is so strongly established that it seems to have become a monstrous incarnation, with allegorical and visceral strengths, both relevant to the rational analysis and to the final contemptuous insult. But once more, hostility is revealed as the end of a slow-dying love. The poem is not simply hostile.

If poems impersonating such different moods and passions all imply this wisdom about the other side of experience, it is not surprising that some of the *Songs and Sonnets* resist this classification into positive and negative. But I want to suggest that those poems which do resist are very rare imaginative achievements; it being rather more common, both in life and in the concentrated form of lyric, to create and act out specialised passions. Passionate experience, however it may possess and transcend knowledge and irony, tends towards singleness. But Donne wrote a few poems which possess a rare and highly disturbing quality, which belong to and imprint that kind of passionate experience which joins extremes, which feels the momentary truth of possession with the possibility of loss, the expectation of denial at the time of recognition. A poem of this kind is 'A Valediction: of my Name in the Window'. Like 'Loves Growth' it is both very intense and very self-reflective, consciously remarking its own flights of wit and fantasy. Donne's very many literary-critical generalisations within his poetry, about wit, feeling, form, fantasy, dream, plain and ornate forms, and art, are of considerable interest, and they are accompanied, like similar large generalisations in Shakespeare, Milton, Keats, Wordsworth, or T. S. Eliot, by illuminating local self-references. Just as Donne observes the connection between subtlety and torment, in 'The Blossome', so in this 'Valediction' he draws our attention to a connection between fantasy and distress. Neither connection belongs exclusively to art or nature, which

explains why at times we may not know whether to call some
of this passionate poetry very artful or very natural.

'A Valediction: of my Name in the Window' begins by creating
a pattern of wit and qualification. The first four lines of the first
stanza argue that the signature scratched in the lady's window
can stand as a sign of his constancy, but its last two lines shift
the argument to assert that what will really give the signature
value is not his quality, but her eye. The second begins by
arguing that the glass of the window can stand for his trans-
parent candour, 'As all confessing, and through-shine as I', but
goes on to say that it can also reflect her image, and, finally
that more important than these separate reflections is the
signature's emblem of their unity, 'Here you see mee, and I am
you'. This setting up and putting down of argument and emblem
does not continue, in such neat stanzaic form, but once estab-
lished as a pattern goes on more irregularly, spreading quali-
fication over the whole of the third stanza and becoming very
self-reflective in the fourth,

> Or if too hard and deepe
> This learning be, for a scratch'd name to teach,
> It, as a given deaths head keepe,
> Lovers mortalitie to preach,
> Or thinke this ragged bony name to bee
> My ruinous Anatomie.

The self-consciousness about 'This learning', arguing for a
change of emblem, draws attention to the poem's shape-
changing, which in itself, as often in Donne, gives the effect of
restlessness and a loose-sitting exercise of choice, 'Take this or
this or this'. But the looseness and eclecticism is compatible
with deep seriousness, as in the analogy with the resurrection
of the body, in stanzas 5, 6, and 7. In the eighth stanza we move
from the pattern of proffered and shifting emblems to a sus-
tained fantasy, in which the signature is cast for certain passive
and active roles. The habit of wit having been established in the
comparisons, the fantasy is perhaps also presented as something
possible, something entertained, a subject for the mind to play
with. The fantasy also involves a change from the early images
of steadfastness to the image of infidelity, all the early emblems

depending indeed on her 'eye', her use of the signature as memorial and promise, the imagined infidelity depending on her neglect of these significances.

The infidelity, or its approach, is imaged in considerable dramatic psychological, and physical detail:

> When thy'inconsiderate hand
> Flings out this casement, with my trembling name,
> To looke on one, whose wit or land,
> New battry to thy heart may frame,
> Then thinke this name alive, and that thou thus
> In it offendst my Genius.

The wit is that of very compressed and various point: the signature's 'trembling' is justified because the scratched characters are irregular, not smooth; because the window itself shakes with the gesture of its opening; because it represents his image, trembling with insecurity, doubt, and fear; because of the shock of the act even of imagined treachery; and because of the imagined new love's energy, 'New battry'. All combine to give physicality to the central idea of a shattered love. There follows the small inset drama, very fully imagined, of the seduction: the maid, the persuasion, the gold, the page, the letter at the pillow, all eloquent and the more eloquent for the central speaking omission of the new lover. Suspension and ellipsis are present also in the penultimate stanza where we are led to expect a sexual climax, but are instead held, with tension and decorum, at the point where she is writing an answer to her new lover's letter

> And if this treason goe
> To'an overt act . . .

It begins, only to be let down, in this poem about writing, in the discovery that the 'act' is writing, sufficiently bad as a betrayal of the significant act of writing, which by now has for lady and for reader been charged with all the argued values and meanings. We also stop short, anguished, of the un-imaginable act. In actual argument, there comes the check as the speaker thinks that perhaps the name's magic will work, not just as fancy or conceit but indeed as a good psychological cause, a pre-Freudian error of guilt and love which will write the wrong name – a marvellous touch, combining fancy and reality in a way utterly typical of Donne:

> So, in forgetting thou remembrest right,
> And unaware to mee shalt write.

It is then as if he stops short in the flight of fancy, realising after all that a mere name is a feeble device and guard against infidelity. So the last stanza undermines the fantasy, as the earlier local wit-points were undermined. Fantasy is questioned, then wit, and ultimately, the whole poetic act:

> But glasse, and lines must bee,
> No meanes our firme substantiall love to keepe;
> Neere death inflicts this lethargie,
> And this I murmure in my sleepe;
> Impute this idle talke, to that I goe,
> For dying men talke often so.

The argument is blatantly disingenuous, still using that same wit and fancy it rejects, arguing the firmness and substantiality of their love from the fragility of the glass, denying and yet incorrigibly keeping up the play of fancy and wit. The rejection of the poem, however, makes the strongest claim after all, as the speaker says that he is talking madly but decorously, not in command but driven to irrationality by the anguish of parting. The argument is of course made most wittily, parting seen as 'death' and the lover dying. The final effect, recasting and revising the total experience of the poem, and taking force and point from the initial habit of self-questioning wit, is to establish a sense of reality by rejecting art. It confers a kind of reality on glass, signature, room, lovers, and parting, in one of those admissions of illusion, like Cressid's speech about her truth, or Hamlet's ghost in the cellarage, or Keat's 'warm scribe, my hand', that oddly but powerfully distinguish art and the live act of creating art. Here in a new last bizarre liveliness is the admission of the poem as artefact and as reality, for 'lines' apply both to signature and verses, while 'murmure', 'idle talke' and 'talke often so' all apply more to the poem than to the local conceit, though taking us out of poetry into talk.

The motion is circular. The poem cannot efface its tracks: poet, lover, woman, reader, have been through the fantasy, and if what the imagination seizes as beauty must be truth, so also what it seizes as horror must also be truth. The inclusiveness and duality of this poem is violent and pathetic, stating both the extreme conviction that love is firm and reliable, needing no emblems or promises, and the opposite vision of doubt, fear, and jealousy. It moves between and joins the need to persuade with the fantasy that explains the act of persuasion. Poet, like lover and lunatic, and here most precisely impersonating all three identities, has both reality and fantasy, and can have both without commitment to either. Or, to put it in a way that makes sense not only of our feeling that this art reveals the torments as well as the riches of imagination, he has to have reality and fantasy, is forced by passion to imagine all the possibilities, and in hateful detail. Urgency, strain, grief, affection, security insecurity, jealousy, faith, strength, and weakness all acted out, in a unity that belongs both to art and to experience. Donne is explicit about such wholeness in another poem, 'A Valediction: of the Booke':

> To take a latitude
> Sun, or starres, are fitliest view'd
> At their brightest, but to conclude
> Of longitudes, what other way have wee,
> But to marke when, and where the darke eclipses bee?

I am very far from wishing to smuggle in an argument about the biographical origins of Donne's poetry. What this range and variety of passionate lyric tells us, if we need to be told, is that the imagination, passion and intelligence which belong to poetry, and which are both displayed and discussed in Donne, do not belong only to poetry.

5

The Dismissal of Love

Or, Was Donne a Neoplatonic Lover?

A. J. SMITH

'You (I think) and I am much of one sect in the philosophy
of love; which, though it be directed upon the mind, doth
inhere in the body, and find pretty[1] entertainment there.'
(Donne, letter to Sir H. Wotton, Amiens, February 1612)

> Stand still, and I will read to thee
> A Lecture, Love, in loves philosophy.
> ('A Lecture upon the Shadow')

There seem to be two opposite ideas current about Donne's
'philosophy of love', both, I think, mistaken. One is that neo-
platonic attitudes crop up often in his verse and that his more
'serious' love poems – by definition, those to his wife perhaps?
– are simply neoplatonic. The other, more in favour with
amateurs of Donne than with scholars, is that his poetry offers
no coherent view of love at all but only a variety of local
impulses, felt in the senses as any virile man feels them and
carried with subtle erotic life in the texture of the verse. I find
this latter view more attractive if only because one does better
to oversimplify one's author than to travesty him. It doesn't
ask one to assume a dramatic conversion or to sort out Donne's
goats from his sheep on the understanding that poems of errant
passion can't *ipso facto* be as good ('sincere'? 'mature'?) as
those written to the woman one devotedly loves.

But a critical liberation is too dearly bought which requires
that one take the incessant mental life of Donne's writing as
mere casual cleverness. For it's not his frankness about sex

---

[1] Given as 'piety' in the early editions of the letters, 1651 and 1654. Gosse alters
that to 'plenty' (*The Life and Letters of John Donne*, 1899, i, p. 291).

that sets the quite distinctive temper of Donne's love poetry but the sensitive play of his intelligence – his wit. Johnson's inexcusable disservice to Donne was to characterise his wit as a random figurative ingenuity. I shall assume in this essay that Donne's wit is purposeful and expresses a settled way of encountering experience which *is* his philosophy of love. The love poems cohere overall. They don't say the same thing by a long way but they don't exclude each other either; they refer back convincingly to the realities of erotic life in which a committed passion will subsume sexuality rather than reject or transcend it. The intelligence that vibrates there so humorously yet so strongly is consistently directed, placing not only this particular relationship or that but the possible kinds of love. In attitude Donne's love poetry is wholly pragmatic, exploratory. If his sect of love is identifiable among the stances of his time it will not be because he has accepted a given set of propositions but because in feeling his way to an understanding of his own proven experience he inevitably fastened on ideas already current which seemed to define or clarify it. These certainly need not have been neoplatonic.

What Donne made of love in *The Songs and Sonnets* decisively revised the understanding which had prevailed in Europe for some four centuries; or he expressed a sexual consciousness undefined till then. The simple schematic terms of his remark to Wotton – love 'though it be directed upon the mind, doth inhere in the body' – put the bones of the matter, if the mere scholastic bones. His distinctiveness emerges sharply when one sets him against other great European love poets. I propose to threaten several birds with one stone by instancing some ways of writing about love before Donne, and by turning my discussion around the handling of one sensitive motif in Renaissance love poetry, the renunciation of love. The Donne poem for scrutiny will be 'Farewell to Love' whose reputation as a tough nut gives me a double interest in trying to crack it. In particular I want to see how Donne stands towards Renaissance neoplatonism; though that must entail a laborious rehearsal of the metaphysic of love one finds in Ficino and Pico, the two great Florentine exponents of Plato and neo-Plato.

Donne is a great metaphysical love poet and Dante is a great metaphysical love poet, but the radical unlikeness in the temper of their verse argues more than a personal disaccord or the transforming power of three centuries. It suggests that they are writing out of quite different orders of experience. Yet Dante's lyrics have many of the qualities we attribute to Donne's, arresting openings, strength of line, a vivid colloquial diction, and above all, a metaphysical sense of drama:

> Angelo clama in divino intelletto
> e dice: 'Sire, nel mondo si vede
> maraviglia ne l'atto che procede
> d'un anima che'nfin qua su risplende'.

[An angel cries out in the divine intelligence and says 'Lord, in the world is seen a marvel, in the act that proceeds from a soul which shines even up to this height'. Heaven, which has no defect save the lack of her, asks her of its Lord, and every saint implores this favour. Only Pity takes our part, for God speaks, and refers to my Lady: 'My loved ones, now suffer in peace, that your hope may be fixed for as long as pleases me there where there is one who waits to lose her, and who will say in the inferno, "O you accursed, I have seen the hope of the blessed" '.]

(*La Vita Nuova* xix, 7-8)

No later hyperbolist of love would match the cosmic inclusiveness of this metaphysical conceit, asserted as simple fact, which takes in heaven, earth, and hell, and brings God himself as well as the angels and the rest of creation to attest the marvel of the lady.

Put only a few hackneyed lines of Donne against that and you are in a different world, as well as on another cosmic plane:

> I wonder by my troth, what thou, and I
> Did, till we lov'd? were we not wean'd till then?
>
> ('The Good-morrow')

The exaltation, the single great arch of the cadence, are gone and the whole reference has shifted to domestic life. A sudden thought breaks in upon a lover's conversation or lovemaking and utters itself as if spontaneously in the lively tentative locutions of familiar talk. The attack directs one firmly to the relation between two people and assumes before the second stanza proclaims it their complete absorption in one another.

Pitched thus, as itself speaking one side of a lovers' dialogue, the voice is peculiarly immediate and peculiarly true to circumstance; it renders the living impulse of the moment, whose nuances of tenderness, fun, wonderment, pleasure, pride, play delicately across the excitement of sexual discovery that kindles the mind to vivid inventive life. One can't doubt that Dante Alighieri knew such moments, but his love poetry is about something else, rigorously fencing out domestic affections so that it can work at all.

It's Donne's sense of our human vulnerableness, frailty in time, that gives the guarded hyperboles of 'The Good-morrow' their brave poignancy:

> If our two loves be one, or, thou and I
> Love so alike, that none doe slacken, none can die.

But the decisive thing about Dante's poem is precisely that it allows the poet no possible turning back upon his great commitment. The love thus poetically enacted is beyond gainsaying because in this one respect the earthly experience is finally continuous with the celestial, the impulse wholly transcendental, the concern truly metaphysical. Dante's progress from the *Vita Nuova* to the *Paradiso* marvellously comprehends the entire creation in a scale of being up which he advances by defined degrees of moral understanding or love, a pattern of successive transcendences. The love of Beatrice is finally one with the love on which the whole creation turns:

> La mente innamorata, che donnea
> con la mia donna sempre, di ridure
> ad essa li occhi piú che mai ardea:

[My enamoured mind, which communed perpetually with my lady, burned more than ever to turn my eyes back to her . . . But she, who saw my longing, began to speak, smiling so happily that God seemed to joy in her countenance. . . . 'this heaven has no other place than the divine mind, in which is kindled the love that turns it and the *virtú* which it rains down. Light and love comprehend it in one circle, as it comprehends all other things. . . .']

(*Paradiso* xxvii, 88-90, 103-5, 109-13)

Yet the love of Beatrice, conducted in that way, is not any love as Beatrice herself points out:

Mai non t'appresentó natura o arte
piacer, quanto le belle membra in ch'io
rinchiusa fui, e sono in terra sparte;

[Neither nature nor art ever presented you with a greater pleasure
than my fair members, which are now scattered in the earth. And if
this consummate pleasure failed you by my death what mortal thing
ought you to have been drawn to desire thereafter! Certainly at the
first arrow of false things you should have risen up after me who
was such no longer.]

(*Purgatorio* xxxi, 49-57)

Dante's associates, the *dolce stil novo* poets, show us that his
singleness of vision was hard won. They aimed at it themselves,
which is why they keep insisting that a true lover needs rare
nobility and understanding – *intelletto d' amore* – and perhaps
why their own poetry seems so rarefied. One can see them
struggling to rise beyond the inner turmoil of their double
allegiance to love – earthly, and divine – tentatively trying out
the powerful idea that the beauty of a particular creature in the
world might itself have something divine in it and be celebrated
as a particle of heaven's beauty. Indeed they prove themselves
by the degree of their willingness to give the idea scope.
Frescobaldi and Guinizelli hover ambiguously between compli-
mentary similitude and hyperbolic assertion – a woman is like
a star/a woman is a star. Frescobaldi:

Un' alta stella di nova bellezza,
che del sol ci to' l'ombra la sua luce,

[A high star of miraculous beauty, whose light takes away the
sun's shadow, shines in the heaven of love with such *virtú* that its
brilliance makes me love it. . . . And as a woman, this new star lets
it be seen that my existence displeases her, so that she has ascended
thus high in disdain. Love, which speaks to me in my mind, makes
arrows of her light, and uses my meagre life as his target.]

Guinizelli:

Così lo cor, ch'è fatto da natura
asletto, pur, gentile,
donna, a guisa di stella, lo inamura

[To the heart which nature has made elect, pure, gentle, a woman
like a star brings love.]

(*Al cor gentil ripara sempre Amore*)

Cavalcanti takes the decisive step:

> veder mi par de la sua labbia uscire
> una sì bella donna, che la mente
> comprender no la può, che 'nmantenente
> ne nasce un'altra di bellezza nova,
> da la qual par ch'una stella si mova
> e dica: la salute tua è apparita.

[It seems to me that there issues from her lips a lady so beautiful that the mind cannot comprehend it, and from this at once is born another of marvellous beauty, from which it seems that a star issues and says, 'Your blessedness stands before you'.]

(Veggio negli occhi de la donna mia)

Dante's sublime vision consummates and in a sense makes intelligible the aspiration of his school, which were otherwise mere hyperbole to us:

> Se quanto infino a qui di lei si dice
> fosse conchiuso tutto in una loda,
> poco sarebbe a fornir questa vice. . . .

[If that which is said of her even up to the highest heaven were all consummated in one act of praise it would be too little to answer the present need. The beauty that I saw transcends all other, and not only what we on earth call beauty; but certainly I believe that only its maker enjoys it completely. . . . From the first day that I saw her face in this life, even up until this present sight of it, my song has never been diverted from following her. . . . She spoke again: 'We have moved out beyond the greater universe to the heaven which is pure light, intellectual light full of love, love of true good, full of delight, delight which transcends every sweetness. . .']

(Paradiso xxx, 16-21, 28-30, 38-42)

After Dante that sense of an unbroken continuum of existence seems no longer possible. When Donne gives metaphysical standing to the innocence and beauty of a young woman the outcome is his definitive dismissal, not of love only but of this world altogether:

> thou hast but one way, not t'admit
> The worlds infection, to be none of it. . . .
> For the worlds beauty is decai'd, or gone,

(The first Anniversary, 245-6, 249)

But the devotion finally apotheosised in the *Paradiso* hardly answers a normal experience of love. Bidding farewell to love is a more human gesture, moral not metaphysical. Courtly lovers might simply reassert their independence after years of unrewarded service by dramatically turning on their lady and the enslaving passion itself:

> Ffarewell Love and all thy lawes for ever:
> Thy bayted hookes shall tangill me no more; . . .
> For hetherto though I have lost all my tyme
> Me lusteth no lenger rotten boughes to clymbe.
>
> (Sir Thomas Wyatt)

Harsher exigencies suggested themselves as Christian asceticism hardened into an uncompromising contempt of the world. Choice becomes imperative when one finds no way to reconcile a compulsion to the life of the senses with the yearning for oneness with God. If Medieval and Renaissance love poetry offers us a paradigm of moral life then an attempt to renounce love might signal an impulse of some moment, even a central human dilemma. Its effect is to put acutely at issue the several allegiances implied in the notion of love itself – ultimately, to raise the whole relationship between earthly experience and eternal reality. St Augustine's example was there:

> To love then, and to be beloved, was sweet to me; but more when I obtained to enjoy the person I loved. I defiled, therefore, the spring of friendship with the filth of concupiscence, and I beclouded its brightness with the hell of lustfulness. . . .
>
> In this so vast wilderness, full of snares and dangers, behold many of them have I cut off, and thrust out of my heart, as Thou hast given me, O God of my salvation.[1]

It is notably St Augustine who in Petrarch's *Secretum Meum*, the *locus classicus* for the moral turn against love, irresistibly condemns the poet's long years of devotion to Laura, that ideal of earthly womanhood, showing the absolute discontinuity of a secular passion with heavenly love:

> From the time you fell victim to love nothing but disconsolate groans issued from your breast; the tears and sighs which the voluptuousness of love stirred up in you kept you from sleep, so that you passed whole nights repeating her name. . . . You loved the

[1] *Confessions* III, i, and X, xxxv, transl. E. B. Pusey, 1838.

laurel, with which poets are crowned as well as emperors, the more
ardently because her name was Laura, and you wrote hardly a line
of poetry that didn't mention it. . . . Such is the effect of love,
miseries unbelievable and indescribable to one who hasn't ex-
perienced it. But the greatest misery of love is the forgetfulness it
produces both of ourselves and of God. Indeed, while the love-
vanquished heart bows under the weight of so many ills, entangled in
the mud, how may it raise itself to God, the one pure fount of well-
being?[1]

Love of a woman, however idealised, cannot finally be reconciled
with love of God; on the contrary it is a damning distraction
from true love. The *Canzoniere* itself, the manual of love for
two following centuries, is framed within a severe judgment
on the thirty-one-year devotion it celebrates:

> del vario stile in ch'io piango e ragiono
> fra le vane speranze e'l van dolore,
> ove sia chi per prova intenda amore,
> spero trovar pietà, non che perdóno.

[by the varied style in which I weep and argue among vain hopes
and vain suffering I hope to find the pity, not to say pardon, of
anyone who knows love by experience. . . . And the only fruit of
my vanity is shame, repentance, and the clear recognition that
whatever pleases the world is a brief dream.]

(*Canzoniere* 1, 'Voi ch'ascoltate')

> Omai son stanco, e mia vita reprendo
> di tanto error che di vertute il seme
> ha quasi spento; e le mie parti estreme,
> alto Dio, a te devotamente rendo,
> pentito e tristo de' miei so spesi anni,

[Now I am tired, and reproach my life with so much error that the
seed of virtue is almost spent in it, and I devoutly give back my
remaining years to you, high God, repentant and sad at my ill-spent
years. . . . Lord, who have closed me in this prison, draw me out
of it safe from eternal torments, for I know my error and I don't
excuse it.]

(*Canzoniere* 364, 'Tennemi Amor anni vent'uno ardendo')

---

[1] *Secretum Francisci Petrarche de Florencia Poete laureati De Contemptu Mundi.* . . .,
Strasburg, ?1470, 32ᵛ-33ᵛ. The work was written about 1342 when Petrarch was
thirty-eight. There is an English translation of it by W. H. Draper, *Petrarch's
Secret: or the Soul's Conflict with Passion*, 1911.

The crux or dilemma Petrach exemplifies seems inherent in a moralistic understanding of love such as the cult of chivalry adopted. Love may be a refining devotion which elevates, ennobles, keeps one chaste; but if it has any reality at all it is still in the end a fixation upon an earthly object and inevitably subject to the laws of desire, the prompting of the senses and passions. Hence it always contains in itself the seeds of its own defeat, existing in necessary self-contradiction, self-frustration:

> So while thy beautie draws the heart to love,
> As fast thy Vertue bends that love to good:
> 'But ah,' Desire still cries, 'give me some food.'
> (Sidney, *Astrophil and Stella* 71)

Court jongleurs seized on the contradiction as a way of praising their Duchess's irresistible beauty yet invincible chastity in the same motion:

> Deh dimme amor se gliè fuor di natura,
> Da un cor di ghiaccio uscir fiamma chincende?

> [Alas, tell me Love if it is something beyond nature that flames which set one on fire should issue from a heart of ice?]
> (Serafino d'Aquila, *Strambotto*)

More highminded poets dramatise it as a dire self-war, the lower faculties against the higher, flesh against spirit, the sensible apprehension against the intelligible:

> L' alma vaga di luce e di bellezza
> ardite spiega al ciel l'ale amorose,
> ma sí le fa l'umanità gravose
> che le dechina a quel ch'in terra apprezza;

> e de' piaceri a la dolce esca avvezza
> ove in candido volto Amor la pose
> tra bianche perle e mattutine rose
> par che non trovi altra maggior dolcezza;

> [The soul, eager for light and beauty, boldly spreads its amorous wings heavenwards; but humanity makes them so heavy that they fall back to that which is valued on earth. And among such pleasures it accustoms itself to the sweet lure which Love has placed in a fair face among white pearls and morning roses, so that one might think it could find no greater sweetness. . . .]
> (Tasso, *Rime per Lucrezia Bendidio* lxvii)

Spenser's inability to sustain his confused vision of a transcendent love and beauty leads him in the end to condemn the attempt as itself corrupt:

> Many lewd lays (ah! woe is me the more!)
> In praise of that mad fit which fools call love,
> I have in th' heat of youth made heretofore
>
> (*An Hymne of Heavenly Love*)

From a dilemma so absolute, so locked in the contradictory terms of our human nature itself, a flat renunciation of love altogether offered the only escape in the end:

> Leave me ô Love, which reachest but to dust,
> And thou my mind aspire to higher things:
>
> (Sidney, *Certain Sonnets* 32)

Such extreme ways of coping with love imply a distinctive conception of man's moral nature, as striking in its omissions as in its assumptions. For the fact is that normal theorising about love, and Renaissance lyric poetry altogether, found no licit place for sexual love as such or even a mutual passion in itself. The woman appears as a kind of angelic apparition leading the mind (but not the senses) beyond. Or she is a paragon of chastity and beauty whom we can't love as we ought, through the mind alone, but must desire in ways that frustrate each other and distract our minds from God.

Either attitude supposes an absolute qualitative difference between the several elements of our nature, sense and intellect or spirit, as between the realms of being in which we act and experience. Sense apprehends the world of matter whose nature is formless chaos, contingency, flux, momentariness, total instability. But mind looks beyond the discrete particularities of matter to the form that alone gives matter coherence, reaching out thus to the realm of absolute and immutable truth whose final consummation is God himself. Our distinctive power of reason enables us to elect our own course and destiny as between the life of sense and the life of mind. But in practice the choice cannot be so conveniently categorical for we apprehend through sense, and the mind must depend upon sense to grasp the world outside at all: *nihil in intellectu quod non prius in sensu.*

What then may span the gap between sense and mind? The answer generally assumed was that the senses themselves are qualitatively ordered, touch being the lowest of them, committed as it is to momentary and indiscriminate impression, and sight the highest, looking to symmetry, order, and in all, the triumph of form over matter that even physical beauty implies. Sexual love as such belongs to the world of matter in so far as the end it proposes is bodily union, the gratification of the most material sense; and it is to that extent unappeasable or self-defeating for it craves impermanence and its own decay. But a love which is prompted by pure beauty and heroically confines its sensual response to a gaze of wonderment already looks to the world of form and may soon transcend sense altogether as it strikes beyond time to the timeless, from seeming to being, false to real.

Petrarch's dilemma, as Sidney's later, implied a living stricture upon his transcendentalising predecessors in favour of a grimmer view of love and human nature. Petrarch admires Laura's chaste and virtuous beauty and repeatedly celebrates it in quasi-Platonic terms as a manifestation of the divine, the universal form of beauty, celestial beauty and the like; but it is precisely these heavenly qualities in her which inflame his sense to the heat of love, so that he finds himself in the hopeless self-frustration of desiring her for that very virtue which she would forfeit altogether if she yielded to him. He is inevitably caught in sum between the contradictory terms of his own nature and of the apparition itself, unable to love incarnate virtue save through his senses or to detach the ideal he apprehends from the woman he craves to enjoy. Even Laura's death offers him no such pattern of successive transcendence as Beatrice's death allowed Dante; and the only alternative to ruin in the end, as St Augustine had foretold him, is renunciation of earthly beauty for heavenly, Laura for the Virgin:

> Mortal bellezza, atti, e parole m'hanno
> tutta ingombrata l'alma.
> Vergine sacra et alma,
> non tardar, ch'i'son forse a l'ultimo anno.
>
> (*Vergine bella*, 85-8)

Succeeding poets evidently found this a more apt rendering of love than Cavalcanti's or Dante's.

The Florentine neoplatonists, however, were *dantisti*. In effect Renaissance neoplatonism emerged out of the idealist synthesising that went on around Il Magnifico at San Marco and Careggi; and the *Commedia*, with its hierarchy of transcendence, was easily accommodated to Diotima's soaring vision and to the mystical platonism of Dionysius Areopagus and the Plotinians. Ficino and Pico are vast and luminous synthesisers but they haven't Dante's grasp of the world or his comprehensive vision of love. They don't set out to show us in what ways love is the seed of all our virtues and vices – 'sementa in voi d'ogni virtute/e d'ogne operazion che merta pene' (*Purgatorio* xvii, 104–5) – or how it subsumes the lover's desire and his will in the force that links and moves the entire creation:

> Nel suo profondo vidi che s'interna,
> legato con amore in un volume,
> ciò che per l'universo si squaderna; . . .

> ma già volgeva il mio disio e il velle
> sì come rota ch'igualmente è mossa,
> l'amor che move il sole e l'altre stelle.

In its profound depth I saw ingathered, bound up by love in one volume, the leaves which are scattered through the universe . . . but already my desire and will were turned, even as a wheel that moves equally, by the love that moves the sun and the other stars.
(*Paradiso* xxxiii, 85–7, 143–5)

What they do offer us is a transcendental religion of beauty whose moving force is love. Beauty is the divine essence and love its attractive power, which draws us up to God 'as if by a hook' Ficino says[1]; and essentially the whole idealist metaphysic of love is an educing of the manner and modes of that intellectual compulsion. In summarising it I shall conflate as far as seems just the arguments of the two prime texts of neoplatonic love, Ficino's commentary on Plato's *Symposium* and Pico's commentary on Benivieni's *Canzona de Amore*.[2]

[1] See *infra*, *1544*, 127 and *1576*, 1341.
[2] M. Ficino, *In Convivium Platonis De Amore, Commentarium*, in *Opera*, Basilaea, 1576, Tom. ii, pp. 1320-61. Italian version, transl. and augmented by Ficino

Love works in us, they assert, as a desire for union with the beloved. But union is stasis, for the pattern of consummated love is the change from movement to rest. So the end of love is the state of contemplation, which is wholly a stasis and hence wholly beyond sense, wholly intellectual.[1] The final object of love is God alone who draws us thus to union with him and the contemplation of his beauty:

> Hence the light and beauty of God, which is wholly pure, and free of every condition, is without doubt infinite beauty. Infinite beauty calls for infinite love. Hence I implore you . . . that you love the creatures with a definite limit and end. But you must love the Creator with infinite love. And take as much care as you can that in loving God you observe no limit or measure whatever.[2]

Any lesser love than this is necessarily imperfect, and will indeed frustrate the true end of love if it is not already committed to the ascent from matter to form:

> The eye alone, then, enjoys [fruitur] bodily beauty. And as love is a desire to enjoy [fruendae] beauty, and one perceives beauty only by one's eyes, the lover of the body is satisfied just to see the bodily aspect of the loved one.[3]

The vision is both dynamic and qualitative for it supposes that the whole contingent creation is in progressive movement

---

himself, *M. Ficino sopra lo Amore*, Firenze, 1544. I give page references to both versions, denoting them by their dates.

Pico della Mirandola, *Commento Del Illustrissimo Signore Conte Johanni Pico Mirandulano sopra una Canzona de Amore composta da Hieronymo benivieni Cittadino Fiorentino secondo la mente e opinione de Platonici,* ?1519.

Ficino's *Commentary* was written in 1469 and first printed in 1484. According to legend it is the outcome of Lorenzo de' Medici's attempt to renew the ancient neoplatonic custom of a banquet on Plato's anniversary, 7th November, when he invited a company of platonists to Careggi to dine and expound Plato. Pico's *Commento* was written about 1490 and first published with his works in 1495. Girolamo Benivieni was a pupil of Ficino, who condensed in one *canzone* his master's theory of divine love. He later went over to Savonarola and transmuted all his secular poetry into religious poetry, becoming more or less the official poet of Savonarola's followers, the *piagnoni*.

[1] Ficino, *1544*, 190; *1576*, 1352.   [2] Ficino, *1544*, 202; *1576*, 1354-5.
[3] Ficino, *1544*, 49; *1576*, 1328.

either upwards towards stasis or downwards towards total flux and chaos. Men can will their course according to the quality of their election in love, the one motive power, which 'causes some to fall as far as bodily touch and others to rise as far as the vision of God'.[1] So that love is moral choice; and the doctrine gets it characteristic moral impetus from the way it discriminates between our contingent loves, disposing them as lower or higher forms of the desire for union with the beloved according as they impede or tend towards the final end of love. Briefly, it posits three distinct orders of amorous union and types of men: animal copulation, sought by voluptuous men, human love, sought by practical men, and celestial love, sought by contemplative men. Animal copulation, the lowest order, isn't really love at all. Its end is the mere conjunction of material objects so that it is wholly subject to the conditions of the world of matter such as momentariness or change; and it is governed by touch, seeking only the satisfaction of that sense:

> I say that sense judges that this beauty has its origin in the body, and therefore the end of all animal love is coitus. But reason, by opposite judgment, recognises that this material body not only is not the fount and principle of beauty, but is wholly diverse from that and corruptive of it; and it recognises that the more one separates beauty from the body and considers it in itself, the more it has of its own nature and proper dignity and presence.[2]

Such a state of slavery to matter can't be transcended for it doesn't aspire beyond itself; there is only the choice, to settle for it (and forgo one's humanity), or renounce it altogether.

Human love, the realm of the earthly Venus in Pico's myth, has a middle status and nature, being a mixture of animal copulation and intellectual contemplation in varying degrees. It is governed by the highest of the senses, sight, and by our specific human faculty of reason. But it leaves us still pulled either way and having to choose one course or the other. Pico says that most men occupy themselves with these two orders of love, not aspiring higher.[3]

---

[1] Ficino, *1544*, 207; *1576*, 1356.
[2] Pico, *Commento*, 32ᵛ.
[3] 36ʳ.

Celestial love, in the realm of the Celestial Venus, is possible only to men

> whose intellect is purified by philosphical study so that they recognise sensible beauty for a mere image of a more perfect beauty; and having abandoned the love of sensible beauty they begin to desire the sight of celestial beauty. . . .[1]

Ficino puts that more drily as a matter of a progressive abstraction of contingent qualities: taking away matter and place one sees the beauty of soul, taking away time one sees the beauty of angelic mind, taking away multiplicity one arrives at the One pure light which is the beauty of God himself.[2] So the end this love proposes is the final goal of all creatures which set out up the long stairway from material chaos to formal order, nothing less than the pure angelic contemplation of Ideal Form itself, static, immutable, absolute.[3]

As a structure of deduced hypothesis the system has an elegant self-sufficiency and it opens an inspiring prospect to us. The account of the amorous life which Pico in particular projects from it is positively enraptured. Love in the lover, he says, is the exalted pursuit of ideal beauty up 'the ladder of amorous stages'[4] towards the source of all beauty. Glimpsing a gleam of it in another human being the lover elects the amatory life which is our only escape from the bondage of body and matter. He commits himself to a heroic way of transcendence, a kind of epistemological pilgrim's progress in effect, passing by a process of successive abstraction and idealisation from lower senses to higher, sensible qualities to intelligible, sight to contemplation, participated apprehension to direct, particular physical beauties to the one pure form of beauty, and lastly to universal form itself.[5] At each stage he leaves his former state behind, drawn by an ever more powerful desire to see again that beauty which his soul glimpsed 'before it was immersed in the body',[6] until he raises himself beyond the human state altogether and dies as man to be born again 'as if purged by the fire of love to the form of an angel'.[7]

This is the one way open to the man of philosophical mind

---

[1] Pico, 36r.   [2] *1544*, 192-3; *1576*, 1354.   [3] *1544*, 190; *1576*, 1352.
[4] 60r.   [5] 59r-60r.   [6] 33r.   [7] 12r.

who finds himself loving a worldly object; and it cannot start in touch or seek its satisfaction there, for 'the libidousness of touch is not part of love or an impulse of the lover'[1] and does not point upwards beyond itself. On the contrary, 'adulterated love is a ruinous descent from sight to touch'.[2] So Ficino finds the highest and best form of a purely human love in a union where sight and mind are all and touch cannot licitly enter, that between an older man and a handsome youth, founded as it must be in the disinterested admiration of beauty:

> Finally the lovers exchange beauty for beauty. The older man enjoys with his eyes the beauty of the younger; and the younger man enjoys with his mind the beauty of the older. And the one, who is beautiful in body alone, by this habit becomes beautiful in soul; and the other, who is beautiful only in his mind, fills his eyes with bodily beauty. This is a marvellous exchange for the one and the other, honest, useful, delightful. . . .[3]

That strikes one as a curious notion of love, even so – beautiful but inhuman, and a perverse way of asserting the essential dignity of man against such as Savonarola. For however much Ficino may urge that a person so loved has the duty of returning love[4] the end cannot be a mutual regard between human beings. In the end the lover leaves particular objects of enjoyment behind altogether and recognises then that the beauty he loved was within himself, that his soul has endowed an external object with its own intrinsic power of beauty which is a function of universal beauty.[5] In the end the lover's striving for union with the beloved, his dying to himself and living again in the beloved, is consummated as the process itself is consummated in the union with God, for 'the fount of all beauty is God. God is the fount of all love':[6]

> Whoever in the present time gives himself with charity wholly to God will finally recover himself in God. For he will return to his own Idea, by which he was created. . . . But joined then by love to our own idea, we shall become whole again; in such a way that it will appear that we first loved God in things so as then to love

[1] Ficino, *1544*, 49; *1576*, 1328.
[2] Ficino, *1544*, 246; *1576*, 1362.
[3] *1544*, 49-50; *1576*, 1328.
[4] *1544*, 47; *1576*, 1328.
[5] *1544*, 193; *1576*, 1353.
[6] *1544*, 193; *1576*, 1353.

things in him; and that we honour things in God so as to recover ourselves above all. And loving God, we have loved our own selves.[1]

One loses oneself to find oneself completely for the first time.

Ficino's account of physical coupling exemplifies the invincibly teleological habit of the neoplatonic school. Bodily union is an absolute impediment to right love, he says, for 'The appetite for coitus and the appetite for love are not only not the same impulses but show themselves to be contraries'.[2] Yet it may be allowed when it isn't itself the end that is sought; thus the begetting of children in marriage is not blameworthy because the end is the begetting and not the mere gratification of sense. However, that has nothing to do with love.[3]

So coldly schematic a resolution (which il Magnifico himself would delicately reject as a practical lover[4]) comes pat out of the uncompromising idealism of a system whose reference is always to ends and norms not to experience. Dante had not laid himself open to the charge of confusing a metaphysical ideal with the domestic practicalities, as the Florentine neoplatonists quite blatantly did in their attempts to live out their rarified notions as a circle of loving brothers around the Medici. The celibate Ficino, judging amorous behaviour simply as it furthers or hinders an end already defined *a priori*, looks just to deductive logic to resolve the moral exigencies of love and no brute imperatives of sexual life resist his imposing it upon them. So we have the central paradox of the whole neoplatonic doctrine

---

[1] *1544*, 203; *1576*, 1355.

[2] *1544*, 18; *1576*, 1323.

[3] *1544*, 18; *1576*, 1323.

[4] 'It seems to me that little blame attaches to what is natural: nothing is more natural than the appetite to unite oneself with the beautiful object, and this appetite was ordained by nature in men for human propagation, a most necessary matter to the conservation of the human species' (Lorenzo de' Medici, *Comento . . . Sopra Alcuni De' Suoi Sonetti* in *Opere*, ed. A. Simioni, Bari, 1913, 1, p. 16). Lorenzo goes on to say that good lovers are those who 'pursuing this end, love one sole thing perpetually both with firm constancy and with faith'. Much later in the *Comento* he speaks of the 'sweet death' he himself hopes for when he transformes himself into his beloved, this being 'that sweetness which human concupiscence can achieve'. He awaits this, he says, 'as the true end of all my desires and my one saving remedy' (1, p. 139).

of love, that love is more truly itself as it purges itself of sense, passion, even a particular human object, and rises free of historical placing and circumstance to an absolute stasis beyond time:

> Hence it comes about that the vehemence of the lover isn't quenched by any touch or aspect of body; for he desires not this body or that one: but he desires the splendour of the supernal majesty shining in bodies, and it is this that he marvels at.[1]

Between that and Donne's figure of ecstasy there is a world of difference – the human world.

One can't discount the sheer poetic power of the neoplatonic vision, or its exalted idea of man's possible moral grandeur. Succeeding writers found it good for a casual head of ardour if somewhat impalpable as a way of life. But the one great European love poet who unmistakably tried to live out this superhuman metaphysic of love in his art, and in a sense redeems its flights from academicism, had sat at il Magnifico's table in his youth and known Ficino and Pico:

> Non vider gli occhi miei cosa mortale,
> allor che ne' bei vostri intera pace
> trovai, ma dentro, ov'ogni mal dispiace,
> chi d'amor l'alma a se simil m'assale;

[My eyes saw no mortal thing when they found their entire peace in your beautiful eyes; but within, where every evil thought displeases, they saw Him who invests my soul with a love like himself.

And if it were not created like God it would seek no other than the exterior beauty that pleases the eyes; but because this beauty is a deceit the soul transcends it in the universal form.

I say that the desire of a living being cannot be satisfied with that which dies; nor can what is eternal wait upon time, where the husk decays. Sense is not love but unbridled will, that kills the soul; and our love perfects friendship here below, but still more, through death, in heaven.]

Michelangelo Buonarroti know no Greek (or Latin either for that matter[2]). But he was a noted Platonist and *dantista*, and

---

[1] Ficino, *1544*, 26; *1576*, 1326.

[2] See Donato Gianotii, *De' giorni che Dante consumò nel cercar l'Inferno e'l Purgatorio*. Given in C. Guasti, *Rime di Michelangelo Buonarroti*, Firenze, 1863, pp. xxvi-xxxiv.

his poetry has a uniquely personal character of idealising ardour and muscular strength:

> Non è sempre di colpa aspra e mortale
> d'una immensa bellezza un fere ardore,

[The fierce ardour for an immense beauty isn't always a harsh and mortal sin, if it leaves the heart so softened that the divine shaft more quickly pierces it. Love awakes and directs and feathers the wings, and doesn't impede the vain *furore* from rising aloft; for the soul finds no satisfaction in that first stage but ascends and rises to its creator.]

His major love poems, as we have them, were written when he was already past fifty. From the late 1520s he addressed a body of sonnets to a young Roman nobleman Tommaso Cavalieri:

> Veggio nel tuo bel viso, signor mio,
> quel che narrar mal puossi in questa vita:
> l'anima, della carne ancor vestita,
> con esso è già più volte ascesa a Dio.

[I see in your beautiful face, my lord, that which can scarcely be grasped in this life: the soul, still dressed in flesh, has by this beauty already ascended to God many times.

And though the malicious vulgar commonly attributes to others its own folly and evil, that doesn't make the intense will less worthy – the love, the faith, the honest desire.

Every beauty we see here, in wise judgments resembles more than any other thing that divine origin from whence we all issue. Nor do we have on earth any other evidence or other fruits of heaven; and who loves with faith transcends to God and makes death sweet.]

Some twelve years later his pious friendship with the widowed Marchesa of Pescara, the poetess Vittoria Colonna, prompted a series of sonnets and madrigals:

> Gli occhi mie vaghi delle cose belle
> e l'alma insieme della suo salute
> non hanno altra virtute
> c'ascenda al ciel, che mirar tutte quelle.

[My eyes, thirsty for beautiful things, and my soul likewise eager for its salvation, have no other power which ascends to heaven than the contemplation of all these. . . .]

Michelangelo himself was well aware how his relationship with Cavalieri would be construed and disdainfully dismissed those who would take it so as creatures bound in by sense, incapable of apprehending universal form; a judgment that as he saw it grows out of his entire life:

> Per fido esemplo alla mia vocazione
> nel parto mi fu data la bellezza
> che d'ambo l'arti m'è lucerna e specchio

[Beauty, which is lantern and mirror of both arts, was given to me at my birth as sign of my vocation. If anyone thinks otherwise he is wrong. This alone carries the eye to that sublime height which prepares me to paint and sculpture here. If bold and foolish judgments attribute to sense that beauty which transports to heaven every sane intellect, one can only say that infirm eyes cannot rise from the mortal to the divine, and must remain fixed there where it would be vain to think of ascending without special grace.]

For he loved, said his pupil and biographer Condivi, 'not only human beauty, but universally every beautiful thing, a beautiful horse, a beautiful dog, a beautiful landscape . . . admiring them with marvellous feeling, abstracting the beauty of nature as the bees gather honey from flowers to use it in their works'.[1] One can't doubt that Condivi had this direct from the master but not knowing Plato himself he hasn't grasped the crucial distinction Michelangelo draws between mortal and ideal beauty[2]:

> Passa per gli occhi al core in un momento
> qualunche obbietto di beltá lor sia,
> e per sí larga e sí capace via
> c' a mille non si chiude, non c'a cento,

[In one moment there passes through the eyes to the heart whatever they deem beautiful, and by so broad and capacious a way that it's open not just to a hundred but to a thousand beauties of every age, of either sex. . . . If an ardent desire remains wholly fixed on mortal beauty it didn't then descend from heaven with the soul, and is therefore human will. But if it passes beyond this then, Love, it

---

[1] A. Condivi, *Vita di Michelagnolo Buonarroti*, Roma, 1553, 42ᵛ.

[2] 'I have often heard Michelangelo reason and discourse upon love, and those who were present then have heard him say no other of love than that which one reads in Plato. I for my part don't know what Plato may say about it . . .'. *Ibid.*, 42ʳ.

disprizes your name, for it seeks a timeless condition – *altro die* – and hence no longer fears what assails so base a husk.]

The friendship with Colonna was not open to mistake. Condivi recalled hearing Michelangelo say 'he regretted nothing more' than that even when 'he went to see her in her passing from this life he didn't kiss her forehead or face as he kissed her hand'.[1] His poems to her represent the purest and most intensely felt attempt in European writing to give a living human relationship a transcendental status, to find in another human being a scintilla of the love and beauty of the First Principle itself, which draws one upwards beyond fleshly appearance:

> L'anima, l'intelletto intero e sano
> per gli occhi ascende più libero e sciolto
> a l'alta tuo beltá; ma l'ardor molto
> non dà tal previlegio al corp' umano
> grave e mortal,

[The soul, the pure and entire intelligence, ascends free and un-bound through the eyes to your high beauty; but great ardour gives no such privilege to the human body, heavy and mortal . . .]

(Ben posson gli occhi)

Evidently this is no academic matter. For Michelangelo art and love are like intellectual activities having the same origin, serving the same end and manifesting the same special grace; they are alike at the opposite pole from sense, transcendental while that remains earthbound. Here is an attempt, which one can only call heroic, to put a personal dilemma in a cosmic setting. Nothing less is in view than the reconciliation of the sensuous basis of art with a transcendental doctrine behind which lurked a Savonarolean *contemptu mundi*. But at the centre is the poet's titanic struggle to reach a truce between his mastering response to sense experience, and what he consciously believed, between, his deepest sensibility and convictions received but profoundly held. It's a possibility hardly glimpsed by other sixteenth-century celebrants of beauty, whose inability to press beyond moral attitudes led them to locate the cause of their frustration in the naked conflict between the ideal and the senses.

[1] 41^{v}.

So it is an event of moment for European thought when even so devoted a platonist fails to sustain his vision and turns at last to dismiss human love altogether, renouncing in the same breath the divine principle of beauty which had been the touchstone of his art and his life:

> Giunto è già'l corso della vita mia,
> con tempestoso mar, per fragil barca,
> al comun porto, ov'a render si varca
> conto e ragion d'ogni opra trista e pia.

[The course of my life, frail bark in tempestuous sea, has reached the common gate where one passes to render account and justification of all one's works, bad and good.

Whereby I now recognise how full of error was the impassioned fantasy by which I made art my idol and monarch, as well as that which every man desires to his own damnation.

The amorous thoughts, once vain and lighthearted – what are they now if I draw near to two deaths! Of one [death] I am certain; and the other menaces me.

No painting or sculpture may satisfy any more the soul turned to that divine love that opens its arms on the cross to receive us.]

This is the record of a personal agony, whether it be St Augustine or Savonarola or the Council of Trent that lies behind it, or just the fear of imminent death: 'l'arte e la morte non va bene insieme'.[1] Michelangelo is one of those few artists who truly stood in a symbolic relation to his time. In European poetry the triumph of piety over beauty is also the triumph of a moral over a metaphysical sense of love, Petrarch and the Council of Trent over Plato and Dante if one likes. There is no reason in neoplatonic thinking why a man need choose between love and Christ. But Pico della Mirandola, the apostle of platonic beauty himself, is said to have declared for Savonarola as he lay dying and asked for burial in Dominican habit.[2] Michelangelo too had heard Savonarola in his youth and never lost the vivid impression the monk made on him – 'the memory of his living voice still remaining in his mind' wrote Condivi, more than fifty years after Savonarola's death.[3] Possibly the harsh imperative of impending death is another actuality the

[1] 'Non può, Signor mie car.'
[2] See P. Villari, *Life and Times of Girolamo Savonarola*, 1897, pp. 244-5.   [3] 42ʳ.

neoplatonic vision couldn't stand up to, even with so heroic a champion. Whatever the reason, Michelangelo's dismissal of love, more momentous than Petrarch's, amounts to a final renunciation of what had offered itself as the most exalted and ennobling of wordly experiences. And its substantial ground is the absolute discontinuity of ephemeral appearance and eternal reality, love of the creature and love of the Creator.

¶

Donne seems on the face of it a very odd bird to look for in this company. His practical understanding of love, early and late, comes agreeably down to earth:

> Who ever loves, if hee doe not propose
> The right true end of love, hee's one which goes
> To sea for nothing but to make him sicke . . .
> Rich Nature hath in woman wisely made
> Two purses, and their mouthes aversely laid;
> They then which to the lower tribute owe
> That way which that exchequer lookes must goe.
> Hee which doth not, his error is as greate
> As who by Clyster gave the stomach meate.
> (Elegy: 'Loves Progress', 1-3, 91-6)

> Licence my roving hands, and let them goe
> Behind, before, above, between, below. . . .
> Then where my hand is set my seal shall be.
> (Elegy: 'To his Mistris Going to Bed', 25-6, 32)

> Thine age askes ease, and since thy duties bee
> To warme the world, that's done in warming us.
> Shine here to us, and thou art every where;
> This bed thy center is, these walls, thy spheare.
> ('The Sunne Rising', 27-30)

> Some that have deeper digg'd loves Myne then I,
> Say, where his centrique happiness doth lie:
> ('Loves Alchymie', 1-2)

> Neither desires to be spar'd, nor to spare,
> They quickly pay their debt, and then
> Take no acquittances, but pay again;
> They pay, they give, they lend, and so let fall
> No such occasion to be liberall.

(An Epithalamion . . . on the Lady Elizabeth and Count Palatine . . . 92-6)

But the issue here is not so much this sentiment or that as the temper of a man's mind and thought, and the test will be the whole tenor of a single important poem such as in some Renaissance love poets might polarise all their writings.

Farewell to Love

Whilst yet to prove,
    I thought there was some Deitie in love,
  So did I reverence, and gave
Worship, as Atheists at their dying houre
Call, what they cannot name, an unknowne power,   5
  As ignorantly did I crave:
      Thus when
Things not yet knowne are coveted by men,
  Our desires give them fashion, and so
As they waxe lesser, fall, as they sise, grow.   10

    But, from late faire
His highnesse sitting in a golden Chaire,
  Is not lesse cared for after three dayes
By children, then the thing which lovers so
Blindly admire, and with such worship wooe;   15
  Being had, enjoying it decayes:
      And thence,
What before pleas'd them all, takes but one sense,
  And that so lamely, as it leaves behinde
A kinde of sorrowing dulnesse to the minde.   20

    Ah cannot wee,
As well as Cocks and Lyons jocund be,
  After such pleasures? Unlesse wise
  Nature decreed (since each such Act, they say,
Diminisheth the length of life a day)   25
  This; as shee would man should despise
      The sport,
Because that other curse of being short,
  And onely for a minute made to be
Eager, desires to raise posterity.   30

    Since so, my minde
Shall not desire what no man else can finde,
  I'll no more dote and runne
To pursue things which had indammag'd me.
And when I come where moving beauties be,   35

> As men doe when the summers Sunne
> Growes great,
> Though I admire their greatnesse, shun their heat;
> Each place can afford shadowes. If all faile,
> 'Tis but applying worme-seed to the Taile.[1]   40

Donne's dismissal of love has none of the animus of the kind, anguish or indignation as may be, though its blunt terse address and muscular wresting of syntax and form give it a force of brusque impatience. But the rhetoric of 'Farewell to Love', so strikingly *sui generis*, is a function of a very complex sense, and the sense is my first concern.

One notes right away that the arrangement of the poem stanza by stanza plots a movement in time, following out the poet's development from inexperienced enthusiasm to experienced rejection and its consequences – past; present; general state now; future. But his case against love here is ironically unlike the courtier's or the moralist's, and it's a very different kind of ruinous obsession that he assumes. The poem shows him thinking his way to the hard truth about a practice long indulged. Love, here, isn't a state of unsuccessful service at all but a repeated fruition which has never lived up to its promise; he now sees through it after long but finally disillusioning experience, coming out the other side a wiser if warier man.

Like the brusque opening itself that sense doesn't so much challenge as contemptuously dismiss the petitioning posture of common love poetry and it makes such slavish petrarchism as Watson's 'My love is past'[2] look like the childish act of a schoolboy sticking his tongue out at what he hasn't grown up enough to have or grasp. Donne's poem assumes as close an experience of sexual life as Shakespeare's Sonnet 129, 'The expense of spirit', though its temper is different; and these two poems are singular in their unsentimental plotting of the drive itself. But Donne doesn't argue a case here or develop a dialectic. The clear logical structure of the poem marks the stages of a process already complete, a realisation now reached and assured, and the argument moves forward only to affirm the resolve that emerges from this new understanding.

---

[1] Text from the 1635 edition save in line 23, where *1635* reads ' . . . pleasures, unlesse . . .'.   [2] *Ekatompathia*, lxxx on.

It's typical of Donne in the ironic posture of this poem to play off his harshness against a very different impression which he may have deliberately fostered. Here the formal stanza pattern suggests a ceremonial lyric elegance which the mordant stabbing phrases will quite brutally contradict. One can imagine too the shock of a reader who anticipates the graces of a love poem and at once finds himself in an atmosphere of abrasive challenge where quite worldly things are going on. Though this is a poem about love rather than a love poem the various intellectual life of the first stanza may take one aback.

The stanza sets out and accounts for his virgin illusions about love. Its argument has the logical form of *leading instance – analogous case – general law*, and the appearance of logical sequence; though plainly the relation between the several elements is not merely sequential and may itself be crucial to the whole sense. The opening lines (1-4a) at once deflate idealising notions of love and of one's mistress as mere projections of inexperience, and imply more radically that the causes of such beliefs altogether may lie in our unfulfilled desire rather than in the nature of their objects. The bizarre leap to the dying atheists (4b-6) with its ambiguous logical connectives, even holds one in momentary doubt how one is to use the analogy so that the resolution in line 6 gets a clinching force. Immediately of course the argument ridicules atheists by simply taking it for granted that their atheism won't carry as far as the ultimate test of their own dying hour. But it also bears upon the motive itself, which might thus be wholly subjective. In fact the lines pointedly don't say whether the atheists' impulse is just: there may really be something there, a power one feels in one's dying hour, or there may be nothing beyond a projection of one's own fears. The atheists' case parallels, or strikingly instances, our tendency to project our own inner desires outward as objects for reverence and worship. Line 6 gives the argument a further sceptical twist. 'As ignorantly did I crave': atheists at the last really want there to be a god, but are as ignorant of the truth as the rest of us.

The remaining lines (7-10) move from these particular instances to the general nature of human desire as it affects our conceit of things and hence our attitude to them. We most reverence what we know least; and as our yearning for the unknown decreases with knowledge and experience (our nature being such that it does decrease thus) so our esteem evaporates. Our controlling desires, in other words, themselves have the nature of appetites, growing the more they are starved and fading with repletion; and it is these inner states that we project outwards as pictures of reality.

This is a poem which in several ways stands for more than it directly says. But one doesn't go beyond the lines to say that Donne is concerned here with the nature of belief and that he coolly sets the cat among the pigeons by accounting for some of our beliefs, at least, in terms of motives and causes, where the schoolmen and neoplatonists explained them in terms of objects and ends. The difference holds for love poetry too. Dante, Petrarch, Michelangelo, undeviatingly refer their love to an end. The question is, How and to what end do I love her?; and the question, Why do I love her?, if it's raised at all, produces an answer in terms of her attributes and origin, as if one may then take for granted the nature of the experience and what one means when one talks of love. The fact is that the Florentine tradition assumes a commitment which precludes disinterested analysis; it would be wholly destructive of the attitude struck to question its grounds. But questioning the grounds is the essence of Donne's attitude, as of his wit. He works to maintain various possibilities in play, to keep things at a properly sceptical distance, to avoid easy commitments. So in this poem he's not even concerned with a particular woman but with the nature of sexual experience itself, or the natural economy of sex so to say; and thus far his concern is dismissive.

One would put the point barbarously to say that he substitutes a positive epistemology for a normative one, psychology for ontology or metaphysics. What really matters is the vision of our human circumstances which these assumptions imply or allow us to glimpse. The argument is that such beliefs in deity as lines 1-6 instance, with their accompanying charges of reverence, worship and the like, merely project our own inno-cent expectations. But our desires and fears are necessarily innocent, and ignorant too, since experience cuts expectation down to human size. So we may gather two complementary lessons, offered to us here as the proven outcome of living. One is that our experience never remotely matches expectation. The other is that we make our gods in the shape of our unproved desires and not our tested experience. The ribald suggestion of the last line, kept discreetly remote in the image of desires which fall and rise, is that these unknown gods we ignorantly worship are specifically projections of erotic craving and as momentary as that.

But if we take up this suggestion, as I think we must, and see our impulses towards worship and the like as expressions or parallel instances of our sexual state, then there's a further implication. For that condition is already fixed in the poem as inherently self-deluding as well as relative, allowing us only the bitter wisdom of exchanging disillusioned satiety for ignorant aspiration. We have the sense of an inherent and hopeless crossgrainedness, which is actually built into man's physical make-up and speaks of some distortion of our nature. Moreover our situation is such that we can't say we know anything absolutely at all, for what we take for knowledge is always relative to the condition of our desire at that moment. Nor could we posit such a state *a priori*. We can grasp it at all only because we find it proved in experience; as the inductive movement of the argument in the stanza persuades us. Donne's management of syntax here is a virtuoso feat but it grows straight out of the attempt to exhibit these apparently separate ideas in their perceived interrelation.

The second stanza at once makes the move from desire to experience which the Florentine tradition never allowed. Donne may consciously run counter to the doctrines of the neoplatonists when he ironically inverts their hierarchy of the senses, putting sight as an instrument of wondering self-delusion and touch as our means to disillusioned reality. But the opening analogy of children's satiety with what had previously amazed them generalises the dismissive comment to take in five centuries of European love poetry. There's a true lover's progress here as in Pico, but this one is a matter of a simple maturing, the passage from childishness to adulthood, innocence to experience, fancy to reality, illusion to disillusion.

'His highnesse . . . ' probably is in the first place a gilt gingerbread effigy from a recent Bartholomew Fair; though the lines may discreetly glance at a real monarch too since their point is the rapid change even a little experience brings, from naive anticipation to repletion and indifference. That this is true of children with a fairing, subjects with a new monarch, and lovers, argues again that for this poet love is just one telling instance of a larger human condition. Here he indicates a general characteristic of human conduct and the several forms of childish fickleness or gross self-delusion it takes; and he also glances at the motives that prompt people to admire, worship, submit to authority, rebel.

But these senses all come back to the lovers' blind admiration and pursuit of 'the thing', whose enjoyment decays once they have had it. 'Decays' is a strong word. It hints at a larger process which the lovers' disillusionment with sex only instances – things are inevitably running down. A nicety of diction brings that home to our intimate experience, the diction between 'pleases' and 'takes', which delicately shows the anticipatory delight of all our senses dwindling down to the mere dull affecting of one of them as toothache or nausea affects us. This 'kinde of sorrowing dulnesse' which the mind feels surely isn't just *post coitum triste*, though that vaguer sense would have served Donne's turn. His qualified preciseness of phrase strikes one as a concern to get things just right, which means being faithful to the feel of the experience as well as its nature; and the following stanza shows that this dulness matters.

Stanza 3 of this poem is as intricate a poetic organism as Donne ever devised and its conclusion, long regarded as a textual crux, has itself prompted much controversy.[1] I shall assume the rightness of the only text with any authority, that in the edition of 1635, and simply offer my reading of it as an implied argument against the various editorial emendations.

From the melancholy fact of our spent virility the poem turns to possible reasons: Why should things be thus? The question

---

[1] See in particular H. J. C. Grierson, *The Poems of John Donne*, Oxford, 1912, ii, pp. 52-3; J. Hayward, *Donne: Complete Poetry and Selected Prose*, 1929, pp. 766-7; G. Williamson, *Modern Philology*, 1939, pp. 301-3; L. Hotson, *The Times Literary Supplement*, 16 April 1949; Helen Gardner *The Times Literary Supplement*, 10 June 1949; T. Redpath, *The Songs and Sonnets of John Donne*, 1956, pp. 145-9.

comes as a lamenting outcry – 'Ah cannot wee . . .?' whose splendid vehemence is partly comic since it suggests that after all his real worry is just his disabling loss of zest. Giving cocks and lions the vital advantage over man inverts Humanist ideas with ribald unconcern, though the diction altogether – 'jocund' 'pleasures' – suggesting lighthearted randiness or an epicureanism of sex, cocks a snook at more elevated ideas of love. But the implied narrowing of concern is the biggest irony of all. It starts the stanza off as a kind of groping towards an explanation of our sexual shortcoming, so that what follows is put forward as a mere exploratory hypothesis; though its force in the poem is not hypothetical.

The argument in lines 23b-30 has been so much confused by discussion of the supposed crux in the last two lines and is so complicated anyway that I had better set out my sense of it baldly, even schematically. The attempt partly defeats itself of course. One does peculiar injustice to the poem by reducing its pattern to mere sequence, since the point of the poetic argument is its specific structure in the stanza, which is partly a matter here of multiple suggestion, the several related senses the locutions imply. But any reading of the lines will wrest the grammatical function of some good English words and the reader had better see what I, for my part, am doing with them.

The general argument follows out an old scholastic idea that the emission of semen drains vitality, here rendered as a popular belief that each sexual act shortens life by a day. If that is so then some check is needed to restrain our indulgence. For the several deficiences of our present conditon impel us to a constant repetition of the act in an attempt to make them all good, and without restraint we would quickly destroy ourselves.

Donne puts these deficiences themselves as cognate forms of a curse – 'that other curse' – which 'desires to raise posterity', that is, which provokes ones need and desire to have children, and to do whatever else 'raising posterity' may suggest.[1] They are (*a*) our 'being short', and (*b*) the assumed fact that we are

---

[1] *O.E.D.* Desire: 3. *trans.* Of things: To require, need, demand.

8b. To invite a course of action, etc.

Posterity: 3. Posteriority *Obs. rare.*

Posteriority: 3. The back, the back parts of the body. *Obs. rare.*

'only for a minute made to be/Eager'.[1] The phrasing is very elliptical, relying on one's willingness to see the several related meanings which such words as 'short' take on as the argument unfolds itself, but what emerges I think is an explanation of the motives of sex that points to our awareness of shortcomings as the stimulus to sexual acts. Several such conscious shortcomings seem to be implied:

(i) the momentariness of sexual pleasure itself

(ii) the short duration of man's sexual keenness, which orgasm dulls, and of his virility altogether in terms of his entire life

(iii) the humiliating physical diminution after coitus, which impugns his masculinity and impels him to reassert it as soon as he can

(iv) the brevity of life, which prompts our pathetic and desperate attempts to prolong our being vicariously by having children.

This manifold inadequacy is the 'other curse', the first curse presumably being the loss of pleasure and dulling of keenness after orgasm. But 'curse' itself suggests that both are consequences of a disastrous disorder of the proper state of things. In fact this 'other curse' would result in man's ruin in no time by accelerating progression: the 'shorter' he feels himself to be, the greater the urgency of the desire, the more 'sport', the faster his self-undoing, the keener his awareness of his brevity . . . and so on by ever shortening stages to speedy self-consumption. Donne doesn't put a name on this larger curse or say straight out that our sexual acts are an ironically urgent attempt to amend the consequences of the Fall. His concern is the truth of the experience, and he starts here from the imperativeness of erotic desire which he derives from our fearful consciousness of brevity. But it follows that the whole world is caught up in this accelerating spiral towards cataclysm and must end itself soon.

[1] *O.E.D.* Eager: *a.* O.F. *aigre* sharp, keen, sour. . . . ii 6. Of persons: Full of keen desire or appetite; impatiently longing to do or obtain something. . . . Also of desires or appetites: Intense, impatient.

119

'Wise Nature' is what works for our survival and the con-
tinuance of life now, the natural economy of things that operates
by whatever means it can in this desperate condition. Here he
conjectures that nature imposes the inhibiting loss of zest after
the sport, with all that it entails, simply as a built-in counter to
the self-destructive urge. One presumes that the 'sorrowing
dulness' damps the process by dulling sentience as well as
eagerness, narcoticising man's haunting awareness of his situ-
tion; for such is the perverse state of things that our best human
capacities now bring us to most harm. Such, too, is our own
condition that one curse has to be counterweighed by another
curse, man's life maintained by the very limitations and de-
privations of his present constitution; so that he suffers loss and
pain both ways, for the destructive force and the saving counter-
force.

Though the whole argument from line 23b on is put forward
as if tentatively the idea of self-frustration pungently develops
and deepens the sense of Stanza 2. The instances of the frailty
of human desire and expectation picked out there are here given
a larger reference as part of a general athwartness and inherent
self-frustration of things, of an economy gone horribly and
irremediably wrong so that only a makeshift adjustment – and
again at man's expense – stays it from grinding itself to dust
in ever-increasing frenzy.

The one way of evading this particular spiral, which one
won't recognise anyway until one has committed oneself to it,
is to keep the resolve the title of the poem announces. As the
final stanza puts them the grounds of the farewell itself are at
least two. The first is that coitus – and hence the sport al-
together – never yields the anticipated pleasure, or amounts
at best to a momentary excitement followed by 'sorrowing
dulnesse'. Nobody else has been able to discover the pro-
mised deity in love or prolong love's pleasure – or even find the
pleasure, which is rather in the anticipation than the having.
Why then should we desire what we certainly won't find? Or
why indeed should the mind expect a divinity in what is thus so
essentially mortal, bound to time and our general ruin? Beyond
the inevitable disillusionment though, and the plain wish to be
undeceived, there's the danger. This makes the second ground of

the dismissal. Engaging in the sport he is only doting and run-
ning after things which would damage him if he gained them,
pursuing his own harm as he has often pursued it up till now.[1]

Saying farewell to love is consciously putting oneself beyond
the cycle of desire by refusing its prompting. It is crucial though
that one can't escape thus until one has seen love for what it is,
which experience alone will show, and gained an independence
of one's own impulses that only repeated disenchantment could
allow. Freedom thus gained, needing to be asserted in the teeth
of one's own nature, is the point of the poem. We're a long way
from a final sense that the world is to be despised or that love
distracts our minds from God. This is a different moral universe.
What we're shown is a kind of self-subsistent economy of
nature to which we can adjust ourselves if we understand it;
and that is our freedom of choice. Dismissing love thus is
not a matter of turning back to the Creator from the worship
of the creature but of coming to recognise the point of
repeated disillusionments, seeing the true state of things
and then exercising the limited freedom we can have by
deliberately standing aside, in full awareness of what that, too,
entails.

The final dismissal appropriately completes the organic
image which has moved the poem. This account of the 'heat' of
'moving beauties' which 'Growes great' like the summer sun
gives erotic force to the game of courtship it describes, making
sexual excitement the acknowledged point of such games.
And the casual last line points that sense, offhandedly pricking
the illusions of mistress-worshipping lovers. You can collapse
the whole gaudy bubble with a little application of wormseed.[2]
The shadowy intimation that our gods take the shape of our
ignorant yearnings or momentary erotic excitements gets a
concrete finality in the image of a shrunken penis.

[1] Helen Gardner, *John Donne: The Elegies and The Songs and Sonnets*, Oxford,
1965, prints and argues for the reading in one of the manuscripts, S96, 'To
pursue things which had, indammage me'. I prefer the reading of *1635* because
it gives a sharper sense of a new realisation, which does matter here – 'I now see
that the consequence of my doting and running would not have been satisfaction
but harm; my eyes are at last fully opened, and so I can be free'.

[2] Wormseed was not an anaphrodisiac but a popular name for such herbs as fennel,
or their dried flowerheads, which were supposed to shrivel up intestinal worms.

¶ 'Farewell to Love' distinctively expresses a distinctive temper
and attitude which one only crudely identifies as positivist, em-
piricist, sceptical, naturalistic[1] or what. The labels might at
least suggest where Donne stood among the sectaries of his
time and where he couldn't possibly have stood while this poem
conveyed his mind. Florentine transcendentalism is as remote
from him as it was from Boccaccio or Chaucer; he would have
found Michelangelo's love poetry, so curiously like his own in
its muscular force, alien to the point of unintelligibleness. The
people whose ideas one encounters in Donne are the Paduan
aristoteleans and the followers of Sextus Empiricus; and the
writers who strike one as thinking at all like him (their temper
is instantly recognisable) are such as Pomponazzi, Montaigne,
Charron, Reginald Scot.[2] Directly or just by the way they think
and proceed they challenge the mystical metaphysics that
Plotinus and the supposed Dionysius Areopagus had developed
out of Plato, and the discrediting of hermetic texts in the
seventeenth century seemed to justify them finally. The neo-
platonic theory of love evaporated with its parent doctrine, and
it is the temper of 'Farewell to Love' that impressed seventeenth
century love poets:

> Fruition adds no new wealth, but destroys,
> And while it pleaseth much the palate, cloys;
>
> (Suckling, 'Against Fruition')

I believe that the man who conceived 'Farewell to Love' could
not have accepted neoplatonic ideas when he wrote it or, with-
out a drastic change of temperament, at any other time. What
one encounters in the poem is a cast of thought not just a par-
ticular view of love. The question really isn't whether other
poems by Donne claim quite different things for love from this
but how much of Donne one finds in it, what one can see here of
the man who wrote the other poems. In point of fact there's no
evidence beyond its emergence in the edition of 1635 that

---

[1] See L. I. Bredvold, 'The Naturalism of Donne in Relation to Some Renaissance
Traditions', *Journal of English and Germanic Philology* XXII, pp. 471-502.
[2] Scot tried to disprove the existence of witches by showing why people professed
belief in them. I owe this example to Dr Sydney Anglo, who tells me, for what it
is worth, that Scot like Donne was at Hart Hall Oxford.

Farewell to Love really is by Donne: one of the Harvard manu-
scripts assigns it to a certain 'Mr An. Saintleger'. Modern
editors have accepted it as Donne's without question because
no one else then or at any other time wrote and thought
just like that. The poem proclaims the man, palpably the same
man who wrote the *Metempsychosis* and the two *Anniversaries*,
to say no more.

If Donne's love poems chart his own experience at all then
it's fair to suppose that this one was written before the great
celebrations of mutual love – while that further possibility,
unglimpsed here, was yet to prove. So that the poem is
singular in its Renaissance kind, if only in the way it relates to
the rest of the poet's work. It comes neither as a random mood
of love among divers such – good for an attitude or a poem
perhaps – nor as a final dismissal of the world in the face of
last things and eternal truths. We must take it as a report on
experience up till then; and this indeed seems to be how Donne
himself saw it – 'Whilst yet to prove . . .'. But to look at
Donne's love poems in that way is to see that they are not con-
ceived like Petrarch's or Sidney's, not like Michelangelo's,
not like Shakespeare's even. The difference is only secondarily a
matter of form, the lack of a story or an overall artistic pattern;
what really decides it is the poet's own idea of how he stood
towards his poems. This poetry pitches itself as open to ex-
perience and seems to move and modulate with that. When a
poem refers us beyond itself at all it's just to what Donne would
make of a different experience elsewhere. And because there is
no finality in our experience there is no absolute end against
which we can measure the poet's progress; each poem is its
own moment and the sharp change from poem to poem simply
brings home to us the relativeness of our sexual experiences
too, love meaning so many things and no one of them ex-
clusively.

We can try this positivism another way, and Donne's alleged
neoplatonism too, by supposing that 'Farewell to Love' might
be Donne's poem of animal love and touch, marking the limits
of a state which his 'later' poems would transcend. The reading
won't stand up, not least because it doesn't account for what is
there. The poem has its own order of truth which is certainly

not superseded by anything Donne wrote elsewhere; as well say that 'Shall I compare thee to a summer's day?' transcends 'The expense of spirit in a waste of shame'. The difference between a man's several experiences of love is part of his under-standing of love and that is the point of his marking it; nor can we, as readers, evaluate these experiences save as they are mediated to us by a mind whose quality and grasp are what really matter. What holds Donne's love poetry together is not the pattern of his sentimental life, such as it may be, but a coherent vision of human nature and a consistent temper of mind.

The way these poems relate to each other is a part of what they say. If we feel that some of them offer a developed account of love (which doesn't necessarily make them better poems) it will be partly because they seem to comprehend other senses Donne expresses if not to build upon them. The attitudes of *Elegy 1* or 'Womans Constancy' are taken up into – say – 'The Good-morrow', or 'The Anniversarie'. or 'The Canonization', though the poet may now claim a more singular experience for himself. The one writing remains uncancelled by the other and may very well be sharply true for the rest of the world, or for the poet himself in other areas of his life; indeed the brave vaunt of the lovers' unalterable interassurance moves one precisely because it seems so fragile in face of the common nature of things and of their own natures. Donne reminds us that in life at least we don't fence off from each other the several modes of our experience or concern, and that a man doesn't have to sublimate his sexual nature – or undertake a new course of reading – to develop an idea of a mutual love. When people say that Donne's poems in some ways uniquely render their own experience of love it is often this diversity, and complexity, they have in mind. For here too is a real truth about love, and about love's relative-ness, easily falsified by our straining for such convenient absolutes as ideal beauty or marriage. The poems resist hierarchical arrangement, whether its principle is transcendental or sentimental.

What then was Donne's 'sect in the philosophy of love'? Threads from the *Dialoghi d'amore* glint everywhere in the texture of his love verse and one may divine his allegiance by the ideas he made his own.[1] Neoplatonic ideas seem by and large to have offered him targets for casual mockery:

> That loving wretch that sweares,
> 'Tis not the bodies marry, but the mindes,
> Which he in her Angelique findes,
> Would sweare as justly, that he heares,
> In that dayes rude hoarse minstralsey, the spheares.
>
> ('Loves Alchymie', 18-22)

But the author of *The second Anniversary* could have found little to his purpose in a doctrine which defines love by an end, its place in a scheme deduced from a picture of the universe overall. That essentially *a priorist* understanding carries an imperative too, for the end thus predetermined stands as the consummate form which actual loves must strive towards, and by which they are to be placed, 'low' or 'high'. Donne places love by the merit he discovers within the relationship itself and will have nothing to do with such definitions as might impose an external end or goal to be attained. Ficino's lovers 'never know what it is they desire or seek'[2]; but only because they don't yet know God himself. Donne points merely to a realised condition which he can understand at all only by negatives:

> If that be simply perfectest
> Which can by no way be exprest
> But *Negatives*, my love is so.
> To All, which all love, I say no.
>
> ('Negative Love', 10-13)

The consciousness that thus, in this positive spirit, refuses received certainties is likely to express itself tentatively, and relatively – wittily perhaps if it poises itself between several possible ways of taking things. To be absolute for final truth is

[1] My articles 'The metaphysic of love', *The Review of English Studies* n.s. IX, 1958, pp. 362-75, and 'New bearings in Donne: "Air and Angels" ', *English* XIII, 1960, pp. 49-53, tried to show that in two of his greatest love poems the school of love Donne drew on was aristotelean not platonic, Paduan or cosmopolitan not Florentine. I have seen both essays cited as evidence that Donne was thoroughly steeped in neoplatonic ideas, and fear that I couldn't have made myself very clear.

[2] *1544*, 26-7; *1576*, 1326.

alien to the temper of Donne's poetry and its movement too, even the religious poetry. Within the poems themselves he puts one thing by another, one order of things against another, inviting a relative placing; and his sense of most experiences of love is that they are wholly relative to the situation in which they have force:

> Then all your beauties will bee no more worth
> Then gold in Mines, where none doth draw it forth;
> And all your graces no more use shall have
>   Then a Sun dyall in a grave.   ('The Will', 48-51)

The lady's beauties have no inherent absolute value at all, only the value of their effect upon the lover while he lives – the value he himself gives them in fact. Voices from the seventeenth century remind us that Donne's followers saw the drift of his anatomising of love:

> Know, Celia, since thou art so proud,
>   'Twas I that gave thee thy renown;
>   (Carew, 'Ingrateful Beauty Threat'ned')

> Nay, 'tis true: you are no longer handsome when you've lost your lover; your beauty dies upon the instant. For beauty is the lover's gift; 'tis he bestows your charms, your glass is all a cheat. . . .
>   (Congreve, *The Way of the World* II. iv. 354-7)

But indeed a love poet whose eye is fixed so sharply on the fine tonalities of sexual conduct hasn't much to do with Plato or Plotinus and no writer seems more absurdly placed among idealists and transcendentalists than Donne.

Izaac Walton's myth of the two Donnes, Jack and the Doctor, does invite one to find such a division in the love poetry too; as though the 'great Visitor of Ladies'[1] with his exuberantly virile imagination and sceptical wit were by some alchemy of the sentiments metamorphosed into the celebrant of mutual love. Yet the one man is recognisable in the other however the occasion and concern may have changed, and essentially the same mind and imagination are at work:

[1] Sir Richard Baker, recalling Donne at Lincoln's Inn, *A Chronicle of the Kings of England* (1643), 1684, p. 427.

> All Kings, and all their favorites,
> All glory'of honors, beauties, wits,
> The sun it selfe, which makes times, as they passe,
> Is elder by a yeare, now, then it was
> When thou and I first one another saw:
> All other things, to their destruction draw,
>   Only our love hath no decay;
>   ('The Anniversarie', 1-7)

Such poems as 'Womans Constancy' and 'The Indifferent' express the strong sense of an unstable world of change – 'For by to morrow, I may thinke so too'. But he seizes delightedly on that momentariness as the condition of his freedom, assuming with cool assurance that truth to the sexual motive, as experience shows it, is all the moral responsibility one could owe. 'The Anniversarie' doesn't deny our common condition at all or seek to transcend it. With 'The Good-morrow', 'The Canonization', 'The Exstasie' it simply assures the lovers that they have already found in their love a condition which will not be subject to time and change. The resolution quite pointedly refuses the neoplatonic assent to a realm of universal form beyond the world of sense and particular embodiments; specifically it is just this unique relationship that distinguishes them, their achieved and embodied mutualness which a disembodied bliss in heaven cannot better:

> And then wee shall be throughly blest,
> But wee no more, then all the rest.
> Here upon earth, we'are Kings,

This is the escape from the dilemma of 'Farewell to Love' which the poet didn't reckon with there ('what no man else can finde'), a condition of love exempt from the common process of the world because uncommitted to the biological cycle.

'The Canonization' shows how that can be though their bodies aren't denied. In this poem it is precisely their confirmed sexual felicity – a miraculous exemption from the common case of alteration after coitus – that attests their rare love and hence their mutual victory over change and decay:

> Wee dye and rise the same, and prove
> Mysterious by this love.   (26-7)

The witty inweaving of the sexual sense in the emblematic
proof of their mutualness shows us directly and recognisably
the nature of their love as he finds it:

> We'are Tapers too, and at our owne cost die,
> And wee in us finde the'Eagle and the Dove;
>   The Phoenix ridle hath more wit
>   By us, we two being one, are it,   (21-4)

His sense of such a love, readily intelligible to us, precisely
marks off a modern sense of sexual passion from the meta-
physics of Ficino and the moralism of Petrarch. For there's
really no doubt of what actually assures their heroic triumph
over our vulnerable human state and fits them to be love's
martyrs and saints, a 'patterne of . . . love' for lesser lovers. It
is the embodied passion of two people whose sexual expressions
only confirm their deeper sense of oneness.

There seems particular point in the way that poems move
from idea to body. In 'The Dreame' the mere dream of his
mistress has to give way in the end to the better reality of
physical lovemaking. 'Aire and Angels' formalises the pro-
gress, following the poet's search down from unlocalised form,
to particular embodiment, to love, where love is neither the
worship of form nor the admiration of beauty but something
that needs an answering love to give it substance. Specifically,
this beautiful poem shows in fact that the proper object of love
is not disembodied form but another human being, and that love
is not love even then unless it is returned, and mutual.

This sense of a maturing from fantasy to reality, intelligible
idea to sensible actuality, defines itself differently in poems
which assume a mutual love. There it shows as a need to be
true to the complexity of a state such as experience proves, in
which the intangible and the physical can't be finally separated.
The force of 'A Valediction: forbidding Mourning' is its
assumption that the lovers will hate physical separation but can
endure it because the 'soul' of their love isn't 'sense'. 'The
Exstasie' dramatises the issue in scholastic terms of the relation
between soul and body, and shows in fact what this under-
standing of love really amounts to. This poem too offers its
Platonic or neoplatonic properties – the lovers' raptness of gaze,

the souls' abandonment of the bodies for a revelation of truth, the bodily stasis, the metaphysical placing of the events. But the disembodied colloquy of souls yields no vision of supernatural truths or universal forms. It simply shows the lovers to themselves.

For Donne, it seems, love is an active state of mutual concern which also entails the effort to know itself, to understand and follow out what is in effect already there. 'The Exstasie' is far from making love a state of pure static contemplation. The lovers seek to understand something that had perplexed them, not to contemplate it; and it's not beauty or the idea of beauty they now see fully but the realised nature of their mutual love itself, what it amounts to and consists in. Acknowledging the truth of their condition as it is they assure themselves of their fidelity to each other, oneness beyond alteration, as well as of the interdependence of soul and body in such a model love. But this is knowledge from which action follows. Hence in the end the ecstatic revelation justifies their bodily union by and from the union of souls. And that's the *coup de grâce* for neoplatonic love; or so succeeding poets seem to have taken it.

In his love poetry as elsewhere Donne's instinct was to subvert, flout, revise the received pieties of the day in the name of hard actuality. The implied polemic was inevitable once he committed himself to the notion that bodily desire isn't an impediment to love but may actually be essential to it. That sense itself though comes through in the poems just as something won out of the experience of an achieved mutual relationship – a way of putting it. His central concern remains the nature of the relationship itself:

> But, now the Sunne is just above our head,
>   We doe those shadowes tread;
> And to brave clearenesse all things are reduc'd. . . .
>
> Except our loves at this noone stay,
> We shall new shadowes make the other way.
>   ('A Lecture upon the Shadow', 6-8, 14-15)

Donne never strikes one as imposing a scheme upon experience. This poem moves from the inside, as if its dramatic fiction is only one way of articulating the inner sense of such a state. The truth that concerns the poet is an objective and precise one – not the feel of being in love or the vehemence of his intimate sensations but the laws of this love itself, its organic constitution as it were, by which it must survive or fail. Seeing these laws is a matter of knowing oneself, generalising one's grasp of a thousand past experiences to a sharp sense of the way the world goes. And that is wisdom of a kind quite undreamt of in your neoplatonic philosophy.

'The Undertaking' and 'The Relique' very consciously proclaim a different kind of relationship with a woman, which has its own claim to singularity:

> First, we lov'd well and faithfully,
> Yet knew not what wee lov'd, nor why,
> Difference of sex no more wee knew,
> Then our Guardian Angells doe; . . .
> These miracles we did; . . .
>
> ('The Relique', 23-6, 31)

> If, as I have, you also doe
> Vertue'attir'd in woman see,
> And dare love that, and say so too,
> And forget the Hee and Shee;
>
> ('The Undertaking', 17-20)

These lines perhaps bring Donne as near as he gets in his writings to Michelangelo's rapport with Vittoria Colonna. Yet they are utterly unlike Michelangelo's sonnets and madrigals:

> Tanto sopra me stesso
> mi fai, donna, salire,
> [Lady, you make me ascend so far above myself . . .]

In Donne's two poems there's no hint of transcendence or of ideal forms; if they pose an ideal for lovers it's certainly not a disembodied ideal. 'The Undertaking', which some manuscripts entitle 'Platonic Love', does claim that in this one unique instance the poet has got beyond the outside appearance to the beauty of the virtue within and loved that for itself, forgetting the 'Hee and Shee'. 'The Relic' describes a strong mutual affection – possibly the same one – which is wholly unsexual and therefore miraculous. 'Platonic love' seems right for this in the popular sense of the term which carries no metaphysical suggestion at all. And a miracle, one recalls, confirms the order of nature by the inexplicable departure from it. Donne is a poet for whom love is intrinsically sexual, but he is true above all to the unprescribed inflections of living. His fine self-surprise as a celebrant of sexless love makes still more vivid his far different understanding everywhere else.

What precisely is one saying, in the end, when one talks of Donne's metaphysic of love? Donne's love poems don't offer us a Lucretius, a Dante, or a Michelangelo. But neither do they display a mere casual explorer of sex with a gift for violently yoking heterogeneous ideas. One can't be surprised that Donne himself spoke of something so formal as his 'sect in the philosophy of love'. The poems themselves show him consciously formalising his experience in a precise scholastic way. Yet I think he'd have been chagrined to find people talking of neoplatonic ideas in his verse. The terms of the remark to Wotton are specific: 'love . . . though it be directed upon the mind, doth inhere in the body'. I've argued that the poems give point to this understanding, which must have mattered crucially for Donne himself and matters now for our idea of his poetry.[1] It's wholly possible of course that I've mistaken him, or the Renaissance neoplatonists, or all of them. But that might be shown by closer definitions and better readings than I've been able to arrive at here, and until they are forthcoming I think we do Donne a service to ask that people who speak of his neoplatonising should at least say what they mean.

---

[1] It mattered for succeeding poets too, though they render it in very simple terms:

> I was that silly thing that once was wrought
>   To practise this thin love;
> I climbed from sex to soul, from soul to thought
>   But thinking there to move,
> Headlong I rowled from thought to soul, and then,
> From soul I lighted at the sex agen.
>
> (Cartwright, *No Platonique Love*, 7-12)

6

The 'Songs and Sonnets' and the Rhetoric of Hyperbole

BRIAN VICKERS

'What they wanted however of the sublime they endeavoured
to supply by hyperbole.'

Johnson, *Life of Cowley*[1]

I

Anyone who comes to Donne through English love-poetry of
the sixteenth century is immediately struck by his novelty.
First the language, that confident, brusque immediacy of tone
and movement which at first sight appears to have liberated
itself from all previous conventions. The power of Donne's
language has been the most exciting discovery for the majority
of readers in our time, although it is now evident that the critics
who did most to promote a new evaluation of it left several
gaps in their argument: they ignored the colloquialism of some
predecessors (Wyatt and Sidney, in a substantial number of
poems); they naïvely equated colloquialism with 'the speaking
voice', with 'reality' and so with 'sincerity', they were ignorant
of Donne's rich use of traditional rhetoric[2]; they ignored the
continued presence of many 'Petrarchan' elements in the poems
– reworked, of course, but not always ironically (sighs, tears,

---

[1] *The Lives of the English Poet*, ed. G. Birkbeck Hill, Oxford, 1905, i, 21.
[2] I have given some examples of Donne's use of rhetoric in *The Songs and Sonnets*
in my *Classical Rhetoric in English Poetry*, 1970, e.g. pp. 123-5, 127-50 *passim*,
153. See also Rosemond Tuve, *Elizabethan and Metaphysical Imagery*, Chicago,
1947; T. O. Sloan, 'A Rhetorical Analysis of John Donne's "The Prohibition" ',
QJS 48, 1962, pp. 38-45, and 'The Rhetoric in the Poetry of John Donne', *SEL* 3,
1963, pp. 31-44; P. Traci, 'The Supposed New Rhetoric of Donne's *Songs and
Sonnets*', *Discourse* 11, 1968, pp. 98-107.

groans, broken hearts); and they failed to see Donne's relation to wider classical and European traditions of logic and serious wit.[1] What contemporary criticism and scholarship must do is to fill these gaps, 'place' Donne's inheritance, without, of course, losing our appreciation of his unique energy and impact.[2]

Less often commented on than the language is Donne's treatment of love and the relationship between the sexes. English sixteenth-century love-poetry is characterised by frustration, unfulfilment, loss; the mistress is unavailable, indifferent ('fair cruelty'); she is worshipped with agonised self-abasement on the part of the lover. One recalls the deadly seriousness of such a typical stanza as this by Wyatt:

> Deathe and dispaire afore my face,
>   My dayes dekaes, my grefe doth gro;
> The cause thereof is in this place,
>   Whom crueltye dothe still constraine
> For to reioise, tho yt be wo
>   To here me plaine[3]

---

[1] See, e.g., Tuve; A. J. Smith, 'Donne in his Time: A Reading of *The Extasie*', *RLMC* 10 (1957), pp. 260-75; 'The Metaphysic of Love', *RES* n.s. IX, 1958, pp. 362-75; H. Gardner, 'The Argument about "The Ecstasy"', in *Elizabethan and Jacobean Studies*, ed. H. Davis & H. Gardner, Oxford, 1959, pp. 279-306; M. Y. Hughes, 'Some of Donne's "Ecstasies"', *PMLA* 75, 1960, pp. 509-18; M. Praz, 'Donne's Relation to the Poetry of His Time', reprinted in *The Flaming Heart*, New York, 1958, pp. 186-203; *Studies in Seventeenth-Century-Imagery*, Rome, 1964; J. Lederer, 'John Donne and Emblematic Practice', *RES* XXII, 1946, pp. 182-200; F. Warnke, *European Metaphysical Poetry*, New Haven, 1961; J. A. Mazzeo, *Renaissance and Seventeenth Century Studies*, New York, 1964; L. L. Martz, *The Poetry of Meditation*, New Haven, 1962.

I cannot recommend unreservedly either D. L. Guss, *John Donne, Petrarchist: Italianate Conceits and Love Theory in the 'Songs and Sonnets'*, Detroit, 1966; or N. J. Andreasen, *John Donne: Conservative Revolutionary*, Princeton, 1967.

[2] In a lively essay called 'The Love Poetry of John Donne: Pedantique Weedes or Fresh Invention'? (in *Metaphysical Poetry*, ed. M. Bradbury and D. Palmer, 1970, pp. 11-39) Patrick Cruttwell has some enlightening comments on his own experience of the poems (pp. 11-26) but then mounts a confused and one-sided attack on 'historical' interpretations of Donne, which he presents as being somehow antipathetic to a full response to the poetry. The argument is too crude to be worth extended discussion, but I mention it to make the point that a 'historical' interpretation and an 'individual response' are not mutually exclusive. But this is an old dispute: Mr Cruttwell has been proved wrong by hundreds of critics.

[3] No. 137, in *The Collected Poems*, ed. K. Muir, 1960, p. 126.

Or we remember the climax of *Astrophil and Stella*, where after dozens of sonnets of idealisation and tortured analysis of the situation Astrophil actually makes a physical, bodily advance to Stella: in the 'Second Song' (between Sonnets 72 and 73) he finds her asleep, resolves to 'invade the fort', but decides to 'refraine' because of 'the danger,/Of her just and high disdaine', and contents himself with a 'stealing kisse'. The songs continue the action of the sequence (and curiously chaste seduction poems they are, too) until the climax is reached in the 'Eighth song' (between Nos. 86 and 87) where Astrophil, having knelt, and prayed before her, makes his final attempt:

> There his hands in their speech, faine
> Would have made tongue's language plaine;
> But her hands his hands repelling,
> Gave repulse all grace excelling.[1]   (65-8)

Both the refusal, and the 'honourable' tone with which it is accepted – providing the material for another sequence of idealisation and tortured analysis – are typical of the genre. Remarkable as it is for wit, rhetoric and eloquence, *Astrophil and Stella* is trapped by its own convention, what we might call the Petrarchan cul-de-sac: 'No Exit to Arcadia'. Given that the lady is unreachable, this form of love-poetry cannot get anywhere: it can merely oscillate between the poles of hope and despair. In the *Amoretti* Spenser goes through the traditional oscillations for eighty-five sonnets, and then suddenly precipitates a lover's quarrel in the last four sonnets (due to some slanderer who 'with false forged lyes . . . in my true love did stirre up coles of yre', No. 86, 7-8) and breaks the whole thing off. What else can he do? (In other genres, and at other times, he abandoned the sterilities of the neo-Platonic abstraction of love with its ladder leading to heaven or ideal beauty by breaking with his continental models and directing the first two of his *Four Hymnes* firmly towards human, married love and procreation; similarly with the *Epithalamion*, that great celebration of nature and fertility.)

---

[1] *The Poems of Sir Philip Sidney*, ed. W. A. Ringler, Oxford, 1962, pp. 202-3, 217-21.

Donne broke through this barrier of unattainable desire (in doing so he partly went back to classical models, notably Ovid[1]) and instead of frustration gives us fulfilment, consummation, an extended analysis of a full sexual relationship. The poems are too familiar to need quoting, but we should just recall some of the settings; poems are written on (or in) the lovers' bed, its sheets, their room with its curtains through which the sun disturbs their – sleep?; Donne records the leisure with which they can lie there and watch, for instance, the movements of a flea over their skin; or he argues that, although they spent the night together they did not make love merely because it was dark, and so there is no reason why his mistress should want to get up and go now that it is light; or he imagines himself ('Petrarchan!') having been killed by his mistress's scorn, returning to her bed and watching her in the arms of a new (and 'worse') lover:

> Then thy sicke taper will begin to winke,
> And he, whose thou art then, being tyr'd before,
> Will, if thou stirre, or pinch to wake him, thinke
> Thou call'st for more,
> And in false sleepe will from thee shrinke,
> And then poor Aspen wretch, neglected thou
> Bath'd in a cold quicksilver sweat wilt lye . . .
> ('The Apparition')[2]

In poems such as these – 'The Dreame', 'The Flea', 'The Good-morrow', 'The Sunne Rising', 'Breake of Day', 'The Exstasie' – the lover's bed is the focus of the action, and in these and other poems the description of love is frankly physical, either directly or by innuendo. (Learned editors refrain from glossing these passages, and I am never sure whether they have

---

[1] See, e.g., Helen Gardner's edition, *The Elegies and The Songs and Sonnets*, Oxford, 1965, pp. viii (acknowledging indebtedness to a doctoral thesis on Ovidian Love-Elegy by J. Carey), xxi ff., and notes *passim*; A. Brilli, 'Gli *Amores* ovidiana e la poesia di J. Donne', *SUSFL* 38, 1964, pp. 100-39.

[2] Quotations are from Helen Gardner's edition (*op. cit.*). I do not accept Professor Gardner's rearrangement of the *Songs and Sonnets* based on a putative autobiographical 'change' in Donne's style and attitude to love following his marriage.

not seen the allusions, or imagine that everyone sees them, or think it indecent to comment on them.) I lack statistics, but I doubt if the bed or the physical celebration of the body had played much part in English love-poetry since *Troilus and Criseyde*. Even the poems of loss are not, like some of his predecessors, those of a fantasy relationship which never materialised: in Donne the loss is (or presents the illusion of) a total physical experience, an overwhelming emptiness.

That, though, is only one way in which he broke with the tradition: I would distinguish three others. First, the masculine assertion. Whereas in the 'Courtly Love' tradition the woman is on a pedestal and the man kneels or grovels before her, Donne often reverses that situation. Man 'gets', 'has', 'casts off' a woman, or picks up again last years 'relict'; the women, some students have complained to me, are hardly ever *there* in Donne's poems: the poems are a description of love from the man's superior position. Secondly, since he can cast her off, and she him, there are poems which invert the whole tradition of loyal, dogged and fruitless dedication to one unattainable mistress by proposing moods of indifference, or a cynicism about male or female faithlessness, a justification, as it were, for having an affair and then moving on. Lastly, and for the purposes of this essay, most important, is the new sense of a relationship between the lovers. They constitute a unit, separated off from the world, not dependent on it, indeed above it. One way of gauging the difference in attitude is to compare the personal pronouns in *Songs and Sonnets* with those in *Astrophil and Stella* and Shakespeare's *Sonnets* (I do have the statistics for this, but their presentation and analysis must wait for another occasion). Whereas in Sidney, one might say, the characteristic pronouns are 'I'/'me'/'mine' and 'she'/'her'/'hers'; and in Shakespeare they are 'I'/'me'/'mine' and 'you'/'yours'/'thou'/'thine', it is noteworthy that in both sequences 'we'/'our'/'us' play a very small role (in Shakespeare indeed, the plural is outnumbered by the other two forms by several hundred to one). In Donne, while we have 'I' and 'you' and 'she' we have, most memorably, 'we'/ 'us'/'our'.

My argument will be that Donne is remarkable in English Renaissance love-poetry for the way in which he presents the two lovers as a race apart, and that one of the most important ways of creating this separation is by use of the rhetorical figure hyperbole. I mean the type of praise which is exemplified in 'The Sunne Rising':

> She' is all States, and all Princes, I,
> Nothing else is.   (21-2)

Before I discuss the rhetoricians' theory of hyperbole, though, this figure must be distinguished from the more general techniques of encomium or panegyric with which it might seem to be linked. Panegyric or *encomium* represents, according to the traditional division of rhetoric into three kinds, the 'demonstrative' or 'epideictic' type. (The other two are 'judicial', used especially in law; and 'deliberative' for politics or debate.[1]) Demonstrative oratory is divided, according to the writer's intention to praise or to blame, into *laus* or *vituperatio*. The *Ad Herennium* distinguishes three categories within which material may be amassed: 'external circumstances' (descent, education, wealth, power, etc.); 'physical attributes' (strength, agility, beauty); and 'qualities of character' (wisdom, courage, justice).[2] By handling his account of a person under these heads, and by using such additional methods as vouching for his personal knowledge of the subject concerned, a writer can easily construct an encomiastic biography, and many classical and Renaissance examples could be cited. I would stress that, although the mock-encomium flourished, often in the form of the paradox (due, I have argued elsewhere,[3] to the practice of arguing for or against a theme which was practised in schools from ancient Greece to eighteenth-century London and indeed nineteenth-century Harvard), the panegyric is essentially a serious genre. It is grounded on fact, realism, historical probability; it is applied to distinguished rulers, soldiers,

---

[1] I have given a concise account of these three types, with references to the wide literature on this topic, in *Classical Rhetoric in English Poetry*, pp. 68-73.

[2] See *Rhetorica Ad Herennium*, 3.6.10 ff.; ed. and tr. H. Caplan, 1954, pp. 173 ff. Subsequent references to this edition will be abbreviated as *Ad.H.*

[3] '*King Lear* and Renaissance Paradoxes', in *Modern Language Review* 63, 1968, pp. 305-14.

politicians.[1] Since it is based on categories of praise and blame it was inevitable that it should have been interpreted in ethical terms, praise being for virtue, blame for vice. Hardison has rightly stressed the significance of post-Aristotelian theory which urged that epideictic oratory should be didactic (*op. cit.*, pp. 30 ff.).

When the Renaissance developed the analysis of literature under the influence of rhetoric and classified genres according to their rhetorical type and intent, it is significant that panegyric was associated with the highest and most serious genres, epic and tragedy. Bernard Weinberg's study of Italian Renaissance literary criticism[2] has shown this process at work time and again. A major influence was Averroës' twelfth-century Arabic paraphrase of Aristotle's *Poetics*, Latin versions of which were widely disseminated before (and indeed after) the publication of the Greek text itself. Averroës saw literature as intended to persuade its audience to good actions: tragedy is the art of praise, comedy that of blame (Weinberg, p. 358). Many other writers associated panegyric with tragedy or with epic,[3] and the poets celebrated for their ethical use of the opposed ends of praise or blame include Homer, Virgil, Dante, Ariosto, Tasso.[4] Nowhere is panegyric associated with love-poetry, which – in the Italian, as in the English Renaissance – attracted mainly ethical disapproval.[5]

[1] A useful survey is O. B. Hardison's *The Enduring Monument. A Study of the Idea of Praise in Renaissance Literary Theory and Practice*, Chapel Hill, N.C., 1962; less useful is Ruth Nevo's *The Dial of Virtue. A Study of Poems on Affairs of State in the Seventeenth Century*, Princeton, 1963, which discusses political panegyric, and divides it into 'reflective', 'historical' and 'polemical' types but without much sharpness in either theoretical or practical analysis.

[2] Weinberg, *A History of Literary Criticism in the Italian Renaissance*, Chicago, 1961. For general references to praise or blame as the characteristic of epideictic oratory and hence of poetry see pp. 43, 148, 185 (the corrective function of the satiric epigram), 215, 237, 304, 368, 384-5, 459, 723-4, 751, 764, 783.

[3] Tragedy: Weinberg, pp. 209, 544-5, 586, 643, 653. Epic: pp. 253, 603, 643, 745, 824, 836, 849, 868, 881-2, 906, 969, 1016, 1055, 1065.

[4] Hardison has shown that some theorists associated both tragedy and what he calls 'admonitory epic' (a rather artifical category) with the exposure and correction of vice: *op. cit.*, pp. 87-8, 93-5.

[5] Given the erotic nature of some of the *Elegies* Donne's critics might agree with Averroës' observation that 'the species of poetry which they call elegy is nothing but an incitement to acts of copulation which they conceal and adorn with the name of love' (Weinberg, p. 359).

Panegyric, then, is an external operation: a description by a poet of a distinguished man or woman (no one writes a panegyric on himself). It will rehearse their education, good deeds, moral qualities, legacy of fame. Donne wrote a number of panegyrics, in the *Verse Letters*, in the *Epicedes and Obsequies Upon the Deaths of Sundry Personages*, and of course, that most metaphysical (with a small 'm') example of the genre, *The Anniversaries*.[1] These encomia are typical of panegyric: it is a public, serious, ethical, external, historical, supposedly factual genre.

Donne's use of hyperbole is almost point-for-point antithetical: it is a non-ethical, witty, irreverent, at times slightly disreputable figure; it is personal, written from the inside, by the actors themselves, not by a hired (or self-appointed) chronicler; it is not concerned with 'fact' or 'history', indeed almost the main characteristic of the figure is that it is excessive, impossible. But the theorists made a number of shrewd distinctions about the figure's form and function, and to these I now turn, to see if we can gain from them any insights into Donne's use of the figure.

II

Hyperbole is a 'trope', one of that group of rhetorical devices which *turn* or alter the meaning of words, rather than affecting – as 'figures' do – their physical or acoustic shape. Rhetoricians discuss it, usually, in conjunction with tropes like metaphor, simile, irony. I want to show, briefly, a continuing interest in hyperbole from Aristotle to the English eighteenth century: and I want to distinguish three main approaches to the figure.

First, hyperbole is not a merely superficial, luxurious affectation, but an expression of energy and intensity. So Aristotle writes in his *Rhetoric* that hyperbole is a type of metaphor: 'e.g. the one about the man with a black eye, "you would have thought he was a basket of mulberries" '; and that the figure has definite psychological associations: 'Hyperboles are for young men to use; they show vehemence of character; and this is why angry people use them more than other people.'[2] To

---

[1] O. B. Hardison (*op. cit.*) has attempted a (in my view) too schematic analysis of *The Anniversaries* according to the traditional structures of panegyric.

[2] Aristotle, *Rhetoric* III, 11 (1413a 19 ff., 27 ff.); tr. W. R. Roberts, in *The Works of Aristotle*, ed. W. D. Ross, Vol. XI, Oxford, 1924.

illustrate this point he quotes two examples from Book IX of the *Iliad* where Achilles rejects the embassy of Odysseus, representing Agamemnon:

> not if he gave me gifts as many as the sand or the dust is
> not even so would Agamemnon have his way with my spirit. . . .
> Nor will I marry a daughter of Atreus' son, Agamemnon,
> not if she challenged Aphrodite the golden for loveliness,
> not if she matched the work of her hands with grey-eyed
> Athene. . . [1]

The author of 'Longinus, *On the Sublime*' similarly writes that hyperboles achieve their effect 'when they are connected with some impressive circumstances and in moments of high emotion. Thucydides' account of those killed in Sicily is an example: "The Syracusans came down and massacred them, especially those in the river. The water was stained; but despite the blood and the dirt, men continued to drink it, and many still fought for it." It is the intense emotion of the moment which makes [this] credible. . . .' Here, as with other figures representing human emotional states, 'acts and emotions which approach ecstasy provide a justification for, and an antidote to, any linguistic audacity'.[2] The intensity of feeling justifies the excess in language.

The second, and I suspect for most people the habitual approach, is to define it as a figure of exaggeration, with an inherent danger of excess. It was in this frame of mind that Johnson complained of Cowley's 'enormous and disgusting hyperboles' and said of the Metaphysicals in general (and we should always remember that he thought that Cowley 'was almost the last of that race and undoubtedly the best') that their amplifications had no limits: they left not only reason but fancy behind them'.[3] Longinus saw this danger most clearly:

> The important thing to know is how far to push a given hyperbole; it sometimes destroys it to go too far; too much tension results in relaxation, and may indeed end in the contrary of the intended effect.

He quotes an assertion by Isocrates about the limitless persuasive power of human speech (actually, a rhetorical common-

[1] *Iliad*, tr. R. Lattimore, Chicago, 1951, IX, pp. 385-6, 388-90.
[2] 'Longinus', *On Sublimity*, § 38; tr. D. A. Russell (Oxford, 1965), pp. 44-5.
[3] *Life, ed. cit.*, i, 27, 35, 21.

place) and comments that this encomium 'is equivalent to an introduction recommending the reader not to believe what he is told'.[1] (Swift understood this technique perfectly, as we see in many passages in *Gulliver's Travels*, the *Short character of Thomas Earl Wharton* and elsewhere.) Longinus agrees with Quintilian and with the author of *Ad Herennium* that hyperbole may be used either to praise or blame.[2] Quintilian's comment, however, bridges the gap which Johnson diagnosed between 'reason' and 'fancy': hyperbole is fantastic, but it must have a rationale. 'For although every hyperbole involves the incredible, it must not go too far in this direction, which provides the easiest road to extravagant affectation' (8.6.73; p. 343).

English Renaissance rhetoricians share this second concept of hyperbole as a valuable trope which risks being overdone. Puttenham's attempt to anglicise rhetoric by giving the Greek figures vernacular equivalents expresses this attitude perfectly: one type of *'false semblant'* is created

> when we speake in the superlative and beyond the limites of credit, that is by the figure which the Greeks call *Hiperbole*, the Latines *Dementiens* or the lying figure. I for his immoderate excesse cal him the over reacher right with his originall or [*lowd lyar*] . . .[3]

---

[1] Longinus, *tr. cit.*, p. 44. In his earlier edition of the Greek text ('Longinus', *On The Sublime*, Oxford, 1964, p. 171) Mr Russell acutely comments that none of the three examples quoted (Isocrates, Thucydides, Herodotus) is actually a hyperbole, or indeed – in the case of the two historians – an exaggeration. I suspect that, like rhetoricians before and since him (I speak from experience), 'Longinus' was occasionally stuck for examples.

[2] Longinus, *tr. cit.*, p. 45; *Ad.H.*, 4.33: p. 339; Quintilian, *Institutes of Oratory* 8.6.67; tr. H. E. Butler (Loeb Library) 1921, III, p. 339.

[3] Puttenham, *The Arte of English Poesie*, ed. G. D. Willcock and A. Walker, Cambridge, 1936, 1970, p. 191. I suspect that many readers will be familiar with this quotation due to the use made of it by Harry Levin in *The Overreacher. A Study of Christopher Marlowe*, 1954, pp. 41-2. Other rhetoricians merely saw the advantages of the figure. Thus Abraham Fraunce: 'But hyperbolicall amplifications & allegories have singular excellencie in a Metaphore, & therefore commonly they are here most usuall: and by these hyperbolicall metaphores the speach is made very loftie and full of majestie, when we attribute life and action, to dead and senselesse things'. *The Arcadian Rhetorike*, [1588] Sig. B⁵; facsimile, Scolar Press, Menston, 1969. And Dudley Fenner, another Ramist, described hyperbole as an 'excesse of this finenesse [of speech]' but said of one of his quotations [*'Those that hate me are moe in number then the haires of my head'*] that it was 'verye high and lofty': see *The Artes of Logike and Rhetorike*, 1584, Sig. D₁ᵛ.

Traditionally, Puttenham stresses its applicability to praise or blame, and urges moderation (p. 192). These traditions (which did not, of course, die out in the Middle Ages[1]) carried on well into the eighteenth century. Joseph Priestley, for instance, who published his lectures on rhetoric two years before Johnson's *Lives of the Poets*, linked, as Johnson was to do, hyperbole with an attempt on the sublime: 'The extravagant hyperbole is the common fault of those writers who aim at the sublime, and the style that abounds with it is generally termed the *bombast*. As the hyperbole is a figure that has a very striking effect, and is extremely easy in itself (for what can be easier than to exceed the truth in description?) writers whose aim was to elevate and astonish their readers have often adopted it. . . .' Such misuse of hyperbole can be detected when 'it be the *expression*, and not the *idea*, that surprises a reader . . .'[2]

Priestley's distinction between 'expression' and 'idea' is a useful transition to my last and most important category, which involves the relationship in hyperbole between truth and falsehood. Puttenham, as we have seen, described the figure as a 'loud lyar' and went on to describe it as 'a great dissimulation' (p. 192). Nashe, in the course of the hilarious satire on Gabriel Harvey in *Have With You to Saffron-Walden*, pokes fun at all rhetoricians (Harvey's much-vaunted profession) who, *though they lye never so grosely, are but said to have a luxurious phrase, to bee eloquent amplifiers, to bee full of their pleasant Hyperboles, or speake by Ironies. . . .*[3] Nashe has a point, of

---

[1] On medieval uses of hyperbole see E. R. Curtius, *European Literature and the Latin Middle Ages*, tr. W. Trask, New York, 1953, pp. 160-4, 444; also L. Arbusow, *Colores Rhetorici. Eine Auswahl rhetorischer Figuren und Gemeinplätze als Hilfsmittel für Übungen an mittelalterlichen Texten*, 2nd. ed., rev. H. Peter, Göttingen, 1963, pp. 24, 84-91, 97.

[2] Priestley, *A Course of Lectures on Oratory and Criticism*, 1777, pp. 244-5. Cf. also William Smith's translation and commentary on Longinus: 'Hyperboles literally are Impossibilities, and therefore can only then be seasonable or productive of Sublimity, when the Circumstances may be stretched beyond their proper size, that they may appear without fail important and great'. *On the Sublime*, 2nd., corr. ed., 1743, pp. 180-1.

[3] Nashe, *Works*, ed. R. B. McKerrow, rev. F. P. Wilson, Oxford, 1966, III, 120. It is surprising that so knowledgeable a student of rhetoric as Heinrich Lausberg should see no more in hyperbole than a 'deutlicher Verfremdungs-Absicht über die Glaubwürdigkeit hinaus'. *Elemente der literarischen Rhetorik*, München, 1963, §212, p. 75.

course, but is himself ironic. The author of *Ad Herennium* avoided the issue of 'lying' by defining the figure as 'a manner of speech exaggerating the truth' (4.33; p.339); Quintilian at one point agreed that it was a bold figure which means 'an elegant straining of the truth' (8.6.67; p. 339). But if it is conceded that hyperbole goes beyond the truth, how are we to distinguish if from falsehood? The most convincing explanation of this phenomenon was given for the first time, as far as I can see, by Seneca in his treatise *On Benefits*, in the passage where he argued that 'We overstate some rules in order that in the end they may reach their true value':

> The set purpose of all hyperbole is to arrive at the truth by false-hood. And so when the poet said:
>
> Whose witness shamed the snow, their speed the winds,
>
> he stated what could not possibly be true in order to give credence to all that could be true. . . . Hyperbole never expects to attain all that it ventures, but asserts the incredible in order to arrive at the credible.[1]

Similarly Quintilian, who may have known Seneca's treatise, added later in his account of the figure that 'It is enough to say that hyperbole lies, though without any intention to deceive' (8.6.74; p. 343).

The importance of this approach will be evident. It suggests that hyperbole is a special kind of language, which goes beyond normal speech – perhaps because of that heightened emotional state behind it which Aristotle and Longinus pointed to – in order to express a supra-normal idea or experience. Hyperbole is an encoding which expects from the reader a decoding. That this statement is not an irrelevant venture into (rather old-fashioned) linguistics can be seen from the way in which discussion of this aspect developed in the Renaissance and after. Erasmus, whose works were disseminated in the Renaissance to a point probably beyond calculation, quoted in his much-used *De Copia* Seneca's definition: 'by this lie we come to truth' and added: 'for hyperbole says more than reality

---

[1] *De Beneficiis*, 7.22.1-7, 23.2; Seneca, *Moral Essays*, tr. J. W. Basore (Loeb Library) 1935, III, pp. 508-11. The quotation is from Virgil, *Aeneid*, 12.84.

warrants, yet what is true is understood from the false'.[1] Among the examples which Erasmus gives are two from Virgil: 'swifter than the wings of lightning' (*Aen.* 5.319) and, describing a flock of starved sheep: 'Scarce cling they to their bones' (*Ecl.* 3.103). Both quotations occur in Quintilian (8.6.69, 73), which shows as usual the eclectic nature of rhetoric-books.

The English Renaissance rhetoricians were equally eclectic, and developed both these points (lies to reach truth; encoding/decoding) without acknowledging their sources, but with a clarity which shows that they fully grasped the point that hyperbole is a special kind of language. In his popular book on logic Thomas Wilson explained that 'There is a figure in Rethorike, called Hyperbole, that is to saie, when a thing is spoken beyonde measure uncrediblie, and yet is not so largelie mente. As when I wil praise a manne for his strength, I wil saie, he passeth Hercules in manhode, meaning that he excelleth in manhode and valeauntnesse. . . . Therefore we must diligentlie take hede, when soche speches are used, that wee take not them as thei bee spoken, but as thei are mente, neither take the whole for the parte, when the whole is expressed in woordes, and the parte mente in understanding.'[2] The always sensitive John Hoskins made a further distinction: 'Sometimes [hyperbole] expresseth a thing in the highest degree of possibility, beyond the truth, that it descending thence may find the truth; sometimes in flat impossibility, that rather you may conceive the unspeakableness than the untruth of the relation'.[3] In addition

---

[1] Erasmus, *De Copia*, I, 28; *On Copia of Words and Ideas*, tr. D. B. King and H. D. Rix, Milwaukee, Wis., 1963, p. 35.

[2] Wilson, *The Rule of Reason, Conteinyng the Arte of Logique*, 1553, fol. 74ᵛ.

[3] Hoskins, *Directions for Speech and Style* (*c.* 1599) ed. H. H. Hudson, Princeton, 1935, p. 29. The full and systematic rhetoric by Henry Peacham, *The Garden of Eloquence*, 1577; much expanded, 1593, gives a by now traditional account: 'it is a sentence or saying surmounting the truth onely for the cause of increasing or diminishing, not with purpose to deceive by speaking untruly, but with desire to amplifie the greatnesse or smalnesse of things by the exceeding similitude' (1593 ed., p. 31). It is either simple or compound, and Peacham lists several categories with examples from the classics and the Bible (pp. 32-3). As ever he concludes with a double summary: the 'Use' of the figure; and the 'Caution' against its misuse; for the first: the figure has 'so high' a 'reach' that 'it mounteth to the highest things, compasseth the widest, and comprehendeth the greatest'; for the second: (i) do not amplify trifles or you will fall into the vice of style

to the going beyond, in order to reach the truth on the other side, as it were, Hoskins sees the figure as being one of the few means there are of expressing the inexpressible.

Since hyperbole has been so often misunderstood and disparaged, I should like to add two quotations from eighteenth-century writers who understood the figure's potential. In his discursive and eclectic *Essay Upon Unnatural Flights in Poetry* (1701)[1] George Granville, Lord Lansdowne, answered the objection that since poetry uses rhetorical figures it amounts 'out of Sight,/Leaves Truth behind', especially, with 'rash Hyperboles, that soar so high' (pp. 292-3). His answer unites reason and fancy:

> Hyperboles, so daring and so bold,
> Disdaining bounds, Are yet by Rules controul'd;
> Above the Clouds, but yet within our sight,
> They mount with truth, and make a tow'ring flight;
> Presenting things impossible to view,
> They wander, thro' incredible, to True;
> Falshoods thus mixt, Like metalls are refind,
> And truth, like Silver, leaves the dross behind.   (p. 293)

Despite his own soaring metaphors, Lansdowne makes again the important point (as he puts it in his prose annotations to the poem) that these figures 'have an intelligible signification, tho' the expression be strain'd beyond credibility' (p. 296). The tradition is still alive, and is most lucidly expressed, by Joseph Priestley in 1777. He defines its 'coding' property; its stylistic effect; the sense of compression which it achieves by replacing analogy with direct statement; and its intellectual fertility due to the processes of association:

---

known as *bomphiologia*; (ii) do not diminish good things, or you will stray into *tapinosis*; (iii) your use should be 'discreetly moderate' (p. 33). Given this last cautious remark, one wonders whether Peacham truly understood the dynamic of the figure.

[1] Reprinted in, and quoted from, *Critical Essays of the Seventeenth Century*, ed. J. E. Spingarn, Oxford, (1908), 1957, III, pp. 292-8. In his notes (p. 337) Spingarn points out that Lansdowne has cribbed most of his poem from Bouhours's *La Manière de bien penser dans les Ouvrages d'Esprit*, Paris, 1687, a work which Oldmixon later paraphrased (*The Arts of Logick and Rhetorick*, 1728).

When any thing that is asserted in a discourse exceeds the truth, an *hyperbole* is said to be used. In fact, in every species of metonymy (and the same may be said of all the other figures) there is a departure from *literal truth*; but, as was explained in the case of Irony, it is in such a manner as that nobody can be imposed upon, or misled by it, and it is attended with advantages to the sense, which could not have been had by a rigorous adherence to truth.

The reason why the hyperbole is, in appearance, a greater violation of truth than most other figures, is only this, that in the hyperbole the untruth lies in the *affirmation itself*, whereas in most other figures it is concealed in an *epithet*, which however (were the sentence resolved into its constituent parts) would also be a direct untruth in the affirmation.

The advantage of using an hyperbole, is, that the idea of one object may be heightened and improved by ideas transferred from other objects, and associated with it. Thus when the Divine Being says to Abraham, 'I will make thy seed as the dust of the earth; so that if a man could number the dust of the earth, then shall thy seed also be numbered,' Gen. xiii. 16; the idea of a number almost infinite is transferred from the dust of the earth to the children, or descendants of Abraham; and by this means we are enabled to conceive a greater idea of them than we could have done by the help of any plain and literal expression. (pp. 241-2).

Further, Priestley improves on Longinus and Aristotle by showing the heightened imaginative state of the writer using hyperbole, and the way in which the reader not only decodes the message but by that process is led into a closer relationship with the writer:

This manner of expression, though not strictly agreeable to truth, is extremely natural when the imagination is raised, and a person is labouring for an expression adequate to his ideas. In such a situation of mind, as no expressions literally true sufficiently answer his purpose, a writer is obliged to have recourse to objects which can supply him with such as will do it. The expressions to which these views give rise, are, however, so circumstanced, that we instantly enter, as it were, into the mind of the writer, we feel the difficulty he was under, and see the reason why he made choice of such hyperbolical language; and as we are led into no mistake by such terms, they are, in fact, to us who enter into his situation and feelings, more true and just expressions of those feelings than any plainer terms could have been. (p. 242)

Finally, influenced by the long tradition in rhetoric which asserted that one of the advantages of tropes in general, and especially metaphor, was that they extended the bounds of language, Priestley applies that principle to this trope:

> Besides, if we consider that, by reason of the narrowness of our faculties, terms expressing the greatest magnitudes and numbers, yea terms denoting infinities themselves, raise only indeterminate and finite ideas in our minds, we may easily conceive that the *state of mind* produced by an attempt to realise hyperbolical expressions, may not be more than barely adequate to the ideas intended to be conveyed. Let us, for example, endeavour to form an idea of a number equal to that of the *dust of the earth:* the conception may not, in fact, reach to a just idea of the vast numbers of the posterity of Abraham. So that hyperboles, thus properly circumstanced, may, by the appearance of falsehood, lead the mind nearer to the truth than any expressions more literally true.   (*Ibid.*)

I have quoted Priestley at some length, because his is such an intelligent account of the figure, and because I believe that the eighteenth century understood rhetoric much better than we do. Mr Cruttwell thinks that Donne 'has been brought back into the fold of rhetorical tradition' and that scholars have adequately documented 'his affinities . . . with everything that is most unreadable and most irreversibly dead in the medieval-Renaissance culture' (p. 36). I would deny both points: the work has yet to be done in depth, the full value of rhetoric as a language is only beginning to be perceived; and rhetoric is neither 'unreadable' nor 'irreversibly dead'.

As a last stage in this discussion of hyperbole, and as a relevant point of transition to Donne, since I began by distinguishing hyperbole from panegyric, and argued that panegyric was a serious public genre with little relevance to love-poetry, I should end by citing some contemporary evidence that, by contrast, hyperbole was thought to be relevant to love-poetry. Puttenham's distrust of the 'over-reacher' was put aside for only one category: 'if we fall a praysing, specially of our mistresses vertue, bewtie, or other good parts, we be allowed now and then to over-reach a little by way of comparison' (p. 192) – and he quotes two rather undistinguished examples from *Tottel's Miscellany*. Although heavily qualified, the allowance is given. In his essay 'Of Love' Bacon remarked casually, as if it were generally appreciated, that 'the speaking in a perpetual hyperbole is comely in nothing but love.'[1] This applies to sacred love, as well as secular. Rosemond Tuve has noted the function of hyperboles in Vaughan's religious poetry (p. 224); and in his remarkable *Centuries of Meditations* Traherne both alluded to the figure and gave a striking example of it, discussing man's relations with God and the intensity of Divine love:

> The true WAY we may go unto His Throne, and can never Exceed, nor be too High. All Hyperboles are but little Pigmies, and Diminutiv Expressions, in Comparison of the Truth.
>
> *   *   *
>
> Lov is infinitly Delightfull to its Object, and the more Violent the more glorious. It is infinitly High, Nothing can hurt it. And infinitly Great in all Extremes: of Beauty and Excellency. Excess is its true Moderation: Activity its Rest: and burning Fervency its only Refreshment. Since therefore it containeth so many Miracles It may well contain this one more, that it maketh evry one Greatest, and among Lovers evry one is Supreme and Soveraign.[2]

III

There is no need to argue the case formally for Donne's knowledge and use of rhetoric – it is evident on almost every page of his prose or poetry. He can hardly not have known about hyperbole. But in any case I do not want to argue for any specific influence on him, rather to show how his own use of hyperbole fulfils all the potential which rhetoricians ascribed to the figure. I would propose two main groups of subjects to which hyperbole is applied: the lovers, and love, considered first as values in themselves; and then considered in relation to the rest of the world.

This first group of poems (which includes many of Donne's most immediate and popular works) makes an assertion of value directly, with no possibility of misunderstanding:

[1] Bacon, *Works*, ed. J. Spedding *et al.*, 1857-74, VI, p. 397.
[2] Traherne, *Century II*, §52, 54; in *Works*, ed. A. Ridler, 1966, pp. 238-9.

> For love, all love of other sights controules,
>   And makes one little roome, an every where. . . .
> Let us possesse our world, each hath one, and is one.
>> ('The Good-morrow').

> Here upon earth, we'are Kings, and none but wee
> Can be such Kings, nor of such subjects bee;
> Who is so safe as wee? where none can doe
> Treason to us, except one of us two.
>> ('The Anniversarie')

But the direct assertion can be sustained with wit,[1] as in the boast which opens 'A Valediction: of my Name in the Window':

> My name engrav'd herein,
>   Doth contribute my firmnesse to this glasse,
> Which, ever since that charme, hath beene
> As hard, as that which grav'd it, was;

Donne's loyalty is so strong that it has converted glass, one of the most fragile of substances, into the ultimate of hardness, diamond. This tactic of juxtaposing zero and infinity is often used to distinguish their experience of love from other intense experiences:

---

[1] The witty assertion of love's value can even embrace a mocking use of hyperbole, what Peacham might have described as *tapinosis* (disvaluing good things) as in 'The Broken Heart', on the infinitely superior power of Love compared to 'other griefes':

> They come to us, but us Love draws,
> Hee swallows us, and never chawes:
> By him, as by chain-shot, whole rankes do dye,
> He is the tyran Pike, our hearts the Frye.

A. J. Smith has sensitively commented on a similar use of mock-hyperbole in Elegy II, 'The Anagram': see 'The Poetry of John Donne' in *English Poetry and Prose 1540-1674*, ed. C. B. Ricks, 1970, p. 142; and on hyperbole in the panegyrical poems, *ibid.*, pp. 157 ff. In the same volume J. Carey remarks of Donne's sermons that 'The same rage for disproportion that in the poems makes a flea into a temple or eclipses the sun with a wink makes its way into the sermons disguised as a teaching-aid' (pp. 402-3): he dismisses Donne's – to me completely convincing – use of the hour-glass metaphor, as 'quite arbitrary'. Mr Carey adds that 'Donne's hunger for disproportion' in the sermons, 'because it cannot be made the central issue, as it can in a poem, has to hook on to any convenient twig of doctrine, and often eclipses it'. To my mind this seriously distorts Donne's beliefs and preaching methods.

> But this, all pleasures fancies bee.
> If ever any beauty I did see,
> Which I desir'd, and got, 'twas but a dreame of thee.
>
> ('The Good-morrow')

> For I had rather owner bee
> Of thee one houre, then all else ever.
>
> ('A Feaver')

Compared to this, *all* other pleasures are *but* dreams, idle fantasies: it is characteristic of hyperbole that it admits of no intermediate stages between zero and infinity.

If their love is infinite, it can never die: the paradox of constant use and constant growth is one which Donne handles at many levels, from the religious to the physiologically erotic. Since 'all' is one of the words most germane to this type of assertive hyperbole it is no accident that a poem called 'Loves Infiniteness' should wring every possible significance out of that word and out of the situations which it could describe:

> If yet I have not all thy love,
> Deare, I shall never have it all. . . .

I lack space to trace all the paths of 'Loves riddles' here, but the opening of the third stanza makes my point most clearly:

> Yet I would not have all yet,
> Hee that hath all can have no more,
> And since my love doth every day admit
> New growth, thou shouldst have new rewards in store . . .

That theme is worked out in even more explicitly sexual terms in 'Loves Growth'. But nowhere is it given greater force than in 'The Anniversarie':

> All other things, to their destruction draw,
> Only our love hath no decay;
> This, no tomorrow hath, nor yesterday,
> Running it never runs from us away,
> But truly keepes his first, last, everlasting day.

Those lines alone would justify all the rhetoricians' claims that hyperbole expresses energy, vehemency, ecstasy, the 'unspeakableness rather than the untruth of the relation'.

Particularly illuminating is Priestley's observation that 'in hyperbole the untruth lies in the *affirmation itself*, whereas in most other figures it is concealed in an *epithet*'. Much of the assuredness, the confidence of Donne's hyperboles derives from their being simple present-tense statements, direct affirmations, not indirect description.

If some poems present the infinite, inexhaustible power of their love, others use hyperbole to contemplate unhappiness and suffering in love, illness, death. In 'A Valediction: of Weeping' the first stanza presents the man – 'Let me powre forth/My teares before thy face', his tears being 'Fruits of much griefe'. The stanza ends with the conceit that the beloved's image is reflected, mirror-like, in the tear as it falls, and the reduction of the image to nothingness is related to the way in which the lovers 'are nothing' when separated (again the simplest of verbal forms is yoked to a statement of ultimate significance). The second stanza takes up again the contrast between zero and infinity: a craftsman pasting maps on to a globe can

> quickly make that, which was nothing, *All*,
> So doth each teare,
> Which thee doth weare,
> A globe, yea world by that impression grow,
> Till thy teares mixt with mine doe overflow
> This world, by waters sent from thee, my heaven dissolved so.

Of this stanza Dr Johnson made the caustic remark: 'The tears of lovers are always of great poetical account, but Donne has extended them into worlds. If the lines are not easily understood they may be read again'.[1] He is critical, but has in fact precisely described Donne's method of amplifying an issue, pushing its extremes as far apart as possible. In the last stanza the conceit is taken to its logical conclusion, in cosmic terms: since she controls his world, she can inundate it:

> O more then Moone,
> Draw not up seas to drowne me in thy spheare,
> Weepe me not dead, in thine armes, but forbeare
> To teach the sea, what it may doe too soone. . . .

---

[1] *Life of Cowley*, ed. cit., i, 26.

This continuation of the trope basic to the hyperbole points up one of the characteristics of Donne's extension of *superlatio* over a whole stanza or indeed poem: once we have assented to the initial identification, that non-literal impossibility which this trope embodies, we tend to forget that we are moving along inside a trope; we do not stop to translate it back into 'literal' statement, for we do not have time; Donne has made us his prisoners. We could remember, in this connection, Helen Gardner's admirable definition of a metaphysical conceit: 'A conceit is a comparison whose ingenuity is more striking than its justness, or, at least, is more immediately striking. All comparisons discover likeness in things unlike: a comparison becomes a conceit when we are made to concede likeness while being strongly conscious of unlikeness.'[1] So Donne juxtaposes literal and figurative meanings in such a way as to remind us of the identity between the two while stretching it as far as possible.

Some other poems which exploit the cosmic analogy in relation to the theme of 'suffering love' show this trapping process at work. In 'A Feaver' his mistress is ill, and in the first stanza the poet begs her not to die, for if she did he would hate all women – her included. But the second stanza at once denies even that possibility:

> But yet thou canst not die, I know;
> To leave this world behinde, is death,
> But when thou from this world wilt goe,
> The whole world vapors with thy breath.

Again no 'epithet', no circumlocution, a simple direct statement of her absolute value: she is the world. But – since this poem, like many of Donne's lyrics, changes direction at the beginning of a new stanza as if something significant had happened in the interval between them – if her death does not perhaps succeed in extinguishing the whole world, what is left would merely be rubbish. Hence Donne can invent more examples of that gap between zero and infinity which defines her value:

---

[1] *The Metaphysical Poets*, 1957, p. 19.

> Or if, when thou, the worlds soule, goest,
>   It stay, 'tis but thy carkasse then,
> The fairest woman, but thy ghost,
>   But corrupt wormes, the worthyest men.

(Again *tapinosis* cuts the competition down to size.) The next stanza makes a dramatic improvement even on that absolute, by launching an attack on those stoic and Patristic writers who disputed just how the world would be consumed by fire:

> O wrangling schooles, that search what fire
>   Shall burne this world, had none the wit
> Unto this knowledge to aspire,
>   That this her feaver might be it?

This is indeed a fantastic brag, that she might be the cause of the ultimate conflagration, but once we have conceded the first hyperbole we would feel, somehow, foolish or unimaginative if we dropped out at this stage. We concede the likeness, but the unlikeness is made dramatically apparent. A similar wit, using the same cosmic, if less grandiose analogies for her death can be seen in 'The Dissolution', but developed with less cheek. No one could ever forget the intensest expression of this cosmic hyperbole in 'A Nocturnall upon S. Lucies Day':

> Oft a flood
>   Have wee two wept, and so
> Drownd the whole world, us two; oft did we grow
> To be two Chaosses, when we did show
> Care to ought else; and often absences
> Withdrew our soules, and made us carcasses.

The insistent 'us two' of line 24 seems intended to challenge the reader, to remind him of the trope within which he is moving, to offer him the possibility of escaping from it – if he wishes – by presenting the simple reality which lies behind it, and which justifies this assertion of absolute value.

Finally, in this first group of hyperboles that assert the infinite power of love, I delight in being able to discuss 'The Sunne Rising', which uses all the tactics so far distinguished –

except, of course, death and cosmic destruction – with un-equalled freedom. There is no need to quote the opening stanza's insolent dismissal of the sun, the universal embodiment of order, time, fruition, who is sent about other and less important business, nor its closing use of *tapinosis* (or perhaps *meiosis* – either way, a belittling figure) to affirm the infinity and eternity of love as against 'the rags of time'. The second stanza begins with a non-hyperbolic statement – I could blot out the sun by closing my eyes – and redeems its speciousness by the wit of the motive for not so doing ('But that I would not lose her sight so long'). This point seems to have been established so that Donne can, by violent contrast, move into hyperbole and so invert reality:

> If her eyes have not blinded thine,
> Looke . . .

And when you have made your tour of the globe next, report back, tell me

> Whether both the'India's of spice and Myne
> Be where thou leftst them,or lie here with mee.
> Aske for those Kings whom thou saw'st yesterday,
> And thou shalt heare, All here in one bed lay.

'Boldest of figures' Quintilian called it, yet the supreme confidence with which Donne invests those two boasts must convince all but the unconvincible. We barely need to 'decode' his message: she sums up all symbols of worth. This is undeniable: lovers' values are subjective, relative, and may therefore legitimately represent infinity; since we do not share the love-relationship, it is immune from our criticism. As if realising that point Donne immediately proceeds to develop it to its ultimate pitch, with the same political/national comparisons which ended the preceding verse:

> She'is all States, and all Princes, I,

and again that remarkable juxtaposition of zero and infinity:

> Nothing else is.

The whole of human, animal, vegetable, mineral existence has been annihilated by the comparison.

> Princes doe but play us; compar'd to this,

– the same phrase as in 'The Good-morrow' – all honour is mere play-acting, all wealth glittering dross. Having diminished all other value-symbols, having drawn a line across experience, put himself and his love above it, everything else at an infinite distance below it, Donne returns to his first target, the sun. He is only 'halfe as happy' as they are (presumably because he can illuminate only half the globe at one time); he is old and needs a rest[1] and finally, most arrogantly of all, having dismissed the sun to less important occupations in the first stanza, Donne changes his mind and recalls him now to his proper 'office':

> since thy duties bee
> To warme the world, that's done in warming us.
> Shine here to us, and thou art every where;
> This bed thy center is, these walls, thy spheare.

And yet, at this extreme point we see how the hyperbole 'asserts the incredible in order to arrive at the credible': it is, as Sir Thomas Browne might have said, 'not only figuratively, but literally true' that – and by decoding the message I risk a banality which Donne transcended – the universe *does* revolve around them; their bed *is* the centre; nothing else *is*; love *is* 'infinitely delightful . . . infinitely high . . . infinitely great in all extremes'. Who can quarrel with that?

*   *   *

The rhetoricians' serious justification for hyperbole included the point that the figure lies without any intention to deceive. True; but Donne is too witty a man not to see other possible intentions, to amuse, say, or shock. Given that the lovers are a unity, a supreme two-in-one; given that they exceed the rest of humanity by whatever metaphor for infinity you care to think

---

[1] Professor Gardner (p. 202) glosses this phrase by a reference to Ovid (*Metamorphoses*, 2.385-7), 'where Phoebus after the death of Phaethon complains of his endless unrequited toil'. It may be that Donne had in mind the famous illustration of analogy which Aristotle used in the *Poetics* and which occurs in a number of sixteenth-century rhetoric books and collections of similitudes: '. . . old age is to life as the evening is to the day; so the evening will be called the dying day, or old age, as Empedocles called it, the evening of life, or the sunset of life': ch. 21; tr. L. J. Potts, Aristotle, *On the Art of Fiction*, Cambridge, 1959, p. 47.

of; then it follows that the rest of us might profitably *look up* to them. I mean, by that phrase, that we are invited to regard the lovers as secular models for love, yet in doing so Donne exploits the religious overtones of this situation of imitation and adoration.

In the middle of the anguished Petrarchan suffering of 'Twicknam Garden' (which shows, I could argue, that Donne – like Shakespeare – saw that that convention was not wholly beyond further extension) Donne suddenly switches from lamenting his own suffering (love ought to turn him into a senseless object like a mandrake or 'a stone fountaine weeping out my yeare') to inviting everyone else to come and test its authenticity:

> Hither with christall vyals, lovers come,
>   And take my teares, which are loves wine,
>   And try your mistresse Teares at home,
> For all are false, that tast not just like mine. . . .

Once more the simplicity of verbal statement – tears 'which *are* loves wine', 'all *are* false' – seems to insulate the hyperbole from the charge of bombastic arrogance which it would be open to if presented as a simile, say. (There are very few similes in *The Songs and Sonnets*.) The same arrogant invitation to use him as a model – 'the real thing' – comes in 'A Nocturnall upon S. Lucies Day . . .':

> Study me then, you who shall lovers bee
> At the next world, that is, at the next Spring:
>   For I am every dead thing,
>   In whom love wrought new Alchimie.

But it is not simply a question of authenticity: he and she are superior to all the rest; she is dead ('nor will my Sunne renew') and all other lovers, who are about to be given new stores of sexuality by 'the lesser Sunne', are dismissed – real love is dead. In 'A Valediction: forbidding Mourning' their own abilities are contrasted sharply with those of 'Dull sublunary lovers . . . (Whose soule is sense)'. Whereas in my first category hyperbole was used to define the mutuality of the lovers, to set them apart from other value-symbols, now the 'Us/Them' dichotomy becomes sharper, their superiority heightened, the rest of us reduced. As A. J. Smith has wittily put it, the 'protagonist' of

the love poems 'enacts the amorous hero in a world of half-men
or lesser lovers – fat-living tycoons, jobbing merchants, place-
seekers and powermongers, sycophants, and parasites'.[1] Donne
elevates the lovers by treading us down.

'The real thing': in 'The Exstasie', that remarkable fantasia
on neo-Platonic love theory and casuistry, Donne twice invites
us to learn from him. Fittingly, given the progress of that poem,
the first time involves the soul, the second the body. While
the two lovers lie motionless 'All day', their souls have gone out
'to advance their state' (a finely ambivalent phrase) and com-
municate, even though the lovers do not speak. So,

> If any, so by love refin'd,
>   That he soules language understood,
> And by good love were grown all minde,
>   Within convenient distance stood,
>
> He (though he knew not which soule spake,
>   Because both meant, both spake the same)
> Might thence a new concoction take,
>   And part farre purer then he came.

They evidently possess the true elixir, which they will generously
dispense to anyone who can come within 'convenient distance'.
Furthermore, when the time comes for them to 'turn' to their
bodies, which have lain so long neglected, the spectator will
indeed be granted a practical demonstration of the true unity of
soul and body:

> To'our bodies turne wee then, that so
>   Weake men on love reveal'd may looke;
> Loves mysteries in soules doe grow,
>   But yet the body is his booke.
>
> And if some lover, such as wee,
>   Have heard this dialogue of one,
> Let him still marke us, he shall see
>   Small change, when we'are to bodies gone.

The hyperbole is not intended to deceive, perhaps, but is
surely meant to amuse and/or shock: Donne and his mistress as

1 'The Poetry of John Donne', *op. cit.*, p. 143.

the means of Revelation to the rest of us 'Weake men' (doubting Thomases) who are invited to look, learn, and inwardly digest. The effrontery, or impudence (I search for a Johnsonian word) of the final invitation, coming as a climax to a long, earnest, and pseudo-deliberately pseudo-philosophical poem, is not only amusing but shows how the trope, once accepted, can be launched beyond credibility or propriety without our being able to protest. Yet again there is a vein of literal truth: if the neo-Platonic concept of the union of the soul and the body means anything at all, it is difficult to see how it could not mean this. Donne achieves the shock-effect, of course, by postulating a spectator on the scene. We are quite happy to observe erotic poetry direct, in the privacy of a study or a library, but to have a third party in between us and it is rather unnerving.

But Donne has not finished with the 'lovers as model' situation yet. A number of poems continue this metamorphosis of them from examples of authenticity to cult-figures, objects of study or worship. 'A Valediction: forbidding Mourning' stresses their cult-quality, yet at that point refuses to disclose it:

> 'Twere prophanation of our joyes
> To tell the layetie our love.

But 'Loves Exchange' has no such qualms. Donne presents his mistress's face as one of Love's secret weapons:

> This face, by which he could command
> And change th'Idolatrie of any land,
> This face, which wheresoe'r it comes,
> Can call vow'd men from cloisters, dead from tombes,
> And melt both Poles at once,

– and cause a number of other cosmic catastrophes. Her power is indeed divine – rather like that of Dionysus, in Greek myth, invading a town and reducing it to his worship – and the conceit of Donne as a model for other lovers is given a witty turn in the final stanza. Love is torturing him, but won't finish him off: then why won't Love do something useful with his body, like making it an object for an anatomy-lesson in love?

> If I must example bee
> To future Rebells; if th'unborne
> Must learne, by my being cut up, and torne:
> Kill, and dissect me, Love; for this
> Torture against thine owne end is,
> Rack't carcasses make ill Anatomies.

The cult-object is sustained longer in 'A Valediction: of the Booke', which achieves some outrageous hyperboles, even for Donne. The opening stanza proposes that the lovers should 'anger destiny' by recording their deeds for posterity, and Donne assures his mistress of a renown exceeding all the famous exempla of women who have aided poets – Corinna helped Pindar, Lucan owed much to his wife, Homer cribbed both his poems from a woman. The boast proper begins with the second stanza, where Donne invites us – frequently the imperatives pull us into the poem, making escape impossible – to perform the services of a Renaissance historian and base a biography (or 'Life of the Saints'?) on their love-letters:

> Study our manuscripts, those Myriades
> Of letters, which have past twixt thee and mee
> Thence write our Annals, and in them will bee,
> To all whom loves subliming fire invades,
> Rule and example found.

He now deliberately compounds his hyperbole by treating their function as models, paragons, in religious terms.

> There, the faith of any ground
> No schismatique will dare to wound,
> That sees, how Love this grace to us affords,
> To make, to keep, to use, to be these his Records.

> . . . Wee for loves clergie only'are instruments.

Here Donne seems to be teasing us, pushing his fantastic claims further and further: the book thus created will be 'as long-liv'd as the elements' or the world-without-end; if the whole of human knowledge were to be destroyed by a new set of barbarians

> Learning were safe; in this our Universe
> Schooles might learne Science, Spheares Musick, Angels Verse.

> Here Loves Divines, (since all Divinity
>   Is love or wonder) may finde all they seeke,
>   Whether abstract spirituall love

— or if, loath 'to amuze/Faiths infirmitie' with abstractions, they want something more easily communicable, then that too can be provided. The approaches of lawyers, politicians – any aspect of love will be found treated definitively here, indeed better than anywhere else.

Perhaps by now the theories of the rhetoricians are coming to seem too solemn – but then no one could have predicted what Donne would do with hyperbole. For me, at any rate, the poem is ingenious, amusing, deliberately outrageous; Donne is making fantastic claims, knows that he is doing so, and expects us to know (he knows that we know that he knows, etc.). Critics who do not see the point complain of a tongue-in-cheek quality, but it seems to me that if we know the rhetorical convention then – like an audience which understands the routines of the music-hall, or the limits within which an eighteenth-century singer or instrumentalist could ornament the repeat of a section or improvise over a cadence – then we are in a very close rapport with the poet. Not, perhaps, Priestley's rapport with the emotionally intense poet, nor the modern naïve 'spontaneity-and-fidelity-to-self' school of poets, but a rapport with the poet as performer, the poet as wit, the poet as clown. Donne played all these roles, and since modern criticism rehabilitated the seriousness of Metaphysical wit some shoals of critics have blinded themselves to its wittiness, i.e. humour, comedy. We ought, in fact, to be in a better position to talk about Donne's humour than Dr Johnson was, since with Freud's theory of jokes, everyone realises the attraction of wit deriving from inhibited areas – sex, death, religion. Donne's bawdy has yet to be properly appreciated, though (the silence of editors may of course represent the taste of publishers: it is not long since an editor was refused permission to print one of Rochester's poems, and there are things in Catullus which do not get past all editorial boards), and this mode of knowing display to a knowing audience falls today on unknowing and unsympathetic ears.

I am discovering, in effect, that the further my analysis

proceeds away from the straightforward hyperbolic assertion of the infinite value of love, towards the presentation of the lovers as cult-objects, the more difficult it becomes for the modern reader to know how to take the poems. The firm connection with reality which one could see in the hyperboles of 'The Sunne Rising' is reduced to a slender, more tenuous thread relating truth to exaggeration, but then almost giving way to pure, uninhibited, fantastic wit. But precisely because of this virtual erasing of the obviously convertible code it becomes more than ever necessary, as Thomas Wilson saw in 1552, that 'we must diligentlie take hede, when soche speeches are used, that wee take not them as thei bee spoken, but as thei are mente'. Joseph Priestley was confident that hyperbole – like metonymy, Irony – departed from literal truth but 'in such a manner as that nobody can be imposed upon, or misled by it'. He was too sanguine. The history of critical reaction to some of Donne's poems, as to *Troilus and Cressida, The Tale of a Tub*, or *Gulliver's Travels* has shown that irony, hyperbole, or any other departure from literal truth which constructs its own language and its own code, – these, of all forms of discourse, are most liable to be misunderstood.

Here, too, the question of the reader's personal taste becomes crucial. We have abandoned many Victorian inhibitions yet even (or especially) in intelligent circles some people experience unease at a 'dirty joke'; 'gallows humour' can reduce some people to hysterics, others to frosty disapproval. Even in our basically irreligious society jokes about religion are often regarded as being in bad taste – Bacon's belief is still prevalent: 'As for jest, there be certain things which ought to be privileged from it; namely religion'.[1] Personally, I feel no inhibitions about humour in any of these areas – I care only whether the joke is a good one or not. Irony is a 'dry mock', as Puttenham called it: some of Donne's critics, for the last 350 years, have felt that some things ought not to be mocked.

To test the reader's reactions, then, to make him aware that his critical response may well be conditioned by his individual sense of propriety, I take a group of poems which push the 'lovers as cult-figures' trope into the realm of what some people

---

[1] Bacon, *Works, ed. cit.*, VI, 455 (Essay, 'Of Discourse').

would call blasphemy. I would exclude such casual, traditional references as 'all my soules bee,/Emparadis'd in you' ('A Valediction: of my Name in the Window') or a discussion of the beloved's angelic properties ('Aire and Angels'), and I would briefly allude to the long Christian tradition of presenting Christ as the spouse, the beloved, that union of religious and sexual imagery which we find in the *Holy Sonnets*, or in Crashaw, or Bernini, and which culture-historians contentedly describe as 'Mannerist' or 'Baroque'. Those two points made, we are left with 'The Dreame', 'The Relique', 'The Funerall' and 'The Canonization'.

In the first of these, within the setting of the man's erotic dream which is interrupted by the woman and then (he hopes) transformed into reality, Donne praises the woman in terms of that recurrent contrast between zero and infinity:

> Thou art so truth, that thoughts of thee suffice,
> To make dreames truth; and fables histories;

I agree with Grierson (contra Gardner,[1] who reads 'so true')

[1] Professor Gardner's main reasons (p. 209) for rejecting 'truth' are (i) 'I find "so truth" a very forced expression and the repetition of "truth . . . truth" unpleasing to the ear'. But is it more forced than many other unconventional and unpredictable grammatical constructions in Donne? The repetition is not unpleasing to me; and moreover the symmetrical placing of 'truth' within the two lines:

> Thou art so truth, . . .
> To make dreames truth;

(symmetrical in terms of placing within the line, in terms of metrical stress on the second iambic foot, and in the placing of both words immediately before a punctuation mark) make this an example of that very popular rhetorical figure *paromoion*, corresponding structure. (ii) 'Also, to impute divinity to the lady at this point is to spoil the fine audacious climax by anticipation'. Professor Gardner presumably refers to the sexual climax anticipated in the last two lines:

> Thou cam'st to kindle, goest to come; Then I
> Will dreame that hope againe, but else would die.

To 'impute divinity' is indeed to give the grounds for the dream in the first place (it is the mistress alone who can make dreams truths); but the climax works on a different plane from this.

(iii) Professor Gardner comments on the use of 'Prophane' in line 20 (It would be profane to describe the mistress in any other terms but her own) and rightly points to the religious allusion: 'Like the Deity she cannot be defined or described: she is only she' (p. 211). This is, surely, the crucial link with 'truth' in the first stanza.

in preferring the reading of the first edition (1633), as printed here, and in glossing 'truth' with the passage which he cites from Aquinas to the effect that truth is not merely possessed by God, but that He *is* truth ('Thou *art* . . . truth': again the simplest verb for this huge idea). Donne is indeed giving his mistress one of the divine attributes. Later in the poem, in the middle of a string of the familiar sexual puns on 'go', 'come' and 'die' Donne adds a parenthesis:

> I doe confesse, it could not chuse but bee
> Prophane, to thinke thee any thing but thee.

Again she has the attributes of the Deity, who 'cannot be defined or described' (Gardner). In 'The Funerall' he begs those who will bury him to leave undisturbed the 'subtile wreath of haire, which crowns mine arme', for ('Petrarchan'!) he has been slain by love and this memorial of her must be interred, in the interest of true faith:

> For since I am
> Loves martyr, it might breed idolatrie,
> If into other hands these Reliques came. . . .

The conceit is repeated in 'The Relique', but not until the second stanza: the first has the marvellous thought of the gravedigger opening up his grave to make room for a new corpse, tossing out the bones and skulls, and then, when he sees

> A bracelet of bright haire about the bone,
>   Will he not let'us alone,
> And thinke that there a loving couple lies,
> Who thought that this device might be some way
> To make their soules, at the last busie day,
> Meet at this grave, and make a little stay?

Since Eliot's famous essay discussions of this poem have often focussed on that one image, to the neglect of the superbly poignant conclusion of the stanza.

Even less discussed is the second stanza, where that tender and humane tone is replaced by irreverent wit:

> If this fall in a time, or land,
> Where mis-devotion doth command,

163

Then, he that digges us up, will bring
Us, to the Bishop, and the King,
    To make us Reliques; then
Thou shalt be'a Mary Magdalen, and I
    A something else thereby;
All women shall adore us, and some men . . . .

Now that we are alerted to Donne's use of the 'lovers as cult
figures' trope, we can see the consistency with which he has
extended the hyperbole, as in 'The Dreame', to give them the
ultimate cult status, that hint (I suppose it dare not have been
more than a hint which could be explained away, if Donne were
not to lose his ears or worse) of Donne as Christ, that final
union of erotic and Christian love.[1] Are we shocked? We ought
to be. Are you offended? or amused? Reader, if you own this
book, write your answer in the margin. For your decision on
that point will indeed determine your evaluation of the poem as
a whole.

'The Canonization' raises that question again, perhaps even
more impudently. The first stanza ('For Godsake hold your
tongue . . .') is a wonderfully rude dismissal of any of us who
might interfere with Donne's love: we, like the sun earlier, are
sent about our business. The second stanza abruptly shifts

[1] R. T. H. Redpath, in his useful annotated edition of *The Songs and Sonnets*, 1956,
after some discussion (pp. 110-11) plumps for the 'blasphemous' interpretation,
and quotes F. L. Lucas, who arrived at the same conclusion independently, and
who cited in support 'Luther's pronouncement that Christ and the Magdalen
were lovers'. Professor Gardner, however, writes: ' "A something else" is contempt-
uous. It has been suggested that Donne intended that his bone would be thought
to be a bone of Christ and this has been supported by the revival of the hoary
canard [why is it a 'hoary canard'?] that Luther said that Christ and Mary
Magdalen were lovers. But however sunk in "mis-devotion" an age was it would
surely be aware that the grave of Christ contained no relics other than his grave-
clothes' (p. 222). I do not agree with Professor Gardner, since Donne makes the
point in such a quick and off-hand fashion that we do not have the leisure to
reflect on the contents of Christ's grave; and indeed if we do so we confuse
hyperbole and literal statement. J. T. Shawcross' note is: '*A something else:*
perhaps a David . . .; perhaps a Christ', *The Complete Poetry of John Donne*,
New York, 1967, p. 142. A. J. Smith's: 'possibly "a Jesus Christ", if the "mis-
devotion" denies his resurrection; but more probably one of Mary Magdalen's
lovers in her riotous youth. Christopher Ricks points out that "a Jesus Christ"
and "a something else" are metrically equivalent', *John Donne, The Complete
English Poems*, 1971, p. 397.

direction, and exploits the gap between hyperbole and literal truth:

> Alas, alas, who's injur'd by my love?
> What merchant ships have my sighs drown'd?

This brilliant passage inverts the convention: whereas in poems like 'A Valediction: of Weeping' or 'A Feaver' or 'A Nocturnall upon S. Lucies Day' such hyperboles of cosmic, seismic or meteorological disaster are seriously used as the only language adequate enough to describe the lovers' mutual value and its potential or real destruction, now the literal statements about sighs and tears are played off against the impossibility inherent in hyperbole:

> When did my colds a forward spring remove?

Any one who suggests that they did is evidently a fool.

Having disposed of his critics Donne turns abruptly to himself and his mistress, and disarms his critics by thinking of some of the names which they might pejoratively apply to this relationship:

> Call us what you will, wee'are made such by love;
>   Call her one, mee another flye,
> We'are Tapers too, and at our owne cost die,

– Donne is coining epithets as fast as he can go, not even stopping to gloss them. But we notice that he *accepts* them all – the lovers have been 'made such by love' – and I presume that 'flye' alludes to the sexual activities of that insect, as in *King Lear*:

> The wren goes to't, and the small gilded fly
> Does lecher in my sight.
> Let copulation thrive . . .[1]

'Tapers', which burn themselves up and 'die' at their own 'cost' are obvious emblems for the sexual act. The tone so far is frank: it evades nothing, it descends to earth; but Donne goes

---

[1] *King Lear*, IV.vi.112-14; but Shawcross cites an article by A.B. Chambers (*JEGP* 65, 1966) which argues for a reference 'to the taper-fly which burns itself to death by approaching a flame' and which 'was considered hermaphroditic and resurrectable. . . .' This would evidently fit the 'Phoenix riddle' better.

on to give the lovers more status, making them 'the'Eagle and the Dove', 'emblems of strength and gentleness' which, joined together, 'symbolize the perfection of masculine and feminine qualities' (Gardner, p. 204). At this more respectable level Donne then reverses the dead-end, self-destructive image of the tapers, and replaces his mock-hyperboles with 'the real thing' again. Having exposed and destroyed the 'literalist' de-coding of hyperbole he has made the trope privileged, immune from criticism, as he launches it to a new height:

> The Phoenix riddle hath more wit
> By us, we two being one, are it,
> So, to one neutrall thing both sexes fit.
> Wee dye and rise the same, and prove
> Mysterious by this love.

Again we note the 'inexhaustible exhaustion' paradox of love, now explicitly sexual; again the simplest of statement-forms, this time exploiting the grammatical incongruity of singular and plural: 'we . . . are it'; again the overgoing – that most remarkable example of self-propagation and eternal form, the phoenix, takes on *more* wit thanks to them; and finally they become 'Mysterious': like saints or other divine entities they have a supra-rational existence, which can only be apprehended by faith.

The third stanza proceeds (like 'A Valediction: of the Booke') to contemplate ways in which their 'Mystery' can be preserved for posterity, here the literary genres which might best be used: not 'tombes or hearse', since epicedes and obsequies would be inappropriately gloomy for two who have died for love in so transcendent a way (Eagle, Dove, Phoenix); nor 'Chronicle', since they are above the historian's mere recording of facts. 'As saints and martyrs of love they have created a "legend" ' (Gardner), but the conceit of a Saint's Life has been used in 'A Valediction: of the Booke'; so Donne concludes that two genres are appropriate: sonnets, as love poems, and hymns, as the proper medium for 'loves clergie':

> We'll build in sonnets pretty roomes;
> As well a well wrought urne becomes
> The greatest ashes, as halfe-acre tombes,

The apparent modesty, scorning the display of 'half-acre tombes', in fact conceals another ultimate assertion of these lovers' eminence: their urn will contain 'The greatest ashes'. No half-measures: *infinitum in parvo*. The religious ceremony finally begins:

> And by these hymnes, all shall approve
> Us *Canoniz'd* for Love.

> And thus invoke us; You whom reverend love
> Made one anothers hermitage. . . .

Into this suitably religious incantation Donne inserts more of those fundamental hyperboles that assert the lovers' supreme excellence: as lovers, when they were alive, they were infinite, all-embracing, summing up the *whole* of the world, *every* main division of society – we recall Ophelia's lament for Hamlet:

> The courtier's, soldier's, scholar's eye, tongue, sword;
> Th' expectancy and rose of the fair state,
> The glass of fashion and the mould of form,
> Th' observ'd of all observers. . . .
>
> (III.i.151-4)

Similarly, Donne and his mistress were the focus of every gaze:

> Who did the whole worlds soule extract, and drove
> Into the glasses of your eyes,
> So made such mirrors, and such spies,
> That they did all to you epitomize,
> Countries, Townes, Courts:

– and this long parenthesis, which includes the last of Donne's hyperboles which I shall quote, ends with the ultimate gesture in this religion, this elevation to cult-figures:

> Beg from above
> A patterne of your love!

They have been promoted to saints, and we lesser mortals are told (again the imperative: 'thus invoke us') to ask them to ask God if He will give us a model of their behaviour – since they are no longer present, as in 'The Exstasie', to give practical demonstrations, and since not even their written records remain, they having been (like some favoured saint or martyr) mysteriously snatched up to heaven. As, in Roman Catholicism, 'men pray to saints to pray for them',[1] Donne and his mistress are now intermediates between us and God. The Pope had better watch out.

IV

'The Canonization' is one of a number of poems in which Donne exploits all the resources of hyperbole, from the supra-literal assertion of value to the fine thread of comic and fantastic wit. Since I set out the rhetoricians' theories relatively fully, and have not grudged space to my analysis of Donne, then the reader may feel that I have completed my contract with him. But there is a corollary to it. Readers who have followed my argument will have no difficulty in spotting Donne's hyperboles, seeing the ingenuity with which he performs variations on them, and will be able to decide for themselves whether to be shocked or amused by his blasphemy or bawdy. Yet, since hyperbole is a trope, like irony or metaphor or metonymy, it is possible to misunderstand it, and a few pages back I juxtaposed Priestley's over-confidence about the figure with Thomas Wilson's insistence that we take such speeches not 'as thei bee spoken, but as thei are mente'. A handy illustration of the possibilities of misunderstanding comes from the recent book on Donne by Dr J. W. Sanders.[2] This is a piece of anti-historical criticism (e.g., one of the books that Donne owned and which he may have referred to in *The second Anniversary* is described as a 'silly volume of pedantic ant-lore', p. 135), based on supposedly 'pure' analysis of the text and leaning heavily on such concepts as 'tone', 'movement' and 'organising centres of the poetry's seriousness'.

Dr Sanders frequently notes the presence of hyperboles in Donne, more so than any recent critic known to me (which is why I choose his work for discussion here), but he is at a loss to

---

[1] Redpath, *ed. cit.*, p. 19, citing a personal communication from H. J. C. Grierson. Professor Gardner offers as little comment on Donne's blasphemy as on his bawdy.

[2] *John Donne's Poetry*, Cambridge, 1971. 'The Canonization' is discussed at pages 21-5, 44, 50-6, 100, 108, 114.

know what to do with them. He is especially bothered by 'The Canonization'. He likens it to 'a maze', finds that it 'combines an extreme earnestness of overt content [is *earnestness* the right word?] with a disconcerting frivolity of manner' (p. 21). 'Frivolity' is just that disapproving Johnsonian-type word which I was looking for earlier to describe the sense of outrage which 'The Exstasie' might arouse in some readers (and does in Dr Sanders: pp. 56-7, 97-104). Faced with attitudes to life or love which he himself would not endorse, the critic confidently assumes that Donne also did not endorse them, and therefore only alludes to them for purposes of parody. Thus Dr Sanders' 'ear' describes the 'tone' of 'we two, being one, are it', as having 'a tantalising air of prim self-parody' (p. 21). That the apparently objective description of poetic 'tone' here is in fact merely a rationalisation of a prior moral disapproval is clear from his discovery of a 'faintly sulky note' in 'at our owne cost die', a 'note' which, he says, is 'disquieting', but is 'offset' – 'intentionally by Donne', as it were –

> by the sanctimonious complacency of 'And wee in us find the Eagle and the Dove', which is surely self-deflating—the close proximity of the two pronouns ('wee in us') seems bent on drawing attention to the acute isolation of the loving pair and questioning very much, as a consequence, any valuation made from within the tight circle of that first person plural.

The assessment of 'tone' has led to a radical failure to read the poem. The proximity of the pronouns may define the man and woman's closeness but it cannot 'question' it: that is a preformed judgment about life which this critic brings to the poem. 'Any valuation' made of each other by a human couple is a valuation which is made on their terms, and far from being, therefore, 'questionable' it is beyond our question. Dr Sanders is willing to grant the validity of this mutual valuation to lovers in a novel by D. H. Lawrence (p. 70) but he will not grant it to lovers in Donne. Therefore he complains of the third stanza of 'The Canonization' that 'the "she" of "she and I do love" gets wholly subsumed into the synthetic "wee" . . .' (p. 52)—and I have no doubt that 'synthetic' is intended pejoratively. So he writes of the great assertions of the mutual value of love in

169

'The Sunne Rising' that they show 'Donne's extreme sensitivity' – which suggests that Donne is criticising what follows – 'to the solipsistic egocentric blasphemy against the *common* reality, which lovers are prone to fall into' (p. 71). Happily he can at once console himself by writing of 'But that I would not lose her sight so long': 'The careless *superbia* quietly deflates itself' (*ibid.*). Where? How? Why should it?

It seems as if, provoked by Donne's hyperboles, Dr Sanders goes on to the defensive. Sometimes he dismisses the trope as 'self-deflating', sometimes he just labels it excessive, without even stopping to think about its function: of 'prove/Mysterious by this love' he complains of 'the exorbitant substance of the claims' (p. 22); in 'The Canonization' Donne is said to fall into the trap of writing elatedly about love in the first person singular and so 'simply making an exhibition of an essentially private matter, showing off for the edification of the less fortunate'; the fact that the poem used 'hyperbolic defiance' only made matters worse, by creating an 'ironic *anticipation* of those lapses' (p. 72: presumably in order to defend itself against them?).

It is fascinating to observe Dr Sanders from time to time perceiving what a hyperbole is being used for, yet still sternly rejecting it. So he writes of 'The Sunne Rising' that in it Donne 'concedes that the lover's vaunt is intrinsically absurd, and concedes it through a cast of hyperbole so monumental that it simultaneously offers us the preposterous richness of the experience, and grants the impossibility of ever talking about it in ordinary language' (pp. 72-3). (Ironically, if we set aside the chimerical 'absurdity' which Donne – caught on the defensive by his critic – is supposed to 'concede', the rest of that sentence unwittingly hits on precisely the rhetoricians' description of the assertive function of hyperbole which I quoted earlier.) 'The Sunne Rising' is duly described as 'self-parody' (p. 73), but it is significant that the critic, despite himself, begins to perceive one function of the hyperboles: the poem has 'an enormously heightened mental activity, a state of tremendous and exuberant stimulation' – we recall the analyses by Aristotle, Longinus, Hoskins, Priestley; Donne is attempting 'to find some form of speech which is exaggerated *enough* to answer to the exaggeration, the opulence of his feelings. The sense of inexhaustible wealth, perfume, spicery, an insane profusion of natural bounty, all in one "bed" (*both* the "India's of spice and Myne" – one isn't enough) almost overwhelms him.' I agree with Dr Sanders that Donne confesses 'the impossibility of ever describing her'; I agree that 'Donne reaches out, with a reckless abandon . . . for the sole remaining hyperbole':

> She'is all States, and all Princes, I,
> Nothing else is.

So I am all the more disappointed that Dr Sanders cannot leave his imaginative response there. It has to be deflated: his moral or logical sense has to burst the bubble to which he has been responding so warmly: 'Into the stunned silence which follows that . . . the subsidiary outrages upon common sense fall with a faint bubble and ripple of laughter:

> Princes doe but play us . . .

. . . We return to the note, slightly parodied, of royal hauteur' (p. 73).

Evidently, then, despite flashes of an intuitive response, Dr Sanders' 'common sense' is unsettled or 'outraged' by hyperbole. He will accept it only if it is conceived of as being *intended* to mock itself. The second stanza of 'The Canonization' ('What merchant ships have my sighs drown'd?') is said to present a 'gleeful pumping-up of stock poetic hyperbole until it bursts under the strain' (p. 51). To me, however, what happens here is that Donne inverts the relationship between hyperbole and literal statement. This is a relationship which Dr Sanders has not reflected on much: 'The cosmic hyperbole dresses up a very simple fact: "she and I do love" ' (*ibid.*): as we have seen, all Donne's cosmic hyperboles affirm fundamentally simple, yet absolute, concepts of human value. Unable to distinguish between the punctured hyperboles in this stanza and the serious and straightforward affirmations in the one following (Eagle, Dove, Phoenix) Dr Sanders is forced to deny the validity of the 'canonization conceit' on which the whole poem is based. For, he finds, it 'entails an inflation of sentiment just as grandiose as the Petrarchan hyperboles Donne has already punctured –

the sigh/gales, the tear/floods and the passion/fevers. *Inevitably we take the canonization as existing on the same level of factitiousness'* (p. 52; my italics). As I have shown above, the hyperboles work at two quite different levels: the mock ones in the second stanza are taken literally, in order to deflate unimaginative critics, thus 'circumstancing' the real ones in the following verse, which are now made immune to such criticism. If a poet uses literary devices to establish their own convention we must alert ourselves to his subtleties.

Finally, there is the issue of taste. I remarked earlier that modern readers have difficulty with wit based on bawdy or on religion, and Dr Sanders not only exemplifies this difficulty but offers an uncommonly violent repudiation of its cause. So he attacks the religious and sexual images which run through 'The Canonization' with a stern and severe hammer:

> Donne appears to argue the quasi-divine status of the lovers on the preposterous grounds that they re-enact the resurrection of Christ ('Wee dye and rise the same'). And that proposition, of course, rests on a pun – no less excruciating for its shop-soiled condition – on the secondary meaning of 'dye' (to pass away in sexual ecstasy). He is thus impertinently confounding mere carnality with a prime mystery of religion. Nor does the poem as a whole provide much guidance to the interpretation of this blasphemous witticism, for it ends, on the same uninterpretable [*sic*] note of rhapsodic unction as this stanza:
>
> > Beg from above
> > A patterne of your love!

It will now be evident how a purely individual sense of shock, an outraged sense of decorum, has controlled Dr Sanders' whole reaction to the poem's argument. When he comes to give a fuller account of 'The Canonization' later, he summarises his earlier argument with more of this indignant Augustan prose: 'the drastic impropriety of the theological conceits throws the reader into confusion' (p. 51); the 'identification of copulation and resurrection serves in fact to drive a wedge between the two ideas. The hyperbolic force of the identification may derive from the impropriety of the comparison, but the impropriety points to the impossibility of the identification.' (pp. 52-3). The comforting classification of hyperbole as 'self-parody' opens the door to the final rejection (or refutation): 'The poem now moves into the last disintegrating [*sic*] stage of its wit, as Donne struts before the ironically [*sic*] postulated congregation of worshippers, in improving attitudes of erotic sanctity'.

It will be obvious that I disagree fundamentally with Dr Sanders' reading of 'The Canonization' and similar poems. But I have quoted him at a fair length not simply to pick a quarrel or score a point but to show how Donne's blend of wit and seriousness in hyperbole has provoked him, got under his skin, made him uneasy (he complains of Donne's 'uneasy impropriety', p. 53; of his 'unsettling . . . erotic theology', p. 56) and has led him to the only response, perhaps, which he can feel sure about: total condemnation. He stops himself at one point from being 'too puritanically graceless' (p. 106), and indeed there are signs of flexibility with some of the poems. But, cornered by Donne's use of this trope which illuminates, shocks, amuses, confuses, he does fall back on a kind of puritanical thundering, a moral denunciation in which grace and humour are absent. Although the protective denunciation may be personal to him, the kind of provocation offered by hyperbole is one that, as we can see from the history of Donne criticism, has been felt in different ways by other readers. From which I deduce my conclusion, which is that Thomas Wilson's injunction of 1552 that we should take such poems and such figures as they are meant, neither to 'take the whole for the parte, when the whole is expressed in woordes, and the parte mente in understanding', is peculiarly relevant when we read Renaissance poetry of this kind. As T. S. Eliot once observed, Donne shares with other poets of this age the technique of elaborating 'a figure of speech to the furthest stage to which ingenuity can carry it'.[1] Once we have noticed this strategy we must be alert to the contexts in which it is used, and although my point of departure has been the teachings of rhetoric my argument has not been dependent upon any specialist technical expertise. I have tried to show that Donne used hyperbole in a variety of ways, demanding that we should decode the internal conventions which he set up in full awareness that this 'figure of excess' needs to be, in Joseph Priestley's words, 'so circumstanced' that 'we are led into no

[1] T. S. Eliot, 'The Metaphysical Poets', in *Selected Essays*, 1951, p. 282.

mistake by such terms' and perceive their unique economy. Despite Priestley's assurances that this could not happen, Dr Sanders has allowed (or caused) himself to be 'imposed upon [and] misled' by hyperbole and irony; he has not been able to 'enter, as it were, into the mind of the writer'; faced with these 'falsehoods' he has been led, not to a new kind of truth but to unease, confusion, and a self-defending moral pompousness. What he has quite failed to see (and he is evidently not alone) can be summed up in the paradoxical language of Traherne: hyperbole, like love, is 'infinitely Great in all Extremes. . . . Excess is its true Moderation: Activity its Rest: and burning Fervency its only Refreshment'.

7

'As Through a Looking-glass'
Donne's Epithalamia and their Courtly Context

MARGARET M. McGOWAN

Works written for a precise occasion, or composed to praise a particular patron, are frequently regarded by critics with some scepticism. They are dismissed as 'insincere' and 'inflated', or as 'not credible'. It is the purpose of this essay to suggest that works such as Donne's verse letters – and two of his *Epithalamia*, in particular – which have received relatively little attention precisely because they fall into this category of occasional verse, should be studied not as anomalous and extravagant pieces but as the natural expressions of a highly self-conscious and literate society which genuinely believed itself to be exactly as its spokesmen depicted it.

In the past, the *Epithalamia* have been subjected to rather narrow comparative studies. They have been examined in relation to other nuptial songs written for the same occasion, or precedents have been sought which might, or might not, have inspired Donne. Close study of parallels and influences has tended to state the obvious in terms of form and theme. For example, McPeek argues lengthily the thematic influence of one poet upon another[1]; while the influence of Catullus is remorselessly traced through the tradition of the Epithalamium by another scholar.[2] Elsewhere, the reappearance of an image is thought to be significant; or the borrowing of a particular

---

[1] J. A. S. McPeek, *Catullus in Strange and Distant Britain*, Harvard Studies in Comparative Literature, xv, 1939. His comments on Donne start on p. 207.

[2] See J. B. Emperor, *Catullian Influence in English Poetry 1600-1650*, University of Missouri Studies, iii, 1928, no. 3. There is a considerable literature on the Epithalamium. For sixteenth-century reflexions on this form consult Scaliger, *Poetices libri septem*, Lyons, 1561, Book III, Ch. 101, and G. Puttenham, *The*

stanzaic form, or an order of treatment is remarked upon.[1] These restricted approaches are unsatisfactory, since the individual character of Donne's own work disappears in a welter of learned and not altogether relevant comment. They also prove that the study of influences (even within one form) is too complex to be handled by tracing a theme, an image, or an author's subsequent fortunes. The criss-cross ramifications of inspiration which were consciously or unconsciously present in Donne's mind when he composed his two Epithamalia certainly owe something to classical examples, to Jonson's learning, and to the healthy spirit of competition which existed between fellow poets.[2] They owe more to the exploration of the form by the Pléiade,[3] a little to Spenser's beautiful poem, and to Sidney's enthusiasm[4]; but, above all, they should be seen as products of the robust atmosphere of James I's Court.

Arte of English Poesie, 1589, Book I, Ch. 26, 'The Maner of Reioysings at Mariages and Weddings' [G. Gregory Smith, *Elizabethan Critical Essays*, Oxford, 1904, ii, p. 52]. For more modern comments, consult L'Abbé Souchay, 'Discours sur l'origine et le caractère de l'épithalame', *Académie royale des Inscriptions et Belles Lettres*, ix, 1736; A. Gaertner, *Die englishe epithalamien-literatur*, Coburg, 1936; T. Greene, 'Spenser and Epithalamium Convention', *Comparative Literature*, 1957, pp. 215 ff.; and L. Foster, *The Icy Fire*, Cambridge, 1969, for an extensive bibliography.

[1] Alastair Fowler, *Triumphal Forms*, Cambridge, 1970, pp. 154, 160 for Frederick and Elizabeth; pp. 71-3, 107, 158 for Somerset and Lady Howard.

[2] Poets were very conscious of each other's work and frequently indulged in poetic rivalry. Jonson, for example, took note in his masques of the copy of King James's poems which he owned (see R. P. Gillies, prefatory memoir, p. xvii, to the 1814 edition of *The Essayes of a Prentise, in the Divine Art of Poesie*); and of John Donne, he reported, 'he wrott that Epitaph on Prince Henry *Look to me Faith* to match Sir Ed. Herbert in obscurenesse'. *Conversations with Drummond*, in *Ben Jonson: Works*, ed. C. H. Herford and P. Simpson, 1925, i, p. 136.

[3] Examples probably known to Donne are: J. Du Bellay, *Epithalame sur le mariage de tres illustre Prince Philibert Emanuel* . . . Paris, 1559; P. de Ronsard, *Epithalame d'Antoine de Bourbon, et Ianne de Navarre*, Paris, 1549; R. Belleau, His Epithalamium for the second day of *La Bergerie* (*Les Oeuvres Poétiques*, Paris, 1578), and Claude de Buttet, *Epithalame aux nosses de Tres magnanime Prince Em. Philibert de Savoie* . . . (*Oeuvres Poétiques*, Paris, 1880, i. pp. 136-160, first published in Paris in 1559).

[4] Sidney's poem, in particular, thrives on a spirit of competition, and recalls many Catullian touches such as the use of the elm and the vine in Book III of *The Countesse of Pembroke's Arcadia*, 1593, pp. 192-3.

In this essay, the intention is not to chart detailed influences, but rather, through the study of specific works, to convey an idea of the spirit of James I's Court, and of the criteria of expectation assumed by poet and audience alike. Donne's *Epithalamia* will be examined against the background of other poems, plays, and masques written to celebrate the same occasions, so that a composite picture of the literature of the Court and the kind of language current there might be built up. The analysis of the festivities for the marriage of the Elector Palatine and Princess Elizabeth (James I's only surviving daughter), and for that of the Earl of Somerset and Lady Francis Howard, might seem over-extended. But it is my contention that the closest attention to detail is first necessary to establish an accurate impression of the general context, and that *only then* should Donne's poems be considered. In this way, I hope that the individual character (if any) of his contributions will be more readily seen.

By 1612-13 King James's Court was well schooled in lavish ceremonial. Already, when the King and his Danish Queen Anne entered London in the spring of 1604, the time was described by a chronicler as 'Triumphant'. So great were the crowds thronging the streets to celebrate the arrival of a new king and the beginning of a new era, that the same observer commented: 'I can compare to nothing more conveniently than to imagine every grass to have been metamorphosed into a man in a moment, the multitude was so marvellous'.[1] Wonder, triumph, and festivity naturally accompanied every public appearance of the King and his family, and they similarly dominated the life of the Court.

The masques and plays, arranged to present views of vigorous and beneficial kingship to an acquiescent Court and to critical foreign ambassadors, were rather different in character from those which had formed the image of Elizabeth I. As the focal point of every spectacle, the unattainable Virgin Queen had inspired poets to stress chivalric attitudes and ideas. She was the Lady of the Lake who released beleaguered knights (Kenilworth, 1575), and the August Queen who presided over tilts

---

[1] J. Savile, *King James his entertainment at Theobalds, with his welcome to London, 1603*, and printed in *An English Garner. Stuart Tracts 1603-1693*, 1903, p. 61.

fought in her honour (Earl of Warwick's marriage, 1565; Kenilworth, 1575; and Count Palatine's Entertainment, 1578). She was Cynthia (Elvetham, 1591); Perfect Beauty (1581); Diana, Goddess of Chastity (Bisson, 1592); and the Fairy Queen who had power to dispel enchantments (1595).[1] Although the centre of everything, Elizabeth had appeared as a still and lonely figure, whose very presence was sufficient to excite achievement. Her incredible loftiness of being was acutely expressed by poets who spoke the adoration felt by courtiers towards their monarch: an adoration which at first glance might seem mere flattery designed for self-profit, but which on closer examination is seen as the only means of describing the fervent emotions generated in subjects by a Queen who guides and orders their lives. In the matter of marriages, however, Elizabeth had become increasingly disapproving. Sir Robert Cary, for example, who had married in 1572 without her consent, reports 'the Queen was mightily offended with me for marrying'. He only managed to ease royal ruffles by elaborate compliments, which he reports as follows: 'Shee herself was the fault of my marriage, and that if she had but graced me with the least of her favours, I had never left her nor her court. . . . She was not displeased with my excuse.'[2] Elizabeth did make one exception: at the age of 67 she danced at the wedding of Lord Harbert![3]

Ostensibly, the relationship of monarch and subject had not altered under James I. He remains the fountainhead of social and political activity, and the principal source of inspiration to poets and artists. But the mood has changed. From his Court Festivals, we receive the impression of a much more dynamic personality. The King is depicted not so much as the aloof pinnacle of State, but as the busy centre towards which all eyes turn and from which all activity begins. He seems closer to his courtiers; and he literally fathers their peace and prosperity by organising their marriages. For instance, the first marriage of Lady Frances

---

[1] Details of these spectacular events may be found in J. Nichols, *The Progresses and public processions of Queen Elizabeth*, Second edition, 1823, *passim*.

[2] Nichols, *op. cit.*, ii, 'The Queen at Windsor, 1593', from the Memoirs of Robert Cary, Earl of Monmouth, pp. 9-11.

[3] Lord Harbert married Mrs Anne Russell in June 1600; see Rowland Whyte's account in a letter, printed by Nichols, *op. cit.*, ii, 'The Queen's Progress', 1600.

Howard to the Earl of Essex, arranged to foster peace and good will between two important rival houses, was celebrated with great pomp in 1606 – Ben Jonson creating one of his most sumptuous and coherent masques, *Hymenaei*, to consecrate the occasion.[1] Campion composed a lengthy masque to celebrate the marriage of Lord Hay and Honora (the daughter of Lord Denny) which took place in 1607.[2] The following year, obeying the King's express command, Jonson brought immortal Gods with nuptial songs to honour the wedding of Viscount Hadding-ton and Lady Elizabeth Ratcliffe[3]; while the years 1612-13 witnessed further royal and noble excuses for solemn ceremony. Without doubt, James was expansive; festivals celebrate his doings, and in festivals his Court revelled in its well-being. There was a robustness about, in comparison with which the atmosphere surrounding Elizabeth seems more like Fairyland.

To praise a learned king, well-versed in the arts of writing and of controversy, was a ticklish business.[4] Samuel Daniel presents the problem in this way:

> Nor shall we now have use of flatterie,
> For he knowes falsehood farre more suttle is
> Than truth; basenesse than libertie,
> Feare than love, t'invent these flourishes:
> And Adulation now is spent so nie
> As that it hath no colours to expresse
> That which it would, that now we must be faine
> T'unlearne that Art, and labour to be plaine.[5]

[1] For an important analysis of this masque (Ben Jonson, *Works, ed. cit.* vii, pp. 203-41) see D. J. Gordon's substantial article: '*Hymenaei:* Ben Jonson's Masque of Union', *Journal of the Warburg and Courtauld Institutes*, 1945, viii, pp. 107-45.

[2] Given in his *Works*, edited by W. R. Davis, 1969, pp. 203-30.

[3] See Jonson's *Works*, vii, pp. 243-63. There is a good analysis of this masque by D. J. Gordon, 'The Haddington Masque', *Modern Language Review*, 1947, pp. 180-9.

[4] James was a prolific writer who prided himself on the extent of his erudition. His tutors, George Buchanan and Peter Young, encouraged him to collect books and to read avidly. One gains a good idea of his scope by looking at his Library holdings: see 'The Library of Mary Queen of Scots and James I', *Miscellany of the Maitland Club*, Edinburgh, 1834, i, and 'The Library of James VI', *Miscellany of the Scottish Historical Society*, Edinburgh, 1893, i.

[5] Samuel Daniel, *A Panegyricke congratulatorie to the Kings Maiestie*, 1603, p. 27.

Call yourself a plain man and people are more inclined to believe you. Assume a diffident tone and people will listen eagerly. King James himself had learned these tricks from George Gascoigne and others, whose advice he paraphrases when he writes on the art of praising:

> Ye shall rather prayse hir vther qualiteis, nor her fairnes or hir shaip . . . and syne say that your wittis are sa smal . . . remitting alwayis to the Reider to iudge of hir.[1]

Here writes a man who, though there were few topics on which he himself did not voice an opinion, appreciated the force of few words and the power of reticence, and understood that the most effective praise is to understate or hide it. Such a man probably smiled at Ben Jonson, who in his very first entertainment composed for James wrote:

> He can neither bribe a grace
> Nor encounter my lords face
> With a plyant smile, and flatter,
> Though this lately were some matter
> To the making of a courtier.[2]

If you declare yourself unworthy to speak, whatever praise you utter thereafter is more readily believed. This technique of self-deprecation advocated by the King, and employed here by Jonson, was often used by Donne in his verse letters. To the Countess of Bedford, for example, he writes:

> When all (as truth commands assent) confesse
> All truth of you, yet they will doubt how I,
> One corne of one low anthills dust, and lesse,
> Should name, know, or expresse a thing so high,
> And not an inch, measure infinity.

('To the Countesse of Bedford, At New-Yeares Tide', 26-30)

Statements of inadequacy were only one means of expression at Court, and certainly not the means most frequently employed

---

[1] *Ane Schort Treatise conteining some Reulis and Cautelis to be observit and eschewit in Scottis Poesie*, 1584, printed in G. Smith, *Elizabethan Critical Essays*, *op. cit.*, i. pp. 220 ff.

[2] *Works*, vii, p. 127, from *A particular entertainment of the Queene and Prince their Highnesse to Althorpe*, performed Saturday, June 25, 1603.

if we are to believe the Earl of Suffolk who in a letter written about 1611 to his friend Sir John Harrington of Kelston, gives us an idea of the King's sense of values rather different from those he had advocated in his *Schort Treatise*:

> You are not young, you are not handsome, you are not finely; and yet you will come to Courte, and think to be well favoured! Why, I say again, good Knight, that your learning may somewhat prove worthy hereunto; your Latin and your Greek, your Italian, your Spanish tongues, your wit and discretion may be well looked unto for a while, as strangers at such a place; but these are not the thinges men live by now-a-days. Will you say the moon shineth all the sommer? That the stars are bright jewels fit for Car's ears? That the roan jennet surpasseth Bucephalus, and is worthy to be bestridden by Alexander? That his eyes are fire, his tail is Berenice's locks, and a few more fancies worthy your noticing.[1]

These, it seems, had to be the aims and expectations of anyone desirous of a successful career at Court, and this was the language which commanded favours. Of course, Suffolk exaggerates; yet his words do confirm other contemporary impressions of the sudden rise to fortune of Robert Carr, in whom the King 'tooke more delight and contentment in his companie and conversation then in any man living'.[2] The following letter from George Calvert to Sir Thomas Edwards captures the spirit of Carr's influence over James; indeed, the terms used to describe the favourite might well be thought more appropriate to the status of a king. 'My lord; You know the *Primum mobile* of our Court, by whose motion all other spheres must move, or else stand still; the bright Sun of our firmament, at whose splendour or glooming all our marygolds of the Court open or shut. In his conjunction all the other Stars are prosperous, and in his Opposition malominous.'[3] The language is deliberately extravagant in so far as it refers to Carr.[4] If, however, one were to

---

[1] Letter printed in J. Nichols, *The Progresses, processions, and magnificent Festivities of King James the First*, 1828, ii, p. 414. (Cited hereafter as *James's Progresses*.)
[2] *The Letters of John Chamberlain*, ed. N. E. McClure, Philadelphia, 1939, i, pp. 448-9.
[3] Letter printed in *James's Progresses*, ii, p. 454.
[4] Arthur Wilson tersely remarked about him: 'the Lords themselves can scarce have a smile without him', *The History of Great Britain, being the Life and Reign of King James the First*, 1653, p. 55.

understand that the King was being referred to here, then neither James nor his Court would have thought it needful to modify a syllable, since the words accurately describe the King's function.[1]

If poets were 'the trumpetters of all praise', as Puttenham had called them[2] (and there were few contemporaries who would disagree[3]) then, when it came to displaying princely magnificence fit to publish the Union between two Protestant powers in Europe – England and the Palatinate – it is precisely the kind of panegyric used here of Carr which would be called for. King James and his Court *expected* a certain tone, in poems, plays and masques, reflecting not their aspirations to greatness but the glory they felt manifest in themselves every day. As Ben Jonson expressed it in *Neptune's Triumph* (1624) 'That were a heauy and hard taske, to satisfie *Expectation*'.[4]

Jonson himself was abroad with the son of Sir Walter Raleigh at the time of Princess Elizabeth's marriage to Frederick of the Palatinate in 1613.[5] There were, however, innumerable poets anxious to replace him. Epithalamia, congratulations, and paeans of praise poured in from every side. In George Wither's nuptial poems all the Gods summoned their noblest wits to honour the marriage; James Maxwell celebrated the event in one hundred stanzas; Henry Peacham elaborated similar hymns of praise; and Thomas Heywood, describing the combined efforts of heaven and earth to do glory, recalls the amazement

---

[1] On the language appropriate to kingship and on the ritual of the masque, W. Todd Furniss, *Jonson's Masques* (in *Three Studies in the Renaissance: Sidney, Jonson, Milton*, Yale, 1969, pp. 89-179) is indispensable.

[2] Smith, *op. cit.*, ii, p. 36.

[3] This fact is well demonstrated in O. B. Hardison's study which examines the literature of praise, *The Enduring Monument*, Chapel Hill, 1962.

[4] *Works*, vii, p. 683. This is part of a conversation between the Poet and the Cook, the whole of which is interesting from the point of view of audience expectation:
POET. That were a heauy and hard taske, to satisfie *Expectation*, who is so seuere an exactresse of duties; euer a tyrannous mistresse: and most times a pressing enemie.
COOKE. She is a powerfull great Lady, Sir, at all times, and must be satisfied: So must her sister, Madame *Curiositie*, who hath as daintie a palate as she, and these will expect.
POET. But, what if they expect more then they vnderstand?
COOKE. That's all one, Mr *Poet*, you are bound to satisfie them.

[5] According to Paul Reyher, *Les Masques anglais*, Paris, 1909, pp. 176-7.

of the massed spectators who marvelled at the beauty of the bridal pair.[1] According to John Taylor, the Water Poet,

> Since the first framing of the worlds vast Rome,
> A fitter, better match was not combinde.[2]

Andrew Willet praised the King for having 'married religion to religion'[3]; and Franchis, developing the same theme, foretold that

> Sceptra Palatinis commixta Britannica Sceptris
> Aurea restituent renovato saecula mundo.[4]

In this context of a Golden Age restored, Donne's offering has a more private touch.

The context of the marriage celebrations extends beyond these Epithalamia which formed but a tiny part of the festivities for the marriage performed on St Valentine's Day 1613. Speculation about the magnificence, the cost, and the participants, had been rife since early November when the Venetian Ambassador reported to the Doge: 'The six hundred thousand crowns destined for these fêtes have grown to a million, and those who know say that even this will not suffice'.[5] Indeed, interest had already reached a high point a month earlier when the Count landed in England, and 'most happily deceived good mens'

---

[1] George Wither, *Epithalamia or Nuptiall Poems upon the most blessed and happy Mariage* . . ., 1633. There was a first printing in 1612. James Maxwell, *A Monument of Remembrance erected in Albion, in honor of the Magnificent Departure from Britannie and honourable receiving in Germany* . . . *of the two most Noble Princes* . . ., 1613. Henry Peacham, *The Period of Mourning* . . . *Together with Nuptiall Hymnes, in Honour of this Happy Marriage* . . ., 1613. Thomas Heywood, *A marriage triumphe solemnized in an Epithalamium, in memorie of the happy nuptials betwixt the High and Mightie Prince Count Palatine, and the most Excellent Princesse the Lady Elizabeth,* 1613.

[2] John Taylor, *Heaven's Blessing and Earth's Joy,* 1613, sig. Di.

[3] Andrew Willet, *A treatise of Salomon's Marriage, or A Congratulation for the Happie and Hopefull Mariage between the most illustrious and noble Prince Frederike the V* . . . *and the Most Gratious* . . . *Ladie Elizabeth* . . . 1612, 'Epistle Dedicatorie', sig. A i.

[4] I. M. Franchis, *De Auspicatissimus Nuptiis,* Oxford, 1613, sig. E ii. Two Scottish additions to honour the princes arrival in Heidelberg should be mentioned: J. Forbesio, *Genethliaca* . . . *Frederici V* . . . *et Du. Elizabethae,* Heidelberg, 1614, and J. Gellio, *Epithalamium et Gratulatio,* Heidelberg, 1613.

[5] *Calendar of State Papers (Venetian),* p. 680, letter of 9 November, 1612.

doubts and ill mens' Expectations'.[1] James and his Court spared no pains to ensure that the news of the festivities and solemnities reverberated around Europe. The *Mercure François* published an account of the ceremonies; extended French and German narratives of the events were printed; and foreign ambassadors resident in England sent their impressions home.[2] The extraordinary splendours displayed in Paris in April 1612, for the publication of the double marriages arranged between France and Spain, were effectively eclipsed by the London shows of 1613.[3] As one account of the English festivities put it: 'Nothing can better set forth the greatnesse of Princes, nor more expresse the affection of friends, together with the dutie, love, and applause of subjects than those solemne and sumptuous Entertainments which are bestowed on great and worthy persons'.[4]

Let us then turn to the detailed calendar of magnificence which stretched out over a fortnight. Five hundred musketeers had been called into London where the bells rang 'generally in every church, and in every street bonfires blazed abundantly'. This was the spirited scene which Donne and his contemporaries experienced every time they walked out. Thursday 11th February witnessed the first of the Fireworks[5]: ordnance pealed like thunder, rockets of fire burst from the water, and the sky seemed filled with blazing sparks. Artificially contrived, a flaming St George on horseback vanquished a dragon, and burning hunting hounds pursued a hart up and down the waters

---

[1] Sir Ralph Winwood's *Memorials of Affairs of State*, 1725, 3 vols, iii, pp. 403-4.

[2] *Mercure François*, iii, pp. 72 ff.; and D. Jocquet, *Les triomphes, entrées, cartels, tournois, ceremonies, et autres magnificences, faites en Angleterre, et au Palatinat, pour le mariage*, . . . Heidelberg, 1613. It is amusing to note that Jocquet has completely muddled up his information. At sigs. H i-H iv^v, for the Tuesday night, he gives a very detailed account of Jonson's *Hymenaei* which was composed for the first marriage of Lady Frances Howard in 1606. G. F. Bondi, the Venetian Ambassador's secretary, sent the British Ambassador in Venice, Sir Dudley Carleton, a copy of the *Epithalamia* written at Oxford. *C.S.P. (Domestic)* 17 March 1613.

[3] There were at least two dozen works published to celebrate these events; the most detailed is François de Rosset's *Le Romant des chevaliers de la Gloire*, Paris, 1612.

[4] *James's Progresses*, ii, p. 612.

[5] Two main sources provide these details: John Taylor's *Heaven's Blessings, op. cit.*, and T. C.'s *The Mariage of Prince Fredericke* . . ., 1613; both are printed by Nichols, *James's Progresses*, ii, pp. 527 ff. and 536 ff.

as realistically as if the hunt had been on land. As the smoke cleared, a Christian navy advanced upon Turkish territory, espying a Turkish fleet, and two towers of defence; and the ensuing sea-fight ended in triumph for the Christians when the towers were 'sacked, burned, and ruinated'. This was a mere prelude to an elaborate naval battle which took place on the Thames on Saturday 13th. Two hundred and fifty vessels guarded the bounds of the contest area where sixteen ships, sixteen galleys, and six frigates prepared to do damage. First, the Venetians and then the Spaniards unsuccessfully assailed the Turks, and, inevitably, it was left to the English Fleet to carry the day. The 'business' cost the King upwards of £9,000.[1] And there were other costs, too: 'as one lost both his eyes, another both his handes, another one hande, with divers others maymed and hurt'.[2] As one of the Captains, Mr Phineas Pett, complained, 'in which jesting business I runn more danger than if it had been a sea service in good earnest'.

The religious ceremony was conducted by the Archbishop of Canterbury. First, from the new Banqueting House specially built for the occasion,[3] came the Palsgrave attired in garments of white satin, richly set with pearls and gold. Elizabeth came next in richly embroidered white, attended by virgin bridesmaids 'like a skye of caelestial starres, [attending] upon faire Phoebe'.[4] The King wore jewels esteemed 'not to be less worth than six hundred thousand pounds', while Queen Anne's gems were valued at four hundred thousand pounds. The solemnities were done in due form in the presence of magnificently clothed princes, earls, barons, and their ladies, the Ambassadors of France, Venice, and the States. This splendid company, carefully observing the rules of precedence, then processed ceremoniously back to the Banqueting House where they 'fell to dancing, masking, and revelling, according to the custome of such assemblies, which continued all the day and part of the night'.[5] It was well

---

[1] *James's Progresses*, ii, p. 525.

[2] Chamberlain, *op. cit.*, i, p. 423.

[3] Sir J. Finett, *Finetti Philoxenis, some choice Observations*, 1656, p. 11, 'a large roome built of purpose for the time over the North Terras next the first Court of Whitehall'.

[4] *James's Progresses*, ii, p. 544.   [5] *Ibid*, ii, p. 549.

that the Spanish Ambassador had refused to be present for he would have had to stare at the wall of the Great Chamber decorated by a new set of Tapestries representing the defeat of the Spanish in 1588.[1]

Thomas Campion was the author of the first of three masques specifically created to celebrate this wedding.[2] Intermingling song and dance, in a décor of moving lights, he presents a mirror of the events we have just described, heightening and intensifying the experience. The bride and groom, the King and Court, are assembled to savour their own great achievements, wrought with propriety, and endorsed by higher beings. As soon as the King is settled, Orpheus, the sweet enchanter, and (in this instance) the messenger of Jove, causes Entheus (or Poetic Fury) to be freed from the entanglements of Madness so that together they might

> . . . create
> Inventions rare, this night to celebrate.

The power of their music and song banishes Mania and her Franticks who disappear after performing bizarre dances, and prepares Entheus for his vision of Prometheus and his dancing lights. Veils are lifted and these lights grow larger and stronger, as Prometheus himself appears to answer the plea:

> In Hymen's place aide us to solemnpize
> These royall nuptials; fill the lookers eyes
> With admiration of thy fire and light,
> And from thy hand let wonders flow tonight.

He turns all eyes to gaze on the 'heav'n borne starres' which he has brought, whose light and beauty aptly fit the place; and he announces 'a Courtly miracle'.

It would be difficult to imagine a sight more splendid than the bridal couple, and James surrounded by his Court, glittering

---

[1] *C.S.P.* (*Venetian*), p. 775, 1 March 1613, 'Passed into a great chamber, especially made for this wedding, . . . and the hangings in the Hall represented the defeat of the Spanish in '88'.

[2] The masques for both Princess Elizabeth's wedding and that of the Earl of Somerset are printed in *James's Progresses, op. cit.*, and all detailed quotations from them used in this essay can be found there; the discrepancies between these texts and the originals are very minor ones.

with satin, brocades and jewels, watching the sudden trans-
formation of stars into human shapes attired in cloth of silver,
embossed with flames of embroidery; and wearing, on their
heads, 'crownes, flames, made all of Gold-plate Enameled'.
Where ends the reality and where does the fiction begin? Like a
hall of answering mirrors, King and Court see embodiments of
their own grandeur wherever they look.[1] The transformation
scene, and all the dances which followed, were interspersed
with music and song expressing vows that this night

> . . . may live in fame,
> As long as Rhenus or the Thames
> Are knowne by either name.

Flames in human shape, led by sixteen fiery spirits bearing
torches, prepare to act out this vow when, unexpectedly, four
noble women, statues of silver, were discovered in a Temple
made of Gold.

Now begins an elaborate courtship sequence, with silver
statues coming to life four by four, and Prometheus' lights
wooing and winning their favour, singing and dancing out their
joy, and reminding the spectators at regular intervals

> . . . Io Hymen
> To the Bride we sing . . .
> These love for Virtue's sake alone;
> Beautie and Youth unite them both in one,
> Live with thy Bridegroome happy, sacred Bride . . .

Thus, the happy couple are the centre of all the festivity; and, to
enforce this notion 'the Princely Bridegroome and Bride were
drawne into these solemne Revels', maskers and audience
intermingling, fused in one glorious celebration. This inter-
changeability is yet further emphasised in the scenes which end
the Entertainment. Gold statues of the Bride and Groom
dominate the final set; beside them, Sibilla stands ready to give
her blessings, and speak her prophecies inspired by Jove. They
tell of the infinite prosperity, peace and plenty of a new golden
age. With gay shouts and trumpetings, song and dance take

---

[1] The sphere of lights and the twelve signs also presided over the Haddington
wedding in 1608, see Jonson, *Works*, vii, pp. 243-63.

off again, more joyful and delirious than ever, to celebrate the triumph of this union. The climax has at last been reached; and just in time, for 'the Cocks alreadie crow'. Time Triumphant had welcomed James on his arrival in London, and triumphant his career continues. Through his agency this newly-wedded pair have attained divinity, and enjoy that glorious self-contemplation given only to the Gods.

Night was consumed, and on Monday there were many famous races at the Ring, before the same glittering company, decked out as gloriously as on the previous day,[1] repaired to a gallery to await George Chapman's masque which was on its way from the Inns of Court.[2] Two hundred Halbardiers accompanied the fifty gentlemen masquers, a mock masque of baboons, and two Triumphal cars in which rode, 'the choice Musitians of our Kingdome . . . attir'd like Virginian Priests', and called Phoebades because they adored the Sun. The chief masquers wore Indian habits 'richly embroidered with Golden Suns', and a third Chariot, 'à la Grotesca', carried Capriccio, the Goddess of Honour, her priest Eunomia, her herald Phemis, and the earthly deity Plutus. At Whitehall, a stage prepared with craggy rocks, a grove and a temple dedicated to Fame, awaited their revels which celebrated the marriage union as symbolic of a greater unity – the joining of the Old World and the New. Human love is shown as the image of the Divine, and as symbolic of a cosmic harmony, the marriage image spiralling out, through a chain of correspondences, till it includes the universe.[3]

The unifying theme of the masque is the desire to celebrate the marriage. This allows for a heterogeneous sequence of entries: Capriccio with his baboons; Plutus desiring to join

---

[1] The Venetian Ambassador informed the Senate that he had to change his dress every day, as did every member of James' Court, and for this reason he demanded more funds from the Senate to cover these extraordinary expenses.

[2] Admission fees and levies raised upon the members of the Inns of Court (the Middle Temple, and Lincoln's Inn) paid for the masque. Financial details are given in E. K. Chambers, *The Elizabethan Stage*, Oxford, 1923, i, p. 211.

[3] Fame, Union, and Concord, were inevitable themes in Court Entertainments, and they frequently imposed the same range of imagery as that used here; see, for example, Jonson's *Hymenaei* (1606) where a similar stress on Religion, Reverence, and Reason occurs.

with Honour 'In purpos'd grace of these great Nuptials'; and the Phoebades called from Virginia,

> To do hue homage to the sacred Nuptials
> Of Law and Vertue, celebrated here.

While the sun worshippers engage in their prayers and ceremonies, Honour and Plutus comment on their movements, their rhythmic dances, and the significance of their hymns. The sun is a Janus-like symbol, representing the light, warmth, and the perfection which normally attaches to it, and signifying also

> . . . our cleare Phoebus, whose true piety
> Enjoyes from Heaven an earthly deity.[1]

Easily and naturally, observers and worshippers turn from the actual setting sun on the stage, to a more powerful Phoebus, who constantly rises, maintaining his light, his honour, and his riches, through fruitful unions. It was indeed fortunate that the marriage of Count Palatine to Princess Elizabeth coincided with the discovery of rich gold mines in the colony of Virginia.[2] This metallurgical fact happily confirmed James's luminous power. Compared to his glory 'that Sun is but a beame', and

> All other Kings in thy beames met
> Are cloudes and dark effects of night.

For these reasons, the Phoebades are urged to abandon their superstitious worship of a planet, and to turn to 'our Britain Phoebus', a more powerful luminary than the Sun, whose Christian piety creates harmony, religious unity, and universal peace. Chapman is in no way making the empty gestures

---

[1] The sphere of the Sun as a Symbol of Perfection is recurrent in the masque. See Jonson's *Hymenaei* (1606), and his masque for the Haddington wedding (1608), where James's Piety, Justice, Prudence, and Virtue are detailed. In Campion's masque for the wedding of Lord Hay (1607) James, as the sun, is referred to in this way: 'Long live Apollo, Britaine's glorious eye'.

[2] The Venetian Ambassador, Foscarini, writes (*C.S.P.* 9 August 1613), 'A ship has arrived here from Virginia which has caused universal rejoicing by the news of success. It appears that the soldiers of the Colony have inflicted a great defeat upon the King of Poitaw, and have taken prisoner one of his daughters by reason of which he has offered friendship, peace, and the knowledge of some rich gold mines.'

expected of a Court panegyrist when he equates James's powerful effects as centre of the social hierarchy with those which emanate from the central planet of the universe. In very truth, James has proved himself worthy of the comparison. Throughout his kingship he had advocated peace and union: on the political level with his joining of Scotland and England, and his encouragement of links between the Old World and the New; on the religious level with his constant appeals to Protestants and Catholics to live harmoniously together. The metaphor of marriage, the King had used more than once in his writings and in his wordy speeches to Parliament, as a way of describing his intentions and aspirations for social, political, and religious concord. So it is without exaggeration that voices in the masque sing,

> A learned King is as in skies
> To poore dimme stars the flaming day!

and, Eunomia, the Virgin Priest of the Goddess of Honour, can congratulate James whose influence has already (through the marriage Union which is being celebrated, as well as through his efforts at oratory) had an impact. She speaks,

> To this our Britain Phoebus, whose bright skie,
> Enlightened with a christian piety,
> Is never subject to black error's night,
> And hath already offer'd Heaven's true light
> To your darke region.

In a symphony of song and dance, the highpoint of the masque is reached as the chief masquers come forward to acknowledge the true shining light, the father of love and beauty (the Bride and Groom) since by their union 'thus the Golden World was made'. Only the harmonies of dance and silence could bring these self-indulgent celebrations to a finish; and, appropriately, a hymn to sleep – 'let stir no aspen leafe' – and a dance, end the revels.[1]

On Saturday night, the Court enjoyed Francis Beaumont's masque, devised at the request of Sir Francis Bacon who 'spared no time nor travail in the setting forth, ordering, and furnishing

---

[1] Jack E. Reese, 'Unity in Chapman's masque of the Middle Temple and Lincoln's Inn', *Review of English Studies*, 1964, pp. 291-305, sets out the different levels of unity in the masque, and draws parallels with Jonson's *Hymenaei* (1606).

of this Masque'. Jupiter and Juno, willing to do honour to the marriage of two famous rivers (the Thames and the Rhine) send down Mercury and Iris for that purpose. The two messengers first try to outdo each other in producing revels worthy of the occasion: Naiades, Hyades, Cupids and Statues, pursue each other, then dance together; even common people rush in and perform their measures, until finally Jove intervenes and sends a troop of Fifteen Olympic Knights whose eminence more fittingly honoured so august an event. Dressed in carnation satin embroidered with blazing stars, and glittering all over with silver, they appear before the luminous altar of Jove. His twelve priests urge them to dance while they accompany their movements with song for

> . . . at the wedding of such a pair
> Each dance is taken for a prayer
> Each song a sacrifice.

Indeed, as the excitement of the masque reaches its height there is little to distinguish the ritual from that of a religious ceremony, where everyone participates in a soaring, uplifting experience. Ladies from the audience rise to share in the dancing before the festivities end in blessings, peace, and silence:

> Peace and silence be the guide
> To the Man and to the Bride.

Tranquillity was hardly an apt description of the days and nights which followed for the newly-married pair. In April, they left for 'the Palsgraves land [that] stands like a Paradise',[1] and in every town they were entertained with banquets, masques, tilts, triumphs, gunshot, military displays, shows, pageants, and fireworks; until finally, in June, they reached Heidelberg where the most sumptuous shows of all awaited. But these belong to another story.[2]

[1] The words are William Fennor's, *Fennor's descriptions* . . ., 1616, sig. B iv^v.

[2] D. Jocquet gives a detailed account of these entertainments in *Les Triomphes, op. cit.* The prose account is illustrated by some interesting engravings of triumphal chariots.

Throughout the celebrations for this marriage the tone has
been precisely that which James and his Court expected. The
occasion and the context naturally called forth certain effects,
recognised forms, and a specific language. The wedding cere-
monies followed a pattern of behaviour and a traditional ritual
of service. Where Kings are 'the most conspicuous beings',[1]
magnificence, rich apparel, and ceremony automatically attach
themselves to them. They receive their most eloquent expres-
sion at particular moments in time (such as a princely marriage)
when not only the Court, but the country as a whole, can con-
template a well-ordered, harmonious structure, working mag-
nificently.[2] The moment might be a particular one, but its
significance is general. Marriages are public affairs, and princely
ones are even more so. They act as a looking-glass reflecting
the prosperity of the State. The songs of the masque 'ravish'
and do not 'rave',[3] however superlative our more democratic
eyes might find the words. We interpret these songs as ex-
pressions of some kind of ideal state to which people merely
aspired, but could never, in fact, attain; but for Donne's con-
temporaries the meaning was much more immediate: the state
celebrated in these songs was an ideal, but it was one which
could be attained by certain beings on certain occasions. James
is the Sun of Britain, and he and his Court are self-consciously
rejoicing *in that fact*.

Modern critics tend to underestimate the power of metaphor.
The allegories of St George, Light, Prometheus, Phoebus, and
Olympus, seem to them mere idealisation, either too remote
to be understood, or too obvious to be meaningful. Indeed, on
one level, they do express a kind of remoteness, for James is an
exemplary figure, and contemplation of his powers is naturally
elevating, intensifying, and expansive. Yet, it is the revealing

---

[1] Jonson, *His Panegyre, On the happie entrance of James* . . ., 19 March 1603.
Works, vii, p. 115.

[2] Jonas A. Barish, *Ben Jonson and the Language of Comedy*, Harvard, 1960, sets out
similar points very forcibly in the second part of his study.

[3] The distinction is made by Meric Casaubon in his *Treatise concerning Enthusiasme*,
1655, p. 142, 'Many men, saith he, [referring to Longinus] whilst they strain their
wits to find somewhat that is very extraordinary, and may relish of some rapture
or Enthusiasme; they plainly rave (or, play the fools) and not ravish.'

force of the allegories,[1] the warm effects of wondrous self-regard which take away all sense of aridity and of distance. There is no need for the verses to describe the figures of the masque: they are well known, and their attributes can be clearly seen. Moreover, even the seemingly obscure areas of allegory – for instance, the Obelisk, and words of Sibilla in Campion's masque – encourage, on the part of the participants, a collaborative effort of thinking and discovery. The moral and symbolic role of these figures is what counts, and, to an audience of initiates, descriptive explanations are superfluous.

Initiates: such a word admirably describes the relationship of members of the Court to the occasion. They are taking part in ceremonies which demand a previous knowledge of their form, rules, language, and purpose. The specific nature of the occasion merely encourages a heightening of the wonder which properly belongs to their mode of life; and this is stressed throughout, not because it is different from usual, but because it presents an elevated version of their everyday being. In a very real sense they share in the exalted experience. In each of the masques we have examined it has been clear that no fine distinction existed between stage and audience. The masquers *are* the spectators, in that the Queen, her ladies, or their Lords, all qualify equally to assume the characters of the masque; conversely, the spectators are the masquers in so far as they dance together frequently throughout the proceedings. Characters call upon 'Ladies' to respond, judge, or comment; they appeal to the King, exalt him, and pay him homage; they point out the qualities of the Bride and Groom, and present their physical doubles to gaze upon. Interchange is fluid and constant in these two spheres which are mere extensions of each other. The poet's role is to re-create the exalted opinions which King and Court already have of themselves. In his task of reproducing their style, he is as conscious as anyone of the formality, the rules and expectation, the appropriateness of metaphor and propriety of language. Jonson expressed this aptly in *Oberon* (1611),

[1] I have found Judith Dundas's comments on the revealing qualities of allegory very enlightening; they are developed in her article 'Allegory as a form of wit', *Studies in the Renaissance*, 1964, pp. 223-33.

This is a night of greatnesse, and of state;
Not to be mixt with light, and skipping sport:
A night of homage to the *British* court,
And ceremony, due to ARTHURS chaire . . .[1]

The poet recognises that his success depends on recognising
the specificity of the event, and on exploiting its general
significance. He knows that he is part of a ritual where strict
adherence to its laws are essential. You may consciously appear
to break the rules – as the irruption of common people into the
middle of Beaumont's noble masque shows – but you must then
justify the violation, and consciously dismiss it as Iris and
Mercury did there. Specific expectation, a shared knowledge, a
high degree of identification, therefore, allows for common
expression of feeling and for collaborative wit. The poet has to
abide by the rules. Within limits, however, he can also play
with them. In this way, for example, Plutus can open Chapman's
masque with the apparently satirical comment 'Rockes! Nothing
but rockes in these masking devices! Is invention so poore shee
must needes ever dwell amongst rocks?[2] But it may worthily
have chaunc'd (being so often presented) that their vaine
custome is now become the necessarie hand of Heaven, trans-
forming into rocks some stonie-hearted Ladies, courted in
former Masks.' Initially, the response might be a little am-
biguous. Is he right? Has he gone too far? It rapidly becomes
clear, however, that Chapman, is operating within a convention:
he is at one and the same time complimenting his female
audience (they are fashioned in heaven, they are beautiful, and
have attracted attention), and criticising them as 'stonie-
hearted'. But, before either impression settles, Capriccio bursts
forth from the rock, with the self-conscious and laughter-
provoking statement: 'How hard this world is to a Man of
Wit!' It is then that the ladies laugh.[3] As Puttenham had
observed some years before, 'the Poet must know to whose
eare he maketh his rime, and accommodate himself thereto'.[4]

---

[1] Jonson, *Works*, vii, p. 352.

[2] They were, indeed, used in most masques at some point or another; to quote but
one example, see Jonson's *Oberon* (1611).

[3] There is a similar, very pointed appeal to the Ladies, and a similar effort at con-
nivance, in Jonson's *Haddington Masque* (1608).   [4] Smith, *op. cit.*, ii, p. 199.

In circumstances where to eulogise the King is to congratulate the society,[1] the problem for the poet seems to be less that of making his art relevant to a particular event,[2] than of ringing the changes so that he and his patrons might with renewed vigour and profit contemplate their achievements. It is interesting to examine how far the criteria we have found controlling a set of masques devised for a royal wedding apply when the marriage is that of the King's favourite and Lady Frances Howard. This notorious pair were married on 26 December 1613 by the Dean of the Chapel Royal, 'which fell out somwhat straungely, that the same man, shold marrie the same person, in the same place, upon the self-same day . . . the former partie yet living'.[3] The occasion was marked with great celebrations undertaken by express command of the King. Poets and nobles alike felt 'they must do something for the Man whom the King loves'.[4]

On the evening of the marriage a masque by Thomas Campion was performed in the Banqueting House. Immediately the King is the focus of attention. Although a seascape, with rocks, beautiful gardens, and a temple, dazzled at one end of the room, all eyes turn towards James as four Squires bow before him and explain how their journey from the four parts of the world to honour the marriage has been hindered, how their vessels are shipwrecked and their knights stand transformed into pillars, by the efforts of 'Deformed Errour, wing tongu'd Rumor', and 'Curiositie' and 'Credulitie'. Only James's 'Majesticke Grace' could protect the world from the prodigious confusion wrought by those four Demons. The extent of the disorder is suggested by the tumultuous appearance of the four winds all blowing and dancing at once, the four elements scrambling around in uproar, and the four parts of the world, turbulent and distraught, joining confusedly in the mêlée. The gloating triumph of the

1 I accept Barish's statement that the 'Masque was designed to emphasise, not the ideals to be achieved by discipline or faith, but ideals which are desired or considered to be already possessed'. *Op. cit.*, p. 243. Such a view is well substantiated by the reading of any masque of the period.

2 To my mind Stephen Orgel, *The Jonsonian Masque*, Harvard, 1965, p. 7, states the problem the wrong way round when he suggests that the poet's problem was to accommodate his ideas to the needs of a particular event.

3 Chamberlain, *op. cit.*, i, p. 495.   4 Wilson, *op. cit.*, p. 72.

forces of turmoil is, however, shortlived. Eternity enters with the Fates, carrying a Tree of Gold. They are followed by Harmony and the nine Muses who speedily banish Confusion. It remains for the enchanted knights to be freed; and this is accomplished by BelAnna who plucks a branch from the Tree of Gold – a gesture symbolising her grace, her virtue, and her compassion,

> . . . for she, she, only she
> Can all knotted spels untye.

The sea perspective disappears and gives place to a vista of London and the Thames in which the twelve knights, magnificently attired, begin the first of many dances, interspersed with song. 'Io, Io, Hymen' echoes all around as they sing of fire and of love's delight. The lady spectators join in the dances which end with the arrival of twelve skippers who come to carry the knights back to their native lands. As they leave in four barges drawn along the Thames, the Squires advance once more towards the King's dais, and speak of blessings,

> . . . plentie, honor, love,
> Power, triumph, private pleasure, publique peace . . .
> Ever attend your Triple Majestie.

To the honoured bridal pair they offer the same blessings granted by the Fates at Peleus' Nuptials; but the entertainment ends abruptly as 'Hymen frownes at your delay'.

The celebrations continued the next day with a Running at the Ring as a preparation for the New Year's Day Tilt. The Challenge prepared by Jonson concerned a dispute between two Cupids, one of whom was thought to be false. Each explains in detail the rites they severally performed at the 'glad solemnities', the one serving the Bride, the other the Groom; and finally, unable to discover any counterfeit, they resolve to fight out the Truth, each one's birth-right to be defended by ten knights.[1] Challenge Day arrives, and Cupid I with Spring, Beauty, and Cheerfulness on his side fights Cupid II supported

---

[1] The use of contention and *débat* in Court Entertainments is very traditional, and probably goes back to the challenges issued in Tournaments as well as to medieval literary examples in morality plays.

by Youth, Audacity, and Favour. They are so evenly matched that neither has lost nor vanquished, when Hymen arrives to settle the affair, complaining that another kind of Tilting would be more appropriate – they should 'crack kisses instead of staves'. It transpires that they are both true Cupids: One Eros, son of Venus and Mars, the other Anteros, Venus's second born, and both are necessary to marriage where concord, mutual respect, interchange of ardour, and not contention, are signs of happiness.[1]

29 December witnessed the first performance of Jonson's vigorous and satirical *Irish Masque*.[2] 'The King being set in Expectation, out ranne a fellow attir'd like a Cittizen', and the first words he utters are: 'For Chreeskes sayk, phair ish te King? Phich ish he, an't be? show me te shweet faish, quickly.' Real or feigned ignorance, this sets a new tone in a masque, for the King is plainly there for all to see. The momentary questioning – Patrick soon locates the King and presents his credentials – is by no means unsettling. From the complacent, settled hierarchy comes laughter, even perhaps astonishment, at the Citizen's obtuseness; and even when Donnell enquires, 'Ish it te fashion, to beate te Imbasheters here?' noble spectators rightly think, not that the Court ceremony is being made fun of, but that the antics of foreign ambassadors are the source of the joke.[3] Patrick and his companions come to dance, having heard of the marriage of 'Ty man Robyne', 'ty man Toumish hish daughter', and 'ty good man, Toumish o'Shuffolke'; they introduce the twelve principal masquers who first dance in Irish mantles (having lost their sparkling clothes in the sea), but soon come forth again as 'new-born creatures all'. The power of the King's presence is such that he can work such miracles as

---

1 D. J. Gordon provides Jonson's sources for the story of Eros and Anteros (mainly Cartari and Giraldi) in Appendix II of his article: 'Poet and Architect: The Intellectual Setting of the Quarrel between Ben Jonson and Inigo Jones', *Journal of the Warburg and Courtauld Institutes*, 1949, xx, p. 177.

2 The King liked this masque so well that it was performed a second time on 10 January 1614.

3 The quarrels of French, Spanish, and Venetian Ambassadors, in particular, were a continuous source of trouble at James I's Court. For details, Guy de la Boderie's *Ambassade*, 1750, the Venetian Ambassador's correspondence, and Mary Sullivan's *The Court Masques of James I*, 1913, should be consulted.

these, can end Ireland's 'most unnatural broils', and, furthermore, can engender a quality of renewal in everything:

> So breaks the sunne earths rugged chaines,
> Wherein rude winter bound her vaines;
> So growes both streames and source of price,
> That lately fettered were with ice.
> So naked trees get crisped heads,
> And cullord coates the roughest meads,
> And all get vigour, youth, and spright,
> That are but look'd on by his light.[1]

On the 31st a letter on behalf of the King was dispatched to the Lord Mayor of London informing him that the King, the newly-wedded couple, and members of the Court, intended to sup with him and the City Fathers on 4 January. At first the Mayor begged to be excused, saying that his house was not big enough for such a large company; he was peremptorily told that he should use one of the large city halls. Thereupon, the Merchant Taylors' Hall was fitted out for the banquet, two masques, and a play. These were devised by Thomas Middleton, but only the title – *Mask of Cupids* – survives.[2] The festivities did not end until Twelfth Night, when Sir Francis Bacon again did the honours, spending £2000 on a *Masque of Flowers*.[3] The dedication suggests that he was 'in effect the only person that did both encourage and warrant the Gentlemen to do their good affection towards so noble a conjunction in a time of such magnificence'.[4] The slender theme of this entertainment, on a night so remarkable,

> . . . when a sonne, a moone, and stars
> Are met within the pallace of a King,

---

[1] Robin-Goodfellow and Cupid give a similar account of James's powers in *Love Restored*, 6 January 1612, *Works*, vii, pp. 382-4.

[2] It is significant perhaps that the City Fathers considered it unimportant to preserve the description of these shows, while Middleton's work, *The Triumphs of Truth*, written to celebrate the installation of the Lord Mayor for the year 1613, survives intact.

[3] The authors of this masque are unknown. The preface of the version printed in 1613 is signed J. G., W. D., and T. B.

[4] Bacon owed the king particular allegiance since he had been named Lord Attorney on 26 October 1613.

concerns the efforts of Winter and Spring (under orders from the Sun) to celebrate 'two noble persons of the greatest island of his universal empire'. Winter's contribution forms the 'anticke-mask', and presents the challenge of Silenus to Kawasha that Wine is more worthie than Tobacco. The burlesque challenge, inspired by the King's own taste,[1] was acted out, in verse, song, and dance, before giving way to a more solemn enterprise, played in a beautiful garden. There, amid exotic trees and brilliantly coloured flowers, sat twelve Garden Gods. As soon as they are revealed and perceive the King – 'the great Sun of our firmament' – they begin their sung entreaty, praying that his power will transform the flowers of the garden into men. Scarcely are their hymns over than thirteen masquers, 'on their left armes a white scarfe fairly embroidered sent them by the Bride, on their hands a rich paire of embroidered gloves, sent them by the Bridegroome,' rise up, transformed before one's very eyes. They dance, and their movements are interrupted by songs which sometimes marvel at their metamorphosis, and sometimes address the ladies of the company urging them to dance with the fairest flowers of manhood. Other songs praise the King's 'vertue soveraigne' which produces such prosperity, and offer the 'lovely couple' flowers of honour, beauty, affection, and duty.

These were the public ceremonies given by order of the King to his favourite. The flavour is often different from that which pervades revels made for Princes. It is significant, for instance, that in all the entertainments, the King remains the principal focus of interest; and that the marriage celebrations are primarily a means of doing honour to him. In Campion's and Jonson's masques, he is the first to be appealed to, and the revels always end at the foot of his dais. In Bacon's masque the King's own opinions provide the inspiration for the anti-mask. His love of wine was well-known and his antagonism towards tobacco smokers had been many times exposed in speeches, writings, and disputations. These writers have their priorities right, for whatever the excuse for a magnificence, the King –

---

[1] James was a great drinker and a vociferous opponent of tobacco; his *Counterblaste to Tobacco* had appeared in 1604, and naturally provoked a spate of supporting pamphlets from his subjects.

frequently depicted in these masques as the sun, the source of light – reigns supreme over his hierarchy. The end of Jonson's boisterous *Irish Masque*, for example, surges into incantation, restoring not only a sense of stateliness and power to James, but also suggesting that his capacities for creating the conditions in which good flourishes are constantly expanding.

In all these celebrations, the bridal couple, the reason for the revels, are hardly mentioned. In Campion's masque they are not named, 'Io, Io, Hymen' referring generally to the sacrament of marriage. In Jonson's *Challenge*, the discussion is again abstract and general, and even the title, *A Challenge at Tilt, at a Marriage*, as Herford and Simpson point out, is expressed in the vaguest possible terms. In the masque, it is customary to use one particular event to discourse more generally on the virtues and qualities of marriage, as, for example, in Jonson's *Haddington Masque* (1608) and in his *Challenge* which, in many ways, comes close to a morality play. Although the framework for the contest seems slight, it does, nevertheless, invite the spectators to reflect on questions of some seriousness: companionship, reciprocal affection in marriage, and mutual respect. In his *Irish Masque*, the family name of Suffolk does occur; but sufficiently surrounded by banter and burlesque. Indeed, it seems that a different language entirely is being used for this occasion, except when the King himself is directly implicated. Obviously, there is a recognised way of writing and talking about the King which is not the same as that used for mere courtiers, however lofty their position; and Jonson probably had this distinction in mind when he criticised Campion's masque with its Catullian overtones[1] which he considered extravagant for the occasion. More properly, he acknowledges, the tone of this series of entertainments belongs to a salon where the kind of *jeu d'esprit* on which Jonson's *Challenge* rests naturally thrives; where words are delicate compliments to superbly dressed ladies and gentlemen who can accept or reject the inherent moral truths; and where the success of the whole depends on drawing the audience into the riddle-solving process.[2]

[1] Campion freely acknowledges his debt to Catullus.
[2] *Love freed from Ignorance and Folly* (3 February 1611) is based on the riddle 'To find a world, the world without', and in *Hymenaei* (1606), despite the solemnity

Or, to take an example from the *Masque of Flowers* where the parallels of transformation are spelt out in light, flattering terms:

> Thrice happy Flowers!
> Your leaves are turned into fine haire,
> Your stalkes to bodies streight and faire,
> Your sprigges to limmes, as once they were,
> Your verdure to fresh bloud . . .

Either the language is socially orientated, abstract, and general, pointing to useful moral implications, with a few compliments thrown in as in the *Challenge*, or it is pugnacious (even contentious) more readily to fit the character of Jonson's Irish blades.

It is noticeable that any references to the circumstances leading up to the marriage are, on the whole, studiously avoided. In fact, the specific nature of the occasion is largely ignored; a few references to Rumour, Envy, and Curiosity at the beginning of the Campion masque are the only elements which might remind the distinguished audience of the divorce of Lady Frances, or the death of Sir Thomas Overbury. The poets' tact (and, perhaps, their integrity) is evident in their refusal to comment specifically, and by their relating the occasion to a general area of human experience (marriage), and their making the event set forth, once again, the infinite glories of the King. It was clear to them that anyone who tried to make too many detailed references to the precise situation between the King's favourite and his wife was doomed both to disappointment and discredit. The unfortunate Chapman, who failed to observe this fact, miserably wrote that his *Andromeda Liberata, or the Nuptials of Perseus and Andromeda*, written to celebrate the marriage, had been 'maliciously misinterpreted'. He insisted that the entire narrative had been inspired by Natalis Comes; and yet, no lengthy justification could undo the harm

---

of the context, Jonson can write more intimately of

> . . . fresh delights
> As courtings, kissings, coyings, oaths and vows,
> Soft whisperings, embracements, all the joys
> And melting toys,
> That chaster love allows.

201

he had already done by his references to the people's con-
demnation of the divorce proceedings, and by his use of the
unhappy adjective 'barren'.[1]

While Donne was seeking secular preferment he came into
daily contact with the kind of language used in Court Festivals.
Since he was, during a major part of his career, a 'courtier', in
the sense that he sought employment from the great and was
willing to serve them for favours,[2] he knew how to distinguish
different levels of language for different occasions. Among his
friends can be counted many writers of masques and related
works dedicated to the glories of the Court: Ben Jonson,
Samuel Daniel, Michael Drayton, George Wither, and Sir
John Davies.[3] He also had close connections with many success-
ful diplomats of whom Sir Henry Wotton is, perhaps, the most
outstanding. Among his patrons Lucy, Countess of Bedford
'the Queenes only favourite',[4] who always danced at her side
in every masque, can be singled out, together with the Countess
of Huntingdon, Mrs Herbert (mother of George Herbert),
Lord Hay, and the Earl of Somerset. Lady Lucy Donne ad-
dressed variously as 'unique', 'the good countess', 'the best
lady', and 'the Happiest and Worthiest lady'; and to Sir Robert
More he wrote, 'no man attends Court fortunes with more
impatience than I do'.[5]
    He seems to have been fully conversant with the ways and
manners of the Court, and, occasionally, in his letters, he sends
friends news of masques and revels: for example, of the Hadding-

---

[1] One example from Chapman's poem suffices to illustrate his insistent clumsiness:
    'Forth then (my Lord) . . .
        Till Scandall pine, and Barre-fed envie burst . . .
        No truth of excellence, was ever Scene,
        But bore the Venom of the Vulgare's spleene.'
                                        Andromeda, op. cit., sig. B ii[v].

[2] See R. C. Bald's *John Donne: A Life*, Oxford, 1970, p. 125.

[3] He probably knew Campion too; in any case, the latter's *Poemata* figures among
several poetic works in Donne's library. (Sir Geoffrey Keynes, *A Bibliography of
Dr John Donne*, 1958.)

[4] Chamberlain, *op. cit.*, i, p. 306. According to Bald's biography, *op. cit.*, p. 173,
she became Donne's patroness about 1607.

[5] Edmund Gosse, *The Life and letters of John Donne*, London, 1899, ii, p. 46.

ton masque in 1608, and of one for which the Duke of Bucking-
ham was preparing in 1614.[1] He attended the three great days
of festivities in Paris in April 1612, rather arrogantly dismissing
them in favour of more vigorous English sports and greater
magnificence.[2] Although, except for his Epithalamia, he was
not personally involved in either of the two great events we
have described in detail, he was nevertheless in close touch.
With the Drurys, he travelled widely in the Palatinate in 1612,
thinking as he went of the Princess Elizabeth for whom he had
considerable regard, describing her as the 'worthiest princess of
the world'. With Lord Rochester, future Earl of Somerset, he
had closer links, and in the matter of the divorce proceedings he
offered specific aid: 'My poor study, having lain that way, it
may prove possible that my weak assistance may be of use in
this matter in a more serious fashion than an epithalamium'.[3]
'Poor' and 'weak': this was the same self-deprecating tone which
he had used so that he might not flatter Mrs Herbert though
praises belonged to her – 'But since to you, who are not only
a world alone, but the monarchy of the world yourself, nothing
can be added, especially by me . . .'[4]; a tone that he had fre-
quently employed in his verse letters to the Countess of
Bedford and which he used (perhaps a little satirically) for his
friends,

> But care not for mee: I, that ever was
> In Natures, and in Fortunes gifts, (alas,
> > Before thy grace got in the Muses Schoole)
> > A monster and a begger, am now a foole.
> > (*To Mr T. W.*, 'All haile sweet Poet,' 13-16)

Protestations of inadequacy were, as we have seen, a means of
preparing the terrain for the praise consciously expected by
listener and poet alike. They reveal, incidentally, an acute
awareness on the part of both poet and patron of the importance
of a certain relationship to be established between them. The
act of recording the virtues of the great meant a sharing in them,

[1] *Ibid.*, i, pp. 182, 192; ii, p. 66.
[2] *Ibid.*, i, p. 302, and R. C. Bald, *Donne and the Drurys*, Cambridge 1959, p. 96.
[3] Gosse, ii, p. 25, and Bald's discussion in his biography *op. cit.*, p. 275.
[4] Gosse, *op. cit.*, i, p. 166.

and a desire to emulate them. The perception of virtue is itself a source of self-congratulation. So Donne addresses the Countess of Bedford, 'Madame, You have refin'd mee . . .', and as he was to express later in another place: 'this is truly to glorifie God in his Saints, to sanctifie our selves in their examples; To celebrate them, is to imitate them'.[1] Here, the flavour of Court Festivals is well caught. The form matters little: whether it be a sermon, a masque, a poem in praise of a countess, or an Epithalamium, the atmosphere which surrounds their composition and the context in which they are conceived are the same.

The Epithalamium shared general similarities and many detailed characteristics with the Court Masque. It celebrated a specific occasion; it had similar religious, political, and social, as well as erotic, overtones; and its role was to praise the bridal pair and offer them tokens of good will. The language was suitably elevated in both forms, which depended in large part for their effects on recurrent images. Yet the Epithalamium is more limited. It lacks the flexibility of the masque, the harmonious effects of song and dance, and the spectacular wonder of the décor. To praise and celebrate without these aids, as one writer on Epithalamia has expressed it, has frequently been 'l'écueil des Poëtes'.[2]

Donne's marriage song for Princess Elizabeth and Count Frederick immediately draws attention to the general context in which this specific happening must be set.[3] The union of these two princes is a significant human fragment of a universal structure built by Bishop Valentine,

---

[1] *The Sermons of John Donne*, ed. G. R. Potter and E. M. Simpson, California, 1953-61, x, p. 190.

[2] Souchay, *op. cit.*, p. 318. It is worth quoting his detailed comments: 'Ce Poëme au reste a deux parties qui sont bien marquées, et qui me paroissent essentielles à tout Epithalame. L'une qui comprend les louanges des nouveaux époux; l'autre qui renferme des voeux pour leur prospérité. La première partie exige tout l'art du Poëte, car il en faut infiniment pour donner des louanges qui soient tout ensemble ingénieuses, naturelles, convenables: et voilà sans doute pourquoy l'on dit si ordinairement que L'Epithalame est l'écueil des Poëtes.'

[3] The texts used for this Epithalamium and the poem written for the Earl of Somerset can be most conveniently found in A. J. Smith's edition (*John Donne, The Complete English Poems*, Penguin, 1971), pp. 135 and 139 respectively. I quote them from this edition.

> . . . whose day this is,
> All the air is thy diocese,

A solemn, religious occasion, is the first suggestion of these words which are quickly underscored with tones of expansiveness, and filled with airy delight. The gaiety of a bird hastening to its mate is heightened by the knowledge that this ceremony is an eternal one, to be renewed every year; and yet, in spite of this eternity, the specific occasion which Donne celebrates has especial brilliance, capable of rebounding back upon Old Valentine and *enflaming even him*.

It is this uniqueness (in all senses of the word), only hinted at here in a general way, which forms the main source of inspiration, and the principal theme of the poem. The general happy mating of bird with bird, annually performed, according to religious rites, 'All that is nothing unto this' – the coupling of two Phoenixes. Now, as Donne well knew, legend decreed that the Phoenix, symbolising flames and passion, was the rarest bird. It was unique, and only reproduced itself by self-destruction – that is to say, out of its ashes a new Phoenix was born. This is how James I defined its nature:

> . . . my Phoenix rare, whose race,
> Whose kynde, whose kin, whose offspring, they be all
> In her alone, whom I the *Phoenix* call
> That fowle which only one at onis did live.

And the King's notes suggest how widespread was the knowledge of this bird.[1] Thus, by the second stanza, Donne's poem begins to turn on a deliberately contrived impossibility. As is his custom, he instantly acknowledges the paradoxical nature of the facts he presents, and stresses the artificial character of the occurrence, by suggesting that the Phoenix is being used here only metaphorically:

> Thou mak'st a taper see
> What the sun never saw,

[1] James I, *Poems*, Scottish Text Society, series 3, no. 22, 1955, p. 95: 'I have insert for the filling out of thir vacand pageis the verie words of Plinius upon the Phoenix [James then quotes at length from Chapter 2 of the *History*, and continues] I helped myself also in my Tragedie thairof, with the Phoenix of Lactantius Firmianus, with Gesnerus de Avibus, and dyvers others, bot I have onely insert thir foresaid words of Plinius, Because I follow him maist in my Tragedie, Fareweill'.

And yet, before we have absorbed the ingenuity of this, he insists:

> . . . what the Ark . . .
> Did not contain, one bed contains, through thee,
> Two phoenixes,

and a few lines later he affirms even more strongly that these two phoenixes shall produce,

> Young phoenixes, and yet the old shall live.

In these ways, the legend is broken twice: phoenixes multiply, while the old live on, and their qualities of love and courage overspill the confines of St Valentine's Day to embrace the whole year. The special character of the occasion increasingly takes on extraordinary overtones.

Flames, light, love, and courage – all these elements are contained in the notion of Phoenix, and the third stanza singles out the fair Phoenix Bride as a source of warmth, activity, and with the power to create of herself extensive constellations of jewels, of brightness, and light. One remembers the prose description of her at the wedding ceremony: 'shining like a constellation, her train supported by 12 young ladies in white garments so adorned with jewels that her passage looked like the milky way'. Donne himself has absolutely succumbed to her dazzling force. He assumes from the start an extraordinary power of light, inspiration, and passion; appeals of 'frustrate the sun' and of 'up', 'call', 'take', and 'make' (the last three gaining more urgency by echoing at the line-end) increase the impression of the active participation of the poet. He himself is personally touched by the vision he is re-creating. As he thinks about her brilliance, associated notions present themselves – 'new star', 'new glory', portentous of 'Ends of much wonder'. And his mind moves from the sphere of the physical presence of light, passion, and riches, to the more exciting speculations about the consequences of such gifts.

The glorious flames grow larger and stronger, and the tone more impassioned and argumentative, as Donne imagines the meeting, mating, and union of Elizabeth and Frederick. Since they are both one and infinite (infinity being incapable of separation), they are doubly and irrevocably joined. The call to Church seems almost impatient, only one way of making one, among 'divers ways', the most urgent seeming 'yourselves to entwine'. Here, Donne brings to the fore a preoccupation which has been lurking throughout the poem: the physical joining of Elizabeth and Frederick. For three stanzas this interest had seemed dominated by more traditional St Valentine references, decorously covering the feather beds introduced at the end of stanza 1, and diverted by the paradox of two phoenixes in stanza 2. Yet, 'one bed contains two Phoenixes' is the central notion of that stanza. The interest was screened by the dazzling light of the Phoenix bride in stanza 3 where the subtle suggestion – 'a great Princess falls, but doth not die' – seemed anticlimactic and even a rather exaggerated and not an entirely appropriate compliment, until one realises that sexual union is the main burden of the poem – and, incidentally, the one way that Donne can solve his paradox, making his two Phoenixes become One, and restoring Nature to herself again (stanza 8).

The traditional chronology of the Epithalamium is largely ignored,[1] telescoped into one stanza to enhance the sense of urgency and unreasonable delay which Donne wishes to convey. He expostulates against the lingering sun – 'Stays he new light from these to get?' – and reprimands the slow steps of the bridal couple in procession from the Church. Food furnishes additional fodder for blame as he dwells lingeringly on its 'gluttonous delays'. Even the masquers are gently upbraided for prolonging their magic till cockcrow, like fairies. One would think it were Donne's own wedding night.

At last, relief and expectation are combined in stanza 6, for night is come. Yet, patience is stretched tauter as the formalities of disrobing the Bride are precisely and punctiliously performed,

> . . . (as though
> They were to take a clock in pieces,)

[1] All writers on the Epithalamium set down their own rules of chronology; but, in general, the poem should start with the time of the marriage, and continue with the company present, a description of the Bride, the Groom, the Revels, the Going to Bed, the ritual of the marriage night, and so on. Donne is more faithful to this kind of scheme in the second Epithalamium, as will be evident from our discussion below.

The incongruity of the simile is a measure of the poet's increased irritation, while his notion of how a bride should be bedded at once describes his ferment and tells us how extraordinarily precious she seems to him:

> A Bride, before a good night could be said,
> Should vanish from her clothes, into her bed,
> As souls from bodies steal, and are not spied.

This sense of spiritual uplift and exaltation while performing a physical act is maintained throughout the rest of the poem. The bridegroom passes 'through sphere after sphere', touching sheets, arms, anywhere and everywhere.

These two are mirrors to each other, reflecting their glories, sharing their riches and generosity, dazzling with truth and courage. A 'she sun', she has dominated the poem with light and warmth, and has communicated her brilliance to others so that they are filled with wonder and awe. Her groom, like the moon, takes all his strength from her. The famous and abused – 'Here lies a she sun, and a he moon here' – sums up the purport of the poem.[1] It points directly and precisely at a contained self-reflecting universe, where two privileged people enflamed with passion seem exemplary. They are models, capable of imparting to others the exhilaration they feel, and of giving such pent-up emotions a spiritual value. The overturning of our normal expectation of a 'she moon' only serves to emphasise the points further. The line appears unseemly and extravagant when wrenched out of the context which has been so carefully prepared for it.

Elizabeth and Frederick outdo all Valentine's birds in a blessed harmony which extends to the universe at large. The last two stanzas celebrate the unique nature of this event, and the poem comes full circle, back to Bishop Valentine and the mating season, back to the problem of the two Phoenixes:

> And by this act of these two phoenixes
> Nature again restored is,

---

[1] Critics have generally followed Johnson – 'Confusion worse confounded' – in their comments on this line and Hazlitt remarks that it 'is an almost irresistible illustration of the extravagances to which this kind of writing, which turns upon a pivot of words and possible allusions, is liable' (*Lectures on the Comic Writers, Complete Works* ed. P. P. Howe, 1930-4, vi, p. 53).

> For since these two are two no more,
> There's but one Phoenix still, as was before.

Just as the golden statues of the bridal pair stared out at excited spectators in Campion's masque, so this sun and moon, these two phoenixes, arrest Donne's gaze as he expresses the enthusiasm of many. The context is the same, the atmosphere produced is identical, and yet, somehow, an individual voice seems to speak.

In the Court performances and in this poem we recognise the same spirit. We are the witnesses of men contemplating themselves and indulging their wonderment. It is not surprising that Elizabeth and Frederick appear as exemplary figures in both, for the enthusiasm which their union provokes can only be conveyed through heightened phrases where their particular marriage serves as a model for others to emulate. Consistent elevation of tone and images matches the feelings of formality and excitement. Poets of masque and epithalamium assume the active participation of an audience. Donne, for instance, is conscious that Epithalamia have rules of structure, tone, language, imagery, and chronology; he assumes that his readers have a similar knowledge of the rules; and his ingenuity depends upon that assumption. Chronology, as we have seen, he abandons, since he can highlight the impression of his own feelings of impatience by doing so. The tone is largely formal, as would be expected, though its harmonies are frequently broken by contorted syntax, as in stanza 2 when Donne wishes to set in relief 'one bed contains . . . two Phoenixes' – the main focus of the poem. The images of light, sun, moon, Phoenixes, and so on, belong to that vocabulary which customarily expressed praise and admiration; yet, in the image of the Phoenix he deliberately plays with the reader's normal expectation of its significance, only to restore the symbol to its rightful form by the end of the poem.[1] Some readers might well have solved the

---

[1] One could compare the structure of this Epithalamium with that of Jonson's *Masque of Blacknesse* (1605) which is founded upon a similar paradoxical ingenuity. The Ladies

> . . . tho' blacke in face,
> Yet are they bright,
> And full of life, and light.

riddle for themselves, long before the end; and it is arguable that, as a consequence, their participation is greater, and their appreciation of the poem is enhanced.

It is noticeable that the tapestry-like descriptions which delight us in Spenser's Epithalamium are nowhere in evidence here. As in the masque, magnificence of mind and body is self-evident: its impact is what is important. Nevertheless, the impact is given a different focus in the two forms. Public harmony, political and religious concord, and a ritual, public celebration were the main preoccupations of the masque. Donne, using similar means, and while speaking for all men ('us' occurs more than once in the poem), has created something much more private. He recognises the general reverberations of the union, is tempted by idealisation, but concentrates the attention of all – bridal couple, and readers alike – on the revelling of two bodies made one.

Expectation seems to play an even more significant role in Donne's second Epithalamium entitled *Eclogue 1613. December 26* – his contribution to the Somerset wedding – which straight-away strikes a strange and contentious note. 'Unseasonable' begins the poem, and raises doubts and questions. The thematic structure is founded on a complex set of contraries: the block 'East, Sun, Warmth, Light, King, and Heaven' opposes a second block 'Winter, West, North, Cold, Night, and Hell', and their contest extends itself through to the end of the poem. Such contraries, and such argument, are of course germane to the Eclogue form which Donne has chosen as the frame of his Epithalamium. The form is loose and freer, allowing the poet considerable room to protect himself while performing his task of praise with due distinction. However, it is important to note that, from the beginning, Donne makes it clear to his alert reader that this is to be no ordinary eclogue. Already, a note of harshness introduces the poem. And then, the idylls of the countryside, the joys of pastoral life, that Arcadia of ease and delights which any reader anticipates with the very sound of the word Eclogue has been metamorphosed into the 'ice', the 'cold and decrepit time' which turns the landscape into a 'frieze jacket'. Allophanes (possibly Donne's friend Sir Robert Ker) remonstrates with Idios (a private man) who is mad enough to retire to such a region of frost, when the centre of heat is where the King is, at Court. From his generous light, so powerful and all pervading that it resembles that light which antedated both sun and moon, comes warmth, good desire, wisdom, honour, blessings, and spiritual expansion. From the beings, who walk in his radiant sphere, emanates the brilliance of stars, so from

> . . . the Brides' bright eyes,
> At every glance, a constellation flies,

which, in turn, kindles the lights of others. In this way, Allophanes persuasively argues the case for being at Court, at the wedding of the Earl of Somerset.

'No, I am there,' is Idios' paradoxical reply. The reader, who has already had his expectation punctured once, starts up perplexed, only to settle back comfortably once more as Idios asserts that Princes animate everything: the physical world of lights and warmth; and, more significantly, the mental world. They 'enlarge' narrow men, allowing them to feel effects from afar, and to surpass themselves in perception.

In the ensuing discussion, it becomes evident that these two are in no way disagreeing with each other. Apparently contrary arguments are used not to prove opposite cases, but to reinforce their shared view that the King is the source of all power and good,

> . . . all tinctures move
> From higher powers; from God religion springs,
> Wisdom, and honour from the use of kings.

There is something almost extravagant about the insistence on the wisdom, justice, trust, liberality, and virtue in the King; such statements extend over virtually the first hundred lines of the poem:

> Hast thou a history, which doth present
> A Court, where all affections do assent
> Unto the King's, and that, that King's are just?
> And where it is no levity to trust.
> Where there is no ambition, but to obey,
> Where men need whisper nothing, and yet may;

Where the King's favours are so placed, that all
Find that the King therein is liberal
To them, in him, because his favours bend
To virtue, to the which they all pretend.

Such lines as these elaborate views on James and kingship
which had been adumbrated by Jonson and Dekker at his Entry
into London in 1604; and they parallel his virtues so frequently
extolled in pamphlets such as Marcelline's *The Triumphs of
King James the First* (1610), and in the detail of the masques we
have examined. In order 'to know and feel all this' more deeply,
Idios has retired from Court, to write; for words are a means of
knowing and feeling more acutely – a way of rediscovering
exhilaration in tranquillity.

In some ways the nuptial song strikes a great contrast with its
lengthy prelude. It is extremely formal: eleven stanzas of
eleven lines, each one given a title. It follows much more closely
the conventional pattern for such poems than Donne's first
Epithalamium, adhering fairly strictly to a chronological
sequence, which moves from the Time of Marriage through the
church ceremony to the Going to Bed[1]; declaring vows and
blessings and, expostulating at delays in an attempt to imitate,
or re-enact, the actual ritual of the ceremony. There is, however,
thematic consistency between the Eclogue and the nuptial song;
the block 'East, Sun, Warmth, Light' continues to provide the
principal source of theme and metaphor, figuring, rather in-
sistently, through the poem in the repetitive last line of each
stanza with 'The fire of these inflaming eyes' and 'this loving
heart'.

Since the content of each stanza is announced in advance, each
stanza constitutes in a sense a specifically defined difficulty to be
overcome. Expectation is screwed up tight as each successive
verse challenges our credulity, proceeds through paradoxes, and
turns received opinions upside down. In stanza 1 the Sun bows
low and withdraws early on the most wintry of nights; but,
amazingly, a mightier fire of Promethean strength prolongs its

---

[1] Fowler, *op. cit.*, pp. 71-3, discusses the number symbolism of the poem at some
length and argues that the *Going to the Chapel* is the centre and therefore the climax
of the poem. Though this might be arithmetically sound, it does not take account
of the shifting tones of the poem.

effects of warmth and love. The second stanza seeks ways of distinguishing the bride and groom; yet they both love equally, and their qualities are such that their persons seem interchangeable: the Bride 'Becomes a man' because of her manly courage which scorns unjust opinion, and 'the Bridegroom is a maid' by virtue of his beauty. Donne is asking a lot, even from his initiates, with this blunt proposition which seems not so much forced, as too startlingly and emphatically stated for the needs of the case. Beauty and courage, insufficiently attached to what Donne has told us about the bride and groom, remain abstract words. Even when we do contemplate the Bridegroom we are allowed no details of physical description. In a stanza, which leaps forward with gathering speed, we catch some glimpse of the strong urges of his passion, as he outstrips the sun with her 'red foaming horses'; and his surging inward flame obscures all other outer characteristics.[1] The Bride is next presented in two stanzas where her coming and her apparelling are evoked. And her form, too, almost disappears behind lustrous radiance. She is akin to Phoebus, and her clothes of silk and gold serve merely to cloud her dazzling form and allow us to glimpse her,

> . . . since we which do behold,
> Are dust, and worms, 'tis just
> Our objects be the fruits of worms and dust;

It is difficult to see quite why Donne interpolates this moralising play on words; it certainly establishes a sense of distance between the onlookers and the Bride, whose ethereal and diaphanous nature has been delicately suggested. Her form is insubstantial, and filled with light; it is unreal, and perhaps Donne is implying that from her lofty height she scorns the golden silks she wears. Certainly the next lines serve to underline both her unreality and her distant purity:

> Let every jewel be a glorious star,
> Yet stars are not so pure, as their spheres are.

[1] In the particular circumstances of this marriage one wonders whether the word 'divorce' in the line
> Though it be some divorce to think of you
has a double meaning.

So we proceed through statement, qualification, or contradiction, on to the religious ceremony where these two suns – the bride and groom – meet, and become one. For two stanzas the contrary movements of statement and denial cease, as a climax of union in Church is reached, and vows for blessings are eloquently made. The King appears once more as the spring of riches, crowned (indeed almost overburdened) with wisdom and honour. The excessive nature of these blessings provides the link to the next verse, which seems strangely distorted with its many short lines of sharp complaint. The food is too abundant, the entire sphere of the world whirls in the dance, the sun is set, eyes are weary, and the revels go on. These events are referred to again in the following stanza, but this time they are used metaphorically to describe the bride's wedding night.

The tone of the poem changes yet again. No longer are there the extravagant comparisons, seemingly unrelated asides, and insistent imagery. In stanzas 9-11 the poet generates the same passionate excitement which was a feature of his first Epithalamium, and which has so far been absent in this poem. The notion of abundance, of whirling dance and revels, readily anticipates the transports of the Bride and Groom as they discover each other, and the husband finds a warm and yielding wife. Joy's bonfire, kindling bright and strong, provided with fuel enough to last an eternity, rounds off this record of passion.

Although it was in Donne's interest at this time to be a committed supporter of the Earl of Somerset, the Epithalamium which he wrote in his honour is not devoid of the sense of strain which Jonson displayed in his compositions for the same occasion. Both use a specific occasion as a way of expressing general notions and reactions. Both, at the outset, give pride of place to the King, introducing extended comment on his beneficence and his power to do good. In Donne's poem, however, the bride and groom figure very prominently. It is true that they might be any bride and groom – the theme is both topical and timeless – yet Donne is careful to write into his work references to the distasteful circumstances surrounding this particular wedding with the words 'unjust opinion' in stanza 2; and he dwells strangely on wisdom and honour (in stanza 7). It is as if he wants the reader to recognise that he himself is conscious that an extraordinarily difficult feat of persuasion is being undertaken, and that he is capable of accomplishing it.

One may, however, have reservations about the degree of his success. His presentation and evocation of the Bride seem especially laboured. By introducing so early in the Eclogue her 'bright eyes' which sow

> . . . the Court with stars, and doth prevent[1]
> In light and power, the all-eyed firmament;

he has given himself the task of maintaining this luminous vision throughout the nuptial song. However ingenious his list of compliments – comparison with Phoebus, clothed in silk and gold to hide her dazzle (as well as to enhance it), pure as a sphere, and so on – they do not complement each other, or provide us with a convincing picture. He is not interested in her physical reality, but only in the sparkling impact she makes on him; and somehow, he has not managed to communicate that effect to us. He has only assumed that we agree with him, while making no effort to ensure this. Only when she seethes with excitement and arouses an answering passion does Donne's pen convey the authenticity of those feelings.

His treatment of the bride reflects his handling of the main theme – the passion of Somerset and Lady Frances for each other. Until he can dispense with particular identities, Donne reels from one extravagant effort to another, opposing contraries, arguing by extremes, while managing fairly successfully to keep the two opposing blocks 'East, Sun', and 'West, Cold' moving consistently through the poem. In no way do the metaphors and superlatives transform these beings into exemplary figures like Elizabeth and Frederick. Such idealisation is either not achieved, through technical deficiency, or is not appropriate to a noble pair beneath the rank of prince.

A further problem arises from the thoroughly defensive stance which the poet assumes from the start. The nuptial song is lengthily prepared. Idios is any private man, not necessarily

---

[1] 'prevent' = outstrip.

Donne (the 'me' of stanza 3 need not apply exclusively to him), and he has to be cajoled and persuaded into speech. He deliberately chooses to speak in a voice not his own; it is an unidentified voice, creating a pleasing ambiguity which both protects the speaker from potential attack, and provokes the reader, leading him into the poem while the poet can maintain (until the last three stanzas of the poem at least) a fairly objective stance. He calls his offering a sacrifice; and, he insists, both immediately before the Epithalamium and after it,

> Read then this nuptial song, which was not made
> Either the Court or men's hearts to invade.

There is an exhausted, rather exasperated note here, as he gives up his poem under pressure. It starts then as a private greeting, but by the end Allophanes has claimed it as part of a public worship,

> Whatever celebrates this festival
> Is common,

Donne seems to have associated his own feelings much less personally with this event than with the wedding celebrated on St Valentine's day; in *Eclogue 1613. December 26* his role as poet is much more stylised.

The relationship between poet, reader, and the work, is again extremely important, but seems much more complex in this poem, partly because there is so much advance preparation, partly because Donne has contrived ambiguities, and partly because the tone of the piece is so uneven. At two moments in particular, during the nuptial song, he seems to interrupt the natural flow of thoughts and events, and speaks in a different voice: in stanza 2 where the bride and groom temporarily change their sex; and in stanza 5 where there is a fairly gratuitous play on worms and dust. One is tempted to say that here is the voice of Donne himself who cannot resist an extravagance or a pun. Such manoeuvres certainly heighten the reader's awareness of what the poet is trying to do; but they seem also to work against the task he has set himself. Donne is perhaps indulging over-dangerously in what Greville called 'Ironia, wherein men commonly (to keep above their workes) seem to make Toies of the utmost they can doe'.[1]

The general assumption behind this essay has been that a poet's individuality cannot be described in a vacuum. The particular character of Donne's *Epithalamia* emerges only when the poems are studied within the context which inspired them. In its turn, this context can only be defined with any accuracy by a study of the individual works which comprised it at any one moment of time. A more general survey might, for example, describe the language of the Jacobean masque, on those occasions when flattery seems a dominating feature, as Petrarchist; or, at other times when Jonson argues his cosmic themes, as neo-platonist. But such descriptions are hopelessly superficial. They depict a succession of masques merely as variations on well-worn themes, elaborated in a familiar language of praise; and they can tell us little about the personal twists which different poets give to the same material, and which mark their work with an individual stamp. For example, the sun image, both in Donne's second Epithalamium and in Chapman's masque, concentrates a vast array of virtues relating to their ideas of kingship; whereas in the poem for Princess Elizabeth, the 'she sun' expresses for Donne the highest attributes possible in a private person.

Participation and celebration are key concepts for a proper understanding of any poetic work of this period when it was the social context, above all, which determined the form. Poet and reader consciously shared certain assumptions about language and metaphor, so that images could simultaneously provide not only a vehicle for general expression which could be immediately comprehended, but also a means of making more private comment. The phoenix legend, for instance, suggests notions of exception, rarity, and preciousness, and the use Donne makes of it both enlarges these qualities and allows him to include (and even to display) his personal emotion. Similarly decorum, a framework of appropriate formality, and fitting vocabulary, may encourage on the part of a reader or spectator general observations on a specific event; they do not, however,

---

[1] Quoted by George Williamson, *The Proper Wit of Poetry*, 1961, p. 27.

prevent him from feeling that his own thoughts are being expressed. The technique of generalising seems to me to be the principal way in which 'court' poets – and Donne is one of them – solved the problems posed by being bidden to write for a particular occasion. And such generalising was accomplished with comparative ease when the poet worked within commonly agreed assumptions about forms, words, and images.

8

Not, Siren-like, to tempt:

Donne and the Composers

BRIAN MORRIS

I

A Dutchman, Constantine Huygens, provides almost the only independent evidence about Donne's interest in music. In a poem about his early life, written in 1678, Huygens recalls meeting Donne in 1622-3 at the house of Sir Robert Killigrew in London, where a circle of musicians, poets, scientists, and diplomats gathered regularly to listen to music provided by Lady Killigrew and her children:

> Tota domus concentus erat: pulcherrima Mater,
> Mater (adhuc stupeo) duodenae prolis, ab illo
> Gutture tam niveo, tam nil mortale sonanti
> Quam coeleste Melos Cytherae sociabat, et ipso
> Threicio (dicas) animatis pollice chordis![1]

Huygens's description of Donne in the poem is not very specific: he calls him 'optime Rhetor, Prime Poetarum', and praises his sermons and his conversation, but it is clear that his primary interest was in the poetry, since in 1629 or 1630 he translated a selection of Donne's privately circulated poems into Dutch.[2] Yet Huygens never tells us that Donne sang, or played an instrument, or had any particular disposition towards music. He says only that about 1622 Donne attended musical evenings

---

[1] Huygens, *De Vita Propria Sermones inter Liberos*, quoted in R. C. Bald, *John Donne: a Life*, Oxford, 1970, p. 441.

[2] See A. G. H. Bachrach, *Sir Constantine Huygens and Britain: 1596-1687*, Leiden and London, 1962, i, p. 5. Volume ii has not yet been published, but the material for it is in Bachrach's D.Phil thesis in the Bodleian Library.

at Killigrew's house. The connection between Donne, Sir Henry Wotton, Huygens, and Killigrew gives grounds for intriguing speculation, but it is possible to add two hints to Huygens's evidence, which may serve to link Donne a little more closely with the musical activities of the Killigrew circle. Firstly, in 1612 or 1613 Huygens probably met the composer and lutenist Giovanni Coperario (born John Cooper: see p. 228), and the connection may have been kept up in later years. Coperario was living as a Court musician in London for several years before his death in 1626, and he composed a setting for Donne's 'Send home my long strayd eyes to mee' which has survived in Tenbury Wells MS. 1019. The point is insubstantial, but it may suggest a personal link between poet and composer. Secondly, in Tenbury Wells MS. 1018 (f.44^v) there is an anonymous setting of Donne's poem 'Sweetest love, I do not goe', followed on the same page by a setting of the unknown poem 'Eies look of theires no beeholdinge', and between the two are written the words 'my lady Killigrewe'. John P. Cutts, describing the MS., says 'it is not clear whether this is intended to refer to this poem or the one above it',[1] but in view of Donne's known association with the musical Killigrews it is quite possible that the anonymous setting originated in the circle which Huygens describes.

The only other evidence to suggest that Donne had any interest in music is provided by Walton. He reports that Donne caused his 'Hymne to God the Father'

> to be set to a most grave and solemn Tune, and to be often sung to the *Organ* by the *Choristers* of St *Pauls* Church, in his own hearing

and that the poet had said

> *that Harmony added to this Hymn has raised the Affections of my heart, and quickned my graces of zeal and gratitude;* and I observe, *that I always return from paying this public duty of* Prayer *and* Praise *to God, with an unexpressible tranquillity of mind,* and a willingness *to leave the world.*[2]

---

[1] 'Early Seventeenth-Century Lyrics at St Michael's College', *Music and Letters*, July 1956, pp. 221-33.

[2] *The Lives of John Donne*, etc., ed. G. Saintsbury, Oxford, 1927, p. 62.

This anecdote does not appear until the 1658 edition of
Walton's *Lives*, but there is no reason to disbelieve it, and it is
worth pointing out that the story only demonstrates that in his
later years Donne recognised the power of Church music to
direct his thoughts to solemn topics, and bring him peace of
mind. It does not imply that he knew anything about music, or
that he delighted in it.

The poems themselves make surprisingly few references to
music, and none that is specially startling or complex. The best
known is obviously the opening of the 'Hymne to God my God,
in my sicknesse', where Donne resolves to 'tune the Instrument
here at the dore', but the *Divine Poems* taken as a group contain
few musical images or allusions. There are none in the *Holy
Sonnets* unless we allow the brief trumpets at the beginning of
'At the round earths imagin'd corners', *A Litanie* contains only
three, and, with one exception, there are none of any signifi-
cance among the 'Occasional Poems' apart from the 'Hymne'
already mentioned. The exception is the poem 'Upon the
translation of the Psalmes', where Donne does elaborate a
musical image in a characteristic way. The translators, Sir
Philip Sidney and his sister,

> Make all this All, three Quires, heaven, earth, and sphears;
> The first, Heaven, hath a song, but no man heares,
> The Spheares have Musick, but they have no tongue,
> Their harmony is rather danc'd than sung;
> But our third Quire, to which the first gives eare,
> (For, Angels learne by what the Church does here)
> This Quire hath all. The Organist is hee
> Who hath tun'd God and Man, the Organ we: (23-30)

Donne is concerned here with the Platonic, the Pythagorean,
aspect of music – the balance of phrases and the syntactical
patterning prove that – not with the ravishing quality of musical
sound. The whole image is dumb; it explores inaudible sound,
and the heavy repetition of the same verb 'hath', 'have' shows
that what attracts the poet is music's part in the great cosmo-
logical order. The image develops the theological argument
from Design, and it is the 'tidiness' of the three Quires, one
Organist, one Organ which is important, not the sounds they

make. When Donne's mind turned to music it was always to illustrate something he considered more important.

But Donne's mind seldom moved that way. I have found only half a dozen allusions to music in the *Satyres*, and only one of them (*IV.* 73-4) is audible. More common is the strictly visual comparison as in *Satyre I*

> And as fidlers stop low'st, at highest sound,
> So to the most brave, stoops hee nigh'st the ground.
>
> (77-8)

The *Elegies* are even more bare of musical reference. There is the image, in 'Jealousie', of the husband

> Drawing his breath, as thick and short, as can
> The nimblest crocheting Musitian, (5-6)

but nothing else apart from passing references to the 'gamut' and the sirens' songs. The *Epithalamia*, where one would expect music to flourish, hardly mention it, and, unexpectedly, the *Verse Letters* are much richer in this respect. In 'The Storme' Donne tells of tacklings 'Snapping, like too-high-stretched treble strings'; in 'To Mr. S. B.' he says

> I sing not, Siren-like, to tempt; for I
> Am harsh; (9-10)

and in a letter to the Countess of Bedford ('Honour is so sublime perfection') he makes one of his very few mentions of an actual composition:

> Care not, then, Madame,'how low your praysers lye;
> In labourers balads oft more piety
> God findes, then in *Te Deums* melodie;
>
> (13-15)

But it is in the *Epicedes*, *Obsequies* and *Anniversaries* – poems concerned centrally with death – that Donne most readily turns to music. I have counted some eighteen passages in these poems, but nearly all refer to the same thing: the heavenly music which awaits the dying soul, and of which he or she will become a part. The longest example occurs in the last fourteen lines of 'To the Praise of the Dead' before *The first Anniversary*, but the habitual direction of Donne's thought can be seen, for example, in *The second Anniversary*, where he writes

> These Hymnes thy issue, may encrease so long,
> As till Gods great *Venite* change the song.   (43-44)

He makes a similar point nearly three hundred lines later:

> Up, up, my drowsie Soule, where thy new eare
> Shall in the Angels songs no discord heare;   (339-40)

In every sense of the word Donne's idea of harmony is that it is 'heavenly'.

The surprising thing is that, from a musical point of view, the *Songs and Sonnets* are silent poems. There are single, trivial references to singing in 'The Indifferent' and 'Goe, and catche a falling starre', but (apart from 'The Triple Foole' to which I will return) that is all. So both the external evidence of Huygens and Walton and the allusions and images of the poems themselves suggest that Donne was not interested in music either as listener or performer, that he thought of it (when he did) primarily in scientific, cosmological terms, and that it moved his imagination only in the most obvious ways. It is striking that Donne's ear should be so unreceptive an organ in an age which produced Dowland, Campion, and Morley, an age whose music so deeply and intimately affected the art of Donne's contemporary, George Herbert. Miss Tuve has shown the intricacy and depth of Herbert's penetration of the relationship between words and music,[1] and the formative impulse which musical patterns gave to so many of the individual poems, and although Herbert stands foremost in this respect one need only think of Ben Jonson to realise the pervasive power which the music of the period exercised over the poets. Donne alone seems to have resisted it.

There is a hint of Donne's attitude to music, and especially to words set to music, in 'The Triple Foole', though the acerbic tone of the poem as a whole warns us against any simple-minded interpretation of what he says. He has drawn his pains 'Through Rimes vexation' in order, he says, to allay them:

---

[1] Rosemond Tuve, *A Reading of George Herbert*, 1952.

But when I have done so,
Some man, his art and voice to show,
    Doth set and sing my paine,
And by delighting many, frees againe
    Griefe, which verse did restraine.
To Love, and Griefe tribute of Verse belongs,
But not of such as pleases when 'tis read,
    Both are increased by such songs:
For both their triumphs so are published,   (12-20)

The thought turns on the ambiguity of 'delighting' and 'pleases', as if, in one sense, music made Love and Grief merely amusing, and the inference of the last two lines is that musical settings in some way inflate and publicise emotions which the poem had succeeded in refining and restraining. The underlying attitude is scarcely complimentary to the composers, whose art is condemned as parasitic by origin and exhibitionist by intent. Of course one must not lean heavily on so casual a reference as this, but the fact that it is casual and solitary, together with the paucity of other evidence, suggests that Donne never conceived his poems in musical terms, and never delivered them as material for a marriage of the arts.[1]

II

Despite the warning several of Donne's poems were set to music by his contemporaries, some of them more than once. Not all the settings have survived, not all that have survived are complete, and the exact number depends on whether one includes incomplete settings and settings of poems which modern editors consider spurious or dubious.[2] In what follows I discuss

[1] Some of Donne's musical images, in the poems and the prose, are discussed in Gretchen Ludke Finney, *Musical Backgrounds for English Literature 1580-1650*, New Brunswick (n.d.).

[2] Twenty-nine settings are listed by Vincent Duckles, 'The Lyrics of John Donne as set by his Contemporaries', in *Bericht über den siebenten Internationalen Musikwissenschaftlichen Kongress Köln* 1958, Kassel, 1959, 91-3; seven are reprinted and discussed in *Poèmes de Donne, Herbert et Crashaw mis en musique par leurs contemporains*, Transcription et réalisation par André Souris . . . Introduction par Jean Jacquot, Paris, 1961 – hereafter referred to as *Jacquot*. See also *The Elegies and the Songs and Sonnets of John Donne*, ed. Helen Gardner, Oxford, 1965, Appendix B.

only those poems which Helen Gardner consider genuine and of which complete settings have survived. Seven texts come into this category, five from the *Songs and Sonnets* and two from the *Divine Poems*, which argues that the composers were principally motivated by what Jacquot calls 'l'inspiration profane'. The *Songs and Sonnets* are as follows:

1. Song 'Goe, and catche a falling starre'
2. Song 'Sweetest love, I do not goe'
3. The Message ('Send home my long strayd eyes to mee')
4. Breake of Day ('' Tis true, 'tis day, what though it be?')
5. The Expiration ('So, so, breake off this last lamenting kisse').

Three of these poems are concerned with the parting of lovers, and the other two with constancy in love, both commonplace themes among the madrigalians and the composers of ayres. All five are metrically interesting, and offer rhythmic opportunities and challenges which the composers took up in various ways.

The setting of 'Goe, and catche a falling starre', which Jacquot prints from British Museum MS. Egerton 2013, is a very undistinguished composition.[1] The composer is unknown, and the music, set for voice and lute, neglects almost all the chances the words offer. The vocal line is unusually plain, plodding steadily, a word to a note, through the opening phrases:

The only rhythmic characteristic of the piece is the dotted quaver-semiquaver figure which appears in the first bar, cutting

[1] *Jacquot*, 4-5.

across the urgency of the speech rhythm and deadening it completely. It would be hard to imagine a more insensitive setting of the first three words of this poem than three equal quavers on the tonic note. The points of melodic climax bear no relation to the sense or movement of the words: they occur on words like 'where', 'the', 'heare' and 'off', and the sudden swoops of a downward seventh to land on 'Divels' and 'envies' seem to be dictated by harmonic requirements rather than the sense of the text. Not that the piece is harmonically interesting. The heavy progress from tonic to subdominant in Example 1 is typical of the obviousness of all its modulations, so that the four-square, predictable harmonic structure emphasises the flatness of the melodic line and destroys all sense of the impatience, the aggressiveness of the poem. Only in the last three lines is there any understanding of the rhythmic problem, where what in modern notation is an interpolated bar of $\frac{2}{4}$ permits the voice to register something of the poet's cynicism and to dwell on the ambiguity of 'honest'. The music is simple enough to allow all three verses to be sung easily to it, but 'regularity' is about the highest claim one could make for it. The composer clearly did not understand, or did not care, what Donne wrote.

The anonymous setting of 'Sweetest love, I do not goe', though musically much more successful, demonstrates even more clearly the composer's attitude to Donne's words and rhythms.[1] The verse form is important, and much of the poem's delicacy and immediacy comes from the way Donne handles the sudden two-stress line which begins the second half of each stanza. The composer, in pursuit of a smooth melodic line and a simple regularity of utterance, overrides Donne's decision, setting the second half of stanza 1 as if it comprised three four-stress lines.

A glance at Helen Gardner's text of the poem will show that it is impossible to sing the remaining four verses to this melody. So the composer varies Donne's words to make them fit. Only in stanza 1 do words and music make any sort of unity, but if we think of the song as a single-stanza setting it has its attrac-

---

[1] *Jacquot*, 1-3. Two versions survive: a plain setting for vocal line and bass in Tenbury Wells MS. 1018, f. 44ᵛ, and an ornamented version in B.M. Add. MS. 10337, f. 55ᵛ. Nothing is known about the connection between the two.

tions, especially in the ornamented version. For example, the setting of 'But since that I/Must dye at last', modulating from G minor to D minor, with the voice rising high over the accompaniment, allows the singer momentarily to retard the cadence and make a sensitive contrast with ' 'Tis best,/To use my selfe in jest' with its top G entry and its decisive key of E flat major.

It is not what Donne intended; it fails to register the tenderness, the intimacy of the moment. But in musical terms it makes a different point quite successfully.

Giovanni Coperario's setting of 'The Message' is a much more serious musical exercise. It is an art-song, obviously written by a composer with the text in front of him, and attempting to find musical expression for the poem's rhythms and meanings. Coperario was an accomplished, professional musician.[1] He was born John Cooper in or about 1575, and his musical reputation seems to date from a visit he made to Italy during the early years of the seventeenth century. When he returned to England, with his italianised surname, he became a prominent figure in London's musical life, as viola da gambist, lutenist, and composer. He later became a member of King James's Private Musick, a group of chamber musicians which included nearly all the great names of the period, from Dowland to Gibbons. Coperario's best works are the series of fantasies for viols he wrote for this group, but he also published two books of lute-songs, *Funeral Teares* (1606) and *Songs of Mourning* (1613), and three more songs appeared in *The Masque of Squires* (1614). He died probably in 1626. It is a mistake to think of Coperario's songs as like those of the other English composers of ayres, men like Dowland, Campion, or Rosseter. He was undoubtedly influenced powerfully by the monodists on his visit to Italy, and if he was anywhere near Florence in 1602 he may have read the epoch-making preface to Caccini's *Le Nuove Musiche* when it was published. Caccini denounced the current style of elaborate madrigals weighed down with long embellishments 'for a certain tickling of the ears of those who do not well understand what it is to sing passionately'. He advocated, and composed, 'a kind of music by which men might, as it were, talk in harmony, using in that kind of singing . . . a certain noble neglect of the song'. Caccini's word for it is 'sprezzatura'.[2] Coperario's settings of texts like 'Deceitful fancy, why delud'st thou me', or the dialogue 'Foe of Mankind' in *Funeral Teares* make clear what he learned from the monodists, and distinguish him

---

[1] *Jacquot*, 6-7, and *The English Lute-Songs*, series I, vol. 17 (Giovanni Coperario), transcribed and edited by Gerald Hendrie and Thurston Dart, 1959, pp. 42-3. For what is known of Coperario's life see Grove's *Dictionary of Music and Musicians*.

[2] A word with a distinguished history. See Castiglione, *Il Libro del Cortegiano*, Book I. Giulio Caccini was one of a famous group in late sixteenth-century Florence, who, among other things, wrote the world's first operas.

sharply from his more thoroughly English contemporaries. Hendrie and Dart make the point that

> With their impassioned declamation, irregular rhythms, bold harmonies, angular and wayward tunes, extravagant lyrics, and melodic polarity between tune and bass, Coperario's songs clearly foreshadow 'recitative musick' and the vocal style of his most gifted pupils, William and Henry Lawes.[1]

Coperario's setting of 'The Message' seems to have been of the first stanza only, though the other verses would fit his music tolerably well.[2] The opening, with its slow, rising melodic line, sets the 'recitative' tone, which is enforced by the jerky setting of 'which O, which O' with its disturbed rhythm and graver rests. The measured language, the almost reproving attitude of the poem, is finely caught in the setting of lines 3-5, with its rising semiquavers on 'learnt' and its rhythmic emphasis (echoing a speech emphasis) on 'forc'd' and 'false'.

---

[1] Hendrie and Dart, *ed. cit.*, p. ii.

[2] The setting seems to have been for the first stanza alone. See the variants listed in the 'Notes Critiques' by Jacquot, p. xvii.

Professor Duckles and Dame Helen Gardner find the song over-rhetorical[1]; perhaps it is a heavy treatment of a comparatively light theme, but there is a genuine attempt to let the music express the words, and the musical idiom is, in its way, as new and urgent as Donne's verbal one. In this song Coperario is more intelligent than sensitive, but one cannot help wishing he had been attracted to Donne's poems more often.

Virtually nothing is known of William Corkine, who set the full text of 'Breake of Day' and published it as the fourth song in his *Second Booke of Ayres* (1612).[2] The *Firste Booke* had appeared two years earlier, and contained settings of poems by Campion and Munday, but the majority of the poems in both books cannot be ascribed to any author. We have neither birth-date nor death-date for the composer, and it is not easy to trace any specific musical influence in his work. From a musical point of view his setting of Donne's words is a routine, predictable piece of composition, though the song, taken as a whole, does catch something of the quick, persuasive urgency, something of the gentle banter of the lady's tone. The total effect is better than the sum of the parts. The routine quality comes in the text-book word-painting. Thomas Morley never had a more obedient pupil. In *A Plaine and Easie Introduction to Practicall Musicke*[3] Morley had written:

> Moreover, you must have a care that when your matter signifieth ascending, high heaven, & such like, you make your musick ascend: & by the contrarie where your dittie speaketh of descending lowenes, depth, hell, & others such, you must make your musicke descend.

Corkine follows the master's precept in the second line of Donne's poem, which offers a paradigmatic opportunity:

[1] Gardner, *ed. cit.*, p. 240.
[2] *Jacquot*, 15-17. Corkine's *Second Booke of Ayres*, 1612, contains a lesson for the lyra-viol with the incipit 'Come live with me, and be my love', which has been thought to have some connection with Donne's 'The Bait'. The *Second Booke of Ayres* has been edited by E. H. Fellowes in *The English School of Lutenist Song-Writers*, second series, vol. 13.
[3] Facsimile reprint by Oxford University Press, 1937, and a modern edition by R. A. Harman, 1952.

The words 'lie downe' in line four produce five descending notes, the rhyme of 'spight' and 'light' is duly honoured, and so on. The general effect is of a simple but intelligent academic exercise in a rather old-fashioned mode of composition. Corkine's technique is deployed on the first verse only, since although the second and third verses of Donne's poem fit the melody well enough, the rising quaver figure quoted in this example is set to the word 'well' in the second stanza, and in the third to the second syllable of 'disease'. The song is typical of many in the *Second Booke of Ayres*, and the temptations to word-painting offered by such phrases as 'My love did rise, did live, did fall' in 'Truth-Trying Time', or 'thou soarest far above thy might' in 'Down, down, proud mind' are seldom resisted. Only in 'Go, heavy thoughts' does Corkine allow the sense and rhythms of the words to penetrate the music, and this is the only fully successful song in the collection. Donne's words are nowhere near so well served.

Two settings of 'The Expiration' survive, one by Alfonso Ferrabosco, the other by an unknown composer. Alfonso Ferrabosco the Younger was born in England, and was 'trained up to Musick' as Wood says, in the court of Elizabeth.[1] After the accession of James I he appears as one of the King's Musicians for the Violins, but he is chiefly remembered as the friend of Ben Jonson and the composer of music for some of Jonson's masques. He continued in Court service under Charles I, and became Composer of Music in Ordinary to the King when Coperario died in 1626. His setting of 'The Expiration' appears in *Ayres* (1609), and it shows the composer taking up a definite interpretative attitude towards his text.[2] It is possible to read the poem as a light-hearted, witty velleity, masking the pain of parting with a gentle bravura, controlling the sentiment by verbalising it, and offering appropriately dignified stances for the lovers. This is certainly the view Ferrabosco takes, and the opening bars of his song treat the situation lightly, almost inconsequentially.

The rising figure on 'lamenting' allows nothing to the meaning of the word, and the crotchet rests in the first two bars suggest a swift, lively tempo, making the 'So, so', gently dismissive and nothing more. The music of this first line, with its plain, steady progress from G major to D major, indicates the general lack of seriousness that Ferrabosco finds in his text. By imposing this simple, almost cheery, overall tone the composer obliterates most of the directives the poem supplies; the line 'Turne thou ghost that way, and let mee turne this' offers several musical invitations, but there is nothing either 'ghostly' or 'turning' about the firm, foursquare handling it gets, in which the only point of surprise is the unexpected drop from C to G sharp on the words 'that way', and that is dictated by the harmonic progression of the line from C major to D major rather than by any response to the dainty discrimination the text makes at that

---

[1] *Jacquot*, 8-9, and *The English School of Lutenist Song-Writers*, ed. Fellowes, second series, vol. 16. See also G. E. P. Arkwright, 'Alfonso Ferrabosco the younger', in Robin Grey's *Studies in Music*, 1901, p. 199.

[2] Ferrabosco's setting marks the first appearance of one of Donne's poems in print.

moment. Ferrabosco responded only to the cavalier note of the lovers' defiance, and it is as if the last two lines of the first stanza directed his setting for the whole verse. In these lines the voice rises to its high register, and the top F natural on 'leave' is the climax from which the rest of the song gently descends, a note to a word, as it has been almost throughout,

to its firm and obvious G major cadence. One might compare his setting of 'The Expiration' with his song 'Shall I seek to ease my grief' in the same volume, which is successful because the mood of the poem is single and uncomplicated; there are no quick, slight shifts of thought, no fine contrasts of feeling. Ferrabosco catches the simple tone and develops it with rhythmic and harmonic logic. The prevailing tenor of Donne's poem is not so easily grasped. It is essentially serious, but the grave gallantry, the delicate concern for another person's feelings, makes itself felt through the formalities devised for parting, the decorum established for it. One might point to the way the imperatives in the first verse soften from 'breake off' to 'nor will we owe', which, though still a direction, is also an act of courtesy, allowing the lady a polite, conceded retreat from the situation. Ferrabosco's music cannot follow Donne's finer modulations; having once set his tone the composer must develop it firmly. He cannot veer with every wind.

The anonymous setting of the same poem is a much finer piece of work, and certainly the most perceptive setting of any of Donne's secular verse.[1] This becomes immediately clear if we compare the opening bars with Ferrabosco's:

The minim in the first bar sets a slower tempo, the crotchet rest imitates the speaking voice and allows the line to breathe, the two semiquavers on 'last' permit a delaying emphasis and prepare for the little figure swelling over a minor third on the

---

[1] *Jacquot*, 10-11. Dating these songs is notoriously difficult, but I suspect this setting is considerably later than Ferrabosco's.

key word 'lamenting', which establishes the full poignancy of
the phrase. The song succeeds because the music expands the
dramatic possibilities of the occasion by allowing full play to
what the sense of the words directs the voice to do. And the
suggestion of 'recitativo' style gives formal control and stylised
presence to the emotion – those very qualities which the poem
goes on to display. Expansion of a perceived dramatic moment
is what the composers of ayres at their best can do supremely
well. One thinks of Dowland's 'Welcome, black night'. In his
setting of the third line of Donne's poem the anonymous com-
poser shows a masterly understanding of its sense and its place
in the developing dramatic ritual:

The wavering, uncertain rhythm, and the indecisive melodic
line of 'Turne thou ghost that way' is balanced by the steady
ascent of 'and let mee turne this', with its emphasis falling as the
speech rhythm dictates on 'mee'. The last two lines give
strength to the 'recitativo' quality of the whole song, flowering

as they do into strangely impressive melismata on the words 'nor' and 'saying'. The striking success of this setting derives from its refusal to impose a musical pattern on the verbal structure. It ignores the metre and pays attention to the rhythm, following the contours of the speaking voice. In seventeeth century vocal music the development of the 'recitativo secco' style provides an essential rhetorical element, and here it allows the composer the freedom which Donne's verbal dexterity and delicacy demand. The comparative failure of the settings of all Donne's *Songs and Sonnets* except this one stems from the mistaken attempt to fit the poetic rhythms into set musical phrases. It is a central quality of Donne's verse that it senses and exploits the unpredictability of human speech. Only with the advent of opera does it become possible for music to treat words rhetorically and freely, and this is what the *Songs and Sonnets* require. Rhythmically, Donne was half a century ahead of the musicians.

To compare the two surviving seventeenth-century settings of 'A Hymne to God the Father' is to compare two generations of musicians. The earlier setting is by John Hilton, junior (?1599-1657), whose musical education was at Trinity College, Cambridge, where his father had been organist.[1] Hilton was for many years organist of St Margaret's, Westminster, a post which must have brought him into contact with many of the Court musicians, but in spite of his ecclesiastical appointment the music he published is not specifically religious. His *Ayres, or Fa La's for Three Voyces* appeared in 1627, and *Catch that catch can*, a collection of Catches, Rounds, and Canons, was published in 1652. But most of his surviving works are still in manuscript, and they include a number of ayres and dialogues in the fashionable mode. The setting of Donne's 'Hymne' is simple and intimate in style, and strophic in form. The poem itself is not without its simplicities and its directness. The first stanza, for example, presents the orthodox, Pauline commonplace of 'the good that I would, I do not; the evil that I would not, that I do' without undue catachresis, and the pun on the poet's name

---

[1] *Jacquot*, 18-19. See also M. C. Boyd, *Elizabethan Music and Musical Criticism*, Philadelphia, 1962, pp. 272 ff., and W. L. Woodfill, *Musicians in English Society from Elizabeth to Charles I*, 1954.

introduces no profound theological paradox. Wilfrid Mellers' close analysis of the poem goes too far when he says of lines 5-6:

> The lines hint either Your act of forgiveness will be useless: or You will always be deceived in thinking I belong to You, because there is no end to the flow of my sins.[1]

Donne was aware of every Christian's propensity to sin, and he knew the need for the variety of confessional formulae available in the Book of Common Prayer. The poem does not go beyond these experiences. As L. A. Cormican says:

> Different interpretations of the words 'Father' and 'sin' do not necessarily result in different estimates of Donne's *Hymne to God the Father* because the experience within the poem does not depend on the technical meaning we assign to them.[2]

Hilton's setting recognises that the poem is not a cry of doubt or anguish. It is the expression of a firm faith, clearly aware of the blighting and sundering effect of personal sin. The opening, with its dotted quaver rhythm, balances 'forgive' against 'sinne' with theological exactness, and the second line moves into a higher register to enforce the repetitive nature of the offence. The song develops soberly, a phrase to a line and a note to a word, modulating only to the obvious key of B flat major, until the last two lines where the pun is allowed to create the only expressive point in an otherwise quiet and austere progress.

plore? When thou hast done, thou hast not done, for

---

[1] Wilfrid Mellers, *Harmonious Meeting*, 1965, p. 119.
[2] L. A. Cormican, 'Milton's Religious Verse', in *Pelican Guide to English Literature*, iii, p. 176.

The simple, falling sequence, and the double dotted crotchet on 'I', secure recognition for the personal quality of the utterance, while the semiquaver rest allows a breath to take the emphasis from the 'thou' and suggests an intimate tone of submission and repentance rather than a confrontation between God and the Sinner. The music exercises this control of tone over each of the three stanzas, and although the strophic form denies the composer any chance to register the greater urgency of the last verse, with its wider horizon and its more complex language, the solemnity it achieves is gentle and apt, and its refusal to overdramatise anything in the text is a notable and valuable abstention. It is unlikely that Hilton's is the setting to which Walton refers in the *Lives*, but its directness and non-dramatic quality make it a fine and sensitive piece of Anglican church music.

Pelham Humfrey was a church musician, and the composer of many anthems for the Chapel Royal in London, but he also wrote for the stage.[1] There is a MS. in the library of the Paris Conservatoire called 'The Vocal Musick in *The Tempest* by Mr. Pelh. Humfrey', and he wrote songs for Dryden's *Conquest of Granada* and *Indian Emperor*, Crowne's *History of Charles VIII of France*, and Wycherley's *Love in a Wood*. His *Harmonia Sacra* (1688) is later than these, but his interest in drama invades his religious music. This is especially true of his setting of Donne's 'Hymne'. Mellers says of it:

> . . . although this is a religious poem, it is also a dramatic dialogue between the Self and the Alter Ego, with God as silent listener: so it

[1] Humfrey's setting has been edited by Tippett and Bergmann, Schott & Co., 1947.

is not surprising that a composer of a later generation than Donne's should set it operatically. For although Pelham Humfrey treats the poem strophically, he also set it in lyrical arioso.[1]

His scrupulous analysis of the piece, which he sees as a key work in the development from Ayre to Arioso, is indispensable. The quasi-operatic treatment of the text reinforces one's sense that only an opera composer can fully do justice to Donne's words, because the song form imposes too strict a constraint on the variety and flexibility of the verse forms. The freer treatment which Humfrey adopts allows all the older techniques to be used: he can emphasise a word by an unusual interval, as he does in the first line when he sets 'that sinne' to a descending diminished fourth; he can let the music shadow the sense, as in the three-quaver setting of 'runne' in line four; he can enforce a point through a vocal register, as when the words 'wallowed in, a score' are sung to low C sharps and D's in the second verse. But he can expand the means of expression. The repeated quavers with which the song begins, suggesting, as Mellers says, both liturgical intonation and operatic recitative, are repeated a fifth higher at the beginning of the second verse, and varied subtly to begin the third. This third stanza opens briefly in G major, in contrast to the pervasive G minor of the first two, and this momentary expansion of the musical range allows the heightened emotion of the last six lines to be celebrated more fully and freely, by longer musical phrases and a wider vocal range. I cannot agree with Mellers that 'the music of the last stanza perhaps fits the defiant better than the simply triumphant interpretation of the poem', since I find little defiance in Donne's words. The allusion in 'Sweare by thy selfe' is surely, as Helen Gardner has pointed out, to the promise to Abraham (Gen. xxii. 16) and the comment on it in Hebrews vi. 13-19, which provides hope 'as an anchor of the soul, both sure and steadfast'.[2] Humfrey's setting of these last lines, with its rising, expanding vocal line and its predominantly major tonality, suggests an esperance and an exultation founded on

---

[1] *Op. cit.*, p. 120.
[2] *John Donne: The Divine Poems*, ed. Helen Gardner, Oxford, 1952, pp. 110-111.

the poet's personal apprehension of the divine promise. But Mellers is surely right when he speaks of the music's 'wide range of emotional reference'. This is a quality which the music of Humfrey's age can express. It is seldom to be found in the work of the composers of Ayres, and yet it is a central feature of Donne's religious poems.

So far as I know the three-part setting of the first two stanzas of Donne's paraphrase of *Lamentations* has never been printed before. It is mentioned by Helen Gardner, by Vincent Duckles, and by Jacquot who does not print it because the 'intérêt poétique nous a paru faible par rapport à celui des chants sacrés publiés dans notre recueil', but the music is neither described nor discussed. The composer is Thomas Ford, and the setting exists among a large collection of his manuscript music in Christ Church library.[1] Ford, who must have been born *circa* 1580 and died in London in November 1648, was a lutenist who wrote music for various combinations of voices and for viols. Nothing is known of his life before 1607, when he published *Musicke of sundrie Kindes, Set forth in two Bookes*, which seems to have established his name as a composer.[2] He was one of the Prince of Wales' musicians in 1611, and was made musician to Charles I in 1626. Two of his anthems appeared in Leighton's collection *The Teares or Lamentacions of a Sorrowfull Soule* (1614), but he is a composer who is now principally remembered for a single work: his four-part setting of the anonymous poem 'Since first I saw your face', which has been reprinted in a number of twentieth-century collections of madrigal music. There is nothing to connect Ford personally with Donne, and so little is known that nothing can be usefully conjectured, except that since Ford was a Court musician and so were most of the others who set poems by Donne, it may have been in the Court musical circle that Ford became acquainted with Donne's work. Donne's paraphrase was probably not written until after his ordination, which would place it within the period of Ford's appointment as musician to the King. The setting survives only

---

[1] I am indebted to the Dean and Fellows of Christ Church for permission to reproduce this part of a manuscript in their collection.

[2] See Boyd, *op. cit.*, p. 146, and Wood, *Athenae Oxonienses*, second edition, vol. i, entry 680.

in the three part-books (Christ Church MSS. 736-8) and these have been edited to provide the version printed here as Appendix I. The grave polyphony of the opening A minor phrase, with its dark harmonic colour and powerful suspensions, sets a tone which is faultlessly sustained throughout the forty-three bars: serious, close-textured, and using for the most part the lower registers of the voices. Ford is alert to the rhythms of individual words, and the dotted crotchet figures on 'populous' and 'perfidiously' are distributed through the three parts in a subdued, muted counterpoint which is contrasted with the longer rhythms at the centre of the piece, where phrases like 'she weeps' and 'her teares fall downe' are permitted to develop through repetition and sequence, and over a stronger harmonic base. The climax, with the repeated phrase 'perfidiously her friends have dealt', is created by shortening the phrases and increasing the complexity of the part-writing rather than by any rise in the register, and it arises naturally as a development of the method used at points of inner tension and climax like 'she weeps' at bar 18, and 'her Louers' at bar 33. Ford's handling of the verbal rhythms – delicate, precise, setting them in one part and varying them in the others – creates a firmness of texture which permits the sliding and shifting harmonies to establish a rich tone of lamentation without loss of emotional control. Only in the last three bars, where the bass approaches the perfect cadence stepwise, in the conventional way, are the upper parts allowed to expand and expatiate musically in the melisma on 'enemyes'. It is a clear indication of Ford's artistry and restraint that this occurs only after the climax has been created by rhythmic means, so that the fuller quality of the music in the final phrases releases the tension, and brings the piece to rest in a properly elegiac tone. It would be wrong to claim that Ford's setting is any kind of undiscovered masterpiece, but it is a characteristically sensitive composition, which enlarges our sense of what a gifted composer could do with Donne's words, and it is admirable for the attention it gives to the phrasing and the word-rhythms at the expense of the line-lengths and the strophic form.

Few contemporary composers seem to have understood that Donne was treating stanzaic construction in a wholly new way, and a radically anti-musical way. Nearly all the Ayres of men like Ferrabosco, Rosseter, Pilkington, and Morley are 'first-verse' settings, written on an assumption of strophic regularity. And for most of the texts they set the assumption held good. Dowland's famous setting of the anonymous 'White as lilies was her face' in *The Second Booke of Songs or Ayres* (1600) is a case in point. There are eight stanzas, of which the first two are as follows:

> White as lilies was her face.
>   When she smiled
>   She beguiled,
> Quitting faith with foul disgrace.
> Virtue, service thus neglected,
> Heart with sorrows hath infected.
>
> When I swore my heart her own,
>   She disdained;
>   I complained;
> Yet she left me overthrown,
> Careless of my bitter grieving,
> Ruthless, bent to no relieving.[1]

The other six stanzas follow exactly the same metrical pattern, and, in addition, the key words recur in the same places. The art which makes this possible, without making it obvious, permits the composer to create a point of climax in the fourth line of the first stanza, confident that it will not be misplaced in the rest of the song (see opposite). In the succeeding stanzas this melodic line, with its emphasis on the top F, is fitted to the following words: 'Yet she left me overthrown', 'Yet she could not be procured', 'To destroy a faithful heart', 'For their pride is to remove', 'Changeless faith with foul despair', 'And the swain that loved most', and 'I will never change my thoughts'. Obviously, the poem is written with music in mind; these are not the accents of any speaking voice. If one compares this

---

[1] The full text is in E. H. Fellowes, *English Madrigal Verse*, revised and enlarged by Sternfeld and Greer, third edition, Oxford, 1967, pp. 473-4. The music is in *The English School of Lutenist Song-Writers*, ed. E. H. Fellowes, first series, un-numbered, under the title John Dowland, *Second Book of Airs*.

custom-built stanzaic pattern with Donne's sense of what a
stanza does in, say, 'The Expiration' it is clear that the com-
posers set themselves an almost impossible task. To find music
which could express the sense and accent of two such lines as

'So, so, breake off this last lamenting kisse' and 'Goe; and if that
word have not quite kil'd thee' is a challenge to ingenuity
rather than to art. The anonymous setting of 'The Expiration'
in fact fares better than Ferrabosco's in this particular test, but
on the whole the contemporary composers failed to see that
Donne's accent and rhythm was dictated by the passionate
speaking voice rather than by the regular lyric metre.

Pelham Humfrey deals with this aspect of Donne better than
any of the others because he is the latest, and in his day the
development from Ayre to Arioso permitted him to sit far more
lightly to the stanzaic pattern, and to let the music follow the

shape of the spoken phrase. The recitativo style is a subtle instrument, if only because it lets a speaking voice speak.

III

It is a matter of accident that the composers, great and small, of the eighteenth and nineteenth centuries ignored Donne.[1] He was not set because he was not read, and we can only muse what a composer like Handel or Elgar might have made of the poems. But when one sees what Pelham Humfrey's proto-operatic style could do with the 'Hymne to God the Father' it is not surprising that the next setting of Donne's verse is by the great English master of opera in the twentieth century, Benjamin Britten. *The Holy Sonnets of John Donne* are the product of an intense moment in the composer's personal life. Peter Pears has written:

> They were written in a week in August 1945, immediately after the composer's return from the German concentration camps whither he had gone as Yehudi Menuhin's accompanist. . . . The *Sonnets* had been planned for some time before this, but it is hard to believe that the horrors of Belsen did not have some direct impact on the creative unconscious, already preparing itself to set John Donne. When Britten returned, he suffered a delayed reaction to an inoculation, and the *Holy Sonnets* were written on a bed of high fever.[2]

But Britten's settings of Donne also have their place in his development as a writer of song-cycles and a composer of operas. The decade before 1945 had seen the publication of *Our Hunting Fathers* and *On this Island*, where Britten had engaged with the contemporary voice and special idiom of Auden, *Les Illuminations*, where Rimbaud's words had encouraged him to achieve a greater control of the melodic line,

---

[1] There is one possible, and strange, exception. (As a boy, Browning) 'wrote music for songs which he himself sang: among them Donne's *Go, & catch a falling star* . . . and his settings, all of which he subsequently destroyed, were, I am told, very spirited' (A. Orr, *Life and Letters of Robert Browning*, 1908, p. 41). I owe this reference to Professor A. J. Smith.

[2] In *Benjamin Britten: A Commentary on his Works*, ed. Mitchell and Keller, 1952, pp. 69-70.

a sparser and more economic utterance, and, above all, *The Seven Sonnets of Michelangelo*, in which the strict metrical form and disciplined development of thought found correlative expression in Britten's 'continental stylisation, a stylisation absolutely purged of affectation or mannerism'.[1] In these major song-cycles Britten had concerned himself with the voice of one poet at a time, but in *Serenade* (1943) he used the work of poets as different as Jonson and Blake to create a musical unity of mood, in which the words subserved an over-arching musical formulation. Britten's song-cycles had never been a simple matter of fitting music to verse; the tension between words and notes had always been creative, expanding and exploring both. But immediately before the *Holy Sonnets* Britten had written his first major opera, *Peter Grimes*, which clearly taught him more about drama than he had ever known before. Emotional patterns are developed on a large scale, which encourages inner complexity and simultaneous contrast (as, for example, in Ellen's 'Nothing to tell me, nothing to say' in Act II, scene i). At the same time the composer is able to develop a degree of dramatic intensity at specific moments which is unparalleled in any of his earlier work. Peter's great aria in Act I, scene ii, 'Now the Great Bear and Pleiades', achieves its concentrated and distilled power by a deliberate display of utter simplicity – the intoning of the repeated E, over the bare harmonies and gentle rhythmic figures in the strings – until the single outburst of the voice in 'Like a flashing turmoil of a shoal of herring' is a release from tension, almost a relief. Dramatic intensity is similarly the quality of Peter's last utterance, 'What harbour shelters peace', where he suddenly tries to find freedom in song, while chorus and foghorn enforce the grim reality.

The success of Britten's *Holy Sonnets* stems from two related perceptions: he saw that the essence of drama in music is the single emotional impact of thematic material to be developed; and he realised that it was not necessary for the rhythms of his vocal line to be limited by those of the poem. There is an example in the first sonnet 'O my blacke soul', where the key word 'summoned' dictates the semiquaver pattern on which the whole accompaniment is based, riding over bar-lines, nagging away

[1] *Ed. cit.*, p. 41.

245

in relentless octaves which only break into chords late in the piece. The voice struggles to get loose from the piano's insistence, from the opening words, with their characteristic descending ninth, to the last phrase 'it dyes red soules to white', which rises in fourths from D sharp to a top F sharp sung pianissimo and conceding the B major tonality of the accompaniment only on the last word. The vocal phrasing shows how Britten overrides Donne's metre in the opening lines. The singer sings

> Oh my blacke Soule!
> now thou art summoned By sicknesse,
> deaths herald, and champion;
> Thou art like a pilgrim,
> which abroad hath done Treason, and durst
> not turne to whence hee is fled,

and then, as the poem assumes a more speculative and meditative tone, falls in with Donne's pentameters. Similarly, in the second sonnet, the word 'Batter' creates the complicated $\frac{4}{8}$ ($\frac{12}{16}$) rhythm, and the violence is enforced by the phrasing 'Batter my heart,/three person'd God;/for, you As yet but knocke, breathe, shine, and seeke to mend'. As in other fine works of art, the basic premises are simple. Britten's achievement lies in the marvellous musical logic he brings to the development of his initial insights. One might instance the 'sighes and teares' of sonnet three, the irritable relationship between voice and piano in sonnet four, or the heavy, relentless tread of the left-hand accompaniment in 'What if this present'. Yet in the centre of the cycle, its climax and one of Britten's finest achievements, stands the setting of 'Since she whome I lovd', which is purely lyrical, and develops from totally different premises. As Peter Pears has remarked 'No one today but Britten could have covered such ground in those first twelve bars, no one but he could have used his material so fully without a suggestion of exhaustion'.[1] Oddly, and probably accidentally, Britten's direction 'Adagio molto rubato' sets the tone for Donne's celebration of the effects of God's 'robbery' of Anne Donne, and the steady $\frac{3}{4}$ movement of the vocal line against the triplets of the accompaniment encourages the singer to make

[1] *Ed. cit.*, p. 70.

Adagio molto rubato (♩ = 33)

VOICE: Since she whom I lov'd _____ hath payd her last debt _____ To Na - ture, and to hers, and my good is dead, _____ And her Soule ear - ly in - to Heaven ra - vish -ed, _____

sost. con molto Ped.

247

his own emphases and climaxes. The accompaniment is built on broken chords, changing at each bar-line and moving downwards away from the voice until the first climax on the richly ambiguous word 'ravished'.

The steadying, supportive quality of the harmony and piano figuration establishes the calm basic mood, and the composer is free to make his points by other musical means: the open, sequential figure on 'Here the admyring her my mind did whett/ To seeke thee God', where the music enacts the comparison; the dotted quaver rhythm which intrudes on 'A holy thirsty dropsy melts mee yett'; and the beautiful, totally dramatic effect of the return of the opening phrase, an octave higher, on the words 'tender jealosy'. This gently climactic moment shows Britten's sure instinct for selecting precisely the crucial words in the poem to fit into his musical structure, since the argument of the sonnet moves from Donne's unexpressed jealousy to the solicitous rivalry of God for the poet's love. Britten can delicately assert this intellectual structure simply by repeating five notes. The seventh and eighth sonnets are more violent and powerful, contrasting sharply with the astringent tenderness of the sixth. The last of the *Holy Sonnets* is a masterpiece of control and restraint. The invitation of 'Death be not proud' to a composer is obvious. It looks like the culminating point of the cycle's theme, and one would expect Britten to treat it as he had treated 'Spirto ben nato' in the *Michelangelo Sonnets*. I find the direction 'Allegro molto moderato e sostenuto' a little puzzling, since in the composer's recording of the cycle with Peter Pears the tempo he sets seems slower than one would have predicted. But the slower speed with the sostenuto effect is unquestionably right. It allows the ostinato bass to pursue its untroubled way, and to control the whole development. The singer's opening phrase 'Death be not proud' is a subtle contraction of the opening phrase of sonnet one. The echo suggests that the emotion explored in the cycle has now been governed and directed towards the central Christian realisation that the last enemy is itself no more than 'slave to Fate'. In this song the voice is slowly allowed to flower into moments of almost seventeenth-century embellishment on key words like 'pleasure', 'warre', and 'sicknesse', establishing both an instinctive confidence and an achieved resolve in the face of Death. The steady, unstoppable movement of voice and piano in the last line, into an openly asserted B major tonality, together with the extended note values, is a plain musical assertion of the plain faith in which the poem comes to rest. But it is a plainness which Donne, and Britten, have won out of real emotional complexity.

In the *Holy Sonnets* Britten treated his text with intelligence and transparent honesty. He has followed the movement of Donne's mind, and gained an intellectual control over his material. But in the technical realm he has also succeeded in finding musical expression for Donne's phraseology. His use of restrained recitativo style to follow the modulations of the speaking voice, holding back the lyrical and dramatic poten- tialities of song until exactly the right moment, is a triumph of timing, and a perfect realisation of the stress between speech rhythm and metre which gives Donne's sonnets their power and life. The cycle shows how a composer who is inward with Donne's unique mode of utterance and his very personal dramatic sense can give them perfect expression. As Donald Mitchell has said:

> The *John Donne Sonnets* make the least concessions to Britten's own social, out-turning tendencies. A song cycle which seems to be the declaration of a creative loneliness finding no remedy or relief in the act of creation, the music appears at times to underline its own withdrawal from humanity and the consolations of human sorrow.[1]

This is fair comment on Britten's music, and equally good criti- cism of Donne's poems.

There are some signs that Donne's verse is once again attracting the attention of composers. There have been some amateur settings in Universities, and, very recently, the BBC broadcast a performance of three of Donne's poems set to music by Elizabeth Maconchy. They were apparently written over a long period, but intended as a triptych, and they show how another very personal idiom, quite different from Britten's, takes up the challenge of Donne's words. All three songs are for tenor and piano, and the broadcast recital by Philip Langridge and Mark Elder was the first performance of one of them ('The

[1] *Ed. cit.*, p. 30.

Sunne Rising'). In her setting of the 'Hymne to God the Father' Miss Maconchy, like Pelham Humfrey, chooses to follow Donne's strophic pattern, and, again like Humfrey, she creates a refrain for the last two lines of each verse, though she subdues the pun until the last verse, where she recognises the greater verbal complexity by making equal points of climax on 'sunne' and 'done', stressing the connection between the poet and Christ. This intellectual control is a feature of the song. It is very much a dialogue between voice and piano. The vocal line is complemented by and interwoven with the piano's melody, accompanied by a slow, chordal progression in the left hand, giving an effect which is meditative, even sombre, without being in any obvious way liturgical. The 'Hymne to Christ' is similar in style, but much freer and more declamatory in manner. The accompaniment is less closely involved with the voice, remaining for the most part in the piano's lower register, where it supports the voice without permitting any basic tonality to emerge. Again, the song is not noticeably liturgical; it resolutely uses the musical vocabulary of a post-Christian age, but uses it with great sympathy and expressiveness. There are moments when the song takes up the invitation of the words, as in the almost jaunty setting of 'the amorousnesse of an harmonious Soule', but the climax follows the poem's sense, occurring on the lines 'O, if thou car'st not whom I love/Alas, thou lov'st not mee'. Here the music breaks free of its restraint to express the poet's passionate words passionately. The last verse gradually releases the emotional pressure, but registers the lesser urgency of 'Fame, Wit, Hopes' with octave leaps which stand out against the untraditional intervals of most of the melodic line. The setting of 'The Sunne Rising' is in some ways more ambitious than that of the Hymns, and it is more reminiscent of Britten's style. The note clusters and powerful rhythms of the piano part give the voice opportunity to make the most of Donne's wit, and phrases like 'saucy pedantique wretch' are skittish and delicate. The humour of country ants at their 'harvest offices' is saluted in some clever syncopation, and the song has a dramatic life and appropriateness which seems to derive from the security in which twentieth-century English opera now finds itself. I have not been able to study the scores of Miss Maconchy's songs, but it is clear from the performance of them that a sensitive instinct is at work, and that she is fully alive to all the complexities and opportunities which Donne's resolutely unmusical voice provides. Much more alive, it seems, than Donne's own contemporaries were.

Appendix I

Thomas Ford's setting of stanzas one and two of Donne's paraphrase of Lamentations.

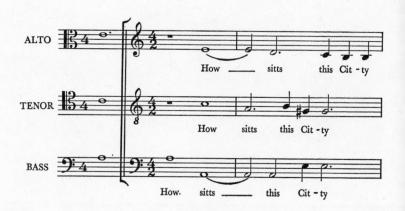

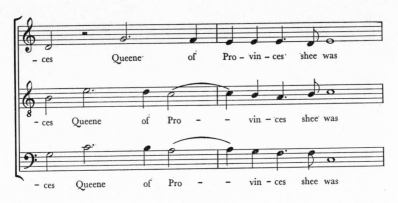

weeps   shee   weeps   and her teares___

___ shee, weeps   shee   weeps   and her   teares   fall:

weeps   shee   weeps,   and her   teares___   fall   downe

___   fall   downe___   by her cheekes   a -

downe   and her   teares___   fall downe   by her cheekes   a -

fall   downe   by   her   cheekes   a -

- long   and her   teares   fall

- long   and her   teares   fall

- long,   and her   teares___   fall   downe

downe_____ fall downe_____ by her cheekes a -

downe fall downe fall downe by her cheekes a -

fall downe fall downe by her cheekes a -

- long, and none of all her

- long, and none of all_____ her; Lou – ers

- long, and none of all_____ her Lou – ers

Lou – ers and none of all her

and none of all_____ her Lou – ers

and none of all_____ her Lou – ers

Lou - ers com — fort her, per - fid - ious - ly   her friends have

com — — fort her,   per' - fid - ious - ly·   her

com — fort her,   per' - fid - ious - ly her

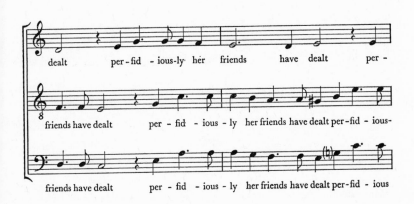

dealt   per - fid - ious - ly· her   friends   have dealt   per -

friends have dealt   per - fid - ious - ly her friends have dealt per-fid - ious-

friends have dealt   per - fid - ious - ly her friends have dealt per-fid - ious

- fid - ious-ly her   friends have dealt   and now   are en - em-

- ly her   friends have dealt   and now are en — em -

- ly her   friends have dealt   and   now are en — em -

9

Donne and the Limits of Lyric

JOHN HOLLANDER

So much has been written about Donne's metrical roughness
that a comprehensive survey of commentary upon what the poet
himself called 'my words masculine perswasive force' would
parallel the whole course of his reputation. Aside from the dis-
agreements of his contemporaries about his metrical style – the
strictures of a Jonson, the complex praise of a Carew – we can
trace even in the revived but canonical twentieth-century phase
of Donne's career a shift from an acceptance of Jonson's famous
'not keeping of accent' to the commendation of it as a positive
and unique virtue. Even though Jonson may have been com-
plaining to Drummond of Hawthornden about the slightly
more than fashionably irregular verse of the satires and even as,
in twentieth-century criticism, a Browningesque rather than a
Tennysonian sense of verbal music in verse began to be praised,[1]
Grierson, writing before 1912, would find it necessary to
apologise for 'a poetry, not perfect in form, rugged of line and
careless in rhyme' as being yet 'a poetry of an extraordinary
arresting and haunting quality, passionate, thoughtful, and with
a deep melody of its own'.[2] That 'deep melody' of speech has
since almost become a cliché of Donne criticism; it is used with
force and clarity by the editor of a recent college text edition:

> To begin with, despite the absence of any facile smoothness of
> versification, the lines have a strange and original music, derived
> largely from an imitation of the accents of emotionally heightened
> conversation . . . Donne's metrical control is of an astounding
> virtuosity, although that virtuosity is generally in the service of
> drama rather than of song.[3]

[1] See for example Sir Herbert Grierson's Introduction to his edition of the *Poems*,
Oxford, 1912, ii, p. xv.   [2] Grierson *op. cit.*, ii, p. lv.
[3] John Donne, *Poetry and Prose*, ed. Frank J. Warnke, New York, 1967, p. xviii.

Whether they 'imitate' or, in fact, embody, and whether they emulate 'the accents of emotionally heightened conversation' or, as I shall try to show, are partly a necessary consequence of a speaker's trying to make himself understood – in any event, Donne's jagged rhythms, when considered against the smoothness usually demanded of strophic song-texts, remain highly problematic, even when highly praised. 'Donne,' says Arnold Stein, 'is a conscious master of harshness',[1] and he is speaking for the literary temper of Modernism, for an age which approves of strong lines not for their wit, their 'tension' alone, but for the rhythmic inisistence upon domination over the metre and its schemata which would place them in a line stemming from Catullus and Villon – the lyric of insistent talk, rather than the lyric of written flow (Horace and Ronsard). The modernist sense of that tradition which makes of the speaking voice the most authentic singing has been one that has found the irregularity of Wyatt's experimental pentameters valuable *per se*.[2] It has found thinness and smoothness in what its Victorian forbears had thought of as lyrical language. And still largely unacquainted or unimpressed with Browning, it has made the rhythms of the *Songs and Sonnets* into touchstones for revisions of prosodic theory.[3]

---

[1] Arnold Stein, *John Donne's Lyrics*, Minneapolis, 1962, pp. 24-5. Here again, it is 'dramatic' expressiveness which is emphasised. Douglas L. Peterson in *The English Lyric from Wyatt to Donne*, Princeton, 1967, pp. 285-7, tries to connect Donne's roughness with the tradition of the plain, as opposed to the courtly, style.

[2] Brought up on the invidious comparison of Tottel's reworking of 'They Flee from Me' with the MS. text – almost a set school exercise in the early 1950s – I now find myself preferring the former. For an interesting discussion of this, see John Thompson, *The Founding of English Metre*, London, 1961, pp. 15-36.

[3] Seymour Chatman, 'Comparing Metrical Styles', in *Style and Language*, ed. Thomas A. Sebeok, Cambridge, Mass., 1960, pp. 149-72, uses the structural linguistic model of English stress, propounded by Trager and Smith in 1951, to compare the style of the *Satyres* with Pope's versions of them. Chatman's analysis was one of the first to try to systematise a description of some of the stress phenomena I shall discuss below. Roger Fowler, '"Prose Rhythm" and Meter' from Essays on *Style and Language*, ed. Roger Fowler, New York, 166, pp. 82-9, is clear and useful. Disagreements with Chatman's methodology have been voiced eloquently and powerfully by W. K. Wimsatt and Monroe Beardsley in 'The Concept of Meter: An Exercise in Abstraction', *PMLA* LXXIV, 1959, pp. 585-98; also, in a revision of his own theory by Chatman in *A Theory of Meter*,

In these second thoughts on the nature of the unmusicality of Donne's lyrics, I should like to consider their roughness in a literally, rather than figuratively, 'musical' context, and to inspect certain features of his rhythmic style, strophic patterning and rhetorical tonality which make the 'songs' of their title so hard to take with an older, Elizabethan literalness. Some of these problems need no new discussion. Certainly the rhythmic variations within the versification of metrically identical strophes is not a problem peculiar to Donne. Composers of monodic airs like Dowland who set a great variety of texts would always work out a setting for the initial stanza and cheerfully ignore the lack of fit in subsequent ones, whether or not the performance of those following stanzas could be made possible with a little melismatic assistance. In the case of a rhythmically active line like the opening one of the great, anonymous peddler's song from Dowland's 1600 Book of Airs,

> Fine knacks for ladies, cheape, choice, brave and new

– the equivalent line of the third strophe gets a weaker setting, requiring displaced word-stress on the line's only two disyllables. Thus

That is, in both cases the iambic norm is stretched by the rhythm of the text, but the *ad hoc* accentual underlining of one which a musical setting provides will not fit the cadences of another. With Donne, this situation is frequent and strongly marked. Let us consider one of the most interesting of the seven

---

The Hague, 1965. A more recent study of English accentual-syllabic metre from the viewpoint of transformational grammar is that of Morris Halle and Samuel Jay Keyser, 'Chaucer and the Theory of Prosody', *College English* XXVIII, December, 1966, pp. 187-219, where they establish linear syllabic position as a schematic unit. I adopt their useful concept of stress-maximum to indicate the iambic handling of relative stress, particularly in groups of monosyllabic words.

settings of Donne lyrics by seventeenth-century composers edited by André Souris and Jean Jacquot,[1] the version of 'The Expiration' by Alfonso Ferrabosco from his 1609 book of airs. Here again, the setting cannot possibly hope to accommodate the second strophe in its rhythmic setting of the first one: 'Any so cheape a death as saying goe'[2] The terminal line of the second strophe, for example, must be sung to this rhythm:

Being   dou - ble dead   go - ing————— and bid - ding goe

It is interesting to note that although the final imperative 'Go!' is meant in both lines, it should be in inverted commas in the first instance – 'saying, "Go!" ' as a quick, easy death – whereas in the second, it is a direct but conditional command of the singer-lover. No matter how 'expressive', by early-baroque or modern standards, the setting is to be, it must surely comprehend the *sense* of the text. For example, the music in a good setting should punctuate the final two lines of the song, with its own rhythms, so as to do something like this:

> Except it be too late to kill me so,
> (Being double-dead—going and bidding), Go!

Now Ferrabosco's setting realises neither the speech-rhythm of the phrase 'saying, "Go!" ' in the first strophe, nor that of the complex syntax of the second. But at the crudest level of rhythmic fitting of musical downbeat to normal word-stress (let alone to phrase-stress among monosyllabic groups, or stress maxima in an iambic context) the second strophe will not work. It is rewarding to contrast Ferrabosco's setting of just

---

[1] *Poèmes de Donne, Herbert et Crashaw, mise en musique par leurs contemporains* transcribed and realised by A. Souris, introduced by Jean Jacquot, Paris, 1961, to whose musical text I shall refer. Helen Gardner gives melodic lines from these in her edition of the *Songs and Sonnets*, Oxford, 1965, pp. 238-47.

[2] The enjambment which leads to this line ('. . . owe? Any . . .') is completely lost in setting. Here as elsewhere, when I am quoting from a text in its setting, I shall use the texts of the songbooks and MSS., as transcribed in *Poèmes de Donne*, etc. These lines are from p. 9.

these lines with another one, from an anonymous musical MS of about the same time.[1]

A - ny so cheape a death—— as say - ing goe

Here, at least the 'saying' "Go!" ' phrase is plausibly treated; the syntax, and, hence, the rhetoric of speech is recognisable in the melodic interpretation of it. I mention syntax only because so much recent discussion of Donne's metrics has concentrated on declamatory and emotional effects of apparently aberrant stress-positioning in Donne's iambic lines,[2] without appeal to the basic complex relations between phrase-stress patterns and syntactic structure in English. But if the anonymous setting handles the terminal line of the first stanza well, its reciprocal is even more distorted than in Ferrabosco's version. It demands two sorts of accentual deformation.

Being dou - ble dead, go - ing—— and bid - ding goe

– the first, on 'going', exacerbated by the long tied, note value on the second syllable, the second, making the phrase 'bidding go' syntactically equivalent – through rhythmic identity – to 'saying go'. But 'bidding' is, as we have seen, part of another, complex parenthetical phrase, the very syntactical existence of which dissolves in song. Or, at any rate, this song.[3]

In other words, Donne's rhythmic modulation of language is such that even the most musicianly attention to word-stress (and this, indeed, is not always Ferrabosco's strongest point) will frequently not suffice to accentuate correctly the textual syntax. In view of the increased attention, in early seventeenth-century

---

1 For lute and voice, from Bodleian MS. Mus. Sch. F. 575. f. 8ᵛ, *Poèmes de Donne*, pp. 10-11.
2 See, for example, Arnold Stein, *Donne's Lyrics*, p. 42.
3 Occasionally, strophic fitting can occur in these settings. Giovanni Coperario's version of 'The Message' takes advantage of the alignment, in successive stanzas, of the word-pairs 'Which O' – 'Which no' – 'That I', for a repeated musical phrase. See *Poèmes de Donne*, pp. 7-8.

monody, given to freeing the text from polyphonic labyrinths, in view of the growing influence outside of Italy of the *stile espressivo* of recitative, the unique problems of English prosody remained a stumbling-block in the way of properly 'committing short and long', not only in strophic settings but in through-composed ones as well.

One of these problems is that posed by contrastive stress. Even in the case of another poet, one who took pride – or at least believed himself undeserving of hanging – in keeping of accent, the accentual properties of English phrase structure posed a difficulty for musical setting. Ben Jonson's friend and collaborator Ferrabosco was, again, the victim; this time, the text in question is the final couplet of the famous seduction song from *Volpone*, out of Catullus, later included in *The Forrest* in 1616.' 'Tis no sinne loves fruits to steale,/But the sweet theft to reveale'[1]

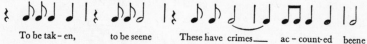

While the purely melodic effect is lovely and sophisticated – a stylistically forward-looking evaded cadence on the chord of the sixth at 'beene', heralding the repetition of the words in a final phrase, etc. – it is almost as if the text laid under it were a fairly clever verse translation of that for which the music was composed. The sense of the couplet becomes clear only when we underline the emphatic stress:

> To be *taken*, to be *seene*,
> *These* have crimes *accounted* been.

'Crimes' needs no added stress, since it refers back to, rather than contrasts with, the 'sinne' of the previous couplet. '*These*'

---

[1] Another problem here is the relation of the two concluding couplets to each other. Jonson's folio text gives the punctuation 'to reveale:/To be taken' and this suggests that Ferrabosco's setting is correct in its reading of the full stop. In that case, the penultimate couplet means 'There's no sin in sex save for to do it openly', and 'but' has the same sense of 'except' that it does in the penultimate line of stanza 1 of 'Drink to me only with thine eyes'. I wonder about this: perhaps 'but' means 'nevertheless' here, and governs all three lines – '*But* (1) to reveal the theft, (2) to be taken, (3) to be seen – *these* are called crimes'.

(i.e. getting caught, not adultery itself) or, more subtly, 'accounted' (morality is mere fashion) are the words which take an implicit contrastive stress in speech. According to the setting, the preceding lines of the text would have had to suggest that these were blessings, and 'crimes' was then given emphatic development.

Ben Jonson's lyric culminates in the moral arguments of seduction which are frequently rhetorically contrastive. But we have only to turn to a far less schematic example, again from Ferrabosco's treatment of Donne's 'The Expiration', to see how fundamental this problem is. Consider the third line of the first strophe:

$$\text{Turne thou (ghost!) } \textit{that} \text{ way, and let } \textit{me} \text{ turne } \textit{this}^1$$

This has been underlined and repunctuated to gloss its meaning in the context of the stanza ('So, so, breake off this last lamenting kisse,/Which sucks two soules and vapours both away,/Turne thou ghost that way, and let me turne this'). We may observe that, as in so many of Donne's lines, the 'roughness' comes about as a result of ambiguities in reading the metrical disposition of stresses. 'Let *me* turne *this*' falls perfectly into iambic position[2] because of the contrast with the preceding 'Turne *thou* (ghost) *that* way'. It also allows 'kisse' and 'this' to rhyme with greater reason, whereas if 'this' were enjambed, for example (as in, say, '. . . . and let me turne this/As yet unbloodied dagger from my heart'), any coherent musical setting would have to avoid a rhythmic ictus on 'this. Similarly, another syntactic version of the line 'Turne thou ghost that way which faces East' would call for a musical downbeat on 'way' to make sense of it. But to emphasise 'way' in the setting of Donne's line would be something like the way certain Romance foreign accents mis-stress English words. Here, then, is Ferrabosco's setting

Turne thou (ghost!) *that* way,   and let *me* turne *this*

---

1 Text from Ferrabosco's song book of 1609 (*Poèmes de Donne*, p. 11). One could also read 'Turne (thou ghost!) that way . . .' with a less archaic imperative form, but the larger problem would still remain.

2 Or, with stress-maxima properly assigned, to use the Halle-Keyser terminology.

which commits just that fault, totally missing, in its rhythmic generations, the point of the line. The other, anonymous setting cited before,[1] incidentally, manages just this problem rather better:

The contrastive stress is pointed up in the setting, and at least gross syntactic grouping – aside from any nuances of expression which might grace that grossness – has been satisfied. But as we might expect, the consequences for the reciprocal line in the second strophe are more disastrous than merely a matter of musical rhythm wrecking word-stress

Here, the gasping rest after the poorly treated 'if it have, let . . .' is grotesque and irrelevant.

The setting of any poem to music recapitulates, in a strange way, the very process of metrical composition in a language; this is especially true in the case of English iambic verse. A particular line will make manifest certain possibilities implicit in the iambic schema (allowable reversals, promotions or demotions in trisyllabic words, heightening of syllabic prominence by means other than stress, such as rhyme, assonance, alliteration, etc.). Just so will a musical setting of that line go one step further and resolve ambiguities that may remain yet exist in the fulfilled rhythmic line. For example, we know that line 21 from 'A Valediction: Of Weeping',

> Weepe me not dead, in thine armes, but forbeare

is not dactyllic only because of our knowledge of its context of versification, of the metrical convention of the poem itself.[2] For

---

[1] See note 1, p. 263, above. With reference to the choice in note 1, p. 265, note that the anonymous setting opts for the grouping 'turn (thou ghost!)'.

[2] Catherine Ing, *Elizabethan Lyrics*, London, 1951, pp. 234-5, considers this line, but her prosodic comments are hampered by her confusion of musical downbeat, word-stress, emphatic stress and metrical position.

if the line had been preceded by a different one, the rhythmic possibilities would have gone the other way, as in, say,

> Sweete though to drowne in the tides of thy haire,
> Weepe me not dead in thine armes but forbeare . . . etc.

A good musical setting, like a proper scansion in the act of reading, or an actual oral performance of the line by a speaker, will resolve the ambiguity.[1] But let us take this back one step further: we know how frequently Donne's lines which look 'rough' (or, in the precisely defined terms of a recent prosodic theory, 'unmetrical'), turn out not be to so if the proper attention is paid to contrastive stress.[2]

A startling case of this occurs in 'A Nocturnall upon S. Lucies Day', in such a way as to suggest an alternative reading of syntax and, thus, of the nature of the image therein embodied. The mourning poet says of the alchemist Love

> He ruin'd mee, and I am re-begot
> Of absence, darknesse, death; things which are not.

In order that the rhyme may function at all, let alone not set off what Milton called 'wretched matter and lame Metre', the final syllable must be stressed; in order that Donne may not really deserve hanging, the semantic phrase-stress must allow that to happen. Now assume for a moment that the phrase 'things which are not' means 'things which aren't, which don't exist'. The rhythmic phrasal paradigm would be that of the phrases from Jeremiah 5:21, 'which have eyes and see not'. 'Things which are not' would in any case give either a truncated predicative, or else a totally existential meaning of the copula. We should then expect, in the first instance, a completion of predication in a

---

[1] The composer Charles Wuorinen carries this analogy a step further into music itself, by considering the 'freezing' of interpretation in taped, electronic music (whatever schematic randomisations may occur), as opposed to the interpretive choices of traditional instrumental performance. See his 'Toward Good Vibrations', *Prose #2*, 1971, pp. 205-9.

[2] A J. Smith, *The Songs and Sonets*, London, 1964, p. 44, observes this, albeit from an inverted viewpoint; I would disagree only in that I am arguing that 'a reading with the natural speech rhythm' will often, indeed, scan, and that such elements as contrastive stress are part of natural speech rhythm.

contre-rejet in a following line (as, say, '. . . thíngs which áre not/Prèsent, brighte, alive . . .'[1] But the stress on 'not' suggests another reading, with a different paradigm of syntax and scansion; 'thíngs which are hót', for example, would take an iambic stress on the final adjective, 'hot' (unless specifically stressed contrastively, of course, viz. 'things which *are* hot'– as opposed to things which *aren't*). If Donne's phrase is modelled on this one, we must take '*not*' as adjectival, rather than as a negative particle, a nonce term meaning 'not x, x being any predicate whatsoever'. The ontological joke about reifying nothing is even stronger in this reading, and Love's alchemy far more impressive – the 'quintessence . . . of nothingnesse' would certainly be, if nothing else, 'not'.

Recent theories of prosody have interested themselves in Donne's emphatic stress for a variety of reasons.[2] The *Songs and Sonnets* and the *Elegies* seem encrusted with examples of lines which become fairly regular iambic pentameter when the purely contrastive stress is recognised:

by that remorse,
Which *my* words masculine perswasive force
Begot in *thee*, and by the memory

('On his Mistresse', 3-5)

– is a self-illustrating case. Pairs of pronouns frequently contrast in Donne; this is basic to the texture of his rhetoric. Phrases like 'my words', normally stressed [. '], are shifted

[1] Warnke in his edition (see note 3, p. 259) omits a full stop after 'not'. I'm not sure whether this is a typographical error, or whether he means to read the enjambment as 'things which are not/All others, from all things draw all that's good,'where 'not' is merely negatively predicative, an enjambment across strophes even more violent than 'And there he lives with memorie and Ben/Jonson who wrote this of him . . .' from Jonson's Cary and Morison Ode.

[2] The most profound treatment of contrastive stress in Donne that I have seen is in an unpublished paper by William B. Krohn. But see, for example, the attempt to apply transformational principles in a somewhat crude way to the treatment of contrastive stress by Joseph C. Beaver in 'Contrastive Stress and Metered Verse', *Language and Style*, ii, 1969, pp. 257-71. His examples from Donne are not too well handled.

to [′ ·]. With the normal iambic option for trisyllables, 'mas-
culine' can be either [′ · ·] or [′ · ′], and with the latter choice,
the line becomes regularised, rather than 'sprung' as in older
ways of scanning Donne ('Which my words masculine persuasive
force', for example). If the line is indeed as potent as the language
it describes, then it is at least normally erect.

A few more examples, perhaps: line 20 of 'The Anniversarie'–

When bodies *to* their graves, soules *from their* graves remove.

– falls into its alexandrine role more adroitly when the double
contrasts of 'to-from' and 'their-their' are realised. Line 24 of
the same poem –

> but wee
> Can be such Kings, nor, *of* such, subjects bee;
> (my punctuation)

– depends upon a contrastive elevation of 'of'. A particularly
delicate effect is gained in 'The Primrose', where, in line 8 –

> I walke to finde a true Love; and I see

– the iambic irregularity obtained by reversal of stress in
positions 7 and 8 rushes on toward an enjambment of 'see'; this
differs sharply from the situation in line 13

> For should my true-Love lesse then woman bee . . .

in the stressing of the compound. In the first instance, 'true
Love' with a plus-juncture, a spondaic accent, the stress pattern
of Christian-name-plus-surname, or however an informal pros-
odic descriptive vocabulary would want to put it, is the usual
adjective-noun pair. In the second instance, the name of the
flower, the stress has regressed to the first syllable of the
compound, and the four or six petals of the false floral emblem
of love are matched by a skewed stress pattern on the words of
its name as well.

It is just these contrasts which in English are far from being
mere nuances, but engage fundamental grammatical relation-
ships. To a French or Italian ear, particularly that of a musician,
they might die away; and since the rhythmic generations of

melodic lines were constantly being influenced by Continental music, the ability of English composers of the seventeenth century to embody and enhance in their settings the basic rhetorical stuff, the compelling speech-music of strong lines markedly decreased. Smoother, post-Jonsonian lyric traditions, moving toward the thinness of Augustan song texts, provided easier materials for song settings than could poetic language rhythmically exciting in itself. Expressive formulae took precedence over rhetorical complexity, which fortunately, texts began to abandon. Can we tell, for example, from John Hilton's (1599-1657) setting of 'A Hymne to God the Father'[2] whether, in the rhythmic realisation of

When thou hast done,   thou hast not done, [for   I   have more]

the composer has 'set' the pun on the poet's name? At least he has not reduced the paradox to the more trivial one by implying with musical ictus a speech rhythm of 'When thou hast done, thou hast not done'.[3]

No matter what the genres of the *Songs and Sonnets* lyrics are considered to be – and they embrace dramatic monologue, emblem verse, implicit dramatic scene (as when the insect is successfully threatened and killed in the white space between successive strophes in 'The Flea'), argument, or whatever – the modulation of personal speech make the sounds of sense, and makes sense of the sound patternings of the metre. It is not the diversity of genres *per se* which makes so many of the songs un-song-like. Many a Jacobean composer, 'his art and voice to show', would set and sing all manner of texts; William Byrd in his 1589 and 1611 books of madrigals set four passages from

---

[1] Even in the more recitative-like monody of the middle seventeenth century, this is evident. See Lawes' setting of 'Sweet Echo' from *Comus*, for example, where the rhetorical music of 'Tell me but where/Sweet Queen of parley, daughter of the Sphere' is turned, in the setting, into something rather strange.

[2] From British Museum Egerton MS. 2013. f. 13^r, transcribed in *Poèmes de Donne*, pp. 18-19. This may be the setting which Walton says that Donne had sung by the St Paul's choir, although it would have had to be in polyphonic form.

[3] Beaver, p. 268, gives this reading, presumably because he never heard of the pun.

Geoffrey Whitney's emblem book, and, in an earlier volume, a quantitative translation of a group of lines from Ovid's *Heroides*. Musical and textual quotations from street-cries and well-known tunes work their way into art-songs by John Daniel and Thomas Campion. And the latter could insist on the similarity of lyrics and epigrams:

> Short Ayres, if they be skilfully framed, and naturally exprest, are like quicke and good Epigrammes in Poesie, many of them shewing as much artifice, and breeding as great difficultie as a large Poeme.[1]

It is ultimately a matter of modality that marks the metaphysical lyric from a musical point of view, a mixture of basic tonalities within a particular song. Whether polyphonic or monodic, the song is at a loss to handle the dialectic between lyric modes, the simultaneous presence of contrary impulses which even the formal musical dialogue (an increasingly popular seventeenth-century form) could only trivialise. This is particularly true in the case of the most complex kinds of post-Petrarchan love poetry. The Petrarchan poem will develop a mode and an emotional tonality of its own, and while it may turn against that tonality (particularly in the sestet of a sonnet) a sequential musical shift could represent it in a setting.

For example, in Thomas Campion's 1601 book of airs, there is a conventionally Petrarchan lyric whose first strophe goes as follows:[2]

> Mistris, since you so much desire
> To know the place of Cupid's fire,
> In your faire shrine that flame doth rest,
> Yet never harbourd in your brest.
> It bides not in your lips so sweete,
> Nor where the rose and lillies meete,
> But a little higher, but a little higher;
> There, there, O there lies Cupids fire.

The lady's eyes, a source of a higher, purer love than is her mouth, are here celebrated in the language of the sonneteers,

---

[1] Thomas Campion, 'To the Reader' from *A Booke of Ayres*, 1601, in *Works*, ed. Walter R. Davis, New York, 1967, p. 15.
[2] Campion, *Works*, p. 41.

and the air of sanctity, the forswearing of mere passion ('So meanely triumphs not my blisse', goes a line in the second strophe) are all familiar enough. But in his fourth book of airs, published *c.* 1618, Campion parodied his own earlier song in some now-fashionable anti-Petrarchan second thoughts. The first strophe:[1]

> Beauty, since you so much desire
> To know the place of *Cupids* fire,
> About you somwhere it doth rest,
> Yet never harbour'd in your brest,
> Nor gout-like in your heele or toe;
> What foole would seeke Loves flame so low?
> But a little higher, but a little higher,
> There, there, o there lyes *Cupids* fire.

This is a satiric reduction, a literal lowering: here love starts, as Donne suggests that it should in 'Loves Progresse', from below, that it may find its home in sex, at the body's centre. Campion's setting for the second song is more chromatic in melodic line than is the first, and the lute part bawdily points up the repeatedly ascending 'But a little higher' with contrapuntal nudging.[2]

These two songs represent two conflicting modalities. The major tradition of European song would have to differentiate between those modalities in setting them. Many of Donne's major lyrics embody a constant process of dialectic between modalities, conducted by an ingenuity masked as a reality principle, juggling hyperbole and abuse, insisting that the truest tenderness is the most feigning, that the most faithful caresses are those of wit and will combined. Art song could not begin to treat such complexity musically until Schumann began to set Heine *Lieder*. The poet of the *Songs and Sonnets*, double fool – perhaps even exponential fool – as he was, seldom ran the real risk of being a triple one.

---

[1] Campion, *Works*, p. 190.
[2] Miles W. Kastendieck, *England's Musical Poet*, Oxford, 1938, pp. 114-15 discusses the sequence of rising repetitions of 'but a little higher', each starting a whole tone above the end of the last one; but he appears to misunderstand the song and its relation, textually and musically, to the earlier one.

10

Courtiers out of Horace

Donne's *Satyre IV;* and Pope's *Fourth Satire of Dr John Donne, Dean of St Paul's Versifyed*

HOWARD ERSKINE-HILL

I

'To my satyrs there belongs some feare . . .', Donne wrote, perhaps to Sir Henry Wotton, perhaps at the very end of the sixteenth century.[1] This is a good, though not total, summary of the spirit of *Satyre IV.* Yet when Donne pioneered the Elizabethan satiric revival with his *Satyre I* (*c.* 1593), he seemed to be setting a very different kind of precedent. Based on a walk through the streets with a ridiculous and wearisome companion, *Satyre I* may, as Milgate observes, have been broadly influenced by the Ninth Satire of the First Book of Horace ('Ibam forte Via Sacra . . .'): the encounter with the Talker (*garrulus* – 1. 33). If we may take *Sat.* I. ix as *one* pattern of Horation satire (for Horace is certainly a more various poet than his image in English literature often allows), other features of Donne's poem may strike us as Horatian. It tells a short, coherent, well-rounded story. Donne's 'humorist'-companion wishes to leave the study for the streets, but is chidden by Donne for his 'headlong, wild uncertaine' behaviour which respects outward appearance before inner merit. Yet the 'humorist' is contrite, and so

I shut my chamber doore, and 'Come, lets goe.'

(52)[2]

---

[1] *John Donne, Dean of St Paul's, Complete Poetry and Selected Prose,* ed. John Hayward, 1930, p. 440.

[2] Quotations from Donne's *Satyres* are taken from *John Donne, The Satires, Epigrams and Verse Letters,* ed. W. Milgate, 1967.

Once outside, however, Donne's reproofs are shown to have been all justified, and are all ignored. The 'humorist's' behaviour gets more and more out of hand until he deserts his steadier companion, and the poem comes to its comic *dénouement*:

> At last his Love he in a windowe spies,
> And like light dew exhal'd, he flings from mee
> Violently ravish'd to his lechery.
> Many were there, he could command no more;
> He quarrell'd, fought, bled; and turn'd out of dore
>   Directly came to mee hanging the head,
>   And constantly a while must keepe his bed.   (106-12)

The progressive self-assertion of the Humorist is broadly analogous to the increasing desperation of Horace with the Talker, until each reaches its sudden reversal and conclusion. The deflation of the Humorist with words, his increasing self-assertion in the streets, and his subsequent deflation with blows, is a small triumph of comic art. As in Horace, *Sat.* I. ix, this comedy arises from a delicate balance of opposing recognitions. Horace's moral and social position, as rendered in *Sat.* I. ix, is entirely secure; yet it is precisely because of this that the importunities of the Talker yield such exquisite comic pleasure, and Horace is able to elicit so much humour from the account of his own discomfiture. In *Satyre I*, the Humorist is in a subordinate position, 'As prentises, or schoole-boyes'; the superior wisdom of the speaker is unchallenged, except implicitly in its failure to make any impact upon ebullient folly. Yet, by virtue of this implicit challenge, a balance is struck in *Satyre I*, lending a degree of astringent irony to what would otherwise have been a simple union of comic perception and firm moral assurance. *Satyre I* is a precocious, and not wholly unsuccessful, attempt to emulate the shaped narrative, the perfect control and the finely shaped balanced assurance of the Latin poem.

There follow, chronologically if we are to believe Drummond of Hawthornden, *Satyre II* and *Satyre III*.[1] *Satyre II* is perhaps one of the less successful of Donne's group of five formal satires. It lacks the immediate narrative and dramatic interest of *I* and *IV*,

---

[1] Milgate, *ed. cit.* p. xlvi.

and is not united, like *Satyre III*, by the exposure of a central theological and human dilemma. The objects of Donne's attack, the abuse of poetry, law, and finally property, are united in the figure of Coscus in a largely formal sense; the union does not seem a source of dramatic or poetic life. Yet there is some effectiveness in the change of Coscus from a figure of mere ridicule to one of menace –

> Shortly ('as the sea) hee'will compasse all our land; (77)

– and the satire abounds in strokes of vigorous and mordant wit. There is also a notable change of tone from *Satyre I*. The basic assurance of outlook, which gives rise to comedy, is here replaced by a mood of somewhat hectoring indignation. Tone and stance are different again, at the opening of *Satyre III*, and are considerably more complex:

> Kinde pitty chokes my spleene; brave scorn forbids
> Those teares to issue which swell my eye-lids;
> I must not laugh, nor weepe sinnes, and be wise,
> Can railing then cure these worne maladies? (1-4)

Thomas Drant, in his *Medcinable Morall* . . . (1566), which it must be remembered was a verse-rendering of *The Lamentations of Jeremiah* as well as the Satires of Horace, had already set out the alternative attitudes to sin of laughter or tears:

> Therfore as it is mete for a man of god rather to wepe than to iest: and not undecent for a prophane writer to be iestyng, and merie spoken: I have brought to passe that the plaintiue Prophete *Ieremie* shoulde wepe at synne: and the pleasant poet *Horace* shoulde laugh at synne. Not one kynde of musike deliteth all passions: nor one salve for all greuances.

The easy symmetry of this resolution is not altogether sustained in Drant's own explanation. The religious hypocrisies of the sixteenth century were something unknown to Horace: 'he neuer se, yt. with the uiew of his eie, which his pensiue translator can not but everuew with the languishe of his soule'.[1] It is

---

[1] Thomas Drant, *A Medicinable Morall, that is, the two Bookes of Horace his Satyres, Englyshed accordyng to the prescription of saint Hierome . . . The Wailyngs of the Prophet hieremiah, done into Englyshe verse. Also Epigrammes*, 1566; To the Reader.

the very point of the opening of *Satyre III* that the alternative attitudes of laughter or tears conflict with and check one another; Donne seems both the 'prophane writer' and the 'man of god'; each role is necessary for a full human response to his subject. *Satyre III*, which at first develops in a free way reminiscent of a dramatic soliloquy, calls each attitude into play at different points, as it explores man's dedication of his courage to worldly ends as opposed to those of 'true religion', and the confusion of conflicting claims with which the seeker after 'true religion' must contend. The moral assurance of *Satyre I* has gone, and is replaced by the less confident but immensely stronger and more resolute aspiration towards the ideal of Truth, on its 'huge hill,/ Cragged, and steep, . . .'. The speaker is strenuously engaged, with all his faculties and responses, in the midst of the conflicts which the satire exposes. *Satyre III* may merit (though not altogether for the same reasons) the term 'Tragical Satyre' which Dryden was later to apply to Juvenal.[1]

II

Satyre IV (*c.* 1597?) brings us back to Horace. This poem has a much closer relation with the Ninth Satire of the First Book than the broad resemblances of *Satyre I*. Not only is the first half of *Satyre IV* a recognisable imitation of Horace's encounter with the Talker, but there are several small though clear echoes of Horace's text. Thus 'Towards me did runne . . .', as Donne's Courtier-Talker makes his appearance, recalls 'accurrit . . .' at the parallel point of Horace's satire.[2] Donne's 'To fit my sullennesse, . . .' (when the speaker fails to shake off the Talker) is a witty play, as Niall Rudd has observed, on Horace's . . . ut iniquae mentis asellus . . .' (like [the ears of] a sullen ass), again at the parallel point in the Latin poem.[3] Donne's l. 94 echoes l. 4 of Horace, and ll. 116-7 recall ll. 10-11. The vain announcement of the Talker in Horace: 'docti sumus' (soon to be

---

[1] Dryden, *A Discourse Concerning Satire*, l. 2225, in *The Poems of John Dryden*, ed. James Kinsley, 1958, ii, p. 657.

[2] *Satyre IV*, l. 17; Horace, *Sat.* I. ix. 3.

[3] *Ibid.*, l. 91; Horace, *Sat.* I. ix. 20. See Niall Rudd, 'Donne and Horace', *Times Literary Supplement*, 22 March 1963.

brilliantly expanded by Jonson in his *Poetaster*: 'we are a scholar, I assure thee . . . Nay, we are new turn'd *Poet* too, which is more; and a *Satyrist* too, which is more then that: I write just in thy veine, I . . . we are a prettie stoick too') is developed by Donne into an account of the Courtier-Talker's parade of linguistic accomplishment.[1] In Donne, as in Horace, the scene fills with a crowd as the poet makes his escape.[2] Trifling through these echoes might seem, they would certainly have been recognised by Donne's contemporary readers, more familiar than we are with the chief literary texts of the Roman Augustan Age. The nature of their response may perhaps be gauged by that of Pope when, in imitating Donne's poem over a century later, he correctly recognised in Donne's 'Not alone/My lonenesse is . . .' an allusion to Cicero's *De Officiis*, III. i. 1, making it more explicit in his own version.[3] The Horatian echoes are signs from Donne to his readers which acknowledge his original as a text to be remembered. In this way, whether Donne follows or departs from Horace, what he does will have a significance relative to the Latin poem. That the relationship which Donne set up was recognisable to his contemporaries may be seen from a revealing couplet in Clement Paman's seventeenth-century imitation of *Satyre IV*: *The Taverne*:

> Oh happy Donne & Horace, you h'd but one
> Deuill haunted you, but me a legion . . .[4]

The common features of *Satyre IV* and Horace, *Sat.* I. ix may be summed up as follows. In each poem the speaker is encountered in a public place by a stranger who runs and engages him in conversation. In each poem the stranger proves an intrusive and tactless talker, who praises his own accomplishment, seizes the speaker by the hand with offensive familiarity, and, because

---

[1] Horace, *Sat.* I. ix. 7; Jonson, *The Poetaster*, III. i. 23-8; *Satyre IV*, 51-65.

[2] *Satyre IV*, 150-4; Horace, *Sat.* I. ix. 77-8. Most of the detailed allusion to Horace, *Sat.* I. ix. in *Satyre IV* has been pointed out by Niall Rudd, 'Donne and Horace', *loc. cit.*

[3] *Satyre IV*, 67-8; Pope, *The Fourth Satire of Dr. John Donne* 91. Quotations from Pope are taken from the Twickenham Edition of *The Poems of Alexander Pope*, iv (*Imitations of Horace . . .*), ed. John Butt, 1939; revised edition 1961.

[4] Milgate, *ed. cit.*, p. 149.

he will not be shaken off, causes the speaker to sweat with exasperation, and feel like a fool and a beast of burden. In each poem almost all the speaker says is an attempt to get rid of his unwelcome companion. In each poem a crowd fills the scene as the speaker is finally free.

Once these common features have been recognised, the many significant differences of Donne from Horace may be seen more clearly. Firstly, his method is different. Horace's art in *Sat.* I. ix is above all concise. It is a model of expressive brevity. And because both narrative and dialogue are pared down to their essentials the overall shape of the encounter is made very clear. As several critics have intimated, the poem is a drama on a small scale.[1] With great skill Horace plays on his hopes of escape. Ordinary pretexts (the sick friend) fail, and the first stage ends when he droops his ears like a sullen ass under a heavy load (20-1). The second stage reveals that the Talker seeks Horace's friendship and ends with the dashing of the latter's hope that the Talker would leave him to attend his case in the law court. The third and final stage then reveals that the Talker's real purpose is to get an introduction to Maecenas, whose character and household he vulgarly misunderstands. The Talker is, in effect, a would-be courtier, in the worst sense of the word. Peripeteia is introduced when Horace's friend, Aristius Fuscus, appears but refuses to save him from the Talker. This is the cruelly comic climax of the satire, immediately following which the Talker is arrested (an outcome prepared for by the legal incident at the centre of the poem), and Horace is released: 'sic me servavit Apollo'.[2] By contrast, Donne's approach to his subject is copious and exuberant. We have already seen how two words of Horace ('docti sumus') release a small fountain of comic invention in Jonson's *Poetaster*. Donne's comedy is more grotesque and dark than Jonson's but the same fertile amplification of Horace is to be seen in *Satyre IV*. Thus Donne does not start into his story, but opens with a long preamble of explosive exasperation, during the course of which a half-line ('Yet went to Court') is allowed

[1] See Eduard Fraenkel, *Horace*, 1957, pp. 113-16; Niall Rudd, *The Satires of Horace*, 1966, p. 75.

[2] I follow Rudd's analysis, *The Satires of Horace*, pp. 75-6.

to set the scene. The first introduction of Donne's Courtier-Talker –

> Towards me did runne
> A thing more strange, then on Niles slime, the Sunne
> E'r bred; . . .   (17-19)

introduces no fewer than nine comparisons to convey his strangeness, and Donne launches into a denunciation of his speech before it has actually begun. The same is true of Donne's handling of the dialogue. Donne introduces a dialogue of deliberate cross-purpose, which may perhaps be seen as an extravagant comic distortion of the one interruption and change-of-subject in Horace:

> ' "invideat quod et Hermogenes, ego canto."
> Interpellandi locus hic erat: "est tibi mater,
> cognati, quis te salvo est opus?" '[1]

Characteristically, Donne uses the device not once but several times.

Donne also introduces fundamental changes into the situation of Horace's satire. While these involve naturalising his original in Donne's country and time, they go much beyond this. The Via Sacra has become the court of Queen Elizabeth. The Talker has explicitly become also a courtier, or at least a pretender to being one. Furthermore the whole theme of Maecenas and his household, which might well seem the heart of Horace's poem, has been dropped. Not only is there no parallel in *Satyre IV*, but Donne has almost reversed the positions. Thus Horace is secure in the good opinion of the noble Maecenas, an opinion which the poem encourages us to see as the just view of a disinterested as well as influential man. By this token Horace's moral and social situation is guaranteed. The Talker, on the other hand, is outside this security, and the clumsiness with which he attempts to break in only emphasises his remoteness from it. In *Satyre IV*, by contrast, the Talker is the one to be, or at least pretend to be, thoroughly conversant with the centre of power, the court, while Donne is the conscious outsider:

---

[1] *Sat.* I. ix. 25-7: ' "Even Hermogenes might envy my singing." This was the place to break in. "Have you a mother or relations dependent on your welfare?" '

He adds, 'If of court life you knew the good,
You would leave lonenesse.' I said, 'Not alone
My lonenesse is.'   (66-88)

In keeping with these changes, Donne has given the conversation of his Talker a marked political aspect:

More then ten Hollensheads, or Halls, or Stowes,
Of triviall houshold trash he knowes; He knowes
When the Queene frown'd, or smil'd, and he knowes what
A subtle States-man may gather of that;   (97-100)[1]

Here it is possible that Donne is reaching behind Horace to the two Characters of Talkers in Theophrastus: ὁ ἀδολέσχης and ὁ λάλος.[2] Theophrastus's ὁ λάλος (Rudd translates as: 'The Loquacious Man') is full of news of the Assembly, reminiscences of speeches made there, including his own important oratorical efforts, and of tirades against "the masses".'[3]

Perhaps Donne's most important change, however, concerns the treatment of the law. In Horace's satire the law combines with the good opinion of Maecenas in guaranteeing the poet's fundamental security. In the middle of the poem it is suggested that the leechlike Talker may have been guilty of some misdemeanour. It is his failure to answer bail which causes his arrest, and the liberation of Horace, at the end. As Niall Rudd points out, the world of law mediates between the immediate

---

[1] Cf. also 119-26.

[2] In the notes to his edition of Horace, *Horatii Flacci Opera Omnia* . . ., Paris 1604, Theodorus Marcilius was to refer to these Characters of Theophrastus in connection with the *garrulus* of *Sat.* I. ix; see pp. 95-9. An edition of Theophrastus, including these Characters, and with a Latin translation, had appeared in 1527, another in 1531; and in 1592 the first of the three editions of Isaac Casaubon (see R. C. Jebb, *The Characters of Theophrastus* . . ., 1870; new edition by J. E. Sandys, 1909, pp. 164-5). The similarities to Horace's *garrulus* are fairly striking, apart from the general probability of Theophrastan influence on Donne. It is also probable that Donne knew, through his early friend Sir Henry Wotton, of Casaubon's preparation of the important edition of Theophrastus which he published in 1598, since Wotton had stayed with Casaubon in Geneva in 1593-4 (see R. C. Bald, *John Donne: A Life*, 1970, p. 284 note 1). Donne's explicitly Theophrastan *True Character of a Dunce* was to be published in Overbury's *Wife* in 1622.

[3] Jebb, *ed. cit.*, pp. 105-6. I am grateful to Mr I. P. Davies, of Jesus College, Cambridge, for his advice concerning this passage, and Theophrastus generally.

realm of the dialogue, and the more distant one of heroic
warfare recalled for us through metaphor and diction. It is
through the instrumentality of the law that Apollo saves Horace.[1]
There has certainly been the undercurrent of something
frightening in Horace's utter inability to shake off his unwelcome
companion; and there is, at the end, a powerful sense of renewed
security as he is saved through the public operations of his own
society. The world is, after all, an ordered and reasonable place.
These important features of Horace's story have no parallel
in Donne. The law certainly plays a part in *Satyre IV* – but of
a very different kind. It is introduced, in the preamble, by an
apparently tangential comparison: Donne's going to court and
suffering for it,

> as Glaze which did goe
> To'a Masse in jest, catch'd, was faine to disburse
> The hundred markes, which is the Statutes curse,
> Before he scapt . . .   (8-11)

The sardonic humour of this seems to focus chiefly on Glaze,
who recalls Donne's list of the ecclesiastically misled in *Satyre
III*. It is, however, important that Donne himself is here, though
only by analogy, made to seem vulnerable to the law. The theme
is picked up again when the Courtier-Talker, 'like a priviledg'd
spie', libels the conduct of the government in every aspect:

> I more amas'd then Circes prisoners, when
> They felt themselves turne beasts, felt my selfe then
> Becomming Traytor, and mee thought I saw
> One of our Giant Statutes ope his jaw
> To sucke me in;   (129-134)

At the end of the encounter with the Talker, Donne runs from
court as one 'Who feares more actions, doth make from prison'
and this seems to link with the 'Low feare' concerning which
Donne communes with himself in the lines which connect the
first half of *Satyre IV* with the more visionary view of the court
in the second half. Even through this vision we find the theme
continued, for here a gallant *protests* to a lady so much as would
have had him arrested and thrown to the Inquisition at Rome;
and swears so often 'by Jesu' that 'A/Pursevant would have

---

[1] Rudd, *The Satires of Horace*, p. 80.

ravish'd him away/For saying of our Ladies psalter' (212-17).
When Donne finally leaves the Court, he goes 'As men
which from gaoles to'execution goe' and, passing the Yeoman
of the Guard, shakes with fear 'like a spyed Spie' (230-8).
Throughout *Satyre IV* Donne emphasises his sense of funda-
mental insecurity. This is conveyed partly through intimations
that the Courtier-Talker is not what he seems (the opening
description likens him to a Jesuit in disguise; while the 'priv-
iledg'd spie' passage suggests he may be leading Donne on to
betray himself), but chiefly through the constant assumption
that the law is an enemy rather than a friend. The reversal of
the Horatian picture could not be more striking and, in view of
the echoes of Horace, *Sat* I. ix, cannot but have been deliberate
on Donne's part.

Horace's satire is autobiographical in the subtly artificial
way also to be found in the satires and epistles of Pope. It may
be that, in recognising the fearful attitude towards the law in
Satyre IV, we have come up against a fact of Donne's biography,
as well as a more general response to the time. It has been
suggested that Donne's satires express, if somewhat covertly,
something of the viewpoint of a Roman Catholic.[1] Born and
brought up in this religion, Donne was still a Catholic in 1591,
but probably not when he joined the Cadiz Expedition in 1596.[2]
It was probably between these dates that Donne undertook his
examination of the *Disputationes* of Cardinal Bellarmine, 'the
best defender of the *Roman Cause*'.[3] *Satyre III* (*c.* 1594-5)
may well seem the outcome of Donne's personal bid to 'Seeke
true religion', and while it would be wrong to interpret
Mirreus in that poem as a satire on the genuinely convinced
Roman Catholic, such a Catholic might seem unlikely to have
written the poem. *Satyre IV* has many Catholic references, but
they are not all pro-Catholic and, whether pro or con, are often
balanced by Protestant references.[4] If Donne is not writing as a
Catholic, this does not mean that he is writing as if he had never
been one. He was himself to testify, in his *Pseudo-Martyr* (1610)

[1] By H. J. C. Grierson; see Bald, *op. cit.*, p. 70.
[2] Bald, *op. cit.*, p. 63; Milgate, *ed. cit.*, p. 139.   [3] Bald, *op. cit.*, pp. 68-72.
[4] Cf. 8-11, 241-4 with 47-8, 200-3. Some such references are balanced in close
pairs, eg. 55-7 and 212-18.

with what gradual deliberation he had moved away from
the Roman faith (no 'violent and sudden determination');
and several commentators have observed how a Catholic
awareness remained as part of his total awareness, for many
years.[1] What is important here is Donne's experience of being
a Catholic in a Protestant state, a member of a Church whose
practices were forbidden by law. Donne's own brother had been
arrested and imprisoned, in 1593, having been discovered with
a priest in his chambers. The priest was condemned to death,
hanged, drawn and quartered. Henry Donne died of the plague
in Newgate.[2] Donne's references to 'the Statutes curse' and the
'Giant Statutes' are sufficiently intelligible in this context, and
we may note that at l. 216 an early MS. reads: 'Topcliff would
have ravish'd him away/For saying our Ladies psalter', Richard
Topcliff being the notorious priest-hunter, whose chief colleague
had been responsible for the arrest of Henry Donne and his
priest.[3] No such references are to be found in the free imitation
of Horace, *Sat.* I. ix, published by Mathurin Régnier in 1608.
His satire is thoroughly Christian and Catholic, the Talker
saluting his victim while the latter is on his knees at mass, but
retains the Horation conclusion in which the satirist is saved by
the law.[4] Doubtless Donne was not much less ready to allude to
his Catholic background, in a Protestant state, than Horace to
refer to his relation with Maecenas. Yet this should not be
allowed to support an unduly restricted reading of *Satyre IV.*
Of the five references in the poem which express fear of the
law only two are explicitly linked with anti-Catholic legislation.[5]
What, by contrast with Horace and Régnier, this poem urges
upon us is the experience of fearing an unjust force in the law
and operations of the established state.

[1] Bald, *op. cit.*, p. 67. And see, for example, E. M. Simpson, *The Courtier's
Library by John Donne*, 1930, p. 12: 'The tone of the Catalogue is indeed more
anti-Protestant than we might expect from the date [c. 1603-11?] which I have
assigned to it.' Her conclusion that Donne's Papist sympathies lingered on to
some degree (pp. 12-13) seems a fair one, though here too a balance is struck by
Donne.

[2] Bald, *op. cit.*, p. 58.   [3] Milgate, *ed. cit.*, p. 162; Bald, *op. cit.*, p. 58.

[4] Régnier, Satyre VIII, 1-12, 211-24; Mathurin Régnier, *Oeuvres Complètes;*
Edition critiques publiée par Gabriel Raibaud, 1958, pp. 80-90.

[5] 8-11, 215-17.

The remaining differences of Donne from Horace, in the first half of *Satyre IV*, are in accord with the intention and tone we have already noticed. The Sabine woman's prophecy of Horace's death from a Talker – a piece of stately mock-heroic – is dropped; so is the appearance of Horace's friend near the end of the encounter; and Donne finally gets rid of his Courtier-Talker in a shabbily ordinary way: the latter asks him for money, and the poet gives him a crown in ransom. By comparison with Horace this is a most anti-climactic ending to the encounter, but it is right, for two reasons. The asking for money is a derisive comment on the Courtier's earlier invitation to Donne to enjoy 'the good' of court life; and Donne is, unlike Horace, preparing for a different kind of climax after the encounter is over. That climax is to arise from the poet's regaining his 'wholesome solitarinesse' after the exasperation and fear of the encounter; the appearance of some 'Fuscus Aristius . . . mihi carus', however unsympathetic to the poet's plight, would have broken this necessary contrast. And indeed the episodes of Fuscus Aristius and the Sabine woman show that for Horace comedy goes almost to the heart of his situation; with Donne it is much more on the surface. Régnier was to introduce the prophecy of 'une Bohemienne' into his satire with propriety; in *Satyre IV* it would have been an intrusion.

What then is Donne's final attitude to his Courtier-Talker? Is it the rather resolute laughter recommended in his Paradox X: That a Wise Man is Known by Much Laughing?

A *fool* if he come into a *Princes Court*, and see a *gay* man leaning at the wall, so *glistering*, and so *painted* in many *colours* that he is hardly discerned from one of the *Pictures* in the *Arras* hanging, his *body* like an *Iron-bound chest*, girt in and thick *ribb'd* with *broad gold laces*, may (and commonly doth) envy him. But alas! shall a *wise man*, which may not only not *envy*, but not *pitty* this *Monster*, do nothing? Yes, let him *laugh*.[1]

---

[1] John Hayward, *ed. cit.*, p. 344. Wilbur Sanders discusses the *Paradoxes and Problemes* in connection with the *Satyres*, in Ch. 2 of his book *John Donne's Poetry*, 1971. I think there is a particularly close relation between Paradox X and *Satyre IV*, but that thei nsights of the poem are nevertheless more complex than those of the Paradox.

The close connection of this Paradox with *Satyre IV* is not to be doubted. Yet Donne's attitude in the poem, though it partakes of the wise laughter of the Paradox, is much more complicated. The opening description, though to the effect that the Courtier is a '*Monster*', conjures up through its exuberant amplification more fantastic shapes even than the Paradox – shapes whose appropriateness in the poem becomes clear in the second half. When Donne makes his Courtier praise 'your Apostles' as 'Good pretty linguists', he gives us something which invites sardonic ridicule, but a tremendous undercurrent of indignation is felt at the same time. Something of the same complexity is found in Donne's magnificent repartee (though here the patronising tones of the Courtier are not, as in Pope, present to provoke anger):

> . . . I was faine to say, 'If you'had liv'd, Sir,
> Time enough to have beene Interpreter
> To Babells bricklayers, sure the Tower had stood.'
>
> (63-5)

The comic extravagance of this conception also sizes up the Courtier effectively in Biblical terms; it tells us, perhaps, that he is not altogether a creature to be dismissed with a laugh. Once the initial exchanges are over, his conversation is by no means unmitigated nonsense. 'When the Queene frown'd, or smil'd, and . . . what/A subtle States-man may gather of that', in the atmosphere of this poem, is not altogether 'triviall houshold trash' and his subsequent remarks are in themselves so clearly a satire on court corruption that we are not surprised to notice the tones of Donne eventually taking over:

> He knowes who loves; whom; and who by poyson
> Hasts to an Offices reversion;
> He knowes who'hath sold his land, and now doth beg
> A licence, old iron, bootes, shooes, and egge-
> shels to transport; Shortly boyes shall not play
> At span-counter, or blow-point, but they pay
> Toll to some Courtier;   (101-7)

That outrageous *enjambement* expresses the very acme of in-credulous contempt – but whether for court gossip, or court abuse, it is hard to say. Certainly the lines have modulated into a comment by Donne at the end. It might seem that in these lines Donne recklessly takes over the Courtier's conversation as a vehicle for his satire on the court – and that that is all. But this is not so, for the subjects of the Courtier's discourse here point unmistakably ahead to the passage in which, 'like a priviledg'd spie' he libels the whole government, and terrifies his listener at the implications of the situation. There is just enough method in the Courtier's conversation to suggest that he may not be altogether what he seems; it is hinted that he talks like an intelligencer, and there the matter is left, most disturbingly and, in view of the sense of danger Donne wishes to create, most successfully, undefined. The situation is consistently dramatic. Neither in the poem, nor, at this time perhaps, in real life, has Donne the security of the mere commentator: the wise man who can just laugh. The exuberant comedy is in dialogue with fear.

III

It is fear which is the theme of the soliloquy to which the satire now mounts. Donne now takes his leave of Horace, *Sat.* I. ix and, given his own very different treatment of its basic situation, it is easy to see why *Satyre IV* had to continue, though Horace had solved all *his* problems with the arrest of the Talker. The somewhat anti-climactic passing of money, which ended Donne's encounter, by no means dispelled the exasperation and fear to which it had given rise, and the general sense of danger with which the writing of poetry about the court had so often been associated in sixteenth- and late fifteenth-century England. We remember Skelton, newly embarked on the 'goodly' ship 'Bouge of Court', confronted by 'Favell, full of flattery,/With fables false that well could feign a tale;' and 'Suspect, which that daily/Misdeemed each man, with face deadly and pale'.[1] Wyatt in his important and successful First Satire ('Myne owne John Poynz . . .'), while in no way scorning 'The powar of them, to whome fortune hath lent/Charge over vs, of Right, to strike the stroke', could still say: 'I am not he that can alow the state/Off highe Cesar and dam Cato to dye,' who 'wolld not lyve whar

---

[1] *The Complete Poems of John Skelton, Laureate,* ed. Philip Henderson (1931), 1948, p. 41.

lyberty was lost'; and could oppose to the values of the court
those of his personal 'libertie', retired 'in Kent and Christen-
dome'.[1] In the 1563 edition of *The Mirror for Magistrates*
appeared the plea of the unhappy poet Collingbourne:

> I thought the freedome of the auncient tymes
> Stoode styll in force. *Ridentem dicere verum*
> *Quis vetat?* . . .
>
> Belyke no Tyrantes were in Horace dayes,
> And therefore Poetes freely blamed vyce.
> Witnes theyr Satyr sharpe, and tragicke playes . . .[2]

But three years later, in the prefatory matter of Drant's
Medicinable Morall, the perennial ideal was reaffirmed:

> The Satyrist loues Truthe, none more than he.
> An utter foe to fraude in eache degree.[3]

A simultaneous awareness of this danger and this challenge
powers Donne's passage of soliloquy:

> At home in wholesome solitarinesse
> My precious soule began, the wretchednesse
> Of suiters at court to mourne, and a trance
> Like his, who dreamt he saw hell, did advance
> It selfe on mee; Such men as he saw there,
> I saw at court, and worse, and more; Low feare
> Becomes the guiltie, not th'accuser; Then,
> Shall I, nones slave, of high borne, or rais'd men
> Feare frownes? And, my Mistresse Truth, betray thee
> To th'huffing braggart, puft Nobility?
> No, no, Thou which since yesterday hast beene
> Almost about the whole world, hast thou seene.
> O Sunne, in all thy journey, Vanitie,
> Such as swells the bladder of our court?   (155-68)

---

[1] 7-9, 37-41, 80-5, 100-3; *The Collected Poems of Sir Thomas Wyatt*, ed. Kenneth
Muir, 1949, pp. 185-7.

[2] 'Howe Collingbourne was cruelly executed for making a foolish rime', 96-101;
The Mirror for Magistrates, ed. Lily B. Campbell (1938), 1960, pp. 350-1.
Pope knew *The Mirror for Magistrates* (see Owen Ruffhead's *Life of Pope*, 1769,
p. 425) and was to refer to the story of Collingbourne, and also to statutes
of Edward VI and Elizabeth, when he in his turn came to discuss the dangers
of writing satire: The First Satire of the Second Book of Horace (*To Fortescue*),
145-9.   [3] To the Reader.

This 'wholesome solitarinesse', prepared for, indeed longed for, in Donne's cryptic remark to the Courtier: 'Not alone/My lonenesse is', with its allusion to Cicero on the retirement of Scipio Africanus, comes with immense relief after the almost intolerable pressure of the court encounter. Yet in the freedom of this respite the mind returns again to the experience, this time fully mastering it, through the allusion to Dante, and suffusing it with an infernal hue. We may recall an entry in Donne's *Catalogus Librorum*: 'The Quintessence of Hell; or, The private apartment of Hell, in which is a discussion of the fifth region passed over by Homer, Virgil, Dante and the rest of the Papists, where, over and above the penalties and sensations of the damned, Kings are tortured by a recollection of the past'.[1] There is a comic ambiguity in this compared with the boldness and plainness of the declaration he makes in the satire:

> Such men as he saw there,
> I saw at court, and worse, and more;

which the poem's mode of sardonic exaggeration should not persuade us to pass over lightly. In the 'wholesome solitarinesse' of his retirement the moral and religious realities triumph over the temporal ones, and therefore over 'Low feare'. From this conviction springs the satirist's heroic dedication of himself to Truth despite the consequences, the emotion of which is utterly different from anything to be found in Horace, *Sat.* I. ix, though it has some affinities with the conclusion of *Sat.* II. i. The need and the energy for this dedication has, through Donne's different treatment of the situation of Horace, *Sat.* I. ix, been building up from the very beginning of *Satyre IV*. This is the centre and the climax of the poem, and is most like the 'Tragical' mode of satire already achieved by Donne in *Satyre III*. From this point the tone begins to descend once more, with the emphasis falling again on hollowness and vanity; scorn and ridicule, major weapons in Donne's satiric armoury in the first half of the poem, now come back into their own. But this central withdrawal and affirmation, which has drawn together all the leading *motifs* in the reflections upon court satire of Skelton,

[1] No. 30, *ed. cit.*, p. 52. Other entries in *Catalogus Librorum* relate to the *Satyres*, e.g. No. 13 with *Satyre II*, 91-6, and, more generally, No. 22 with *Satyre III*.

Wyatt, the *Mirror for Magistrates* author, and Drant, has structured Donne's poem, and given us, in dramatic fashion, intimations of that source of dedication and defiance which animates much of the finest satire between the Roman Lucilius and the English Pope.

'Tis ten a clock and past . . .' (175) returns us to the court. It is hard, on the level of strict literal interpretation, to tell whether what now follows is a continuation of that 'trance/Like his, who dreamt he saw hell' which has been so crucial to Donne's satiric resolve. I am inclined to think that it is, and that the intervening lines between that and this point are another example of the eager self-anticipation, with which, at the beginning of the poem, Donne described the manner and matter of the Courtier's speech before he gave us his opening remark. Certainly once the infernal comparison has been made it is hard to forget, and this is the most important point. The comparison links readily with certain details in the latter part of the poem: 'As if the Presence were a Moschite . . .', '. . . his face be'as ill/As theirs which in old hangings whip Christ . . .', '. . . through the great chamber (why is it hung/With the seaven deadly sinnes?)' (199, 225-6, 231-2). Perhaps, the answer is implied, because this is like Hell. Perhaps that quality of the grotesque/fantastic, in the appearance of the original Courtier –

> A thing more strange, then on Niles slime, the Sunne
> E'r bred;

– not to mention Macrine, Glorius, and the giant Askaparts, is consonant with the same trancelike effect.

However the chief logic relating this part of *Satyre IV* to the earlier part is one of expansion. At first an individual encounter with a courtier is almost too much for the satirist, and at the sudden sight of 'All the court fill'd with more strange things then hee' he flies. After self-communing in 'wholesome solitarinesse', he is able, either literally or more probably in vision, to return and confront a full gathering of courtiers in the Presence Chamber. His renewed fortitude is not, however, a simple heroic defiance. This indeed comes first, in the central passage of soliloquy, but hard on the heels of his resolution comes a supporting – in the circumstances almost a comforting –

conviction of the essential hollowness of the court. 'High borne, or rais'd men' are succeeded, if not replaced, in his awareness by 'th'huffing braggart, puft Nobility'. The stress on hollowness stretches quite far into the satire's second description of the court, and Donne's gift for remarks of sardonic realism, already deployed against the courtier, is an effective satirical resource here:

> 'For a King
> Those hose are,' cry the flatterers; And bring
> Them next weeke to the Theatre to sell;　　(181-3)

Indeed Donne's 'All are players' is a limiting judgement, lacking the philosophical resonance this famous metaphor has in More's *Utopia*, or in (the perhaps roughly contemporaneous) *As You Like It*, not to mention the forthcoming *Macbeth*. The figures of the court, at this point, are grotesque, jerking puppets. So absurd are they that even Heraclitus would laugh. Yet this reference to the Weeping Philosopher suggests an underlying conflict which is for the moment being resolutely simplified. We are reminded, as we were at the opening of *Satyre III*, of laughter and tears, the alternative attitudes to sin. In Drant 'not a thousand *Democrati*, coulde suffice to laugh' at fools that have been praised and revered, 'nor a thousand *Heracliti* be enough to wepe' at wise men discredited and prophaned.[1] Donne's resolution in Paradox X ('*Democritus* and *Heraclitus*, the *lovers* of these *Extreams*, have been called *lovers of Wisdom*. Now among our *wise men*, I doubt not but many would be found, who would laugh at *Heraclitus* weeping, none which weep at *Democritus* laughing') is further condensed at this point in *Satyre IV*.[2] The *picture* of Macrine is absurd enough to make even Heraclitus laugh; the infidel associations which are stressed immediately after ('As if the Presence were a Moschite . . .') tell us that this laughter is almost inseparable from weeping at sin.

From this point the sense of fear and horror begins to make itself felt once again. Laughter at the absurd 'protests protests protests', in the paying court to the ladies, is of no easily secure kind when followed so promptly by references to Roman

---

[1] Drant, *op. cit.*, To the Reader.
[2] John Hayward, *ed. cit.*, pp. 343-4.

Inquisitors and Elizabethan pursuivants. The portrait of Glorius, related to the *'firebrand'* of Paradox X as the Courtier is to the *'gay* man . . . *glistering,* and . . . *painted'*;

> if one of these *hot cholerick firebrands,* which nourish themselves by *quarrelling,* and kindling others, spit upon a *fool* one *sparke of disgrace,* he, like a *thatcht house* quickly burning, may be *angry* . . .[1]

is done with an especially appropriate defiant vigour:

> But here comes Glorius that will plague them both
> Who, in the other extreme, only doth
> Call a rough carelessenesse, good fashion;
> Whose cloak his spurres teare; whom he spits on
> He cares not; His ill words doe no harme
> To him; he rusheth in, as if 'Arme, arme,'
> He meant to crie. And though his face be'as ill
> As theirs which in old hangings whip Christ, yet still
> He strives to looke worse, he keepes all in awe;
> Jeasts like a licenc'd foole, commands like law.
>
> (219-28)

Glorius, by comparison with the summarised satiric *type* in the Paradox, is a dramatic presence; Donne's style seems to emulate 'a rough carelessenesse' here, though in fact his control is sure. The phrase 'good fashion' takes its quiet stand at the end of the third line to create a symmetry of opposites, and this sense of balance within vehement movement assures us of the continuance of Donne's judgment. But what the satire perceives morally is brilliantly conveyed in the visual detail which follows ('Whose cloak his spurres teare . . .') which at once enforces the judgment and renders the figure of Glorius immediate to the eye. A familiar balance and control may be seen in the whole portrait. On the one hand there is a reckless bravura of description (' . . . as if "Arme, arme,"/He meant to crie . . .'); on the other, the pattern of the verse, frequently through skilful use of *enjambement,* keeps some disturbing recognitions in reserve. The manner of the contemptuous satirist seems well away with 'His ill words doe no harme', but is sharply qualified by '/To *him'* (my italics), while the lurid and macabre comparison with those who 'in old hangings whip Christ', which we

---

[1] *Ibid.,* p. 344.

have already seen to add to the infernal atmosphere, is similarly followed up by: ' . . . yet still/He strives to look worse . . .'. There is here a strange mingling of hyperbolic sarcasm and the sense of evil. The most disturbing touch of all, however, is undoubtedly the end, where another strongly symmetrical line, promising a powerful and well-rounded conclusion, associates with this barbarian, by its last word, all that sense of danger from the law which this satire has cumulatively built up.

'Tyr'd, now I leave this place' (229) marks not the end but the final intensification of the nightmare. Deadly sins loom from the walls, the guards stand like giants, massive in their loyalty to a sovereign whose power is not less dreadful if she has herself been absent from the vision of the court which the satirist has rendered. Amid the *grotesque* of the nightmare, the note of confidence just advances once more, as the 'Askaparts' become 'barrells of beefe, flaggons of wine', but then the *motif* of danger, fear and the sense of guilt felt if unearned, a *motif* which has run through the satire, is stressed for the last time:

> I shooke like a spyed Spie . . .　　　　　(237)

It is in this context, I think, that the conclusion of the satire must be read. Confident and powerful judgment upon the court, vehement and energetic ridicule, are one side only of the satirist's human response. Fear, whether, as in the central soliloquy of the satire, 'Low', or as here at the end, justified and religious, has been equally if not more emphasised, has mingled with the wit, hyperbole and exaggeration, and is the other side. This is the development, in *Satyre IV*, of those antitheses of laughter and tears which conflicted at the opening of *Satyre III*, and which had been set out schematically by Drant. The concluding appeal that 'Preachers' rather than satirists should 'Drowne the sinnes of this place' (237-41) is thus something more than the boyish 'hot flush of modest sanctimony' which a recent critic has found it, just as the poem to this point has been more than '240-odd lines . . . passionately denouncing that bladder swollen with vanity, the Court . . .'.[1] Not only has the satire been much more complex than this judgment allows but

---

[1] Sanders, *op. cit.*, p. 36.

its conclusion marks the completion of an expressive structure. Donne has dramatised a double-exposure to the court, divided by a passage of self-communing which regenerates his moral strength for the second bout, but concluded by the overcoming both of his erected wit and his moral resolution to withstand.[1] In the fiction of the satire, the satirist passes his pen and his scourge over to the divine. This is his final taking of the moral measure of the court. The tone, with its '*Macchabees* modestie' (242), now becomes one of controlled understatement. The final allusion, at once a graceful disclaimer of merit, an acknowledgement that his subject has in a sense been too much for him, a delicate reminder of Papist and Protestant differences, and suggestion that his views as those of a one-time Papist are urged with diffidence, nevertheless lays its chief stress on the inconspicuous but firm contention that it is the truth which the satirist has told.

IV

Many English translations and imitations of Horace, *Sat.* I. ix, appeared between the last decade of the sixteenth century and the first decade of the eighteenth century, but none so bold, extravagant and significant an adaptation as Donne's *Satyre IV*. One work stands out, however, partly because of intrinsic interest, partly because Pope commended it, and recalled it when he came to write his verson of Donne's poem. This is John Oldham's *Imitation of Horace. Book I. – Satire IX*.[2] Oldham's poem is a genuine imitation. It follows the outline of Horace's story, ending where Horace did, and embodies all its major features. On the other hand the rendering is free in points of detail, including passages for which there is no parallel in Horace, and the situation has been transposed to the London

---

[1] Sanders' view (*op. cit.*, p. 39) that: 'Satirical activity of this kind . . . can have no structure beyond the episodic. . . . Most of the *Satyres* go on too long . . .' is, I think, questionable in general, but certainly wrong in respect of *Satyre IV*.

[2] Pope marked his approval of this satire in his copy of *Oldham's Works*, 1679-93 now in the British Museum (pressmark: C. 45. q. l) calling it one of 'The Most Remarkable Works in this Author'; and he echoed 16-17 of it ('. . . wild to get loose . . .') at the parallel point of his imitation of *Satyre IV* of Donne (116-17)

of 1681: the Mall, Westminster Hall, Rochester recently dead,
and the Popish Plot crisis just dying down. The Plot is in fact
the subject of some of the most interesting lines:

> Next he begins to plague me with the plot,
> Asks, whether I were known to Oates or not?
> 'Not I, thank Heaven! I no priest have been;
> Have never Douay, nor St. Omer seen.'
> 'What think you, sir; will they the Joiner try?
> Will he die, think you?' 'Yes, most certainly.'
> 'I mean, be hanged.' 'Would thou wert so,' wished I!
> Religion came in next, though he'd no more
> Than the noble peer, his punk, or confessor.
> 'Oh! the sad times, if once the king should die!
> Sir, are you not afraid of popery?'
> 'No more than my superiors: why should I?
> Come popery, come anything,' thought I,
> So heaven would bless me to get rid of thee!
> But 'tis some comfort that my hell is here . . .[1]

It is convincing that this, more than topics of poetry and music,
represented the current talk of the town. Furthermore the con-
versation of the Talker is doubly unwelcome here because it is
dangerous. The Talker asks politically leading questions, and
the satirist, having spotted and avoided the trap in the first ('I
no priest have been . . .') is soon confronted, at that precarious
turning-point in British politics when support for the succession
of the Catholic Duke of York was beginning to rally, with a trap
of the opposite kind ('Sir, are you not afraid of popery?'). The
evasiveness of his answer only stresses the danger. It is interes-
ting that an English imitator of Horace, *Sat.* I. ix has again
responded to the Roman poem in a political way, and has under-
lined Horace's extreme discomfort and exasperation with the
Talker by adding to it the sense of insecurity and danger. This
may suggest that Oldham knew *Satyre IV* (last republished in
the 1669 edition of Donne's poems) and there are other signs
in the passage quoted (the wilful misunderstanding of the

---

[1] *An Imitation of Horace. Book I. – Satire IX*, 106-20; *Poems of John Oldham*,
intro. Bonamy Dobrée, 1960, pp. 137-8 (not a complete or entirely reliable
edition, but the only modern one available).

question about College, the Protestant joiner; the declaration in the last line that 'my hell is here') that this was so.[1] But whether Oldham remembered Donne or not, his poem can only have contributed to Pope's awareness of how the imitation of Horace, *Sat.* I. ix might be turned to political ends.

It is this point which ought first to be borne in mind when we ask the question: why, in 1733, did Pope choose to imitate Donne's *Satyre IV* when he might, had he so wished have included a direct version of Horace, *Sat.* I. ix among his current *Imitations of Horace?* Pope's reasons are intimated in the Horatian epigraph he chose for his versions of Donne:

> Quid vetat, ut nosmet Lucili scripta legentes
> Quærere, num illius, num rerum dura negarit
> Versiculos natura magis factos, & euntes
> Mollius?[2]

These lines from Horace, *Sat.* I. x suggests to the reader that the relation between Horace and the earlier Roman satirist Lucilius, and that between Pope and Donne, are intended to be seen in parallel. This, coupled with the fact that much of what Horace says about Lucilius consists of praise for his wit and blame for his rough versification and poor craftmanship, has encouraged critical investigation of the more technical differences and similarities between Donne's satires and Pope's imitations of them. Attention has been paid particularly to rough and smooth rhythm, open and closed couplets, the nature and

---

[1] It is interesting that Donne's *Ignatius His Conclave* (1611) was republished (in the original Latin) in 1680, at the height of the anti-Jesuit *furore* of the Popish Plot crisis, shortly after the publication of the first, and apparently after the composition of all, of Oldham's own celebrated *Satires Upon the Jesuits* (1679, 1681). This might have prompted Oldham to look at Donne's *Satyres*.

[2] Pope, *Imitations of Horace, ed. cit.*, pp. 23, 129 (Horace, *Sat.* I. x. 56-9): 'And as we read the writings of Lucilius, what forbids us, too, to ask whether it was himself, or the harsh nature of his material, that denied him more finished and smoother verses?' On Pope's idea of Donne as an English Lucilius, see Pope, *Horatian Satires and Epistles*, ed. H. H. Erskine-Hill, 1964, pp. 14-17. The second half of the present essay is an expanded version of what was first suggested there.

handling of images.[1] There is, however, another aspect of the Lucilius-Donne parallel which was, if anything, more important to Pope. The poem which Pope published immediately before his version of *Satyre IV* was his imitation of Horace, *Sat.* II. i. In this satire Horace praised Lucilius for his bold attack upon vice in high places. When Pope comes to render the lines in which this tribute occurs, he departs from the procedure of Horace and assumes the role of Lucilius himself.[2] Horace, *Sat.* II. i, together with Pope's imitation, tells us that if indeed Pope sees Donne as the Lucilius to his Horace, it is as much because he admired Donne's daring and dedication to truth, as because he longed to polish his rough numbers.

Pope's purpose in seeking to command and redirect the moral qualities of *Satyre IV* may be seen from the sub-title he gave his imitation, when it first appeared late in 1733: *The Impertinent, Or a Visit to the Court . . .* [3] Pope could find a pattern in Horace

---

[1] See Ian Jack's valuable essay 'Pope and "The Weighty Bullion of Dr Donne's Satires" ', PMLA, 66, 1951, pp. 1009-22; and, for a somewhat different approach, A. C. Bross, 'Alexander Pope's Revisions of John Donne's *Satyres*', *Xavier University Studies*, 5, 3, 1966, 133-52. When, in 1735, Pope published his versions of Donne's *Satyre II* and *Satyre IV* together, he invited detailed comparison by printing his original alongside them. Pope's text of Donne diverges from all previous editions (except, possibly, the rare 1649 edition, which I have been unable to check). It seems probable that Pope constructed his own critical text of the satires concerned, as we know he did with the Horatian originals which he printed alongside his imitations (see Lillian Bloom, 'Pope as Textual Critic: A Bibliographical Study of his Horatian Text', *Journal of English and Germanic Philology*, Vol. 47, 1948, pp. 150-55).

[2] Horace, *Sat.* II. i. 62-79; The First Satire of the Second Book of Horace (*To Fortescue*), 105-42.

[3] That Pope should have originally called his poem *The Impertinent* suggests he was well aware of the Latin text behind *Satyre IV*. This term seems first to have been applied to Horace's *garrulus*, in English translations of *Sat.* I. ix, by Alexander Brome, who entitled his version: 'A description of an impertinent prating Fool' (*The Poems of Horace . . . Rendred into English Verse by Several Persons*, 1666, p. 227). Creech followed: 'The Description of an Impertinent Fop . . .' (Thomas Creech, *The Odes, Satyrs, and Epistles of Horace. Done into English*, 1684, p. 410); so did Dunster: 'The Description of an Impertinent' (S. Dunster, *The Satires and Epistles of Horace, Done into English . . .*, 1709, p. 95). Pope himself, in the MS. note in his copy of *Oldham's Works*, refers to Oldham's version as 'The Impertinent from Hor. Sat. 9 lib. 1'. Other relevant uses of the term 'Impertinent' may be found in Thomas Shelton's translation of *Don Quixote*, Part I, 1612, iv. 6: 'Wherein is rehearsed the History

for much of what he wished to say about contemporary England in the third decade of the eighteenth century; he could make much of Horace's praise of a Lucilius who ' . . . primores populi arripuit . . .' (*Sat.* II. i. 69) but he could find no precedent in that many-sided poet for so direct an attack upon the court as Donne's. In the Advertisement with which Pope, two years later, was to preface his versions of Horace and Donne, he spoke of having versified the satires of Donne ' . . . *at the Desire of the Earl of* Oxford *while he was Lord Treasurer, and of the Duke of* Shrewsbury *who had been Secretary of State; neither of whom look'd upon a Satire on Vicious Courts as any Reflection on those they serv'd in.*'[1] A satire on a vicious court was thus Pope's aim, and the mildly equivocal nature of the statement quoted (though Pope versified Donne's *Satyre II* while Oxford was Treasurer there is no other evidence that he then versified *Satyre IV*) leaves us with the implication that there was a significant difference between the court of Anne and that of George II and Queen Caroline. This, with some justification, Pope firmly believed. This is not the place to enter into Pope's motives for wishing to mount an attack upon the English court at this time. Suffice to say that Pope held it to be corrupt, responsible for the prolongation in power of a corrupt and corrupting régime – that of Sir Robert Walpole – and that corruption was for Pope, not just localised maladministration that could be halted at any time but the process by which commonwealths are ruined and civilisations decay. *Satyre IV* was to be pressed into the service of a vision which had already, in Book III of the 1729 *Dunciad*, offered a prospect of the fall of earlier civilisations, and in the Epistle *To Bathurst* (published January 1733) depicted the financial corruption of contemporary Britain.[2] Thus while Pope

---

of the Curious-Impertinent' (his role is almost entirely destructive) (*The History of . . . Don Quixote . . .* , intro. A. W. Pollard, 1900, i, 312 - ii. 11); and in L'Estrange's digest of Seneca: 'Epist. VII. *Of Impertinent Studies, and Impertinent Men*' (*Seneca's Morals . . . By Sir Roger L'Estrange*, 1705 edition, pp. 412-15).

[1] *Imitations of Horace, ed. cit.*, p. 3.

[2] *The Dunciad* (1729), iii, 59-110; *Epistles to Several Persons*, iii (*To Allen Lord Bathurst*) 25-151, 339-402. Studies which throw light on Pope's concept of 'corruption' are: Isaac Kramnick, *Bolingbroke and his Circle*, 1968; Maynard Mack, *The Garden and the City*, 1969; and Howard Erskine-Hill, *Pope: The Dunciad*, 1972, Ch. 6.

opens his imitation in a tone of easy Horatian equanimity (remembering, perhaps, the closing lines of Horace, *Ep*, II. ii), he follows Donne in his initial attribution to the court of various sins and faults: pride, vanity, falsity and debt; and thus the moral of Donne's cryptic and sardonic allusions to Spartan drunkenness, and to Aretino, is proclaimed by Pope in rollingly clear and confident couplets:

> . . . Tho' in his Pictures Lust be full display'd,
> Few are the Converts *Aretine* has made;
> And tho' the Court show *Vice* exceeding clear,
> None shou'd, by my Advice, learn *Virtue* there.
>
> (94-97)

Pope has certainly made himself 'exceeding clear', if he has abandoned the more subtly inflected accents of Donne.

At a later point Pope shows how well he can use Donne's poem to speak to his own time. Donne's reference to Queen Elizabeth bore witness to the awesome power of the sovereign, and the significance which might be attributed to her every gesture. Pope, with the air of an *ingénu*, follows the reference literally (as also Donne's expressive, colloquial *enjambement*):

> When the *Queen* frown'd, or smiled, he knows; and what
> A subtle Minister may make of that?   (132-3)[1]

to produce a more specific and somewhat different meaning. Queen Caroline's influence over the king was notorious, as was the fact that it was through her Walpole retained the backing of the court. In the context of the 1730's the 'subtle Minister' is Walpole himself, and 'what he makes of' Caroline's smiles or frowns is richly ambiguous. Something of what he makes of them is now detailed by Pope's Courtier-Talker, and a succession of regular end-stopped couplets provides a glib catalogue of the corruptions of the time:

> Who, having lost his Credit, pawn'd his Rent,
> Is therefore fit to have a *Government*?
> Who in the *Secret*, deals in Stocks secure,
> And cheats th'unknowing Widow, and the Poor?
> Who makes a *Trust*, or *Charity*, a job,
> And gets an Act of Parliament to rob?   (138-43)

[1] In 1735 and after, the reader would see Donne's reference to the Queen on the facing page.

Pope's rhythms in this poem, though certainly more regular and rapid than those of Donne, are not without their colloquial inflexions; here, however, as Pope expands on his original, the easy symmetry of the couplets is notably appropriate to the blandness of the Courtier-Talker's delivery. The catalogue seems endless, and the satirist's expression of a moral nausea, when it comes, has more point, is more of a relief, than in Donne. Pope now comes to the 'priviledg'd spie' passage; again he is able to follow the main lines of Donne, while adding and altering in detail to give contemporary point. Walpole is again at the centre of the picture:

> Then as a licens'd Spy, whom nothing can
> Silence, or hurt, he libels the *Great Man;*
> Swears every *place entail'd* for Years to come,
> In *sure Succession* to the Day of Doom:
> He names the *Price* for ev'ry *Office* paid,
> And says our *Wars thrive ill,* because delay'd;
> Nay hints, 'tis by Connivance of the Court,
> That *Spain* robs on, and *Dunkirk's* still a Port.
>
> (158-65)

These were the reiterated criticisms of the Opposition to Walpole. Coming from the Courtier, they arouse the same sense of danger in the satirist as had been hinted at by Oldham and dramatised by Donne. But after Pope has followed Donne almost exactly in the crucial line (' . . . methought I saw/One of our Giant *Statutes* ope its Jaw!') he introduces his one significant change to the story-line of Donne's poem:

> In that nice Moment, as another Lye
> Stood just a-tilt, the *Minister* came by.
> Away he flies. He bows and bows again;
> And close as *Umbra* joins the dirty Train.
> Not *Fannius* self more impudently near,
> When half his nose is in his Patrons' Ear.   (174-9)

Since 'the *Great Man'* has been alluded to so often in Pope's imitation of *Satyre IV* it is appropriate that he should make this brief appearance at the climax of the satirist's encounter with the Courtier-Talker. It is of more interest, in Pope's context, than the passing of money would have been, though it plays down the possibility that the Courtier-Talker was really a 'licens'd Spy'. But if he thus appears less dangerous as an individual, he is the symptom of something more dangerous: he is the man of no values, *Umbra*, the shade, the shadow of all men, the creature and parasite, entirely corrupted. Pope might well compare him with Lord Hervey (*Fannius*), the pliable go-between of Walpole and Caroline, whose current political role was soon to be expressed in the Sporus portrait of *To Arbuthnot*.[1] At this point it is clear that Pope, in deviating from Donne, has been fully aware of Donne's Horation original. For the Courtier-Talker's pursuit of 'the *Great Man*' is precisely how the Talker in Horace proposes to ingratiate himself with Maecenas ('. . . non, hodie si/exclusus fuero, desistam; tempora quaeram,/ occurram in triviis, deducam.').[2] And this, as so often in Pope's poems, leaves us with the implied comparison between a Roman ideal and a fallen contemporary reality. The corrupt great minister is seen in the light of Maecenas, of whose household Horace could say to the Talker:

> domus hac nec purior ulla est
> nec magis his aliena malis; nil mi officit, inquam,
> ditior hic aut est quia doctior; est locus uni
> cuique suus.[3]

V

So much for the political daring of *Satyre IV* and what Pope was able to make of this for his own time. Pope was drawn to *Satyre IV* for at least two other reasons. The first is its Christianity. The second is its wit.

In his Advertisement to his Imitations of Horace, Pope was to speak of the '*Example*' of '*Freedom in so eminent a Divine as Dr. Donne,*' which '*seem'd a proof with what Indignation and Con-*

---

[1] *To Arbuthnot*, 305-33; and see the relevant notes, not only in *Imitations of Horace, ed. cit.*, pp. 117-19, but also John Butt, ed. *An Epistle to Arbuthnot*, 1954, pp. 36-7.

[2] *Sat.* I. ix. 57-9: 'If shut out today, I'll not give up; I'll enquire the right time; I'll meet him in the streets; I'll escort him home.'

[3] *Ibid.*, 49-52: 'No house is cleaner or more free from such evil intrigues. It doesn't hurt me, I say, if someone is richer or more learned than I am. Each of us has his own place.'

tempt a Christian may treat Vice or Folly, in ever so low, or ever so high, a Station'.[1] This statement prompts a question about Pope's knowledge of Donne's life. Did Pope, in some confused way, believe that Donne wrote and published his *Satyres* as an eminent divine? And was part of Pope's attraction to this Christian satirist the quiet knowledge that the form of Christianity in which Donne had been brought up was Roman Catholic? These questions cannot be answered with certainty. From the text of *Satyre IV* itself, however, Pope must have realised that it fell within the reign of Elizabeth, while if he had seen Walton's *Life* (most recently published in its complete form in 1675) he would have known at least the broad outline of Donne's career.[2] I am inclined to think that the statement in Pope's Advertisement is deliberately disingenuous: designed to suggest for satiric freedom a respectability in Donne's lifetime which it never possessed. Where Donne's early Catholicism is concerned, Warburton was later to remark: 'About this time of his life Dr. Donne had a strong propensity to Popery, which appears from several strokes in these satires'[3]; and when the texts of *Satyre II* and *Satyre IV* are taken together, Ian Jack's comment that Pope must have been quick to notice features 'which suggest a Catholic background' is a fair one.[4] He adopted most of these references, and while they are not meant to proclaim a Catholic commitment on the part of the still Catholic Pope, any more than they were on the part of the no-longer Catholic Donne, they have a personal appropriateness, and somewhat strengthen that aspect of Pope's imitation, fainter than in *Satyre IV*, which emphasises isolation and danger.

Pope would, however, almost certainly have agreed with Donne when he wrote that the Anglican and Roman churches,

---

[1] *Imitations of Horace, ed. cit.*, p. 3.

[2] A Life was prefixed to Tonson's 1719 edition of Donne's *Poems*. It is based on Walton, but omits any reference to Donne's Papist upbringing.

[3] *The Works of Alexander Pope* . . ., ed. William Warburton, 1751, iv, 265. But Pope certainly knew of Donne's early Roman Catholicism, for he possessed and indexed a copy of *Pseudo-Martyr* (1610), in the Preface of which the fact is acknowledged. (Geoffrey Keynes, *A Bibliography of the Works of John Donne*, 1914, p. 7).

[4] Ian Jack, *art. cit.* p. 1017.

indeed Rome, Wittenburg and Geneva, 'are all virtuall beams of one Sun' and 'connaturall pieces of one circle'.[1] For both poets the Catholic background is subsumed in the Christian poem. Pope follows Donne in 'placing' almost every figure by means of biblical allusion. Thus the Courtier-Talker excels the apostles as a linguist, and might have translated for the builders of Babel; thus the chaplain is 'Sweeter than *Sharon*' and the captain like '*Herod's* Hang-dogs in old Tapestry' (76-7, 81-5, 252-3, 266-7). Donne's stress, at the centre of his satire, on 'wholesome solitarinesse' is enriched by echoes of Christian poems by Milton (*Comus*) and Marvell (*The Garden*) which speak of a spiritual freedom from temptation and taint.[2] Donne's vision of the court as a court of the damned, with its allusion to Dante, its comparison of the presence chamber to a mosque, and the seven deadly sins lining the wall, is all accepted by Pope; indeed his 'See! where the *British* Youth . . .' (replacing Donne's 'Tis ten a clock and past . . .') more effectively assimilates the later part of the poem into the Dantesque trance to which perhaps it belongs. It is in the context of this, almost medieval, vision that the satirist's courageous self-dedication to Truth occurs, and Pope seeks to emulate this un-Horatian passage:

> Not *Dante* dreaming all th'Infernal State,
> Beheld such Scenes of *Envy, Sin* and *Hate.*
> Base Fear becomes the Guilty, not the Free;
> Suits Tyrants, Plunderers, but suits not me.
> Shall I, the Terror of this sinful Town,
> Care, if a livery'd Lord or Smile or frown?
> Who cannot flatter, and detest who can,
> Tremble before a *noble Serving-Man?*
> O my fair Mistress, *Truth!* Shall I quit thee,
> For huffing, braggart, puft *Nobility?*
> Thou, who since Yesterday, has roll'd o'er all
> The busy, idle Blockheads of the Ball,
> Hast thou, O *Sun!* beheld an emptier sort . . .

> (192-204)

---

[1] Donne to Sir H. R. (before 1610?), *Letters to Several Persons of Honour*, 1651, p. 29. Cf. Pope's *Universal Prayer.*
[2] See the discussion of the passage in Maynard Mack, *op. cit.*, pp. 89-91.

It is fair to say that Pope has some success. The two-line apostrophe to Truth (though altered from Donne) has a rising directness, a dramatic inflexion, and a plainness of diction ('Shall I quit thee . . .'), worthy of the tragic soliloquy-style of the earlier poet. The connectedness of the last three lines reaches this style, and 'Scenes of *Envy*, *Sin*, and *Hate*' strike the right note of blunt religious attack. But in other places Pope has an unfortunate tone. 'I, the Terror of this sinful Town' has an air of self-righteous complacency (Pope as John Knox, or Savanarola?) absent in those other places in his epistles and satires where he expresses an heroic personal pride. Furthermore, Pope's contempt for the nobility of the court appears to have a fair tinge of plain snobbery. On both counts, the terse strength of Donne's 'Shall I, nones slave, of high borne, or rais'd men/Fear frownes?' is far more effective.

More effective than Pope, also, is Donne's handling of the conclusion, closely connected with the Christian vision of the damned at court. This is, I think, one of the places (less frequent than a cursory reading of the poem might suggest) where Pope has simply regularised away the careful inflexions of the speaking voice. The handing over of the satirist's weapons to the preacher has lost its urgency, the final lines their subtle blend of satisfaction and caution. But Pope brings off one elegant sleight of hand, for his 'bold *Divine*' sounds very like the terms in which he was, in his Advertisement, to speak of '*so eminent a Divine as Dr*. Donne . . .'. It is possible that Pope is here doffing the mask of Pope-Donne, and yielding up his attack to the unmediated roughness and force of the Elizabethan satirist. What is very plain, however, from an examination of the latter part of the later poem, is that Pope was strongly attracted to the heroic stance of this Christian satirist; that he made an intelligent and not wholly unsuccessful attempt to re-create this stance; and that this was a major reason why he sought to imitate Horace, *Sat*. I. ix, not directly, but through the mediation of *Satyre IV*.

Pope's remark to Spence that Donne had '. . . as much wit as any writer can possibly have' is celebrated, and may be supported by the very early judgment of Pope to Wycherley (10 April 1706) that 'Donne had infinitely more Wit than he wanted Versification: for the great dealers in Wit, like those in Trade, take least Pains to set off their Goods . . .'[1] What Pope took to be the wit of Donne's *Satyres* may be said to be a vital and pervasive intelligence, seizing upon relationships through trenchant and concrete expression, often coloured by a sardonically comic exaggeration: the blood in the body of the poem, as Pope put it.[2] In this sense, much of what has already been said about the two poems has involved their wit. Since, however much emphasis has fallen on the aspects of bold political attack and of the Christianly heroic stance, it is right to conclude this essay by recognising the comic aspect of Pope's achievement.

In speaking of the earlier part of *Satyre IV*, I suggested that it showed exuberant comedy in dialogue with fear. Donne's stress on danger and fear is felt throughout, and is necessary if (by contrast) a vivid sense of the satirist's courage and defiance is also to be conveyed. Pope saw this, for he has actually increased the number of expressions designed to convey fear (e.g. Donne's 'Tyr'd, now I leave this place . . .' becomes 'Frighted, I quit the Room . . .'). Yet this sense of fear is not convincingly conveyed in Pope's poem, partly owing to his change of the story-line, partly to his occasional note of vanity, partly to his faster and more regular metre. But chiefly this failure is the necessary opposite side of the coin to a brilliant success. In amplifying the cryptic strokes of Donne's comic wit, setting off his 'Goods' more prominently, Pope upset the balance in *Satyre IV* between mockery and fear; but he came near, in the first half of the poem, to creating a comic masterpiece. Consider what the Courtier-Talker is made to say about languages:

> Nay troth, th'*Apostles*, (tho' perhaps too rough)
> Had once a pretty Gift of Tongues enough.
> Yet these were all *poor Gentlemen*! I dare
> Affirm, 'Twas *Travel* made them what they were.'

(76-8)

---

[1] Joseph Spence, *Observations, Anecdotes, and Characters of Books and Men*, ed. J. M. Osborn, 1966, Item 434 (1734?); *The Correspondence of Alexander Pope*, ed. George Sherburn, 1956, i, p. 16.

[2] *An Essay on Criticism*, 303-4; for the meaning and background of Pope's ever-memorable definition of wit (297-8), see E. N. Hooker, 'Pope on Wit: The *Essay on Criticism*', *The Hudson Review*, 2, 1950, pp. 84-100.

Pope had his cue from Donne's 'Nay, your Apostles were/Good pretty Linguists' especially in the word 'pretty' which has the air of a parlance at once polite and vacuous. But, expanding from this, Pope's rendering is triumphant: the mingling of blasphemy with the patronising and empty civility of a 'polite' age, which sought to polish roughness, is itself done with such appropriately polished rapidity of metre that the effect is quite breathtaking. The Courtier has waved a negligent hand –'a pretty Gift of Tongues enough' – and the apostles are dismissed. Pope has not only clarified but amplified the comedy. Or again:

> Thus other Talents having nicely shown,
> He came by sure Transition to his own:
> Till I cry'd out, 'You prove yourself so able,
> 'Pity! you was not Druggerman at *Babel*:
> 'For had they found a Linguist half so good,
> 'I make no question but the *Tow'r* had stood.'
> 'Obliging Sir! for Courts you sure were made . . .'
>   (80–85)

Phrases such as 'nicely' and 'sure Transition' convey the complete control, and thus the complete security, of the satirist; he has his comic subject in the palm of his hand. The rhyme of the second couplet is brilliantly pointed, and if we regret the disappearance of Donne's 'bricklayers' we can only applaud the appearance of the fittingly exotic yet undeniably trenchant 'Druggerman'. But Pope most enriches the comedy here by making his Courtier-Talker, in insufferable vanity, take the satirist's devastating repartee for a compliment. Pope further amplifies the comedy in the satire by making additions in the spirit of his original. The comparison of the Courtier-Talker to a 'Blunderbuss' discharging a miscellaneous 'Shot of Dulness' (64–5) is not in Donne, but it has all his trenchancy, aptness and ludicrous exaggeration. And (another addition) perhaps nothing is more expressive than the civil nothingness of the following line:

> 'Oh! Sir, politely so! nay, let me dye . . .'   (112)

Pope has profited from the century of theatrical fops, from Jonson's Fastidious Brisk to Congreve's Witwoud, which elapsed between the writing of *Satyre IV* and his own time. With the possible exception of Jonson in *The Poetaster*, no English writer has made anything so richly ridiculous out of Horace's Talker. A final example, comedy of a different kind, may be taken from the second half of the poem. The courtiers advance upon the ladies:

> How each Pyrate eyes
> So weak a Vessel, and so rich a Prize!
> Top-gallant he, and she in all her Trim,
> He boarding her, she striking sail to him. (228-31)

The bare idea only is in Donne. The *double entendre* of the simile works out perfectly to each detail, the antithetical couplets perform a stylised ritual – and one of the best examples of what Rochester would have called the 'mannerly obscene' has been brought off with consummate skill.

Though we have all descried Donne's 'huge hill,/Cragged, and steep,' on which 'Truth stands', comparatively little attention has yet been paid to his *Satyres*, still less to reading them, as they ask, in their intellectual and social context. It is still possible for some or all to be dismissed in a sentence or two. They deserve better. I have tried to suggest here something of the impressive human complexity of *Satyre IV*, the way it uses and changes Horace, its synthesis of classical and Christian, its tension between laughter and tears, or, more precisely, between mockery and fear, each reined in and checked so that one does not outrun the other. I have suggested too that, far from being a shapeless and over-long denunciation, this satire possesses an expressive unifying structure.

Horace and Donne are not names very commonly linked, but *Satyre IV*, belongs to a traditon of translation and imitation of the Ninth Satire of the First Book of Horace which connects it with Oldham and Pope, the latter of whom certainly recognised the dual challenge when he wrote his *The Impertinent, Or a Visit to the Court*, later entitled *The Fourth Satire of Dr John Donne, Dean of St Paul's, Versifyed*. Pope was then at a crucial stage in his poetic development. He had recently composed, in a few days, and as a largely unpremeditated effusion, his imitation of the First Satire of the Second Book of Horace (*To*

Fortescue), with its personal identification by Pope with the bold satire of Lucilius. Dryden, in his Discourse Concerning Satire, had argued that in defining formal satire the 'Majestique way of *Persius* and *Juvenal*' should be taken into account as well as the ways of Horace.[1] Pope, in his handling of the Lucilius passage in Horace, *Sat.* II, i, began to respond to this challenge. He next proceeded to expand and enrich his satiric approach through an attempt to assimilate the qualities of Donne's sardonic yet heroic Christian satire, seeing Donne at once as an English Lucilius, and probably, one who could reach the heights of what Dryden had termed the 'Tragical Satyre' of Juvenal. A part of this attraction towards Donne was Pope's growing sense that the highest role of the satirical poet, and the one which his age was to warrant from him, was, (far from the secure voicing of a consensus of enlightned opinion) isolated, dangerous and, partly for this reason, courageous and heroic. Pope attempted to express, though he did not manage to convey, the vivid sense of fear in *Satyre IV*; he attempted with better success the bold attack, and the lonely heroic manner of Donne's central soliloquy; and he succeeded, at some cost to the total effect he was working for, in reaping a comic harvest from Donne's satiric wit.

Brilliant and remarkable as it is, Pope's imitation of *Satyre IV* is not wholly a success; rather it is a poem of growth, a stage in that poetic development which was to culminate in *To Arbuthnot* and the two Dialogues of the *Epilogue to the Satires*. Yet each of the two poems considered is humanly admirable in its courage and independence: in being so intimately of its time yet so bravely against it, with all the intelligence, misgiving, principle and skill which that took.

[1] A Discourse Concerning Satire, 2324-59; *ed. cit.*, ii, pp. 660-1.

307

11

Donne and the Poetry of Patronage

The *Verse Letters*

PATRICIA THOMSON

There are sound economic reasons for the existence of a 'poetry of patronage' in the Elizabethan and Jacobean period. He who pays the piper calls the tune. The poets had to sing for their supper. This 'sheer survival' motive behind literature can, however, be emphasised in the wrong way. It is true that poets 'produced what their sponsors demanded, or what they hoped possible patrons might like'.[1] But it is not true that mere flattery of patrons or mere pandering to their tastes always followed. Indeed, it is much to be doubted whether Spenser, Shakespeare, Jonson, Donne or any other good poet of their time found his genius seriously cramped by the aristocratic élite, even by its demand for laudatory poems such as complimentary sonnets, epigrams or epistles, masques, epithalamia and elegies.

In the maze of bitter complaint and warm gratitude,[2] it is often only possible to guess at the feelings of the original participants in a system of patronage which was itself so necessary a part of a hierarchical society. Guess-work would suggest that the substance and form of the complimentary sonnet were at least as congenial to Shakespeare as to the noble youth he addressed, and that Spenser was uniformly on congenial ground. He explored the common ground of social, intellectual and literary experience shared by his patrons and himself. He had had an education at school, at university, and in government circles

---

[1] Hiram Haydn, *The Counter Renaissance*, New York, 1950, p. 12.

[2] Contrast, for example, the excessive disappointment of Spenser's 'But ah *Mecoenas* is yclad in claye' (*The Shepheardes Calender* (1579), October Eclogue) with Jonson's satisfied praise of the Sidneys' hospitality at Penshurst, 'Where comes no guest, but is allow'd to eate' (*The Forrest* (1616), II).

similar to that of many of the 'gentlemen or noble persons' for whom he wrote. He catered for the patron class in so far as he was, not of it, but prepared to identify himself with its interests. That *The Faerie Queene* was a bid for patronage is another matter. In making that bid Spenser did not have to go out of his way. Again, it is only possible to guess at what Shakespeare and Spenser would have written had patrons not existed. But they would probably not have written at all without a demand of some kind. The fact that the 'demand' came from patrons is no more to be regretted than if it had come from any other section of the community.

He who pays the piper has a right to call the tune. But the patron who wants to get the best from his piper knows that he must not be the ignorant dictator. If they had more than a perfunctory or fashionable interest in literature, Renaissance patrons were likely to become arbiters of taste and, sometimes, leading spirits of literary groups. Like any other audience they could stimulate those who wrote for them. This is especially true of those patrons who wrote themselves and shared a practical interest in poetry with their protégés. Various members of the Sidney-Herbert family provide outstanding examples. Only a little behind them falls Lucy Harington Russell, third Countess of Bedford, the most brilliant patroness of the court of James I and one of whom something will be said later. Of course, even interested, stimulating patrons such as these could not make silk purses out of sows' ears. Their effect on the quality of the 'poetry of patronage' was, at most, indirect. The relationship with patrons was a vitally important element in the life of a non-dramatic poet, and his success or failure, happiness or unhappiness in that relationship, would influence his state of mind and hence his manner of writing. No more than this – and it is, after all, enough – can reasonably be claimed.

In the early seventeeth century, to which the focus will now be narrowed, the verse letter holds a high place amongst the poems written for or about patrons. Jonson, Daniel and Donne, all by now mature poets, made particularly distinguished contributions to this 'kind'. Though less formal than the complimentary sonnet, it absorbed some of the Petrarchan mannerisms and was used for similar purposes. Yet, while they give interesting insights into poet-patron relationships, Jonson, Daniel and Donne rarely use the verse letter merely to pay compliments. Furthermore there are differences between the three poets, differences which correspond to their differing experiences of and attitudes to patrons, and as might be expected, even more to their differing individualities.

The 'differences' must be briefly stated, if at the risk of over-generalisation. Like most Jacobean (that is, post-feudal) poets, Jonson, Daniel and Donne courted many patrons, and also kept an eye on the centre of patronage, the court. But whereas Jonson and Daniel were successful professional poets, Donne was an amateur. His social position was above that of the city poets and apart from that of the court poets who sought print and publicity. Jonson, with one foot in the London theatre and the other in the court, printed as much as he could. Daniel, who under Elizabeth had been a humble yet respected protégé of the Herberts, also entered the court world after the accession of James, and he too suffered from no gentlemanly inhibitions about print. Literary patronage provided, more or less, for those who belonged to Jonson's and Daniel's social and professional group. And, though Jonson was sometimes angry at supercilious individuals, it left them with no sense of outraged human dignity or consciousness of inferiority. The gentleman-amateur such as Donne could hardly fit in here. He belonged with his own kind, with Sir Henry Wotton, Sir Henry Goodyer, Sir Thomas Roe, and his other courtier friends, and had his place in a scheme of social rather than of literary patronage. This eventually led him not to poetry but to the pulpit. Meanwhile, Jonson was the only professional poet whom Donne acknowledged, a sign, perhaps, of the uniquely high status the former achieved at court. For many years before his entry into the Church, Donne's misfortune was that while he could call Goodyer and other gentlemen his friends, and their patrons his, he remained outside the court circle to which they belonged.[1] When, in his letters, he talks

[1] At Christmas 1605-6, for example, three of Donne's future patrons and friends, the Countess of Bedford, Sir Robert Drury, and Goodyer, were at court, taking part in the Twelfth Night celebrations. He himself was not included in such festivities. Jonson and Daniel, the former particularly, provided the masques which graced them.

of being 'brought to a necessity of printing'[1] his poems, and
then of 'descending' and 'declining' to print,[2] he seems to be
contemplating a dreadful step into some no-man's-land between
the amateur and professional kingdoms.

That these anxieties and preoccupations contribute something
to the distinctive manner of Donne's complimentary verse
letters may be tentatively suggested. Jonson's and Daniel's,
whatever the reason, breathe an air of greater security. In
Epigrammes, The Forrest and *The Vnder-wood*, Jonson uses the
form as a means of talking, in friendly style and on intellectually
equal terms, to his patrons and about himself, themselves or
affairs in general. Daniel's *Epistles* are philosophic musings on
subjects more important than the poet-patron relationship,
though touching on that indirectly. Donne's *Verse Letters* to
patrons, though sometimes friendly in tone and often exploratory
of 'philosophy', are distinguishable from both as being ex-
ceedingly witty discourses showing at once the patron's worth
and the poet's skill.

Other reasons for the differences between the three poets,
reasons outside their experience of patronage, are not, of course,
far to seek. Jonson was by nature assertive. Hence he accounts
himself superior to supercilious patrons, equal to good ones.
'Gifts stinke from some' he asserts in the Epistle to the Earl of
Dorset, before working towards his concluding admonition to
this patron:

> Keep you such
> That I may love your Person (as I doe)
> Without your gift, though I can rate that too.
> (*The Vnder-wood*, XIII, 156-8)

Daniel, in sharp contrast, was a retiring person, inclined to
retreat into lofty thoughts. He treats his patrons to moral
exhortations appropriate to their circumstances. A sermon on
justice and law is delivered to Sir Thomas Egerton, the Lord
Keeper, and one on endurance to the Earl of Southampton when
he is released from the Tower. 'Height of the minde' and 'This
Concord . . . of a wel-tun'd minde', as described in the epistle to

---

[1] *Letters to Severall Persons of Honour*, London, 1651, p. 196.
[2] *Ibid.*, p. 255.

the Countess of Cumberland, are favourite areas in which both patron and protégé, *au dessus du mêlée*, survey together 'This rowling world, and view it as it is'. Donne is unlike both in his intellectual restlessness and in being, for many years, unsure of his loyalties, his prospects, and his vocation.

Most of Donne's *Verse Letters to Several Personages*, notably those addressed to patrons, belong to the middle period of his life, between about 1601, the year of his marriage, and 1615, the year of his ordination. He was no longer 'a rash and temerarious youth', as Elizabeth called the Earl of Essex, on whose expeditions Donne himself had served in the 1590s. The *Satyres*, the Ovidian elegies, and, probably, most of the *Songs and Sonnets* were behind him. Ahead lay those few *Divine Poems* written after his wife's death in 1617. In this phase he was inevitably more circumspect – even, more worldly – than he had been and was to be. His rashest act, his marriage, with the consequent family responsibilities, made urgent the existent need to carve out a career and hence to find influential patrons, especially those close to the throne. Always demanding, Donne was now so in what may be called a social style. The author of *Songs and Sonnets* and *Holy Sonnets* either bullies or asks to be bullied, a fact reflected in the prominent imperative mood:

> For Godsake hold your tongue
> > ('The Canonization')

> Take heed of loving me
> > ('The Prohibition')

> Spit in my face yee Jewes
> > (*Holy Sonnets*, 1633, 7)

> Batter my heart, three person'd God
> > (*Ibid.*, 1633, 10)

Donne's relationships with patrons and friends, though personal, will obviously differ from those of his most private life, with his 'profane mistresses' and with God. With patrons he prepares to meet the faces that he meets. His demands are now expressed in a much more cautious, oblique or complicated way:

Others by Testament give Legacies, but I
Dying, of you doe beg a Legacie.
> ('Epitaph on Himselfe *To the Countesse of Bedford*' 5-6)

For so God helpe mee, I would not misse you there (i.e., in
Heaven)
For all the good which you can do me here.
> (*To the Countesse of Bedford*, 'Reason is our Soules left
> hand', 37-8)

The contrast with Jonson's disarmingly direct manner is
obvious.[1]

Donne's addresses to friends are in a class apart from all his
other addresses. One reason why is that, having few or no
extreme demands to make, he is here at his most relaxed. 'A
Frend', Bacon remarked, 'may speak, as the Case requires, and
not as it sorteth with the Person'.[2] Hyperbole, histrionics,
melodrama, all signs of strain or intensity, are virtually absent
from the *Verse Letters* to friends. Sir Henry Wotton, who first
became Donne's friend at Oxford, was later with him on the
Cadiz and Islands expeditions. This 'case' could be said to
'require' the letter contributing to the debate, current among
Essex's followers, about the best *modus vivendi*, whether in the
country, at court, or in town:

> Life is a voyage, and in our lifes wayes
> Countries, Courts, Towns are Rockes, or Remoraes;
> (*To Sir Henry Wotton*, 'Sir, more then kisses,' 7-8)

And again there are letters to Wotton on his service in Ireland
and on his going to Venice as ambassador. Friendship trans-
mutes the imperative passion of *Songs and Sonnets* into con-
fident, poised sentiment. Contrast the use of a common motif
in a love poem,

> So, so, breake off this last lamenting kisse,
> Which suckes two soules, and vapours both away
> ('The Expiration')

and in the letter to Wotton already quoted

> Sir, more then kisses, letters mingle Soules;
> For, thus friends absent speake.

---

[1] 'Make it your gift' concludes Jonson's request, to the same court patroness, for a
buck (*Epigrammes*, LXXXIV).   [2] 'Of Friendship', *Essays* (1625).

Donne treats Wotton as Wyatt, first imitator of the classical verse epistle, treated his friend John Poins: the Horatian intimacy, the easy intercourse of kindly minds and of men equal in education and experience, is proper not only to the relationship but to the traditional form. Donne is here at his closest to Jonson's mode of address. He is perfectly at ease when, without condescension, he proffers Wotton advice. That he does so at all is a sign of the security of friendship, besides being, in itself, a compliment. Direct compliments, though relatively few, are manly and courteous when they do come. At the end of the same address to Wotton, Donne compliments the man he 'throughly loves':

> But, Sir, I 'advise not you, I rather doe
> Say o'er those lessons, which I learn'd of you: (63-4)

Absence of hyperbole, so common in the poems of courtship or praise, is a distinctive feature of this poem, as it is also of the verse letters of both Jonson and Daniel.

Common motifs of Renaissance love poetry, now with the heightening of hyperbole, are also carried over into Donne's *Verse Letters* to patrons. For obvious reasons the Petrarchan stance is uniquely well adapted to his relationships with patronesses, the great countesses and ladies of James I's court. For here it has not only a personal basis but a social one; that is, a basis in the proprieties of a hierarchical society. Thus the stance adopted by the humble lover towards the lofty heroine of Petrarch's *Canzoniere* or of certain Elizabethan sonnet sequences, such as Drayton's *Idea*,[1] becomes the stance adopted by protégé to patroness. Queen Elizabeth, willing Laura of her court, had already set the precedent for this kind of adoration.[2] Religious adoration of *la princesse lointaine* combines with self-depreciation in a recognisable idiom. In the sonnet 'To Mr C. B.', Donne adores some unknown mistress as 'the Saint of his affection',

---

[1] Many of the sonnets are believed to be addressed to Anne, daughter of Drayton's early patron, Sir Henry Goodyer the elder, in whose household at Polesworth he was employed as a page and educated.

[2] Raleigh's adoration of his sovereign provides perhaps the most striking example, in such poems as *The Booke of the Ocean to Scynthia* and in the sonnet, in which she is said to outdo Laura, prefixed to *The Faerie Queene*.

'Heavens liberall, and earths thrice-fairer Sunne', while he
remains the conventional 'martyr' to Love. It is but a short step
to 'Here, where by all, all Saints invoked are', a verse letter
written in Amiens in 1611-12 'to the Lady Carey, and Mris
Essex Riche': these courtly sisters are two 'Saints', Donne
their 'Convertite' explaining the insights gleaned from his
'Apostleship'. It is indeed, with him, a common motif. In 'Man
to Gods image,' a letter of unknown date to the Countess of
Huntingdon, he extravagantly asserts

> I was your Prophet in your yonger dayes,
> And now your Chaplaine, God in you to praise.   (69-7)

The unfinished address, 'Though I be *dead*', to the Countess of
Bedford (1611-12), takes the form of a religious confession to
her. And again, in another address[1] to her, Donne develops a
religious argument starting

> Reason is our Soules left hand, Faith her right,
> By these wee reach divinity, that's you;   (1-2)

Further letters to the same 'divinity' illustrate the lengths to
which Donne, here at his furthest from Jonson and Daniel, is
prepared to carry the self-depreciation of the Petrarchan
tradition. In 'Honour is so sublime perfection', a letter of un-
certain date, he argues that praise of the high must, like herbs,
come from the 'despis'd dung': 'Care not then, Madame,'how
low your praysers lye' (1. 13). Simultaneously he is edgily
aware that too much attentiveness might bear the impression of
toadying, while lack of it would suggest ingratitude to his
bountiful patroness. Yet another letter to the Countess of
Bedford, probably of 1609 and a reply to some communication
of hers, opens

> T'have written then, when you writ, seem'd to mee
> Worst of spirituall vices, Simony,
> And not t'have written then, seemes little lesse
> Then worst of civill vices, thanklessenesse.   (1-4)

But within a few lines this anxious protégé, who now calls him-
self a 'nothing', ingeniously settles the conflict of 'spiritual' and
'civill' claims:

[1] Written probably at some time between 1608 and 1612.

In this, my debt I seem'd loath to confesse,
In that, I seem'd to shunne beholdingnesse.
But 'tis not soe; *nothings*, as I am, may
Pay all they have, and yet have all to pay.   (5-8)

Readers, and not necessarily cynical ones, may well eventually
ask who this patroness of Donne's is and whether she measures
up to the praise he confers on her. Perhaps the subtlest part of
his complimentary addresses to the Countess of Bedford lies
not in his 'Petrarchan' divinisation of her, but in his assumption
that, on his level, she could follow the intricacies of such ingenious
arguments as have been described above. There is good reason
to conclude not only that this was the case but that Donne knew
it to be so. They had much in common, so that the years of their
closest acquaintance, from about 1608 to 1615, were, in their
way, fruitful to his genius.[1] The Countess, an active patroness of
numerous poets, was, according to Jonson, 'a learned, and a
manly soule' (*Epigrammes*, LXXVI). She also earned his further
compliment: 'Rare poems aske rare friends' he states in an
epigram he sent to her with a copy of Donne's *Satyres* (*Epi-
grammes*, XCIV). Daniel too addressed an epistle to this
'learned Lady'. Florio praised her skill in French and Italian,
languages she learned in her girlhood. Later she developed an
interest in classical antiquities and painting. Though no poetry
of her own survives, she seem to have written some. Donne
himself says that she showed some of her 'verses' to him in her
garden at Twickenham,[2] that haven from his home cares which
he termed a 'balm' and 'True Paradise' ('Twicknam Garden').
In his prose letters to his close friend Sir Henry Goodyer, who
acted as her agent and confidential servant, he stresses not only
the material advantages of courting this important patroness
but her influence over him: 'I have made her opinion of me,
the ballance by which I weigh myself'.[3] He even claims that she
is his inspiration, that she 'only hath power to cast the fetters
of verse upon my free meditations'.[4] Then there is the evidence

---

[1] For a fuller account of their relations, see Patricia Thomson, 'John Donne and
the Countess of Bedford', *Modern Language Review*, xliv, 1949, pp. 329-430.

[2] *Letters*, pp. 64 and 67.

[3] *Ibid.*, p. 151.

[4] *Ibid.*, p. 117.

of the *Verse Letters* themselves. Donne addressed to the Countess of Bedford no less than seven, that is, more than to any other patron. Besides, he wrote elegies for members of her family, her cousins Cecilia Bulstrode (d. 1609) and Lady Bridgit Markham (d. 1609), and her brother Lord Harington (d. 1614).

There is therefore no reason to be unduly cynical about such praise, exaggerated and conventional though it may appear, as is expressed in the lines already quoted:

> Reason is our Soules left hand, Faith her right,
> By these wee reach divinity, that's you;

This poem really has two subjects: the Countess of Bedford and Reason/Faith. Donne simultaneously flatters the Countess and defines the relative importance of belief in, and understanding of, God. In this way it is, like other of his verse letters, distinguishable from the average Elizabethan Petrarchan poem, such as his own sonnet 'To Mr C. B.' The latter is confined to a simple, ostensible subject, and, in fact, works upon the one level, that of love-longing. Donne's method in the verse letters has a queer effect. There are certainly moments when he degrades his greater subject by referring it too closely to his lesser one: his 'that's you', in the second line of 'Reason is our Soules left hand', comes as a shock. The poem as a whole, while it contains not a single flippant or unorthodox remark, perhaps leaves an opening for cynicism. At least the voice of the circumspect, worried, ambitious Donne of the middle years is heard. Take the concluding stanza:

> Since you are then Gods masterpeece, and so
> His Factor for our loves; doe as you doe,
> Make your returne home gracious; and bestow
> This life on that; so make one life of two.
> For so God helpe mee, 'I would not misse you there
> For all the good which you can do me here.   (33-38)

In proffering religious advice to the Countess, Donne speaks with a manly authority reminiscent of his letter to Wotton. The emphasis falls strongly on the need to devote the earthly to the heavenly life, to make the former harmonise with the latter, and 'so make one life of two'. The last line, with its reminder of the actual relationship of patron and protégé on earth, is only slightly disturbing. Donne does not let himself forget permanently, however far his religious speculations carry him, the practical aspect of the situation, 'all the good which you can do me here'. The Countess is a 'Factor for our loves', giving access to God, and she is also, it may be cautiously suggested, fulfilling a similar role on earth, giving access to the benefits of James I's court; for there she was certainly an influence, which Donne once tried to use when angling for a post in Ireland. In his poem he plays disturbingly with the contrasting perspectives: his own small one on the poet-patron relationship and the larger one on ultimate destinies.

A more clear-cut, hence less questionable, case is the address to the Countess of Bedford, 'This twilight of two yeares' (? 25 March 1610). It is, again, in Petrarchan vein. Donne, in humble style, is 'One corne of one low anthills dust' (l. 28). The Countess is, he claims, given 'just praise', and it is true that the praise here is less high-flown than usual. He is secure enough in the relationship to offer further religious advice to one who, for all her learning, was in constant attendance at a gay, pleasure-loving court. This, it may be recalled, is a charmed circle from which, during the years of his acquaintance with her, he feels himself cut off. 'Turne to God', he advises the great court lady,

> Hee will teach you, that good and bad have not
> One latitude in cloysters, and in Court;   (41-42)

He is mindful of the social obligations of the great. God, he reminds the Countess,

> will best teach you, how you should lay out
> His stock of *beauty, learning, favour, blood*;   (36-7)

No doubt he himself has a stake in the 'stock of . . . *favour*', for the poem starts with the assumption that the poet owes 'thankes' to his patroness. Hard upon this he proceeds to transform, with lively wit, the usual commonplaces. For example, to this situation, itself inevitable in an age of aristocratic patronage, a stock response, found in numerous Elizabethan sonnets, is to remind the reader of Horace's doctrine that thanks are also owing to the poet who will enshrine his patron's name for ever in immortal verse.[1] Accordingly Donne says

> In recompence I would show future times
>   What you were, and teach them to 'urge towards such.
> Verse embalmes vertue; 'and Tombs, or Thrones of rimes,
>   Preserve fraile transitory fame, as much
>   As spice doth bodies from corrupt aires touch.   (11-15)

The divergence from the conventional statement begins to come in the last line. It suggests that, after all, the effect of 'rime' is not to defeat Time, as Shakespeare supposes:

> His beauty shall in these black lines be seen
> And they shall live, and he in them still green.
>
> (*Sonnets, 63*)

Here Shakespeare suggests that poetry can work miracles and confer life. Donne, by contrast, knows that the corpse can only be embalmed and that his verses can only arrest decay:

> Mine are short-liv'd; the tincture of your name
>   Creates in them, but dissipates as fast,
> New spirits; for, strong agents with the same
>   Force that doth warme and cherish, us doe wast;
>   Kept hot with strong extracts, no bodies last:
>
> (16-20)

Where Shakespeare makes the potent verse absorb the 'name', Donne reverses the process, making the 'name', like a 'tincture' or 'strong agent', absorb into itself the weaker substance of the verse. This argument leads him to something more than a humble acceptance of his own inferiority. Though, as usual, notions of his inferiority *vis à vis* the great are present, Donne now shows that, in relation to ultimate truth, the local truth of his poem of praise will be found deficient:

> When all (as truth commands assent) confesse
>   All truth of you, yet they will doubt how I,
> One corne of one low anthills dust, and lesse,
>   Should name, know, or expresse a thing so high,
>   And not an inch, measure infinity.

[1] One of the most familiar examples of this *exegi monumentum* motif is Shakespeare's 'Not marble, nor the gilded monuments / Of princes shall outlive this powerful rime' (*Sonnets, 55*).

I cannot tell them, nor my selfe, nor you,
  But leave, lest truth b'endanger'd by my praise,
And turne to God, who knowes I thinke this true,
  And useth oft, when such a heart mis-sayes,
To make it good, for, such a prayser prayes.

(26-35)

Donne again contrasts two perspectives: his own limited one ('One corne of one low anthills dust') and the completer vision ('All truth') of posterity. The turning to God, who alone has a perfectly complete vision of truth, and who understands the partial truth of human 'mis-sayings' follows logically. In this way the doctrine common in poetry of praise from classical to Elizabethan times is transformed, and without being actually contradicted is given a diminished value. The lines

Verse embalmes vertue; 'and Tombs, or Thrones of rimes,
  Preserve fraile transitory fame,

suggest that Donne has the conventional *exegi monumentum* doctrine in mind, and that he is therefore consciously offering his comment on it.

Donne certainly does not use the clichés of praise in an unthinking way. Truth, he acknowledges, may be 'endangerd by my praise'.[1] Therefore in the *Verse Letters* he rejects as much as he accepts from the Petrarchan common market. If the conventional hyperbole is there, much is omitted as untrue to the social relationship of patroness and protégé. Obvious examples are the lover's hankerings during enforced absence from his

---

[1] At about the time that or not long after this phrase was penned (?1610) Donne was forced to consider yet more alertly the possibility of misinterpretation of his praise as untruthful because both exaggerated and wrongly directed. In 1611 he published the first of his two *Anniversaries*, 'A Funeral Elegy' prefaced by 'An Anatomy of the World', on the anniversary of the death (1610) of Elizabeth, fifteen-year-old daughter of his patron Sir Robert Drury. Jonson's well-known condemnation of this extravagant eulogy of a girl the poet had never met does not stand alone. While abroad in 1611-12 Donne heard 'many censures' of it (*Letters*, p. 74): 'since I never saw the Gentlewoman, I cannot be understood to have bound myself to have spoken just truths' (*Ibid.*, p. 206). Evidently some of his patronesses must have objected: the incomplete 'Though I be *dead*' to the Countess of Bedford and 'Here, where by all, all Saints invoked are' to Lady Carey and Mris Riche attempt to explain away praises directed to 'other Saint, then yow'.

mistress, the favourite of the Petrarchan topics used in *Songs and Sonnets*, and also such of Love's sufferings and cruelties as are expressed in 'When by thy scorne, O murdresse, I am dead' ('The Apparition'). Donne's alertness to the use and limitations of Petrarchanism is perhaps best illustrated from 'That unripe side of earth' (?1605 or later), addressed to the 'other Countesse' of his prose letters to Goodyer, that is, to the Countess of Huntingdon. He engages immediately with convention and cliché. He adopts, most successfully, the convention of unconventionality through which the poet-lover asserts his own integrity by mocking, and thus dissociating himself from, the cliché-ridden Petrarchans. The most comic of his immediate English predecessors in this very popular vein is Sidney, who delights to go on parade in his fictitious guise as the simpleton Astrophil:

> Some Lovers speake when they their Muses entertaine,
> Of hopes begot by feare, of wot not what desires:
> Of force of heav'nly beames, infusing hellish paine:
> Of living deaths, dear wounds, faire stormes and
> > freesing fires
>
> . . . .
> I can speake what I feele, and feele as much as they.
> > (*Astrophil and Stella*, 6)

In the witty opening discourse of 'That unripe side of earth', Donne also dissociates his present sentiments from the 'fever' and 'paine' of 'sighing Ode' or 'crosse-arm'd Elegie'. He is not the stock lover, with wreathed arms, pleading for 'pitty' from a mistress who shows nought but 'disdaine'. He is not, that is, in this context, the Donne of 'The Apparition', not of that class of lovers who strive 'through womans scornes, women to know' (l. 65). Like Astrophil, he is less literary, more himself: 'The honesties of love with ease I doe' (l. 75). Needless to say, the purpose of his poem is different from Sidney's in that the love he feels for the Countess of Huntingdon is not the erotic passion Astrophil suffers for Stella. Donne shares with the Countess his joke at the impropriety of addressing an aristocratic patroness as 'A weather-beaten Lover' addresses 'every girle' (63-4). And then, at line 77, he proceeds to define how far above her *Zani's* she really stands:

> But (madame) I now thinke on you; and here
> Where we are at our hights, you but appeare,
> We are but clouds you rise from, our noone-ray
> But a foule shadow, not your breake of day.   (77-80)

Her admirers are legion and distant. Donne repudiates flattery as strongly as Jonson and Daniel are wont to do.[1]

> You are a perfectnesse, so curious hit,
> That youngest flatteries doe scandall it.   (83-4)

The repudiation of flattery itself flatters. Donne is ready with his answer to this objection in another address to the Countess of Huntingdon. In 'Man to Gods image, *Eve*, to mans was made' (?1608-9), he spins the ball back into the court of the great lady he praises. The Petrarchan images of praise abound: for him she is a star, gold, 'heavenly things', one from whom 'all vertues flow'. And then, in a subtly argued tail-piece, he prevents all reply from her:

> If you can thinke these flatteries, they are,
> For then your judgement is below my praise,
> If they were so, oft, flatteries worke as farre,
> As Counsels, and as farre th'endeavour raise.
>
> So my ill reaching you might there grow good,
> But I remaine a poyson'd fountaine still;
> But not your beauty, vertue, knowledge, blood
> Are more above all flattery, then my will.
>
> And if I flatter any,' tis not you
> But my owne judgement, who did long agoe
> Pronounce, that all these praises should be true,
> And vertue should your beauty, 'and birth outgrow.

---

[1] See, for example, Jonson's 'An Epistle to Master IOHN SELDEN' (*The Vnderwood*, XIV) in which he promises a new vein in hard-won praise, turning 'a sharper eye' upon those earlier poems in which, he admits, he has 'too oft preferr'd/ Men past their terms, and prais'd some names too much'; and also Daniel's epistle 'To the Lord Henry Howard' in which he asserts that only 'Vertue and Desart' can make a poet's compliment valid, for 'Praise, if it be not choice, and laide aright, / Can yeeld no lustre where it is bestowde, / Nor any way can grace the giuers Arte'.

Now that my prophesies are all fulfill'd,
   Rather then God should not be honour'd too,
And all these gifts confess'd which hee instill'd,
   Your selfe were bound to say that which I doe.

So I, but your Recorder am in this,
   Or mouth, and Speaker of the universe,
A ministeriall Notary, for'tis
   Not I, but you and fame, that make this verse;

I was your Prophet in your yonger dayes,
And now your Chaplaine, God in you to praise.

                           (49-70)

12

Hermetic Elements in Donne's Poetic Vision

ELUNED CRAWSHAW

Holy Alkimy was based on a set of firm *a priori* beliefs about the nature of the universe which were never subjected to rigorous scrutiny by the adepts themselves. When, later in the seventeenth century, experimental science as we understand it began to develop, the demand for demonstrable proofs rather than blind adherence to ancient authority meant that the *slidynge science* rapidly lost ground. But Donne's physics is still very much in the alchemical tradition, and where he turns its language to metaphysical ends he does not depart from that tradition, for while on one level alchemy has undoubtedly deserved its reputation for charlatanism most serious writers considered it to be as much a spiritual exercise as a physical operation. Even Sir Thomas Browne remarked

> The smattering I have of the Philosophers stone, (which is something more than the perfect exaltation of gold) hath taught me a great deal of Divinity, and instructed my beliefe, how that immortall spirit and incorruptible substance of my soule may lye obscure, and sleepe a while within this house of flesh.[1]

There is nothing incongruous then in the appearance of alchemical imagery in Donne's meditative and religious verse, but before I look at the way he uses some individual images it is necessary to consider how some of the broader issues of Hermetism bear on Donne's vision of things.

One of the distinguishing characteristics of alchemy was that it was qualitative, unlike modern chemistry, and a qualitative

---

[1] *Religio Medici*, London, 1643, pp. 17-18.

theory of matter does more than provide an objective definition of chemical properties. It recognises not only the variations in appearance and behaviour between substances but differences in value, classifying things according (for instance) to their purity – a simple physical description which clearly has strong moral overtones. Transmutation can only be meaningful when some substances are considered superior to and more desirable than others. This way of seeing matter is a development of the old notion of a hierarchy of being where 'all things are linked together, and connected one with another in a chain ascending from the lowest to the highest'.[1] This chain was a minutely graduated order of material forms and spiritual essences 'which is extended *a non Gradu ad non Gradum*, From that which is *beneath* all *Apprehension*, to that which is *above* all Apprehension.'[2] This order, however, is not established once and for all but allows for the possible movement of things up or down and although individual alchemists differed on details they all believed that their work would raise matter to a higher level and described the changes base metals underwent as they ascended through higher forms to gold. Indeed the very point of such an order is that everything should be involved in the movement upwards, including man, since 'the aim of Hierarchy is the greatest possible assimilation to and union with God'.[3]

Alchemy did not draw hard and fast lines between the material and the spiritual. The qualities ascribed to matter often had moral connotations, and, since 'the whole external world with all its creatures is an indication or figure of the inner spiritual world',[4] the physical process of purifying metals was thought to be paralleled by a spiritual one, the adept undergoing purgation simultaneously with the metals. Thus the significance of the work extended far beyond the confines of the crucible, and spiritual attainment might be expressed in terms of the material hierarchy.

---

[1] *Asclepius*, 3, in Sir Walter Scott, *Hermetica*, Oxford, 1924, i, p. 327.

[2] Thomas Vaughan, *Lumen de Lumine*, London, 1651, p. 44.

[3] Ps. Dionysus, *De Coelestia Hierarchia*, in Migne, *Patrologiae Graecae*, iii, col. 171.

[4] Jacob Boehme, *De Signatura Rerum*, cap. 9. in *Sämtliche Schriften*, ed. W. E. Peuckert, Stuttgart, 1955-60, vi, p. 96.

till death us lay
To ripe and mellow there, we'are stubborne clay
Parents make us earth, and soules dignifie
Us to be glasse; here to grow gold we lie.

(*Epitaph on Himselfe*, 11-14)

In his *Elegie on the Lady Marckham* Donne envisages a refinement through clay, porcelain and precious stones while the grave as the limbeck, the vessel of purification, serves as a reminder that this order of purity is achieved only at the resurrection of the body. The idea recurs in these poems:

The ravenous earth that now wooes her to be
Earth too, will be a *Lemnia;* and the tree
That wraps that christall in a wooden Tombe,
Shall be took up spruce, fill'd with diamond.

(*Elegie. Death,* 57-60)

Death here is not a sudden transformation but the completion of a process initiated in life, for the chain passes unbroken from life to death even though the links take on a new degree of purity.

The alchemists' universe was wholly permeated by the divine spirit so that, according to one adept, 'if we open any *Natural Body,* and *separat* all the *parts* thereof *one* from *another,* we shall come at *last* to the *Prester,* which is the *Candle,* and *secret Light* of God'.[1] The graduation of matter was based on the amount of spirit it was held to contain since 'into all things he [God] infuses spirit, assigning it to each in larger measure, in proportion as the thing stands higher in the scale of being'.[2] To perfect a substance the alchemist had to discover and 'multiply' this spirit. So the worlds of physics and metaphysics overlap and intermingle, and refinement is at once material and spiritual:

Her Soule is gone to usher up her corse,
Which shall be' almost another soule, for there
Bodies are purer, then best Soules are here.

(*Elegie on Mris Boulstred,* 46-8)

Even the alchemists had to admit that this spirit is invisible under normal circumstances when '*the Light* appears not, it is

---

[1] Thomas Vaughan, *op. cit.,* p. 88. [2] *Asclepius,* 3, *ed. cit.,* 1, 317.

Ecclips'd with the *Grossenesse* of the *matter*.[1] But the purer a substance is the more likely it is that the light will shine through, and lack of density therefore both denotes purity itself and reveals the spirit. This sort of thinking lies behind Donne's praise of beauty which is 'all colour all Diaphanous'.

> wee understood
> Her by her sight; her pure, and eloquent blood
> Spoke in her cheekes, and so distinctly wrought,
> That one might almost say, her body thought;
> (*The second Anniversary*, 243-6)

Physical beauty then is not an accidental attribute of some women but an outward sign

> Through which all things within without were shown.
> (*To the Countess of Bedford*, 'Honour is so', 30)

Moral goodness alone can dare present a 'through-shine front,' having no need to deceive by obscuring or assuming false colours. This equation of transparency with purity is confirmed and illustrated by other images of glass, crystal, amber and specular stone whose very clarity implies their high standing in the order of being.

But the possibility of advancement in this hierarchy is counterbalanced by that of decline. Virtue may promote but sin demotes, and if on the one hand the body can become 'almost another soule'

> Whilst in our soules sinne bred and pamper'd is,
> Our soules become wormeaten carkases;
> (*Epitaph on Himselfe*, 15-16)

So all things in the universe are in a state of flux, but man has a unique position since his rational soul is endowed with the ability to choose the direction it will take. At the creation God, according to Pico della Mirandola, 'took man as a creature of indeterminate nature' and gave him 'a place in the middle of the

---

[1] Thomas Vaughan, *op. cit.*, p. 41.

world'[1] whence he might move at will. Like so many Humanists Pico believed he was living at the dawn of the new Golden Age. Man is 'a great miracle' he declared, citing the Hermetic *Asclepius,* and when he added 'we can become what we will'[2] the implication was that we would choose advancement. Many of the Hermetic texts are concerned with a fall and regeneration of man which syncretists seized on as foreshadowings of Christian doctrine, but however ambitious the alchemists were they never quite shared the enthusiasm of the Florentine Neoplatonists for the imminence of this renewal. Thomas Vaughan commented that the rational soul ' . . . adheres sometimes to the *Mens,* or *superior portion* of the *Soul,* and then it is filled with the *Divine Light,* but most commonly it descends into the *aethereal inferior portion,* which Saint *Paul* calls *Homo animalis'.*[3] Indeed one of the reasons for the alchemists' elitism was that they believed most men to be unworthy of knowledge so that it was 'not *safe,* nor *convenient* that all *Eares* should heare even the *mysteries* of *Religion'.*[4] For Donne too this was no returning age of gold. Through sin we have forfeited any dignity conferred on us by our place in the hierarchy, and the exalted terms of praise lavished on mankind by the Humanists are bitterly ironic when they come from Donne.

> Thus man, this worlds Vice-Emperour, in whom
> All faculties, all graces are at home;
>
> · · · · · · · · · ·
>
> This man, whom God did wooe, and loth t'attend
> Till man came up, did downe to man descend,
> This man, so great, that all that is, is his,
> Oh what a trifle, and poore thing he is!
>
> (*The first Anniversary,* 161-70)

Donne's position here is absolutely antithetical to that of the Florentine Neoplatonists. Man is not Vice-Emperor but Lord of Misrule, and the age, far from being golden, is iron 'and

---

[1] Pico della Mirandola, *Oration on the Dignity of Man,* in *The Renaissance Philosophy of Man,* ed. E. Cassirer, P. O. Kristeller, J. H. Randall, 1963, p. 224.

[2] *Ibid.,* p. 223.

[3] *Anthroposophia Theomagica,* London, 1650, pp. 40-1.

[4] Thomas Vaughan, *Aula Lucis,* London, 1652, p. 29.

rustie too' (line 426). Our continuing depravity perpetuates the decline initiated by Adam's sin:

> mankinde decayes so soone,
> We'are scarce our Fathers shadowes cast at noone:
> Onely death addes t'our length: nor are wee growne
> In stature to be men, till we are none.
>
> (*Ibid.*, 143-6)

We should be engaged on realising our potential, taking advantage of the possibility of moving upwards towards the infinite. According to Ficino 'the mind cannot fail to strive after that end',[1] but Donne sees that we can and do fail in this. Our aim should be to re-achieve the prelapsarian condition, 'to rectifie/Nature, to what she was'.[2] This was also the business of the alchemists since they sought the untainted *prima materia* of the Creation. All matter had been debased by the Fall but it remained susceptible to external influences, from the planets for instance, and even from men who, as adepts, had a sufficient knowledge of the occult processes of the cosmos to gain control over them and manipulate them in order to regenerate material things.

Thomas Vaughan in his treatise *Euphrates* shows how alchemical work might be a kind of applied natural theology:

> For my own part, I have this Assurance of *Philosophy*, that all the *Mysteries* of *Nature* consist in the *knowledge* of that *Corruption*, which is mention'd in *Scripture*, and which succeeded the *Fall*; namely to know what it is, and where it resides principally: as also to know what Substance that is, which resists it most . . .[3]

Alchemy had incorporated the Aristotelian notion of a world in which nature has been frustrated and things fall short of their true perfection, so that while in Eden 'things ripened sooner and did longer last', they now neither mature nor endure. The Philosophers' Stone in fact 'does no more than hasten a purification for which Nature requires ages, and which in some cases

---

[1] Marsilio Ficino, *Five Questions concerning the Mind*, in *Renaissance Philosophy of Man*, p. 211.

[2] *To Sir Edward Herbert, at Julyers*, 34-5.

[3] *Op. cit.*, pp. 13-14.

Nature could not effect at all in the absence of an active purifying agent'.[1] So the alchemists aimed to expedite the movement of immature substances to gold, heating them for months in the laboratory in an effort to 'ripen' them. Paracelsus defined alchemy as 'that which brings the incomplete to completion', and as 'that alone which prepares the impure by fire and makes it pure'.[2]

Christian alchemists were extending the problem of repairing the Fall into the physical plane when they sought the *Terra Adamica*, the uncorrupted *prima materia*, in a tangible form. But they did not lose sight of the moral and spiritual processes of recovery which ran parallel to material reparation and without which it would have been impossible. The true adept must therefore be exceptionally pious, and he had to make a spiritual commitment almost equal to that of one pursuing a contemplative religious life.[3] Most Christian alchemists interspersed their descriptions of the *opus* with prayers for divine assistance, while in some cases the religious aspect of the work was developed to a very high degree, and Melchior Cibinensis in fact produced an alchemical parody of the Mass, *Addam et processum sub forma missae*. Such alchemists whose interests transcended the mere manufacture of gold used the language of chemistry as a veil for spiritual arcana. They saw nothing anomalous in talking of such matters in material terms and they consciously intended that their symbols should

> represent *two things*, according to the capacity and understanding of them that behold them; First, the *mysteries* of our future and undoubted *Resurrection*, at the day of Iudgement, and coming of

[1] A. J. Pernety, *Dictionnaire Mytho-Hermetique*, Paris, 1787, p. 153.

[2] *Labyrinthus medicorum errantiun*, Ch. 5. in *Sämtliche Werke*, ed. Sudhoff, München and Berlin, 1922-33, xi, pp. 188-9.

[3] Thomas Vaughan wrote 'Thou must prepare *thy self*, till thou art conformable to Him, whom thou wouldest entertain. . . . Fit thy *Roofe* to thy *God*. . . . When thou hast set thy *House* in *Order*, do not thinke thy Guest will come without *Invitation:* Thous must *tyre* him out with pious importunities. . . . *This is the way thou must walk in*, which if thou doest thou shalt *perceive a sudden Illustration*.' (*Anima Magica Abscondita*, London, 1650, pp. 46-7).

According to many alchemists, Thomas Norton among them, 'He must have Grace that would for this Arte sue.' (*The Ordinall of Alchimy*, in *Theatrum Chemicum Britannicum*, ed. Elias Ashmole, London, 1652, p. 9).

good *Iesus* . . . And secondly, they may signifie to them, which are skilled in Naturall *Philosophy*, all the principall and necessary operations of the *Maistery*. These *Hieroglyphicke figures* shall serue as two wayes to leade vnto the heauenly life: the first and most open sense, teaching the sacred *Mysteries* of our saluation . . . the other teaching euery man, that hath some small vnderstanding in the *Stone*, the lineary way of the worke.[1]

The physical terms of alchemy thus have a simultaneous moral application, and we are urged to purify and concentrate what is good on both levels. Yet Donne sees that we expedite decay not growth, dissipate what we should preserve and leave our-selves less not only in quantity but more important, in quality. And while the alchemists treasured the wisdom of ancient sages as revelations of knowledge which would assist regeneration, Donne sees rather that we neglect all such aid and become active in our own destruction.

> this were light, did our lesse volume hold
> All the old Text; or had wee chang'd to gold
> Their silver; or dispos'd into lesse glasse
> Spirits of vertue, which then scatter'd was.
> But 'tis not so: w'are not retir'd but dampt;
> And as our bodies, so our mindes are crampt:
> 'Tis shrinking, not close weaving that hath thus,
> In minde, and body both bedwarfed us.
>
> (*The first Anniversary*, 147-54)

While occult philosophers established clear distinctions be-tween the ranks of the hierarchy of being they did not envisage a universe which was fragmented or compartmentalised. It was on the contrary a highly complex structure with layer upon layer of corresponding planes held together in a dynamic relationship, which Thomas Vaughan, for instance, described a 'a vitall magneticall series'. This magnetism is a sort of sympathy between the parts of the universe causing them to reflect and represent each other. The storms in *Lear* and the unnatural

---

[1] Eirenaeus Orandus, *Nicholas Flammel, His Exposition of the Hieroglyphicall Figures which he caused to be painted upon an Arch in St Innocents Church-yard*, Paris, 1624, pp. 34-5.

events in *Macbeth* show just this sense of a sympathetic inter-action between the worlds of man and nature, and they show too the cosmically destructive nature of human sin in such a universe.

This mode of seeing a correlation between the moral and physical planes is fundamental to Hermetic speculation. The *Tabula Smaragdina* attributed to Hermes Trismegistus stated that 'what is below is like that which is above, and what is above is like that which is below', and Hermetic writers consequently drew elaborate analogies between things terrestrial and celestial. Some of the alchemists also embraced astrology since it postulated definite relationships between the planets and material forms.[1] So nothing is without significance in this sort of universe and virtually everything may be symbolic, however abstrusely, of something else; just as for Donne man's head-first birth becomes a figure of his headlong fall into confusion.

The notion of correspondence gave a symbolic force to alchemical operations since the metals might represent the alchemist and the degree of purity they reached would con-

---

[1] Astrological talismans derived power from the fact that they were made of materials 'ruled' by certain planets at a time when those planets were strongly placed in the heavens. Donne uses this image in 'A Valediction: of my Name, in the Window'.

> As all the vertuous powers which are
> Fix'd in the starres, are said to flow
> Into such characters, as graved bee
> When those starres have supremacie,
>
> So since this name was cut
> When love and griefe their exaltation had,
> No doore 'gainst this names influence shut;

Alchemists similarly aimed to entrap specific planetary influences by selecting the appropriate materials and time for the purpose. It was held that substances 'reduced' to their first matter might be reformed and that at this stage they would be more susceptible to formative influxes from the planets.

> With *Astrologie* joyne Elements also,
> To fortune their Workings as theie goe:
> Such simple kindes unformed and unwrought,
> Must craftily be guided till the end be sought.
> All which season theie have more obedience,
> Above formed Natures to Sterrs influence.
>
> (Thomas Norton, op. cit. pp. 60-1)

sequently indicate the adept's own level of spiritual attainment. According to Thomas Norton the adept had already to be in state of grace if he were to achieve anything in the laboratory. So the alchemist had to prepare himself as well as his materials, and while the rituals and verbal formulae vary from one writer to another, the principle obtains in all cases that the spiritual condition of the man may have actual physical repercussions. Nature had originally been corrupted by man's moral lapse and it continues to be affected by sin. Donne, in the *Anniversaries* faces the problems of transience and corruption which were central to alchemy and sees that

> as mankinde, so is the worlds whole frame
> Quite out of joynt, almost created lame:
> (*The first Anniversary*, 191-2)

This is reinforced by the comparisons drawn between man as the microcosm and the universe. The image of man as 'a little world made cunningly/Of Elements' was a commonplace one, but it had considerable significance for alchemical writers since according to their theories it was literally true. All things were produced from one *prima materia*, so that there was a fundamental unity in the universe, and 'the difference between the great world and the microcosm consists only in this . . . that man is disposed and created in another form, image, figure and substance, and that earth is flesh in man, water his blood, fire his heat and air his balsam'.[1] And because the world was animated by the Divine Spirit 'man is the microcosm not just in form or bodily substance but is in all powers and virtues like the great world.'[2] It is not a piece of wild hyperbole then when Donne asserts that Elizabeth Drury's death injures or diminishes the world. Her death is at once cosmic in its implications and symptomatic of the state of things:

> She to whom this world must it selfe refer,
> As Suburbs, or the Microcosme of her,
> Shee, shee is dead; shee's dead: when thou knowst this,
> Thou knowst how lame a cripple this world is.

---

[1] Paracelsus, *Ein mantische Entwurf*, in Sudhoff, x, p. 648.
[2] Paracelsus, *Opus Paramirum* in Sudhoff, ix, p. 308.

> And learn'st thus much by our Anatomy,
> That this worlds generall sickenesse doth not lie
> In any humour, or one certaine part;
>
> (*The first Anniversary*, 235-41)

Alchemical writers tended to use the microcosm symbolism to extol the great potential of man who contains all things. But Donne uses it savagely, seeing man as an undeveloped mass of base prima materia, 'a lumpe, where all beasts kneaded bee'.[1] And the notion of an animal soul takes on new force when Donne describes the inner conflict of sin in which 'all which was man in him, is eate away'. This state of spiritual anarchy where proliferating passions 'on one another feed/Yet couple'in anger, and new monsters breed' is in brutal contrast to the vision of bodies of crystal, diamond and gold. Against our potential for progress is the reality of our decline, and it is clear that our position in the hierarchy is at best tenuous since we can and do 'adde weight to heavens heaviest curse', and our mobility becomes instability. Here again Donne's position is very different from the Neoplatonists', for when they speak of what they vaguely call *man* they picture a being capable of and inclined to almost infinite progress. Some of the Hermetic texts such as the *Pimander* and the *Asclepius* which exerted considerable influence on them imply that man is even to re-achieve a divinity lost at the Fall. But Donne, while he conceives of progress in terms of a few specific individuals, sees mankind in general as bent on a downward course.

The macrocosm/microcosm relationship was not confined to man and the cosmos, but might be held to exist on one hand between man and society, and on the other between society and the universe. Social structure thus becomes comparable with the order of nature, and again the moral force of alchemical language comes through its physical imagery:

> As in the first Chaos confusedly
> Each elements qualities were in the'other three;
> So pride, lust, covetize, being severall
> To these three places, yet all are in all,
>
> (*To Sir Henry Wotton*, 'Sir, more then kisses,' 29-32)

---

[1] *To Sir Edward Herbert* at Julyers, i.

Here Donne takes the Paracelsian theory of the *tria prima* to illustrate the corruption of society. Paracelsus said that 'every element is divided into three parts . . . into salt, which is also known as balsam, into resin, known as sulphur, and into liquid, known as mercury'.[1] Salt, sulphur and mercury were not, in this context, the substances we recognise as such, but represented the principles of solidity, combustibility and liquidity from which the four elements sprang. And these divisions had their counterparts in spiritual or 'transcendental' alchemy since salt represented the body, sulphur the soul and mercury the spirit. So Donne uses these pseudo-chemical classifications in relation to moral qualities here, and adds a sting by replacing the essentially pure *tria prima* with three vices.

It was a commonplace of much contemporary political writing that human society should be organised according to the divinely established pattern of the macrocosm. Ulysses reinforces his argument on degree with the assertion that

> The heavens themselves, the planets, and this centre
> Observe degree, priority and place.

This does not run counter to the notion of progress which is so deeply rooted in the hierarchical scheme, but serves to uphold the necessity that any progress must be merited so that the constituent parts of the universe remain in a right relationship to each other. But as soon as we begin to falsify the scheme of things or deny its existence we 'untune that string' and the structure begins to crumble:

> 'Tis all in peeces, all cohaerence gone;
> All just supply, and all Relation:
> Prince, Subject, Father, Sonne, are things forgot,
> For every man alone thinkes he has got
> To be a Phoenix, and that then can bee
> None of that kinde, of which he is, but hee.
>
> (*The first Anniversary*, 213-18)

This failure to grasp how things should be in our own world is just part of our general inability to make sense of things as a

---

[1] *Labyrinthus medicorum errantium*, Ch. 3 in Sudhoff, xi, 179-80.

whole. Christian mystics had stressed the prime necessity of self-awareness for, as Walter Hilton wrote, 'it nedeth a soule that wolde have knowynge of ghostly thynges for to have firste knowynge of itself'.[1] And those alchemists whose main concern is their own regeneration come close to the religious mystical tradition here. If there is to be a recovery of the Fall it must begin with an understanding of the nature of corruption and its source in us. Agrippa shows how at this point practical and transcendental Hermetism are finally bound together:

> Whosoever . . . shall know himself, shall know all things in himself, especially he shall know God . . . and Geber in his summ of Alchimy teacheth, that no man shall come to the perfection of this art, who shall not know the principles of it in himself.'[2]

Yet Donne sees that we are unable to come to an understanding of our decline:

> Poore soule, in this thy flesh what dost thou know?
> Thou know'st thy selfe so little, as thou know'st not,
> How thou didst die,
>
> *(The second Anniversary, 254-6)*

And this failure extends to all our attempts at knowledge, for, as Montaigne remarked, 'hee who hath no understanding of himselfe, what can he have understanding of'.[3] We are not inadequate only in the face of 'ghostly thynges', but because all our faculties have been debased by the Fall. Sense perception is delusive, yet we lack the means to

> shake off this Pedantery,
> Of being taught by sense, and Fantasie[4]   (291-2)

---

[1] Walter Hilton, *Scala Perfectionis*, London, 1494, 2.30.

[2] H. C. Agrippa, *De Occulta Philosophia Libri Tres*, trans. J. F., *Three Books of Occult Philosophy*, London, 1651, p. 460.

[3] *An Apologie of Raymond Sebond*, *The Essayes of Michael Lord of Montaigne*, trans. John Florio, 1891, p. 284.

[4] The senses are not only inadequate themselves but have to deal with a mutable world which may rapidly invalidate conclusions based on perception. '. . . seeing all things are subject to passe from one change to another, reason, which therein seeketh a reall subsistence, findes her selfe deceived as unable to perceive any thing subsistent and permanent.' (Montaigne, *Sebond*, p. 309).

The discussion of astronomy in *The second Anniversary* illustrates this unreliability of experience. The 'perplexed course' of the heavens is a projection of our own perplexity, for we construct theories from what we at best incompletely and often wrongly observe, and further observations force us to modify our conclusions until we end in confusion. The Ptolemaic view of the universe which began with simple planetary spheres and ended in a tangle of cycles and epicycles added to accommodate newly discovered phenomena becomes a type of our efforts to systematise things without understanding them.

But astronomy only deals with one relatively straightforward aspect of the heavens and does not take into account the hidden sympathies which bind earth and heaven together. The *Asclepius* states that 'by all the heavenly bodies . . . there is poured into all matter an uninterrupted stream, emanating from God and holding all things together unseen'.[1] And the correspondences which exist between heaven and earth in a sympathetic cosmos are a hidden aid to man in his efforts at recovery. But if the mechanical processes of the universe are beyond us we cannot hope to probe its occult workings, and sin, which clouds our vision, finally accomplishes a slow deterioration in the cosmic structure:

> Nor in ought more this worlds decay appeares,
> Then that her influence the heav'n forbeares,
> Or that the Elements doe not feele this,
> The father, or the mother barren is.
>
> (*The first Anniversary*, 377-80)

For Hermetic philosophers these correspondences are a vital source of knowledge, and of power too since natural magic rests on the ability to interpret and manipulate them. Paracelsus discussing his notion of *das Buch des Firmaments* says that 'just as every word has its particular meaning but is not a sentence in itself, so the stars of the heavens must be put together like the perfect words which make a complete sentence, and we must draw the heavenly sentence from them'.[2] But Henry Vaughan, brother of the Hermetist Thomas, looking at the book of nature

---

[1] *Ed. cit.*, p. 291.
[2] *Labyrinthus medicorum errantium, ed. cit.*, p. 176.

sees that sin diminishes our ability to piece things together and interpret them so that they become

> Hyeroglyphicks quite dismembred,
> And broken letters scarce remembred.[1]

So in an age when virtue is 'ebb'd out to a dead low tyde', Donne also sees a 'booke of creatures' which is falling apart, for sin precludes us from knowledge and at the same time destroys its channels:

> The art is lost, and correspondence too.
> For heaven gives little, and the earth takes lesse,
> And man least knowes their trade and purposes.
> (*The first Anniversary*, 396-8)

Our inner chaos is projected onto the universe and we are again faced with a loss of coherence:

> The Sun is lost, and th'earth, and no mans wit
> Can well direct him where to looke for it.
> And freely men confesse that this world's spent,
> When in the Planets, and the Firmament
> They seeke so many new; they see that this
> Is crumbled out againe to his Atomies.
> (*Ibid.*, 207-12)

Donne does, it is true, raise the Galen/Paracelsus, Ptolemy/ Copernicus controversies, but the question of whether he favoured the old or new philosophy is largely irrelevant here because as far as he is concerned we cannot arrive at any definitive truth:

> one Soule thinkes one, and another way
> Another thinkes, and 'tis an even lay.[2]
> (*The second Anniversary*, 267-8)

Donne derides the scientific mode of empirical enquiry because

---

[1] *Vanity of Spirit*, 24-5.

[2] cf. Montaigne: 'The question is now, if Ptolemey was heretofore deceived in the grounds of his reason, whether it were not folly in me to trust what these late fellowes say of it, and whether it be not more likely that this huge body which we terme the worlde is another manner of thing than we judge it.'

we lack the faculties for it. Since reason and the senses have been debased by the Fall we can be sure neither of our perceptions nor of what we deduce from them, The *tria prima* may or may not be an advance on the four elements but finally this is not what matters, for all our systems are arbitrary and short-lived. All that has been achieved is an 'infinite confusion of opinions and sentences which this goodly humane reason by her certainty and clear-sighted vigilance brings forth in whatsoever it meddleth withal'.[1] And our debates are as trivial as our attitudes are petty, 'a hundred controversies of an Ant', because we are concerned with superficial explanations of 'matters of fact'. These are 'unconcerning things' since we approach them in a way which does not bear on our regeneration, and we waste our small abilities on an unstable phenomenal world where the *facts* change and we fail to examine the underlying moral issues. And it seems that Donne's scepticism must come ultimately to this declaration that we can establish nothing absolutely and that everything, including our notion of morality, is relative, 'an even lay':

> Ther's nothing simply good, nor ill alone,
> Of every quality comparison,
> The onely measure is, and judge, opinion.
>
> (*Metempsychosis*, 518-20)

But such a conclusion runs counter to the movement of Donne's thought in these poems where he is attempting to define the nature of good and evil. So he does not end with a counsel of despair but with the need for a constant awareness of human fallibility and the ease with which pride can lead to unyielding dogmatism where we are 'too stiffe to recant'. And when he

---

[1] Montaigne, *Sebond*, p. 275. Montaigne complained that 'Men only debate and question of the branch, not of the tree: they ask not whether a thing be true, but whether it was understood or meant thus. They enquire not whether Galen hath spoken any thing of worth, but whether thus, or so, or otherwise.'

Hermetism was particularly bedevilled by this approach, since it was based on the transmission of secret knowledge from master to pupil; and authority and age therefore carried great weight. The seventeenth century saw a shift of emphasis with the decline of this appeal to authority and the rise of empirical scientific method.

asks 'in this thy flesh what canst thou know?' he is pointing not to our inability ever to know anything but our incapacity while we are unregenerate. Montaigne remarked that 'all things are hid from us: there is not one thing that we may establish, how and what it is'.[1] So there are absolutes but they are concealed from us in this life just as for the Hermetists they were concealed in the arcane symbols of the book of the universe or obscured by the veils of sin.

It would be a gross misrepresentation to suggest that Donne would have embraced Hermetism as a complete philosophical system since his position is that no system can be either complete or free of error. So Donne goes 'about it and about', and if he is interested in the notions of regeneration which pervade it, it is clear from poems such as 'Love's Alchymie that he has no time for practical Hermetism. He remains uncommitted too when he talks of Hermes, even though the whole issue of the existence of such a sage was being called in question. In 1614 Isaac Casaubon published his conclusions on the writings attributed to Hermes Trismegistus arguing that they were not survivals from ancient Egypt but were much later works showing Christian and Platonic influences.[2] So the Hermetica were slowly being discredited and, with the authenticity of the texts in dispute, Hermetism was greatly weakened in the course of the seventeenth century. Some of its adherents like Fludd and Vaughan simply ignored Casaubon, but many others, including the Cambridge Platonists, More and Cudworth, modified their acceptance of the texts, admitting that 'though some of the Trismegistick books were either wholly counterfeited, or else had certain suppositious passages inserted into them by some Christian hand', yet there were 'others of them wholly Egyptian'[3]. So Hermetism no longer enjoyed the respect it had in preceding centuries. In one of his sermons, however, Donne still ranks Hermes with Plato and Zoroaster as one of the pristine sages in whose writings might be found foreshadowing of the teachings

---

[1] *Sebond*, p. 258.

[2] *Exercitationes XVI. Ad Cardinalio Baronii Prolegomena in Annales. . . . Londinii*, 1614.

[3] Ralph Cudworth, *The True Intellectual System of the Universe*, London, 1743, p. 333.

of the Gospels.[1] This is very much in line with the attitude of earlier Renaissance writers who attempted to trace the descent of wisdom through the major figures of antiquity and for whom Hermes was as solid as Plato.[2] Yet Donne is aware that this view has been threatened, for, a year later, he describes Hermes as 'elder (as some will have it) then any but some of the first Secretaries of the Holy Ghost in the Bible'.[3] This is explicitly someone else's opinion, and Donne does not involve himself in the debate, perhaps itself another controversy of an ant, because he has no interest in defending or destroying Hermetism and the historical origins of notions or images which attract him are to a large extent immaterial.

In the *Songs and Sonnets* Donne uses alchemical imagery dramatically and flamboyantly and twists it into striking paradoxes.

> For I am every dead thing,
> In whom love wrought new Alchimie.
> For his art did expresse
> A quintessence even from nothingnesse,
> From dull privations, and leane emptinesse:
> He ruin'd mee, and I am rebegot
> Of absence, darknesse, death; things which are not.
>
> (*A Nocturnall upon S. Lucies day, being the shortest day* 12-18)

But in the funeral poems he is more subdued, relying often on the associative value of single words such as 'balm' or 'elixir'. Alchemical language is distinctive and such words which belong almost exclusively to it evoke immediately the whole world of Hermetic speculation. The alchemists were acutely aware of transience and corruption, of the need for regeneration, and they felt that the final cause of mutability in the universe was moral rather than purely physical. And since

---

1 ' . . . in *Trismegistus*, and in *Zoroaster*, and in *Plato*, . . . there seeme to be clearer, and more literall expressings of the Trinity, then are in all the Prophets of the Old Testament.' *The Sermons of John Donne*, ed. G. R. Potter and E. M. Simpson, California, 1953-62, viii, p. 55. (*Preached at St Dunstan's Upon Trinity Sunday, 1627, on Revelation 4.8.* No. 44 in *LXXX Sermons.*)

2 For a detailed discussion of this see D. P. Walker, 'The Prisca Theologia in France', *Journal of the Warburg and Courthauld Institutes, XVII*, 1954, pp. 204-59.

3 *Sermons*, ed. cit. viii, p. 255. (*Preached at St Paul's upon Whitsunday, 1628, on John 14.26.* No. 29 in *LXXX Sermons.*)

these are the dominant themes of the funeral poems Donne can formulate the basic questions through the imagery of Hermetism and suggest a way in which things might work.

So Donne looks for some source of permanence in a changing universe just as the alchemists, like Thomas Vaughan, were always seeking some substance which would withstand the corrosion of time. One quality of gold which had caused it to be so highly valued was its apparent resistance to all the natural processes of decay. And *fixatio* was an important stage in the alchemical work, since at this point the base metals cease to be volatile and seem to take on this perfect durability. Gold, as the *elixir vitae*, was again able to overcome the depredations of time, although it only rejuvenated, slowing down the decay not conferring immortality. Faced with the problems of mutability Donne sees that one possibility is to 'forget this rotten world', but he presents this as a wholly negative act, a gesture of indifference born of hopelessness.

> Be not concern'd: studie not why, nor when;
> Doe not so much as not beleeve a man.
> For though to erre, be worst, to try truths forth,
> Is far more businesse, then this world is worth.
>
> (*The second Anniversary*, 51-4)

If evil cannot be overcome the only wise course is to avoid becoming tainted with it, so that 'thou hast but one way, not t'admit/The worlds infection, to be none of it.' (*The first Anniversary*, 245-6). But as 'wee/All reape consumption from one fruitfull tree' (*Elegie, Death*, 37-8) we cannot opt out and must finally come to terms with corruption. Donne suggests that we may do this through virtue which he sees as the analogue of balm. And this single image does much to explicate Donne's notion of virtue. Balsam was the indestructible and regenerative spirit which preserved and strengthened matter and which the alchemists worked to find and 'multiply'. Henry Vaughan, meditating on his younger brother's death, himself finds consolation in this belief that when all seems crumbled away

> a preserving spirit still doth pass
> Untainted through this Masse.
>
> (*Resurrection and Immortality*, 31-2)

So balm belongs both to the physical and the spiritual worlds, and in giving it moral application Donne is not diverging from the traditional double interpretation of alchemical language:

> In every thing there naturally growes
> A *Balsamum* to keepe it fresh, and new,
> If 'twere not injur'd by extrinsique blowes;
> Your birth and beauty are this Balme in you.
> (*To The Countesse of Bedford*, 'Reason is our Soules left hand', 21-4)

And virtue, as balm, is revealed as a spiritual force which, incorruptible itself, strengthens those who possess or come into contact with it. So good men are as 'lumps of Balme', and the language Donne uses of Elizabeth Drury's death becomes in a sense literally true:

> Sicke World, yea, dead, yea putrified, since shee
> Thy'intrinsique balme, and thy preservative,
> Can never be renew'd, thou never live,
>   (*The first Anniversary*, 56-8)

Donne's preoccupation with balm imagery shows that his constant search for a prophylactic against evil has led him to see how virtue may act as a dynamic force resisting the disintegration brought about by sin. And poetry itself, which has a moral force not only because it may speak of virtue but because it may so do long after the poet and his subjects have gone, is part of this search for something which will endure:

> Verse embalmes vertue; 'and Tombs, or Thrones of rimes,
> Preserve fraile transitory fame, as much
> As spice doth bodies from corrupt aires touch.
> (*To the Countesse of Bedford*, *At New-Yeares Tide*, 13-15)

Balm pervaded the whole of a body, and virtue similarly must affect every aspect of our being. This is reinforced by images of gold and transmutation, for to be good in one sphere is to be but 'parcel guilt', to have merely the superficial colouring of virtue. Only

> to Golde we'are growen,
> When vertu ys our Soules Complexione;
> (*A Letter to the Lady Carey, and Mris Essex Riche, from Amyens*, 31-2)

Two of the main processes of purification in the alchemical work were *separatio* and *distillatio* by which the dross was drawn off so that the spirit dispersed in the matter might be drawn into the quintessence. Moral dissipation is a failure to achieve an analogous concentration of goodness because we have not 'dispos'd into lesse glasse/Spirits of vertue,' So against the images of crumbling, falling apart, loss of coherence, Donne sets those of a preservation which is not passive resistance to decay but a vital force pulling things together. Elizabeth Drury's power had precisely this quality,

> The Cyment which did faithfully compact,
> And glue all vertues,
> > *(The first Anniversary*, 49-50)

And her innocence endues her with

> all Magnetique force alone,
> To draw, and fasten sundred parts in one;
> > *(Ibid.*, 221-2)

All the physical properties of gold which made it so valuable in the eyes of the earliest metal-workers and raised it to its height in the alchemical hierarchy find their moral analogues in virtue which remains undiminished though working in a world of evil:

> as no fire, nor rust can spend or waste
> One dramme of gold, but what was first shall last,
> Though it bee forc'd in water, earth, salt, aire,
> Expans'd in infinite, none will impaire;
> So, to your selfe you may additions take,
> But nothing can you lesse, or changed make.
> > *(To the Lady Bedford*, 'You that are she', 35-40)

This may at first sight seem hyperbolic, but the imagery in fact exerts a limiting influence here. Just as the gold produced in alchemy can be 'multiplied' so the friends here are explicitly admitted to be capable of 'additions' of virtue. Donne's praise of Elizabeth Drury goes much further:

> Shee whose Complexion was so even made,
> That which of her Ingredients should invade
> The other three, no Feare, no Art could guesse:
> So far were all remov'd from more or lesse.
> > *(The second Anniversary*, 123-6)

344

She typifies the harmony of true virtue, which owes its strength to overall, balm-like goodness, so that like gold, which was described as *corpus aequale*, it cannot be weakened by the dominance of any one element. Here again Donne's imagery belongs very much to the world of the alchemists since they adhered to the old Galenist notion that matter decayed as a result of a disproportion between its consituents. But it is clear that Donne sees innocence which reflects man's pre-lapsarian state as much more than virtue:

> as in Mithridate, or just perfumes,
> Where all good things being met, no one presumes
> To governe, or to triumph on the rest,
> Only because all were, no part was best.
>
> (*Ibid.*, 127-30)

The key to resistance to evil lies in this innocence which is not simply self-preserving but dynamic and out-going, as his imagery suggests, in the manner of an antidote.

While Donne's alchemical images often seem just a mode of elaborate praise, he does in fact use them very sensitively to stress delicate distinctions between degrees of virtue or between virtue and innocence. His flattery of the Countess of Huntingdon is extravagant, but it also defines the nature and extent of her influence:

> She [virtue] guilded us: But you are gold, and Shee;
> Us she inform'd, but transubstantiates you;
> Soft dispositions which ductile bee,
> Elixarlike, she makes not cleane, but new.
>
> (*To the Countess of Huntingdon*, 'Man to Gods image', 25-8)

The Countess is the substance to be purified, the base matter on which virtue must work. She must be in a fit state for that purification since even the Philosophers' Stone was rarely claimed to transmute wholly unprepared metals to gold. But, according to most alchemists, the gold thus produced was not capable of acting as the ferment or transmuting agent itself, and the Countess has indeed this passive role since men may 'vertue know' by knowing her but they are not made virtuous by the contact. Yet her transmutation sets her above them in the hierarchy so that she becomes an intermediary pointing the way of ascent, being thus God's 'Factor for our loves'. (*To the Countesse of Bedford,* 'Reason is our Soules left hand'). Elizabeth Drury, however, is

> shee that could drive
> The poysonous tincture, and the staine of *Eve,*
> Out of her thoughts, and deeds; and purifie
> All, by a true religious Alchymie;
>
> (*The first Anniversary,* 179-82)

Virtue is the best we can hope for once we have taken on the full sinfulness of human nature, but in Elizabeth Drury, Donne sees that it is possible 'not t'admit/The worlds infection', for her innocence is a type of the pre-lapsarian condition which we should be striving to recover. But despite her considerable purity she remains subject to disease and death and the minute graduation of substances in alchemy allows Donne to show how things may fall fractionally short of perfection. If her soul is as gold her body is as electrum which 'is like gold in its resistance to corruption, unspent and undiminished, and its undimmed brightness; and is like silver in its shining and heavenly lustre'.[1] The fact that Donne applies the term gold to lesser people does not detract from its significance in the *Anniversaries,* for just as there are degrees of electrum (as he acknowledges) so there are degrees of gold, and even degrees of the Stone, each with its own powers. And although Elizabeth Drury is gold, having great influence for good through her innocence, her power is not boundless. She could have done so much 'But that our age was Iron, and rustie too'. This criticism, though aimed directly at the people around her, nevertheless imposes a definite limitation on the force of human innocence in a fallen world. So while Donne seems extravagant in his praise, the terms in which he expresses it keep that praise under strict control. Even allowing for this element of restraint within the imagery, the *Anniversaries* may still seem rather fulsome flattery addressed as they are to a young girl Donne had never met. But like the other funeral poems these are essentially meditations on morality and mortality so that their concern is far broader than the individual deaths on which they are based.

[1] Ps. Dionysus, *De Coelestia Hierarchia,* cap. XV. in Migne, *Patrologiae Graecae,* iii, col. 359.

And far from trying to present Elizabeth Drury in vivid detail Donne depersonalises her so that she becomes a type of innocence, a figure through whom he may explore the nature of virtue.

Donne does push praise to the limits in his alchemical imagery but he simultaneously defines those limits unequivocally. The comparison with gold might seem to be the ultimate which could be made, but the alchemists made nice distinctions even here, and in fact Donne never applies the imagery of the final stage of the work to the people or things of this world. But he writes of Christ

> Hee was all gold when he lay downe, but rose
> All tincture, and doth not alone dispose
> Leaden and iron wills to good, but is
> Of power to make even sinfull flesh like his.
>
> (*Resurrection, imperfect,* 13-16)

This parallel between Christ, the *Filius Dei*, and the Stone, the *Filius Philosophorum*, pervades Christian alchemy, though few writers are as explicit as Basil Valentine.

> From God the Father was born his own Son Jesus Christ, who is God and man, and is without sin, and who also had no need to die. But he died of his own free will, and rose again for the sake of his brothers and sisters, that they might live with him without sin for ever. So, too is the gold without flaw, and is fixed . . . Yet, for the sake of its imperfect and sick brothers and sisters, it dies and rises again glorious and redeemed, and tinctures them to eternal life, making them perfect like to pure gold.[1]

The climax of the work then produces a 'gold' which, when projected onto base metals, has the power of transmutation.[2] 'Salvation it self'. wrote Thomas Vaughan, 'is nothing else but transmutation'.[2] And only Christ can be spoken of as gold when it reaches this degree and becomes the *tincture* or agent of transmutation for He alone is the Saviour whose regenerative power is unbounded.

Much of the vocabulary of alchemy pertains exclusively to the processes of that art, but since Hermetism was based on texts heavily influenced by Gnosticism and Platonism many of

---

[1] *Chymische Schriften*, Hamburg, 1700, p. 364.
[2] *Lumen de Lumine*, p. 93.

its ideas ultimately derive from other sources. So picking Donne's work over for scraps which might be Hermetic could yield a great deal and give a very false picture because of these accretions which belong also to far more widely current bodies of thought. But there are points at which one can be quite sure that Donne's source is not Hermetic. I consider it mistaken to suggest for instance that the Phoenix, Eagle and Dove of 'The Canonization' are 'an example of the use of alchemico-zoological symbolism'.[1] These are common alchemical terms but as Donne uses them here they make as much sense ornithologically as alchemically. And Donne's sensitivity to the shading of his Hermetic language so evident in his *gold* imagery would preclude such a casual approach. I would also suggest that in the *Holy Sonnet* 'Oh my blacke Soule!' Donne employs straightforward liturgical colour symbolism and that an alchemical reading makes nonsense of it for the alchemical sequence is unequivocally black, white and red.[2] Donne does not play with his imagery nor is he careless of its precise meaning. Alchemy offers him a sort of symbolic shorthand whose terms evoke a certain way of approaching some of his major preoccupations, and when he uses its language he does it with the seriousness and precision of the alchemists themselves.

[1] See E. H. Duncan, 'Donne's Alchemical Figures', *Journal of English Literary History*, 1942, pp. 269-71 and J. A. Mazzeo, *Renaissance and Seventeenth Century Studies*, London, 1964, Ch. 4. The Eagle and the Dove have many interpretations in alchemy but they both represent volatile substances as do most bird images and would not be joined to produce the Phoenix or Stone. Donne here uses the Eagle for its suggestions of masculinity, strength and power, while the Dove suggests feminine attributes which could be united in the hermaphroditic Phoenix.

[2] Mazzeo suggests that 'we find the Hermetic progression from black to white, but red, for human beings, is not the highest state of perfection. Red in this instance corresponds to Christ's grace, whose operation was compared to that of the elixir. Instead of completing the analogy Donne has made a conceit of the term "red" and developed it in the poem in at least three of its possible symbolic meanings' (pp. 81-2). This leaves the impression that Donne has somehow allowed various 'possible' interpretations of his symbolism to become hopelessly entangled and that the end of the sonnet finds him undecided about the meaning to be put on it. But the only confusion here is in the appeal to Hermetism at all. Donne is in fact using Isaiah i. 18, for his colour sequence: '. . . though your sins be as scarlet, they shall be as white as snow; though they be red like crimson, they shall be as wool.'

13

More Machiavellian than Machiavel

A Study of the Context of Donne's *Conclave*

SYDNEY ANGLO

In 1611, when John Donne published his *Ignatius His Conclave*, the Society of Jesus had been going strong for more than seventy years; and the literature concerning its virtues and vices, achievements and crimes, had swollen to a monstrous bulk. Indeed, eight years earlier Thomas Bell – whose doleful knell was subsequently tolled by the Jesuit, Robert Parsons – had already complained that the works produced merely in one area of controversy, relating to the activities of the Society in England alone, were so numerous that 'to read all the said books is a labour both tedious and painefull. To buy them is too chargeable for manie. To understand them, as they are confusely published, is a thing not easie for the greater part'.[1] With regard to my own task of elucidating the *Conclave* via 'this pratling fellow Machiavell', I cannot, like Bell, confidently promise that the 'defect herein, my annotations and compendious observations will supplie'; but I hope that an examination of what might be termed the penumbra of ideas surrounding Donne's pamphlet may lead to a helpful appreciation of the text itself.

As far as clarifying the precise points of the controversy touched upon by Donne, and the numerous texts cited in the course of his work, are concerned there is little, I imagine, which could be added to the thorough annotations of Father Healy.[2] However, satirical pamphlets of a semi-popular kind

---

[1] Thomas Bell, *The anatomie of popish tyrannie*, 1603, sig. B4$^{\text{r–v}}$.

[2] John Donne, *Ignatius His Conclave*, ed. T. S. Healy, Oxford, 1969. All references are to this edition, cited as 'Healy'.

make their effect not solely by such precise references. Their effectiveness must also, in large part, depend upon a more general atmosphere of controversy within which an allusion – or even a word – might alert a reader to countless other, similar ideas. And this is certainly the case with the *Conclave*.

The immediate context of Donne's work was the paper war provoked, in May 1606, by the Oath of Allegiance imposed on the Roman Catholic community in England. The Oath was largely inspired by the hostility and fear aroused by the Gunpowder Plot, and Catholics were required to swear that the Pope had no authority to depose the King, or to interfere with his affairs in any way whatsoever; that they would remain loyal whatever attempts were encouraged by the Pope against the King; and that they did 'abhor detest and abjure as impious and hereticall this damnable Doctrine and Position, that Princes which be excommunicated or deprived by the Pope may be deposed or murthered by their Subjectes or any other whosoever'.[1] English Catholics were somewhat taxed by the situation. Their Archpriest, Blackwell, was inclined to regard the Oath as a 'civil' document; advised that it should be taken; and himself set an example to that effect, which was followed by many of his co-religionists. On the other hand, Pope Paul V issued two breves forbidding the taking of the Oath, and subsequently engaged Robert Bellarmine, his 'grand-master of controversies',[2] to set out the Jesuit position which was to regard the Oath as no merely civil act, to recognise that it called into question the foundations of the Catholic faith, and to urge that it be utterly refused. Everybody who was anybody in the world of religious controversy joined in the fray, and volumes poured from the presses both in England and on the Continent, defending the Crown's right to impose such an oath, and defending those Catholics who accepted it; or attacking the whole affair root and branch. Among the first group were two works by King James himself, the *Triplici nodo, triplex cuneus*, and its later reworked form, *An apologie . . . together with a Premonition*; while outstanding on the Jesuit side were

[1] Act 3. Jac.I, c. 4. ix.
[2] David Owen, *Herod and Pilate reconciled: or, the Concord of Papist and Puritan . . . for the Coercion, Deposition, and Killing of Kings*, Cambridge, 1610, p. 38.

the *Responsio* and *Apologia*, in which Bellarmine sought to crush his royal adversary. Healy has shown that the arguments touched upon in Donne's *Conclave* were intimately related to the whole Oath of Allegiance controversy in general, and to these four works in particular; and his general conclusion that the pamphlet was devised as a 'satirical mockery of Bellarmine's two works against James' seems to me completely convincing.[1] However, the problem remains of how this 'satirical mockery' really functions; and to understand this it is necessary to consider a wider context of controversy than that relating merely to the Oath of Allegiance. And here 'Machiavel' provides a clue.

Innovation and innovators

Controversialists have always relished the opportunity to take an opponent's own words and use them against him. The technique was much favoured in the early seventeenth century by enemies of the Catholic cause, who delighted in collecting, tabulating, and commenting upon damaging maxims drawn from the writings of Jesuits and Seculars. As one delighted Protestant inscribed on the fly-leaf of his copy of *The Jesuites Catechisme*: 'Whin knaves fall out, the truth is discovered and honest men come into their own. Here is an unnaturall combat papist against papist.'[2] Thomas Bell was but one of many who undertook to read the work of Catholic adversaries, draw out their principal points of contention, and enable readers to comprehend them with a minimum of labour and cost. Indeed, Bell was so impressed by one of his own efforts that he was convinced that his enemies dare not even name the work: 'their hearts pant so often as they remember it'.[3]

Donne's *Conclave* is, I think, to be regarded partly as a work within this genre: that is, as a confutation of one's enemies who are seen to condemn themselves out of their own mouths. However, instead of the customary tedious apparatus – generally set out in a bewildering variety of type-faces, where points are

---

[1] Healy, p. xxvi. The controversy is summarised at pp. xix-xxix.
[2] Etienne Pasquier, *The Jesuites Catechisme*, n.p., 1602. The copy referred to is in the British Museum, press mark 860.i.4.
[3] Thomas Bell, *The Popes funerall*, 1605, sig. D2ᵛ.

cited paragraph by paragraph, sentence by sentence, and even phrase by phrase, before being laboriously refuted – Donne has conceived a far more striking method. In an '*Extasie*', the author's soul wanders through the heavens; then it suddenly arrives in Hell, and proceeds to a secret place where Lucifer, accompanied by only a few great *innovators*, is enthroned. Boniface III and Mahomet contend for the 'highest roome', although it is clear that the latter is no match for his papal adversary, and has to be content 'to sit (as yet hee doth) at the Popes feet'.[1] Apparently the gates of this inner sanctum are opened but 'once in an Age' when all contenders for admission come forward to plead their causes. The author's soul has arrived at just the right moment, and he recognises the first challenger as Copernicus who impresses Lucifer, until Ignatius Loyola – who is already firmly ensconced – destroys his argument. This sets the pattern for the rest of the work. One after another the claimants come forward; and one after another each has his claim torn to pieces by Ignatius who finally hurls Pope Boniface from the place next to Lucifer and occupies it himself.

Donne's vision of Hell is simply a means of bringing together all the standard accusations against the Jesuits within the compass of one small pamphlet; and the matter is very ingeniously handled. Apart from Machiavel, there are five principal aspirants whose pretensions are crushed by Loyola – and not one is allowed by Donne either to make out more than a token case for himself, or to occupy Ignatius much time in refutation. Only Machiavel makes a real speech on his own behalf, and Ignatius's answer occupies almost exactly a third of the entire pamphlet. The reason for this is patent: Machiavel is the only *innovator* who comes near to challenging Ignatius within the specific terms of *innovation* as defined in the *Conclave*. And one cannot begin to understand the *Conclave* without considering precisely what Donne means by *innovation* and *innovators*. The greater part of the vision is taken up with a contest for admission to Lucifer's secret place; and this admission depends entirely upon the extent to which a claimant can prove, or Ignatius can disprove, his right to be regarded as an innovator.

Throughout the sixteenth century *innovation* and *novelties*

[1] Healy, pp. 9-13.

had carried religious connotations – and invariably bad ones. In January 1536, when the English Reformers were getting out of hand, and when ardent preachers were moving on from attacking the Pope to more fundamental religious issues, Thomas Cromwell had sent a letter to the Bishops pointing out that the people should not be charged with 'overmuch novelties' which could breed 'contention, division and contrariety of opinion in the unlearned multitude'.[1] Such attempts to suppress *novelties* became a commonplace; and *novelties* simply became equated with views other than one's own which were, perforce, regarded as long-established and hallowed by custom. It was such fear of change in any order, once established, which led Nashe to cite Machiavelli – 'a pollitick not much affected to any Religion' – as one who had exposed just 'howe odious and how dangerous innovations of Religion are'; which led Richard Cosin to accuse factions within the reformed Church of mistaking 'seditious innovation, for lawfull reformation', and to argue that it was a poison which would endanger both Church and Commonwealth; and, more specifically concerning the Jesuits, which led Anthony Copley to write that the Society had grown so haughty that 'wheresoever in all Christendome it sets footing it straight seeks to innovate all, and to captivate as well the Laitie as the Cleargie to her hommage'.[2] Thinking of this kind resulted in continual battling as to which Church was the more truly primitive, that of Rome or that of England, and induced controversialists such as Bell to set before the eyes of his readers 'as cleerly as in a glasse of Cristall, the original and daily excrements of Popery, and that it is not the Old but the New Religion'.[3] *New* very clearly equalled illegitimate and unauthorised; and innovation was, therefore, unequivocally a bad thing.

---

[1] *Letters and Papers, foreign and domestic, of the Reign of Henry VIII*, x, p. 46; printed in Gilbert Burnet, *The History of the Reformation of the Church of England*, ed. N. Pocock, Oxford, 1865, iv, pp. 394-5.

[2] Thomas Nashe, *The Returne of the renowned Cavaliero Pasquill of England*, London, 1589, in R. B. McKerrow, *Works of Thomas Nashe*, London, 1904-10, i, p. 79; Richard Cosin, *Conspiracie for pretended reformation: viz. Presbyterial discipline*, London, 1592, sig. B2^r; Anthony Copley, *Another letter of Mr A. C. to his dis-jesuited kinsman*, 1602, p. 21.

[3] Thomas Bell, *The tryall of the new religion*, 1608, sig. Bl^r.

Something of these conventional attitudes are to be discerned in the *Conclave*. In particular, the question of the original state of the Church occurs when Ignatius is considering Lucifer's proposal that he should go to establish his own Church on the Moon. Recalling that a woman governs there, Ignatius points out that those who have attempted any religious innovation have always profited from that sex. The only exception he can call to mind is Elizabeth of England; and even she was not free from all innovation, 'for the ancient *Religion* was so much worne out, that to reduce that to the former dignity, and so to renew it, was a kinde of *Innovation*'. On the other hand, Ignatius hastily corrects himself, he dare not recognise this sort of thing as truly innovatory, lest he should thereby 'confesse that *Luther* and many others which live in banishment in *Heaven* farre from us, might have a title to this place, as such *Innovators*'.[1] Elsewhere, on three occasions, Donne speaks of innovation in a more purely political sense: that is, as a revolution following a power struggle in Hell itself. Machiavel, prior to his own speech, considers the possibility of undermining Jesuitical influence by making Lucifer suspect that '*Ignatius*, by winning to his side, politique men, exercised in civill businesses, might atempt some innovation in that kingdome'; and subsequently Lucifer does indeed come to fear such a takeover bid and the introduction of innovations into Hell.[2]

However, such interpretations of *innovation* are only incidental to the purpose of the *Conclave* where, for the most part, Donne offers a highly idiosyncratic, and very circumscribed, view of the matter. His very first statement of the theme seems straightforward and related to accepted ideas: only those have access to Lucifer's secret place, who have 'so attempted any innovation in this life, that they gave an affront to all antiquitie, and induced doubts, and anxieties, and scruples, and after, a libertie of beleeving what they would; at length established opinions, directly contrary to all established before'.[3] This suggests that *innovation* is to be equated with intellectual revolution and the subversion of established beliefs. But the idea is quickly qualified by the short, sharp contest between Boniface

[1] Healy, pp. 83-7.   [2] Healy, pp. 25, 65, 71.   [3] Healy, p. 9.

III who had 'expelled an old Religion', and Mahomet who had founded a new one. Mahomet is overmatched because he had 'attributed something to the old *Testament*'; whereas Boniface had destroyed the entire monarchical system established in the Old Testament and had 'prepared *Popes* a way, to tread upon the neckes of *Princes*'. Moreover, Mahomet compares unfavourably because, since his time, his followers have lived in 'idle concord'; whereas the successors of Boniface 'have ever beene fruitfull in bringing forth new sinnes, and new pardons, and idolatries, and King-killings'. Thus, though both Turks and Papists daily come to Hell in droves, the latter have the more ready access to the innermost room, 'reserved for especiall Innovators'.[1] Already *innovation* is assuming a rather unusual meaning which is further defined when Donne points out that not only those who have innovated in matters directly concerning the soul attempt to gain access to the room but also those who have done so 'either in the Arts, or in conversation, or in any thing which exerciseth the faculties of the soule, and may so provoke to quarrelsome and brawling controversies: For so the truth be lost, it is no matter how'.[2] Here, *innovation* is limited to the promoting of dissension and, above all, to the destruction of truth – which is a long way from merely upsetting established opinion. This is further emphasised by Ignatius when dealing with Copernicus's claim based on having 'turned the whole frame of the world'. How, asks Ignatius, has this theory affected men's beliefs concerning God? What advantage is it to Lucifer whether the earth moves or stands still? Moreover – and this is the vital point – Copernicus's right to entrance is derogated because his opinions 'may very well be true'. Thus, if these astronomical questions give anyone the right to enter Lucifer's room, Clavius – who had opposed Copernicus 'and the truth', and had caused 'contentions, and schoole-combats in this cause' – had the better claim. Finally,

[1] Healy, pp. 11-13.
[2] Healy, p. 13. Cf. Owen, *Herod and Pilate*, p. 42. Owen – having shown how from the same example of Chilperic, the Papists argue for the Pope's power to depose, and the Puritans argue for the people's power to do likewise – writes: 'Men cannot say (as it is in the proverbe) *nimium altercando veritas amittitur*, seeing that in this opposition, the truth is not lost, but divided among them'.

Ignatius tells Copernicus that he must content himself with a less exalted place, with other philosophers, and not aspire 'to this place, reserved onely for *Antichristian Heroes*'.[1] This last would seem a very curious qualification for recognition as a great innovator; but it is, in fact, the *sine qua non* of the whole satire, and is even further stressed when Machiavel comes on the scene to acknowledge that 'entrance into this place may be decreed to none, but to Innovators, and to onely such of them as have dealt in *Christian* businesse; and of them also, to those only which have had the fortune to doe much harme'.[2]

Antichristian subversion of the truth, fomenting of discord, gratuitous harm – these are the criteria by which innovators are to be judged at the portals of Lucifer's inner sanctum. And it is obvious that, given such criteria, neither Copernicus with his heavenly motions, Paracelsus with his uncertain medical experiments, Aretine with his pornographic pictures, Columbus with his geographical discoveries, nor Nerius with his sermons on the Saints, was likely to cause a stir in Hell, nor to present Ignatius with opposition much sterner than the motley crew of those who had 'but invented new attire for woemen', or had invented porcelain dishes, spectacles, quintains, stirrups, and *Caviari*. But Machiavel could; and did. He came armed with excellent credentials: described by Pole as the 'finger of Satan'; by Cosin as an 'imp' of Satan; and by Covell as 'polluted Machiavel', and as an instrument fashioned by Satan to disgrace religion. Richard Harvey had even recommended him as 'that secretary of hell, not only of Florence'.[3] And his relevance can be comprehended not so much within the context of the Oath of Allegiance controversy which was the immediate occasion for the *Conclave*, but within the context of contemporary anti-Machiavelli literature and its relation to the far greater mass of anti-Jesuit polemic.

[1] Healy, pp. 17-19.
[2] Healy, p. 29.
[3] Reginald Pole, *Apologia ad Carolum Quintum* printed in *Epistolae Reginaldi Poli*, ed. A. M. Quirini, Brescia, 1744-57, i, p. 137; Cosin, *loc. cit.*; William Covell, *Religions speech to Englands children* in *Polimanteia, or, the meanes to judge of the fall of a common-wealth*, Cambridge, 1595, sigs. Y3r-Bb4v; Richard Harvey, *A theological discourse of the Lamb of God and his Enemies*, 1590, p. 97.

Donne's Machiavel; and Machiavelli

Machiavel makes his appearance immediately after the discomfiture of Copernicus and Paracelsus; and, having observed how Ignatius has taken upon himself the 'office of *kings Atturney*' to destroy their case, he first prepares some 'venemous darts, out of his *Italian Arsenal*' to cast against the foe. However, in view of the latter's evident authority, Machiavel deems it more prudent to 'sweeten and mollifie' him – a tactic which would have the advantage of making Lucifer fear that his lieutenant might himself 'atempt some innovation in that kingdome'. Therefore Machiavel addresses himself both to the 'Dread *Emperour*' and to his 'watchfull and diligent *Genius*, father *Ignatius*'. He flatters their 'stupendious wisedome' and government; parodies the Trinity by likening Lucifer, Ignatius, and the Pope, to the Father, Son, and Holy Ghost; and goes on to praise the 'sonnes of *Ignatius*' for having created a 'new art of *Equivocation*', and for having reintroduced the language of the Tower of Babel, whereby people have again been brought to misunderstanding. Compared with the work of the Jesuits, Machiavel admits, his own achievements are but childish. Nevertheless, he hopes that one honour will not be denied him: that he has 'brought in an *Alphabet*, and provided certaine Elements, and was some kind of schoolmaister in preparing them a way to higher undertakings'.

Machiavel is ashamed that he should have to sue for admittance in the company of such creatures as Copernicus and Paracelsus, although the latter is the more endurable, and the more likely to enjoy the Jesuits' favour in that he was practised in the 'butcheries, and mangling of men':

> for I my selfe went alwaies that way of bloud, and therefore I did ever preferre the sacrifices of the *Gentiles*, and of the *Jewes*, which were performed with effusion of bloud (whereby not only the people, but the Priests also were animated to bold enterprises) before the soft and wanton sacrifices of *Christians*. If I might have my choyce, I should rather have wished, that the *Romane Church* had taken the *Bread*, then the *Wine*, from the people, since in the wine there is some colour, to imagine and represent blood.

This, Machiavel feels, should be a special attraction since Ignatius himself, having begun as a soldier, went on to wage spiritual war against the Church, and had even opened ways 'into Kings chambers' for his executioners. Though others outside the Society of Jesus might be involved in king-killing, Machiavel believes that the foundation and 'nourishment' of the doctrine is peculiar to Ignatius. Now, since only antichristian innovators, who have had the 'fortune to doe much harme', are allowed into Lucifer's room, Machiavel insists that, after the Jesuits, his own claim must be regarded as the best:

> since I did not onely teach those wayes, by which thorough *perfidiousnesse* and *dissembling of Religion*, a man might possesse, and usurpe upon the liberty of free *Commonwealths*; but also did arme and furnish the people with my instructions, how when they were under this oppression, they might safeliest conspire, and remove a *tyrant*, or revenge themselves of their *Prince*, and redeeme their former losses; so that from both sides, both from *Prince* and *People*, I brought an aboundant harvest, and a noble encrease to this kingdome.

This is an interesting speech which poses several interpretative problems. Only two earlier English Machiavels have survived – Gabriel Harvey's epigram, *Machiavellus ipse loquitur*; and Marlowe's Prologue to the *Jew of Malta* – and neither of these had much to do with Machiavelli[1]. What of Donne's Machiavel? That Donne had some acquaintance with Machiavelli is apparent from his *Pseudo-martyr* published in the year prior to the *Conclave*. There he discusses papal claims to jurisdiction outside Rome, and writes that, 'as an Author which lived in profession of that Religion, informs us', the citizens of Rome itself were always prepared to defend themselves against Papal usurpations: 'and this, at that time when England under Henry the second, and the remoter parts trembled at him, who trembled at his owne neighbours, and Subjects, as he pretended'. A marginal note cites Machiavelli's *Florentine History*: 'f. 34. Edit. Picen. An. 1587'. This is, in fact, the edition printed in

---

[1] Gabriel Harvey's sequence of poems relating to Machiavelli (*Machiavelli himself speaking: the Mercury of Florence, or the divinisation of Machiavelli;* and *the Hymn of the Medici*) are included in his extraordinary *Gratulationum Valdinensium libri quatuor*, 1578. As a series they afford an interesting parallel with Donne's *Conclave*. For Harvey, however, the scene is Olympus; Machiavelli's rival is Mercury; and the Florentine is recognised, ultimately, as a king among the Gods.

London, with the false Piacenza imprint, by John 'Machiavel' Wolfe; and, since the reference is accurately given, we may, in this instance, presume first-hand knowledge on Donne's part.[1] Unfortunately, one can travel no further in this direction.

Father Healy, suggesting that Donne was 'no victim of the "myth of Gentillet" ' and that he had not taken his knowledge of Machiavelli 'from his critics, Catholic or Protestant,' adds that the original texts were easily available to Donne 'in Italian, even in English printings'.[2] But what does Donne's Machiavel really amount to? He reveals cunning in attempting to create a rift between Lucifer and Ignatius. He claims to have provided elements for the Jesuits' evil doctrines and practices, and emphasises his preference for the 'way of bloud' through an unfavourable comparison between Christian and pagan sacrifice. He boasts that he has taught how, by dissembling religion, a man might usurp a commonwealth; and how, conversely, people might overthrow princes. Now it is certainly true that these few simple propositions could have been drawn from an uncritical reading of Machiavelli's own writings; but it is patent that Donne *need* not have read a single word by Machiavelli himself in order to write what he has written in the *Conclave*. Donne's Machiavel expresses all the sentiments popular opinion would, at that time, have expected of him. And here, it must be stressed, Gentillet's importance in moulding such opinion was no 'myth'.[3]

Gentillet and some Jesuits

There are nine things which must be borne in mind when considering the extent of Gentillet's relevance.[4] First, that up to

[1] John Donne, *Pseudo-martyr*, London, 1610, sig. B4ᵛ. On Wolfe, see A. Gerber, *Niccolò Machiavelli. Die Handschriften, Ausgaben und Übersetzungen seiner Werker im 16. und 17. Jahrhundert*, Gotha, Munich, 1912, 1913, i, pp. 83-91.

[2] Healy, p. xxxii.

[3] The source for this idea of the 'myth of Gentillet', and for much other misinformation, is F. Raab, *The English Face of Machiavelli*, 1964, which, in its earlier chapters, leans heavily though with scant acknowledgement on an equally inaccurate, but far more serious and valuable study – the unpublished London University thesis by J. W. Horrocks, *Machiavelli in Tudor Political Opinion and Discussion*.

[4] On Gentillet's life and work, see P. D. Stewart, *Innocent Gentillet e la sua polemica antimachiavellica*, Florence, 1969; C. Edward Rathé, 'Innocent Gentillet and the

and including the year 1611, his *Discours sur les moyens de bien gouverner . . . un royaume . . . Contre Nicolas Machiavel*, first published in French in 1576, went through a further nine French editions or variant versions, and five Latin, one German, and two English editions. Secondly, that its bitter denunciation of the Italianisation of the French court under Catherine de' Medici, and the association of this political development with the ready availability of Machiavelli's writings, seemed to make very good sense in the years following the Massacre of St Bartholomew's Eve, not only in France but also in England where the proposed marriage between Elizabeth and Alençon led many to speculate about the spread of this 'infection' across the Channel. Thirdly, that Gentillet's detailed, if prolix, refutation of Machiavelli stands alone in the sixteenth century and early seventeenth century in its citation and close examination of the actual text of the Florentine's work – principally of the *Prince* and *Discourses*, but also in the French editions of 1585 and 1609, heavily augmented with material drawn from the *Art of War* and the *Florentine History*. Fourthly, that this detailed critique confirmed, rather than challenged, existing prejudices concerning Machiavelli. Fifthly, that Gentillet's method of argument – drawing maxims and aphorisms from Machiavelli's work, demonstrating their implications, and then refuting them with a mass of classical, biblical, and historical exempla – seemed, to contemporaries, both convincing and thorough. Sixthly, that this historical method, crude and biased though it undoubtedly appears, is really no more so than Machiavelli's selective use of historical exempla to substantiate his own political assumptions. Seventhly, that several writers were so stung by Gentillet's condemnation of Machiavelli that they felt it necessary to draft something by way of reply. And eighthly, that there is ample evidence to show that Gentillet's criticisms of Machiavelli did, in fact, become accepted – by

---

first Anti-Machiavel', *Bibliothèque d'Humanisme et Renaissance*, xxvii, 1965, pp. 186-225; and Rathé's edition, *Anti-Machiavel. Edition de 1576 avec commentaires et notes*, Geneva, 1968. I am at present completing a book on the reception of Machiavelli in Tudor England, which will elaborate on the points mentioned below. For some preliminary remarks see my article, 'The Reception of Machiavelli in Tudor England: a Re-assessment', *Il Politico*, xxxi, 1966, pp. 127-38.

many of those who had occasion to discuss affairs of state, and especially the relationship between policy and religion – as what Machiavelli had himself written; and this despite the availability in print of Machiavelli's own writings. There is nothing remarkable about this. The availability of a literary text in its original form does not automatically eliminate a reader's desire for critical studies of the same work; if it did, the world of scholarship would wear a vastly different aspect. People enjoy reading books about books. Even now they find it simpler to read books about Machiavelli than to read the greater part of Machiavelli's own writings. In the sixteenth century Gentillet was widely read; and his interpretations were deemed convincing because they seemed politically relevant, and because they systematised an unsystematic and naughty writer. He is, therefore, important to us for these reasons; and for one other especially pertinent to a consideration of Donne's *Conclave*.

Among the most bitter, and most often published, late sixteenth-century attacks on Machiavelli, were those by Antonio Possevino and Pedro de Ribadeneira; while the fullest native English denunciation of the Florentine was published early in the seventeenth century by Thomas Fitzherbert. This has a twofold interest. In the first place, Possevino had never read Machiavelli, but summarised and condemned his doctrines solely on the basis of what Gentillet had written; Ribadeneira, though citing Machiavelli thrice, derived many of his opinions very obviously, but without acknowledgement, from Possevino; and Fitzherbert derived many of his opinions, just as obviously, and also without acknowledgement, from Ribadeneira. In the second place, all three were Jesuits.

In 1592 Possevino first published his *Iudicium* which included an attack not only on Machiavelli but also on Machiavelli's Huguenot opponent, Innocent Gentillet.[1] Gentillet was an

---

[1] Antonio Possevino, *Cautio de iis, quae scripsit tum Machiavellus, tum is, qui adversus eum scripsit Antimachiavellum, qui nomen haud adscripsit*, in his *Iudicium de Nuae militis Galli scriptis etc.*, Rome, 1592. A version of this *Cautio* was included in Possevino's *Bibliotheca selecta*, Rome, 1593, and was reprinted, with other critical material, in the edition of Telius's Latin translation of Machiavelli, *Princeps*, published by Cornelius Sutor, Oberursel, 1600. Another edition of the *Iudicium* was published by I. B. Buysson, Lyons, 1594.

uncompromising critic of the Papacy which, he claimed, had been rightly condemned by Machiavelli but for the wrong reasons. It was no wonder that his Calvinist beliefs should have vexed Possevino. The ironic thing, however, is that the Jesuit's summary of Machiavelli's pestilential doctrines consists merely of selected chapter headings from the Huguenot enemy. Moreover, Possevino has so misunderstood Gentillet's tripartite classification of maxims, that he believes Machiavelli's *Prince* to have been itself divided into three sections. This is really all there is to Possevino's Machiavelli; but just three years later, Ribadeneira – friend and biographer of Loyola, hagiographer and vituperative historian of the English Reformation – was able to expand these same few propositions into an immense work almost approaching Gentillet's own *Discours* in magnitude.[1]

Introducing his *Tratado de la religion y virtudes* to the Christian Reader, Ribadeneira writes that, though Machiavelli had devoted himself to the study of politics, he was an impious and godless fellow whose doctrines, like water flowing from an infected fountain, were like to poison all those who drank thereof. Ribadeneira then enunciates the principal points of Machiavelli's political theory, by summarising Possevino's summary of a few of Gentillet's chapter headings. Furthermore, Ribadeneira argues, there are other authors similar to Machiavelli, who take as their oracle Tacitus's account of the very worst of the pagan emperors, Tiberius; and he specifically condemns Bodin, La Noue, and Du Plessis Mornay – all of whom had been adversely judged, also in association with Machiavelli, by Possevino.[2]

Throughout the two books into which his work is divided, Ribadeneira sets out the true criteria for his Christian prince; and these prove to be little different from the old catalogue of princely virtues familiar to every student of the genre *de*

[1] Pedro de Ribadeneira, *Tratado de la religion y virtudes que debe tener el Principe Christiano para govenar sur Estados. Contra lo que Nicolas Machiavelo y los politicos deste tiempo ensenan*, Madrid, 1595. Other Spanish versions: Antwerp, 1597; Madrid, 1601. Latin translations: Antwerp, 1603; Cologne, 1604; Mainz, 1603; Mainz, 1604. Italian translations: Genoa, 1598; Brescia, 1599. French translation: Douai, 1610.

[2] Ribadeneira, *Tratado*, 1595, sigs. †† 3ʳ-6ʳ.

regimine principum. In particular the Jesuit contrasts two methods
of government. One, advocated by the 'politici', and founded
merely on human prudence, is false and diabolical: it accom-
modates religion to the state; and it assumes that God has no
concern for human affairs, and that the world is governed by
the malice and cunning of mortal men. On the other hand, the
true mode of government derives from God Himself; it accom-
modates the state to religion; and it recognises that divine
providence watches over the good rulers and punishes the bad.[1]
All this could have come from almost any medieval treatise on
kingship; but Ribadeneira's aim is principally to establish that
proper care for religion means the destruction of heresy. It is
impossible, he says, for true Catholics ever to come to terms
with the heretics, who must be completely extirpated, for they
are the prime cause of revolutions, the fall of states, and the
death of princes.[2] In his second book Ribadeneira discusses the
virtues – justice, wise choice of advisers, clemency, liberality,
prudence, and all the rest – which his Christian prince must
possess. Here Machiavelli is cited as the great advocate of
simulated virtue; and such hypocrisy is refuted at considerable
length. Inevitably, Ribadeneira is led to a consideration of
Christian fortitude and to the dreaded Machiavellian maxims
which had angered Gentillet and Possevino: that Christianity
had corrupted pagan fortitude by demanding patience rather
than activity, by foregoing blood sacrifice, and by emphasising
humility, abjection, and poverty, rather than human valour.[3]
In his refutation Ribadeneira shows an acquaintance not only
with Possevino, and possibly with Gentillet himself, but also
with Machiavelli's *Discourses*, and, more especially, with
Osorio's *De nobilitate christiana*, the first important published
attack on Machiavelli, which is heavily paraphrased in this
section of the *Tratado*.[4] There is little acuity of thought, little
originality, and certainly little knowledge of Machiavelli, in
Ribadeneira's work. Nevertheless, the Spanish Jesuit was a
historian of European reputation; and, up to the appearance of

[1] *Ibid.*, sig. †† 7^{r-v}. [2] *Ibid.*, pp. 180-93. [3] *Ibid.*, pp. 468-89.
[4] *Ibid.*, p. 469, citing Machiavelli, *Discourses*, ii, 2. Geronimo Osorio, *De nobilitate
christiana*, Lisbon, 1542, was reissued in at least a dozen different versions before
the end of the century.

Donne's *Conclave*, his *Tratado de la religion y virtudes* went through three Spanish, four Latin, one French, and two Italian editions. And at least one Englishman had read the work with close attention.

In 1606 there appeared the *First part of a treatise concerning policy and religion* by the English Jesuit controversialist, Thomas Fitzherbert. In 1610 the *Second Part* appeared; and in the same year a Latin treatise, substantially similar in argument to his English works, was published by Fitzherbert at Rome.[1] In these books Fitzherbert, like Ribadeneira, was concerned to demonstrate the fallaciousness of Machiavelli's doctrines, both on religious and on utilitarian grounds; and, like Ribadeneira, he sought to implicate Protestants as heretics and Machiavellians. These tasks had been in Fitzherbert's mind as early as 1602 when, in his *Defence of the Catholyke cause*, he had argued that Protestants, following the 'absurd and pestilent doctrin of Machiavel', had sought to strengthen Elizabeth's position by rigour, cruelty, and injustice; whereas reason and experience taught that it is the Christian virtues which preserve princes, so that 'these most cruel and bloody devises of our persecutours, are not only impious, but also foolish in that very point wherein they will have them seeme most wyse'.[2] His three long works of 1606 and 1610 constitute an immense expansion of these ideas. Human affairs are so complex and variable that it is beyond the wit of man to devise any system of politics capable of meeting every possible contingency; but, of all political doctrines, those of Machiavelli are the most ruinous, to princes and to states alike.[3] Fidelity is especially praised by Fitzherbert as the basis of successful government; and, naturally, Machiavelli's advice concerning the efficacy of deceit comes in for heavy criticism; though this leads Fitzherbert into the difficulty faced by virtually every writer on princely virtue. There simply are occasions when rulers, bearing the heavy responsibility of their subjects'

---

[1] Thomas Fitzherbert, *The first part of a treatise concerning policy and religion, wherein the infirmitie of humane wit is amply declared*, Douai, 1606; *The second part of a treatise etc.*, n.p., 1610; *An sit Utilitas in Scelere: vel de Infelicitate Principis Macchiavelliani, contra Macchiavellum et politicos ejus sectatores*, Rome, 1610.

[2] Thomas Fitzherbert, *A defence of the Catholyke cause*, n.p., 1602, fol. 32^r.

[3] *Policy and religion*, i, 1606, p. 51; *An sit Utilitas*, p. 60.

welfare, cannot afford to be honest with their sworn enemies. What then are they to do? The answer had generally been to draw a hairline distinction between dissimulation and simulation: between white lies and nasty falsehoods. Ribadeneira had himself devoted a chapter to this knotty problem, and had come up with a crass distinction: between lying without cause and without profit, which, not unreasonably, he deemed always bad; and merely giving people to understand one thing when another is meant – and this only when necessity and utility require it! In the Spaniard's opinion, the latter course is justifiable; though he wisely refrains from trying to clarify what he means by necessity and utility.[1] Fitzherbert was equally taxed over this matter, and largely borrows from Ribadeneira in order to reach his conclusion that there is a great difference to be noted 'betwixt telling a lye, and concealing the truth'. Simulation, 'or fiction', is never lawful; but dissimulation 'is both lawful and commendable, yea and some tymes so necessary in princes, that it may wel and truly be sayd; *Qui nescit dissimulare, nescit regnare*'.[2]

Fitzherbert discusses, point by point, what he considers to be the principal tenets of the Machiavellist: to practise extremity in both virtue and vice; to foment factions; to divide and rule; never to trust those to whom offence has been given; to destroy all those likely to trouble the state; to take Cesare Borgia as a model for political action; and to regard Christianity unfavourably in comparison with the pagan religions.[3] He claims to have obtained a faculty to read Machiavelli's works which were on the Index of Prohibited Books and therefore not normally available for consultation[4]; but he never cites a text directly; his summaries of Machiavelli's assumed positions are

---

[1] Ribadeneira, *Tratado*, 1595, pp. 283-92.

[2] *Policy and religion*, i, 1606, pp. 342-8.

[3] Fitzherbert's refutation of Machiavelli's view of Christianity is in *Policy and religion*, ii, 1610, pp. 345-57.

[4] *An sit Utilitas*, sig. † 3ʳ. On the benefits of the Index, see Robert Parsons, *The Warn-word to Sir Francis Hastinges Wast-word*, n.p., 1602, Part II (*The second encounter about Falshood and Lying*), fols. 67ᵛ-68ʳ. Parsons argues that Catholics are forbidden works such as 'the Turks *Alcaron* it self, *Machevile* and *Bodin* tending to Atheisme, and baudy *Boccace*, with the most *pestilent English Pallace of Pleasure*': all of which poison those not protected by the Index.

redolent of Gentillet; and the detail of his refutations is largely derived from Ribadeneira whose very words are frequently pressed into service. Moreover, like Ribadeneira, and like Gentillet before him, Fitzherbert sees in history irrefutable evidence of Machiavelli's incapacity in practical politics. Had Machiavelli and other contemporary 'politikes' been the first inventors of such notions, and had these never been put to the test, then, says Fitzherbert, there might have been some excuse for believing in their efficacy. But they have been practised by all tyrants; and they have almost invariably proved ruinous.[1]

I would not wish to suggest a simple, unilinear relationship between Gentillet, Possevino, Ribadeneira, and Fitzherbert. Ribadeneira's work, though singularly obtuse, was extensive and learned, and drew upon a range of material far greater than was possible in Possevino's slim pamphlet; while Fitzherbert, similarly, draws on material not employed by his Spanish colleague. There were, in addition, many other writers at this period condemning Machiavelli *en* generally *passant*, and generally without showing first-hand knowledge of his writings —despite their availability. Nevertheless, the three Jesuits are especially important in that their criticism of Machiavelli was not contained in merely passing allusions. Possevino and, more notably, Ribadeneira and Fitzherbert were specifically concerned to combat a Machiavelli who bears strong evidence of Gentillet's paternity. Possevino was popular in the period prior to the appearance of Donne's *Conclave*; Ribadeneira was more popular still; and Fitzherbert was an Englishman whose books against Machiavelli appeared just prior to Donne's own controversial works. Moreover, for Fitzherbert, Machiavelli – despite the staleness of his maxims – is an innovator almost within the terms of reference subsequently specified by Donne. Machiavelli, he writes, 'to make good his new doctrin (which was devised, no dout by the divel for the destruction of men, and common welths) not onlie impugneth, the Christian religion, Which he him selfe professed, but also frame than other morall philosophy, then hath hetherto bene heard of in the world, all

---

[1] *Policy and religion*, i, 1606, p. 384.

tending to the establishment of an inhumane barbarous and tirannicall pollicy'.[1]

It is, of course, possible that Donne had heard neither of Possevino's *Iudicium* nor of any of Fitzherbert's three anti-Machiavelli treatises; and it is likewise possible that he had not heard of Ribadeneira's treatise on the virtues of a Christian Prince, despite its numerous editions, and despite the fact that he used others of Ribadeneira's writings in the course of his own controversial works. Such things are possible; but they are not very likely. In any case, to debate the question of Donne's knowledge of these books would be to confine oneself merely to the possible intention of the *Conclave*; whereas if one considers probable effect, rather than possible intention, then it is obvious that many of Donne's readers could well have known these current Jesuit anti-Machiavelli writings. Not to take them into account is to divest the *Conclave* of some of its choicest ironies.

Donne's Machiavel finds himself face to face not merely with Jesuits in general, but with the very father of all Jesuits, Ignatius Loyola; and this Machiavel, too, is torn to pieces by an irate antagonist. Like Fitzherbert, Donne's Ignatius scorns Machiavel's claims to originality, and tells him that his precepts are so stale and obsolete that Serarius had even called Herod, 'who lived so long before *Machivell*, a *Machiavellian*'.[2] Like Possevino's Machiavelli, and those of Ribadeneira and Fitzherbert, Donne's Machiavel is taken to task for daring to extol the 'way of bloud'; for comparing Christianity adversely with paganism; for advocating the dissembling of religion for political purposes; and for showing princes how to usurp power. But here everything has been turned upside down. Jesuit scholars may write their highly moral books against Machiavelli; but they fool nobody. Here in Hell the truth is revealed. Machiavel is rejected not because he is evil but because he is not evil enough; and because Ignatius is too clever and too wicked for

---

[1] *Policy and religion*, ii, 1610, p. 357.

[2] Healy, p. 55. An even better example, from the Protestant side, is Thomas Bell, *The anatomie of popish tyrannie*, p. 72, where he exposes Parsons as a bastard, a drunkard, and as an incestuous, seditious traitor: 'being thus qualified with supernaturall gifts, and extraordinarie graces proceeding from *Beelzebub* that notable Machivell'.

him. Donne's *Conclave* is the apotheosis of a cliché of contro-
versy: the Jesuit is more Machiavellian than Machiavelli.

More Machiavellian than Machiavelli

The first Jesuit mission to England had arrived in June 1580,
and, less than seven months later, a Proclamation issued for
their arrest accused them of deceiving and abusing simple folk
under the 'color of a holy name'; of entering the kingdom to
corrupt and pervert the Queen's subjects in 'matter of con-
science and religion'; of drawing them from their 'loyalty and
duty of obedience'; and of provoking them to 'attempt some-
what to the disturbance of the present quiet'.[1] A Proclamation
of the following year put the finishing touches to the picture,
when it accused the Jesuits not merely of 'stirring up of re-
bellion within their natural countries' but also of the 'en-
dangering of her majesty's most royal person'.[2] These, sub-
stantially, were to remain the principal elements of the Jesuits'
official and popular character-reference: they were renegades
who, under a pretended religion, sought to subvert the state,
and even threatened the person of the sovereign. It was in vain
that a Jesuit such as Campion protested that he was concerned
with religion and nothing more. How could this be possible,
demanded William Charke, voicing the incredulity of many.
In England, religion and policy were one life and one spirit;
and anybody taking away one inevitably procured the death of
the other. No Jesuit could come to alter religion, 'but he must
attempt the change of the state, to the lamentable destruction of
the lande'. Nor was it possible to reinstate Papal authority, 'but
he must take awaye from her royall Maistie, her just supreme
soveraintie, and deprive her at one clappe of the authoritie shee
hath over all persons and ordinances'. The Jesuit may say that
matters of policy appertain not to his vocation, 'yet it is so
sayde onely to cover his purpose, which is to the contrary'.[3]

---

[1] P. L. Hughes and J. F. Larkin, *Tudor Royal Proclamations*, Yale U.P., 1969,
II, No. 655 (p. 483): Proclamation of 10 January 1581.

[2] *Ibid.*, No. 660 (p. 489): Proclamation of 1 April 1582.

[3] William Charke, *An answere to a seditious pamphlet by a Jesuite*, London, 1580,
sigs. C1ʳ-2ʳ. Cf. Meredith Hanmer, *The great bragge and challenge of M. Champion
a jesuite*, 1581, fols. 17ᵛ-18ʳ.

It was, of course, normal for one party to accuse its opponents of using religion for political ends. This was the most common form of abuse – hurled by Anglicans at Catholics and Puritans; by Puritans at Anglicans and Catholics; and by Jesuits both at Protestants of all persuasions, and at fellow Catholics less extreme than themselves – and it was commonly associated with a charge of Machiavellism. This was nothing new. As early as the mid-1560s Roger Ascham had heaped abuse on those Italianate Englishmen who counted the Christian mysteries as mere fables to serve civil policy, and had pointed out that such creatures were prepared to countenance either Papistry or Protestantism; whichever better served their turn. Nevertheless, he thought that they most commonly associated themselves with the 'worst Papistes' with whom they shared three fundamental opinions: open contempt of God's word; a 'secret securitie of sinne'; and a 'bloodie desire to have all taken away, by sword or burning, that be not of their faction'. Anybody, said Ascham, who cared to read 'with indifferent judgement *Pygius* and *Machiavel*, two indifferent Patriarches of thies two Religions' would know that he was speaking the truth.[1] These were strong words, often repeated, and with greater frequency towards the end of the century as the religious controversies grew increasingly complex and bitter.

Most vindictive, perhaps, of all the controversies was the internecine struggle between Jesuit extremists and Catholic moderates. As we have seen, the Jesuits in England were immediately recognised as proponents of political revolution, seeking to restore Catholicism by subversion and force. They enjoyed some early success in stirring their co-religionists; but the execution of Mary Queen of Scots gave pause to many Catholics who began to wonder whether it might not be advantageous to come to terms with the establishment. Those Catholics who did seek toleration within the Anglican system were attacked for subordinating their religious duty to matters of secondary importance (either public interest or private commodity) and were dubbed 'Politici in schola

---

[1] Roger Ascham, *The Scholemaster*, 1570, fols. 28ᵛ-29ʳ.

Mahiavelliana [*sic*]'.[1] On the other hand the Jesuits were regarded by their more patriotic co-religionists from a viewpoint similar to that of the government itself, and were condemned for seeking to overthrow Elizabeth by raising a Spanish claimant to the throne. With such goings-on, the moderates felt, how was it possible for Catholicism ever to be tolerated in England? A work such as Parsons's *A conference about the next succession*, advancing the claims of the Spanish Infanta, sent patriotic Catholics into transports of wrath; and Parsons's pious refutation of Machiavelli's alleged dictum, that religion and piety hinder wise government, cut little ice.[2] The constant accusations of being arch-politicians worried the Society, and in 1596 Thomas Wright complained of the difficulties faced by the Jesuits in convincing critics that they did not seek to promote foreign invasion, and that they did not seek to procure Elizabeth's death. He wrote to the Jesuit Garnet at Rome, urging him to resist 'any such Machiavelian treasons', and to let the Queen know that ambition, covetousness, and pretence were 'far from us, whose vocation is religion, and not suppressing of princes'; for, if she could not be convinced, Wright feared 'lest of all our priests be rather put to death for matters of state then religion'. The Jesuits, he says, in their last general congregation had decreed that, under pain of mortal sin, they should not deal in any affairs concerning the state.[3]

But the Jesuits could swear what they liked. Their opponents were not going to believe them, and, as Wright suspected, they deemed the decree 'rather a cover of craft and policy than a sincere rule and law'. Anger concerning Jesuitical activities, real and alleged, boiled up in the controversy over the appointment of an Archpriest to direct the Catholic mission in England.[4]

---

[1] Thomas Stapleton, *Oratio Academica: an Politici horum temporum in numero Christianorum sint habendi?*, Munich, 1608, p. 28. Horrocks, *op. cit.*, pp. 157-8, demonstrates that this work must have been written between the years 1589 and 1590.

[2] Robert Parsons, *A conference about the next succession to the croune of Inglond*, n.p., 1594, p. 41.

[3] See Thomas Birch, *Memoirs of the reign of Queen Elizabeth, from the year 1581 till her death*, 1754, pp. 359-60.

'See T. G. Law, *A historical sketch of the conflicts between Jesuits and Seculars in the reign of Queen Elizabeth*, 1889.

Was it not singular, demanded one Catholic writer, Anthony Copley, that the Jesuits sought not only to rule over the secular clergy but also to bring 'armes and conquest into the Catholicke church', thus managing affairs of state 'more machiavelianlie then Machivell himselfe?' The Jesuits, he said, used the sacrament of confession to probe into a man's private conscience to see whether he was apt to serve their seditious turns: 'could Machiavell himselfe have beene so prophane?' Indeed, since they were capable of such sacrilege, it was no wonder that they scorned to come an ace behind 'either Machiavell or his Maister' in any other matter against either religion or morality. As for believing their protestations of honesty: how was it possible? They were the masters of deceit, and Copley would be ashamed to weary his reader with all that he knows concerning their 'lying legierdemaines' consisting of 'infinite querks & quiddits; as mentall evasions in their speech, interpretative colloguings, half fac'd tearmes, tergiviersations, tentative speeches, whole and demie-dublings, the vulpecular-fawne, detraction with sighes, buttes, and the shrugge, circular calumniations, holding it lawfull to be forsworne in too manie cases, intercepting, rasing, and forgerie of letters, and such like'.[1]

Accusations such as these were a commonplace; and it is impossible to cite here every relevant instance at length. Nevertheless, one writer should not be passed over in any attempt to distil the essence of this controversy. William Watson, secular priest, bitter antagonist of the Jesuits – and in particular of the much-execrated Parsons whom he accused of writing more spitefully than 'Don Lucifer the wittiest fiend in hell' – was a prolific controversialist; and three of his publications are especially valuable for their identification of Jesuitism with a Gentillet-type Machiavellism. In his *Sparing Discoverie*, Watson denounces the Jesuits who have become corrupted since their original foundation. Through their 'haughtie-aspiring-touring-wits', they are due for a 'Luciferian fall'. The 'Jesuiticall ghosts' are wicked spirits who, 'transforming themselves into angels of light', lead more souls to Hell than the ugliest fiends acting under their own colours.

---

[1] Anthony Copley, *An answere to a letter of a Jesuited gentleman by his cosin, maister A. C.*, 1601, pp. 92-3.

Watson says that he could set forth a 'triple alphabet intire of Machivilian practises used by the Jesuites', setting down their 'rules atheall in order of their platforme layd for a perpetuity of their intended government despoticon, and mock-weale publick oligarchicall'; and he rails against their conception of religion as a mere political device upheld by human wisdom and 'sleights of wit'. They are the men 'that by Machivels rules are raysed up to mayntayne it by equivocation, detractions, dissimulation, ambition, contention for superioritie, stirring up strife, setting kingdomes against kingdomes, raising of rebellions, murthering of princes, and by we know not how many stratagems of Sathan, comming out of hell, and tending to confusion'.[1] These same 'rules' are likewise denounced in Watson's *Important Considerations*, where he protests that true Catholics wish to acknowledge that they really *are* the Queens' subjects 'without all Jesuiticall equivocation'; and warns against 'novelties and Jesuitisme' which are nothing but a 'very vizard of most deepe hypocrisie'. The Jesuits, he writes, following their Spanish founder Loyola, 'being altogether Hispaniated, and transported into those humours', seek to establish a Spanish monarchy, and to this end they are ready to practise every mischief which they can devise, or learn in the 'very schoole of Machiavellisme'.[2]

Watson's most striking work is the *Decacordon of ten quodlibeticall questions*, where his conventional views of Jesuitism and Machiavellism converge to give us a perfect focus for Donne's *Conclave*. Within the pages of the *Decacordon* the Jesuits commit every one of their familiar crimes: they use religion as a mere 'Atheall devise'; they practise equivocation and sedition; they set kings against kings, and states against states; and they murder princes. Can such creatures be called religious? 'No, no', cries Watson: 'their course of life doth shew what their study is: and that how-so-ever they boast of their perfections, holinesse, meditations, and exercises . . . yet

[1] William Watson, *A sparing discoverie of our English Jesuits*, n.p., 1601, sigs. a1v-2r, pp. 6-7, *et al.*
[2] William Watson, *Important considerations which ought to move all true catholikes to acknowledge that the proceedings of Her Majesty have bene mild*, n.p., 1601, pp. 3, 8, 37, 39, 42.

their platforme is heathenish, tyrannicall, Sathanicall, and able to set *Aretine, Lucian, Machiavell,* yea and *Don Lucifer* in a sort to school'. Neither the foul fiend himself, nor all the infernal furies, nor the Devil with all his art, could have deceived people as the Jesuits have done while yet preserving their own seeming innocence. Was there anybody who could take precedence over the Jesuits in matters of policy and prudence? Well, says Watson, it all depends on what you mean by prudence. In true policy which is derived from Christian prudence there are many superior to the Jesuits; but

> take pollicie as it is now a dayes taken by common phrase of speech, in the subject wherein it is inherent: as we say that a right Polititian is a very Machiavell, a very Machiavell is an upright Atheist, and an upright Atheist, is a downeright dastardly coward, void of all religion, reason, or honestie: so by consequent it may be said, that in politicall government or Machivilean pollicie none goeth beyond the Jesuits at this day.

For the Jesuits, *Politia* is but a 'nose of waxe' which may be turned in any direction a man pleases, for it is always pliable and 'fit to receive all impression: fresh and faire, or foule and filthie'. And in this kind of policy the Jesuits 'do farre passe Machiavell, and I verily thinke any whomsoever of and in this age'.[1]

King-killing

In 1602, the French historian, Etienne Pasquier, crowned a lifetime's antagonism towards the Jesuits with a treatise which was immediately translated and issued in England as *The Jesuites Catechisme.* Like Watson, Pasquier identifies Jesuitism with Machiavellism, and even devotes a chapter to 'Ignace his Machiavellismes, used to set his Sect afloate' where he compares the disruptive influences of Luther, Calvin, and Loyola. Luther merely made 'uproare' in Germany, and Calvin merely troubled France; but Loyola 'hath made a pudder' not only in Spain and the Spanish dominions, but in many other nations, too. Moreover, he had achieved this distinction without writing a

---

[1] William Watson, *A decacordon of ten quodlibeticall questions concerning religion and state,* n.p., 1602, pp. 33, 59, 61-4, 69, 70-3, 84, 91, 109, 244, 247, 314-15 *et al.*

word, but had simply feigned heavenly inspiration, like Minos, Lycurgus, Numa Pompilius, and Sertorius. These, writes Pasquier, are the 'Machiavellismes of which the old world was delivered before *Machiavell* was borne'; just as, at the present time, there are a great many 'Machiavells' who have 'never read his bookes'. 'I think', Pasquier continues, 'the same devises glided through the soule of this great *Ignace*'. The very vows taken by the Jesuits contained 'heresie and Machiavellisme'; their deceit and hypocrisy proved them to be 'brave schollers of Machiavell'; and, in their handling of affairs of state, and especially in their 'murthers and killings' of kings and princes, they had 'intermingled' a lesson from Machiavelli's *Prince* – in the 'chapter of wickedness'. And Pasquier devotes several chapters to proving that, whatever the Jesuits may say to the contrary, they have specialised in King-killing, and have learnt to kill, or cause to be killed, 'all such as stand not to their opinions'.[1]

This was the most constant and most serious of all the charges levelled against the Jesuits at this period. Already, as we have seen, in 1582 an English Proclamation had expressed fears for the safety of Queen Elizabeth; and subsequent events, and the interpretation thereof, served to heighten alarm. The Jesuits were thought to have been implicated in the murder of William of Orange in 1584; while the assassination of Henry III of France in 1589 – 'a murder written in Tymes forehead by the pen of aeternitie to astonish all posteritie'[2] – offered even more striking evidence to contemporaries that the Jesuits were the protagonists of a veritable doctrine of King-killing. Henry was freely denounced by Catholics as an atheist, a devil-worshipper, and, above all, as a Machiavellist; and his character as an unmitigated tyrant was advanced as sufficient justification for his murder.[3] It was in these terms that Ribadeneira had condoned the act, denouncing the King as a detestable Machiavellist, and euphemising the assassin as a poor, simple, and young

---

[1] Pasquier, *The Jesuites Catechisme*, 1602, fols. 63^v-65^r, 99^r-100^v, 132^r, 148^r-159^v, 210^v, *et al.*

[2] William Covell, *Polimanteia*, sig. F4^r.

[3] On the pamphlets which poured forth, first after the murder of the Guises, and then after the assassination of Henry III, see Anna Maria Battista, 'Sull' antimachiavellismo francese del secolo XVI', *Storia e Politica*, i, 1962, pp. 413-47.

religious.[1] Even more startling was the stand taken by another Spanish Jesuit, Juan de Mariana, who devoted a chapter of his *De rege* to the defence both of the revolt against Henry III and of the assassination itself, and went on to enunciate more general principles concerning the right of subjects to depose and slay not only usurpers, but even legitimate rulers who had degenerated into tyrants.[2] Mariana was not alone in his views on the derivation of regal authority from the commonweal, his emphasis on the duties as well as the rights of kings, and his extreme solution to the problems posed by tyranny. There were other Catholic political theorists holding similar views; and, of course, there existed a strong tradition of anti-Catholic political writing which placed great emphasis on contractual theory and on the dire consequences for rulers who violated their vows.[3] Indeed, for some observers, the more violent views of Catholic and Protestant alike were indistinguishable, and such hostility is well summarised in a small treatise, published in 1610, by David Owen, illustrating the concord between religious extremists on the doctrine of King-killing. Such opinions have spread like a 'gangrene'; and daily the kings of Christendom are crucified, like Christ, between two thieves – Papist and Puritan – 'which have prepared this deadly poison for Princes whom they, in their own irreligious and traiterous hearts, shall condemn for tyrannie'.[4]

Nevertheless, in popular opinion, the Society of Jesus had almost exclusive rights to theories of political murder. Even before the accession of Henry of Navarre, Catholic pamphleteers had denounced him as a tyrant intent on filling the kingdom with 'heretiques Machiavellistes et Athees'[5]; and his career as

---

[1] Ribadeneira, *Tratado*, 1595, p. 90. Cf. Fitzherbert, *Policy and religion*, i, 1606, p. 338. This passage in Ribadeneira was later singled out for specially violent attack by the Protestant controversialist David Hume, *Le Contr'Assassin*, n.p., 1612, pp. 37-8.

[2] Juan de Mariana, *De rege et regis institutione libri III*, Toledo, 1599, Caps. vi, vii.

[3] For an interesting and relevant survey of the evolution of these doctrines, see J. H. M. Salmon, *The French Religious Wars in English Political Thought*, Oxford, 1959.

[4] David Owen, *Herod and Pilate*, p. 56.

[5] *Advis aux princes, seigneurs, gentilshommes, et autres Catholiques de France*, Paris, 1589, p. 18.

King of France was punctuated by attempts on his life, commonly attributed to the encouragement of the Jesuits. In England, too, where the Queen was similarly subject to threats and plots, feeling against the Society of Jesus ran high. The Bull of Pope Pius V against Elizabeth was an especial irritant and led writers such as John Hull – yet another antagonist of Parsons whom he describes as a 'Machivillian Turkish practiser' – to regard the Society as a progeny issuing from a 'murdering Spanish souldier *Ignatius de Laoila*', and as traitors who laid their 'bloody hands upon the Lords annointed'.[1] The situation was further aggravated, early in James I's reign, by the Gunpowder Plot which was interpreted as the diabolical fruit of a league between Satan and the Jesuits – 'or rather Jubusites and Satanical Seminaries'.[2] This conspiracy was the immediate occasion for the drafting of the Oath of Allegiance which resulted in those further tensions, between moderate Catholics and Jesuit extremists, briefly alluded to at the beginning of this essay, together with a reiteration of the whole complex of abuse and counter-abuse, already evident in the last decade of the sixteenth century. The Society of Jesus was branded as a collection of ruthless villains who would kill anybody who stood in their way. The paranoid Thomas Bell even claimed to have irrefutable personal evidence for this. The Jesuits had been trying to silence him for his writings against their 'rotten Poperie' – but, as so often, their pamphleteers cloaked themselves in anonymity. His latest adversary, who might well have been some 'bloody cut throate', had promised to provide Bell with a winding sheet for his 'blacke Funerall'. Furthermore, Bell had received a 'friendly letter (but without name),' containing a silver packet; but the circumstances were so suspicious that neither he nor others 'durst open the Packet; as having apparent inducements to suspect Poyson, Pestilence, or other like infection Diabolicall'.[3]

---

[1] John Hull, *The unmasking of the politique atheist*, 1602, sig. A4^{r-v}, pp. 53-4.

[2] *The araignement and execution of the late traytors*, 1606: passage cited, from the text reprinted in Lord Somers, *A Collection of Scarce and Valuable Tracts*, ed. Walter Scott, 1809-15, ii, p. 115.

[3] Thomas Bell, *The catholique triumph*, 1610, p. 418. Cf. *A discoverie of the most secret and subtile practises of the Jesuites. Translated out of French,*

This was the way the Jesuits went about to eliminate their enemies!

The last straw came on 14 May 1610, when the assassin Ravaillac struck down Henry IV. The uproar was colossal, and the Jesuits were regarded as instigators of the crime despite the murdered king's well-known regard for the Society. So violent were the denunciations that Pierre Coton, one of Henry's Jesuit confessors, felt obliged to issue a letter condemning the murder and attempting to show that the doctrine of tyrannicide and the murder of princes was not maintained by the Jesuits, but had been peculiar to Mariana who had been condemned by the Society itself. His defence was in vain, and provoked angry accusations that it was a mere colour to hide Jesuitical glee.[1] In England, Coton's letter was published; but it was swiftly followed by an English translation of the Decree of the Sorbonne against tyrannicide, and of the Paris Parlement's sentence that Mariana's work should be publicly burnt. A 'Preamble' to the translations argues that the majority of men are desirous of 'novelties', and that the Jesuits cunningly exploit this desire to engineer their dastardly plots. When the Oath of Allegiance was made and confirmed by Act of Parliament it was likely that 'all the Recusants in England would willingly have taken it, as sundry of them began, had not the Jesuits opposed themselves, and procured the Pope to command the contrary'. As a result of this interference, even the moderate Catholics have refused the Oath because it describes the doctrine of deposing, or killing princes, as heretical. But, the

---

1610, sig. C2ʳ, which claims that the Jesuits employ 'certaine murtherers and poysoners, to poyson the Principall Doctors of the Churches aswell Lutherans as Calvinists'.

[1] Pierre Coton, *Lettre Declaratoire de la doctrine des Peres Jesuites conforme aux decrets du Concile de Constance*, Paris, 1610. T. Owen, *A Letter of a Catholicke man beyond the seas, written to a friend in England: including another of Peter Coton etc.*, n.p., 1610, which claims, at p. 41: 'Rebellious doctrine proper unto Protestants, and condemned by Catholicks'. *Anticoton, ou refutation de la lettre declaratoire de pere Cotton*, n.p., 1610. *Anti-Coton, or a refutation of Cottons Letter Declaratorie*, 1610. *The Hellish and horribble Councell, practised and used by the Jesuites . . . when they would have a man to murther a King*, 1610. The arguments of the last work were expanded by David Hume in his *Contr'-Assassin* which was, probably, the principal work against Coton.

author demands, why should this doctrine not be regarded as heretical? And he bitterly points out that such 'false, lewd and traiterous' opinions have been openly published by the Jesuits, and most especially by the iniquitous Mariana. In a postlude, a second author hastens to supply one point omitted from the 'Preamble'. Ravaillac, who gave the accursed stroke which 'hath made all France to bleed', had confessed that he had long deliberated the question of assassination before he could resolve that it was lawful to kill the King; but 'falling upon that booke of *Mariana*, he found his conscience (as he said) cleard of all scruple in that point'. Thus, whoever it was who put the knife into the assassin's hand, it was evident that its 'metall had been tempered in the forge of the Jesuits', and that it was their books 'gave edge unto it'.[1]

Donne's Ignatius

For John Donne – writing so soon after the assassination of Henry IV, amidst an increasing flood of anti-Jesuit invective, and within the context not only of the Oath of Allegiance controversy, but also of those other longer-standing traditions sketched above – it was the doctrine of political revolution, to be accomplished by any means, which gave the Jesuits pre-eminence amongst evil-doers. Father Healy has suggested that regicide provides the 'unifying theme' of the *Conclave*[2]; but this is not exactly so. The unifying theme of the work is implicit in its very structure. Ignatius is, within the special limits of *innovation* enunciated by Donne, too powerful for a series of contestants; and he is too powerful not merely because of the Jesuits' special distinction with regard to King-killing. Rather it is because the Jesuits are the arch-enemies of monarchies, and because they are prepared to enforce age-old papal claims against foreign states, by all means, fair or foul. King-killing is certainly their most extreme shift – and is regarded as peculiarly theirs – but it is only one of a series of iniquities in their armoury. It is the rigorous application of these criteria which

[1] *The copie of a late decree of the Sorbone at Paris, for the condemning of that impious and haereticall opinion, touching the murthering of princes: generally maintained by the Jesuites, etc.*, 1610, sigs. B1r-2r, B3r, E3r, E4v.
[2] Healy, p. xxxviii.

enables Donne's Ignatius so easily to demolish rival claims to a coveted seat within Lucifer's inner sanctum.

Copernicus, for instance – who has put his hopes in the reorganisation of the heavens and the added lustre thereby given to Lucifer's namesake, the Morning Star – is sharply corrected by Ignatius. What honour, asks Ignatius, is to be derived from the star Lucifer which is merely Venus? If one were going to have regard to namesakes then surely the work of Lucifer the *'Calaritan Bishop'* must be recognised as far more valuable, because 'he was the first that opposed the dignity of Princes'. Paracelsus is even more severely rebuked. His followers 'abuse and prophane' the precious minerals which belong to Lucifer himself. Their 'physicke' wastes resources which would be better employed by Lucifer's brother and colleague, the Pope: gold and precious stones, to 'baite and ensnare the *Princes* of the earth'; iron to make engines of war; minerals for poisons; and the elements of gunpowder to 'demolish and overthrow Kings and Kingdomes, and Courts and seates of Justice'.[1] Later, when Lucifer himself tentatively advances the claims of Nerius, he does so principally on the grounds that the Oratorian Friars have 'used a more free, open, and hard fashion against *Princes'*, and have better provided for direct papal jurisdiction, than have Jesuits such as Bellarmine whose complexities are beyond ordinary men's understanding. Ignatius's reply is withering. What kingdom, he demands, have the followers of Nerius ever 'cut up into an *Anatomy'*? If mere scholarly writings are to be deemed sufficient for entrance into this room reserved for innovators, then Reformers such as Beza and Calvin might equally well have qualified. However, their purpose was not to 'extirpate *Monarchies'*; nor have their disciples ever 'done any thing upon the person of his soveraigne'. A few Oratorians have followed the Jesuit example of disturbing the peace of some states; but since they have performed 'nothing with their hands', they can scarcely ever aspire to this 'secret and sacred *Chamber'*. Lucifer intends to counter this argument by suggesting that, perchance, all those whose hands had been 'imbrued in the bowels of Princes' have not necessarily been armed by the Jesuits – an answer, Donne is quick to stress, which would have

[1] Healy, pp. 17, 23-5.

been made by Lucifer as 'Father of lies', in which capacity he might say anything – but he thinks better of it, and refrains from advancing Nerius's slender claim against Ignatius and his bristling followers.[1]

Even Machiavelli cannot match Ignatius in such matters; though Donne does his best for the Florentine who argues that he has armed the people against princely oppression, and shown them how to conspire against, and even overthrow, tyrants. This is the final point of Machiavel's speech; but it does not, I think, represent a recognition on Donne's part of any truly republican element in Machiavelli's own writing, as Healy suggests.[2] In so far as it represents anything more than an attempt by Donne's Machiavel to vie with the Jesuits, it may be compared with a minority view of the *Prince* which was first tentatively advanced in the 1530s, when Reginald Pole had reported that some Florentines were defending Machiavelli as a lover of liberty who had written the *Prince* to overthrow the Medici, who must inevitably be ruined when following his precepts. Pole's work remained unpublished until 1744; but its interest lies in the suggestion that contemporaries were already seeking a hidden meaning in Machiavelli. The idea was repeated by Matteo Toscano in 1578, and, more important, by Alberico Gentilis in his *De legationibus* of 1585, where he wrote that Machiavelli was a 'eulogist of democracy and its most spirited champion', and that, as the supreme enemy of tyranny, Machiavelli had devised his *Prince* not to instruct tyrants but to expose them to the 'suffering nations'. Fitzherbert, in his *Policy and religion*, though totally unconvinced by such a theory, cites some of Machiavelli's own countrymen who confess that the *Prince* is contrary to true reason of state, and assert that the author himself knew this, but, desiring the downfall of the Medici, 'published his pestilent doctrin, hoping that they wold embrace it and ruine theym selves by the practise therof, wherby the state of *Florence* might returne to the ould *Democracy*'.[3]

---

[1] Healy, pp. 75-9.   [2] Healy, p. xxxiii.

[3] Pole, *op. cit.*, i, pp. 151-2; M. Toscano, *Peplus Italiae*, Paris, 1578, p. 52; A. Gentilis, *De legationibus libri tres*, 1585, p. 109, and trans. by G. J. Laing, Classics of International Law, New York, 1924, p. 156; Fitzherbert, *Policy and religion*, i, 1606, p. 412.

Despite this tradition, it was difficult to identify Machiavelli very closely with the monarchomachs. It was true that he had devoted a long chapter of the *Discourses* to conspiracies, which had been recognised as 'fort bonne instruction tant pour les princes que pour les sujets'.[1] Some interpreters went further. The idea, for example, of using religion as a cloak to win a people's allegiance in plots against their princes was regarded by John Leslie, Bishop of Ross, as 'extractit out of the *Discourses*'; and he also thought that the 'fyne witted clerkis of Machivellis scoole' are never content with the present state, but 'employ thair braynes for altering of commoun wealthes and depriving and setting up of Princes at thair plesour'.[2] For Bishop Morton, even the theory that people might, in their primitive state, have lived without kings, tasted 'too much of Machiavellisme'[3]; and Pasquier, as we have seen, suggested that the doctrine of king-killing itself had been developed by the Jesuits from Machiavelli's *Prince*. But these views, and especially the last, were scattered reflections, and were not generally taken up. Machiavelli was certainly identified with political murder; but generally at a different level. The Machiavellian prince might, it seemed, murder his opponents; but the merely Machiavellian opponent rarely murdered his prince. In popular estimation you needed to be something more than a Machiavellian to do that. You had, in short, to be a Jesuit.

Donne's Machiavel advances his claim as a deposer of princes without much conviction; and, like the rest of his arguments, it is relentlessly brushed aside, or rather totally disregarded, by Ignatius whose speech in answer to Machiavel forms the core of the *Conclave*. Lucifer had been impressed by the Florentine, and was considering the possibility of using him as a counterpoise to Ignatius; but the latter is more subtle than the devil

---

[1] Hierosme de Chomedy, *L'Histoire de la conjuration de Catilin*, Paris, 1575, sig. A3ᵛ. The chapter is *Discourses*, III. 6.

[2] *Calendar of the State Papers relating to Scotland*, III, 27, p. 813. The first of these documents is assigned to 1569, and is said to be in Leslie's hand. It is entitled 'Ane breiff declaratioun of the wikit and ungodlie proceedingis of certane inveterat conspiratoris aganis ye quenis majeste' (that is, Mary Queen of Scots). The second is a letter from Leslie to Queen Elizabeth, dated 22 June 1571.

[3] Thomas Morton, *A full satisfaction concerning a double Romish iniquitie, hainous rebellion and more than heathenish equivocation*, 1606, p. 28.

himself and sees through this stratagem. His first concern, therefore, is to castigate Machiavel for even daring to think that he might entrap Lucifer by flattery; especially when he had attributed 'so much to his own wit' that he never once acknowledged the Devil – nor even believed in the Devil's existence. It had to be conceded that Machiavel had not believed in God either – nor in any other religion – and might on that account be deemed worthy of entrance. On the other hand, the very sincerity of Machiavel's unbelief constituted a drawback; for, since he 'beleeved that those things which hee affirmed were true, hee must not be rancked with them, which having beene sufficiently instructed of the true God, and beleeving him to be so, doe yet fight against him in his enemies armie'. The Jesuits, Ignatius acknowledges, themselves speak ill of the Devil, but this is done 'out of a secret covenant' and out of '*Mysteries*' which may not be revealed to a mere catechumen of their '*Synagogue*'.[1]

Machiavel is also indicted for the great injuries which he has inflicted on the Bishop of Rome. These injuries, in the topsy-turvy world of the *Conclave*, consist of 'weake praising'. The sins attributed by Machiavel to the Papacy are really too feeble to do justice to truly colossal iniquities – a circumstance which enables Donne, through Ignatius's mouth, to catalogue some choice papal peccancies, culminating in the story of the alleged rape committed on the venerable Bishop of Fano by Pier Luigi, son of Pope Paul III. In the face of such crimes, this 'pratling fellow *Machiavell* doth but treacherously, and dishonestly prevaricate, and betraie the cause' if he considers it sufficient for papal dignity to accord them sins 'common to all the world'. The characteristic, and really noteworthy crimes of the Papacy, are the 'transferring of Empires, the ruine of Kingdomes, the Excommunications, and depositions of Kings, and devastations by fire and sword'; and it was precisely these which the Jesuits had encouraged and attempted to justify by distorting the '*Canons and Histories*'.[2]

---

[1] Healy, pp. 33-5. The problem posed by this section – that is the degree to which sincere atheists might be deemed less sinful than perverse believers – is illuminated in Anthony Raspa, 'Theology and Poetry in Donne's "Conclave" ', *Journal of English Literary History*, xxxii, 1965, pp. 478-89.   [2] Healy, pp. 37-43.

At last, having dwelt on Machiavelli's failure even to recognise the true state of affairs in Hell and on earth, Ignatius moves on to examine the things which 'this man, who pretends to exceed all Auncient and Moderne *States-men*' boasts about. And here, Ignatius is even more scathing. That the matters which have been 'shoveld together' by Machiavel are of no consequence is evident from the way in which they have been universally condemned and nowhere defended. Not, Ignatius hastens to add, that this would necessarily make his doctrine any the worse; but it does mean that it is 'the lesse artificially caried' and, therefore, the less able to achieve its desired ends. The Jesuits, by contrast, are subtle and effective, using historical and theological evidence in whatever way best suits the needs of the moment. They can lull a kingdom, such as Britain, with their '*Opium*', into believing that there is no danger of a deposition; and then, when the time is ripe, they will reinterpret their sources 'to awake that state out of her *Lethargy*, either with her owne heat, intestine warre, or by some *Medicine* drawne from other places'. The security of princes is at the mercy of the Jesuits' interpretation of the *Canons*, and may be 'diminished, revoked, and anulled' as the Society wishes. The Jesuits, unlike other religious orders, have rules which might be 'applyed to times and to new occasions'; and, unlike Machiavel, whose 'Mine' has been perceived by the enemy, their own flexibility and cunning has enabled them to receive the Church 'as a ship', and to 'freely saile in the deep sea'. It is not that Machiavelli's work contains nothing of value. It is simply that the Jesuits do not require his advice. In particular, the business of dissembling, in which he glories, is as old as Plato and 'other fashioners of *Common-wealths*', and the Church Fathers themselves had allowed the liberty of lying. In any case, the Jesuits had gone beyond this 'free lying' with another less suspicious doctrine: 'which is *Mentall Reservation*, and *Mixt propositions*'.[1]

Machiavel is clearly not in the same class as Ignatius who now delivers the final blow which will destroy his rival once and for all. Machiavel's books have all been conceived for the sole purpose of ruining the Roman Church, removing people's liberty, destroying 'all civility and re-publique', and reducing

[1] Healy, pp. 47-55.

all states to monarchies. In truth, everywhere Kings have either withdrawn from allegiance to the Church or have damaged its power in some way. On the other hand, to the Jesuits the very name, *Monarch*, is 'hatefull and execrable'; and, having done its utmost to undermine royal power, their Society has been termed the *Sword* of the Roman Church, as a name most apt for the '*Jesuites Assassinates*, and *King-killings*'. This is the greatest glory of the Society. They are prepared to murder kings 'voluntarily, for nothing, and every where'; and their art of divination far exceeds in subtlety that of the ancient Romans, in that 'wee consider not the entrails of *Beasts*, but the entrails of souls, in confessions, and the entrails of *Princes*, in treasons; whose hearts wee do not beleeve to be with us, till we see them'. In view of all this it would be better for 'this pratling *Secretary*' to hold his tongue, rest content that his work has enjoyed some temporary reputation, and recognise that he cannot compare with the Jesuits whose achievements are world-wide. Indeed, in Ignatius's estimation, poor Machiavel cannot aspire to anything higher than an honourable place 'amongst the *Gentiles*'. This is the final thrust at Machiavel's own claim to have merited recognition as an innovator who has 'dealt in Christian businesse'; for, as Ignatius remarks, 'in all times in the *Romane* Church there have bene *Friers* which have farr exceeded *Machiavel*'.[1] So, in his vision, Donne sees Machiavel 'often put forward, and often thrust back, and at last vanish'. The only serious contender for a place in the inner sanctum has been vanquished; and Ignatius, having quickly disposed of the other aspirants, turns his attention to the principal seat next to Lucifer's own throne. Boniface is in possession. But not for long; and Donne's last vision, before his soul returns to its body, is of the Pope being hurled down by Ignatius with eager assistance from Lucifer who fears that otherwise 'his owne seate might bee endangered'. If the Devil himself is so terrified of Ignatius, what chance could mere mortals stand – even if they be as cunning and as evil as Machiavel himself?

[1] Healy, pp. 55-63.

14

The *Devotions* Now

D. W. HARDING

The *Devotions* record a man wrestling to persuade himself of his acceptability to God in spite of a deep and pervasive sense of sin. But what meaning can the work have now? The biographical material and the glimpses of medical and social practices three and a half centuries ago are certainly of interest but of course entirely peripheral to the book's appeal; its central importance is the sight it offers of an intellectually subtle and a strongly emotional man struggling with problems that still assail us. But 'us'? If the book could be appreciated only by Christians of Donne's doctrinal persuasion, even by Christians generally, its readership would now be sharply restricted. In fact, regardless of the framework in which he sets his experiences, they can be recognised as human experiences by people of different religious faith or of none. But they will not have force for everyone.

The biographical illumination that the book offers is relevant to the question of its continuing significance; the sort of man he was defines the readers who can, and those who can not, meet Donne here in the *Devotions*. There are many people so fortunate in disposition that they can feel nothing but a detached wonder, perhaps some distaste, at the sight of a seventeenth-century divine abasing himself with biblical fervour for public edification. They include at the simplest level the people who perform their social role and pursue their pleasures without question and with eyes averted from death; for them it is not Donne but the Hostess who can speak – 'So 'a cried out "God, God, God!" three or four times: now I, to comfort him, bid him 'a should not think of God, I hoped there was no need to trouble himself with any such thoughts yet.' There are also people of less restricted consciousness – sensitive and intelligent

readers among them – who are more or less content with them-
selves, not unaware of their shortcomings but able to accept
themselves as they are, not afraid to fear death but not needing
constantly to test their capacity to tolerate the fear. For these
psychologically fortunate people Donne's wrestling with his
guilt and his fear will be a distant thing, to be understood if at
all by an effort of clinical empathy.

It is to those who have felt despair and horror at themselves
and their waste of life that the book can still speak, those in the
state that Scott Fitzgerald for instance tried to convey – but
how faintly and feebly compared with Donne's intensity – in
The Crack-Up. For most who confront it the devastating ex-
perience of three o'clock in the morning is dissipated as rapidly
as the misery of seasickness; when day returns with the sound
of lavatories being flushed in adjoining flats and early radios
beginning to flow it becomes no more than a fact of memory,
irrecoverable as experience. Donne's effort as he convalesced
was to set down the experience.

The illness he records, probably relapsing fever, was severe;
there was an epidemic, and he listened to burial bells from the
nearby church, and even more poignantly to the passing bell
for another man and then the death knell, knowing that his own
life was in great danger. In the *Devotions* we have a man of very
high achievement and learning and of brilliant and unresting
creative intelligence confronting the prospect of death, a man
too of such unsparingly honest self-criticism that his failures
and unworthiness are as vivid to him as death. An agnostic
reader is not debarred from entering into Donne's fear of death
and his remorse and regrets: imminent death ends all the
opportunities – for trying again, making amends, choosing
better; it presents the finished picture and asks what you think
of it. The sense of failing to live up to your own standards, of
constant relapse in spite of regrets and good resolves, and of
having made poor use of a life now running out is not confined
to religious people.

Donne divides his illness and his reflections on it into twenty-
three stages (perhaps because he recovered and the last hour
for him was still to strike), and since he was a poet of concrete

situations and of sharply realised metaphor and simile he tied his reflections to the actual events of the illness. It is not to be believed that while he lay seriously ill his thoughts came to him in their present form, elaborated with well marshalled biblical allusions and with each stage organised into the three divisions of Meditation, Expostulation and Prayer. But it is likely, given such a man, that the essential quality of the thinking – the nature and the sources of his fears and hopes – was present in the more disorganised and desperate reflections that really came to him in his states of high temperature, sleeplessness, drenching sweat and extreme debility.

[At each stage the Meditation starts (and may end) with a fact of his physical condition or some social incident of the illness (such as the King's sending his own physician to consult in the treatment), and it usually proceeds to the spiritual state with which the fact can be compared. In the Expostulation (the word having overtones of respect and friendliness in argument which seem to be fading from modern usage) Donne addresses God, exclaiming and lamenting, trying to understand his affliction, at times almost protesting: 'But comes not this *Expostulation* too neere a *murmuring?*' (Expostulation 4)[1]; at times exclaiming at the seeming impossibility required of a Christian, for instance both to fear God and to come to him in prayer at any time: 'But, *O my God*, can I doe this, and *feare* thee; come to thee, in all places, at all houres, and *feare* thee?' (Expostulation 6); but always ending with a reasoned acceptance of God's will. There is no mechanical submission, and if in the end he can say 'God's will be done' it is much more than a conventionally pious formula; he has to exercise his alert and learned and ingenious mind to discover a sense in which his wretched condition can be rationally interpreted as part of a beneficent purpose. Only after this submission can he see what to ask for in the Prayer.]

From the factual detail with which he commonly begins his Meditation (and sometimes his Expostulation) Donne's thinking often pursues a tangential association of some emblematic or metaphorical significance. So in Expostulation 3, for instance, he sets out from the facts that he is as weak as an infant and has

[1] *Devotions upon Emergent Occasions*, ed. J. Sparrow, Cambridge, 1923.

had to get to bed, and that Jesus said *Suffer little children to come to mee:*

> *O Lord,* I am a sucking childe, and cannot eat, a creeping childe, and cannot goe; how shall I come to thee? Whither shall I come to thee? To this bed? I have this weak and childish frowardnes too, I cannot sit up, and yet am loth to go to bed; shall I find thee in bed? Oh, have I alwaies done so? The bed is not ordinarily thy *Scene,* thy *Climate: Lord,* dost thou not accuse me, dost thou not reproach to mee, my former sinnes, when thou layest mee upon this bed? Is not this to hang a man at his owne dore, to lay him sicke in his owne bed of wantonnesse?

The method is not unlike that of free association in psycho-analysis, in that his path of thought is determined by seeming accidents. They have of course been selected, sifted and organised by critical scrutiny in the final writing, but they often retain something of their arbitrariness and logical unpredictability.

At first glance the writing may seem highly rational; it is always intellectual in manner and range of reference. Yet the manner and the materials very often serve primarily to in-tensify the emotional response. His pursuit of the idea (Expostu-lation 2) that 'No man is so little, in respect of the greatest man, as the greatest in respect of *God . . .*' leads him through successive elaborations to its human limits, not in order to develop or clarify the thought but to enforce the emotional impact:

> He that hath no more of this world but a *grave,* hee that hath his grave but lent him, til a better man, or another man, must bee buried in the same grave, he that hath no *grave,* but a *dung-hill,* hee that hath no more *earth,* but that which he carries, but that which hee is, hee that hath not that *earth,* which hee is, but even in that, is another's slave, hath as much proportion to God, as if all *Davids Worthies,* and all the *worlds Monarchs,* and all *imaginations Gyants* were kneaded and incorporated into one, and as though that one were the suvivor of all the sonnes of men, to whom *God* had given the world.

Or he can give the impression of a reasoned statement by what is really a play on language; his serious condition affrights his beholders:

they conceive the worst of me now, and yet feare worse; they give me for dead now, and yet wonder how I doe, when they wake at midnight, and aske how I doe to morrow. (Meditation 3.)

Here the effect is gained entirely by his pretending to take literally the idiomatic exaggerations 'conceive the worst' and 'take me for dead'.

The technique of associative thinking that he uses could be seen as a development of the familiar exercise of elaborating a sermon from a text, when a well-known saying has to be developed into something new and unexpected enough to hold attention, but Donne allows it to express highly personal characteristics. Meditation 8, for instance, opens with a statement of the technique, the possibility of exploring further aspects of the comparison (from Meditation 4) between man and the world; but this time they lead not to intellectual dissection but to a crescendo of gloom:

Stil when we return to that *Meditation*, that *Man* is a *World*, we find new *discoveries*. Let him be a *world*, and him self will be the *land*, and *misery* the *sea*. His misery (for misery is his, his own; of the happinesses of this world hee is but *Tenant*, but of misery the *Freeholder*; of happines he is but the *farmer*, but the *usufructuary*, but of misery, the *Lord*, the *proprietary*) his misery, as the *sea*, swells above all the hilles, and reaches to the remotest parts of this *earth*, *Man*; who of himselfe is but *dust*, and coagulated and kneaded into earth, by *teares*; his *matter* is *earth*, his *forme*, *misery*.

The free associative nature of his reflections, arbitrary, 'accidental', following personal preoccupations rather than a strictly logical train of thought, can be seen in the ending of the famous Meditation 17. He has worked up rationally, through the principle of the Church's catholicity, to the recognition that 'No man is an *Iland* . . .' with the conclusion that when the bell tolls it tolls for each of us. And immediately he wonders if this is needlessly borrowing others' misery 'as though we were not miserable enough of our selves'. He denies it, indeed, but then adds that even so it would be excusable because (contradicting the implication of what he has just said) scarcely any man has enough: affliction is a treasure, maturing us and making us fit for God. Then his thought jumps to the idea that treasure in the form of bullion, uncoined, is no use on our journey towards Heaven. The dying man's affliction lies in his bowels like gold in a mine; the passing bell coins that treasure and makes it currency that Donne can put to his own use: '. . . by this consideration of another's danger, I take mine owne into contemplation, and so secure my selfe, by making my recourse to my God, who is our onely securitie'.

He could well have ended, as the hackneyed quotation always does, 'It tolls for *thee*'. Instead, the pseudo-rational argument about treasure and currency springs from his afterthought that perhaps he is wilfully adding to his own affliction by reinforcing it with another's, this doubt being immediately rebutted by the assertion (reflecting his personal outlook as much as conventional Christian thought) that 'affliction is a *treasure*'. Then the alert, exploratory mind seeks its way back to the bell, his starting point, and he reaches the conceit that the passing bell mints the bullion of misery into usable current coin.

The mechanics of writing in the *Devotions* is influenced by the sermon technique. What seems an over lavish italicising stems from its use not only for the abundant biblical quotations and allusions but in order to indicate the speech emphases that clarify the sense and show which ideas he wanted to bring out most forcefully. His repetitions, rhythmically cumulative without being mechanical, keep the pattern of speech as he tries to communicate his crescendo of conviction:

> *Thy Sonn went about healing all manner of sicknesses.* (No disease incurable, none difficult; he healed them *in passing*.) *Vertue went out of him, and he healed all,* all the multitude (no person incurable) he healed them *every whit* (as himselfe speaks) he left no relikes of the disease; and will this universall *Phisician* passe by this *Hospitall*, and not visit mee? not heale me? not heale me wholy? (Prayer 4)

Or again, with a crescendo followed by a falling movement to emphasise his submission:

> O Eternall and most gracious *God*, who hast beene pleased to *speake* to us, not onely in the *voice* of *Nature*, who speakes in our *hearts*, and of thy *word*, which speakes to our *eares*, but in the speech of *speechlesse Creatures*, in *Balaams Asse*, in the speech of *unbeleeving men*, in the confession of *Pilate*, in the speech of the *Devill* himselfe, in the

recognition and *attestation* of thy *Sonne,* I humbly accept thy *voice*
in the sound of this sad and funerall *bell.* (Prayer 17)

The rich resourcefulness of the thought, its close planning
and organisation, and the variety and springy force of the
sentence structure make the *Devotions* an extraordinary product
of convalescence, written as they were in the month immediately
following his illness and turned to as an alternative occupation
when the doctors thought the strain of reading would be
dangerous and forbade books.

Although he intended his book as devotional reading for
others Donne conveys himself as a unique person undergoing
the reality of a particular illness. In comparison with the
Devotions Jeremy Taylor's *Holy Dying,* also discussing sickness
and the possible approach of death, offers advice from the out-
side, benign undoubtedly but almost school-masterly in its
detachment. Donne gives no advice except through his example;
he invites us only to realise what he has gone through, to
overhear him as he struggles with his problems. The reader is
not directly addressed.

Part of what he has gone through is the great physical dis-
comfort of the disease and the suddenness of its onset:

> In the twinckling of an eye, I can scarse see, instantly the tast is
> insipid, and fatuous; instantly the appetite is dull and desirelesse:
> instantly the knees are sinking and strengthlesse; and in an instant,
> sleepe, which is the *picture,* the *copie* of *death,* is taken away, that the
> *Originall, Death* it selfe may succeed, and that so I might have death
> to the life. (Meditation 2)

But it is his anxiety rather than his bodily distress which mainly
demands his attention and his effort after insight. In trying to
bring the discipline of religion to bear on his fear he faces
himself honestly, examining the natural facts before he tries to
get them into a religious perspective. Meditation 6, in which he
tries to understand his fear, exhibits his psychological insight
and the closeness of his natural observations. He notes that
because the physician tries to conceal his fear 'I see it with
the more sharpnesse . . .':

He knowes that his *feare* shall not disorder the practise, and exercise of his Art, but he knows that my *fear* may disorder the effect, and working of his practice.

He points out that as disturbances of the spleen will complicate every other bodily infirmity, or 'the *wind* in the body will counterfeit any disease', so fear will explain mental attitudes that look superficially quite other. He has observed specific phobias, for instance of the sound of a particular musical instrument in an otherwise valiant soldier who is 'not afraid of the sound of Drummes, and Trumpets, and Shot, and those, which they seeke to drowne, the last cries of men'. And in himself, now, he recognises the conflict between his own natural fear and the attitude his religion inculcates:

> . . . I know not what it is that I fear now; I feare not the hastening of my *death*, and yet I do fear the increase of the *disease*; I should belie *Nature*, if I should deny that I feared this, and if I should say that I feared *death*, I should belye *God* . . .

He concludes by realising that he can submit to God's will without denying his fear. Prayer 6 asks for 'a *feare*, of which I may not be *afraid*'. It goes on

> Many of thy blessed *Martyrs*, have passed out of this life, without any show of *feare*; but thy *most blessed Sonne* himselfe did not so. Thy *Martyrs* were known to be but *men*, and therefore it pleased thee, to fill them with thy *Spirit*, and thy *power*, in that they did *more-*than *men*; Thy *Son* was declared by thee, and by himselfe to be *God*; and it was requisite, that he should declare himselfe to be *Man* also, in the weaknesses of man. Let mee not therefore, *O my God*, bee ashamed of these *feares*, but let me feele them to determine, where his feare did, in a present submitting of all to thy will.

The courage and honesty with which Donne examines his natural fear make it so real and vivid that by contrast the re-assurance he finds in his religious faith, after the long argument with himself in Expostulation 6, may seem less convincing. It is, at any rate, achieved only by an evident effort of faith:

> *A wise man wil feare in every thing.* And therefore though I pretend, to no other degree of wisedome. I am abundantly rich in this, that I lye heere possest with that feare, which is *thy feare*, both that this

sicknesse is thy immediate correction, and not meerely a *naturall accident;* and therefore fearefull, because *it is a fearefull thing to fall into thy hands,* and that this feare preserves me from all inordinate feare, arising out of the infirmitie of Nature, because thy hand being upon me, thou wilt never let me fall out of thy hand.

And in fact Meditation 7 opens with an increase in the natural fear as the physician brings in consultants and so confirms Donne's conviction of the seriousness of his condition.

Throughout the work his bodily ills are taken as an emblem, even a consequence of his sins; '*sinne* is the *root,* and the *fuell* of all *sicknesse* . . .' (Expostulation 22). The anxiety engendered by the unheralded onset of his illness is extended to the unobserved encroachment of sin:

> I fall sick of *Sin,* and am bedded and bedrid, buried and putrified in the practise of *Sin,* and all this while have no presage, no pulse, no sense of my *sicknesse* . . . (Expostulation 1)

A sense of guilt, a conviction of sin that threatens to engulf him, is the recurrent burden of the book.

This was presumably a more compelling theme in the first half of the seventeenth century than for the next two hundred years, to judge by the fact that after five editions of the *Devotions* between 1624 and 1638 the work was not reprinted until 1839 (and then as part of a six volume edition of his works). Apart from the puritans' antagonism to the kind of church doctrine Donne adhered to, they presumably had a much stronger and more optimistic (however grim) commitment to the avoidance of sin than to dealing with the condition of sinfulness. Donne devotes much of his rhetoric to bringing himself and us to realise the ocean of guilt that threatens him:

> I have, O *Lord,* a *River* in my *body,* but a *Sea* in my *soule,* and a *Sea* swoln into the depth of a *Deluge,* above the *Sea.* Thou hast raised up certaine *hils* in *me* heretofore, by which I might have stood safe, from these *inundations* of *sin* . . . but this *Deluge,* this *inundation,* is got above all my *Hills;* and I have sinned and sinned, and multiplied *sinne* to *sinne,* after all these thy assistances against *sinne,* and where is there *water* enough to wash away this *Deluge?* (Prayer 20)

'Sin', as a broad and vague, and safe, generalisation is not enough for Donne. Without being exhibitionist he is a good deal more explicit and specific about his personal sins than we might have expected, considering that he intended the *Devotions* for immediate publication and that he filled a prominent position in the London of his time. In Expostulation 1 he names his sins as lust, envy and ambition, a self-accusation he repeats in Expostulation 11. (He adds sloth at one point but glancingly, with little emphasis.) He records the changes of sin that occur with increased age – 'This *transmigration* of sinne found in my selfe . . .' 'Our *youth* dies' he says

> and the *sinnes* of our *youth* with it ; . . but still the *soule* lives, and passes into another *sinne*; and that, that was *licentiousnesse*, growes *ambition*, and that comes to *indevotion*, and *spirituall coldnesse* . . . (Expostulation 23)

It seems evident that Donne, once the young poet for whom sex had been a preoccupying excitement, and Donne the sick man of fifty-one who had taken orders (at the King's suggestion) only eight years before and risen in six years to be Dean of St Paul's, is accusing himself personally, not in the sweepingly vague terms of the General Confession. He owed his deanery, R. C. Bald suggests, 'largely to the successful employment of the courtier's arts . . .' and may even, though Bald thinks not, have had to pay Buckingham for it. There are other places in the *Devotions* where he shows concern about ambition and the consequences of worldly success. He remarks in Meditation 16

> We scarce heare of any man *preferred*, but wee thinke of our selves, that wee might very well have beene that *Man;*

Expostulation 20 opens

> My *God*, my *God*, the *God* of *Order*, but yet not of *Ambition*, who assignest *place* to every one, but not *contention* for place . . .

And in Meditation 21 he discusses the dangers and uncertainties of preferment:

> But is every *raising* a *preferment*? or is every present *preferment* a *station*? . . . How many *men* are raised, and then doe not *fill* the place they are raised to? No *corner* of any place can bee *empty*; there can be

no *vacuity*; If that *Man* doe not fill the place, *other men* will; complaints of his *insufficiency* will *fill* it . . .

And along with Donne's suggestion that in the transmigration of sin ambition gives way to indevotion and spiritual coldness we can put his self accusation in Prayer 15:

> I have sinned *behind thy backe* (if that can be done) by wilfull absteining from thy *Congregations*, and omitting thy *service*, and I have sinned *before thy face*, in my *hypocrisies* in Prayer, in my *ostentation*, and the mingling a respect of *my selfe* in preaching thy Word; I have sinned in my *fasting* by repining, when a penurious fortune hath kept mee low; and I have sinned even in that fulnesse, when I have been at thy table, by a negligent examination, by a wilfull prevarication, in receiving that heavenly *food* and *Physicke*.

The sins he feels and confesses are the sins of one real man. And, as in *A Hymne To God the Father*, also written 'during' this illness (presumably in the convalescence), his remorse is specially keen for relapsing into the sins he has once repented. 'My returning to any sinne,' he writes in Prayer 4, 'if I should return to the abilitie of sinning over all my sins againe, thou wouldest not pardon'. However, the last Meditation starts from the physicians' warning '*of the fearefull danger of relapsing*', and the whole work ends with the prayer that he may never '*make shipwracke of faith, and a good conscience*, and then thy *long-livd*, thy *everlasting Mercy*, will visit me, though *that*, which I most earnestly pray against, should fall upon mee, a *relapse* into those *sinnes*, which I have *truely repented*, and thou hast *fully pardoned*'.

Like *A Hymne To God the Father*, again, the *Devotions* record Donne's struggle to conquer his anxious depression through faith. Just as he came to terms with his fear, without denying it, so he reveals a sombreness of outlook which always tends towards the dejection and despair that he recognises as sins and strives against. 'Every thing', he says, 'serves to *exemplifie*, to *illustrate* mans misery' (Meditation 21); but he also prays 'let those *shadowes* which doe fall upon mee, *faintnesses of Spirit*, and *condemnations of my selfe*, bee overcome by the power of thine irresistible *light*' (Prayer 14); and after persuading himself that for all God's severity against relapses into old sins he is still capable of mercy, Donne writes 'But I speak not this, O my *God*, as *preparing* a way to my *Relapse* out of *presumption*, but to *preclude* all accesses of *desperation*, though out of *infirmity*, I should *Relapse*' (Expostulation 23). The accesses of desperation are what he has to guard against.

But he makes no attempt to resist, or to conceal, his gloomy view of things:

> We say, the *Elements* of man are *misery*, and *happinesse*, as though he had an equal proportion of both, and the dayes of man vicissitudinary, as though he had as many *good* daies, as *ill*, and that he liv'd under a perpetual *Equinoctial*, *night*, and *day* equall, good and ill fortune in the same measure. But it is far from that; hee *drinkes misery*, and he *tastes happinesse*; he *mowes misery*, and he *gleanes happinesse*; he *journies in misery*, he does but *walke in happinesse*; and which is worst, his misery is *positive*, and *dogmaticall*, his happinesse is but *disputable*, and *problematicall*; All men call *Misery*, *Misery*, but *Happinesse* changes the name, by the taste of man. (Meditation 13)

And in Meditation 12 he reflects resignedly, almost defiantly, on his melancholy:

> But what have I done, either to *breed*, or to *breath* these *vapors*? They tell me it is my *Melancholy*; Did I infuse, did I drinke in *Mellancholly* into my selfe? It is my *thoughtfulnesse*; was I not made to *thinke?* It is my *study*; doth not my *Calling* call for that?

The seeming rationality of his writing might conceal the strong bias towards a gloomy view of life's possibilities. Thus in Meditation 13, again, he writes

> A woman is comforted with the birth of her *Son*, her body is eased of a burthen; but if shee could *prophetically* read his *History*, how *ill a man*, perchance how *ill a sonne*, he would prove, shee should receive a greater burthen into her *Mind*.

The surely larger number of women whose prophetic glimpse of their son's future would add to their pleasure or at least not diminish it is silently ignored. 'I would not' he begins Meditation 14 'make *Man* worse then hee is, Nor his Condition more miserable then it is. But could I though I would?'

Yet there is nothing debilitated about his gloom, and his own

assessment seems justified when, after surveying biblical
references to good hearts and evil hearts, he writes

> The first kind of heart, alas, my *God*, I have not; the last are not
> *Hearts* to be given to thee; What shall I do? Without that present
> I cannot bee thy *Sonne*, and I have it not. To those of the first kinde
> thou givest *joyfulnes of heart*, and I have not that; To those of the
> other kinde, thou givest *faintnesse of heart*: And blessed bee thou,
> *O God*, for that forbearance, I have not that yet. (Expostulation 11)

In spite of one, almost perfunctory, mention of sloth, there is no
sign that Donne suffered from the inert, apathetic condition,
the sense of the worthlessness of oneself and everything else,
that seems to have been covered by the notion of *accidie* (and
would now probably be described as depression with retardation).
His thinking is alert and infinitely resourceful and his writing
has a springy energy even while he is expressing his melancholy
view of things. Apart from the fact that despair would have been
a denial of his faith, a sin to be strenuously resisted, there was
also in Donne an intense appreciation of bodily life, and this
ran counter to any debilitating tendency in his sombre outlook.

His great vitality, evident in what he wrote in the weakness
of this convalescence, is a facet of that bodily life which for
Donne was the object of such complex, or perhaps confused and
fluctuating attitudes. One passage of the *Devotions* (Meditation
16) touches on the preoccupations of *Biathanatos*:

> If man knew the *gaine of death*, the *ease of death*, he would solicite,
> he would provoke *death* to assist him, by any hand, which he might
> use. But as when men see many of their owne professions preferd, it
> ministers a hope that that may light upon them; so when these
> hourely *Bells* tell me of so many *funerals* of men like me, it presents,
> if not a *desire* that it may, yet a *comfort* whensoever mine shall come.

But the living body too set up a conflict of attitude in Donne's
mind. On the one hand it is seen with loathing as the source of
sin, on the other its resurrection in a glorified form is an
essential part of the ultimate bliss for which he hoped:

> When therefore I took this *farme*, undertooke this body, I under-
> tooke to *draine*, not a *marish*, but a *moat*, where there was, not water
> *mingled* to offend, but all was *water*: I undertooke to *perfume dung*,

where no one part, but all was equally *unsavory* . . . To cure the
sharpe accidents of *diseases*, is a great worke; to cure the *disease it selfe*
is a greater; but to cure the *body*, the *root*, the *occasion* of *diseases*, is
a worke reserved for the great *Phisitian*, which he doth never any
other way, but by *glorifying* these *bodies* in the next world.
(Meditation 22)

Like others of his period, Donne was very far from discarding
the body as a deplorable clog upon the soul and contemplating
its dissolution with satisfaction. He is intensely concerned for it.
In Meditation 18, after touching on the conflicting ingenuities
of surmise about the generation of the soul and putting that
problem on one side, he gives himself up to a fervent lamenta-
tion for the doomed body with all its faculties and skills. He
prays for the unknown man whose death knell he has listened to:

> . . . so I doe *charitably*, so I do *faithfully* beleeve, that that *soule* is
> gone to everlasting *rest*, and *joy*, and *glory*. But for the *body*, how
> poore a wretched thing is *that*? wee cannot expresse it *so fast*, as it
> growes *worse* and *worse*. That *body* which scarce *three minutes* since
> was such a *house*, as that that *soule*, which made but one step from
> thence to *Heaven*, was scarse thorowly content, to leave that for
> *Heaven*: that *body* hath lost the *name* of a *dwelling house*, because
> none dwells in it, and is making haste to lose the name of a *body*,
> and dissolve to *putrefaction*. Who would not bee affected, to see a
> cleere and sweet *River* in the *Morning*, grow a *kennell* of muddy land
> water by *noone*, and condemned to the saltnesse of the *Sea* by *night*?
> And how lame a *picture*, how faint a *representation* is that, of the
> precipitation of mans body to dissolution? *Now* all the parts built
> up, and knit by a lovely *soule*, *now* but a *statue* of *clay*, and *now*, these
> limbs melted off, as if that clay were but *snow*; and *now*, the whole
> *house* is but a *handfull* of sand, so much *dust*, and but a *pecke* of
> *rubbidge*, so much *bone*. If *he*, who, as this *Bell* tells mee, is gone
> now, were some *excellent Artificer*, who comes to him for a *clocke*,
> or for a *garment* now? or for *councaile*, if hee were a *Lawyer*? If a
> *Magistrate*, for *Justice*?

So Donne laments the doom of the body and its skills. In the
Prayer (18) which follows this passage he argues that the
living are able to pray for the saints because we know that the
saints still lack bodies; and he prays for the dead man:

> For though hee bee by *death* transplanted to thee, and so in posses-
> sion of inexpressible happinesse there, yet here upon earth thou

hast given us such a portion of heaven, as that though men dispute, whether thy *Saints* in heaven doe *know* what we in earth in particular doe stand in need of, yet without all disputation, wee upon earth doe know what thy *Saints* in heaven lacke yet, for the *consummation* of their *happinesse;* and therefore thou hast affoorded us the *dignitie*, that we may *pray* for them. That therefore this *soule*, now newly departed to thy *Kingdome*, may quickly returne to a joifull *reunion* to that *body* which it hath left, and that *wee* with *it*, may soone enjoy the full *consummation* of all, in *body* and *soule*, I humbly beg at thy hand, O our most mercifull *God*, for thy *Sonne Christ Jesus sake.*

Although the resurrection of the body is part of his Christian faith on which Donne puts such emphasis (even in Expostulation 2 balancing the quickness of the resurrection against his terror at what threatened to be the rapid approach of death), still it was the death of the body, the ending of this life, and the final accounting of what he had made of it, with which he was struggling to come to terms in much of the *Devotions*.

The other focus of intense emotion in the work is separation:

> As *Sicknes* is the greatest misery, so the greatest misery of sicknes, is *solitude;* when the infectiousnes of the disease deterrs them who should assist, from comming; even the *Phisician* dares scarse come. *Solitude* is a torment which is not threatned in *hell* it selfe. (Meditation 5)

It is significant that he chose, in convalescence, to elaborate at great length this early fear, although in fact he experienced no such isolation. He had several physicians in attendance, including one sent by the King, his servants (as he records with gratitude later) never failed in attendance on him, and Walton reports that Henry King visited him every day. In the same Meditation he exclaims that infectiousness 'is an *Outlawry*, an *Excommunication* upon the *Patient*, and seperats him from all offices not only of *Civilitie*, but of *working Charitie*'. That he had in mind his own personal dread of loneliness seems clear; in Meditation 7, for instance, when he has discussed at some length the advantages of having several physicians he is checked by his customary self observation and asks himself

But why doe I exercise my Meditation so long upon this, of having plentifull helpe in time of need?

and reminds himself of the distress of those who have none. The need for others is so fundamental, he argues, that

> *God* himself wold admit a *figure* of *Society*, as there is a plurality of persons in *God*, though there bee but one *God*; and all his externall actions testifie a love of *Societie*, and *communion*. (Meditation 5)

And he goes on in the same Meditation to say that God was never so near seeing a defect in any of his works

> as when he saw that it was not good, for man to bee *alone*, therefore *hee made him a helper*; and one that should helpe him so, as to increase the *number*, and give him *her owne*, and *more societie*.

As for religious recluses, whom he strongly condemns, he asserts in this Meditation that their choice of solitude 'is a disease of the *minde*'.

The intense awareness of a need for others, expressed in its personal, dependent way in the first miserable anxiety about his infectiousness, comes to its stronger and more impersonal expression in the passage 'No man is an *Iland* . . .' of Meditation 17. But even in the early statement of the theme he expresses it in the ultimate Christian form of horror and distress at the possibility of separation from God:

> *O my God*, it is the *Leper*, that thou hast condemned *to live alone*; Have I such a *Leprosie* in my *Soule*, that I must die alone; alone without thee? Shall this come to such a *leprosie* in my *body*, that I must die alone? Alone without them that should assist, that shold comfort me? (Expostulation 5)

Separation from God is closely linked for him with separation from man, and even in Prayer 5, in terms that again recall *A Hymne To God the Father*, he associates the opinion of others with his own faith when he prays God to

> preserve this *soule* in the faculties therof, from all such distempers, as might shake the assurance which myselfe and others have had, that because thou hast loved me, thou wouldst love me to my *end*, and at my *end*.

In Donne's hands the Christian idiom is shot through with the realities of a sensitive and intelligent man's experience, and the whole plan of the *Devotions* gives the religious concepts a firm anchorage in human events and emotions. Readers who can enter into the sombreness that marked his outlook – in spite of the robust vigour of his mind – will probably have no difficulty, however far they are from accepting his doctrines, in following him in his self accusations and regrets. It may seem altogether more difficult, if not out of the question, for the non-believer to find any parallel to the affirmations, centrally his faith in the redemption, through which Donne achieves his reassurance. For it is a reassurance, something far more positive than mere resignation in the face of death, that he achieves.

We have to see that what his faith does for Donne in his sickness, for Donne in this world, is to convince him that his self-condemnation need not and must not be total and final. And non-Christians too, suffering from a deep sense of worthlessness, do in favourable circumstances, or with the right kind of help, come to terms with it, not by condoning what they have cause to deplore but by coming to believe that in spite of everything they can accept themselves, that there remains some worth in being the person they now are. Reconciliation to himself, though not to his past failures, is what in terms of human experience Donne achieves through his faith.

The need for some such self-acceptance emerges from the few studies that psychotherapists have undertaken of the process of dying. Thus, for example, a fifty-year-old American patient reported on by H. R. Greenberg and H. R. Blank[1] had much to regret in his life, especially his wretchedly unsatisfying homosexuality. At times his depression was a matter of concern to the hospital staff, but the psychotherapist saw it as a not excessive form of 'grief in advance – a necessary precondition for his death'. Dreams expressed both his fear of loss and his resignation and readiness to let go; waking fantasies of a move to the country were encouraged by the therapist as expressions of 'his unconscious perception of death as a calm and peaceful

[1] 'Dreams of a dying patient', *British Journal of Medical Psychology*, 43, 4; December 1970.

resolution to a highly conflicted life'. The patient managed to make a real peace with a brother with whom he had been on bad terms, and with the therapist's help he 'gradually came to think of himself as a person invested with dignity and self-respect' in spite of his bodily distresses and embarrassments, including the loss of sphincter control. With the details of the very subjective psychoanalytic interpretations on which these studies rely we are of course plunged into a morass of uncertainty, but even if they partly represent the therapists' own projective fantasies about the situation they may be none the less a reflection of deep human needs and fundamental mechanisms in meeting with death. The construction made by the patient and the therapist between them and accepted by them both has its significance.

The reconciliation with himself that a dying retail store executive could achieve took, of course, a simple form, aided very largely by the continuing interest and support of his friends and the therapist. The assurance of being accepted by someone else as valuable enough to be given care and attention is a vital aid towards accepting oneself. It is at the same time a postponement of the final separation that death entails, a postponement until the moment when the patient has separated himself and is not aware of it.

The emotional need for the ordinary attentions of physicians, friends and servants which Donne felt so poignantly can be seen as a facet of a much more general need for acceptance and love, with a dread of worthlessness that would reach its nadir for him in a sense of separation from God:

> It was for thy blessed, thy powerfull *Sonne* alone, *to tread the wine-presse alone, and none of the people with him;* I am not able to passe this agony alone; not alone without *thee;* Thou art thy spirit; not alone without *thine;* spirituall and temporall *Phisicians,* are *thine;* not alone without *mine;* Those whom the bands of *blood* or *friendship,* hath made *mine,* are *mine;* And if *thou,* or *thine,* or *mine,* abandon me, I am alone, and woe unto me, if I bee alone. (Expostulation 5)

The conviction of having worth in spite of all that we have reason to regret seems to answer a basic human need, one that the more fortunate are not aware of because they never doubt their worth. In Donne's idiom and frame of thinking that necessary conviction was expressed in the knowledge that he was one of God's Elect (though not of course in the Calvinistic sense of unconditional election). Like any of us he is striving for the sense of having value as a person when he writes in Prayer 15

> But, as I know, O my gracious *God*, that for all those sinnes committed since, yet thou wilt consider me, as I was in thy *purpose*, when thou wrotest my name in the *Booke of Life*, in mine *Election*: so into what deviations soever I stray, and wander, by occasion of this sicknes, O *God*, returne thou to that *Minute*, wherein thou wast pleased with me, and consider me in that *condition*.

15

John Donne's *Critique of True Religion*

DOMINIC BAKER-SMITH

At the close of his essay on Lancelot Andrewes, T. S. Eliot allows himself some rather unfavourable comments on John Donne's religious objectivity.[1] Of the two men we are told, 'Andrewes is the more medieval, because he is the more pure, and because his bond was with the Church, with tradition . . . Donne is the more modern'. Clearly this modernity is not viewed with approval: Donne is guilty of a personality-cult and his sermons are a means of self-expression. While 'Andrewes is wholly absorbed in the object and therefore responds with the adequate emotion' Donne uses religion as a convenient vehicle for his own emotional outpourings. Now Eliot's judgment does not survive any careful reading of Donne, though it is perhaps applicable to that fictional Donne inflicted on several generations of readers by Logan Pearsall Smith. Its inadequacy will emerge, I hope, in the course of this essay. But it should not be totally disregarded, for in it there is undoubtedly some element of truth. After all Andrewes and Donne aren't quite the same: there is a difference which emerges in spite of their many common interests, beliefs and tastes. One can see what Eliot means by calling Andrewes 'medieval' – there is a scholastic tautness, a vigilant check on personal exposure in his sermons that reinforces the impression of a professional divine. But in Donne the epithet 'modern' is more puzzling. What, apart from 'post-medieval', does it actually mean? Something more substantial than kinship to Huysmans is required. Certainly there is a difference in tone when we hear Donne preach, the theological formulations are controlled by mood and feeling in a relatively subjective manner. But this can be explained as the voice of the

[1] *Selected Essays*, 1951, pp. 351-2.

layman, the late-vocation, whose intellectual formation was completed outside the divinity school. If we are to arrive at a precise sense of Donne's modernity it will surely be helpful to probe the highly sensitive issue of his religious allegiance where the keenest needs of his intellectual and moral being manifest themselves.

There is no certainty as to when Donne first became dissatisfied with the recusant Catholicism of his family. As he asserts in *Pseudo-Martyr* it had paid a price: 'I beleeve, no family (which is not of farre larger extent, and greater branches,) hath endured and suffered more in their persons and fortunes, for obeying the teachers of Roman Doctrine, then it hath done.'[1] The sharpest pang was probably the death of Donne's brother Henry in Newgate prison where he had been committed for sheltering a priest. That was in 1593 when Donne had already been at the Inns of Court for two years; at some date between that loss and the Cadiz expedition of 1596 he had moved far enough from a recusant position to write *Satyre III*. It must also have been at this stage that he undertook his survey of divinity 'as it was then controverted betwixt the *Reformed* and the *Roman Church*'. From the preface to *Pseudo-Martyr*, as well as from Walton's account, it is clear that Donne determined to devise criteria that would ensure objectivity and it is these criteria that provide the frame for the *Satyre*. During this period of 'indifference' Donne posed questions in the hope of resolving his personal uncertainty. When his uncertainty passed and he was able to adopt a public stance in religion the questions did not lose their force or relevance, they remained an essential part of his religious consciousness throughout his life. Vigilance was to be the price of spiritual health, and in the criteria that are projected in *Satyre III* we encounter an important aspect of the poet's mind.

The poem opens with the time-honoured contrast between Christians and the 'blinde Philosophers' of pagan antiquity: the opposition is between the Christians who are saved by faith – to whom virtue is a consequence rather than a cause of salvation – and the sages of antiquity whose ethical discipline may be

---

[1] *Pseudo-Martyr*, London, 1610, sig. ¶r.

accepted in lieu of faith.[1] The discrepancy between Christians who have the means to virtue and the pagans who actually achieve virtue is, after all, the starting point of Thomas More's *Utopia*. Once Donne has set up this contrast he can go on to expose the base motives, gain or honour, for which men will suffer danger and inconvenience, while retaining in the background echoes of the persecution of the just ('Children in th'oven, fires of Spaine') and of pagan devotion to the one God

> (who made thee to stand
> Sentinell in his worlds garrison)

In both cases suffering is borne for a valid motive: resisting the three enemies, 'The foule Devill', 'the worlds selfe' and the 'Flesh' which promote confusion of values.

After this vigorous but obvious attack on vice Donne turns to pseudo-religious motives. The five characters portrayed have all failed to base their religious position on an objective assessment of evidence. Their criteria are simply inadequate. Mirreus the papist and Crants the sectarian are straightforward cases, but Graius is an example of a man adopting Anglicanism for the wrong reasons, while Phrygius and Graccus both show the dangers of scepticism and indifference, though in opposing directions. The section seems to reveal that Donne is less concerned, at this stage at least, with the public stance adopted than with the process of enquiry behind it. Thus Graius's bogus Anglicanism – bogus because passively accepted – is particularly interesting. Moreover, it seems that Donne always laid stress on personal responsibility in religious affiliation since this is the theme of his letter to Sir Toby Mathew in 1619 after the latter's conversion to Rome,

> . . . it is true, That we are fallen into so slack and negligent times, that I have been sometimes glad to hear, that some of my friends

---

[1] Cf. 'If we be too weak to follow the apostles, the martyrs, to follow the virgins, at the least way let us not commit that the Ethnykes or heathen men should seem to over-run us in this plain or lists', Erasmus, *Enchiridion*, Tyndale's translation, 1905, p. 232. Donne's syncretistic suggestion that the pagans 'merit/Of strict life may be'imputed faith', is not so impudent as Milgate implies – such a view is proposed by e.g. Lefèvre d'Etaples *Epistolae Pauli*, Paris, 1515, fol. 69ʳ and is matched by Donne's reference to the 'morall mans holy Ghost, *Seneca*', *The Sermons of John Donne*, ed. G. R. Potter and E. M. Simpson, California, 1953-61, vii, 216.

have differed from me in Religion. It is some degree of an union to be united in a serious meditation of God, and to make any Religion the rule of our actions.[1]

But this should not be taken to indicate indifferentism on Donne's side:

> but unmoved thou
> Of force must one, and forc'd but one allow;
> And the right;

Clearly he is thinking here of a position that will emerge inevitably from any examination of the Churches and their claims provided that the proper criteria are applied. In a sense, according to Donne, a man is a Christian before he is a member of a particular Church.[2] If he lives in the light of the Gospel and in the tradition of the Apostles he will possess criteria that will enable him to discriminate between the various Churches, discerning the essential features while detecting the corruptions introduced by human practices. Obviously such a distinction is artificial, the priority is one of responsibility, not of time; every Christian in so far as he has a social being is involved in some Church. When Donne ceased to be a Papist and became an Anglican it is unlikely that he thought of it as a 'conversion': it was simply a purer realisation of his Christian conviction, an advance in self-awareness. Really, then, Mirreus and Graius stand in the poem as discarded *personae*, their satiric exposure the echo of a personal decision. It is true that the following lines (71-73) suggest a context for this personal decision in terms of revelation and the tradition of the early Church, but there is no question of an automatic possession of truth. The emphasis falls on the area of personal responsibility, on the actual quest for truth:

> Be busie to seeke her, beleeve mee this,
> Hee's not of none, nor worst, that seeks the best.
> To'adore, or scorne an image, or protest,

[1] *John Donne: Selected Prose*, ed. Helen Gardner and T. Healy, Oxford, 1967, p. 153. All references to the letters are to this collection.

[2] This is presumably what he means in a letter to Sir Robert Ker in 1627: 'My Tenets are always, for the preservation of the Religion I was born in, and the peace of the State, and the rectifying of the Conscience' (*Selected Prose*, p. 160). Donne was not born an Anglican.

> May all be bad; doubt wisely; in strange way
> To stand inquiring right, is not to stray;
> To sleepe, or runne wrong, is.

The compression of statement and the urgent rhythms point to the poet's engagement here. External standards, represented by the attitudes towards 'an image', are shown to be inadequate precisely because they set up inadequate criteria. Indeed there is a remarkable continuity between *Satyre III* and Donne's mature treatment of this theme in the Sermons,

> *Vae Idolatris*, woe to such advancers of Images, as would throw down Christ, rather than his Image: But *Vae Iconoclastis* too, woe to such peremptory abhorrers of Pictures, and to such uncharitable condemners of all those who admit any use of them, as had rather throw down a Church, then let a Picture stand.[1]

Running through the whole sermon is the theme of *odium religiosum*: the hatred of a man for his religion which ultimately destroys all religion. Among its consequences Donne depicts the 'miserable impotency to be afraid of words . . . We dare not name *Merit*, nor *Penance*, nor *Sacrifice*, nor *Altar*, because they have been abused'.[2] 'To sleepe, or runne wrong', to be indifferent to these labels or to confuse them with the core of religion, is to miss the point; what the *Satyre* advocates is an alert and sensitive act of discrimination, to 'doubt wisely', 'To stand inquiring right'. When a man doubts wisely he sweeps aside those obstacles – conventions, stock responses, persuasive definitions – which block the way to an authentic appraisal of values. It is an attitude of mind very close to that of Montaigne who wished to ally Christ's teachings with the sceptism of Pyrrho.[3] But the emphasis is on the adverb, one must doubt wisely. This involves a demanding form of intellectual ascesis:

> and hee that will
> Reach her, about must, and about must goe;

There is no place in Donne's writings where we are more poignantly aware of man's role as *viator*, travelling towards a

---

[1] *Sermons*, vii, 433. [2] *Ibid.*, 429.

[3] '. . . moi qui, au dogme du Christ, alliai le sceptisme de Pyrrhon', cited in M. Dreano, *La Religion de Montaigne*, Paris, 1969, p. 273.

future perfection. While the Papist or the sectarian may seem to confuse time with eternity Donne can calmly accept the flux of human affairs; this maturity of historical awareness which flashes out at moments in his controversial work, as in that of Thomas Morton, is part of the Anglican debt to humanism. Its essence can be detected in Newman's adage: 'In a higher world it is otherwise, but here below to live is to change, and to be perfect is to have changed often'. In the sermons Donne speaks of the man who 'doubts with an humble purpose to settle his owne faith, and not with a wrangling purpose to shake another mans'.[1] To doubt wisely means the sacrifice of easy consolation and self-justification; it finds its fulfilment in the act of discrimination between the human and the divine. The history of the Church is, to Donne, a gradual confusion of these two and to escape from the confusion is a testing process of self-definition. Scepticism is not employed in a purely negative function since its end is to ensure an authentic faith rather than one in an idol held up as divine, so there is no tension for Donne between appealing to personal judgment and appealing to the Church's teaching. There is a revealing analogy here between Donne's treatment of ecclesiological dilemmas and his biblical exegesis as summarised in the Christmas sermon for 1621.[2] To explore the Scriptures does not mean acquiring a purely technical familiarity with verse and chapter; rather, a personal involvement is envisaged,

> This is *Scrutari Scripturas, to search the Scriptures*, not as though thou wouldest make a *concordance*, but an *application;* as thou wouldest search a *wardrobe*, not to make an *Inventory* of it, but to finde in it something fit for thy wearing.

Revelation and the Church are the visible means of salvation. But both can be vitiated by a partial use, their healing work thwarted by human short-sightedness. It is this danger that Donne anticipates in *A Litanie*,

> May they pray still, and be heard, that I goe
> Th'old broad way in applying; O decline
> Mee, when my comment would make thy word mine.
>
> (79-81)

---

[1] *Sermons*, v, p. 38.   [2] *Sermons*, iii, p. 367.

Underlying Donne's quest for the true Church, Christ's 'spouse, so bright and cleare', is a highly disciplined analysis of motive which is far removed from Eliot's insinuation of emotional indulgence.

This conception of an intellectual mortification is supported by the parallel (86) between 'Hard deeds' and 'hard knowledge': both are won at a price. The mysteries of revelation are known to all but should, like the biblical texts, be assimilated into a Christian's life and the personal vision which results – a union of data with experience – must be preserved against the pressure of human laws whether secular or ecclesiastical. So Donne is able to introduce the conclusion of the *Satyre* where the theme of discrimination refers to bounds between power and idolatry. The final couplet contains the germ of his case against the Papacy in *Pseudomartyr*, but it equally well applies to any human assumption of divine authority:

> So perish Soules, which more chuse mens unjust
> Power from God claym'd, then God himselfe to trust.

Satyre III, then, manifests a particular habit of mind that Donne appears to have developed out of his search for a satisfying church allegiance. As with Dryden's conversion to Rome it is easy to point to the temporal advantages of his decision, but that does not seem to be the whole story. Donne, after all, was only human and did not always attain the standards he set himself (particularly in controversy) but there can be no doubt of the sincerity and coherence of his views. It seems indeed, as I have already argued, that we cannot talk about a 'conversion' so much as an evolution. Nor is this to suggest that every Papist is an Anglican *in potentia* – though Donne might think so – but rather that Donne, given the particular circumstances, could have done little else and preserved his integrity. His emergence as an Anglican is clearly indebted to just the sort of critical procedure outlined in the *Satyre*. A reference has already been made to Montaigne, but perhaps the most useful analogy here is with Bacon. Isn't Donne's approach to divinity very similar to Bacon's approach to natural philosophy? The aim in both cases is to escape the baneful influence of those Idols which distort our native perception,

For the mind of man is far from the nature of a clear and equal glass, wherein the beams of things should reflect according to their true incidence; nay, it is rather like an enchanted glass, full of superstition and imposture, if it be not delivered and reduced.[1]

For Bacon the result is our tendency to project a non-existent harmony onto our experience of nature:

> ... the spirit of man, being of an equal and uniform substance, doth usually suppose and feign in nature a greater equality and uniformity than is in truth.

The extreme consequence of such a tendency he discerns in the sect of Anthropomorphites who clothe the Deity in human shape. For Donne, too, the root of all intellectual error lies in this sort of appropriation, and the heresy of the Anthropomorphites is very close to his satirical presentation of Popery. As he wrote in his verse letter *To Mr Rowland Woodward*,

> There is no Vertue, but Religion:
> Wise, valiant, sober, just, are names, which none
> Want, which want not Vice-covering discretion. (16-18)

This is 'meer morality' implying an external criterion, in contrast to which the Christian turns inward – 'Seeke wee then our selves in our selves'. But he does not do so in order to instigate a monologue: the ensuing image of a lens concentrating the sun's beams accords the self a dependent role, the light comes from God.[2] There can be no question of making 'thy word mine'. This withdrawal into the self is not an escape into fantasy but a stern imposition on the soul of its limitations, in direct contrast to the projection outwards of private harmonies. Donne's frequent references to the role of memory in the Christian life

---

[1] *The Advancement of Learning*, II, xiv, 9.
[2] Milgate glosses line 22 with a quotation from Augustine, 'Noli foras ire, in teipsum redi, in interiore homine habitat veritas' (*De Vera Religione*, xxxix, 72). It is worth recalling Petrarch's account of ascending Mt. Ventoux, climaxed by his quotation from Augustine: 'And men go to admire the high mountains, the vast floods of the sea, the huge streams of the rivers, the circumference of the ocean, and the revolutions of the stars – and desert themselves' (*Confessions*, x, 8, 15), the theme in fact of *The first Anniversary*. The fascination of Augustine for Petrarch, Montaigne and Donne is a sign of their 'modernity', their heightened self-awareness. It is no accident that Augustine emerged as the virtual patron saint of humanism and its related intellectual concerns.

emphasises its function in relating the inner history of each Christian to the cycle of salvation history presented in the Bible. Typology is more than an intellectual game.[1]

This pruning of the ego is an epistemological parallel to the doctrine of justification by faith which provides the vehicle for the verse letter to Woodward. Justification by works appears to have been an obnoxious doctrine to Donne; one great benefit he attributed to the Reformation was learning 'how to doe good works without relying upon them, as meritorious'.[2] To Woodword he writes how

> If our Souls have stained their first white, yet wee
> May cloth them with faith, and dear honestie,
> Which God imputes, as native puritie.   (13-15)

This overturns the egotistical criteria of classical ethics and makes of moral achievement a consequence, a 'declaratory justification', rather than a cause of virtue. While such a view of justification was fundamental to Reformed theology it is certainly implicit in St Paul and was widely shared by radical Catholics, even after the anathema of Trent. Two such Catholics to whom we shall return were George Cassander and Paolo Sarpi.

But such justifying faith, centred on imputed justice, is far from mere intellectual assent – it subsumes the entire Christian life. As an illustration we can take Donne's outline of the process of salvation in one of his Whitsunday sermons: there can be no separating of links in a chain, he argues,

> for though in that sense of which we spoke, *Fides justificat sola*, Only faith do justifie, yet it is not true in any sense, *Fides est sola*, that there is any faith, where there is nothing but faith.[3]

Faith, in other words, is meant here in an existential sense as personal commitment, just as the true exegete goes beyond chapter and verse to relive sacred history in his own blood and nerves. This faith is really *fiducia*, trust, rather than notional assent, and as such it must spill over into love, into works.

---

[1] On memory see e.g. *Sermons*, ii, pp. 238-46; viii, pp. 261-2. Again memory is central to Augustine's view of the spiritual life.

[2] *Sermons*, x, p. 102.

[3] *Ibid.*, vii, pp. 228-9.

The emphasis is typically Pauline and it is appropriate that Donne should demand that a true understanding of Paul entails amendment of life. Religious experience is never allowed to remain purely discursive as in the scholastics, but embraces the whole range of human emotion: 'let us make *Ex scientia conscientiam*, Enlarge science into conscience'.[1] All this may seem far removed from the injunction to 'stand inquiring right' but the common bond is an appreciation of the personal response. In his quest for authentic doctrine, in his exegesis and in his interpretation of religious faith Donne admits an element of subjectivity which is an inheritance from the humanism of the Renaissance.

This goes a long way to explain Donne's contempt for 'quomodo theology', a hateful monosyllable as he called it in echo of Luther's 'Odiosa et exitialis vocula',

> He that can finde no comfort in this Doctrine . . . till he can expresse *Quo Modo*, robs himself of a great deale of peaceful refreshing.[2]

It was the question *quomodo* which elicited the fatal answer of transubstantiation and to Donne the Roman Church as he understood it came to be the Church of *quomodo*, translating the Gospel into definitions and formulae that seemed indifferent to human response. In the same spirit he objects to an insensitive theology which presents sacraments *ex opere operato*, as automatic and self-contained means of grace. It is revealing that he should speak in his funeral oration for Sir William Cokayne of a tendency to 'imprison Christ *in Opere operato*'[3] which turns the Church into a self-perpetuating mechanism, almost independent of God and of man. Man is not saved by a system but by a personal relation with God expressed in assurance of mercy; seen in this perspective every moment in the life of every individual can assume a rich significance. In fact that awareness of the immediate and the momentary which has been so admired in Donne's secular poems plays an equally vital role here in his formulation of religious experience, and 'To stand inquiring right' is to exercise this awareness. The individual must expose

[1] *Sermons*, ix, p. 248. [2] *Ibid.*, vii, p. 227.
[3] *Ibid.*, vii, p. 267. To Donne sacraments work '*ex pacto*, and *quando opus operamur*' (*Sermons*, ii, 258): the subjective emphasis is clear.

himself to reality – and this means ultimately to God – with an arduous passivity.

There is, then, a remarkable consistency in John Donne's personal development, a consistency that springs from this concern with authenticity. To arrive at authentic experience demands this disciplined availability that is so similar to Baconian perception. The paradox reveals the two dangers that threaten our intelligence, excessive passivity on the one hand and excessive self-reliance on the other. Thus, returning to exegesis, Donne distinguishes between presumption which goes beyond the word of scripture and doubt which falls short. Between is the mean approach that sifts the evidence with sensitive discrimination and fully accepts the reading that emerges unscathed. A particularly clear exposition of this sifting process occurs during one of Donne's attacks on Bellarmine, in this case the Commemoration of Lady Danvers.[1] Bellarmine, he argues, endeavours to present a Church

> endow'd with these and these, with those and those, and such and such, and more and more Immunities and Privileges, by which, that particular Church must bee *Super-Catholicke*, and *Super-universall*, above all the *Churches* in the world . . .

The Anglican retort, that is to say Donne's, is here

> *Ubi libellus*, Where is your *evidence* . . . for *such a Church?* For we content not our selves, with such places of *Scripture*, as may serve to *illustrate* that *Doctrine*, to them, that beleeve it aforehand, without *Scripture*, but wee aske such places of *Scripture*, as may prove it to them, who, till they see such Scriptures, beleeve, and beleeve truly, that they are not bound to beleeve it;

This sort of doubt is not that of the man who doubts 'with a wrangling purpose' but of the man who 'doubts with a humble purpose to settle his own faith':

> to come to a doubt, and to a debatement in any religious duty, is the voyce of God in our conscience: Would you know the truth? Doubt, and then you will inquire: And *facile solutionem accipit anima, quae prius dubitavit*, sayes S. *Chrysostome*.[2]

This, in other words, is to 'doubt wisely', to practise a modest objectivity in contrast to those who worship 'an imaginary

[1] *Sermons*, viii, pp. 64 and 73-4. [2] *Ibid.*, v, p. 38.

Jesus, in an illusory sacrifice, in another Church'. Not that Donne denies the real presence, he goes far beyond the majority of contemporary Anglicans in this respect, but the entire system of the Roman Church appears to him as built on a confusion of the metaphorical and the literal. It is again a sign of his acute awareness of the human and his intuitive grasp of history, both part of the inheritance of humanism, that he always resists the temptation to parade the human as the divine, the temporal as the eternal. There is something distinctly nominalist about this reluctance to reify abstractions which is reminiscent of Ockham's razor, as well as Ockham's hostility to the temporal power of the Papacy. But it is a different exponent of nominalist attitudes, Nicolas of Cusa, whose *docta ignorantia* Donne echoes in his depiction of 'a profitable, a wholesome, a learned ignorance, which is a modest, and a reverent abstinence from searching into those secrets which God hath not revealed in his word'.[1]

Those were the words that Donne used at the funeral of Sir William Cokayne in 1626 but they demonstrate exactly the same mental attitude revealed in the *Satyre* some thirty years before. In that sermon Donne castigated the very human tendency to obscure truth by some convenient idol, the consequence either of a too facile acceptance of authority, looking on nature 'but with *Aristotles* Spectacles, and upon the body of man, but with *Galens*, and upon the frame of the world, but with *Ptolemies* Spectacles', or of a distorting projection of 'imaginary revelations'.[2] This propensity for obfuscating divine law is one of the ground-themes of *The Anniversaries* also, poems which are usually regarded as sceptical or pessimistic. But though these qualities are present it would be wrong to over-emphasise them. If a criticism could be directed at *The Anniversaries* it would be that Donne fails to maintain full control of mood; there is an occasional shrill vehemence distorting the poet's quest for authenticity. When something like Pyrrhonic scepticism is invoked – 'Doe not so much as not beleeve a man' – the reasoning offered

> For though to erre, be worst, to try truths forth,
> Is far more businesse, then this world is worth.
> (*The second Anniversary*, 53-54)

[1] *Ibid.*, ix, p. 234.   [2] *Ibid.*, vii, pp. 260, 263.

directly contradicts the quest outlined in *Satyre III*. But this is, after all, an elegy: the extreme view of the world as mere 'fragmentary rubbidge' can be explained, if not excused, on rhetorical grounds. The diverse readings of *The Anniversaries* result from Donne's failure at times to coalesce theme and tone, and the perverse ingenuity of some conceits may indicate technical strain,

> The world is but a carcase; thou art fed
> By it, but as a worme, that carcase bred;
> (*The second Anniversary*, 55-6)

It is not difficult to be impressed by his dualistic rejection of the transistory and oversimplify the statement of the poems; but it is necessary to reflect on the sense of 'world' since Donne and Christian tradition use the word in several different ways.[1] Here it suggests an option rather than a place, an attitude rather than an experience.[2] It is certainly not that *liber creaturarum* which, in *Essayes in Divinity*, Donne admits as a prelude to the Scriptures (p. 8). This trying of truths that is condemned as 'more businesse, then this world is worth' should be associated with distraction from essential truth. It is not the exercise of the mind as such which is condemned but its absorption in the secular learning exemplified by astronomy:

> For of Meridians, and Parallels,
> Man hath weav'd out a net, and this net throwne
> Upon the Heavens, and now they are his owne.
> (*The first Anniversary*, 278-80)

The image of the net vividly summarises the process by which an idol is projected onto reality. The most sustained attack on secular learning occurs in *The second Anniversary* but again it is not reason that is attacked but abuses of it: the scholar who starves and sweats

> To know but Catechismes and Alphabets
> Of unconcerning things, matters of fact;   (284-5)

---

[1] For this point see D. Quinn, 'Donne's *Anniversaries* as Celebration', *Studies in English Literature*, ix, 1969, p. 100.

[2] Cf. the pun on 'whirld' in 'Goodfriday' (8) which is associated with business and pleasure.

and with peculiar relevance the figure of the 'spungie slacke Divine' who contrives to

> Drinke and sucke in th'instructions of Great men,
> And for the word of God, vent them agen
> (*The second Anniversary*, 329-30)

The crucial passage contains a question and an exhortation,

> When wilt thou shake off this Pedantery,
> Of being taught by sense, and Fantasie?
> Thou look'st through spectacles; small things seeme great
> Below; But up into the watch-towre get,
> And see all things despoyl'd of fallacies: (291-5)

Again man's intelligence is not rejected but the materials on which it operates are seen as all important. Thus learning as the amoral accumulation of facts and theology as a cerebral parade of authorities are condemned together with all the irrelevancies of 'quomodo' speculation. To get 'up into the watch-towre' seems to require the same sort of inner discipline that we have already seen in that *Satyre* and particularly in the verse letter to Woodward,

> So wee, if wee into our selves will turne,
> Blowing our sparkes of vertue, may outburne
> The straw, which doth about our hearts sojourne. (22-4)

This straw about the heart is identical with the 'world' of *The Anniversaries* which lulls the mind into forgetfulness and distracts it from its essential relation with God. The common feature of the poems so far discussed is their insistence on a return to the self, the seat of memory, breaking through 'that circle, in which we compasse, and immure, and imprison ourselves'.[1] Only by reduction to the self, to the ground of consciousness, can the believer like the Cartesian philosopher discern reality; and at the centre of the self is memory – 'the Holy Ghosts Pulpit' – containing the collective history that is the Bible and the private history that is the individual. *The Anniversaries* are about this recollection of the past which is the condition of future growth. Without this recognition of the

---

[1] *Sermons*, x, p. 79.

authentic self, divinity becomes an intellectual game and the Church a self-perpetuating system. In *The second Anniversary* Donne uses seventeen lines to depict the *persona* of Elizabeth Drury as the autonomous self, 'being to her selfe a State' (359-75). If we place these lines against the critique of religious motivation in *Satyre III* we can appreciate the crucial import-ance Donne allots to individual response. It is, of course, response within a defined context. The means of salvation are the Bible and the Sacraments; the Church interprets the former and administers the latter. In both cases the Church is providing the occasion, the composition of place as it were, for contact with God, but the final step, the colloquy, remains the responsi-bility of the individual.

So much seems clear from Donne's stress on the subjective element in the eucharist. His hostility is directed against any attempt to make grace automatic or substitute the sign for the reality, both ways of cutting out the individual. But this does not entail neglect of the Church: 'God loves not singularity; the very name of Church implies company; It is *Concio, Con-gregatio, Coetus* . . .'.[1] What emerges is an extremely delicate relationship between Church and believer designed to allow a maximum of personal responsibility within a framework of Catholic tradition. As such it is directly indebted to the concept of the *via media* outlined by such Henrician apologists as Thomas Starkey and John Bekinshaw and massively fulfilled in Hooker. But the *via media*, so often dismissed as genial compromise, can demand the kind of alert discrimination that emerges from Donne's habit of mind. His awareness of himself as primarily a Christian rather than a member of a specific Church is itself an Anglican characteristic. But to grasp his religious position comprehensively we must place it in a wider European context.

Donne's recusant background could never be entirely thrust from his consciousness: as he admitted in the 'Advertisement to the Reader' which concludes *Pseudo-Martyr*, 'I have beene ever kept awake in a meditation of Martyrdome, by being derived from such a stocke and race'. It would be quite wrong

---

[1] *Sermons*, ii, p. 279.

to interpret this as evidence of a guilty conscience. Donne wishes to assure the Catholic reader that his dilemma is understood. *Pseudo-Martyr* is, of all Donne's prose, the work which obviously relates to the concerns of *Satyre III* and reveals most about the intellectual basis of his religious faith. Its immediate occasion was the controversy stimulated by the Oath of Allegiance imposed on Catholics as a consequence of the Gunpowder Plot and intended, in James I's own words, 'for making the difference between the civilly obedient Papists, and the perverse disciples of the Powder-Treason'.[1] The debate has been fully described by McIlwain and more recently by Professor Bald,[2] but it is in its European dimension that it becomes particularly interesting. The Crown's intention was simply to drive a wedge between those Catholics who confined Papal authority to spiritual matters and those who allowed the Papacy control over secular governments either, like the moderate Bellarmine, indirectly, or, as with Baronius and Carerius (who thought Bellarmine a heretic), by direct right.

Needless to say, that the Papacy had some power to control secular affairs whether directly or indirectly was the official viewpoint of post-Tridentine Catholicism, braced as it was in the stance of counter-reformation. On the other hand the Catholic radicals who attempted to confine Rome to a purely spiritual authority were the heirs of a complex tradition, nourished in part by late-medieval nominalism and in part by the evangelical humanism of the Renaissance. The former position was championed primarily by the Jesuits while the radicals included laymen like William Barclay and the Benedictine Thomas Preston *alias* 'Roger Widdrington'. Such radical authors were not necessarily on James's side – they could hardly view his secular power as more spiritual than the Pope's – but they shared his desire to distinguish religious adherence to Rome from any political allegiance. Preston even seems to have enjoyed royal protection from the Jesuits.

In many respects this controversy was a revival of the medieval squabble over investitures, and some certainly saw it

---

[1] *An Apologie for the Oath of Allegiance* in *The Political Works of James I*, ed. C. H. McIlwain, Cambridge, Mass., 1918, p. 85.
[2] *John Donne: A Life*, Oxford, 1970, Ch. ix.

this way. In two enormous volumes printed in 1611 and 1614 Melchior Goldast made a collection of texts that upheld the independence of the secular and imperial arm from the Papacy.[1] A glance at the texts included is very revealing. Apart from early writers like Ambrose and Hincmar of Rheims Goldast includes the entire political output of William of Ockham and Marsiglius of Padua[2], with other nominalist works by Giles of Rome, Jean Gerson and even Jan Hus. There is a selection from Petrarch ('Epistolae de iuribus Imperii Romani adversus Papam') and several evangelical humanists including the Catholic Georg Witzel, the Reformer Beatus Rhenanus and Gianfrancesco Pico della Mirandola's *Apologia pro Savonarola*. Two of the texts printed are by defenders of the Henrician Church: Stephen Gardiner's *De Vera Obedientia* (1536) and John Bekinshaw's *De supremo & absoluto Regis Imperio* (1546); while out of contemporary material he includes an account of the Sorbonne's condemnation of pro-Papal works at the instigation of Edmond Richer and the text of Isaac Casaubon's *De Libertate Ecclesiastica*.[3] Three common features can be discerned in this strange collection: antipathy to the Papacy's temporal claims, a complimentary Conciliar inclination, and a typically nominalist distrust of universals. The emphasis is local and sceptical, more favourable to history than to metaphysics.

Sometime during 1609 Donne wrote to Sir Henry Goodyer, asking him to obtain a book, and Professor Bald has argued that this letter records the earliest stages of Donne's work on *Pseudo-Martyr*. The book is described incorrectly as *Baldvinus de officio pii hominis in controversiis;* in reality Donne wished to see the *De Officio pii ac publicae tranquillitatis vere amantis viri in hoc religionis dissidio* by Georgius Cassander. 'Baldvinus' or François Baudouin had been instrumental in arranging the

---

[1] *Monarchia S. Romani Imperii, sive tractatus de iurisdictione imperiali seu Regia* I (T. Willer for C. Bierman, Hanover, 1611); II (N. Hoffman for C. Bierman, Frankfort, 1614).

[2] The far-sighted Thomas Cromwell had had Marsiglius' *Defensor Pacis* put into English to support Henry's breach with Rome.

[3] On Richer's association with Donne see Bald, *Life*, p. 255. It is interesting that Donne also cites Petrarch as an anti-papal author, *Pseudo-Martyr*, p. 339. Casaubon made use of Goldast's first volume while staying with Lancelot Andrewes in 1611.

publication of Cassander's book at Basle in 1561, hence Donne's error[1]; but it is obvious that such a title would appeal to the author of *Satyre III*. Cassander, like Georg Witzel, represented the survival into the mid-sixteenth century of the Christian humanism of Erasmus.[2] Consequently he tended to play down the 'opus operatum' aspect in sacramental theology and to lay stress on an inner personal response. From Witzel he derived the title *via regia* to describe the mean between the Protestants and 'papistici' and his refusal to accept the divisions of Christendom as definitive, with its consequent shunning of entrenched positions (including disregard for the Council of Trent) led to a flexibility close to Donne's ideal. Certainly Donne was not the only Anglican to feel this interest. In *A Catholike Appeale for Protestants* (London, 1610) his close associate Thomas Morton devotes considerable attention to Cassander whom he calls 'a choice divine'. Similarly the whole text of the *De Officio* is printed as an appendix to the *De Republica Ecclesiastica* of Marcantonio de Dominis, the refugee Archbishop of Spalato, who saw in the Church of England – for a time at least – the realisation of his ideals.[3]

In ecclesiastical terms Cassander lived dangerously, endeavouring to establish a position from which the widest possible range of options would remain open. Like Erasmus and Melanchthon he thought in terms of a limited number of fundamental doctrines that would be acceptable to all Christians, while other details of religious practice would be open to personal choice and local custom. The individual could adopt his own attitude to images without having to 'adore, or scorne' since they are far from the centre of the Christian faith. This is exactly the way Donne approaches ceremonies and images: 'Rituall, and Ceremoniall things move not God, but they exalt that Devotion, and they conserve that Order, which does move

---

[1] Bald, *Life*, p. 219; P. G. Bietenholz, *Basle and France in the Sixteenth Century*, Geneva, 1971, ch. vii gives an account of the collaboration between Baudouin, then a Protestant, and the Catholic Cassander.

[2] To Cassander he was 'Erasmus Roterodamus, qui pro singulari sua in rebus ecclesiasticis prudentia prope mihi vates fuisse videtur'. Cited by Bietenholz, *op. cit.*, p. 150.

[3] *De Republica Ecclesiastica*, pars tertia, Hanover, 1622. The first two parts, dedicated to James I, were printed in London in 1617 and 1620.

him'.[1] Underlying this moderate view is a respect for the complexity of human motivation, and an idea of the Church as a spiritual rather than a legal community. To Cassander the source of Christian truth is the Scriptures as properly understood, that is, as interpreted by the general consensus and public testimony of the Church since the Apostles.[2] It may seem a vague formula but it does avoid the excesses of those Calvinists or Papalists who diverged from the *via regia*. Where they constructed rigid, if coherent, systems Cassander retained flexibility and left a wide responsibility in 'indifferents' to personal and local need.

Cassander's flexibility comes from his Augustinian view of the visible Church as drawn from the two cities, from God's enemies as well as his friends. In these circumstances no simple line can be drawn between elect and damned. Significantly the feature of Cassander's book which most excites Morton's sympathy is his discussion of Church membership: those who break with the public Church may have sound reasons, such as the correction of abuses. Though Cassander regrets the Reformers' decision to break with the Church he admits the justice of their complaint, and he is at least as critical of those who deny faults in the Church. Extreme reactions on either side can result in the loss of precious insights. But on Cassander's terms leaving the Church is an obscure step since the Church is given such a spiritual character. Christ is the head and the body, one only severs oneself from the head by false and unscriptural doctrine and from the body by a defect of charity. The qualification for membership is simply to desire the true Church and to work for it. Thus Cassander will admit as members those who even if they lack some opinions (i.e. non-essential doctrines) and practices of the Church, are bound to it by charity and fundamental Christian faith.[3]

Although Cassander considers that the Reformers overreacted he lays the blame at the door of the *pseudocatholici* who have raised the Pope's authority above Councils and even

---

[1] *Sermons*, vii, 430.

[2] *De officio*, Basle, 1562, p. 6.

[3] *Ibid.*, p. 19. Christian piety is summarised: 'fide in Christe mortuum & resuscitatum pro nobis collocanda, & charitate Deo & proximo exhibenda', p. 30.

Scripture, treating his utterances as divine oracles and infallible rules of faith. Nor does he see any prospect of reunion until the Papists be 'contented that manifest abuses of the Church be reformed according to the direction of Scripture, and the custome of antiquitie, from whence they are departed', a point that Morton is anxious to relate to the situation of the Anglican Church.[1] But for Cassander, as for Donne, this moderate stance is not a weak compromise. At the close of the *De officio* he warns against a deceptive tranquillity which is not the peace of Christ but the peace of evasion. Similarly he warns against the subordination of religion to political advantage. The true moderate must undergo a severe discipline, learning to sacrifice wealth and even friends in his prophetic quest for truth.[2]

By the turn of the sixteenth century those who wished to argue the catholicity of the Anglican Church could find support in such diverse places as late medieval scepticism, with its ecclesiological counterpart in the conciliar movement, in propaganda of the Imperial interest in the Investiture debate, and in the varied and complex attitudes of evangelical humanism. Common features that can be isolated are resistance to the encroachment of spiritual authority on the temporal, hostility to any abstract application of universal law in violation of local need, scepticism about the status of ecclesiastical pronouncements and – almost as the foundation – a developed sense of history and the human. None could be said to promote the kind of confidence that sustained the Counter-Reformation and its particular agents the Jesuits. On the whole the Jesuits gave little attention to historical studies, and the Oratorian Baronius, the chief historian of the Roman party, had not absorbed the lessons of humanist scholarship.[3] What is the relevance of history when the answers are immediately available? The Roman

---

1 *De officio*, pp. 27-8; the translation is Morton's, *A Catholike Appeale*, 1610, p. 454. Morton, who emphasises Cassander's Catholicism, continues, 'We wish no more, if by *abuses* we shall vnderstand as well their new doctrines, as their corrupt constitutions.'

2 *Ibid.*, pp. 35-8.

3 W. J. Bouwsma, *Venice and the Defence of Republican Liberty*, Berkeley, 1968, p. 312. Those Jesuits like Gretser who dealt with the past were rather antiquarians than historians.

Church placed authority above evidence and tended to merge the Church militant with the Church triumphant; in the struggle for Christendom external criteria increasingly outweighed inner disposition. Theology, deprived of its historical roots, shrank into formulae: as Professor Bouwsma comments, 'The articulation of Catholic belief . . . became almost an administrative problem'.[1] Only in three parts of Europe did political and cultural conditions allow the delicate poise of the *via regia*: Venice, England and, to a lesser extent, France. Even here it did not last very far into the seventeenth century.

An interesting product of this comparative freedom of mind is Sir Edwin Sandys' *A Relation of the State of Religion*, completed in 1599 and published in London in 1605. Sandys, a former pupil of Hooker at Oxford, was an acute observer possessed of enough self-control to restrain his Anglo-Saxon irritation at Italian religious practice, and enough irony to entertain his reader.[2] His criticism is aimed at both sides of the debate, both 'having by their passionate reports much wronged the truth, abused this age, and periudiced [*sic*] posterity'. The Protestants in particular are cudgelled for sliding 'from an Historiographers into an Oratours profession'.[3] On the whole Sandys' complaints about the Papacy comprise a familiar list: temporal ambition, hostility to secular Princes, greater concern with its own laws than those of Christ, determination to shed everything (however good) that is held by the Protestants. Similarly, with an irony close to Hooker's, he notes the Protestant's 'negative and contradictorie humour of thinking they are rightest, when they are unlikest the Papacy, and then nearest to God when furthest from Rome'.[4] The impressive feature of the book is that Sandys does not simply note faults, however justified he may be, but endeavours to penetrate beneath the surface. Thus he is able to discern in the Roman

---

[1] *Op. cit.*, p. 297. The same could be said of much Protestant theology, though there were exceptions on both sides.

[2] '. . . if the worst fall out, that a man be so negligent as to droppe into Purgatory at the time of his decease, which but by very supine negligence can hardly happen . . .' *A Relation*, sig. B2ᵛ.

[3] *A Relation*, sig. Kᵛ.

[4] *Ibid.*, sig. Tᵛ; cf. 'They which measure Religion by mislike of the Church of Rome', Hooker, *Laws*, IV, viii, 2.

Church an effort to transmute faith into science which ultimately destroys it. His major concern is to urge a reconciliation on grounds of charity, and as agents of this he detects in each country 'A kind of men . . . not many in number but sundry of them of singular learning and pietie'. These are the wise judges who pick the truth out of both sides, refusing to allow either side to be wholly right or wrong. This element of ambivalence in all religious data comes in fact from the very nature of man himself:

> Ignorance and error, which seldome goe severed, being no other than vnseparable companions of man, so long as he continueth in his terrestriall pilgrimage.[1]

Once again responsibility rests squarely on the individual.

Sir Henry Wotton was appointed ambassador to the Serene Republic of Venice in July 1604 and before he sailed Donne sent him a verse letter. It cannot have been long before Wotton encountered there a leading Anglophile, Fra Paolo Sarpi. Sarpi was already a friend of Edwin Sandys and certainly approved of *A Relation of the State of Religion* since he helped to translate it into Italian. Professor Bald has suggested that Donne might have visited Venice during the following year, 1605, and in this case he must surely have met Sarpi. Certainly both would count among Sandys' 'kind of men', but the only concrete link is a picture of Sarpi that Donne hung in the Deanery at St Paul's.[2] English relations with Venice became particularly close during Wotton's term, in part as a result of several startling events: in November 1605 came the Gunpowder Plot, at Christmas the Papal Nuncio delivered an ultimatum to Venice over matters of ecclesiastical jurisdiction in the city, and in the spring of 1606 the city was laid under an Interdict, while in September the same year Rome formally condemned the Oath proposed to English Catholics. Just a year later Sarpi, who had emerged as the intellectual champion of Venice, was attacked and nearly killed by assailants whose weapon he drily described as 'lo stilo romano'. To many

---

[1] *Ibid.*, sig. S4ᵛ, Tᵛ.

[2] Bald, *A Life*, pp. 150-1. The possible relationship is also discussed by Dr Frances Yates, 'Paolo Sarpi's *History of the Council of Trent*', *Journal of the Warburg and Courtauld Institutes*, vii, 1944, pp. 123-43.

contemporaries it seemed that the true nature of the Roman threat had been laid bare.

Sarpi was a man of prodigious learning who established his European reputation by his extensive correspondence but chiefly by fierce opposition to the Papal Interdict. The celebrated *Istoria del Concilio Tridentino*, first printed at London in 1619, was in reality his testament. The principles on which he built his vision of a Christian 'republic' were simple and familiar. He is sceptical of all universals and in place of metaphysically based natural law he appeals to actual experience, to history. As we might expect, all systems are suspect to him as nets woven by men and thrown onto phenomena. In this respect his admiration for William of Ockham is revealing; he rates him 'a very judicious Writer, excepting the barbarousness of his Stile. I have ever valued *him* above all the *School-men*. In contrast Aquinas is dismissed as 'an easy writer . . . that does not intangle ones Mind in Doubts and Perplexities, but over-resolves his Reader'.[1] 'Over-resolves' is the key word, inviting comparison with Bacon's hostility to 'perfection or completeness in divinity'.[2]

An important factor in Sarpi's reading of history is his extremely pessimistic interpretation of human nature. In part this is due to a vivid awareness of the flux inherent in natural things. Such an awareness of instability in creation complements his insistence on the transcendence of God. Thus any attempt to identify human institutions too closely with the working of grace is blasphemy; whereas Roman historians like Baronius encourage a triumphalist view of history, Sarpi presents the Council of Trent as a collision of human factions, each endeavouring to imprison the divine within its particular vision. The

---

[1] *The Letters of Father Paul*, tr. E. Brown, 1693, pp. 412 ff.; text in *Lettere ai Gallicani*, ed. B. Ulianich, Wiesbaden, 1961, pp. 173-5. For a comparison between astronomical and theological devices 'per salvar le apparenze' see *L'Istoria*, ed. G. Gambarin, Bari, 1935, i, p. 363.

[2] *Advancement*, II, xxv, 13. The enthusiasm of Sarpi's circle for Bacon has been explored by V. Gabrieli, 'Bacone, La Riforma e Roma', *English Miscellany*, VIII, 1957, pp. 195-250. Sarpi's excitable amanuensis Fra Fulgenzio Macanzio, whose portrait also hung on Donne's wall, called Bacon '*l' Angelo del Paradiso*'. Other English contacts are explored by G. Cozzi, 'Paolo Sarpi e l'Anglicanesimo', *Rivista Storica Italiana*, lxviii, 1956, pp. 559-619.

truth of the Gospel may survive in the basic consensus of Christians but it cannot be tied to any visible bloc; it is an occasional flicker in the murky swirls of human history. The Papacy of the Counter-Reformation appears to him as a clerical conspiracy. Thus alert to the dangers of 'creeping infallibility' Sarpi distinguished between the Pope's utterances 'according to Christ' when he expresses the mind of the Church and those 'according to his owne private opinion and passions'. As he concludes.

> ... whosoever supposeth any humane will to be infallible, committeth great blasphemie, in ascribing to the creature a propertie onely divine.[1]

Two of Sarpi's replies to the Interdict were published in London within months of their appearance in Venice: *Considerations Vpon the Censure of Pope Paul* was printed by John Bill in 1606 and the *Apology to the objections of Cardinal Bellarmine against certaine treatises of John Gerson* in 1607. Donne almost certainly used them in the preparation of *Pseudo-Martyr*. Since the Venetian issue concerned the right of the secular power to limit church-building and to punish clergy for secular offences it had an immediate relevance to James's efforts to ensure the secular loyalty of his Catholic subjects, and James's admiration for Sarpi would not have been lessened by the latter's insistence that it was sin for a prince to allow his prerogative to be infringed. With his usual abrasive humour Sarpi argued that the only thing that Venice had taken from her clergy was 'but a libertie of doing evill'. If one were to accept Roman claims to jurisdiction over all church land why not admit that 'every cloth, all metall, wood, or any other thing, should belong unto the state ecclesiastical':

> And not only these persons, but all which appertaines to them, becomes spirituall; and by a new Alchimy, they doe not only extract spirit out of everything, but transmute it all into spirit, and by their possessing them, *Houses, Horses*, and *Concubines* are spiritual.[2]

A similar argument *ad absurdam* underlies Donne's account of clerical immunity.[3]

[1] *An Apology to the objections of Cardinall Bellarmine*, 1607, p. 6.
[2] *Considerations*, pp. 73, 13.   [3] *Pseudo-Martyr*, p. 94.

Sarpi's principal target, then, is ecclesiastical government in so far as it tends to displace secular authority; like Donne he complains that 'we give power to the Prelate over matters temporall, and transforme the ecclesiasticall ministry into a secular Court iudiciall'.[1] The divisions of Christendom are products of clerical self-interest. In a letter to Jerome Groslot written in July 1609 he gives a remarkable statement of his views,

> I do believe that many of the Differences amongst us, are merely *verbal*, and they make me sometimes laugh at them: Others of them there are that might be indured without breaking any Peace for them: And others there are that might be easily composed. But the main of all is, that both Parties are agreed in this, but they will not have them composed.

There can be no hope of peace when each side assumes that it is entirely right and the other entirely wrong. Sarpi proposes two courses to alleviate this situation: in the first place to 'mind the Defence of the Liberty of Princes, and curb the exorbitancy of the Roman Power', in the second to oppose the Jesuits, 'There is not a greater Work can be undertaken, than to bring the Jesuits into discredit'.[2]

Sarpi's two recommendations were closely linked. The English reaction to the Gunpowder Plot instinctively placed all blame on the subtle machinations of the Jesuits, regardless of evidence. While the Archbishop de Dominis fled to James's protection, a Catholic parallel to the Protestant Casaubon, Sarpi refused at any time to compromise his Catholicism despite invitations for the English Court. Yet he was extremely hostile to the English recusants who supported the Jesuit mission. His two-pronged attack was that used by the Scots Neo-Latinist John

---

[1] *An Apology*, p. 93; cf. Donne to Goodyer in 1609, 'the Divines of these times, are become meer Advocates, as though Religion were a temporall inheritance', *Selected Prose*, p. 136.

[2] *Letters of Father Paul*, pp. 121, 305, 255; texts in *Lettere ai Protestanti*, ed. M. D. Busnelli, Bari, 1931, i, pp. 86, 218, 183. Sarpi's hostility to the Jesuits was not simply political; in the 'De Auxiliis' controversy which rocked Catholic theology between the late 1580s and 1607 he supported the Dominican Banez against the Jesuit Molina. This was also Donne's feeling (*Pseudo-Martyr*, p. 100). Banez' Augustinian view of grace was called crypto-Lutheran by his enemies.

Barclay who became a Gentleman of the Bedchamber to James around 1606. Barclay had already published his *Euphormionis Satyricon* at Paris in the previous year. Although a Catholic he effectively satirised Papal secular ambitions and attacked all attempts to confine religion within party interest, attempts he particularly associates with the Puritans and the Jesuits. Barclay makes clear his sympathy with the Venetians and there is evidence that he included Sarpi among his correspondents. In 1609 he edited a treatise *De Potestate Papae* by his father William, a jurist who had had to vacate his chair at the Jesuit university of Pont-a-Mousson on account of his radical views. This work, like the *Satyricon*, was speedily placed on the Index – an indication of its effectiveness – while James posted Barclay off to the courts of Europe with copies of his own *Premonition to all Christian Monarches*. It is a sad comment on the power of patronage that by 1616 Barclay was resident at the Papal Court where he produced nothing more virulent than his romance *Argenis*.[1]

Sarpi's two concerns, 'to mind the Defence of the Liberty of Princes' and 'to bring the Jesuits into discredit' are precisely those of *Pseudo-Martyr* (1610) and *Ignatius his Conclave* (1611). The earlier work is essentially a legal discussion, despite the occasional flash of satire, while the fact that *Ignatius* is a satirical fiction originally composed in Latin suggests that Donne aimed it at the same European readership that had been diverted by Barclay's *Satyricon*. But in both his books Donne seeks to establish a moderate stance from which he can expose 'the *Mythologie* of the Roman Church'. This is a theme to which he returns frequently since it relates to his admonition to 'doubt wisely': Rome has not only extended the corpus of Christian doctrine beyond the bounds of traditional consensus, she even insists that there can be no salvation outside her ranks. While Rome was originally awarded a primacy of honour among the Churches this has been lost by doctrinal distortions – clerical privilege, justification by works, Purgatory – which encourage

---

[1] See the articles by D. A. Fleming, 'John Barclay', *Renaissance News*, xix, 1966, pp. 228-36; 'Barclay's *Satyricon*', *Studia et Textus Neolatini*, ed. J. Ijsewijn, Louvain, 1968, pp. 83-116.

self-glory and ultimately pseudo-martyrdom. These distortions of the schoolmen came from over-presumption, from spying 'even into Gods secret Cabinet of his *Essence* and his *Counsails*', and Donne, adopting a conceit from 'Aire and Angels', finds their symbolic expression in the Papacy:

> And then because these sublime and ayrie meditations must have some body to inhere in, they vsed to incorporate their speculations of God, in the Pope; as it were to arrest and conserve them the better, being else too spirituall and transitorie.[1]

The Jesuits, then, with their special vow of obedience to the Pope become whipping-boys for the whole 'super edification'; they do not preach Christ but his Vicar. The argument is handled with such abstract precision and wit that it comes as a shock to realise that its practical issue for some disputants would entail public disembowelling.

Like all his contemporaries, Lancelot Andrewes not excluded, Donne could adopt a coarse tone in controversy, even from the pulpit. But his intellectual assault on Rome does have its source in deeply-felt and humane convictions, the gibes are invariably elicited by political issues. Behind the mineral brilliance and the irony lies Donne's image of the true Church, an image that holds in delicate relation the values of personal judgment and Catholic tradition. It is indeed a microcosm of the individual's response to the Given. To veer one way leads to Geneva, the other leads to Rome; and the middle way may entail lumpishness or discrimination. At the heart of the Church is truth:

> That therefore is Catholique faith, which hath beene alwaies and every where taught; and *Repentance*, and *Remission* of sinnes, by the *Death* and *Resurrection* of *Christ*, and such truthes as the *Gospell* teaches, are that *Doctrine* which coagulates and gathers the Church into a body, and makes it *Catholike*.[2]

If this truth is distorted by addition or subtraction the coagulation is dissolved. Thus Catholics are urged to adopt 'a more humane and civill indifferencie', so that the Roman Church may shed

---

[1] *Pseudo-Martyr*, p. 141.
[2] *Ibid.*, p. 373. Cf. Donne's praise of Lady Danvers' 'mediocrity', *Sermons*, viii, p. 90.

doctrinal innovation and once more assume her role as the 'exemplar member' of God's Catholic Church,

> (for I am ever loth, to seeme to abhorre, or abstaine from giving to that Church, any such Stiles and Titles, as shee is pleas'd and delighted in, as long as by a pious interpretation thereof, her desire may thereby be satisfied in some measure, our Churches not iniur'd nor preiudiced, and the free spirit of God, which blowes where it pleaseth, not tied nor imprison'd to any place or person).[1]

If *Satyre III* is about anything it is about the free spirit of God.

When Donne's writings are placed in relation to his vigilant critique of pseudo-religion they demonstrate a clear unity. About a quarter of a century separates the *Satyre* from the sonnet on the Church, 'Show me deare Christ, thy spouse, so bright and cleare'. It has been argued that the two poems raise different questions: the problem of authority in the satire, the marks of the Church in the sonnet. If one sees them as expressions of responsible discrimination in religious matters then, I believe, the difference fades. The sonnet could, in terms of attitude, have been written by any of Edwin Sandys' 'kind of men'; it is in effect a refusal to imprison the spirit in a single place. The features of the Church that most impress us are often the *adiaphora*, the transitory features, 'the peace of the Church, the plenty of the Church, the ceremonies of the Church, they are *sua*, but not *illa*, they are hers, but they are not she'.[2]

It was fittingly at a christening that Donne preached on the theme of the pilgrim Church. On earth she will always be rent by earthquakes and schisms, 'the Church is in a warfare, the Church is in a pilgrimage, and therefore here is no setling'. But out of this flux and confusion the Church grows in heaven 'by continuall accesse of holy *Soules*', in anticipation of the marriage day:

> to setle such a glorious Church, without spot, or wrinkle, holy to *himselfe*, is reserved for the Triumphant time when she shall be in possession of that beauty, which Christ foresaw in her, long before when he said, *Thou art all faire my love, and there is no spot in thee;*[3]

In the course of his pilgrimage the Christian, through the word and the sacraments, maintains a direct contact with this heavenly

---

[1] *Pseudo-Martyr*, p. 135.   [2] *Sermons*, ix, p. 332.   [3] *Ibid.*, v, 126.

Church. Donne's sonnet is a prayer for spiritual discernment, so that he can penetrate local manifestations and view the essential truths around which the glorious Church 'coagulates'. In one sense, then, it refers to his hopes for Christian unity as expressed in the *Essays in Divinity*,[1] but it refers equally to inner union with this glorious Church beyond the reach of time. Perhaps the most effective gloss on the sonnet is a letter sent by Sarpi to Isaac Casaubon in June 1610, some three months before the French scholar settled in England. Sarpi places the glorious Church, free of blemish, in a future beyond the reach of mortals; here the best that can be found is that which is least disfigured. When the structures that men have erected on the foundation of Christ are finally tested by fire not much will emerge unscathed:

> I am deceived if the Church of Corinth which Paul founded, instructed and called holy, was less corrupt than the Churches of this day. Where men are involved you will more easily find something to blame than to praise. Wherever we are the perfect is an idea, something we must aspire towards.[2]

For Donne too the seeker for truth 'about must, and about must goe'. The quest for true religion involves constant self-discipline, a refusal to settle for an idol or pseudo-Church which relieves the individual of his obligations. The emphasis on personal response, the awareness of subjectivity, the broad historical perspective, all these characteristics find a common source in the experience of Renaissance Humanism. Donne's 'modernity' is, when analysed, the expression of a new mode of religious sensibility; one which differs from the 'medieval' certainly but is not less rooted in tradition.

---

[1] *Essays*, pp. 51-2.
[2] *Lettereai Protestanti*, ii, pp. 217-18. The passage is a remarkable echo of Sandys' words.

16

Donne's Sermon to the
Virginia Company

13 November 1622

W. MOELWYN MERCHANT

On 1 December 1622, a fortnight after his sermon to the Honourable Company of the Virginian Plantation, Donne wrote to Sir Thomas Roe, ambassador at Constantinople and representative of the Levant Company:

> A few days after that, I preached, by invitation of the Virginian Company, to an honorable auditory, and they recompenced me with a new commandment, in their Service, to printe that: and that I hope, comes with this:[1]

This tortuous sentence will become clearer when we examine the letter in some detail; meanwhile it is interesting to have Chamberlain's extension of Donne's phrase 'an honorable auditory':

> On Wensday night the Virginia companie had a feast or meeting at Marchant-taylors Hall, whether many of the nobilitie and counsaile were invited but few came. They spent 21 does and were between three and fowre hundred at three shillings a man:[2]

It is pleasant to know that this sermon, of about an hour's duration, was regarded as an acceptable commonplace on such an occasion: 'the Deane of Paules preached, according to the common custome of all feasting nowadays'.[3]

---

[1] *John Donne, Complete Poetry and Selected Prose*, ed. John Hayward, 1929, p. 478.
[2] *The Letters of John Chamberlain*, ed. N. E. McClure, Philadelphia, 1939, ii, 464; cited *The Sermons of John Donne*, ed. G. R. Potter and E. M. Simpson, California, 1959, iv, p. 36 f.n.   [3] *Ibid.*, p. 36 f.n.

The letter to Roe and its historical context deserve closer examination.[1] Sir Thomas Roe had been for some years a friend of Donne and the recent biography by Professor M. J. Brown gathers together the matter of a varied and influential career.[2] His activities touch those of Donne at many points and illuminate in unexpected ways the sermon to the Virginia Company. For Roe, in about his thirtieth year, had been a leading member of the Guiana expedition which left Dartmouth in February 1610. This venture, in which Raleigh and Prince Henry shared the initiative with Roe, was a significant union of commerce with religion and politics, for the voyage was manifestly directed in part against Spanish interests. Professor Brown indicates the mixture of motives over Guiana which we shall find so constantly also in the Virginian venture:

> The conclusion is unavoidable: in giving their full (but secret) support to Roe's venture, the king and his adviser [Salisbury] were taking a calculated risk in trusting that the discovery of gold would precede any possible clash with Spain. For the benefit of the Spanish representatives at the English court, stories were circulated that Roe's fleet was destined for Virginia.[3]

After the qualified success of the Guiana expedition, Roe was successively engaged in Europe, on embassage to the Great Mogul, as a remarkable ambassador at large of the East India Company, and involved over a period of four years in considerable journeyings. Then, in the years 1619 to 1621, he was in England and closely connected with the affairs of the Virginia Company which formed the background to Donne's sermon.

The tentative beginnings of the Virginian settlement extended into the sixteenth century: Raleigh was granted letters patent in 1584,[4] and in 1587 'the Reverend Thomas Hariot baptised the first white English child' with the almost emblematic name of Virginia Dare.[5] This moment in the history

---

[1] Public Record Office, S. P. Domestic, James I, Vol. 134, No. 59; item 381 in *Records of the Virginia Company of London*, ed. S. M. Kingsbury, Washington, 1906, i.

[2] M. J. Brown, *Itinerant Ambassador*, The Life of Sir Thomas Roe, Lexington, 1970.

[3] *Ibid.*, p. 13.   [4] Kingsbury, *op. cit.*, i, p. 12.

[5] S. P. Dorsey, *Early English Churches in America, 1607-1807*, N.Y., 1952, p. 2.

of the settlement has its happy coda during the long and con-
tentious 'Extraordinary Court held for Virginia' on 12 April
1623, in the records of which we read:

> Mr Deputy propounded Sr Walter Rawleighes sonne to be ad-
> mitted into this Company, wch in reguard his father was ye first
> discouerer of Virginia was generally well liked of.[1]

Despite the difficulties of the early years, it would be as idle to
deny the idealism of its establishment as it is necessary to pre-
serve a proper scepticism about the mixture of its motives.
Captain John Smith writes of the early days of settlement:

> When we first went to Virginia, I well remember, wee did hang
> an awning (which is an old saile) to three or four trees to shadow
> us from the Sunne, our walles were rales of wood, our seats un-
> hewed trees, till we cut plankes; our Pulpit a bar of wood nailed to
> two neighboring trees: in foul weather we shifted into an old
> rotten tent, for we had few better, and this came by way of adventure
> for new. This was our Church, till wee built a homely thing like a
> barne, set upon cratchets, covered with rafts, sedge, and earth; so
> was also the walls; the best of our houses of the like curiosity, but
> the most part farre much worse workmanship, that could neither
> well defend wind nor raine, yet wee had daily Common Prayer
> morning and evening, every Sunday two sermons, and every three
> moneths the holy Communion, till our Minister died. But our
> Prayers daily, with an Homily on Sundaies, we continued two or
> three yeares after, till more Preachers came.[2]

This adds substance and reality to the aspirations consistently
expressed in the early charters, articles and instructions, and
reflected even among the mercantile (and quarrelsome) pre-
occupations of the *Records of the Virginia Company*. Donne in
1622 is echoing, in his sermon to the Council and friends of the
Company, the earliest desire of its founders, that the officers of
the Plantation

> with all diligence, care and respect doe provide that the true word,
> and service of God and Christian faith be preached, planted and
> used, not only within every of the said several colonies, and

[1] Kingsbury, *op. cit.*, ii, p. 362.
[2] W. S. Perry, *The History of the American Episcopal Church*, Boston, 1885, i, pp.
45-7, cited Dorsey, *op. cit.*, p. 1.

plantations, but alsoe as much as they may amongst the salvage people which doe or shall adjoine unto them, or border upon them, according to the doctrine, rights, and religion now professed and established within our realme of England.[1]

Indeed, as the *Records* amply show, the evangelising impetus was never wholly lost in the bickering greed; Prebendary Richard Hakluyt was third in the list of patentees and titular rector of Jamestown with Robert Hunt as resident vicar; and as late as 18 April 1622, a crucial moment in the tragic background to Donne's sermon, Patrick Copland preached to the Company: *Virginia's God be Thanked, or A Sermon of Thanksgiving for the Happie successe of the affayres in Virginia this last yeare.*[2]
This was one of the last buoyant expressions of faith in the spiritual life and commercial integrity of the Virginia Company before the chartered proprietary company established in 1609 became a royal province in 1624, 'the most important transition in American history previous to the colonial revolt'.[3] These years, when John Donne and Sir Thomas Roe became most intimately concerned in the affairs of the Company, had a complexity of troubles which very accurately reflected in the New World some of the most characteristic problems of the Stuarts in England and Europe. At the moment when Church and State in the Jacobean and Laudian sense were being challenged by a growingly self-conscious parliament and by 'Non-conformitans' in religion (in Donne's phrase), the affairs of Virginia were torn with faction and accusations of corruption in the field and by divisions in the Council of the Company in London. 'A "court party" led by Sir Thomas Smythe and Sir Robert Rich advocated the established church and the continuation of the martial law in Virginia. They were opposed by a "country party" whose leading lights were Sir Edwin Sandys and the earl of Southampton who

---

[1] W. W. Hening, *The Statutes at Large*, Being a Collection of all the Laws of Virginia, ... N.Y., 1823, i, pp. 68-9, cited Dorsey, *op. cit.*, p. 2. The passage quoted is the third article of the letters patent granted by James I to the Company.

[2] Stanley Johnson, 'John Donne and the Virginia Company', *ELH.*, xiv, 1947, p. 130. This valuable article was the first to draw attention to certain aspects of the Company's affairs and in particular to the *Poem on the Late Massacre in Virginia*, 1622, by Donne's friend, Christopher Brooke, which will be quoted below.

[3] Kingsbury, *op. cit.*, i, p. 16.

were in favour of allowing freedom of worship and the exercise of political rights by the colonists.'[1] In Europe the Thirty Years War was throwing a wide shadow, and English policy was motivated by two opposed matters: the Elector Palatine, King James's son-in-law, was defeated at Prague in the autumn of 1620 by the coalition of Austria and Spain; yet James was inhibited from the most efficient way of assisting the Elector, an attack on Spain, by his tortuous desire to secure a wider peace through the marriage of Prince Charles to the Spanish Infanta.

All these matters find direct or indirect reflection in the sermons which Donne preached between Easter and Advent 1622 and especially in the sermon to the Virginia Company on 22 November; and they find unexpected reflection in the apparently miscellaneous and ill-assorted topics of the letter to Roe. Half the letter has the oblique intimacy of assured friendship; Donne alludes to the troubles Sir Thomas had experienced between his employment in the interests of the East India Company and his ambassadorship to the Porte[2]; the interim in England (1619-21) involved him in delicate and even bitter relations with his fellows in the Virginia Company and with the Court, and Donne's pastoral concern for his friend quietly related Roe's personal and public troubles to his own recurring spiritual concerns:

> Many graines make up the bread that feeds us; and many thornes make up the Crown that must glorifie us; and one of those thornes is, for the most part, the stinginge calumny of others tongues. . . . I never heard your private, nor publique actions calumniated; so you have the lesse thorns to make up that Crowne.[3]

This was indeed true but Roe, though never 'calumniated', had nonetheless experienced in May 1620 the humiliation of being nominated with three others by King James to replace Sir Edwin Sandys as Treasurer of the Virginia Company and of being summarily rebuffed by its Council, who preferred Sandys, despite the integrity and distinction of Roe's career hitherto.

---

[1] M. J. Brown, *op. cit.*, p. 109.

[2] *Ibid.*, pp. 108-18; the *Records of the Virginia Company* for these years contain constant reference to Roe's concerns.

[3] Hayward, *op. cit.*, p. 476.

Donne had himself ample experience of such various fortunes in public life and now deflects these matters in Roe's case towards an interior piety; he writes:

> But, Sir, since that Crown is made of thorns, be not without them when you contemplate Christ. . . . Finde thorns within; a woundinge sense of sin; bringe you the thorns, and Christ will make it a Crown,

The letter then proceeds to more public theological affairs and their associated political implications, in the Spanish Marriage proposals. In this delicate matter, even in a personal letter, Donne becomes evasively elaborate in manner:

> You know, Sir, that the Astronomers of the world are not so much exercized, about all the Constellations, and their motions, formerly apprehended and beleeved, as when there arises a new, and irregular meteor. Many of these, this treaty of the Mariage of the prince hath produced, in our firmament, in our Divinity, and many men, measuringe publique actions, with private affections, have been scandalized and have admitted suspicions of a tepidnes in very high places. Some civill acts, in favor of the Papists, have been with some precipitation over-dangerously mis-applyed too.

'Mis-applyed' clearly implies 'mis-interpreted'; Donne was no friend of 'Papistry' and indeed, in examining Jesuit political manoeuvres in *Ignatius His Conclave*, he showed no surprise at their 'colonising' cruelties:

> *Ignatius* staid him, and said: 'You must remember, sir, that if this kingdome [Spain] have got any thing by the discovery of the *West Indies*, al that must be attributed to our *Order*: for if the opinion of the *Dominicans* had prevailed, *That the inhabitants should be reduced, onely by preaching and without violence*, certainly their 200,000 of men would scarce in so many ages have beene brought to a 150 which by our meanes was so soone performed.'[1]

When therefore in this letter to Roe he counsels diplomatic moderation in interpreting the King's 'civill acts, in favor of the Papists' we have an indication of a judicious temper in Donne and not a change of theological stance. He tells Roe that he encloses a new-printed sermon which Donne had preached 'by commandement' on 15 September 1622, on the occasion of one

---

[1] Hayward, *op. cit.*, pp. 392-3.

of those 'civill acts' which had been too hotly misinterpreted, namely James's directions to preachers that they should not meddle in affairs of state or theology in which they were rarely competent. Donne's sermon is a long and deeply-felt meditation on the office of preaching, on which he concludes, in the first part of the sermon:

> Preaching then being *Gods Ordinance,* to beget Faith, to take away preaching, were to disarme *God,* and to quench the spirit; for by that *Ordinance, he fights from heaven.*[1]

But the second half of the sermon is a coolly appraising examination of the king's justification for regulating this office of preaching: that the king has been 'grieved at the heart' that, under 'liberty of prophesying', many of his subjects should have been misled by preaching so that 'every day' there were 'so many defections from our religion to Popery and Anabaptisms'; that the king had undoubted authority to regulate preaching, so that his *'so well grounded Directions, might,* (as himselfe sayes) *bee receiv'd upon implicite obedience'*; that the king nevertheless had supplemented his absolute authority by communicating to all 'the *Reasons* that mov'd him'; and that Donne, as Dean of St Paul's and commanded to defend the king's intentions, 'was not willing only, but glad to have any part therein', concluding his sermon with 'a Psalme of Confidence in a good *King'.*

But if we are to assess this sermon truly (and through it to appraise the temper of Donne's preaching in the autumn of 1622), it is as well to turn to the epistle dedicatory to 'George, Marquesse of Buckingham'. There Donne distinguishes carefully between the first part of the sermon (the high office of preaching) and the second part (the circumstances in which that office may be limited by the royal prerogative); he writes:

> For the first part of the *Sermon, the* Explication *of the Text, my profession, and my Conscience is warrant enough, that I have spoken as the* Holy Ghost *intended. For the second part, the* Application *of the Text, it wil be warrant enough, that I have spoken as his Majestie intended . . .*

---

[1] *Sermons, ed. cit.,* iv, p. 195.

This is a nice discrimination and it is clear that with whatever reasonable assent Donne regarded the king's Divine Right, it scarcely carried for him the authority of the Holy Spirit.

We see the delicate path he trod as Dean when we consider the next sermon of which he writes to Roe:

> Some few weeks after that, I preached another [sermon] at the same place: upon the Gun-powder day. Therin I was left more to mine owne liberty; and therfore I would I could also send your Lordship a Copy of that; but that one, which, also by commande-ment I did write after the preachinge, is as yet in his Majesties hand, and, I know not whether he will . . . command it to be printed; and, whilst it is in that suspence, I know your Lordship would call it Indiscretion, to send out any copy thereof;

He did indeed take his 'owne liberty' in this sermon on 5 November, and a Dean of St Paul's must be secure in his profession who proceeds in a sermon by way of these propositions:

> That man must have a large comprehension, that shall adventure to say of any King, *He is an ill King* . . . [yet]

> Many times a Prince departs from the exact rule of his duty, not out of his own indisposition to truth, and clearnesse, but to counter-mine underminers . . .

> If . . . [the King's] good intentions are ill executed by inferiour Ministers, this must not be imputed to him . . .

> hee [the king] is a most perfect Text-man, in the Booke of God, (and by the way, I should not easily feare his being a *Papist*, that is a good *Text-man*) . . .

> A Prince, that lives as ours, in the eye of many Ambassadors, [Gondomar of Spain being the most prominent at James's court] is not as the *children of Israel*, in the midst of *Canaanites* . . . But then all strangers in the land, are not noble, and candid, and in-genuous *Ambassadors* . . .

> as you would make one son a Lawyer, another a Merchant, you will make one son a Papist, another a Protestant. Excuse not your own levity, with so high a dishonor to the Prince; when have you heard, that ever he thanked any man, for becoming a Papist?

It was an uncomfortable sermon, not least in its recurring and ambiguous ironies, and one can scarcely wonder that James omitted to command its publication, at this most delicate time in relations with Spanish power.

Finally Donne tells Roe of the sermon to the Virginia Company, 'to an honorable auditory, and they recompenced me with a new commandment, in their Service, to printe that'. We have now sketched some of the historical context to that sermon; more significantly we can estimate Donne's tone and temper at this time, that he was prepared to be judicious in theology where that was demanded of his office, to be diplomatic to political power where that did not compromise his profession; but no civil power, no diplomatic consideration curbed him from truth where that was demanded. So it was on 22 November as he preached to the council and friends of the Virginia Company. We have seen some of the political and religious affairs, in the New World as well as in Europe, which dominated the decade before Donne's becoming a member of the Company in 1622. Now the Council was faced with a new and dramatic danger. We first meet it in the entry in the *Records* in May (n.d.) noting a 'letter from Sir Francis Wiat [Wyatt] governor of Virginia, describing the massacre;'[1] on 10 July, a lost work *Mo[u]rninge Virginia*, is recorded in the Stationers Register[2]; three days later John Chamberlain writes to Sir Dudley Carleton of a ship 'arrived from Virginia with news that savages have by surprise slain 350 (circum) of the English;'[3] the next day Sir Thomas Wilson reports that 'Indians have killed in Virginia 300–400 English, and but for accident man, mother and child had all been slain'.[4] But the proceedings of the Council in London are still filled with concern for trading difficulties and with charges and counter-charges of malpractice in the Plantation, until, on 10 September, it is recorded that a Commission has been issued by the governor and captain-general of Virginia to Sir George Yeardley to make war on the Indians,[5] and on 7 October a letter was sent to the governor and council in Virginia with further advice about 'destroying the Indians'.[6]

This then is the immediate context of Donne's sermon. He

---

[1] Kingsbury, *op. cit.*, i, p. 155, item 318. This letter is published in summary in *Purchas, His Pilgrimes*, iv, Bk. ix, Ch. 15, Sec. iii.
[2] *Ibid.*, p. 158, item 346.   [3] *Ibid.*, item 349.
[4] *Ibid.*, item 350.   [5] *Ibid.*, p. 159, item 362.   [6] *Ibid.*, p. 160, item 367.

was now a member of the Council; he was wholly aware of the correspondence and the concern of the Company and there is every reason to suppose that he knew of (had probably read) the poem by his friend Christopher Brooke, *A Poem on the Late Massacre in Virginia*. Professor Stanley Johnson draws attention to the temper which this poem reveals:

> For, but consider what those creatures are,
> (I cannot call them men) no Character
> Of God in them: Soules drown'd in flesh and blood;
> Rooted in Euill, and oppos'd in Good;
> Errors of Nature, of inhumane Birth,
> The very dregs, garbage, and spawne of Earth.[1]

The emotional pressure is somewhat high and one could expect Brooke to underpin the Council in their resolution of 'destroying the Indians':

> What feare or pittie were it, or what sin,
> (The rather since with vs they thus begin)
> To quite their Slaughter, leauing not a Creature
> That may restore such shame of Men, and Nature?

It was clearly no easy task for a clergyman however brilliant or powerfully placed, to preach at this moment on the duty of carrying the grace of the Holy Spirit to 'the uttermost parts of the earth'. Yet the structure of this sermon is tight and the tone assured; though the occasion is festive and brings out little of Donne's passion when engaged in a subject wholly personal to him, the Passion of Christ or the power of death, yet there are passages where the cool rhetoric takes fire in moving and eloquent language.

It has frequently been noted that Donne showed such early interest in the Virginia Company as to try in 1609 to become its secretary; since at this period in his life he was making urgent attempts to obtain employment of profit, it is perhaps more significant to judge his engagement in its welfare by the tone of the reference in the *Verse Letter* to the Countess of Bedford[2]:

---

[1] Johnson, *op. cit.*, p. 133.

[2] Usually assigned to 1607-9, see A. J. Smith, *John Donne, The Complete English Poems*, Penguin English Poets, 1971, p. 548.

First seeds of every creature are in us,
What ere the world hath bad, or pretious,
Mans body can produce; hence hath it beene
That stones, wormes, frogges, and snakes in man are seene:
But who ere saw, though nature can work soe,
That pearle, or gold, or corne in man did grow?
We'have added to the world Virginia,'and sent
Two new starres lately to the firmament;
Why grudge wee us (not heaven) the dignity
T'increase with ours, those faire soules company?

('T'have written then', 61-70)

The argument is tolerably clear and places the Virginian plantation high in the scale of fallible man's activity. Donne maintains the possibility that man can match creatures, the world and nature, in producing all things, both 'bad, or pretious'; yet fallen man in fact more often produces vile than valuable things: worms, frogs, snakes, rather than pearl, gold, corn. Nonetheless man has achieved two recent glories, adding Virginia to the civilised territories of this world and 'two new starres' to the other realm of heaven. Since the 'new stars' were almost certainly Lady Markham and Cecilia Bulstrode (who died 4 August 1609), of whom Donne wrote so feelingly in *Epicedes and Obsequies*, the excitement of the Virginian venture is placed at a point of substantial significance. Too much need not be made of these early references as we approach the sermon of some thirteen years later but neither need they be underestimated.

The most striking fact about the manner of this sermon is its close rhetorical structure, allowing itself only the rarest moments of emotional pressure, despite Donne's handling of highly-charged themes; for the occasion gave opportunity for the most delicate intellectual and spiritual deployment of Donne's wit. He addresses a company of businessmen and their friends, as, just two months earlier he had addressed them directly and formally in the course of his sermon on James's ordinance on preaching (15 September):

for the Merchants of the *West*, we know that in divers forraine parts, their *Nobilitie* is in their *Merchants*, their *Merchants* are their *Gentlemen*. And certainly, no place of the world, for Commodities and Situation, is better disposed then this *Kingdome*, to make

443

Merchants great. . . . you cannot have a better *debter*, a better
pay-master then *Christ Iesus*: for all your Entayles, and all your
perpetuities doe not so nayle, so hoope in, so rivet an estate in your
posteritie, as to make the *Sonne of God your Sonne too* . . . .
many noble families derived from you; One, enough to enoble a
World; *Queene* ELIZABETH was the great grandchild of a *Lord
Maior of London.*[1]

In the Virginia Company he addresses these men not as a
distinct part of his auditory among many, but exclusively, as
merchants devoted by their Charter and avowals to the spiritual
welfare of the Indian. In his sermon on Easter Monday of that
same year Donne had already expressly shown the concern he
develops in his sermon exactly seven months later:

A man is thy Neighbor, by his Humanity, not by his Divinity; by
his Nature, not by his Religion: A Virginian is thy Neighbor, as
well as a Londoner; and all men are in every good mans Diocess,
and Parish. *Irrides adorantem lapides*, says the Father [St Augustine];
Thou seest a man worship an Image, and thou laughest him to
scorn; assist him, direct him if thou canst, but scorn him not:[2]

Now, in his sermon to the Company, 'a Virginian' was no less
their 'Neighbour', even though the Indian had been so recently
the bloodiest threat hitherto to their prosperity. An examination
of the sermon in these circumstances leads to some interesting
conclusions; for Donne was walking delicately: he spoke in a
situation in which his anti-papal feelings, focussed upon Spanish
relations in the New World, were engaged in making a political
statement which could scarcely please the king; and at the same
time he preached words of comfort to the businessmen of the
Virginia plantation while yet deploring their harsh reaction to
the massacre. The native Virginian, whatever his actions, was
still 'in every good mans Diocess'.

Donne's text was from the opening of the book of *Acts* (i. 8):

But yee shall receive power, after that the Holy Ghost is come upon
you, and yee shall be witnesses unto me both in Jerusalem, and in
all Judaea, and in Samaria, and unto the uttermost part of the earth.

The sermon opens with witty virtuosity; the book from which
his text is chosen is 'not called the *Preaching*, but the *Practise*,

[1] *Sermons*, iv, pp. 188-9.   [2] *Ibid.*, p. 110.

not the *Words*, but the *Acts* of the *Apostles'*. 'Acts' initiates a new pattern: 'Beloued, you are *Actors* upon the same Stage too: the vttermost part [*sic*] of the Earth are your *Scene*: act over the *Acts* of the *Apostles'*. But this figure, in its natural develop-ment ('bee you a light to the *Gentiles'*) introduces a more sombre image which is at the heart of his listeners' concerns:

> be you content to carry him ouer these *Seas*, who dryed vp one *Red Sea* for his first people, and hath powred out another *red Sea*, his owne bloud, for them and us.[1]

The Red Sea is a figure of baptism and as a 'heavenly washing' prefiguring the blood of Calvary it was a commonplace; here Donne uses it with great power to link their spiritual duty to the Gentile-Indian with his later reference to the *'Flood, a Flood of bloud'* which had so tragically overwhelmed the planta-tion in the recent massacre.[2]

Again the metaphoric argument shifts and the three-fold occupation of God in the action of redemption ('Taylor' in clothing fallen man, 'Carpenters Sonne' in Nazareth, and 'Ship-wright' in modelling the Ark) is turned to its converse in the christian act of mission and in his hearers' concern for Virginia:

> Now, as *GOD* taught us to make cloathes . . . to cloath him in his poore and naked members heere; as *God* taught us to build houses . . . to house him, in erecting *Churches*, to his glory: So *God* taught us to make Ships, not to transport our selves, but to transport him, . . . *unto the uttermost parts of the Earth.*[3]

His text is thus firmly established in their 'interests' 'who are concernd in this *Plantation* of *Virginia*' and with an exegesis so casual as to be scarcely noticeable he proceeds to open up the whole subsequent pattern of the sermon, by a grammatical quibble which turns to a pun:

> The first word of the Text is the *Cardinall* word, the word, the *hinge* upon which the whole *Text* turnes; The first word, *But*, is the *But*, that all the rest shoots at.[4]

Donne's nervous speech-rhythm in this whole passage, so sharply contrasted with the occasional elaboration of rhetorical

[1] *Ibid.*, p. 265.   [2] *Ibid.*, p. 271.   [3] *Ibid.*, p. 265-6.   [4] *Ibid.*, p. 256.

structure, is characteristic of the whole sermon. Through the
jerky syntax, implying asides which invite assent, he elaborates
this 'cardinal' word *but*, as it applied both to the Apostles and to
the members of the Virginia Company. If we transcribe the
passage in what may be called 'a homiletic pointing', to render
the living speech-rhythm, we may detect the argumentative
urgency of the phrases. They begin smoothly enough:

> And it [*but*] is an inclusive word; something *Christ* was pleasd to
> affoord to the *Apostles*, which they thought not of . . .

but with this reminder by implication of what in fact the
Apostles 'thought of' (namely the temporal kingdom they had
constantly demanded) the pace and rhythm change:

> not that – not that which you beat upon, – *But* [*butt*] – but yet –
> something else – something better than that – you shall have.

As he develops the two elements in his pun on '*but*/butt', as a
conjunction and as the aim or centre of a target, he gives himself
the freedom to assume the whole of the passage in *Acts* 1 which
precedes his text:

> That which this but, *excludes*, is that which the *Apostles* expresse in
> the *Verse* immediately before the *Text, a Temporall Kingdome; Wilt
> thou restore againe the kingdome of Israel?*

Donne denies to the Company this worldly aim, as Christ had
denied it to the apostles; but – and with this the argument is
locked up – '*But;* there enters the *inclusive* [part]; *You shall
receive power, . . . and you shall bee witnesses unto mee . . . unto
the uttermost parts of the Earth.*' Though Donne thus early
warns his listeners that the temporal world of Virginia is not
for mere exploitation, he elaborates their missionary privileges
in terms which must have seemed disconcerting at that un-
comfortable moment. For the areas mentioned in his text are
expounded in such language as truly to make his Jacobean
audience 'apostolic' in function: '*Jerusalem*' is 'this *Citie*' of
London; '*Iudæa*' includes 'all the parts of the *Kingdome*';
'*Samaria*' (and this could scarcely have pleased King James at
this delicate time) embraces 'them who are departed from the
true worship of *God*, the *Papists*'; while the final phrase,

'uttermost part of the Earth', establishes the greatest privilege of the Company, their declared 'witnesse' to 'those poore *Soules*, to whom you are continually sending'. The preacher has now prepared the ensuing structure of his sermon and concludes his introduction with a familiar mnemonic figure of rhetoric:

> And so you have the *Modell* of the whole frame, and of the partitions; we proceede now to the furnishing of the particular roomes.[1]

Both parts of his exposition are closely related in theme, handling the two major topics, 'the power of the kingdom' and 'the leisure of God' in a subtle inversion. In Part One the Kingdom of God is related to an ideal temporal order which is slowly revealed to man; in Part Two this leisurely revelation in history is related to the actual, the present kingdom, as it is revealed in the mundane doings of man. In this consistent relation of the immediate concerns of political man (and especially of his fellows in the Virginia Company) to profound abstractions, Donne is able to maintain the tenour of his sermon above the current rancours which tore the country. This will be seen more clearly in particular passages in each part.

Part One swiftly handles the theological basis of the argument, in contrasting the covetous 'love of this world' with the power of God's kingdom:

> GOD, as hee is three persons, hath three Kingdomes; There is *Regnum potentiæ*, The Kingdome of power; and this wee attribute to the *Father* . . . There is *Regnum gloriæ*, the Kingdome of glorie; this we attribute to the *Sonn*, and to his purchase . . . And then betweene these there is *Regnum gratiæ*, The kingdome of Grace, and this we attribute to the *Holy Ghost*;[2]

Since Christ says to his chosen *'Come ye blessed of my Father, inherit the Kingdom . . .'*, his alone is the kingdom 'thats in heaven' and 'though to good men, this world be the way to that kingdom, yet this kingdom is not of this world'. In this temporal sphere within which all men's work is determined and tested, the power of the Father and the grace of the Holy

---

[1] This is a simple example of the elaborate mnemonic forms explored by Frances Yates in *The Art of Memory*, 1966.

[2] *Ibid.*, p. 268.

Spirit are available as men seek a temporal kingdom; '*But* sayes
the Text, stop there, A kingdome you must not have'.

For here we reach the crux of the First Part as it addresses in
particular the Council of the Virginia Company; their work is
tested by the nature of Christ's kingdom:

> Beloued in him, whose kingdome and Ghospell you seeke to advance,
> in this Plantation, our *Lord* and *Sauiour Christ Iesus,* if you seeke to
> establish a temporall kingdome there, you are not rectified. . . .
> The *Apostles* were not to looke for it, in their employment, nor you
> in this your Plantation.[1]

The first part closes with an extended exploration of 'the
leisure of God,' for 'it belongs not to us to know *Gods* times'.
In the course of nature we must be patient and how much more
in the affairs of God:

> Beloued, vse godly meanes, and give *God* his leisure. You cannot
> beget a Sonne, and tell the Mother, I will have this Sonne born
> within five Moneths;[2]

So with Christ's kingdom of which 'GOD cast the promise . . .
in Paradise'; the seed was scattered, hedged and watered over
the millennia of history; men must be as patient in their affairs.
And here, long delayed, and slipped almost as an aside into his
theological exegesis, is Donne's full comfort in their present
predicament; when God's providence seemed on the way to
fulfilment, 'the *Flood* washed all that away, and GOD was
almost to begin againe vpon eight persons'. So with the
immediate affairs in Virginia:

> Bee not you discouraged, if the Promises which you have made to
> your selues, or to others, be not so soone discharg'd; though you
> see not your money, though you see not your men, though a *Flood,*
> a *Flood* of *bloud* have broken in vpon them, be not discouraged.
> Great Creatures ly long in the wombe;[3]

And so Donne leads to his first peroration, in which, if their
'principall ende, bee the propagation of the *glorious Gospell,*' they
shall carry that power '*unto the uttermost parts of the Earth*'.

Having thus delayed and then triumphantly passed the crux
of Virginian affairs, their mercantile insecurity and their peril

---

[1] *The Art of Memory,* p. 269.   [2] *Ibid.,* p. 270.   [3] *Ibid.,* p. 271.

after the massacre, Donne's tone is more assured and the argument still more firmly marked in Part Two. It begins, where the first part had virtually ended, with the leisurely providence of God. Though 'the Plantation shall not discharge the Charges, nor defray it selfe yet; but yet already, now at first, it shall conduce to great uses'. Donne here nimbly turns phrases from the early Charters concerning the transportations of malefactors, orphans and the destitute to the plantations, upon the present company; Richard Hakluyt had already in 1584, in a secret document for the Queen, suggested that 'many men of excellent wit . . . overthrown by suretyship, by sea or by some folly of youths' might be sent to the colonies to 'the saving of great numbers that for trifles may otherwise be devoured by the gallows'.[1] Hakluyt further thought that soldiers may 'there be unladen, to the common profit and quiet of this realm' and that there also the children of wandering beggars might be 'better bred up'. Donne expands these aims very significantly; he can see the place in the plantations for felons, idle and destitute people to be reformed, and 'if the whole Countrey were but such a *Bridewell*, to force idle persons to work, it had a good use'. But characteristically Donne proceeds to a physical metaphor and thence to theological truth.

> But it [the Plantation] is already, not onely a *Spleene*, to draine the ill humors of the body, but a *Liuer*, to breed good bloud;

Indeed, if the members of the Company but knew it, all their expedient and material aims were turned providentially to grace; for God despises no instrument:

> The *Sonne of* GOD did not abhorre the *Virgins* wombe, when hee would be made man; when he was man, he did not disdaine to ride vpon an *Asse* into *Ierusalem* . . . but if thou doe but *Post-pose* the consideration of temporall gaine, and studie first the aduancement of the *Gospell* of *Christ Iesus*, the *Holy Ghost* is fallen upon you, for by that, *you receive power*, sayes the *Text*.[2]

The word *Power* directs Donne to the central argument of Part Two, the properties of power, in nature and grace, and the

---

[1] *The English Colonization of North America*, Documents of Modern History, ed. L. B. Wright and E. W. Fowler, 1962, p. 26.
[2] *Sermons*, iv, pp. 273-4.

nature of 'witness' in 'the City and the Wilderness'. The development of these themes is a profound contribution to the political debate of his day.

The exploration of power opens with the distinction between the Law of Nature and of Nations on the one hand and the Law of Grace on the other. By the former, 'A Land neuer inhabited, by any, or utterly derelicted and immemorially abandoned by the former Inhabitants, becomes theirs that wil possese it'. The classical maxim, '*Interest reipublica ut quis re ua bene utatur, The State must take order, that euery man improove that which he hath . . .*' justifies seizure of ill-cultivated land and its colonisation, 'And for that, *Accepistis potestatem*, you have your *Commission*, your *Patents*, your *Charters*, your *Seales*' from the civil power. But there is a greater power, the Law of Grace, the power of the Holy Spirit:

> that your principall ende is not gaine, nor glory, but to gaine Soules to the glory of GOD, this Seales the great Seale, this iustifies Iustice it selfe, this authorises Authoritie, and gives power to strength it selfe.[1]

This power of the Spirit by which '*Seales*, and *Patents*, and *Commissions*, are wings . . . to flye the faster,' fulfils the ultimate aim of any temporal society, 'to bee *witnesses unto Christ*'. With this transition Donne begins the final argument of the sermon, which has been long postponed, though implicit in much that has gone before. For we have now an exhaustive and subtle account of the relation of the 'City' and the 'Wilderness' as types of the witnessing Body of Christ; and it is the theological core of the whole sermon, for he addresses a City Company concerned with the Wilderness. Their concern is consciously and avowedly material, mercantile; Donne has throughout the sermon led the argument to the point where mercantile enterprise in a temporal kingdom becomes the foundation and occasion for witness in the kingdom of grace. This is the logical end of his careful handling of delicate problems and its success demonstrates his maturity in the art of sermon rhetoric.

The development of this concluding theme is given room to expand, something approaching a fifth of the whole sermon.

[1] *Sermons*, iv, pp. 274-5.

But it is concentrated and summed in one most moving passage

> *Christ* left the *Ninetie and nine* for one Sheepe; populous *Cities* are for the most part best provided; remoter parts need our labour more, and we should not make such differences. . . . The *Angell* that shall call vs out of that dust, will not stand to survay, who lyes naked, who in a Coffin, who in Wood, who in Lead; who in a fine, who in a courser Sheet. . . . *Christ* was not whip'd to save Beggars, and crown'd with Thornes to save Kings: hee dyed, he suffered all, for all; and we whose bearing witnesse of him, is to doe as hee did, must conferre our labours vpon all, vpon *Ierusalem*, and vpon Iudea too, vpon the *Citie*, and vpon the *Country* too.[1]

There are few passages in Donne's Sermons where his presiding concern with death and resurrection, passion and glory, is more feelingly handled; but unlike the great 'meditative' sermons, the present occasion demanded a strict harnessing of religious devotion to immediate concerns:

> You, who are his witnesses too, must doe so too; preach in your just actions, as to the *Citie*, to the *Countrey* too. Not to seale vp the secrets, and the misteries of your businesse within the bosome of *Merchants*, and exclude all others; to nourish an incompatibility between *Merchants* & *Gentlemen*; that *Merchants* shall say to them in reproach, you have plaid the *Gentlemen*, and they in equall reproach, you have plaid the *Merchant*;[2]

and lest this should too sourly probe the wranglings of recent months in the affairs of the Company, Donne again raises the immediate matter in hand to a worthier level: after a long and sometimes caustic examination of their ills, he returns to a theological centre:

> Before the ende of the world come, before this mortality shall put on immortalitie, before the Creature shall be deliuered of the bondage of corruption vnder which it groanes . . . and the last Enemy Death destroied, the Gospell must be preached to those men to whom ye send; to all men.[3]

Now, with their mercantile hopes dashed, with fears of further massacre, with charges of corruption at home and with doubts of the king's intentions, Donne's audience is given its charge in terms for which the argument has throughout prepared:

[1] *Ibid.*, p. 277.   [2] *Ibid.*, p. 277.   [3] *Ibid.*, p. 280.

Preach to them Doctrinally, preach to them Practically; Enamore them with your *Iustice*, and (as farre as may consist with your security) your *Ciuilitie*; but inflame them with your *godlinesse*, and your *Religion*. Bring them to *loue* and *Reuerence* the name of that *King*, that sends men to teach them the wayes of *Ciuilitie* in this world, but to *feare* and *adore* the Name of that *King of Kings*, that sends men to teach them the waies of Religion, for the next world.

Rhetoric was here the temporary servant of a political situation, as in the greatest preachers it regularly has been. It was the servant of no ignoble end that finally saw this vision of Europe and the Americas:

You shall have made this *Iland*, which is but as the *Suburbs* of the old world, a Bridge, a Gallery to the new; to joyne all to that world that shall neuer grow old, the Kingdome of heauen. . . . . .

Index (1)

The Writings of John Donne

SONGS AND SONNETS

Text, and general reputation, 16-18, 27, 29, 31-2, 37-8, 42-4

Aire and Angels, 41, 125, 162, 430

The Anniversarie, 16, 41, 124, 127, 149, 150, 269

The Apparition, 40, 135, 321

The Blossome, 12, 74-82, 84

Breake of Day, 34, 39, 40, 135, 225, 229-31

The Broken Heart, 6, 40, 149

/The Canonization, 12, 124, 127-8, 162, 164-73, 312, 348

The Computation, 79

The Dissolution, 153

The Dreame, 39, 128, 135, 162-4

The Expiration, 34, 225, 232-5, 243-4, 262-3, 265-6, 313

The Exstasie, 12, 16, 41, 125, 127, 129, 135, 157-8, 167, 169

Farewell to Love, 90, 112-24, 127

A Feaver, 24, 39, 150, 152-3, 165

The Flea, 40, 135, 270

The Funerall, 162-3

The Good-morrow, 13, 39, 40, 41, 64, 79, 91-2, 124, 127, 135, 149-50, 155

The Indifferent, 223

A Jeat Ring Sent, 38

A Lecture upon the Shadow, 79, 129

The Legacie, 40, 82-4

Love(r)s Infiniteness, 150

Loves Alchymie, 39, 111, 125

Loves Deitie, 12, 52

Loves Diet, 40, 79-81

Loves Exchange, 158

Loves Growth, 39, 75-9, 84, 150

The Message, 34, 39, 40, 225, 228-9, 263

Negative Love, 125

A Nocturnall upon S. Lucies Day, 153, 165, 167-8, 341

The Paradox, 79

The Primrose, 12, 269

The Prohibition, 312

The Relique, 12, 14, 79, 130-1, 162, 163

Song: Goe, and catche a falling starre, 14, 34, 40, 223, 225-6

Song: Sweetest love, I do not goe, 16, 34, 39, 40, 79, 220, 225, 226

The Sunne Rising, 39, 52, 64, 71, 111, 135, 137, 153-5, 161, 170-1, 250

The Triple Foole, 33, 53, 223-4

Twicknam Garden, 39, 40, 41, 156, 316

The Undertaking, 12, 13, 130-1

A Valediction: forbidding Mourning, 6, 8, 12, 39, 40, 41, 128, 156, 158

INDEX (1): THE WRITINGS OF JOHN DONNE

A Valediction: of the Booke, 88, 159-60, 166

A Valediction: of my Name in the Window, 82, 84-8, 149, 162, 332

A Valediction: of Weeping, 153, 165, 267-8, 341

The Will, 12, 40, 126

ELEGIES

Text; and general reputation, 29-31, 33-4, 38, 42, 44

Jealosie, 54-7, 65, 67, 222

The Anagram, 39, 40, 42, 51, 149

Change, 76

The Perfume, 39, 40, 49, 53, 58, 61, 65, 67-8

His Picture, 40, 41

Natures lay ideot (Tutelage), 40, 53-4, 60-2, 70

The Comparison, 40, 49

The Autumnall, 39, 40

The Bracelet, 28, 39, 40, 42, 65, 66, 68-9

On his Mistris, 40, 71-2, 259, 268

Loves Progress, 55-6, 64, 67, 76, 111, 272

To his Mistris Going to Bed, 56-7, 62-4, 68, 70, 76, 111

Loves Warre, 55, 58-9, 67

EPIGRAMS,

19, 28, 30, 38, 40

SATYRES

Text; and general reputation, 19, 28, 30-1, 33-4, 37-9, 41-4

Satyre I, 34, 273-4, 276

Satyre II, 6, 274-5, 296, 297, 301

Satyre III, 6, 274-6, 282, 288, 292, 306, 405-8, 410, 415-20, 431

Satyre IV, 6, 30, 222, 273-4, 276-307

The Progresse of the Soule (Metempsychosis), 8, 12, 15, 18, 24, 39, 74, 339

VERSE LETTERS

General, 33, 38, 41, 43, 139, 311-12, 317

The Storme, 30-1, 42-3, 222

To Mr C. B., 314-15, 317

To Mr. S. B., 222

To Mr Rowland Woodward, 411, 412, 417

To Mr T. W. ('All haile sweet Poet'), 203

To Sir Henry Wotton ('Sir, more then kisses'), 313-14, 334

To the Countesse of Bedford At New-yeares Tide, 180, 318-20, 343

To the Countesse of Bedford ('Honour is so sublime'), 222, 315, 326

To the Countesse of Bedford ('Reason is our Soules left hand'), 313, 315, 317-18, 343

To the Countesse of Bedford ('Though I be *dead*'), 315

To the Countesse of Bedford ('T'have written then'), 315-16, 442-3

To the Countesse of Bedford ('You have refin'd mee'), 204

To the Lady Bedford ('You that are she and you'), 41, 344

454

Epitaph on Himselfe, 40, 313, 326, 327

A Letter to the Lady Carey, and Mris Essex Riche, 315, 320, 343

To the Countesse of Huntingdon ('Man to God's image'), 315, 322-3, 345

To the Countesse of Huntingdon ('That unripe side of earth'), 13, 321-2

EPTHALAMIONS

General, 23, 222

Epithalamion made at Lincolnes Inne, 38

An Epithalamion . . . on the Lady Elizabeth, and Count Palatine . . . on St Valentine's Day, 41, 111, 204-10, 216-18

Eclogue. 1613. December 26, 210-18

EPICEDES AND OBSEQUIES

General, 422

A Funeral Elegy ('Sorrow, who to this house'), 42, 64

Elegie. Death ('Language thou art too narrow'), 326, 342

Elegie on Mris Boulstred ('Death I recant'), 15, 317, 326, 443

Elegie on the Lady Marckham, 40, 317, 443

Obsequies to the Lord Harrington, 317

An hymne to . . . Marquesse Hamylton, 41

ANNIVERSARIES

General, 13-14, 25, 33, 139, 346-7, 415, 417

The first Anniversary (An Anatomy of the World), 94, 222, 320, 328-9, 331, 333-5, 337-8, 342-4, 346, 411, 416

The second Anniversary (Of the Progresse of the Soule), 12, 15, 125, 223, 327, 336-8, 342, 344-5, 415-18

DIVINE POEMS

Text, 31-2, 41, 43-4

La Corona, 31, 34-5, 37-8, 43

Holy Sonnets
Text 35-8, 43
Benjamin Britten's settings of, 244-9
Elizabeth Maconchy's settings of, 249-51
Oh my black Soule!, 245-6, 348
Death be not proud, 16, 247, 249
Spit in my face, 312
What if this present, 246
Batter my heart, 246, 312
Since she whome I lovd, 246-8
Show me deare Christ, 431

A Litanie, 31-2, 221, 409

The Crosse, 41

Resurrection, imperfect, 347

Goodfriday, 1613. Riding Westward, 416

Upon the translation of the Psalmes, 221

The Lamentations of Jeremy, 240-1, 252-8

A Hymne to Christ, 250

Hymne to God my God, in my sicknesse, 221

A Hymne to God the Father, 7, 40-1, 220, 235-9, 250, 270

PROSE WORKS

Paradoxes and Problemes, 33, 38, 44, 284, 290-1

True character of a Dunce, 280

Letters, 32-3, 406-7, 420, 428, 433-4, 437-40

Ignatius his Conclave, 295, 349-84, 438

Biathanatos, 32, 397

Pseudo-Martyr, 358, 405, 410, 418-20, 427-8, 430-1

Essays in Divinity, 416, 432

Devotions, 385-403

SERMONS

(denoted by the volume and number in the Simpson and Potter edition)

General	437
II, 13	418
III, 17	409
IV, 3	444
IV, 7	439, 444
IV, 10	439, 443-52
V, 1	409, 414
VII, 8	406, 412-13
VII, 10	415
VII, 17	408, 422
VIII, 1	341
VIII, 2	341, 414, 430
IX, 10	413, 415
IX, 14	431
X, 2	417
X, 3	412
X, 8	204

Index (2)

General Index

Academy, The, 1897, 1899 (anonymous articles in), 19-20

Advis aux princes etc. (anon. in), 375

Agrippa, H. C., 336

Alençon, Duc de, 360

Alexander, Sir William, 2

Alford, Henry, 17

Allen, A. W., 51

Allen, J. W., 26

Ambrose, St, 420

Anderson, Robert (*Poets of Great Britain*), 2, 5, 9,

Andreason, N. J., 133

Andrewes, Lancelot, Bp. of Winchester, 404, 420, 430

Anglo, Sydney, 122, 360

Anne of Denmark, Queen of England, 177, 185

Anne, Queen of England, 297

Aquinas, St Thomas, 163, 426

Arbusow, L., 142

Aretino, Pietro, 298, 356 (in *Ignatius his Conclave*

Ariosto, L., 138

Aristotle, 138, 155 (*Poetics*), 139-40, 143, 146, 170 (*Rhetoric*)

Arkwright, G. E. P., 232

Ascham, Roger, 369

Asclepius (Hermetic text), 325, 326, 328, 337

Athenaeum, The, 1873, 1899 (anonymous articles in), 19, 22

Auden, W. H., 244

Augustine of Hippo, St, 95, 99, 110, 411, 412

Austen, Henry, 12

Austen, Jane, 12

Averroës, 138

Bachrach, A. G. H., 219

Bacon, Francis, Lord Verulam, 148, 161, 190, 198, 199, 313, 410-11, 414, 426

Baker, Sir Richard, 66, 126

Bald, R. C., 36, 202, 203, 219, 282, 283, 394, 419, 420, 421, 425

Bañez, Fr. Domingo, 428

Barclay, John, 429-30

Barclay, William, 419, 429

Barish, Jonas A., 192, 195

Baronius, 419, 423, 426

Bartholomew Massacre (Massacre of St Bartholomew's Eve, 1582), 360

Battista, Anna Maria, 374

Baudouin, François (Baldvinus), 420, 421

Beardsley, Monro, 260

Beaumont, Francis, 190, 194

Beaver, Joseph C., 268, 270

Bedford, Lucy Russell, Countess of, 30, 35, 180, 202, 203, 204, 222, 309, 310, 315, 316, 317, 318, 320

Bekinshaw, John, 418, 420

Bell, John (*The Poets of Great Britain*), 2, 5

Bell, Thomas, 349, 351, 353, 367, 376

Bellarmine, Cardinal Robert, 282, 350-1, 379 (in *Ignatius his Conclave*), 414, 419

Belleau, R., 176

Bellew, J. C. M., 20

Benivieni, Girolamo, 100-1

Bergmann, W., 238

Bernini, Giovanni Lorenzo, 162

Beza, Theodore de, 379

Bietenholz, P. G., 421

Birch, Thomas, 7, 370

Bisson, (Queen Elizabeth at), 178

Blackwell, George (Archpriest), 350

Blake, William, 245

Blank, H. R., 401

Bloom, Lilian, 296

Boccaccio, Giovanni, 122

Bodin, Jean, 362

Boehme, Jacob, 325

Bondi, G. F., 184

Boniface II, Pope (in *Ignatius his Conclave*), 352, 354, 384

Borgia, Cesare, 365

Bouhours, Dominique, 145

Bouwsma, W. J., 423, 424

Boyd, M. C., 236, 240

Bredvold, L. I., 122

Brilli, A., 135

Brinkley, R. F. (*Coleridge on the Seventeenth Century*), 11, 17

Britten, Benjamin (Settings of Donne's *Holy Sonnets* etc.), 244-50

Brome, Alexander, 296

Brooke, Christopher and Samuel, 34, 436, 442

Brooke, Rupert C., 26

Bross, A. C., 296

Brown, E., 426

Brown, M. J., 434, 437

Browne, Moses, 7

Browne, Sir Thomas, 32, 155, 324

Browning, E. B., 13, 15

Browning, Robert, 12-15, 17, 65, 259-60

Browning, R. W. B., 15

Bryan, R. A., 28-9

Brydges, Sir E., 10

Buchanan, George, 179

Buckingham, George, Marquis of, 203, 394, 439

Bulstrode, Cecilia, 317, 443

Burnet, Gilbert, 353

Butt, John, 300

Buxton, John, 29-30

Byrd, William, 270

Caccini, Guilio, 228

Cadiz (expedition against), 282, 405

Caesar, 49

Calvert, George, 181

Calvin, Jean, 373, 379

Campbell, Thomas, 10

Campion, Edmund, 368

Campion, Thomas, 179, 186, 189, 193, 195, 199, 200-2, 209, 223, 228, 230, 271, 272

Careggi (Palace of), 100

Carerius, 419

Carew, Thomas, 3, 46, 126, 259

Carew/Carey, Lady, 315, 320

Carey, John, 135, 149

Carey, Sir Lucius, 32

Carleton, Sir Dudley, 184, 441

Caroline, Queen, 297, 298, 300

Carpenter, F. I., 20

Carr, Robert (later Earl of Somerset—see), 181, 182

Cartari, Vincenzo, 197

Cartwright, William (anonymous editor of), 3

Cary, Sir Robert, 178

Casaubon, Isaac, 122, 280, 340, 420, 428, 432

Casaubon, Meric, 192

Cassander, George, 412, 420-3

Castiglione, Baldassaro, 228

Cattermole, R., 16

Catullus, 52, 160, 175, 176, 200, 260, 264

Cavalcanti, Guido, 94, 100

Cavalieri, Tommaso, 107, 108

Cavendish, W., 1st Earl of Newcastle, 35

Chalmers, Alexander (*Works of the English Poets*), 2, 22-3

Chamberlain, John, 45, 181, 185, 195, 202, 433, 441

Chambers Cyclopaedia of English Literature 1844, (anon. in), 18, 24

Chambers, A. B., 165

Chambers, E. K., 17, 19, 20, 21, 188

Chapman, George, 188, 189, 194, 201-2, 217

Charke, William, 368

Charles, Prince (later King Charles I of England), 437

Charron, Pierre, 122

Chatman, Seymour, 260

Chaucer, Geoffrey, 122, 136 (*Troylus and Criseyde*)

de Chomedy, Hierosme, 381

Christ, Jesus, 347, 388, 430, 442, 446-7

Cibinensis, Melchior, 330

Cicero, 277, 288

Clavius (in *Ignatius his Conclave*), 355

Cleveland, C. D., 11

Cockayne, Sir William, 413, 415

Coleridge, S. T., 10, 12, 20-4, 48, 75

Collier, J. P., 16-17

Collingbourne, William, 287

Collop, J., 3

Colonna, Vittoria, Marchesa of Pescara, 107, 109, 130

Columbus, Christopher (in *Ignatius his Conclave*), 356

Colvin, Sir S., 15

Comes, Natalis, 201

Condivi, Ascanio, 108-10

Congreve, William, 126, 305

Conway, Sir Edward (later 1st Viscount Conway), 36

Conway, 2nd Viscount (Edward), 35, 36

Coperario, Giovanni (John Cooper), 220, 228-9, 232, 263

Copernicus (writings), 338 (in *Ignatius his Conclave*), 352, 355, 356, 357, 379

Copland, Patrick, 436

Copley, Anthony, 353, 371

Corkine, William, 229-31

Cormican, L. A., 237

Cosin, Richard, 353, 356

Coton, Pierre, 377

Courthope, W. J., 25

Covell, William, 356, 374

Cowley, Abraham, 3, 5, 7, 8, 10, 23, 140
Cowper, William, 9
Cozzi, G., 426
Crashaw, Richard, 162
Creech, Thomas, 296
Cromwell, Thomas, 353, 420
Crowne, John, 238
Crum, Margaret, 37
Cruttwell, Patrick, 46, 133, 147
Cudworth, Ralph, 340
Cumberland, Countess of, 312
Curtius, E. R., 142
Cutts, J. P., 220

Dacier, André, 296
Daniel, John, 271
Daniel, Samuel, 179, 202, 309-11, 314, 315, 322
Dante Alighieri, 90-5, 99-100, 105, 110, 115, 131, 138, 302
Danvers, Lady (see Herbert, Mrs Magdalen)
Dare, Virginia, 434
Dart, R. Thurston, 229
Davenant, William, 6
Davies, I. P., 280
Davies, Sir John, 202
de Buttet, Claude, 176
de Dominis, Marcantonio, Archbishop of Spalato, 421, 428
Dekker, Thomas, 15, 30, 212
de la Boderie, Guy, 197
de la Mare, Walter, 26
Democritus, 290
Denbigh, Earls of, 36
Denny, Honora, 179
Dent, R. W., 2
De Quincey, T., 12, 18, 19, 22, 26
de Rosset, François, 184
Descartes, 417 (Cartesian philosophy)

The Dial 1896 (anon. in), 19
Dialoghi d'amore, 124
Dickens, Charles, 68
Dionysius Areopagus (Pseudo Dionysius), 100, 122, 325, 346
Dionysus, 158
Donne, Anne, 246
Donne, Henry, 283, 405
Donne, John (later Dean of St Paul's), see separate list of writings discussed
Donne, John (Junior), D.C.L., 45
Dorset, Earl of, 35, 311
Dorsey, S. P., 434-6
Dowden, E., 17, 19, 24
Dowland, John, 223, 228, 235, 242, 261
Drake, Sir Francis, 64
Drake, Nathan, 9
Drant, Thomas, 275, 287, 289, 290
Draper, W. H., 96
Drayton, Michael, 202, 314
Dreano, M., 408
Drummond, William, 2, 28, 31, 34, 35, 45, 259, 274
Drury, Elizabeth, 94, 320, 333, 343, 344, 346-7, 418
Drury, Sir Robert (and family), 203, 310, 320
Dryden, John, 3-5, 8, 238, 276, 307, 410
Du Bellay, Joachim, 176
Duckles, Vincent, 224, 229, 240
Duncan, E. H., 348
Duncan, J. E., 1
Dundas, Judith, 193
Dunster, S., 296
Du Plessis Mornay, P., 362
Dyce, A., 16, 17

East India Company, 434, 437
Edward VI, King of England, 287

Edwards, Sir Thomas, 181
Egerton, John (1st Earl of Bridgewater), 36
Egerton, Sir Thomas, 36, 44, 45, 311
Elder, Mark, 250
Eldredge, F., 1
Elgar, Sir Edward, 244
Eliot, George, 12-13, 74
Eliot, T. S., 27, 46, 74, 84, 163, 173, 404, 410
Elizabeth, Princess (daughter of James I), 177, 182, 185-6, 189, 203, 204, 206-10, 215-17
Elizabeth, Queen, 177-8, 179, 279, 287, 298, 301, 310, 312, 314, 354, 360, 364, 370, 374, 376, 381, 449
Elvetham (Queen Elizabeth at), 178
Emerson, R. W., 13
Emerson, William, 13
Emperor, J. B., 175
Empson, William, 78
Erasmus, Desiderius, 143, 144, 406, 421
Erskine-Hill, Howard, 297
Essex, Earl of, 179, 312
d'Etaples, Lefèvre, 406
The Expiration, anonymous musical setting of Donne's poem, 234-5, 263

Fano, Bishop of, 382
Fellowes, E. H., 229, 232, 242
Fenner, Dudley, 141
Fennor, William, 191
Ferrabosco, Alfonso, 232-4, 242-3, 262-5
Ficino, Marsilio, 90, 100-6, 125, 128, 329
Field, Barron, 11, 17

Finett, Sir J., 185
Finney, Gretchen Ludke, 224
Fitzgerald, Edward, 13
Fitzgerald, F. Scott, 386
Fitzherbert, Thomas, 361, 364-7, 375, 380
Fleming, D. A., 429
Florentine neoplatonists, 100-6, 116, 125, 131, 328
Florio, John, 316, 336, 338, 339
Fludd, Robert, 340
Forbesio, J., 183
Ford, Thomas, 240, 241, 252-8
Foster, L., 176
Fowler, Alastair, 176, 212
Fowler, E. W., 449
Fowler, Roger, 260
Fraenkel, Eduard, 278
Franchis, I. M., 183
Fraunce, Abraham, 141
Frederick, Elector Palatine, 177, 182, 183-6, 189-91, 204, 206-10, 437
Frescobaldi, Dino, 93
Freud, Sigmund, 86, 160
Fry, J., 10
Furniss, W. Todd, 182

Gabrieli, V., 426
Gaertner, A., 176
Galen, 338, 345
Gambarin, G., 426
Gardiner, Bishop Stephen, 420
Gardner, Dame Helen, 28, 32, 34-6, 39, 41, 50, 60, 62, 63, 82, 117, 121, 133, 135, 152, 155, 162, 163, 166, 168, 224-5, 226, 229, 239, 240, 261
Garnet, Fr. Henry, 370
Garrod, H. W., 208
Gascoigne, George, 180
Gellio, J., 183

Gentilis, Alberico, 380
Gentillet, Innocent, 359-63, 366, 371
George II, King of England, 297
Gerber, A., 359
Gerson, Jean, 420
Gianotti, Donato, 106
Gibbons, Orlando, 228
Giles of Rome, 420
Gilfillan, Rev. George, 24
Gillies, R. P., 176
Giraldi, G. B., 197
Goldast, Melchior, 420
Goodyer, Anne, 314
Goodyer, Sir Henry (the elder), 314
Goodyer, Sir Henry (the younger), 32-5, 45, 302, 310, 316, 321, 420, 428
Gordon, D. J., 179, 197
Gosse, Sir Edmund, 17, 20, 22, 24, 25, 47, 51, 65, 89, 202, 203
Granville, George, Lord Lansdowne, 145
Gray, Thomas, 14
Great Mogul, 434
Greenberg, H. R., 401
Greene, T., 176
Gretser, J., 423
Greville, Fulke, 57, 216
Grey, Robin, 232
Grierson, H. J. C., 15, 20, 21, 24-6, 31, 36, 38, 117, 162, 168, 259, 282
Grosart, Rev. A. B., 16, 17, 19
Groslot, Jerome, 428
Grove, George (*Dictionary of Music and Musicians*), 228
Guardian, The, 5
Guasti, C., 106
Guiana, expedition to (1610), 434

Guilpin, Everard, 30, 34
Guinizelli, Guido, 93
Guises (family of), 374
Guss, D. L., 133

Haddington, Viscount, 179
Haddington wedding (1613), 187, 189
Hakluyt, Prebendary Richard, 436, 449
Hall, Joseph, 34
Hall, S. C., 16
Hallam, H., 11
Halle, Morris, 261, 265
Halleck, R. P., 11
Hamilton, Marquis of, 41, 45
Handel, George Frederick, 244
Hanmer, Meredith, 368
Harbert, Lord, 178
Hardison, O. B., 138, 139, 182
Harington, Lord, 317
Hariot, Rev. Thomas, 434
Harrington, Sir John, 181
Hart Hall, Oxford, 122
Harvey, Gabriel, 142, 358
Harvey, Richard, 356
Hawkins, Sir John, 64
Hay, Lord, 179, 189, 202
Haydn, Hiram, 308
Hayward, John, 28, 117, 284
Hazlitt, William, 10-11, 12, 72, 208
Hazlitt, W. C., 17
Healy, Fr. T. S., 32, 349, 351, 359, 378
Heidelberg, 191
Heine, H., 272
Hendrie, Gerald, 228, 229
Hening, W. W., 436
Henry III, King of France, 374, 375

Henry of Navarre (later Henry IV, King of France), 375, 376, 378
Henry, Prince of Wales, 240, 434
Heraclitus, 290
Herbert family, 309, 310
Herbert, Sir Edward, 35
Herbert, George, 65, 202, 223
Herbert, Mrs Magdalen (later Lady Danvers), 35, 202, 203, 414, 430
Herford, C. H., 200
Hermes Trismegistus, 332, 340-1
Herod, 367
Herodotus, 141
Herrick, Robert, 48
Hervey, Lord, 300
Heywood, Thomas, 182, 183
Hilton, John, 235-8, 270
Hilton, Walter, 336
Hincmar of Rheims, 420
Hofsmannswaldau, H. von, 5
Homer, 138, 140 (*Iliad*), 159
Honora (daughter of Lord Denny), 179
Hooker, E. N., 304
Hooker, Richard, 418, 424
Horace, 260, 273-84, 288, 293-8, 300, 303, 306-7, 318
Horrocks, J. W., 359, 370
Hoskins, John, 34, 144, 145, 170
Hotson, Leslie, 117
Houghton, Baron, 17
Howard, Lady Frances (later Lady Somerset), 177-9, 184, 195, 201, 210-17
Howarth, R. G., 1
Hughes, Merritt Y., 133
Hughes, P. L., 368
Hull, John, 376
Humanists, 118, 327-8

Hume, David (Protestant controversialist), 375, 377
Hume, David (philosopher and historian), 7
Humfrey, Pelham, 238-40, 243, 244, 250
Hunt, Leigh, 20, 23
Hunt, Rev. Robert, 436
Huntingdon, Countess of, 33, 202, 315, 321, 322, 345-6
Hurd, Richard, Bishop of Lichfield and Coventry; Bishop of Worcester, 8
Hus, Jan, 420
Huygens, Constantine, 2, 44, 219-20, 223
Huysmans, J. K., 404

Infanta of Spain, 437, 438
Ing, Catherine, 266
Inns of Court, 188
Isocrates, 140, 141

Jack, Ian, 296, 301
Jacquot, J., 2, 224-5, 226, 229, 232, 240, 262, 263
James I, King of England (and VI of Scotland), 2, 176-90, 192, 195, 197-200, 205, 212, 309, 310, 314, 318, 350, 394, 399, 419, 421, 427, 429, 437-40, 443, 446
Jameson, Mrs A. B., 18
Jebb, R. C., 280
Jeremiah, Lamentations of, 240-1, 252-8, 267, 275
Jessop, Augustine, 17, 19
Jesus, Society of, 349, 351, 356, 357-8, 367-74, 376-8, 381, 383-4, 419, 428-30, 438
Jocquet, D., 184, 191

Johnson, Samuel, 4, 8, 11, 20, 90, 132, 140-2, 151, 160, 208
Johnson, Stanley, 436, 442
Jonson, Benjamin–
General: 46, 176, 180, 202, 232, 310
Comments on Donne: 2, 28, 30, 31, 42, 45, 176, 259, 320
Court entertainments and masques. General: 199, 202, 217, 232, 310
Masque of Blacknesse, 209
A Challenge at Tilt, 196, 200
Haddington Masque, 187, 189, 194, 200, 202-3
Hymenaei, 184, 188-90, 200-1
Irish Masque, 200
The Kings Entertainment in Passing to his Coronation, 212
Love freed from Ignorance, 200
Neptunes Triumph, 182
Oberon, 193-4
A particular entertainment (1603), 180
A Panegyre, 192
For the Somerset-Howard marriage (1613), 214
Plays:
The Alchemist, 60
Every Man Out of his Humour, 305
The Poetaster, 277-8, 306
Volpone, 264
Poems: 223, 245, 264, 265, 268, 270, 308, 309, 313-15, 322
Juvenal, 276, 307

Kastendieck, Miles W., 272
Keats, John, vii, 20, 84, 87

Kenilworth (Queen Elizabeth at), 177-8
Ker, Sir Robert (later 1st Earl of Ancrum), 32, 35, 47, 210, 407
Keynes, Sir Geoffrey, 1, 45, 202, 301
Keyser, Samuel, J., 261, 265
Killigrew, Sir Robert and family, 219-20
King, Alice, 19
King, Henry, 37, 399
Kingsbury, S. M., 434-5, 441
Kippis, A., 8
Knox, John, 303
Knox, Vicesimus, 8-9
Kramnick, Isaac, 297
Krohn, William B., 268
Kyd, Thomas, 66

Laing, G. J., 380
Lamb, Charles, 12, 20, 23, 72
Landor, W. S., 13
Langford, J. A. (*Working Man's Friend*), 19
Langridge, Philip, 250
La Noue, F. de, 362
Larkin, J. F., 368
Lausberg, Heinrich, 142
Law, T. G., 370
Lawes, Henry, 229, 270
Lawes, William, 229
Lawrence, D. H., 73, 75, 169
Lectures on the English Poets (anon., 1841), 13
Lederer, J., 133
Lee, S. Adams, 20
Leighton, Sir William, 240
Leishman, J. B., 29, 48, 56, 62
Leslie, John, Bishop of Ross, 381
L'Estrange, Sir Roger, 297
Levin, Harry, 141
Lewes, G. H., 11

Lewis, Clive Staples, 55, 70
Literary World, The (New York), 21
Longfellow, H. W., 13
'Longinus', 140, 141, 142, 143, 146, 170
Lord Mayor of London (1612-13), 198
Lowe's Edinburgh Magazine, 1846 (anon. in), 18
Lowell, J. R., 13-14, 17
Loyola, St Ignatius, 352, 354-6, 359, 362, 367, 372-3, 376, 378-84
Lucan, 159
Lucas, F. L., 164
Lucifer (in *Ignatius his Conclave*), 352, 354-9, 379-80, 384
Lucilius, 289, 295-7, 307
Lucretius, 131
Luther, Martin, 354, 373, 413
Lycurgas, 374

Macanzio, Fra Fulgenzio, 426
MacColl, A., 35, 38
MacDonald, George, 19
Machiavelli, Nicolo, 351-3, 356-68, 374, 380-4
McIlwain, C. H., 419
Mack, Maynard, 297, 302
Maconchy, Elizabeth, 249-51
McPeek, J. A. S., 175
Maecenas, 279, 280, 283, 300
Mahomet (in *Ignatius his Conclave*), 352, 355
Marcelline, George (*Triumphs of James 1st*, 1610), 212
Marcilius, Theodorus, 280
de Mariana, Juan, 375, 377, 378
Markham, Lady Bridgit, 317, 443

Marlowe, Christopher—
Elegies, 48-50, 70-1
Massacre at Paris, 66
Prologue to *The Jew of Malta*, 358
Marsiglius of Padua, 420
Marsus, Domitius, 48
Martz, Louis L., 133
Marvell, Andrew, vii, 302
Mary Stuart, Queen of Scots, 179, 369, 381
Masque of Flowers (anon., 1613), 198, 201
Mathew, Sir Toby, 406
Maxwell, James, 182, 183
Mayne, Jasper, 46
Mazzeo, J. A., 133, 348
Medici, family of, 380
Medici, Catherine de', 360
Medici, Lorenzo, de', Il Magnifico, 100, 105, 106
Melancthon, Philip, 421
Mellers, Wilfred, 237-40
Melton, W. F., 22
Merchant Taylor's Hall, 198
Mercure François, 184
Meres, Francis, 46
Metaphysical poets, 140
Michelangelo Buonarroti, 106-11, 115, 122-3, 130-1
Middleton, Thomas, 198
Milgate, W., 1, 28-9, 30, 36, 43, 273, 282-3, 406, 411
Milton, John, vii, 8, 12, 36, 84, 267, 270, 302
Minos, 374
Minto, W., 19, 24
della Mirandola, Gianfresco Pico, 420
della Mirandola, Pico, 90, 100-6, 110, 116, 327-8
Mirror for Magistrates, The, 287
Mitchell, Donald, 249

'M.M.D.' (*European Magazine*, 1822), 11
Molina, L., 428
Montaigne, Michel de, 122, 336-40, 408, 410-11
Monthly Review, The, 1756 (anon. in), 7
More, Sir George, 35
More, Henry, 340
More, Sir Thomas, 290, 406
Morley, Thomas, 223, 230, 242
Morton, Bishop Thomas, 381, 409, 421-3
Moulton, C. W., 1
Munday, Antony, 230

Nashe, Thomas, 142, 353
Nation, The, 1913 (anonymous article in), 15, 21, 26
Nerius (In *Ignatius his Conclave*), 356, 379-80
Nethercot, A. H., 1
Nevo, Ruth, 138
Newman, Cardinal John Henry, 409
Nichols, J. (*Progresses. . .*), 178, 181, 184-6
Nicolas of Cusa, 415
Norton, C. E., 17, 22, 24
Norton, Thomas, 330, 332, 333
Notes Theological (1853), 12
Numa Pompilius, 374

Oath of Allegiance, 1606 (and Gunpowder Plot, 1605), 350-1, 356, 376-8, 419, 425, 428
Ockham, William, of, 415, 420, 426
O'Flaherty, Rev. T. R., 17
Oldham, John, 293-5, 299, 306
Oldmixon, J., 6, 145
Orandus, Eirenaeus, 331

Oratorian Friars, 379
Orgel, Stephen, 195
Orr, A., 14, 244
Osborne, J. M., 6
Osorio, Geronimo, 363
Overbury, Sir Thomas, 201, 280
Ovid, 4, 47-65, 70-2, 135, 155, 271
Owen, David, 350, 355, 375
Owen, T., 377
Oxford, Earl of, 297

Paduan aristoteleans, 122, 125
Palatine, Count (entertainment for, 1578), 178
Palgrave, Francis, 16
Paman, Clement, 277
Paracelsus, 330, 333, 335, 337, 338, 356, 357, 379
Paris Parlement, 377-8
Parnell, Thomas, 5
Parsons, Robert, 349, 365, 370, 371, 376
Pasquier, Etienne, 351, 373-4, 381
Paul, St, 413
Paul V, Pope, 350
Peacham, Henry, 144, 149, 182, 183
Pears, Peter, 244, 246, 247
Penny Cyclopaedia of the Society for the Diffusion of Useful Knowledge, The (anon. in), 23
Percy, Henry, 9th Earl of Northumberland, 35, 36
Pernety, A. J., 329
Perry, W. S., 435
Pestell, T., 3
Peterson, Douglas L., 260
Petrarch, Francesco, 95, 96, 99, 110, 115, 123, 128, 314, 411, 420
Pett, Phineas, 185

Phillips, E., 4
Pier Luigi (son of Pope Paul III), 382
Pilkington, Francis, 242
Pimander (Hermetic text), 334
Pindar, 159
Pius V, Pope, 376
Plato, 90, 100, 101, 108, 122, 126, 221, 340, 341, 383
Plotinians, 100, 122, 126
Plume, Archdeacon, 2
Poetical Works of Dr John Donne, Boston, 1855 (Anon.), 17
Poins, John, 314
Pole, Cardinal Reginald, 356, 380
Pomponazzi, Pietro, 122
Pope, Alexander, 5, 6, 260, 277, 287, 289, 293, 295-307
Popish plot, 294-5
Possevino, Antonio, 361-3, 366-7
Potts, L. J., 155
Pound, Ezra, 46
Praz, Mario, 133
Preston, Thomas (alias Roger Widdrington), 419
Priestley, Joseph, 142, 145-7, 151, 160-1, 168, 170, 173-4
Printer to the Understanders (1633 edn. of Donne's poems), 3
Propertius, 48-9, 50-5, 59, 63-4, 70, 72
Ptolemy, 338
Puckering, Sir Thomas, 36
Purchas, His Pilgrimes, 441
Puttenham, George, 141, 142, 147, 161, 175-6, 182, 194
Pyrrho, 408, 415
Pythagorean harmony, 221

Quarles, Francis, 5
Quarterly Review, The, 1897, 1900 (anonymous articles in), 11, 20

Quinn, D. 416
Quintilian, 66-7, 141, 143-4, 154

Raab, F., 359
Raleigh, Sir Walter (and family), 46, 182, 314, 434, 435
Raspa, Anthony, 382
Ratcliffe, Lady Elizabeth, 179
Rathé, C. Edward, 359, 360
Ravaillac, Fr. J. F., 377, 378
Redpath, Theodore, 117, 164, 168
Reese, Jack E., 190
Régnier, Mathurin, 283, 284
Retrospective Review, The, 1823 (anonymous article in), 18, 22
Reyher, Paul, 182
Rhetorica Ad Herennium, 137, 141, 143
Ribadeneira, Pedro, de 361-7, 374-5
Rich, Essex, 320
Rich, Sir Robert, 436
Richer, Edmond, 420
Ricks, Christopher B., 164
Rimbaud, Arthur, 244
Rochester, Earl of (John Wilmot), 294, 306
Roe, Sir John (and family), 34
Roe, Sir Thomas, 34, 310, 433-4, 436, 437-8, 440, 441
Ronsard, P. de, 176, 260
Rosseter, Philip, 228, 242
Rossetti, D. G., 13
Rossetti, W. M., 13, 15
Rudd, Niall, 276-8, 280-1
Ruffhead, Owen, 287
Russell, Ann, 178
Russell, D. A., 140

Saintleger, An., 123
Saintsbury, George, 17, 23, 24, 27

St Valentine's Day marriage, (1613), 183-92, 204-10, 213
Salmon, J. H. M., 375
Sanders, H. M., 24
Sanders, J. Wilbur, 64, 168-74, 284, 292-3
Sandys, Sir Edwin, 424-5, 431, 436, 437
Sanford, E., 17
San Marco (Garden of), 100
Sarpi, Paolo, 412, 425-9, 432
Savile, J., 177
Savonarola, Girolamo, 101, 104, 109, 110, 303
Scaliger, J. C., 175
Schelling, F. E., 11, 20, 25
Schumann, Robert, 272
Scipio Africanus, 288
Scot, Reginald, 122
Seccombe, T., 26
Selections from the Works of John Donne DD (Anon.), 16
Seneca, 143, 297
Serafino d'Aquila, 97
Serarius, 367
Sertorius, 374
Sextus Empiricus, 122
Shakespeare—
    General: vii, 8, 12, 46, 72, 84, 123
    Sonnets, 75, 113, 123, 124, 136, 156, 308, 309, 319
    As You Like It, 290
    Hamlet, 87, 167
    Henry V, 385
    King Lear, 165, 331
    Macbeth, 290, 332
    Troilus and Cressida, 57, 87, 161, 335
Shawcross, J., 164, 165
Shelton, Thomas, 296
Shipman, Thomas, 3

Sidney family, 308, 309
Sidney, Mary, 221,
Sidney, Sir Philip, 2, 8, 46, 97-99, 123, 132, 134, 136, 176, 221, 321
Simeon, Sir John, 16
Simpson, Mrs Evelyn M., 32, 283, 288
Simpson, Percy, 2, 200
Skelton, John, 286, 288
Sloan, T. O., 132
Smith, A. J., 125, 133, 149, 156, 164, 204, 244, 267, 442
Smith, H. L., 260
Smith, Captain John, 435
Smith, Logan Pearsall, 404
Smith, William, 142
Smythe, Sir Thomas, 436
Somers, Lord, 376
Somerset, Earl of, 35, 186, 195-204, 210-17
Song: Goe, and catche, anonymous musical setting of Donne's poem, 225-6
Song: Sweetest love, I do not goe, anonymous musical setting of Donne's poem, 226-8
Sorbonne, 377-8, 420
Souchay, L'Abbé, 176, 204
Souris, A., 2, 224-5, 226, 229, 232, 240, 262, 263
Southampton, Earl of, 311, 436
Southey, R., 10, 27
Spanish Ambassador to England, 186
Sparrow, J., 3
Spectator, The, 1913 (anon. in), 25
Spence, J., 6, 303, 304
Spencer, Theodore, vii
Spenser Edmund, 8, 25, 46, 98, 134, 176, 208, 308, 309

Spingarn, Joel E., 145
Stapleton, Thomas, 370
Starkey, Thomas, 418
Stein, Arnold, 260, 263
Stephens, W. R. W., 12
Sterne, Lawrence, 20, 260
Stewart, P. D., 359
Suckling, Sir John, 122
Suffolk, Earl of, 181
Sullivan, Mary, 197
Swift, Jonathan, 7, 82, 141, 161
Swinburne, A. C., 14
Symons, Arthur, 23-4, 26

Tacitus, 362
Taine, H. A., 11
Tasso, Torquato, 97, 138
Taylor, Jeremy, 391
Taylor, John, 183, 184
T. C. (*The Mariage of Prince Fredericke*), 184
Telius, 361
Temple Bar, 1861; 1876 (anonymous articles in), 19
Tennyson, Lord Alfred, 13, 259
Theobald., L., 7, 22
Theophrastus, 280, 296
Thomas, Edward, 18
Thompson, Francis, 20
Thompson, John, 260
Thomson, Patricia, 316
Thoreau, H. D., 13
Thucydides, 140, 141
Tiberius, 362
Tibullus, 48-50, 52, 54, 55, 60, 61
Tillotson, Mrs K., 1
Times Literary Supplement, The, 1913, 1921, (anonymous reviews in), 21, 26, 27
Tippett, M., 238
Topcliff, Richard, 283
Toscano, Matteo, 380

Tottel's Miscellany, 147, 260
Traci, P., 132
Trager, G. L., 260
Traherne, Thomas, 148
Trent, Council of, 110
Tuve, Rosemond, 132, 133, 148, 223
Tyndale, William, 406

Valentine, Basil, 347
Vaughan, Henry, 148, 337, 342
Vaughan, Thomas, 325-31, 337, 340, 342, 347
Venetian Ambassador to England (Foscarini), 183, 188, 197
Vickers, B. W., 132, 137
Villari, P., 110
Villon, François, 260
Virgil, 3, 4, 138, 143, 144
Virginia Company (and Colony), 189, 433-7, 441-51

Waldron, F. G., 16
Walker, D. P., 341
Waller, E., *The Second Part of Mr Waller's Poems*, 1690 (anonymous preface to), 4
Walpole, Sir Robert, 297-300
Walsh, W., 4
Walton, I., 3, 7, 30-2, 74, 126, 220-1, 223, 238, 270, 301, 399
Warburton, W., 6, 301
Warnke, F., 133, 259, 268
Warton, J., 7
Warwick, Earl of (marriage, 1565), 178
Waterhouse, G. (*The Literary Relations of England and Germany in the Seventeenth Century*), 5

Watson, Thomas
(*Ekatompathia*), 113
Watson, William, 371-3
Watts-Dunton, T., 14
Webster, John, 2, 57
Weinberg, Bernard (*A History of Literary Criticism in the Italian Renaissance*), 138
Welsh, A., 11
Wernicke, C. (*Auf die Schlesische Poeten*), 5
Wesley, John, 7
White, Kirke, 10
Whitney, Geoffrey, 271
Whyte, Rowland, 178
Willett, Andrew, 183
William of Orange (d. 1584), 374
Williamson, George, 117, 217
Wilson, Arthur, 181, 195
Wilson, F. P., 28-9
Wilson, Thomas, 144, 161, 168, 173
Wilson, Sir Thomas, 441
Wimsatt, W. K., 260
Winwood, Sir Ralph, 184
Wither, George, 182, 183, 202
Witzel, Georg, 420, 421

Wolfe, John, 359
Wolseley, R., 4
Wood, Anthony, 232, 240
Woodfill, W. L., 236
Woodward, Rowland (and family), 34, 36
Wordsworth, William, vii, 13, 16
Wotton, Sir Henry, 34, 47, 89, 90, 131, 202, 220, 273, 280, 310, 313-4, 317, 425
Wright, L. B., 449
Wright, Thomas, 370
Wuorinen, Charles, 267
Wyatt, Sir Francis, 441
Wyatt, Sir Thomas, 46, 53, 95, 132, 133, 260, 286-7, 289, 314
Wybarne, J., 30
Wycherley, W., 5, 238, 303

Yates, Frances, 425, 447
Yeardley, Sir George, 441
Yeats, W. B., 13, 26
York, Duke of, 294
Young, Peter, 179

Zoroaster, 340-1